Iran's Foreign Policy, 1941–1973

*A Study of Foreign Policy
in Modernizing Nations*

Iran's Foreign Policy 1941–1973

A Study of Foreign Policy in Modernizing Nations

Rouhollah K. Ramazani

University Press of Virginia
Charlottesville

THE UNIVERSITY PRESS OF VIRGINIA
Copyright © 1975 by the Rector and Visitors
of the University of Virginia

First published 1975

Library of Congress Cataloging in Publication Data

Ramazani, Rouhollah K.   1928-
    Iran's foreign policy, 1941-1973

    Bibliography: p.
    1. Iran—Foreign relations.   I. Title.
DS274.R34 1975   327.55   74-16467
ISBN 0-8139-0594-X

Printed in the United States of America

TO THE
UNIVERSITY OF VIRGINIA
FOR ITS ABILITY TO ADAPT TO
THE IMPERATIVE OF CHANGE IN TUMULTUOUS TIMES
WITHOUT FORFEITING THE STABILITY
OF ITS JEFFERSONIAN TRADITION

Preface

IRAN'S FOREIGN POLICY from 1941 to 1973 contains remarkable contrasts. When President Nixon stated in 1973 that Iran is a bridge "between the East and West, between Asia and Europe, and for that matter Africa," he was reiterating what every president of the United States has said about the strategic significance of Iran in the international system since the Second World War when President Roosevelt characterized Iran as the "Bridge to Victory" in the Allied war efforts against Hitler's Germany. But the continuity of the idea of Iran's strategic position contrasts significantly with changes that have been taking place in Iranian society within the past thirty years or so, particularly the past decade. The foreign-occupied, economically backward, socially explosive, politically chaotic Iran of some sixteen million people of 1941 emerged by the end of 1973 as a nation of thirty-two million enjoying one of the world's fastest rates of economic growth, regarded as the "Japan of the Middle East," sitting, as the predominant power in the Persian Gulf, astride the strategic Strait of Hormuz, through which the energy-poor world receives some twenty-five million barrels of Arab and Iranian oil a day, and playing an active role in world affairs, ranging from serving on the Vietnam Truce Commission to administering a newly established foreign aid program of its own.

The primary objective of this study is to analyze empirically Iran's foreign policy for the period 1941-73, following my earlier study *The Foreign Policy of Iran, 1500-1941: A Developing Nation in World Affairs*. Yet this study, like its companion volume, is not intended to be the kind of single-country description and analysis that might interest only area specialists interested in Iran and the Middle East. It also represents a kind of case study of foreign policy in modernizing societies that will interest general foreign policy analysts. This broader concern is reflected in the Introduction, which discusses relevant conceptual problems, in the kind of questions that are raised for analysis throughout this volume, and in the tables that have been especially prepared for a statistical comparison of Iran's social, economic and military developments with those of numerous other nations.

Some fifteen years ago I first broached my idea of doing research on Iran's foreign policy to Professor T. Cuyler Young, then chairman of the Department of Oriental Studies at Princeton University. His solid encouragement led to my earlier study of Iranian foreign policy, and the warm reception of that book by the international community of scholars lies behind the completion of this one. I hope this study will satisfy the high expectations raised by the earlier one. This study would have appeared earlier had I not been initially denied an entry visa for field research by the Iranian government. Furthermore, it seemed advisable to prepare first a separate study, *The Persian Gulf: Iran's Role;* its reception encouraged completion of this study without further delay.

Field research for this study was made possible by a Social Science Research Council grant, a Fulbright grant, and a fortuitous one year's study and observation in the Arab Middle East. The Social Science grant made it possible to travel in the Middle East for research purposes. The year before my research in Iran I was invited to visit the American University of Beirut as the holder of the Aga Khan Chair of Islamic Studies. My association with Arab and American faculty, the diversity of the student body, the library facilities, and the proximity of Lebanon to other Arab countries provided valuable opportunity for firsthand acquaintance with Arab perspectives on a great variety of issues. The year in Iran provided the opportunity for research in the libraries of the Majlis, the Senate, the University of Tehran, the National Iranian Oil Company, the Central Bank, and the Ministry of Foreign Affairs and for lectures at Tehran, Pahlavi, and Isfahan universities.

This study draws almost totally on primary sources. These are partly cited in footnotes as well as in the Bibliography, which also includes selected secondary sources. I have generally tried to follow the transliteration system of the Library of Congress. Given the primary conceptual concern of this study, the interactions between political modernization and foreign policy, I hope that besides the empirical analysis in the text the comparative statistical data compiled especially for this study will be found useful by two kinds of students. Foreign policy analysts can find the statistical tables useful for purposes of comparing the major and quantifiable components of Iran's international capabilities with those of other nations; students of political modernization can use them for their purposes in comparing demographic and economic changes in Iran with those in other societies over spans of time. Two years of field research and observation, of course, provided in part the opportunity for data collection, verification, and interpretation.

First and foremost I would like to acknowledge with gratitude the assistance of those Iranian officials who managed to overcome the chauvinistic impulses of others and grant me an entry visa after a year of painful delay. They, as well as those I interviewed in Iran informally, will remain anonymous. But I do wish to thank Premier Amir Abbas Hoveyda for the opportunity to talk to him and to mention others who facilitated my research in Iran in one way or another. Among them I would like to mention Dr. Amir Shilaty, former Director General of Cultural and Social Affairs of the Ministry of Foreign Affairs; Dr. Khodadad Farmanfarmaiyan, former governor of the Central Bank; Dr. Parviz Mina, Mr. Taqi Musaddiqi, and Dr. Bahador Haq joo of the National Iranian Oil Company; and Dr. Iraj Afshar and Dr. Shaul Bakhash. I would like especially to register my gratitude to Dr. Kayvan Tabari, who invited me to participate in his seminar; Dr. Manuchihr Ganji, for giving me the opportunity to meet many Iranian students of international relations through my lectures and research at the Institute of Advanced International Studies; and Dr. Hamid Zahidi, former Dean of the Faculty of Law and Political Science of the University of Tehran, for inviting me as a Fulbright consultant to assist in innovative efforts aimed at emancipating the political science curriculum from the apron strings of the study of law.

Among American officials in Iran I would like to acknowledge first and foremost the assistance of former Ambassador Armin Meyer; Mr. Robert H. Harlan, former Acting Deputy Chief of Mission; and most particularly Dr. Richard T. Arndt, former American Cultural Attache; Miss Lois Roth, former Assistant Cultural Affairs Officer; and Dr. Charles Boewe, former Executive Director of the Fulbright program. In the United States I would like to acknowledge Ambassador George C. McGhee's willingness to share generously with me his insights on the oil nationalization crisis of 1951-53. My indebtedness to Ambassador Raymond A. Hare for sharing his intimate knowledge of the Middle East with me over the years can hardly be adequately acknowledged.

Within the international community of scholars, in addition to Iranian scholars already mentioned, I wish to express sincere thanks to Professors Elie A. Salem, Nicola Ziadeh, Zein Zein, Constantine Zurayk, Kamal Salibi, Mahmud Zayid, and Joseph Malone, who shared with me their intimate knowledge of the Arab Middle East during my year at the American University of Beirut. I would also like to mention Professor Majid Khadduri, Mr. William Sands, Dr. John Duke Anthony, Dr. Harry Howard, Dr. John C. Campbell, and Professors Peter Avery, J. C. Hurewitz, Roger M. Savory, Oles M. Smolansky, James A. Bill, Hafez Farman Farmayan, Nikki Keddie, Sepehr Zabih, and Marvin Zonis for their sustained interest in my scholarly pursuits over the years. I remember with gratitude Professor Gabriel Baer's assistance in providing the opportunity to discuss with Israeli students Iran's foreign policy at Hebrew University in Jerusalem in 1969.

My gratitude to my colleagues in the Woodrow Wilson Department of Government and Foreign Affairs, the staff of the University Press of Virginia, the Social Science Research Committee of the University of Virginia, the staff of the University of Virginia library, and my research assistants, Miss Natalie Ferringer, Messrs. Charles G. MacDonald, James P. Piscatori, Howard M. Hensel, and Marion D. Tunstall, is expressed by the dedication of this work to the University of Virginia. To my beloved wife I am indebted more than ever before for assisting me selflessly with this study at a time when she herself was about to emerge as an author in her own right.

As is customary I would like to emphasize that none of the individuals or institutions I have mentioned are in any way responsible for facts and interpretations in this study. The responsibility for these is solely mine.

R.K.R.

Charlottesville, Virginia
January, 1974

Contents

Maps

Appendix Tables

Introduction

Toward the Study of Foreign Policy
in Modernizing Societies

A Theoretical Discussion

IN MY PREVIOUS study of the foreign policy of Iran, I suggested a theoretical
approach for the study of the foreign policy of developing nations.[1] Although
I admitted at the time that the approach was "general" and "crude" and that
I claimed no expertise in "theory building," a number of concepts and propositions were briefly advanced for three principal reasons. The theoretical
notions (1) had been generated partly as the result of making the first systematic empirical analysis of the foreign policy of Iran over a span of some four
centuries; (2) had in turn significantly guided the empirical analysis; and
(3) had been inspired by a consciousness of the general need for the comparative study of foreign policy. The principal theoretical propositions of the
study were these: (1) given the special nature and scope of the problems of
modernization in the new nations, the development of their foreign policy
requires conceptualization; (2) any such conceptualization should emphasize
the particularly intimate interactions between foreign policy (in substance
and process) and political development, on the one hand, and the international system, on the other. The application of these notions and propositions to the study of Iranian foreign policy from 1500 to 1941 was
characterized as "dynamic triangular interaction."

The principal purpose of this discussion is twofold. First, to suggest that
in spite of some progress in political science since 1966, the two propositions
stated then continue to be valid. Second, to attempt to conceptualize, in
greater detail than I did in 1966, toward the study of foreign policy in
developing nations in the light of this empirical analysis of Iranian foreign
policy from 1941 to 1973 and with a view to relevant conceptual contributions made by others since then.

The Need for Conceptualization

Why does the foreign policy of developing nations require a special plea for
conceptualization? For this there are two principal reasons: (1) the study of

[1] See Rouhollah K. Ramazani, *The Foreign Policy of Iran, 1500-1941: A Developing
Nation in World Affairs* (Charlottesville: University Press of Virginia, 1966), pp. 3-10.

the foreign policy of developing nations presents special problems for foreign policy analysts, and (2) students of comparative politics and international politics do not pay sufficient attention to conceptual needs in meeting these problems. It is generally recognized that the processes of modernization in new nations give rise to complicated intellectual, social, political, economic, and psychological problems. Students of political science are engaged in conceptual and methodological discussions regarding the study of "political development" or "political modernization" concerning the domestic politics of developing societies, but to date no sustained systematic effort has been directed at conceptualization about the foreign policy of developing nations. Yet without implying that the analysis of the foreign policy of late modernizing societies should be set aside as a separate field in foreign policy analysis, I believe that it is important to realize that special problems beset analysts interested in the foreign policy of these societies. The reason for this lies in several propositions: (1) the international system is historically and culturally Western: (2) new nations of Asia and Africa are largely newcomers to the international system; (3) as such they do not share the premises, assumptions, traditions, and experiences of the Western nation-states; and (4) these differences in cultural and historical experiences are reflected in their foreign policy values, attitudes, processes, instruments, strategies, and styles.

The Muslim Middle East nations, for example, like other developing states, have only in recent times become acquainted with the very concept of "foreign policy." This is no place to trace the traditional Islamic concept of state, law, nation, and the world. Suffice it to state that for the Muslims of classical times, Islam was not only the "one true, final, and universal religion" but also the foundation of their conception of the "international system." The world was seen as consisting of two poles—the house of Islam (*dar al-Islam*), and the house of war (*dar al-harb*). The Muslim believers resided in the former and were ruled by the caliph, and the unconquered infidels in the latter. Between the two worlds there could be no lasting peace, and a state of permanent war prevailed.[2] This basic division between believers and nonbelievers as the principal perspective from which the Muslims viewed the world survived the crusades and subsequently was passed on to the Ottoman Empire, for which no question of foreign policy arose so long as it retained overwhelming military power *vis-à-vis* Christendom.[3] For all practical purposes the Ottoman Turks viewed the Shi'i Muslims of Iran in the same way they

---

[2]See Majid Khadduri, *War and Peace in the Law of Islam* (Baltimore: Johns Hopkins University Press, 1955) and his *Islamic Law of Nations: Shaybani's Siyar* (Baltimore: Johns Hopkins University Press, 1966).

[3]Bernard Lewis, *The Middle East and the West* (Bloomington: Indiana University Press, 1964), pp. 115-40.

perceived nonbelievers. The two Muslim empires waged intermittent wars with each other from the rise of Safavid Iran at the turn of the sixteenth century into the nineteenth century. The foreign policy of Iran was significantly influenced by Shi'i influences not only in waging inconclusive wars with the Ottoman Empire,[4] but also with Russia.[5] Despite the conclusion of treaties with European powers during the sixteenth and seventeenth centuries, not until the eighteenth and nineteenth centuries did the Ottomans and the Persians establish resident embassies abroad.

To be sure, the transplantation of Western concepts of "nationalism" and "independence" in the Middle East has been associated with the rise of the modern concept of foreign policy, but the popularity of their use could hardly mean the identity of meaning with their Western counterparts. The concept of "foreign policy," states Bernard Lewis, like most of the paraphernalia of modern public and political life, "is alien and new in the world of Islam."[6] In assessing the transplantation of the kindred concepts of independence and nationalism in the non-Western world in general, while admitting their "elusive" nature in the Western world, Adda B. Bozeman states that in the democratic West they were closely related to securing "individual liberties," whereas in the non-Western world they are fastened to "the interests of groups of individuals rather than individuals."[7] It may be argued that the non-Western nations today are the members of the United Nations and a multitude of specialized agencies, have signed numerous international bilateral and multilateral agreements encompassing all aspects of modern international activity, and hence believe and behave in the same way as modern Western nations. That is to say, they too are guided by the dictate of the "national interest."[8] The ambiguity of this concept and the ancient debate about its utility as a way of conceptualizing foreign policy aside, unless the *content* of the "national interest" or any other concept such as "power"

---

[4] See Ramazani, *Foreign Policy of Iran*, pp. 13-32.

[5] See Hamid Algar, *Religion and State in Iran, 1785-1906:* (Berkeley and Los Angeles: University of California Press, 1969), pp. 73-102.

[6] Lewis, p. 115.

[7] Adda B. Bozeman, *Politics and Culture in International History* (Princeton: Princeton University Press, 1960), pp. 454-57. For an assessment of the difficulties in applying Myres S. McDougal and Harold D. Laswell's postulate of the concept of "human dignity" of a universal world order to the cultural and historical experience of Iran, see R. K. Ramazani, "The Shi'i System: Its Conflict and Interaction with other Systems,"*Proceedings of the American Society of International Law,* 1959, pp. 53-59.

[8] Wolfgang Friedmann, *The Changing Structure of International Law* (New York: Columbia University Press, 1964), pp. 297-316.

or "process" is examined in the relevant intellectual, social, economic, and political context, it can mean anything to anybody.

Seldom do developing nations reveal a more clearly divergent attitude from Western nations in foreign affairs than in regard to international law. Given the vast divergence of economic, social, political, and intellectual conditions, legacies, and structures of developing nations, it is obviously difficult to generalize about their attitude toward international law. Nevertheless, it is generally admitted that while the leaders of the Third World do not officially deny the tenets of international law, they do display distinctly different attitudes toward a variety of traditional norms of the law of nations, basically on the ground that in the last analysis it is the product of Western civilization.[9] To be sure, developing nations abide by a variety of international legal norms, but at the same time their perspectives differ from those of Western nations on a wide variety of subjects, such as the treatment of foreign investments and nationals in their territories, the width of the territorial sea, the relative significance of various sources of international law, and the regulation of the threat and the use of force.[10]

The special plea for conceptualization in regard to the foreign policy of developing nations also derives from the insufficient concern of students of comparative and international politics with foreign policy in these new nations. Let us first take note of students of comparative politics. Among standard works in comparative politics, for example, are seven Studies in Political Development sponsored by the Committee on Comparative Politics of the Social Science Research Council. The value of the series for the study of political development is generally acknowledged. Various volumes, as is well known, focus on communications, bureaucracy, political modernization, education, political culture, political parties, and crises and sequences and political development. But none focuses on foreign policy and political development. These studies are useful in varying degrees to the study of foreign policy in developing nations, and I shall argue later that the study of foreign policy in developing nations could hardly be accomplished without establishing conceptual bridges with the study of political development. The point is that in conceptualizing the problems of development in new nations,

[9]See, for example, Jorge Castaneda, "The Underdeveloped Nations and the Development of International Law," *International Organization* 15 (Winter 1969): 38-48; A. A. Fatouros, "International Law and the Third World," *Virginia Law Review* 50, no. 5 (1964): 783-823; George M. Abi-Saab, "The Newly Independent States and the Rules of International Law," *Howard Law Journal* 8 (1962): 95-121; and Richard A. Falk, "The New States and International Legal Order," Academie de Droit International, *Recueil des Cours* 2 (1966): PRIO-95.

[10]See Oliver J. Lissitzyn, *International Law Today and Tomorrow* (New York: Oceana Publications, 1965), pp. 72-101.

students do not consider systematically the intimately connected problems of foreign policy. For example, on the problems of "democratic nation-building," Gabriel Almond has suggested that the new nations are undergoing simultaneously four revolutions: a *national* revolution, an *authority* revolution, a *participation* revolution, and a *welfare* revolution.[11] This formulation lacks any conceptual allowance for what we may call now, and elaborate later, the concept of "*autonomy* revolution" *vis-à-vis* the international system. This disallowance is probably in part a result of the attainment of "independence" by new nations as the end of the line of the quest for "autonomy." And yet "independence" is a static and legal concept that does not encompass the *continuous postindependence quest of developing societies for autonomy.* This is not the same problem as "nation-building" or "national identity," although these concepts are related to the concept of autonomy. In subsequent formulations Professor Almond has paid attention to the importance of external variables in discussing the notions of "an international accommodative capability"[12] and a "consociational-tutelary international system,"[13] but these attempts primarily represent the important but general concern with the international system's impact on the domestic political system rather than conceptualization of the relationship between political development and foreign policy in developing societies *in all respects,* including the relationship between domestic capacity and international capability.[14]

Secondly, students of international politics or international relations, in spite of the proliferation of approaches, like the comparativists, fail to allow

[11] *Political Development: Essays in Heuristic Theory* (Boston: Little, Brown & Co., 1970), pp. 223-33.

[12] Gabriel A. Almond, "Political Systems and Political Change," *American Behavioral Scientists* 6, No. 10 (1963): 6. See also note 14.

[13] The contribution in which this concept of the international system is suggested by Almond was admittedly inspired by the writing of James N. Rosenau. Responding to Rosenau's criticism of the general neglect of the international system by students of comparative politics, Almond argues that "the international environment effects the development of national political systems whether they are cohesive or conflict ridden, and whatever be the structure of the international system" ("National Politics and International Politics," in Albert Lepawsky, Edward H. Buehrig, and Harold D. Lasswell, eds., *The Search for World Order* (New York: Appleton-Century-Crofts, 1971), pp. 283-97. This essay, however, is not intended to probe systematically the linkages between the concepts of political development and foreign policy in developing nations.

[14] Almond and Powell do allow conceptually for the interplay between domestic capacity and international capability, but my argument is that all major aspects of foreign policy, which will be identified below, interact with the major problems of political development. See Gabriel A. Almond and G. Bingham Powell, Jr., *Comparative Politics: A Developmental Approach* (Boston: Little, Brown & Co., 1966), pp. 203-12.

systematically for the study of the foreign policy of modernizing nations. Given the concentration of attention at the international level, the foreign policy of developing nations receives little attention, if any. Some analysts deal in a general way with small states, developed or developing, implying their relative impotence in world power politics.[15] Some treat developing nations as areas of the world where power politics (of the great powers) take place.[16] Some discuss them imaginatively with a view to the strategy of non-alignment, or their attitudes and "biases."[17] And a few analysts mention specifically but briefly the foreign policy of a single developing nation, such as India.[18] Examples could be easily multiplied, but this should suffice to indicate that the study of the foreign policy of developing nations is effectively bypassed.

One of the approaches at the international level does concentrate on a specific variable in a large variety of nations, including developing nations, as it affects external as well as internal behavior. This kind of "macroscopic" approach is evidenced in the work of Ivo K. and Rosalind L. Feierabend. Since this approach focuses on levels of socioeconomic development and their impact on the behavior of nations in the domestic and international system, its main hypotheses should be of interest in a general way to students of the foreign policy of developing nations. Briefly stated, by building on the sources of "systemic frustration"—that is, the discrepancy between socioeconomic wants and socioeconomic satisfaction, a high rate of change on socioeconomic indicators, and the coercive level of the political regime—the Feierabends hypothesize that "the greater these three sources of systemic frustration, the higher the level of external as well as of internal aggression." But as the authors themselves admit, in their broad and general approach "a great many nuances of international and national behavior are lost, including styles and varieties of foreign policies, actions and reactions in the international arena,

[15] See, for example, Hans J. Morgenthau, *Politics among Nations* (New York: Alfred A. Knopf, 1960).

[16] Frederick H. Hartmann, *The Relations of Nations* (New York: Macmillan Co., 1967).

[17] See, for example, K. J. Holsti, *International Politics* (Englewood Cliffs, N.J.: Prentice-Hall, 1967). Leonard Binder developed a number of general ideas especially about the attitudinal aspects of the "new states" in international affairs as early as 1965. See his "The New States in International Affairs," in Robert A. Godwin, ed., *Beyond the Cold War* (Chicago: Rand McNally, 1965), pp. 195-214.

[18] See, for example, Norman D. Palmer and Howard C. Perkins, *International Relations* (Cambridge, Mass.: Riverside Press, 1957).

specific idiosyncracies of nations, and their unique physical, social and historical backgrounds." [19]

When I first called attention to this persistent inattention to the study of
the foreign policy of developing nations in 1964, I offered two reasons as an
attempt at explanation.[20] It was suggested that this oversight might be
attributable to what Annette Baker Fox has called a "traditional great-power
stereotype" of the small state as a "helpless pawn in world politics," on the
one hand, and the small-power view that the great states were "cynical
manipulators of power and the small states . . . virtuous and law-abiding
countries," on the other. Two years later Quincy Wright added his voice to
mine, but, as already noted, neither the students of comparative politics nor
those of international politics have focused sufficient attention on conceptualization about the new nations' foreign policy even since 1966.

It might appear that the Northwestern Conference on Comparative Politics
and International Relations did tackle this problem, but hardly so. The Conference was concerned with the neglect of the study of the interaction
between "domestic and foreign politics" in all types of societies without
focusing on developing nations. Quite rightly the conferees believed that "the
comparative study of the interaction of domestic and foreign politics has
quite often been a no-man's-land—neglected not because students of politics
have thought the topic unimportant but because the divisions between the
two fields have tended to foster this neglect." [21] In other words "conceptual
jails," to borrow Professor Rosenau's words, have impeded conceptual rein-
forcements needed between the two fields. Insofar as the study of the foreign
policy of developing nations is concerned, however, the otherwise valuable

[19] See Ivo K. and Rosalind L. Feierabend, with Frank W. Scanland III and John
Stuart Chambers, "Level of Development and International Behavior," in Richard
Butwell, ed., *Foreign Policy and the Developing Nations* (Lexington: University of
Kentucky Press, 1969), pp. 137-88.

[20] Ramazani, *Foreign Policy of Iran*, p. 4. Reference to the year 1964 indicates when
the manuscript was completed and awarded the prize of the American Association for
Middle East Studies. In the above discussion of the need for conceptualizing about the
foreign policy of developing nations, I have been generally inspired by Rosenau's incisive
criticism of students of comparative politics and international politics in overlooking the
"national-international linkage" in their studies in general. I have had a somewhat similar
interest in such a linkage, but more specifically in regard to interactions between foreign
policy and political development, on the one hand, and foreign policy and the international system, on the other. See James N. Rosenau, *The Scientific Study of Foreign
Policy* (New York: The Free Press, 1971), pp. 307-38.

[21] R. Barry Farrell, ed., *Approaches to Comparative and International Politics*
(Evanston, Ill.: Northwestern University Press, 1966), p. vi.

outcome of this Conference did little to cope with problems of conceptualization.[22] Nevertheless, the fact that the Conference did specifically concern itself with the study of foreign policy in *developing nations* confirms my preceding proposition that the problem does require a special plea for conceptualization.

The Concept of Autonomy

Granted the need for conceptualization, I must first clarify an assumption before going on to propose *autonomy* as the key concept for the study of foreign policy in modernizing societies. I have so far assumed that modernization is a more useful concept than nonalignment as the basis for classification of "new nations" for the purpose of studying their foreign policy. This assumption is based on two major reasons: (1) the inadequacy of the traditional concept of nonalignment and (2) the comprehensiveness and special utility of the concept of modernization.

Let us take up the concept of nonalignment first. The traditional way of conceiving the foreign policy of modernizing nations almost exclusively in terms of nonalignment or as a "third world" has gone unchallenged for too long. Although the concept of nonalignment has been of some use, its uncritical and prolonged acceptance has done much to preempt efforts at conceptualization regarding the study of foreign policy in new nations for three basic reasons: first, a given strategy, be it alignment or nonalignment, is a poor basis for conceptualizing the foreign policy of a group of nations because in the last analysis it is predicated on a static conception of the international system, namely, bipolarity and the primacy of the cold war. Second, the emphasis on strategy tends to exclude most other aspects of the foreign policy of modernizing nations from systematic study, such as objectives, instruments, style, process, and the like. And third, the emphasis on a particular kind of strategy, namely, nonalignment, tends to exclude totally from consideration the foreign policy of some developing nations. As is well known, even at the height of the cold war a number of modernizing nations in the Middle East and South and Southeast Asia, for example, aligned themselves with the West through bilateral or regional arrangements or a combination of both.

Whether aligned or nonaligned, developing nations, both old and new, share the common problem of modernization, which is a broad basis for classifying these nations in regard to the study of foreign policy. To be sure, modernization is a universal phenomenon embracing human activity in all

---

[22] A general discussion of the perspectives of developing nations, however, is found quite useful. See ibid., pp. 120-61.

societies. In a broad assessment of the "modern era," Cyril E. Black identifies five characteristics common to all modern societies. These include the processes of modernization in the intellectual, political, social, economic, and psychological realms.[23] We are, however, concerned with the *late modernizing societies.* That is, those societies that are characterized by (1) economic underdevelopment, though some are developing more rapidly than others; (2) historical and cultural experiences quite different from those of Europe, Russia, and North America; and (3) recency of attainment of formal political independence, though some nations, such as Egypt and Iran, enjoyed nominal independence for a long time and are heirs to ancient civilizations.[24] Admitting the difficulty in determining when a society has become "modern," Black nevertheless finds it possible to describe societies as more or less advanced in the processes of modernization on the basis of a variety of criteria that appear to be "most satisfactorily reflected in the fundamental social feature of modernization that is represented by the gradual transfer of the bulk of the population from agrarian to urban employment. It is only under industrial and urban conditions that the integration of various discrete groups that make up a society can take place effectively, and that the problems of political modernization are fully faced."[25]

No matter what criteria are favored, the concept of modernization is not only more comprehensive than nonalignment as a basis for identifying a larger group of new nations, but it is also essential, I suggest, in studying their foreign policy. The reason for this is the peculiarly intimate relationship between the problems of foreign policy and political modernization in the late modernizing societies. This important point will be taken up separately below in the discussion of interactions between problems of political modernization and foreign policy. In anticipation of that discussion, I shall first propose my key concept for the study of the foreign policy of developing nations, just as general foreign policy analysts have suggested such concepts as "power," "national interest," "decision making," "calculated control," and others.

[23] Cyril E. Black, "Challenges to an Evolving Legal Order," in Richard A. Falk and Cyril E. Black, eds., *The Future of the International Legal Order,* vol. 1, *Trends and Patterns* (Princeton: Princeton University Press, 1969), pp. 3-31.

[24] These characteristics generally correspond with Walter C. Clemens, Jr., ed., *World Perspectives on International Politics* (Boston: Little, Brown & Co., 1965), pp. 10-11.

[25] In 1969 Cyril E. Black spoke generally of some fifty or more societies with a population of some 2.5 billion that are "primarily concerned with economic and social transformation and have not yet made the full transition from a predominantly agrarian to a predominantly industrial way of life" (Black, "Challenges," pp. 10-11). All of these societies may be considered as constituting the bulk of developing nations of concern to us.

"Autonomy" is the key concept. For the moment I shall simply define it as optimization of freedom of action in the international system. A question immediately arises: how would autonomy differ from such general concepts as independence, nationalism, state building, and nation building? First, it should be stated emphatically that these concepts are kindred and interrelated, but none is as useful a concept as autonomy for the study of *foreign policy* in modernizing societies. Let us see why.

The distinction between the concept of autonomy and that of "independence" is important in a number of ways. First, historically the concept of independence in modernizing societies has been largely associated with the process of emancipation from colonial rule. The expression "struggle for independence" is familiar to students of Asian, Latin American, and African nations, as are the related expressions "the advent of independence," "the attainment of independence," and similar phrases. All of these point up the inadequacy of the concept of independence for purposes of foreign policy analysis because they reveal the static notion of a legal and political status in the international system. The most interesting indication of this inadequacy is to be found in expressions "true independence," "complete independence," "greater independence," and the like, which are often used by leaders of developing nations as an inchoate way of expressing one or another aspect of the postindependence dynamic quest for optimization of freedom of action in the international system. The Iranians, for example, spoke of the goal of "complete independence" throughout the Constitutional Movement early in the century and during the nationalization of the Anglo-Iranian Oil Company, as did the Egyptians during the Suez Canal crisis. Besides Iran and Egypt, other modernizing nations, such as Indonesia, India, and Turkey, try to convey the dynamic nature of the continuous quest for autonomy by some variations of the concept of independence. Furthermore, as already seen, the concept of independence has historically been associated, in the West, with securing, to borrow Adda B. Bozeman's words, "individual liberties" as well as national freedom.[26] The concept of autonomy would have the advantage of no such specific cultural association and could be used as the key concept in analyzing the foreign policy of modernizing political regimes, be they authoritarian, democratic, or any other type.

The notorious confusion surrounding the concept of "nationalism" and the kindred concepts of "nation," "nationhood," "nation-state," and "nationality" need not detain us here. Other scholars have ably dealt with these in

[26]Bozeman, p. 455.

varying contexts.[27] Suffice it to state, however, that nationalism is an all-encompassing concept and is inadequate for foreign policy analysis for other reasons as well. First, like independence, it is closely associated more with the struggle for emancipation from colonial control than with the postindependence quest for optimization of freedom of action in the international system. Even a cursory look at the relevant literature would reveal the far more extensive concern of social scientists with the concept of nationalism before the 1950s than after, when the concept of modernization, political or economic, has received the lion's share of attention in spite of the noteworthy exception of a few who insist on the important interrelationship of modernization and nationalism.[28] One could, of course, argue that "maintenance" or "strengthening" of the nation-state would perhaps resemble the concept of autonomy, but this would still be open to serious objections, not only because these terms are too general, but also because they overlap considerably the concepts of "state building" and "nation building," customarily used in comparative politics. By now these concepts have acquired quite specific meanings. Almond and Powell, for example, suggest that state building "is primarily a matter of the differentiation of new roles, structures, and subsystems which penetrate the countryside. Nation building, on the other hand, emphasizes the cultural aspects of political development. It refers to the process whereby people transfer their commitment and loyalty from small tribes, villages, or petty principalities to the larger political system."[29]

So far I have spoken of autonomy as a key concept for the analysis of the foreign policy of developing nations. Does the concept refer to any basic underlying value? Metaphysical questions of free will or determinism aside, it is generally recognized in the theory of action that the reality of "choice" is

[27]Even those social scientists who would envisage a world of increasing interdependence are not oblivious to the pervasive force of nationalism at the present time. This speaks for the relevant concept of autonomy. Deutsch, for example, states emphatically that "*not before the vast poverty of Asia and Africa will have been reduced substantially by industrialization, and by gains in living standards and in education—not before then will the age of nationalism and national diversity see the beginning of its end*" (Karl W. Deutsch, *Nationalism and Social Communication* [Cambridge, Mass., M.I.T. Press, 1953, 1962], p. 165 [italics original]). For the first anthology of writings and documents by Asian and African nationalists with a useful introduction by the editor, see Elie Kedourie, ed., *Nationalism in Asia and Africa* (New York: World Publishing Co., 1970).

[28]See especially Dankwart A. Rustow, *A World of Nations: Problems of Political Modernization* (Washington, D.C.: Brookings Institution, 1967).

[29]See Almond and Powell, *Comparative Politics,* p. 36.

imbedded in human action, that of the individual or collectivity.[30] And it is also generally recognized in the study of domestic and international politics that leaders, rulers, or decision makers act in the name of the nation-state, although customarily one may designate the nation-state as an "actor." Given the fact that one is, in the last analysis, speaking of human choice rather than an abstraction called the "state," the choice of alternative modes, means, or ends of action is influenced by values. As such, what is the common value that developing societies seem to share in the quest for autonomy? An answer may lie in the proposition that the quest for autonomy in all developing societies is urged by the need for the construction or restoration of self-respect. In regard to the Muslim world, for example, a distinguished observer states that nationalism is primarily concerned "with foreign policy," and "independence and national prestige are more directly needed for the restoration of self-respect, collective as well as individual." He then quotes the Tunisian leader, Habib Bourguiba, to this effect: "Our young men are inspired, above all, by an immense need for personal dignity."[31] Whether it is the "charismatic" and "passionate" Nasir, the "pragmatic" Sadat, the shah of Iran, or the fiery Sukarno, the meaning of Bourguiba's words is one of those "secret fountains of action," to borrow Winston Churchill's phrase, in the foreign policy of developing nations.

Viewed in the light of the above analysis, the foreign policy of developing nations may be defined in terms of its nature. As such, foreign policy consists of efforts at optimization of freedom of action in the international system for the attainment of external objectives. The adjective *external* requires clarification because one may argue that in the observable world foreign policy decisions and actions in developing nations are frequently motivated by "internal" or "domestic" considerations. The word external in this definition does *not* imply the denial of such motivations. It simply refers to objectives rather than motivations of action. As such, external objectives not only coexist but conflict with, or reinforce, internal objectives in the allocation of resources, probably more in developing than developed societies. For this reason I shall first pay attention to conceptualizing interactions between domestic and foreign policy.

[30]See especially Clyde Kluckhohn et al., "Values and Value-Orientations in the Theory of Action," in Talcott Parsons and Edward A. Shills, eds., *Toward a Theory of Action* (New York: Harper & Row, 1951), pp. 388-433.

[31]G. E. Von Grunebaum, *Modern Islam* (Berkeley and Los Angeles: University of California Press, 1962), p. 226.

Political Modernization and Foreign Policy

The foreign policy of all nations interacts with the environment. Objectives, capabilities, strategies, instruments, techniques, tactics, style, and machinery as well as decisions, actions, and consequences of foreign policy are all involved in this interaction. Previously I spoke of "situation" rather than environment.[32] I divided it into "internal" and "external" situations and emphasized the importance of modernization as "the basic factor in the internal situation." Although the theoretical formulation was too crude and general, my consciousness of the interrelationship between the environment, both domestic and international, significantly assisted research. Since 1966 James N. Rosenau has innovatively called attention to "national-international linkages."[33] My concept of interactions is generally akin to his concept of linkage. The preceding argument and the succeeding discussion on relating the concept of autonomy to key concepts in political development would show that the linkage between the national and international system is all the more important in the study of the foreign policy of developing nations. In fact, I submit that such a linkage would help the study of political development as well. In a broad analysis of the White Revolution as a problem of political development in Iran, for example, I have attempted elsewhere to show the intimate and far-reaching interactions between Iranian foreign policy and the objectives of political development during the past half a century.[34] Both political modernization and foreign policy in developing nations could be better understood in the light of such interactions.

The really difficult question, therefore, is how to work out conceptually these important interactions. As a starting point I should like to resort to the concept of autonomy. Students of comparative politics and political development have left out of their "modernization syndrome" the intimately related concept of autonomy. In terms of its basic underlying value, it may be recalled, the concept of autonomy involves the construction or restoration of self-respect in the international community. But restoration of self-respect abroad is inextricably interrelated to redefinition of self at home. In other words, the studies of political modernization and foreign policy in developing nations are so crucially intertwined that when they are rigidly compartmentalized neither can fully benefit from the other.

If there is any validity to this argument, then the next problem is how to

---

[32] Ramazani, *Foreign Policy of Iran,* pp. 3-10.

[33] See Rosenau, *Scientific Study of Foreign Policy,* pp. 307-38.

[34] "Iran's 'White Revolution': A Study in Political Development," *International Journal of Middle East Studies* 5, no. 2 (1974), pp. 124-39.

relate political development to foreign policy conceptually. According to several leading comparativists, contemporary usages of the notions of political modernization and development could be usefully reduced to the three key concepts of *equality*, *capacity*, and *differentiation*, which are collectively called the "development syndrome," although they have also called it "modernization syndrome." They also identify five "crises" of political development. These are the crises of *identity*, *legitimacy*, *participation*, *penetration*, and *distribution*.[35] Students of the foreign policy of developing nations could adopt these three concepts along with the concept of autonomy proposed here for the purpose of conceptualizing their vital interactions. They could also juxtapose the major components, or "problems," of foreign policy analysis against those of the five major crises of the study of political development. These problems are as follows: *objectives, capabilities, strategies, instruments, styles, and foreign-policy-making processes.*[36] Students of political development find it useful, for analytical purposes, to note the interplay among the three key concepts of equality, capacity, and differentiation, between these concepts and the five crises, and among the five crises. Although these various kinds of interplay might prove of interest to foreign policy analysts in a general way, the interactions that would interest them most would fall into four major categories: First, autonomy's interactions with the three key concepts of modernization. Second, autonomy's interactions with the five crises of political development. Third, interactions of the six problems of foreign policy with the three key concepts of modernization. And fourth, interactions of six problems of foreign policy with five crises of political development.

The first category consists of the smallest, and the fourth the largest, number of interactions. In the first category autonomy interacts with equality, capa-

_____

[35] See Binder et al., *Crises and Sequences in Political Development* (Princeton: Princeton University Press, 1971).

[36] These concepts are generally known among foreign policy analysts and despite slight variations in definitions most of them are similarly understood. This is especially true of the concepts of objectives, strategies, instruments, foreign-policy-making processes and styles. The concept of capabilities, however, presents problems. In this regard I believe the best way of perceiving "capabilities" is to try to pay attention simultaneously to the efforts of the Sprouts and K. J. Holsti. In preparation of tables for this study, I have tried to do so insofar as quantifiable aspects of international capabilities are concerned. The intangible aspect of influence, on the other hand, is imbedded in the recurrence of actions and reactions discussed throughout the text. See Harold and Margaret Sprout, *Foundations of International Politics* (Princeton: Van Nostrand, 1962) and K. J. Holsti, *International Politics* and his "The Concept of Power in the Study of International Relations," in Peter A. Toma and Andrew Gyorgy, eds., *Basic Issues in International Relations* (Boston: Allyn & Bacon, 1967), pp. 105-18.

city, and differentiation, while in the fourth category each of the six foreign policy problems (objectives, capabilities, strategies, instruments, styles, and foreign-policy-making processes) interacts with each of the five political development crises (identity, legitimacy, participation, penetration, and distribution). These interactions give rise to a large number of useful questions. To cite an example from the first category, how does the quest for equality affect the drive for autonomy? To cite examples from the second category, how does each of the problems of identity, legitimacy, participation, and the like affect the quest for autonomy? How does equality, capacity, or differentiation, to cite from the third category, affect the problem of selection of objectives, strategies, or instruments or international capability? How does each of the crises of legitimacy, participation, or identity, to cite examples from the fourth category, affect each of the problems of foreign policy just mentioned?

All these and similar questions can be illustrated by a variety of examples, but a few will be drawn from this empirical analysis of the foreign policy of Iran. Did the demand for political democratization (participation) in the early 1960s influence the adoption of the policy of normalization of relations with the Soviet Union? To what extent does Iran's more active role in the Persian Gulf today reflect the inability of the shah's regime to respond to the demand for political participation? To what extent does this international activity stem from a spectacular rise in the level of economic development? To view these questions from the standpoint of political development, how does the unprecedented increase in Iran's military capability for the avowed purpose of defense affect the quest for economic development and participation? To cite examples from other Middle Eastern nations, how true is the proposition that the emergent active policy of Iraq in the Persian Gulf reflects the problem of national identity (in terms of the continuing Kurdish problem) or political stability (in view of repeated coups since the 1958 revolution)?

Foreign Policy and International System

Enough has been said to show the importance of conceptualizing the interplay between activities directed toward the domestic environment (political modernization) and those coexisting, and at times competing with, or reinforcing, activities directed toward the international environment (the international system). We need not dwell so much on interaction between the activities originating outside the domestic environment and the foreign policy of developing nations. Professor Rosenau's six subenvironments could prove quite useful.[37] These six subenvironments could be easily interrelated to the six

---

[37] The six subenvironments are: contiguous, regional, cold war, racial, resource, and organizational. I believe that greater emphasis on the dynamic nature of these subenvironments may prove helpful. For example, it would appear useful either to add another

problems of foreign policy identified above for purposes of greater specificity and research utility. The juxtaposition of these problems vis-à-vis the six subenvironments would produce thirty-six interplays. For example, what is the impact of the "contiguous environment" on objectives, capabilities, strategies, or style of a given nation's foreign policy? The same kinds of questions could be asked about interactions between each of the other subenvironments and each of the components of foreign policy.

A few examples may be cited for illustration from this study. Iran has provided, at times, a classical example of a "penetrated political system."[38] My previous study of the foreign policy of Iran shows how immediately in the aftermath of the Constitutional Revolution the British and Russian policymakers participated, for all practical purposes, in the decision-making process. This study reveals how great powers at times participated for all practical purposes in Iran's decision-making process both with and without its approval. This does not mean that the Iranian polity is, or has always been, "penetrated," but the environmental element has often ranked high in its foreign policy largely through various nondiplomatic missions and embassies.

The single most important subenvironment of concern to Iran has been the character of East-West relationships. Iran has, in empirical terms, *reacted* repeatedly to this subenvironment by pursuing varying strategies. For example, it favored a third power, such as the United States, between 1941 and 1951, and Germany in the interwar period, primarily as a means of counterbalancing pressures from the Soviet Union. It has also allied itself with the West since

subenvironment, called simply "détente," or perhaps more appropriately substitute "East-West" for the "cold war" subenvironment because it would include cold war, détente, or any other pattern of the state of East-West relations. See Rosenau, *Scientific Study of Foreign Policy,* pp. 335-38.

[38]The concept of the "penetrated political system" is suggested in a nonevaluative sense by Rosenau and can refer to an authoritarian or democratic, dynamic or static, and modern or primitive system. It is defined as follows: *A penetrated political system is one in which nonmembers of a national society participate directly and authoritatively, through actions taken jointly with the society's members, in either the allocation of its values or the mobilization of support on behalf of its goals"* (*Scientific Study of Foreign Policy,* pp. 95-149 [italics original]). Rosenau's ranking of five sets of variables, namely *"individual," "role," "governmental," "social,"* and *"systemic,"* in regard to small and underdeveloped economies could greatly aid analysis of the foreign policy of modernizing nations. Iran, for example, has oscillated between a penetrated and a nonpenetrated system ever since its rise to power at the turn of the sixteenth century as can be seen from my empirical analysis of its foreign policy from 1941 to 1973 in this study, and from 1500 to 1941 in *The Foreign Policy of Iran.* The "relative potencies" of the individual and systemic variables have accordingly oscillated from one period of Iran's history of foreign policy to another. It may be proposed, in the light of the empirical analysis of its "independent national policy" since the early 1960s in this study, that by the early 1970s the individual variables outweighed the systemic ones.

1955 principally as a counterbalance to Soviet pressures and enticements. One of the most interesting aspects of contemporary Iranian foreign policy has been the convergence of the East-West subenvironment and the "contiguous" subenvironment as a result of the Soviet Union's extensive boundaries with Iran. The same could be said, for example, about Afghanistan and Turkey. Since the British decision of 1968 to withdraw forces from the Persian Gulf, the "regional" subenvironment has gained prominence for Iran not only because of the activities emanating from other gulf powers, but also because of the convergence of the East-West and regional subenvironments. The same could be said about all other Persian Gulf states, such as Saudi Arabia, Iraq, and Kuwait. On this basis one may hypothesize that the more the convergence of subenvironments, the greater the complexity of coping with the international system.

A Plea for Historical Context

In concluding this discussion, I should point out that this kind of conceptualization could assist foreign policy analysts in a number of ways. The conceptual allowance for interactions between the activities directed toward political development and foreign policy, on the one hand, and between activities in the international environment and foreign policy, on the other, would facilitate research in attempts at examining the sources of foreign policy, the contents of decisions and actions, the consequences of these and their effectiveness, and the development of foreign policy. This is all based on the important assumption that the study of these interactions requires research *over a span of time*. Given the different cultural and historical experiences of developing societies, the analysis of their foreign policy could benefit considerably from a greater consciousness of the historical context. For example, study of the "*development* of foreign policy" would suffer considerably without observing patterns of foreign policy over a long span of time. As stated at the outset, the very concept of foreign policy is alien and new to developing societies. As such, the study of continuity and change in patterns of components of foreign policy would especially interest researchers. In acknowledging such a special interest in the historical context, one would not need to imply that it is inevitable that the foreign policy of developing nations will, or ought to, change from traditional to modern patterns either because this kind of typology is adopted or because it is assumed that it is a historical necessity. According to James S. Coleman both the "historical" and the "typological" approaches are vulnerable to criticism because they exaggerate aspects of traditionality, imply irreversibility of movement from traditionality to modernity, and suggest an "ethnocentric, Western-parochial normative bias." But the "evolutionary perspective" allegedly frees observers from these shortcomings because it views the development process as "interminable and indeterminate."[39]

Whether any observer can escape his values totally is, of course, an open question, but this contentious point need not detain us here. What should be emphasized is that the study of the foreign policy of developing nations at this stage of our conceptual and empirical poverty could gain a great deal from attempting to combine analytical and empirical approaches within a loose and general chronological context. This suggestion, of course, runs counter to the current prejudice among some social scientists that when a work is cast in any kind of chronological context, it is by definition of little interest to theorists. The real question is whether a given empirical analysis is of such a nature that can produce useful generalizations for purposes of advancing hypotheses by theorists. One of the useful tasks that foreign policy analysts of developing societies can perform is to study continuity and change with a view to suggesting features observable in the foreign policy of developing nations. A few of these are set forth below.

Major Characteristics of Modernizing Foreign Policy

The quest for autonomy in developing nations seems closely associated with efforts made in acquiring a relatively more *active, responsive, diverse, congruent, complex,* and *effective* foreign policy. *Active* refers to patterns of persistent efforts directed at seeking to take initiative in the international system. These efforts are only in part reflected in establishing new bilateral ties with other nations. They are also reflected increasingly in establishing, or participating in, various regional and international organizations and groupings and creating ventures with foreign corporations. Since participation in international organizations is too obvious to require elaboration, note, for example, the creation of the Regional Cooperation Development (RCD) by Iran, Turkey, and Pakistan, and Iranian and Indian joint ventures with foreign oil companies. International and regional organizations, however, are often perceived, in spite of the rhetoric, more as a means of playing an active role in the world arena than engaging in efforts directed at supranational, regional, or worldwide community building.

Responsive refers to increasing recognition of need for international capabilities generally as a means of influencing the activities of other nations in the international system. More particularly, however, these activities are limited to regional subsystems, such as the Persian Gulf and the subcontinent or the Maghrib (North Africa). Few actions in developing nations, however,

[39] James S. Coleman, "The Development Syndrome," in Binder et al., pp. 73-100.

are taken purely for external ends, including regional objectives. Many foreign policy decisions and actions aim at the fulfillment of domestic objectives. Division and specialization of roles in foreign and domestic spheres of activity is increasing, however. Increase in international military capabilities, for example, is nevertheless still sought as a two-edged sword of insuring domestic political control as well as the optimization of freedom of action in the international system. Responsiveness also refers to an increase in alertness to foreign opportunities as a result of improvement in various governmental functions such as what the Sprouts call the "information-providing function," or intelligence.[40]

Diverse refers to efforts aimed at modifying, diversifying, or even disrupting the old ties with former colonial powers, foreign companies, and international organizations. Note, for example, Indonesia's withdrawal from the United Nations, nationalization of the oil industry by Iran (1951), Iraq, Libya, and the like, or Chilean, Peruvian, and Cuban expropriations. Ties with foreign corporations are either totally disrupted, such as the Iraqi nationalization of IPC; significantly modified, such as the Iranian discontinuation of the operations of the consortium along with the continuation of oil sales to it; or replaced by other foreign interests, such as the Soviet interest in Iraqi oil, which in fact replaced Western operations. When applied to foreign corporate interests, diversification could mean either removing the so-called vestiges of imperialism, or introducing such modifications in the established interests that would optimize national freedom of action, especially in vital industries. The catchword among most Arab oil-producing nations today is "participation," and the plan is to reduce the control of foreign oil companies to less than 50 percent by the 1980s, if not sooner.

Congruent refers to greater correspondence between the ends and means of policy. The notion itself is new, but the increasing interest in selection of more "realistic" objectives and more "pragmatic" policies is generated by either (1) the imperative of interaction with the international system or subsystem; (2) the increase in domestic capacity and "differentiation;" or (3) the conjunction of both. Note, for example, the retreat of the Arab states from an initial position of a rigid oil embargo in 1973 to a more flexible posture under considerable international pressure. To cite another example, Iran's more "pragmatic" policies in the Persian Gulf reflect both the change in the subsystem as the result of the British departure and Iran's own increasing domestic capacity and international capabilities since the early 1960s.

Complex refers to multiplication of functions vis-a-vis other nations, international and regional organizations, and foreign private or public corporations.

[40] See Sprout, pp. 136-77.

Functions extend far beyond diplomatic exchanges; they encompass trans-actions related to complicated military, political, economic, legal, and technical activities through receiving or sending missions, experts, delegations, observers, and the like. The more obvious such functions are performed by developing nations at regional and international conferences. Most developing nations also have to cope with a variety of foreign missions they receive, and a few, such as Iran, Egypt, and India send their own aid missions abroad.

Effective refers to stable and continuous patterns of formulating and implementing foreign policy decisions and actions. The rise of the urban middle class and the increase in number and quality of "technocrats" is paralleled by the incorporation of skill and talents into the foreign policy making process. Positions, most particularly at the level of implementation rather than formulation of policy, are increasingly filled by career diplomats. The control of foreign policy by the political elite varies considerably, but the influence of an individual leader is often observable, as in Nehru's India, Nasir's Egypt, and the shah's Iran. The shah is the supreme decision maker in both domestic and foreign affairs, but in the latter he is less impeded by domestic pressures. The increase in international capabilities does gradually involve *indirect* input by the nonelite even at the inception of foreign policy. In highly technical matters the initiating role of the technocrats becomes particularly visible. Parliamentary control of foreign policy is the rare exception, and where it does exist the speed of decision and action diminishes considerably. Parliamentary bodies act more as arms of political elites. As such they do perform important roles in postponing, criticizing, reneging on, modifying, and even rejecting foreign policy proposals on which the elite does not itself wish to take a public stand. The Iranian Parliament was useful to the political elite in all these respects from 1925 to 1940 and from 1954 to 1973.

Part One

Third-Power Strategy

I
Aborted Neutrality and Resurgence
of Interest in the United States

AFTER THE OUTBREAK of the Second World War Iran formally adopted a policy of neutrality, but the vicissitudes of European power politics produced serious strains on that policy, leading eventually to the Anglo-Soviet invasion of Iran August 25, 1941. The first signs of serious strains became visible after the Russo-German and Russo-Estonian treaties, particularly the Pact of Mutual Assistance between the Soviet Union and Germany signed September 28, 1939. Ever since 1927, when the American advisers withdrew from Iran, Riza Shah had cultivated the involvement of Germany instead of the United States, partly as a counterbalance against the traditional rivalry of Great Britain and Russia. Hence, the German friendship with Iran's traditional bête noire, Russia, was resented, and the developments in Europe at the time exacerbated Iranian apprehensions. The partition of Poland and the virtual loss of independence of the Baltic States created fear that the Soviets would next turn their attention to the Black Sea and the Caspian Sea and that crucial days were ahead for Iran.[1]

Iran's own relations with the Soviet Union caused no less concern during the Nazi-Soviet entente. The outbreak of the war aggravated Iran's traditional transit problem over Soviet territory as transportation was then possible only by way of Russia. By 1939 Germany had become Iran's main trade partner, and Iran tried to persuade Germany to assist Iran's attempts at solving its transit problem with the Soviet Union. In a German-Soviet trade agreement signed February 11, 1940, Russia promised, among other things, to facilitate the transport of goods to Germany from Iran, and on March 25, 1940, Iran and the Soviet Union signed the most comprehensive treaty of commerce and navigation between the two countries to that date.[2] Although this treaty was hailed "as a pleasant surprise and as a welcome sign of definite easing of tensions," it was generally believed that certain promises had been made in

---

[1] U.S., Department of State, *Foreign Relations of the United States, 1940*, Diplomatic Papers, vol. 3, *The British Commonwealth, the Soviet Union, The Near East and Africa* (Washington, D.C.: Government Printing Office, 1958), p. 621 (hereafter cited as *Foreign Relations of U.S.*).

[2] For details see my *Foreign Policy of Iran*, pp. 223-28.

return by the Iranian government, such as the release of "Communist prisoners." Subsequent events indicated that such prisoners were not, in fact, freed until after the Anglo-Russian invasion in 1941. It seemed "practically certain," however, at the time, that the Iranian government had been "obliged to put several flying fields at the disposal of the Soviets." No such promise was included in the treaty mentioned above as it would have been in open contradiction of the Iranian policy of neutrality, but there is little doubt that the Soviet Union was increasing pressures on Iran, and Germany was inciting the Soviets "to adopt greater aggressive policy toward Iran and Afghanistan in the hope of weakening and perhaps eliminating British influence." [3]

Iran's alarm at the implications of Soviet-German rapprochement for its policy of neutrality was further intensified at the time of Molotov's visit to Berlin November 12-13, 1940. Something "near panic swept the country when Molotov's visit to Berlin was accompanied by rumors that, in return for a free hand in the Dardanelles, Germany was offering Russia an equally free hand in Iran."[4] The Iranian prime minister, 'Ali Mansur, took up the matter with the German ambassador, who replied that he knew nothing regarding the conversations in Berlin about Iran. Iranian officials made similar inquiries in Berlin, but were told by Freiherr von Weizsacker, state secretary of the German Foreign Ministry, that he knew of no such bargain about Iran, attributed the rumors to "English intrigues," and instructed the German ambassador to say as much to the Iranian government. Parenthetically, the subsequent capture and publication of an undated secret protocol related to the Four-Power Pact drawn up in Berlin between Hitler and Molotov revealed that the rumors were not without foundation. In this now well-known instrument Germany had conceded that "the area south of Baku in the general direction of the Persian Gulf is recognized as the center of the aspirations of the Soviet Union."[5] Even before Molotov's visit to Berlin it had become "reasonably certain" that the Soviet government had formulated definite demands, including the cession, or at least occupation by Soviet troops, of northern Azerbaijan (including Tabriz) and portions of Gilan and Gorgan, control of the trans-Iranian railway to the Persian Gulf, and use of all Iranian landing fields.[6]

---

[3]*Foreign Relations of U.S., 1940*, D.P., 3: 629, 630, 631.

[4]*Economist*, Jan. 11, 1941. See also U.S., Department of State, *Documents on German Foreign Policy, 1918-1945*, Series D (Washington, D.C.: Government Printing Office, 1962), 12: 531-32.

[5]The text is in J. C. Hurewitz, *Diplomacy in the Near and Middle East* (Princeton: Van Nostrand, 1956), 2: 228-31.

[6]*Foreign Relations of U.S., 1940*, D.P., 3: 634.

Strains on Neutrality

In spite of the strains of the Nazi-Soviet rapprochement on Iran's policy of neutrality, its pursuance seemed tenable until the German invasion of Russia June 22, 1941. The Soviet Union did not oppose Iran's policy; Germany actively supported it, and the British objections to the presence of a large number of Germans in Iran were not pressed too seriously. But once British troops entered Baghdad toward the end of May and the pro-German Iraqi prime minister, Rashid 'Ali, escaped into Iran, the British believed that the center of diplomatic activity in the Middle East had shifted to Iran, where pro-Axis sentiment in the area would be fomented.[7] More important, the German invasion of Russia and the common cause of Great Britain and the Soviet Union against Germany posed a serious challenge to Iran's policy of neutrality because then the Soviet Union as well as Great Britain opposed the presence of a large number of Germans in Iran. Iran's response to this momentous and swift change in external circumstances between June 22, 1940, and August 25, 1941, followed two major lines, both in determined pursuance of the policy of neutrality. I shall consider these separately.

In the wake of the German invasion of Russia, German activities in, and joint Soviet-British pressures on, Iran increased while Iran persistently claimed a policy of strict neutrality. From the beginning of the German-Russian war, German activities increased, particularly among White Russians, Armenians, and disaffected elements in the north. It was known in July 1941 that storm troopers Roman Gamotta and Franz Mayer, ostensibly in the employ of Shenkers Transport Company, headed an efficient Nazi party organization with branches throughout the country and with members strategically placed, although it was believed by some that the size and strength of the German fifth column had been exaggerated. The Iranian prime minister placed the number of Germans in Iran at seven hundred, the British at two to three thousand. Both Britain and Russia required expulsion from Iran of 80 percent of the Germans by August 1941, but the Iranian prime minister, 'Ali Mansur, informed the two powers that he could not accede to their demand, although he would expel any German national for engaging in "illegal activities." On August 16, 1941, the Soviet Union and Great Britain delivered parallel notes to the Iranian government, expressing dissatisfaction with Iran's failure to heed their previous warnings of the danger to Iran from Germans residing there and nonadherence to Anglo-Russian demands for the expulsion of a large number of Germans. The Soviet-British representatives also told Iran orally

[7] *Economist*, Aug. 2, 1941.

that about four-fifths of all the Germans should be expelled by the end of August, and certainly not later than the middle of September.[8]

Iran's overall response to the Anglo-Russian demands was essentially dilatory. By the middle of August 1941 the American minister in Iran, Dreyfus, believed, on the basis of "reliable facts," that (1) there were between two thousand and twenty-five hundred Germans in Iran, seven hundred of whom were in the employ of the Iranian government; (2) fifth column activities were directed from the German legation; (3) two of the German leaders were storm troopers Mayer and Gamotta; (4) propaganda was largely directed by Eilers, a German archaeologist; (5) Germans were strategically placed in the radio station, railway, and other public services; and (6) they were scattered throughout the country as agents of commercial organizations, such as Shenkers and Ferrostahl.[9] In response to the British note Iran's acting minister of foreign affairs, Javad Ameri stated to the British minister in Tehran that (1) the number of German residents in Iran was not so great as pretended; (2) it scarcely touched the figure seven hundred; (3) the Iranian government was sure they could not foment any fifth column activities; (4) Iran was reducing the number of foreign specialists in its employ anyway; and (5) the Iranian government believed that the expulsion of Germans from Iran without any logical reason was against the neutrality of the country.[10] Iran's defiant attitude toward the Soviet and British notes was further revealed in the remarks of its ambassador to the American ambassador in Moscow on August 23, 1941. He stated that Iran had flatly rejected the demand for the expulsion of the Germans because the subject was "distinctly the internal affair of the Iranian Government and that the demand constituted an infringement of the Sovereignty of Iran." He also added, in part, that (1) Iran would defend itself as best as it could against any attempted violation of its sovereignty by either the Soviet Union or Britain or both; and (2) the Soviet-British demand for the expulsion of all Germans was a pretext for occupying Iran inasmuch as the expulsion of all Germans, and transit rights through Iran if desired, "could

---

[8] U. S., Department of State, *Foreign Relations of the United States, 1941, Diplomatic Papers,* vol. 3, *The British Commonwealth, the Near East and Africa* (Washington, D.C.: Government Printing Office, 1959), pp. 383-97.

[9] Ibid., p. 402. For subsequent revelations about the German activities in Iran, see B. Shulze-Holthus (a German agent in Iran), *Daybreak in Iran* (London: Staples Press, 1954). For a well-known Iranian account see the articles of Ahmad Namdar, the Iranian secretary of the German embassy, in *Khandaniha,* Seventh Year, no. 4, pp. 12-15, 20; no. 5, pp. 10-11, 20-21; no. 9, pp. 18-20; no. 13, pp. 7-10; no. 16, pp. 7-8; no. 19, pp. 10, 20; no. 21, pp. 10-11; no. 23, pp. 14-15.

[10] *Foreign Relations of U.S., 1941,* D.P., 3:405.

have been amicably discussed and arranged" without offending the *amour propre* of the Iranian government and people. [11]

Iran's insistence on its policy of neutrality, however, was not confined to the defiance of the Soviet-British representations. The second course of action pursued by Iran was the search for sympathy, mediation, and even intervention by the United States in support of Iranian resistance to Soviet-British pressures. On August 11, 1941, the Iranian minister in Washington, Shayesteh, called at the State Department upon the chief of the Division of Near Eastern Affairs, Murray, declaring that (1) present developments had an ominous resemblance both to the situation leading up to the partition of Iran in 1907 between Czarist Russia and Great Britain and to the disregard of Iran's neutrality in the First World War by the same two countries; (2) Iran might become a victim of Anglo-Soviet aggression; and (3) in such an eventuality his country would expect to receive moral support and even material assistance from the United States. When he was asked whether he believed the shah would consent to a request from either Great Britain or Russia for the passage of troops across Iranian territory, he said, "The Shah's pride and character was such that he would be incapable of accepting any such demand, even though a refusal might mean disastrous defeat." But when asked if Iran would allow the passage of arms and munitions, he said he was unable to answer that question. Later, on August 19, 1941, when he was asked the same question regarding the passage of arms and munitions, he pointed out that the Iranian railway was not equipped to carry heavy arms such as tanks and the like. In writing to the secretary of state on the same day, the American minister in Tehran stated: "I gained the distinct impression in a long conversation yesterday with the Foreign Minister [of Iran] that the Iranians are temporizing and parrying without realizing the seriousness of their situation. Unless they abandon their search for a magic formula and face immediately the realities of the situation they will perhaps within the next few days find it is too late."[12]

In his repeated visits to the Department of State, the Iranian minister reiterated Iran's historical predicament vis-à-vis Great Britain and Russia in support of Iran's policy of neutrality. In his call on the secretary of state, Cordell Hull, on August 22, 1941, only three days before the Anglo-Russian invasion, he asked the secretary hypothetically about the attitude of the United States in case of such an invasion. He was told politely that no one could tell when or just where such invasion would finally develop and that the American government could not define any new policy, in a contingent way, upon a purely theoretical military situation. Secretary Hull tried to impress

[11] Ibid., pp. 412-13.
[12] Ibid., pp. 394-404.

upon the minister that the Germans had no respect for neutrality, but the minister repeatedly talked as though his country would fight if the British undertook by force to occupy it for any purpose. Although the minister did not press further for a promise on the part of the United States to intercede, he concluded by saying that if the United States would say but one word to the British they would not invade Iran. Minister Shayesteh's failure to persuade Secretary Hull to promise American intervention was followed by the shah's own belated and desperate appeal to President Roosevelt at the start of the Anglo-Russian invasion on August 25, 1941, to interest himself in this incident, which brought into war "a neutral and pacific country which had no other care than the safeguarding of tranquility and the reform of the country."[13]

Anglo-Russian Invasion

The Anglo-Russian campaign against Iran for opening, according to Winston Churchill, "the fullest communication with Russia" through Iranian territory was launched at dawn on August 25, 1941. The British, under the command of Wavell, who was directing the operations from Simla in India, made their first major landing at Bandar Mashur (presently Bandar Mah Shahr), deploying 3,000 troops striking into the interior of Iran at three points along a six hundred-mile front from the Persian Gulf to the Turkish frontier. Two other columns struck into Iran from British-controlled Iraq—from Rawanduz, twenty miles south of the Iraqi-Irano-Turkish border junction, and from Khanqin, about eighty miles northwest of Baghdad. The Russian forces struck in three areas, in the northwest, pushing toward Tabriz and Pahlavi, and in the northeast, advancing toward Meshed.

By the time of the Allied invasion Iran had ordered some one hundred and twenty thousand troops to stand guard against attack. Two divisions were located at the capital and the others in strategic areas such as Tabriz, Rizaiyih, Kurdistan, Khuzistan, Khorasan, Gilan, Kermanshah, and Ardabil. There were also five independent brigades, plus an infantry regiment, an artillery regiment, a few antiaircraft guns, two hundred to three hundred planes, and a few escort vessels. The suddenness of the invasion, characterized as "somewhat abrupt steps"[14] by Winston Churchill, the poor preparation of the Iranian forces, and the unrestrained Soviet bombing of various Iranian cities in Azerbaijan and Gilan caused utter confusion, fear, and even desertion among

[13]Ibid., pp. 406-19.

[14]This characterization was made in a review of the war in the House of Commons. See the *New York Times*, Oct. 1, 1941.

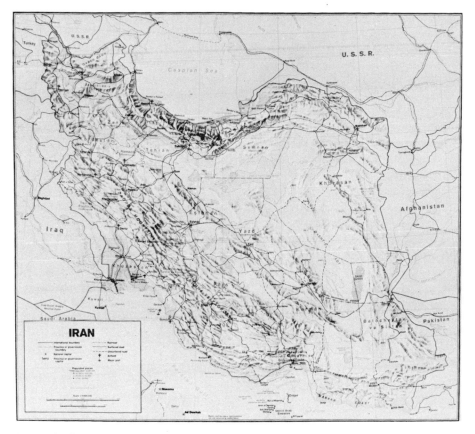

Iran. U.S., Central Intelligence Agency, Washington, D.C.: Government Printing Office,
March 1973.

Iranian officers.[15] The Iranian forces in the path of the British advance to Kermanshah were caught unaware while asleep in their barracks, but those defending Abadan, under the command of General Shahbakhti, proved to be the main exception in the general breakdown of army morale. According to an official British account, at the Abadan refinery the loyalty of Iranian soldiers was "strikingly demonstrated at the pumping stations, where Persian soldiers who had a post on the roof resisted with the highest bravery and a duel of fire went on for four hours before they were dislodged."[16]

In spite of such isolated shows of bravery, however, within forty-eight hours after the invasion, the Iranian military staff realized the impossibility of resisting the Allied forces. On August 27, in a detailed report to the shah, General Zarghami set forth the fate of the Iranian forces on all fronts, and simultaneously the cabinet of 'Ali Mansur resigned. On August 28 the new prime minister, Muhammad 'Ali Foroughi, introduced his cabinet to the Twelfth Majlis.[17] During this extraordinary session of the Majlis, Premier Foroughi announced Iran's cease-fire decision on the basis of the recommendations of the "High National Council" (*Shura-ye Ali-ye Kishvar*), which stated that "whereas the strategic areas of defense were already occupied by foreign troops and because the defense of the capital by the first and second divisions will probably fail to serve any purpose it would probably be more beneficial to order a cease-fire and to continue with the diplomatic negotiations already in progress."[18]

The Allied invasion presented Iran with a newer and more far-reaching problem vis-à-vis Great Britain and Russia. Before the invasion Iran had tried to resist first the British and, after the German invasion of Russia, the Anglo-

---

[15] For detailed accounts of the breakdown of the morale of the Iranian army, the charges against individual officers, and the discredit that fell on the army in general, see Muhammad Riza Khalili 'Araqi, *Vaqay'a-i Shahrivar* (Tehran: Zarbakhsh, n.d.) vol. 2.

[16] Great Britain, Central Office of Information, *Paiforce: The Official Story of the Persia and Iraq Command, 1941-1946* (London: H. M. Stationery Office, 1948), p. 64.

[17] Muhammad 'Ali Foroughi, known as Zaka al-Mulk, was the son of Mirza Muhammad Husain Isfihani, a well-known Iranian scholar and literary figure. Muhammad 'Ali Foroughi was born in 1878/79 (1257 of the Iranian calendar) in Iran; for many years he was a deputy in the Majlis and served his country as ambassador to various countries. His appointment as prime minister in 1941 was ended in 1942 with his resignation. He was subsequently appointed the minister of the court, and died shortly thereafter. Nowadays he is remembered in Iran for his masterful part in the negotiations of the Tripartite Treaty of 1942, as will be seen in the following chapter, but according to those who knew him at the time, he was one of the very few Iranian statesmen who believed in the ultimate defeat of Germany from the very outset of the Second World War. He is also renowned in Iran for his literary and scholarly work.

[18] For the text see 'Araqi, p. 387.

Russian demands for the expulsion of German agents in Iran. While these demands continued, as will be seen, Iran now faced the fact of the Anglo-Russian occupation of its territory. In trying to cope with these two problems from August 25, 1941, to the signing of the treaty of alliance with Great Britain and the Soviet Union on January 29, 1942, Iran pursued two major courses of action. On the one hand, it engaged in negotiations with the British and Soviet representatives, and, on the other, it continued to seek the intervention of the United States as a counterbalance against the joint Anglo-Soviet presence on its territory.

On the day of the Anglo-Russian invasion, Iran was given two separate notes by the Allied powers. The statement of the British Foreign Office reminded Iran that during the past months the British government had repeatedly warned the Iranian government of the potential dangers of an excessively large German colony in Iran; pointed out that in Iran, as in other neutral countries, Germany had pursued a policy of infiltration that could not fail to constitute a serious danger to Iranian neutrality, to the British interests, to India, to Iraq, and to Soviet Russia; reiterated the formal and emphatic representations of Sir Reader Bullard and the Soviet ambassador of August 16 that the German community in Iran should leave without further delay; and concluded that since friendly representations had served no useful purpose, Great Britian and the Soviet Union decided to have recourse to "other measures to safeguard their essential interests." [19]

The note of the People's Commissariat for Foreign Affairs of the USSR of the same date, August 25, was more detailed than the British one. It referred to historical examples of Soviet friendship for Iran, such as its notes of January 14, 1918, and June 26, 1919, its treaty of February 26, 1921, and a number of other instruments on fisheries, water utilization, and trade concluded with Iran in the interwar period; it dwelt at large on the nature and extent of German penetration in Iran and singled out such agents as Von Radanovich, Gamotta, Mayer, Wilhelm Sapow, Gustav Bohr, Heinrich Kellinger, and Trappe, all of whom allegedly organized "terrorist groups to be smuggled into Soviet Azerbaijan—above all into the principal Soviet oil district of Baku—and into Soviet Turkmenistan" and prepared also "for a military coup in Iran"; it referred to its notes of June 26, July 19, and August 16, 1941, calling Iran's attention to the activities of German agents; and stated in conclusion that since Iran had refused to take the necessary measures against the German agents, the Soviet government "found itself obliged to take the necessary measures and immediately to exercise the right belonging to the

---

[19] For the full text see Leland M. Goodrich and Marie J. Caroll, eds., *Documents on American Foreign Relations* (Boston: World Peace Foundation, 1942) 4:674-76.

Soviet Union under article 6 of the treaty of 1921 of temporarily sending its troops into Iranian territory in the interests of self-defense."[20]

In the Iranian perspective the important point in the two notes was the stated assurances of the Allied powers regarding Iran's "independence and territorial integrity." The British note stated: "These measures will in no way be directed against the Iranian people: His Majesty's Government have no designs against the independence and territorial integrity of Iran, and any measures they may take will be directed solely against the attempts of the Axis Powers to establish their control of Iran."[21] In light of the subsequent events, it is interesting to note that the Soviet statement, in addition to a sentence identical to that in the British note just quoted, declared: "As soon as this danger threatening the interests of Iran and of the U.S.S.R. has been removed, the Soviet Government, in discharging of its obligation under the Soviet-Iranian Treaty of 1921, will at once withdraw the Soviet troops from the confines of Iran." [22]

Yet given the historic divergence of Iran's interpretation of article 6 of the 1921 treaty from that of the Soviet Union, its invocation in justification of Soviet military action was not forcefully rejected by Iran.[23] Muhammad Sa'id, Iran's plenipotentiary ambassador to Moscow, took the view that article 6 presented "in principle a guarantee of the territorial inviolability of Iran"; characterized the Soviet representations of June 26, July 19, and August 16 not in conformity with diplomatic custom governing the relations of sovereign states; expressed the personal belief that on September 15 the Germans considered dangerous by the Soviet Union would have left Iran; regretted that the Soviet government had not awaited the result of the Iranian action taken as a neutral power; requested a stop to the advance of Soviet troops; and

[20] For the text of the Soviet note, see ibid., pp. 676-81.

[21] Ibid., p. 676.

[22] Ibid., p. 681.

[23] Article 6 of the treaty of 1921 provides: "If a third party should attempt to carry out a policy of usurpation by means of armed intervention in Persia, or if such power should desire to use Persian territory as a base of operations against Russia, or if a foreign Power should threaten the frontiers of Federal Russia or those of its allies, and if the Persian Government should not be able to put a stop to such menace after having been once called upon to do so by Russia, Russia shall have the right to advance her troops into the Persian interior for the purpose of carrying out the military operations necessary for its defence. Russia undertakes, however, to withdraw her troops from Persian territory as soon as the danger has been removed."

For a discussion of the divergent Iranian and Soviet interpretations of this article, see Ramazani, *Foreign Policy of Iran,* pp. 234-40.

suggested, in return for Iran's expulsion of Germans, the recall of the Red Army to the Soviet frontier.[24]

On August 30, 1941, Great Britain and Russia handed separate notes to the Iranian government setting forth a number of demands and assurances.[25] The British note, however, was more like an Anglo-Russian joint note as it raised points of concern to both powers. It reiterated at the outset that (1) the Allied powers had no designs against the independence and territorial integrity of Iran; (2) they had been compelled to take military actions because Iran had not paid attention to their friendly representations; and (3) their operations were aimed against the threat of possible German action. It then stated that now, when Iran was prepared to fulfill the Allied "just demands" (*taqazaha-ye adilanih*), it must order its troops to retreat, without resistance, from the north and east of a line, stretching from Khanqin-Kermanshah-Khoramabad-Masjid-e Sulaiman-Haftgel-Gachesaran to Bandar Daylam on the Persian Gulf. In the north the Iranian forces must retreat from the following points: Ushnu-Haidarabad-Miandoab-Zanjan-Qazvin-Khoramabad-Babol-Zirab-Semnan-Shahroud-Aliabad. The British note also demanded that Iran expel within one week all German nationals except the "genuine personnel" of the German embassy and a few technicians other than those in military and communication centers and provide a list of those mentioned to the Allied diplomatic representatives. Iran also had to undertake to remain neutral and not commit any act contrary to the Allied interests in the struggle against German aggression.

The Allied powers also demanded that Iran undertake to facilitate the transport of "such materials" (war materials) by road, railway, and air; in return the Allied powers would agree to the following: (1) continued payment of oil royalties (obviously by the British); (2) facilitation of economic materials needed by Iran; and (3) halting further advance by the Allied forces and their withdrawal "as soon as the military situation would allow."[26]

The Soviet note of the same date (August 30, 1941) differed from the

---

[24]For an English Translation of the text of Sa'id's note, see *Foreign Relations of U.S., 1941*, D.P., 3:429-31.

[25]For the full texts of these notes, see Husain Kuhi Kirmani, *Az Shahrivar 1320 ta Faj'ih-ye Azarbaijan va Zanjan* (Tehran: Mazahiri, n.d.), 1:91-93. This source is mostly a collection of documents concerning Iran during the wartime period, although it does not appear so from the title. It contains numerous documents not available elsewhere in English. Professor George Lenczowski's summary of these notes in English is useful (*Russia and the West in Iran, 1918-1948* [Ithaca, N.Y.: Cornell University Press, 1949], pp. 170-73), but I have relied on the Persian texts in order to report a more detailed account.

[26]Kirmani, 1:91-93.

British note in a number of ways. Regarding the transportation of materials, it clearly specified "war materials" destined for the Soviet Union; regarding the list of German citizens it specified that it should contain those German personnel who would remain in Iran; and regarding the continuation of Iran's neutrality, it added that Iran must not allow entry of German citizens into Iran in the future. More important, it differed from the British note on the following points: (1) Iran was required to facilitate the expansion of oil operations at Kavir Khorian, "according to Irano-Soviet agreement," and the fisheries operations in the Caspian Sea," according to the Soviet-Iranian fisheries agreement,"[27] (2) the Soviet government agreed to continue the payment of fisheries royalties according to the October 1, 1927, agreement.

Iran's reply of September 1, 1941, first referred to the British and Russian assurances, stating firmly that "it will take formal note of their official statement, and will expect, that no harm will come from their measures to Iran's political independence and territorial integrity as the two governments have explicitly promised." [28] The Iranian note then made the following major points:

1. Iran in principle would agree to the retreat of its forces for the duration of the war from the areas mentioned in the Allied notes but would request that the cities of Khoramabad and Dizful in the south and Qazvin, Semnan, and Shahroud in the north be excluded from the occupation zones.

2. The food, housing, and other needs of the Allied forces, wherever they happened to reside in Iran, would be met by their own governments, and whatever had to be acquired locally must be done according to the country's regulations, and without causing hardship.

3. The Allied governments would order their forces to have as little contact as possible with local people in order to avoid unpleasant incidents.

4. Iran would accept the Allied request regarding the Germans in Iran but would take measures to insure their safe passage through the areas occupied by the Allied forces.

5. Iran would accept the request to facilitate the transport of Allied war materials as far as possible and in a manner that would not cause hardship for the Iranian government and people.

6. No difficulty could exist in barring the entry of German nationals into Iran, but obviously this condition would obtain only during the course of hostilities between the Allied powers and Germany.

7. In regard to the fisheries the operations would continue under the

---

[27] Ibid., pp. 92-93.

[28] For the full text of the Iranian note, see ibid., pp. 93-99.

existing agreement, but with respect to the Kavir Khorian oil field no concession on it was included in the Soviet-Iranian treaty (that is, the 1921 treaty); and no other agreement was intended, because no action had been taken over a number of years; it had been abandoned. "Therefore the Iranian Government would be willing to enter into negotiations concerning the conclusion of an agreement on Kavir Khorian oil for mutual benefit."[29]

8. Iran understood that in giving assurances on economic aid, the Allied powers, among other things, certainly intended favorable measures to expedite the transport of Iranian goods now held up in their territories and dominions destined for Iran.

9. Concerning the explicit assurances of both governments that the advance of British and Soviet forces would be halted and that these forces would be withdrawing from Iranian territory as soon as the conditions of the present war would allow, "the Government of Iran takes formal note of these and expresses confidence in their words."[30]

10. Iran would expect the return of the arms, ammunition, and other Iranian materials that might have fallen into Allied hands and would hope that the Allied powers would show "friendly and equitable intentions" in regard to the human and material losses suffered particularly after Iran had ordered the cease-fire.

Given the overwhelming fact of the occupation of its territory and the consequent limitations on its freedom of action, Iran nevertheless sought to minimize its disadvantages vis-a-vis Great Britain and the Soviet Union, as seen from the above correspondence. While the government of Foroughi conceded the expulsion of Germans, it sought to insure their safe treatment; while it accepted, in principle, to retreat from the areas delineated by the Allied powers, it sought to make certain exceptions; while it showed a conciliatory attitude toward the opportunistic expression of Soviet oil interest, it flatly denied that Iran had agreed to any oil concession to the Soviet Union; while it acknowledged the occupation of the Allied troops, it tried to specify the burden of responsibility for their maintenance; and while it accepted responsibility to facilitate the transport of war materials to the Soviet Union, it sought to impress upon the Allied powers the limitations of its ability to do so. But above all, it tenaciously clung to Allied assurances of Iran's "political independence and territorial integrity," particularly with a view to the withdrawal of Allied troops. Not that Iran's overriding concern with its independence and territorial integrity was anything new, as I have tried to show elsewhere, but the alertness and agility the old prime minister, despite his

---

[29] Ibid., p. 95
[30] Ibid., p. 96

poor health, could bring to bear on these negotiations seem remarkable. This will become even more evident in light of subsequent developments in the Irano-Allied negotiations and the overall course of Iranian diplomacy during these critical months.

On September 6 the Allied powers responded to the Iranian notes of September 1.[31] Many of the points raised in these notes resembled the previous correspondence, and I shall here confine myself to a contrast between the British and the Soviet notes as perhaps the earliest indication of some of the crucial problems that arose subsequently between Iran and the Soviet Union. The British nine-point note proved altogether conciliatory, both in substance and tone. It generally accepted most of the points raised by the Iranian note. With respect to the Iranian exceptions to the areas falling within the British zone of occupation, Great Britain was not prepared to make any exceptions but did not, in principle, object to an arrangement between the Iranian security forces and the British military authorities in Dizful, Khoramabad, and Kermanshah for the maintenance of order, although such an arrangement would be subject to review in light of military necessities.

In contrast, the Soviet note of September 6 flatly rejected the Iranian request for the exclusion of Qazvin, Semnan, and Shahroud from the Soviet zone of occupation. In regard to the return of the arms and ammunition fallen into the hands of the Allied powers, Great Britain agreed to consider the Iranian request at an appropriate time and declared its readiness to study Iran's "legitimate demands" for compensation of losses suffered by Iranian citizens at the time of the withdrawal of British forces from Iran. But the Soviet Union stated that it would consider the question of the return of captured war materials to Iran "when the necessity of the Red Army's presence in Iran has ceased" and categorically rejected the Iranian demand for indemnity because "the war continued so long as the Iranian troops resisted our forces."[32] In point of fact, however, the Soviet Union had continued the bombing of Iranian cities, including the southern sections of Tehran, after the Iranian cease-fire order and the actual cessation of resistance.[33] And finally, while the British expressed sympathetic interest in Iran's understanding that the term *economic aid* extended to the release of its goods held up in British territories, the Soviet note followed up its more or less similar response on this point with a shrewd invocation of the Iranian statement on Kavir Khorian, stating that "it takes note of the Iranian preparedness to conclude a new agreement for the exploration of the Kavir Khorian oil the progress on which

---

[31] For the full texts of the British and the Soviet notes, see Kirmani, 1:90-104.

[32] Ibid., 99-101.

[33] See *Foreign Relations of U.S., 1941*, D.P., 3:444-45.

has been suspended by Iran over a number of years."[34] This was certainly a self-serving twist of the Iranian statement mentioned above.

Iran replied to the Allied powers on September 8, expressing dissatisfaction with the Allied "rejection" of its request regarding exceptions to the occupied areas.[35] But it insisted, in its note to the Soviet Union, on indemnity on the ground that Soviet forces had begun hostilities without prior notice and that Iran's action had been "naturally in self-defense." More particularly, Iran claimed that "the main part of the damages incurred had taken place after the cease-fire ordered by Iran." As for the return of war materials, Iran did not see any reason for the Soviet retention of these now that good relations between Iran and Russia were being established. But if the Soviet Union insisted on doing so, Iran would prepare a list of these materials for their return after the war or at an appropriate time before the end of the war.

Revival of Interest in the United States

Besides trying to resist the Anglo-Russian pressures and minimize the consequences of occupation by means of direct negotiations with the Allied powers, Iran continued after the invasion, as during the previous months following the German attack on Russia, to counter the Anglo-Soviet pressures by interesting and, if possible, involving the United States in Iran. The invasion eliminated Germany as the third-power that had been favored during most of the interwar period, partly in order to assist Iran against the traditional Anglo-Russian control,[36] and revived interest in the United States. As early as 1910 Iran had made its first try in the twentieth century to interest the United States in its affairs and had made an even more serious bid in the early 1920s; in 1927 Riza Shah turned to Germany. Even if Riza Shah had acted differently with Arthur C. Millspaugh in the 1920s, it is uncertain whether the overall isolationist thrust of American foreign policy at the time would have allowed the United States to become as involved in Iran as the Iranians wished. But during the period examined here, from August 25, 1941, to January 29, 1942, the overall trend in American foreign policy seemed to favor increasing involvement in Iran. Although President Roosevelt did not

[34] See Kirmani, 1:100

[35] For the text of Iran's note, see Kirmani, 1:101-4.

[36] See Ramazani, *Foreign Policy of Iran,* pp. 277-300.

find "the defense of Iran to be vital to the defense of the United States"[37] until March 10, 1942, there is no reason to doubt that the United States was becoming seriously interested in Iran during this period that coincided with President Roosevelt's well-known steps "short of war," such as the "destroyers-for-bases deal" with Great Britain and, above all, the Lend-Lease Act (March 11, 1941). Furthermore, this period coincides with the Japanese attack on Pearl Harbor and the German-Italian declaration of war on the United States (December 11, 1941).

As seen previously, on the day of the Anglo-Russian invasion, Riza Shah sent a message to President Roosevelt requesting him "to take efficacious and urgent humanitarian steps to put an end to these acts of aggression."[38] On the same day the director general of the Iranian Ministry of Foreign Affairs called personally on the American minister in Tehran to urge the legation to communicate to the Department of State the official request of the Iranian government that the president of the United States use his good offices with Great Britain and Russia in order "to bring about the immediate cessation of hostilities, looking to an amicable settlement of the present dispute." On August 26 the Iranian request was discussed in the secretary of state's office, where diverse views on the course of action to be pursued by the United States were expressed; the secretary himself believed that the discussants were handling "a red-hot iron." At the end it seemed to be agreed, however, that three things might be done: (1) to suggest to Iran that the Iranians make every effort to come to an amicable settlement with the British and that the United States keep in close touch with a view to helping the Iranians; (2) to notify the British of the Iranian request; and (3) to point out to the British "that the present Anglo-Soviet invasion of Iran has aroused nationwide attention and discussion in this country; that the situation is a delicate one politically; and that we desire to be informed by the British Government without delay." It was further agreed that a number of questions be raised with the British: possible Nazi aggression against Iran; indemnification for Iranian losses and damages; the extent of the Soviet-British occupation; the possibility of widespread Soviet oppression, persecution, confiscation, and the purge of upper-class Iranians; and an alliance with Britain.[39]

On August 26 the Iranian minister in Washington and the Iranian foreign

[37] U.S., Department of State, *Bulletin* 6, no. 149 (May 2, 1942): 383 (hereafter cited as U.S. State Dept. *Bulletin*), and U.S., Department of State, *Foreign Relations of the United States, 1942*, Diplomatic Papers, vol. 4, *The Near East and Africa* (Washington, D.C.: Government Printing Office, 1963), pp. 289-90.

[38] For the English translation of Riza Shah's message, see *Foreign Relations of U.S., 1941*, D.P., 3:419.

[39] Ibid., pp. 418-21.

minister both urged the United States to do something about the cessation of hostilities. The Iranian minister called upon the chief of the Division of Near Eastern Affairs of the State Department for that purpose, predicting that if the United States sat passively in the face of "the Anglo-Soviet aggression," it "will suffer a great loss in moral authority." The foreign minister, on the other hand, called personally on the United States minister in Tehran, urging American efforts to stop hostilities and stating that the Iranian government in its anxiety to arrive at a settlement was willing "not only to deport the Germans but to meet any reasonable British request such as possible Cabinet changes." Although the American minister was moved "to pity by the Foreign Minister in his agitation and dejection," he reported to the secretary of state that "the Iranians have arrived at this predicament by their failure to recognize and face realities." On August 27 the Iranian minister called upon the secretary of state, repeating substantially what he had so often stated to the American officials about the preservation of his country's sovereignty and independence and emphasizing America's historical idealism and morality. He believed that the United States "as a champion of the rights and sovereignty of small nations and of the principles which underlie world order under law, should have something done about the matter [the Anglo-Russian invasion] without delay." The secretary of state, Cordell Hull, told him frankly that the United States had no intention of listening to Hitler discuss the merits of neutrality while conquering all other areas and eventually attacking the United States. He told the Iranian minister, "I must warn Iran against Hitler's stealthy approach, which is always based on a pledge of his supposed honor that he would not for the world attack a neutral country."[40]

On September 2 Riza Shah received a reply to his message of August 25 to President Roosevelt. On August 31 the Iranian foreign minister had told the American ambassador that the shah "was most disappointed" that his request for American good offices had received no reply.[41] The president's message indicated that he had taken careful note of the shah's remarks; was persuaded that the "situation is entitled to serious consideration of all free nations,"[42] including the United States; and hoped that the shah would concur with him in believing "that we must view the situation in its full perspective of present world events and developments." After remarking on the expansionist ambitions of Hitler's Germany, noting that Hitler must be stopped by military force, the president continued: "It is equally certain that those countries which desire to maintain their independence must engage in a great common

[40] Ibid., pp. 422-33.

[41] Ibid., p. 443.

[42] For the text of the President's reply, see ibid., pp. 446-47.

effort if they are not to be engulfed one by one as has already happened to a large number of countries in Europe." The president declared finally that the United States had "noted the statements to the Iranian Government by the British and Soviet Governments that they have no designs on the independence or territorial integrity of Iran." And the United States had already sought information from the British and the Russians "as to their immediate as well as long-range plans and intentions in Iran, and has suggested to them the advisability of a public statement to all free peoples of the world reiterating the assurances already given to Your Majesty's Government."[43]

The United States suggestion to the British and the Russians for a public statement of assurances regarding Iran was communicated to the British. The secretary of state requested the American ambassador in London to express the hope that "sympathetic consideration" may be given to the suggestion. The ambassador, in response, quoted a speech at Coventry in which Anthony Eden had stated: "We have no territorial claims against Iran. We covet no square inch of Iranian territory." The Soviet ambassador in Washington told the secretary of state regarding the suggestion for a proclamation on the temporary nature of their occupation in Iran that "he thought they were doing so to sufficient extent." And the American ambassador in Moscow was told that the Soviet note of August 25, which contained assurances regarding the territorial integrity and national independence of Iran, had "received the widest possible publicity," and reiteration of the Soviet position might be misunderstood. He also added that the work of the German agents "cannot be undone at once," and at that point it was "too soon" to reaffirm the Soviet assurances of eventual withdrawal but added that "the assurances that were given in the note will be kept scrupulously."[44]

Iran's belief at the time that the United States could have been persuaded to intervene *against* the Anglo-Russian campaign seems to be in keeping with the inability of some of its policymakers to take a broader view of the global nature of the German threat that was so often impressed upon the Iranian representative in Washington as well as other Iranian officials, including Riza Shah, as evidenced by President Roosevelt's own message to him. Yet the Iranian efforts probably were not totally an exercise in futility; they did seem to contribute to the quickening of American interest in the preservation of Iranian independence and territorial integrity. Furthermore, these efforts may well have sown the seeds of the idea of an alliance subsequently concluded between Iran, on the one hand, and Great Britain and Russia, on the other.

[43]Ibid., p. 447
[44]Ibid., pp. 449-54.

The Abdication of Riza Shah

The abdication of Riza Shah was closely tied to the developments just discussed. Given the shah's policy of procrastination, the British view of extensive German influence on his policy, and the decline of the shah's prestige at home, his abdication was anticipated soon after the invasion. But the crucial question is, What finally precipitated it? In the absence of sufficient reliable evidence, it is appropriate to consider two major points of view on the subject. Some Iranians then believed, and many still do, that the British set in motion the events that brought about the abdication. They argued that as early as September 6 the British began a relentless campaign against Riza Shah from radio stations located in London and Delhi that told the Iranians about the "tyranny of silence," cruelty, and injustices the Iranians had suffered at the shah's hands. In countering this, Riza Shah tried to manipulate the press, an effort that miscarried, because the newspaper articles supporting him only intensified Allied suspicion that he was inciting the public against them. The Allied powers then believed that he was "incorrigible and watched for the opportunity to do the surgery."[45] These controlled articles were the final stroke.

Sir Reader Bullard, however, implies that the shah's abdication was perhaps prompted by his fears consequent to a Russian move toward the capital. Bullard states that it is not true that the Allies asked the shah to leave. The Iranian government had been slow in securing the departure of the Axis diplomats, and in order to hasten this, the Allied troops moved to occupy the outskirts of Tehran temporarily. "The Russians at Qazvin," he continues, "were nearer to Tehran than any part of the British forces and when they started for the capital Riza Shah thought that it meant a Russian move to overthrow him, so he abdicated in favor of his eldest son and left the country."[46]

Riza Shah's son, Muhammad Riza Shah, in a much later account of his father's abdication, expressed a different view. He rejected the view that his father abdicated in order to save the throne for him. He recalled his father's telling him "in vivid language" that people had always known him as "an independent monarch, respected and strong, representing the interests of his country as he saw them." He then states that his father said "it was humanly

---

[45] This is my understanding of sometimes ambiguous allusions of A. Khajih-Nuri, *Bazigaran-i 'Asr-i Tala'i* (Tehran: n.p., n.d.), pp. 450-51.

[46] "Persia in Two World Wars," *Royal Central Asian Journal* 50, pt. 1 (Jan. 1963):13.

impossible for him, who had such prestige and such a hold over his people, to act as the nominal ruler of an occupied country."[47]

In any event, in an official statement read by Premier Foroughi to an extraordinary session of the Majlis on September 16, 1941, Riza Shah declared his own rationale for abdication. He resigned because he felt that the time had come for a "younger force" (*qovvih-ye javantari*) to look after national affairs; therefore he left the throne to his heir and successor.[48] On September 19 the American minister in Iran was informed that the British and Soviet governments had agreed to succession of the new shah to the throne. "This approval is contingent in both cases on Shah's [*sic*] future good conduct."[49] On September 23, however, the British advised the American under secretary of state "that the British Government had decided to support the new Shah and to recognize his government because of the wishes expressed thereto by the Iranian Government itself." The "new Shah had given assurances that the Iranian Constitution would be observed, that the properties taken by his father would be restored to the nation and that he would undertake to carry out all of the reforms considered necessary by the British Government." On September 25 the secretary of state informed the American minister in Tehran that since the British and the Soviets had recognized the new shah, he should take appropriate steps to indicate United States recognition.[50]

---

[47] Mohammad Reza Shah Pahlavi, *Mission for My Country* (New York: McGraw-Hill, 1961), p. 74.

[48] For the text of Riza Shah's resignation, see Kirmani, 1:111.

[49] Quoted from the report of the American minister to the secretary of state, *Foreign Relations of U.S., 1941*, D.P., 3:461.

[50] Ibid., p. 462.

II

Tripartite Treaty to
Tripartite Declaration

IRAN'S SIGNING OF the Treaty of Alliance with Great Britain and the Soviet Union on January 29, 1942, marked the beginning of a momentous change in Iranian wartime foreign policy. The change, however, was not so sudden as it might appear. As we have seen, the policy of neutrality had come increasingly under attack by Great Britain until the German invasion of Russia on June 22, 1941, and it had thereafter come under greater pressures from the Soviet Union as well as Great Britain. Allied opposition to the activities of the German agents in Iran had been given almost exclusively before as the principal reason for the Allied dissatisfaction with the Iranian policy of neutrality. Only after the invasion did the Allied powers broach in writing their need for full communications with the Soviet Union over Iranian territory. According to Winston Churchill's account, this need seems to have been the principal factor underlying the decision to launch a joint campaign against Iran.[1]

Yet the failure of Iran's policy of neutrality and the concomitant Allied invasion and occupation of Iran (and the abdication of Riza Shah) do not by themselves shed adequate light on the formal change in Iranian foreign policy from neutrality to a "defensive alliance" (*ittihad-i tadafo'i*), to borrow Premier Foroughi's designation.[2] The genesis of the alliance must be sought in the developments during the months before January 1942.

The persistent Iranian efforts to get the United States to intervene, first against Anglo-Russian pressures and then invasion, bore no fruit, but Iran's resultant appeal to the United States for assurances regarding its political independence and territorial integrity received full support from the United States after the Anglo-Russian armed attack. This was signaled by conversations of Secretary Hull with the Soviet ambassador and the British charge d'affaires to Washington as early as August 27, 1941, in which he referred to

---

[1] See his *The Second World War*, vol. 3, *The Grand Alliance* (Boston: Houghton Mifflin Co. 1948), pp. 476-77.

[2] Premier Foroughi, in defending the Tripartite Treaty against an attack by Deputy Habibullah Nobakht, replied to the deputy's charges, among other things, by stating that if he had to label this alliance in any way he would call it a "defensive alliance." For the text of his speech see Kirmani, 1:268-77.

the military occupation of Iran by the British and Russian forces "and particularly to the assurances given by these Governments to the Government of Iran that they were in that country solely on account of the war with Hitler and that they had no purpose to infringe on their sovereignty."[3] In these very conversations Secretary Hull said that the British and the Russians should repeat this same assurance "to all peaceful nations."[4] And, as we have already seen, this suggestion was mentioned by President Roosevelt in his letter of September 2, 1941, to Riza Shah; was subsequently taken up with the British and the Russians in London and Moscow; and received an openly negative response from the Soviet Union at the time.[5] In his *Memoirs* Cordell Hull clearly links this early American suggestion for a declaration of assurances with the subsequent Tripartite Treaty of alliance by stating that although the British and the Russians did not at that time issue the declaration that he had suggested, they did so later in the treaty.[6]

Although the assurances regarding the political independence and territorial integrity of Iran had been given in the Allied notes of August 25, August 30, and September 6, 1941, the developments subsequent to the Allied invasion not only intensified Iran's interest in acquiring additional assurances but also sharpened the interests of both the United States and Great Britain in the matter. The principal development was the behavior of the Soviet Union. The first postinvasion indication of the Soviet activities in Iran was the bombing in the vicinity of Tehran on August 31, 1941, three days after the cease-fire had been ordered by Iran. The American military attaché examined the bombed areas; the American minister in Tehran had "definite knowledge" that there were some casualties; he wondered why the Russians had done so after the cessation of Iranian resistance and reported the terror that the bombing had caused. The Soviet propaganda campaign apparently began at the same time the Russian bombing planes dropped leaflets telling the Iranian peasants and farmers what the Russians had done for theirs. In September, it was reported, the Russians printed a newspaper in Persian called *Thoughts of the People*, criticizing the Foroughi government and asking the people to stop living such an impoverished life.[7]

---

[3]For the texts of the memoranda of the secretary of state's conversations with the Soviet and British diplomatic representatives, see *Foreign Relations of U.S., 1941*, D.P., 3:434-35.

[4]Ibid.

5Ibid., pp. 450-51 and 453-54.

[6]Cordell Hull, *The Memoirs of Cordell Hull* (New York: Macmillan Co., 1948), 2:1502.

[7]*Foreign Relations of U.S., 1941*, D.P., 3:445-65.

The growing British concern over the Soviet activities in Iran was paralleled by the more active United States interest. On October 3, 1941, the secretary of state told the American ambassador in London of reports about the Russian intrigues in the occupied zone, their propaganda, their open sympathy toward the Armenian and other separatist movements, and the Russian ambassador's suggestion to the Iranian government for a greater autonomy for certain areas in Iran. The secretary told the American ambassador to inform Eden that in view of the Soviet-British assurances regarding the political independence and territorial integrity of Iran, the United States "views with concern Russian political activities in Iran and is extremely apprehensive of the effect upon Turkey of any display of Russian sympathy toward an Armenian separatist movement in Iran." The following day the American ambassador in London informed the secretary that he knew "for a fact that Mr. Eden has considered Russian interference in Iran [*sic*] affairs or efforts toward separatist movements by them as harmful and unwarranted." The American concern was also directly communicated to the Soviets in Moscow, but A. Vyshinski, Soviet deputy people's commissar for foreign affairs, denied the Soviet political activities, propaganda, and sympathy with the separatist movements and stated that the Soviet authorities in the occupied zone of Iran were interested in "the maintenance of law and order." Later, in October, the on-the-spot American observation in Azerbaijan seemed to show that the Russians discouraged separatist movements, but Communist propaganda was being spread.[8]

While Iran's alarm at the Soviet activities continued, the Iranian undertaking regarding the departure of Germans (included in its notes of September 1 and 8) was being implemented by September 21. By this time the British had taken 400 German suspects and the Russians about 60, although two of the German secret service agents, Roman Gamotta and Franz Mayer, had escaped.[9] By late September the negotiations with Great Britain and Russia for a treaty of alliance had begun, but they dragged on because, according to a British account, Iranian sympathizers with Germany still remained in official positions.[10] But the negotiations were slow probably more because of Iran's age-old tactic of procrastinating in hopes of getting favorable concessions in return for the signing of the treaty. This interpretation is supported not only

[8]Ibid., pp. 466-74.

[9]Royal Institute of International Affairs, *Survey of International Affairs, 1939-1946*. (London: Oxford University Press, 1952), p. 138 (hereafter cited as Royal Inst. Intl. Affairs, *Survey*).

[10]Ibid., p. 139.

by the traditional patterns of Iranian diplomacy but also by the frank statement of Premier Foroughi before the Majlis in December 1941 and the
Iranian demands for changes in the proposed treaty.[11]

In a dispassionate speech during the Ninth Meeting of the Thirteenth
Majlis, Premier Foroughi described meticulously the nature of the Allied
proposal for a treaty of alliance and the reasons for the delay in signing it. He
told the Majlis that the proposal had been discussed by his government with
the Allied powers for nearly three months because he believed it was in the
interest of Iran; explained the Allied interest in Iran as a supply route to
Russia; reported the Allied suggestion that in return for such an alliance the
Allies would guarantee the political independence and territorial integrity of
Iran; acknowledged "in all fairness" (*bayad insaf dad*) the economic aid
already given to Iran by the Allied powers and the promise of more to come
after the signing of the treaty; and concluded by stating that "the conclusion
of an alliance treaty resembles a transaction between two individuals, each
party trying to maximize its advantages, and this is why the negotiations have
taken as long as they have; are nearly finished; and when the treaty is ready it
will be brought before the Majlis for consultation and discussion and if
approved [by the Majlis] then it will be signed." [12]

Premier Foroughi's remarks prompted Deputy Musa Javan's strong opposition to the suggested change in Iranian foreign policy. He praised the prime
minister for continuing Iran's policy of neutrality after taking over the
government shortly after the Allied invasion; claimed that Iran's policy of
neutrality in the First World War spared Iran from such dangers [of hostilities]
and returned to the country its independence; engaged in a discussion of the
legal advantages of neutrality; cited the example of Sweden with approval; and
stated that there was no in-between status for a nation—one is either a belligerent or a neutral.[13] Foreign Minister 'Ali Sohaily expressed appreciation of
Deputy Javan's views; admitted that Iran had adopted a policy of neutrality;
but declared that considering the global nature of the war and the special
circumstances of Iran at the time, "no nation from East to West can claim to
be completely neutral."[14]

---

[11]I have identified "procrastination" as one of the techniques of Iranian diplomacy.
See *Foreign Policy of Iran,* p. 309.

[12]For the text of the speech see Kirmani, 1:195-98.

[13]Deputy Javan was better known in Iran as Dr. Javan. For the text of his criticism
of the Tripartite Treaty, see ibid., 1:235-47.

[14]For the text of Sohaily's remarks, see ibid., 1:239-41.

The vehement opposition to the draft treaty, however, was launched by Deputy Habibollah Nobakht.[15] In a long, point-by-point discussion of the draft treaty, he considered its terms contrary to the interests of Iran and particularly to its obligations under the 1921 and 1927 treaties with the Soviet Union; claimed that the undertakings of the Allied powers in the proposed treaty were, in the last analysis, contrary to Iranian interests and that Iran's own undertakings "will naturally benefit the other Parties, will prove detrimental to Iran's interests, and will cause her misfortune." He then stated that "worst of all, this treaty will create enemies [for Iran]; of course, so far Germany and its allies have not declared war [on Iran] as Germany and Japan have concluded treaties of friendship with [Iran]," implying that the treaty of alliance with the Allied powers would turn the Axis powers against Iran.[16]

Prime Minister Foroughi's major defense of the proposed treaty took place during the Seventeenth Meeting of the Thirteenth Majlis in January 1942. The meeting began with an ominous note as a spectator attempted to assault the prime minister with a rock, and, failing that, got into a brief scuffle with him. After the removal of the assailant from the parliament building and the reconvention of the meeting, the prime minister calmly took the floor to discuss the various annexes to the draft treaty that had been considered in part as the result of the criticism in the Majlis in the course of the first reading. I shall consider these changes below in connection with the terms of the treaty, but a brief examination of the prime minister's supporting remarks is appropriate here. In a frank statement (rare in the annals of Iranian diplomacy) he first recalled the unhappy events of August 1941 and the Allied invasion and then stressed that in all fairness one must admit that the "mistakes which we made in the past led to this happening, and if we had not committed those past mistakes these developments would not have occurred; but now that they have what should we do?" He then went on: "The harm must be minimized and the interests [of Iran] maximized as far as practicable. For this, and for no other, reason this treaty should be concluded. This treaty would not obviate Iran's sovereign rights, but rather would make up for what harm might have come to Iran's independence and sovereignty and would change the status of the forces now on Iranian territory so that they would no longer be there as forces of occupation." The government, Premier Foroughi continued, "in introducing this draft treaty to the Majlis [for approval] has believed that by this means the harm incurred as the result of recent events might be

[15] Deputy Nobakht was suspected of pro-German sympathies by the British, who subsequently demanded that the Iranian government waive his immunities and arrest him.

[16] For the text of his criticism of the Tripartite Treaty in the Majlis, see Kirmani, 1:257-58.

minimized and [even] some advantages might accrue [to Iran] as the result."[17]

On January 26, 1942, the Majlis finally approved the treaty as amended by the exchange of letters on three annexes. Eighty Deputies voted for the treaty out of a total of ninety-three present.[18] On January 29, 1942, the treaty was signed by Sir Reader Bullard and M.A. Andreewich Smirnov, on behalf of the United Kingdom and the USSR, respectively, and by 'Ali Sohaily, Iran's minister of foreign affairs. There is little doubt that Premier Foroughi played a major part not only in negotiating with the Allied powers but also in getting the treaty approved by the Majlis. Iran's ambassador to Moscow, Muhammad Sa'id, claimed in an interview that he had suggested the idea to Soviet and British diplomatic and other officials.[19] Muhammad Riza Shah Pahlavi stated years later that his "able and scholarly Prime Minister," Muhammad 'Ali Foroughi, "deserves most of the credit for negotiating for us the Tripartite Treaty of Alliance."[20] But the Shah's own interest in the treaty at the time is also attested by his conversation of October 8, 1941, with the United States minister, Dreyfus.[21] According to the available records, the draft treaty had been worked out by the British and first proposed to Iran some time in late September 1941.[22] But Iran, both before and after the signing of the treaty, tried to get the United States to adhere to it. In his conversation with the American minister the shah had stated that "he would be very happy to be an ally of America."[23] We know now that the Iranians subsequently pursued the idea of American adherence to the treaty, but the British told the United States that it would be helpful to them if "the idea was scotched as soon as possible."[24]

The main provisions of the Treaty of Alliance together with the terms of related annexes may be summarized under the following categories:

1. *Political Independence and Territorial Integrity*: Great Britain and the Soviet Union undertook jointly and severally "to respect the territorial

---

[17]For the text of this defense of the Tripartite Treaty by Premier Foroughi, see ibid., 1:320-24.

[18]Ibid., 1:359. There were apparently eight abstentions. It is difficult to assess the number of absentees, for there were some vacancies in the total number of 136 deputies. See Royal Inst. Intl. Affairs, *Survey, 1939-46*, p. 139, n. 4.

[19]For the text of this interview, see Kirmani, 1:243-45.

[20]*Mission for My Country*, p. 75.

[21]See *Foreign Relations of U.S., 1941*, D.P. 3:470.

[22]Ibid., p. 464.

[23]Ibid., p. 471.

[24]*Foreign Relations of U.S., 1942*, D.P. 4:264-65.

integrity and political independence of Iran";[25] not to adopt an attitude that is prejudicial to "the territorial integrity, sovereignty, or political independence of Iran, nor to conclude treaties inconsistent with the provisions of the present Treaty";[26] and to consult Iran in all matters affecting the direct interests of Iran. They interpreted this last provision as being applicable to any peace conference or conferences held at the end of the war, or other international conferences, and bound themselves not to discuss at such conferences anything affecting the direct interests of Iran without consultation with its government.[27]

2. *Withdrawal of the Allied Forces*: The Allied powers undertook to withdraw their forces from Iran "not later than six months after all hostilities between the Allied Powers and Germany and her associates have been suspended by the conclusion of an armistice or armistices, or on the conclusion of peace between them, whichever date is the earlier. The expression 'associates' of Germany means all other Powers which have engaged or may in the future engage in hostilities against either of the Allied Powers."[28]

3. *Economic Aid*: The Allied powers undertook jointly "to safeguard the economic existence of the Iranian people against the privations and difficulties arising as a result of the present war." Discussions for the best methods of implementing this undertaking were to be opened as soon as the treaty entered into force.[29]

4. *Defense*: The Allied powers jointly and severally undertook to defend Iran from all aggression on the part of Germany "or any other Power."[30]

5. *Status of Forces*: The Allied powers "may maintain in Iranian territory land, sea, and air forces in such number as they consider necessary."[31] But it was understood that "the presence of these forces on Iranian territory does not constitute a military occupation and will disturb as little as possible the administration and the security of forces of Iran, the economic life of the country, the normal movements of the population, and the application of

---

[25] Article 1 and article 6(i) of the Treaty of Alliance between the United Kingdom, the Union of Soviet Socialist Republics and Iran, signed at Tehran, Jan. 29, 1942. For the text of this treaty and the attached annexes, see Goodrich and Caroll, *Documents* 4:681-86.

[26] Ibid.

[27] Annex (a).

[28] Article 5.

[29] Article 7.

[30] Article 3(i).

[31] Article 4(i).

Iranian laws and regulations."[32] Iran will bear the cost of no works carried out by the Allied powers for their own military ends.[33]

6. *Iranian Obligations:* Iran undertook: (*a*) to cooperate with the Allied powers "with all the means" at its disposal for defense of its territory (see paragraph 4, "Defense"), although the assistance of the Iranian forces was limited to the maintenance of internal security,[34] and the Iranian forces were not required to participate "in any war or military operation against any Foreign Power or Powers";[35] (*b*) to secure to the Allied powers, for the passage of troops or supplies, "the unrestricted right to use, maintain, guard, and, in case of military necessity, control in any way that they may require all means of communication through Iran";[36] (*c*) to assist in obtaining labor and material for maintaining and improving the means of communication,[37] (*d*) in collaboration with the Allied powers, to establish measures of censorship control, as the Allied powers may require, for all the means of communication; and (*e*) not to adopt in its foreign relations an attitude, nor to conclude treaties, inconsistent with the treaty.[38] Iran would in this respect consider it contrary to its obligations to maintain diplomatic relations with "any State which is in diplomatic relations with neither of the Allied Powers."[39]

7. *Duration*: The treaty was to come into force on signature and remain in force until the date fixed for the withdrawal of the Allied forces from Iranian territory; but it was to remain in force insofar as the obligations of the Allied powers in regard to conferences held at the end of the war, and before the conclusion of peace, were concerned (see paragraph 1, "Political Independence").[40]

The signing of the Tripartite Treaty marked a formal shift in Iran's wartime policy. Neutral Iran accepted the status of an ally of Great Britain and the Soviet Union. But what was important about this shift was the diplomatic bargain that an occupied Iran was nevertheless able to drive:

1. The Allied interest in the treaty was to regulate and facilitate the supply of war materials to the Soviet Union. Iran capitalized on this interest to get

[32]Ibid.

[33]Annex c(2).

[34]Article 3 (ii a).

[35]Annex c(1).

[36]Article 3(ii b).

[37]Article 3(ii c).

[38]Article 6(ii).

[39]Annex b.

[40]See article 9 of the treaty and its annex a and annex c(3).

the Allied powers to spell out as clearly and concretely as possible their repeated assertion of respect for Iran's political independence and territorial integrity both before and after the invasion. Iran's slowness in signing the treaty and its request for changes made in it were directed toward this end.

2. Militarily and politically, Iran maximized its interest by obtaining the Allied obligation to withdraw their forces at a specific time rather than generally "after the war"; not to interfere in Iranian affairs; and to consult Iran in matters directly affecting its interests even after the expiration of the treaty and before the conclusion of peace. The significance of these terms will become clear in regard to the Soviet demand for an oil concession and the subsequent refusal of Soviet troops to withdraw from Iran. In historical perspective the treaty shows that Iran tried to apply the lessons it had painfully learned from its experience in the First World War when its insistence on a neutral course hardly prevented its becoming a battlefield or furthered its admittance to peace negotiations.

3. Economically, Iran tried to impress upon the Allied powers the sacrifices that it had to bear in the long run and looked forward to future economic assistance.

Considering that the treaty, as such, was concluded during the Allied occupation and, to borrow Sir Reader Bullard's words, "under duress,"[41] the extent to which Iran did manage to bargain suggests that the assertion that it is a "misnomer" to speak about Iran's "foreign policy" during the war does not completely coincide with the facts. To be sure, the occupation of the country narrowed, but did not eliminate, Iranian choices entirely. The same resilience that so greatly made up for Iran's lack of material power during the course of these events will be noted in subsequent events. Iran knew that the problems of occupation would remain despite the Allied treaty obligations, but it was also aware that it could legitimize its demand for Allied, particularly Soviet, withdrawal of troops in the future. Before such time, Iran had to cope with other wartime problems.

Continuing Problems of German Activities

As noted previously, the departure of Germans unacceptable to the Allied powers was well underway by September 1941 when the British and the Russians interned nearly five hundred German suspects. Roman Gamotta and Franz Mayer had escaped by that time. The conjunction of the internal tribal situation and the actual developments of the course of the war increased the British concern with the residual German activities as early as January 1942.

[41] Bullard, p. 14.

On January 5 the commander-in-chief, Middle East, considered seriously the possibility of a German break through the Caucasus and a drive toward the Persian Gulf and the Suez Canal.[42]   At the same time (January, 1942), Franz Mayer together with some Iranian sympathizers organized a movement called "Nationalists of Iran" (*Milliyun-i Iran*), which included a cabinet minister, three members of the Majlis, eleven generals, and other senior officers and aimed at stirring up revolts among the Kurds and other tribes in northern Iran.[43]   According to Berthold Schultze, the other major German agent escapee in Iran, he and Mayer divided their task between them.[44]   He was to incite the Qashqa'i tribesmen in the south.

The tribal situation had become a serious menace to the internal security of the country as well as a problem for the British forces after the Anglo-Russian invasion and particularly after the abdication of Riza Shah. The first wartime Kurdish uprising was signaled by the revolt of Hama Rashid, a Kurdish leader from the Danoh tribes, who had escaped capture by the Soviet forces after the invasion. This revolt resulted in wresting various towns from the control of the Iranian forces in Kurdistan. Subsequently, however, the government forces, under the supervision of the British, reached an agreement with the Kurdish khan. He was appointed governor of Baneh "on behalf of Tehran and allowed to keep his arms, while the Iranian military and police forces were to keep outside the Baneh-Sardasht region."[45]   Meanwhile the Kurdish revolt had in part led to the resignation of Premier Foroughi on February 28, 1942.[46]   The Mayer assignment to incite the Kurds, who had already risen in revolt, alarmed the British.

However, the tribal unrest that particularly troubled Iran's good relations with the British, took place in the south. Berthold Schultze was to incite the Qashqa'i revolt. The principal figure in this uprising was the well-known Nasir Khan Qashqa'i. After the Allied invasion he had escaped from his long-term exile in Tehran to Semirom, a strategic region between Isfahan and Fars and a place of seasonal migration by the Qashqa'i, Bakhtiari, and Buir Ahmadi tribes.[47]   The name *Semirom* is associated in the annals of Iran's modern political history with the protracted and fierce fighting between the Iranian forces and the Qashqa'i and Buir Ahmadi tribes beginning in May 1943. According to a British account, in 1942 Mayer had gone to Isfahan and made

[42] See Royal Inst. Intl. Affairs, *Survey, 1939-46,* p. 51.

[43] Ibid., p. 157.

[44] Shulze-Holthus, p. 150.

[45] See Hassan Arfa, *The Kurds* (London: Oxford University Press, 1966) pp. 67-70.

[46] Royal Inst. Intl. Affairs, *Survey, 1939-46,* p. 156.

[47] For details see Kirmani, 2:477-89.

"plans with General Zahidi . . . for the co-operation of the southern tribes and for revolt when German troops arrived on Persia's frontiers; final details were to be worked out after the fall of Stalingrad."[48]

The firsthand account of the German activities in collaboration with General Zahidi, Nasir Khan, and Deputy Nobakht was made available in 1954 by Berthold Schultze, who traveled in Iran as Doctor Bruno Shulze and adopted Saba as his Iranian name during the war. Khosrow Khan, the brother of Nasir Khan, who captured the fort at Semirom, faced the Iranian forces under General Shahbakhti, who had replaced General Zahidi after the latter had been arrested in Isfahan. According to official Iranian sources the forces of the central government finally brought the Qashqa'i tribesmen under control, and with the fall of Firuzabad (the center of Nasir Khan's activities), he and his supporters fled into the mountains.[49] The main event in these developments that adversely affected Iran's relations with Great Britain was the British capture of certain documents "providing a useful Who's Who of the Persian fifth column."[50] The British were led to these documents by an Iranian who, among others at Isfahan, took fright when the German army failed before Stalingrad and at al-Alamain.[51]

The "Mayer documents," as they were called, became a source of friction between the British and the Americans. In a memorandum of the British Foreign Office dated January 4, 1943, the British acknowledged Iranian displeasure with the British authorities and their complaints to the Americans; claimed that there were still German agents throughout Iran who had organized a widespread conspiracy with the help of "a number of influential Persians, involving definite plans for sabotage against Allied communications, and rising against the Allies in the event of a German invasion of Persia," and stated that the British government regarded "it as absolutely essential to take such steps against German agents as may be required to safeguard the Allied troops and communications in Persia."[52] After the British had arrested Franz Mayer, they demanded in August 1943 that the prime minister of Iran have the Majlis waive the immunity of Deputy Nobakht for his arrest by the govern-

---

[48]Royal Inst. Intl. Affairs, *Survey, 1939-46*, p. 157.

[49]This account was given by the army in a published note for the public. For the text see Kirmani, 2:485.

[50]See Royal Inst. Intl Affairs, *Survey, 1939-46*, p. 157.

[51]Cf. ibid. and Shulze-Holthus, p. 186.

[52]For the full text of the British memorandum on the subject, see U.S., Department of State, *Foreign Relations of the United States, 1943*, Diplomatic Papers, vol. 4, *The Near East and Africa* (Washington, D.C., Government Printing Office, 1964), pp. 320-25.

ment;[53] and requested the arrest of 137 Iranians suspected of collaboration
with the German agents.[54] Meanwhile Deputy Nobakht had begun an interpellation of the government in regard to its military campaign against the
Qashqa'i tribe. The deputy stated in the Majlis that the government had sent
two thousand troops against the Qashqa'i, the Bakhtiari, and the Buir Ahmadi
tribesmen without any legal justification; and demanded that the government
explain what "supreme national interest" (*maslahat-i ali baray-i kishvar*) had
prompted this internal war contrary to national unity.[55] The prime minister
gave the British a "half-hearted promise" to have the Majlis waive Nobakht's
parliamentary immunity and proceeded with his arrest because, he claimed, he
wished to have a chance to answer Nobakht's interpellation and obtain a vote
of confidence on this score.[56]

The American minister in Tehran sent to the secretary of state three
strictly confidential documents furnished by the British on the German fifth
column in Iran and a fourth document containing case histories of 137
Iranians "alleged to belong to the German fifth column organization in Iran."
He commented in a message dated August 20, 1943, that one gains the
impression from the documents "that the Iranians in question were at worst
playing at espionage rather than working seriously in German interests"; and
that without criticizing the British some documents contained "vague accusations." However, he did not see how the United States could oppose the
arrests to be made but suggested that the United States should stress to the
Iranian authorities "the military necessity of restraining any person potentially
harmful to the war effort." On the same day the minister was instructed to
proceed with his own suggestion in mind, should the Iranians approach him
on the subject.[57] Sir Reader Bullard stated that the post-Tripartite Treaty
cooperation of some Iranians with Germany "is understandable, since the tripartite treaty had been signed under duress; but it was our business to stop
them if we could." This was one of his tasks, which became "invidious" when
it had to be performed at the request of the Americans, who had no agreement
with Iran about the presence of their 30,000 noncombatant troops. So when
an American general produced a list of over thirty suspected Iranian railway
workers to be removed, it was the British Embassy that had to secure their
removal.[58]

[53]Ibid., p. 374.

[54]Ibid., p. 380.

[55]For the text of Deputy Nobakht's interpellation, see Kirmani, 2:492-94.

[56]*Foreign Relations of U.S., 1943,* D.P., 4:381.

[57]Ibid., p. 380-84.

[58]See Bullard, p. 14.

American Troops in Iran

The other major problem facing Iran between the signing of the Tripartite Treaty and the Tripartite Declaration stemmed from the arrival of American troops in Iran. The low capacity of Iranian ports, railway, and roads together with adverse local conditions, the British shortage of manpower, and the increase of the daily target for aid to Russia through Iran revealed by fall 1942 that the British troops available for transport duties were inadequate. It was, therefore, decided that the United States army should take over the operation of the ports, the railway, and the bulk of the road haulage in Iran; the commanding general, Persian Gulf Command Service (PGCS), and advance elements of his staff arrived in Iran in October 1942 and the first United States troops landed in December.[59] The Iranian government consented to American operation of the southern section of the Trans-Iranian Railway subject to British and Russian approval as required by the Tripartite Treaty and suggested that since operation necessitated presence of American forces in Iran, their presence should be regularized by signing an agreement between the two governments. But the United States took the position that it would prefer not to conclude any general, overall agreement but would rather sign individual ad hoc agreements to cover specific problems. Furthermore, it preferred to prepare a separate draft agreement on the question of jurisdiction over offenses that might be committed by members of American armed forces.[60]

On two occasions Premier Ahmad Qavam told the Americans of Iran's desire to have the United States adhere to the Tripartite Treaty. In a note dated January 6, 1943, the Iranian Ministry of Foreign Affairs put the suggestion in writing after having complained of the arrival of thousands of American troops in Iran without prior negotiations. The note said shrewdly that since the American action was inconsistent with the spirit of cooperation between the two countries and with Iranian territorial integrity and independence, the ministry had reason to believe that by this action the United States had shown its intention of adhering to the Tripartite Treaty. It then concluded by declaring Iran's preparedness to seek to alter the treaty to a four-power pact,to include the United States.[61] Because of American reluctance to become a party to the Tripartite Treaty, subsequent negotiations centered on the conclusion of a separate agreement between the two countries. Iran's interest in such an agreement, like its previous suggestion that the

[59] See Royal Inst. Intl. Affairs, *Survey, 1939-46,* p. 150.

[60] *Foreign Relations of U.S., 1942,* D.P., 4:315-16.

[61] *Foreign Relations of U.S., 1943,* D.P., 4:454.

United States adhere to the Tripartite Treaty, clearly aimed at greater involvement of the United States in Iran as a counterbalance to Great Britain and Russia.

This objective is evidenced by all the relevant negotiations. On March 18, 1943, the Iranian prime minister urged the American minister that the prospective agreement include a guarantee by the United States of the territorial integrity and sovereignty of Iran; and frankly stated that such a formal pledge would be most "helpful in counteracting the ever growing Soviet menace to Iran."[62] A draft agreement was finally prepared about four months after the arrival of American troops in Iran as a result of work by various divisions of the State Department and consultation with the Iranian minister in Washington and the United States War Department, and was presented to Iran by early April.[63]

In a long preamble the first United States draft linked the presence of the United States troops in Iran principally to the fact of American association with Great Britain and Russia and Iran's alliance with the Allied powers, on the one hand, and the adherence of both Iran and the United States to the principles of the Atlantic Charter of August 14, 1941, on the other.[64] Under the agreement the United States (1) undertook to respect the territorial integrity, sovereignty and political independence of Iran in the future as in the past; (2) understood that its presence in Iran did not constitute occupation; and (3) would consult the Iranian, British, and Soviet authorities in regard to any action affecting privileges and obligations contained in the Tripartite Treaty. Iran agreed in return (1) to the entry, operation, and passage of the armed forces of the United States, the agencies found necessary by these forces, and the civilians employed by the forces or the agencies for the prosecution of the war; (2) to exempt all imports into its territory by these units and agencies from all Iranian taxes, levies, duties, and the like; (3) to grant, upon request, to the United States, the right to use, maintain, guard, and control any of the means of communication within Iran found advantageous for the prosecution of the war; (4) to allow the reexport of any relevant American property that the United States might find desirable to take out of Iran without taxes and other charges; and (5) to conclude agreement with the United States about the disposition of American installations that the United States might not find desirable to remove. The agreement would come into force upon signature and be submitted for the approval of the Majlis; and

[62]Ibid., p. 463.

[63]Ibid., p. 459n.

[64]For the text of the American draft agreement, see ibid., pp. 459-62.

would remain in force until six months after the cessation of hostilities between the United States and "its enemies in the present war," unless the parties terminate it by mutual agreement in advance.

In response to the American proposed draft treaty, Iran sought in part to bring it more nearly into line with the Tripartite Treaty. It requested the United States (1) to spell out the withdrawal of its forces from Iranian territory "not later than six months after the cessation of hostilities, and (2) to undertake to consult Iran in all matters affecting the direct interests of Iran and not to discuss such matters at international conferences without consultation with the Iranian government. Both these provisions were to secure obligations from the United States almost identical to those of the British and the Russians under the Tripartite Treaty. But careful reading of the proposed Iranian additions and alterations seems to reveal clearly that the more important objective to be served was to secure greater United States involvement in Iran, both politically and economically. Politically, Iran requested the insertion of a new article that would commit the United States to protect Iran against not only German aggression but also aggression by any government.[65] Economically, Iran sought, on the one hand, to secure United States commitment to giving its permanent installations to Iran gratuitously and to selling movable property not needed by the United States to Iran, and, on the other hand, to obtain American promise to use its best efforts to safeguard the economic life of Iran, probably with a view to the future.

In part because of the differences between the War and the State Departments, the pace of negotiations was extremely slow.[66] This slowness prompted the Iranian prime minister to address a somewhat strongly worded note to the United States on August 21, 1943, which repeated that the arrival of American troops in Iran "is in violation of international laws and principles and without the previous consent of the Iranian Government. It is inconsistent with the friendly relations between the two countries."[67] It also claimed that the government's position was "undetermined" because of the questions raised by the Deputies of the Majlis in regard to the presence of American troops under the circumstances. Despite a revised American draft agreement, however, no final agreement was reached and the matter dragged on.[68] Moreover, the

[65] For a summary of the Iranian counterproposals, see *Foreign Relations of U.S., 1943,* D.P., 4:464-65.

[66] For evidence of the American interdepartmental differences, see ibid., pp. 471-72. Other related documents can be found in this same source.

[67] For an English translation of the Iranian note, see ibid.

[68] For the text of the revised American draft, see ibid., pp. 473-79.

related problem of the conduct of American forces in Iran became an additional point of friction, although by no means as important as their presence as such.[69]

Declaration of War on Germany

The Tripartite Treaty had formally changed the status of Iran from a neutral to a noncombatant ally of Great Britain and the Soviet Union, but the fundamental attitudes that had precipitated the adoption of the policy of neutrality after the outbreak of the war did not change overnight. The age-old distrust and fear of Russia and the dislike of Great Britain as Russia's traditional rival in Iran rather than any ideological affinity with the Nazis had undergirded Iran's previous friendly relations with Germany. From the Iranian perspective, rapprochement had been a matter of tactical policy, namely, a counterbalance to the British and Russian policies in Iran. For this reason rather than any other, Iran was slow in declaring war on Germany. But the Iranian attitude underwent a significant shift with the Allied successes in the North African campaign and the Russian defense of Stalingrad, both marking a definite turning point in favor of the Allies during the war (November 1942). Apart from its direct impact on the Iranian attitude, the Allied success undermined the activities of the German agents in Iran and led to the capture of the Mayer documents and the arrest of many Iranians suspected of pro-German activities. Officially, however, Iran played down the effect of the Allied successes on its belated declaration of war on Germany because it did not want it to appear that its eventual decision to throw its lot with the United Nations was opportunistic.

Iran's request for adhering to the United Nations Declaration of January 1, 1942, was lodged with the United States because it was the depository of the declaration. It was reported on December 23, 1942, that Iran strongly desired to adhere to the United Nations Declaration; it inquired about the conditions for adherence on January 26, 1943; and it presented the American, British, and Soviet officials with a memorandum on July 5, 1943, setting forth the Iranian position on the subject. Iran claimed that the matter had been under consideration since September-October 1942 but that a propitious moment was not at hand because the government had been preoccupied with internal questions, such as famine and epidemic, and "did not have sufficient strength to take such decisive action in matters of foreign relations," and raised specific questions about additional obligations that adherence would entail and the

[69]Many of the differences regarding the conduct of American soldiers were trivial. For details see ibid., pp. 487-510.

advantages and guarantees that would accrue to Iran. The Iranian foreign minister also stated that since his country had already contributed more toward the Allied cause than many signatory powers, he felt Iran should not in any way be placed in an inferior position.[70] Later, the prime minister, 'Ali Sohaily,[71] in requesting an early and favorable American reply to the Iranian inquiries, expressed regret that Iran had not been able to enter the war before the fall of Mussolini since the Iranians desired to avoid giving the impression that they had deliberately waited until the defeat of the Axis seemed assured beyond question; and even volunteered to go to Washington for discussions on Iran's adherence. The American minister felt this move was a "bid by Sohaily to strengthen his tottering position by a spectacular and successful journey to Washington to align his country officially on the side of the Allied powers."[72]

The secretary of state finally instructed the American minister on August 26 to reply to Iran, after having ascertained that his British and Soviet counterparts had similar instructions, along the following lines: (1) that Iran would become eligible for adherence when it entered a state of war with any of the Axis powers; (2) that adherence as such would not entail new economic or military obligations for Iran, although it was hoped that Iran would take the most energetic possible measures in the war for victory over Hitlerism; (3) that Iran's advantages would be the same that would result from partnership with the thirty-two countries known as the United Nations in the war; and (4) that Iran would have equal rights with the other United Nations to participate in conferences dealing with the peace settlement.[73]

On September 9, 1943, Iran declared war on Germany by a *farman* ("royal decree") of the shah,[74] and on the same day the Majlis approved the declaration by a vote of 73 to 4. The Majlis listened to the text of the *farman*

---

[70]Ibid., pp. 428-30.

[71]'Ali Sohaily is generally regarded as an able Iranian statesman, particularly renowned for his part in the conclusion of the Tripartite Treaty, when he acted as Iran's foreign minister during the government of Mohammad 'Ali Foroughi, and his role as prime minister in the declaration of war on Germany and the issuance of the Declaration of the Allied Powers regarding Iran. He was born in Iran in 1893/94 (1274 in the Iranian calendar), was educated at the well-known "School of Political Science" (*Madrisih-ye 'Ulum-i Siyasi*), and served most of his life in the Iranian foreign service, including posts at Kabul and London and membership in a special mission to Moscow during the interwar period. He was first appointed prime minister after Foroughi and then for a second time during the Second World War.

[72]*Foreign Relations of U.S., 1943,* D.P., 4:431-33.

[73]Ibid., p. 435.

[74]For the text of the shah's *farman,* see Kirmani, 2:496.

"amidst unprecedented applause and commotion" and after an interesting introductory speech by the prime minister. The premier recalled Iran's policy of neutrality after the outbreak of the war and subsequent developments (the Anglo-Russian invasion); and stated that the Tripartite Treaty constituted the basis of Iran's foreign policy, it clarified Iran's attitude toward the belligerent powers, and hence Iran had expected that the Axis powers, conscious of Iran's particular circumstances and its obligations toward the Allied powers, would not do anything contrary to the Iranian policy. But, the prime minister continued, the more recent events (alluding to the capture of the "Mayer documents"), the documents and testimonies in his possession, the German incitement of the tribes against the government, the sabotage and espionage activities of the German agents and their organizations against the railway and the communication lines, and the activities aimed at internal dissension, revolution, and chaos prompted the Iranian government to consider these illegitimate activities of the German government within Iranian territory as hostile acts and to feel compelled to terminate them, for the maintenance of the higher interest of Iran, by declaring war on Germany by the *farman* of His Imperial Majesty.[75]

This was the most unequivocal official admission of German activities in Iran to that date. By making this timely admission and by declaring war on Germany, Iran insured its place among the United Nations. To the Iranians the declaration of war on Germany assured, most importantly, Iran's participation in conferences dealing with the peace settlement, an objective that Iran had set for itself in the light of its disappointing experience at the end of the First World War when it had been refused admission to peace negotiations.

United States Public Support of Iran
The Tripartite Declaration

The next and last important opportunity for Iran to seek to insure worldwide recognition of its wartime contributions to the Allied cause and particularly to secure public assurances from the United States regarding the protection of its political independence was presented by the Tehran Conference. This conference occurred at a propitious time insofar as Iran had just recently declared war on Germany and was therefore in a better position to be considered for a favorable public statement by the United States as well as Great Britain and the Soviet Union.

The genesis of the Tripartite Declaration on Iran must be sought in the previous developments, beginning with the Foreign Ministers Conference at

[75] For the text of Premier 'Ali Sohaily's speech, see ibid., 2:495-96.

Moscow. On October 23, 1943, a British memorandum for common Allied policy toward Iran was circulated at the Moscow Conference. The memorandum stated that the general policy towards Iran must stand the test of whether it conformed to the engagements the Allies had entered into in the Tripartite Treaty; called attention to the fact that in return for maintaining military forces in Iran and using its communications, the Allied powers had guaranteed the territorial integrity and the independence of Iran; declared that so long as Iran granted the Allies their desiderata in the financial and economic field there was a "moral obligation on the Allies to do all that they can to ensure that their utilization of these facilities causes least hurt to [the] Persian economy"; and suggested the adoption of a declaration that, bearing in mind Iran's adherence to the cause of the United Nations (Iran's declaration of war on Germany), committed the American, British, and Russian governments "to safeguard the people of Iran from the privations and difficulties which the present war must bring to them, in common with all other peoples engaged in the conflict."[76]

On October 24 the matter was taken up during the general meeting of the foreign secretaries when Eden referred to the British memorandum. Molotov said that before the conference the Iranian ambassador to Moscow, Ahy, had stated to Soviet officials that Iran was entitled to be represented at any discussions concerning Iran according to the Tripartite Treaty, and that he had been told the Soviet authorities did not expect to make decisions regarding Iran. It was decided, however, to refer the subject to a subcommittee that considered a British memorandum with two declarations that differed from the first British memorandum in that it included statements on the withdrawal of British and Russian forces, according to the Tripartite Declaration, and on the withdrawal or reduction of American as well as British and Soviet non-military governmental organizations as soon as possible after the cessation of hostilities. The American members of the subcommittee also presented a memorandum that committed the three governments to the support of the various foreign advisers, groups, and agencies working with the Iranian government to relieve economic difficulties by strengthening the Iranian government's authority and committed the United States to the withdrawal of its forces from Iran as soon as their presence was not needed and in no case later than six months after the cessation of hostilities between the United States and its enemies in the war.[77]

[76] For the text of the British memorandum, see U.S., Department of State, *Foreign Relations of the United States,* Diplomatic Papers, *The Conferences at Cairo and Tehran, 1943* (Washington, D.C.: Government Printing Office, 1961), pp. 113-15.

[77] For the British draft declarations and American proposed amendments, see ibid. pp. 118-20.

On October 27 and 30, the subcommittee held further meetings. These failed to produce agreement on the necessity or desirability of any declaration on Iran at the time. The opposition that led to this disagreement came from the Soviet Union, which claimed that the Iranian government and people were "entirely satisfied with the intentions of the three governments" and which stated that the proposed declaration repeated the assurances already given Iran under the Tripartite Treaty. In a report to the secretary of state, George V. Allen, a member of the American delegation to the subcommittee, stated on November 4, 1943, that during the meetings of the subcommittee the American and British members were in substantial agreement while the Soviet members held "to a negative attitude." They "answered evasively or ignored questions designed to draw out any specific objections they might have to the policies set forth in the British and American draft texts. They showed no disposition to compromise or to put forward alternative proposals."[78] On October 30 the subcommittee's proposal was adopted. The committee had been unable to agree on the "expediency" of any immediate declaration on Iran, but the proposal stipulated that the issue might be further considered in Tehran, after the signature of the proposed Irano-American agreement (on the presence of troops) and consultation with Iran.[79] Secretary Hull recalled subsequently that the declaration on Iran that he and Eden had supported at Moscow "ran aground on the rocks of Soviet opposition." Eden, Molotov, and Hull then agreed to its subsequent consideration, although Hull and Eden "should have preferred to continue the discussion at Moscow."[80]

The conference at Tehran was primarily concerned with the Allied strategy, but the presence of Churchill, Roosevelt, and Stalin in the Iranian capital provided an unprecedented opportunity for Iran to pursue its main wartime objectives. Armed with its recent declaration of war on Germany, Iran sought more confidently to secure (1) confirmation of the Anglo-Russian assurances concerning its political independence and territorial integrity embodied in the Tripartite Treaty, (2) public support of the United States for these assurances, and (3) favorable indications of great-power economic assistance to Iran in the future. My identification of these major objectives is supported not only by Iranian policy statements and actions already recorded, and others that will be discussed in the following chapters, but also by Iran's own efforts before the issuance of the Tehran Declaration.

On November 25, 1943, Premier Sohaily and Foreign Minister Muhammad Sa'id spoke to the American minister and General Hurley about the proposed

[78] See *Foreign Relations of U.S., 1943,* D.P. 4:400-05.

[79] *Foreign Relations of U.S., 1943 (Cairo and Tehran Conferences),* p. 133.

[80] Hull, 2:1506.

declaration at the Moscow Conference. In his report of December 9, 1943, to the secretary of state about the circumstances of the drawing up of the joint declaration, the American minister stated that he did not know how the Iranians had learned about the proposal at Moscow, but assumed that the British had informed them.[81] It is possible, however, that Iran also learned from the Americans about at least some of the discussions at Moscow in a subsequent meeting between the shah, the American chargé d'affaires, George V. Allen, and John D. Gernagan, in which the American minister was not present. In a memorandum dated November 6, 1943, on the subject of the "Moscow Conference as it Affected Iran," the American chargé in Iran reported Allen's remarks on the conference where Iran had been mentioned and his belief that "it seemed to him inevitable that there should have been some informal conversations regarding Iran at a meeting such as the one in Moscow, since Iran was the one place in the world where the three nations concerned came most closely together."[82] In any event, regardless of how Iran had been informed about the proposal, the fact remains that Iran had known about the notion of a declaration before the Tehran Conference. More important, Iran set forth its own request for a declaration before one was actually approved at the conference.

On November 29, 1943, when the American minister called at the Iranian Ministry of Foreign Affairs regarding some other matter, Prime Minister Sohaily told him that he had seen Eden and put forward the request that the conference should issue a joint communiqué regarding Iran. The major points of the Iranian proposal were these: (1) Allied recognition of Iran's help in the prosecution of the war; (2) confirmation of the pledges embodied in the Tripartite Treaty regarding Iran's independence, sovereignty, and territorial integrity; and (3) assurance that the economic needs of Iran would be considered when the peace treaty was negotiated.[83]

Premier Sohaily also stated that Eden had agreed to these in principle but had requested that he approach the Soviet representatives and the American minister. And on November 30, Sa'id informed the American minister that Stalin and Molotov had expressed willingness to meet the request for a declaration. However, it appeared that Soviet concurrence was not certain, and the following day General Hurley requested that the president speak to Stalin on the matter.[84]

Iran was not only involved in the negotiations preceding the issuance of a

[81]*Foreign Relations of U.S., 1943 (Cairo and Tehran Conferences)*, p. 841.

[82]*Foreign Relations of U.S., 1943*, D.P., 4:408-10.

[83]*Foreign Relations of U.S., 1943 (Cairo and Tehran Conferences)*, pp. 840-41.

[84]Ibid., p. 842.

declaration (an American draft of which was also given to Iran); it also set forth its own aide-memoiré on the subject, dated December 1, 1943, according to both Iranian and American sources.[85] The published version of this instrument in Persian contained the following major points:

1. The holding of the Conference in Iran provided the opportunity to bring to the attention of the three powers "the aspirations of the Iranian people" (*arizooha-ye millat-i Iran*).

2. Iran should be certain that the Allies "will not refrain from lending Iran any kind of assistance at the present and in the future."

3. The Allies would take into consideration "all hardship and damages which have been inflicted on Iran through conditions of war."

4. In return for its cooperation in the war effort and its declaration of war on Germany, Iran expected that the Allies would make a special effort to restore the maintenance of Iranian security to Iran's own forces.

5. Iran confidently hoped that the Allied written and oral promises and assurances about the integrity and full independence of Iran would be strengthened through moral and material help in all political and economic matters.

6. And Iran expected the leaders of the three big powers to issue a declaration (*i'lamiyih*) "specifying once more the good will that they have repeatedly shown toward Iran orally and in writing."

The "Declaration of the Three Powers Regarding Iran" was signed on December 1, 1943, on the last day of the meeting at Tehran, by Churchill, Roosevelt, and Stalin, and a copy of it was initialed by foreign minister Sa'id, on the same day, indicating its acceptance by Iran.[86] The main points of the declaration may be summarized as follows:

1. The three Allied powers recognized the assistance of Iran in the prosecution of the war, "particularly by facilitating the transportation of supplies from overseas to the Soviet Union."

2. They realized that the war had "caused special economic difficulties for Iran" and agreed that they would "continue to make available to the Government of Iran such economic assistance as may be possible."

3. With respect to the postwar period, they agreed with Iran that any economic problems confronting Iran at the close of hostilities "should receive full consideration" along with those of other members of the United Nations, by conferences or international agencies dealing with international economic matters.

---

[85] For the text of this aide-mémoire in Persian, see Kirmani, 2:507-9. For the full text in English with notes on the differences between the original text and the "published" text, see ibid., 2:627-28.

[86] For the text of the declaration in English, see ibid., 2:646-47.

4. And they were "at one with the Government of Iran in their desire for the maintenance of the independence, sovereignty and territorial integrity of Iran." They also "count upon the participation of Iran" in the establishment of international peace, security, and prosperity after the war, in accordance with the principles of the Atlantic Charter, "to which all four Governments have subscribed."

The secrecy surrounding the conference was not broken in Iran until December 5. Foreign Minister Sa'id had agreed that no publicity would be given the declaration until it was released by the three signatory governments.[87] Iran had wished all along to publicize the occasion as a matter of international prestige, but it abided by the wishes of the Allied powers. At a reception given by the Ministry of Foreign Affairs on December 5, the prime minister took advantage of the occasion to impress upon the diplomatic representatives of Great Britain, the Soviet Union, and the United States how much Iran had wished to extend its hospitality to the leaders of the Allied powers, but referred tactfully to the secrecy of the conference by pointing out specifically to the Allied representatives that the secrecy had been from the very beginning "decided" by Iran as well as the Allied powers (*tasmim-i ma va shoma*).[88] Probably this statement was aimed at dispelling the rumors that Iran was unaware of the meeting on its own soil; as seen, it had been aware and involved.

On the following day, December 6, the shah sent a message to President Roosevelt. He assured the president that the friendship of the American people was "very precious" to Iran and that his "constant desire will be to foster closer ties between Iran and the United States of America which have already been brought so near to one another in the common struggle for freedom."[89]

Somewhat different roles have been emphasized in the actual preparation of the declaration. The report of the American minister to the Department of State, dated December 9, seems to give a large share to the legation's role, although that of General Hurley is also admitted. On the other hand, the account of Gernegan, third secretary of the American embassy in Iran, to General Hurley's aide, dated December 3, speaks of a rough draft of a declaration "which I had worked up in anticipation that the question might be broached at the conference and to which General Hurley suggested certain

---

[87] Ibid., p. 843.

[88] For the texts of the speeches of Prime Minister Sohaily and the American, British, and Soviet diplomatic representatives in Iran, see Kirmani, 2:514-26. This particular reference is to be found at page 523.

[89] For the text of the shah's message in English, see *Foreign Relations of U.S., 1943 (Cairo and Tehran Conferences)*, pp. 806-7.

changes."[90] However, Don Lohbeck seems to give all the credit to General Hurley who, according to Lohbeck, was entrusted by President Roosevelt with the task of securing reaffirmation by Great Britain and the Soviet Union of the principles and objectives of the Atlantic Charter: "The solution that Hurley prepared and presented to the Tehran conferees was the Declaration Regarding Iran."[91] The shah's message to President Roosevelt, just mentioned, and the *Memoirs* of Cordell Hull both give credit to the role of the American legation in Tehran.[92]

From all the evidence, however, it appears that a number of individuals played significant parts in preparing the declaration from the very inception of the idea to its final acceptance by the conference. As may be recalled, the British prepared the first memorandum on the subject during the Moscow Conference. Gernegan, according to his own account, had prepared a draft in anticipation that the question might be broached at the conference; the American minister in Tehran and General Hurley worked together on a draft; and the Iranian government presented its own request for a communiqué or declaration. But with the uncertainty about the attitude of the Soviet Union at Tehran in the wake of its strong opposition to a declaration at the Moscow Conference, it would seem that the role played by General Hurley, and particularly by President Roosevelt and Iran, proved decisive in the *final acceptance* of the declaration. General Hurley's request that the president talk to Stalin, and the president's intervention in person, on the one hand, and the request coming from the Iranians themselves, on the other, probably exerted decisive influence in overcoming the Soviet opposition. According to the American minister's report, the Soviets may have felt that they "could not well oppose it [the proposal for a declaration] without placing themselves in an unfavorable light vis-à-vis the Iranian Government, especially after both the American and British representatives had indicated agreement."[93] His report also presented other contributing reasons, but this reason seems more important because at this particular time the Soviet Union was bending every effort to impress Iranian opinion.

In any event, what is also of particular interest to this study is the fact that Iran was not as uninformed and uninvolved an actor in the decision to issue a declaration as has been generally portrayed. To be sure, its role was not that of the initiator of the declaration, but the strength of Iranian diplomacy at

[90] See ibid., pp. 648-49 and pp. 840-43.

[91] See Don Lohbeck, *Patrick J. Hurley* (Chicago: Henry Regnery, 1956), p. 215.

[92] Hull, 2:1506.

[93] For the full text of this report see *Foreign Relations of U.S., 1943 (Cairo and Tehran Conferences)*, pp. 840-43.

this time lay in the alertness of its actors to what was happening around them. Secretary Hull's words about what the declaration meant to Iran aptly sum up the Iranian aspirations: "This declaration was of the highest importance to Iran because, in addition to the pledges it contained of economic assistance, it gave the Iranians what they had so much wanted; namely, a formal expression of American desire for the maintenance of Iran's sovereignty, and a renewal of the assurances previously given by Russia and Britain."[94] It may also be added, in light of this study, that Iran wanted pledges of both economic assistance and maintenance of political independence with a view not only to the wartime period but also, and more especially, the postwar era. The declaration came closer than any previous instrument to the recognition of Iran's expectations as an independent and sovereign state deserving future economic assistance from the Allied powers, particularly the United States.

[94]Hull, 2:1507.

III

Reaching for the United States

EVER SINCE THE early nineteenth century, when Iran was sucked into the whirlwind of European power politics, Anglo-Russian rivalry constituted the international sub-system of particular concern to Iran. One of Iran's most favored techniques in coping with this concern had been reliance upon a third power as a counterweight to the two rival powers. France had been favored as such a power for a short time in the early nineteenth century; the United States was selected twice before the Second World War, first in 1910-11, when Morgan Shuster was employed, and second in 1922-27, when the services of Arthur Millspaugh were acquired. In 1927 Germany became Iran's favored third power, and this was the case when the Second World War broke out.

In the bipolar Anglo-Russian context, Iran's reliance on a third power always began as a strategy of counterbalancing the influence of Great Britain and Russia. The employment of this strategy over time produced extensive ties with the third power, as was the case with Germany during the interwar period. Something similar to this occurred with the United States. What began as a third-power strategy early in the Second World War soon developed into increasing ties with the United States during, and particularly after, the war. In the Iranian perspective the Anglo-Russian alliance against Germany wrought no fundamental change in the traditional patterns of Anglo-Russian rivalry in Iran. The United States could be a most helpful counterweight against both.

Iran's diplomatic reliance upon the United States as a third power has been already seen in previous discussions. These will be brought together in this chapter as backdrop to a discussion of Iran's creation of ties, in addition to diplomatic ones, with the United States as its favored third power during the Second World War. In doing so, I shall examine all major occasions that Iran used to involve American power in order to counter British, and particularly Soviet, influence, except for the Soviet bid for oil concessions, which will be taken up in the following chapter.

The discussion in the previous chapters of Iran's foreign policy from the outbreak of the Second World War to the issuance of the Tripartite Declaration has been sprinkled with references to the development of its third-power strategy. Briefly summarized, three distinct phases may be identified in this development. The beginning of the first phase was marked by the increasing pressure of Great Britain and the Soviet Union on Iran after the German attack on Russia. As this pressure grew, Iran sought the sympathy of the United States by relying heavily on diplomatic channels in defending its policy of neutrality against charges of pro-German bias. The American response, though sympathetic, proved inconclusive.

The Anglo-Russian invasion of Iran signaled the beginning of the second phase. The invasion, for all practical purposes, eliminated Germany as Iran's favored third power, although pro-German sentiments continued in some circles both within and outside the government. The attraction of the United States as the third power began to increase with the invasion. Riza Shah unsuccessfully sought American intervention as a means of minimizing the consequences of the invasion. Although no intervention was, or could have been, forthcoming, the American expression of concern with Iran's independence produced some salutary effects. American insistence just after the invasion that the Soviet Union and Great Britain issue a declaration guaranteeing Iran's independence and insuring the temporary nature of their occupation was significantly influential in the conclusion of the Tripartite Treaty.

The arrival of United States forces in Iran in late 1942 marked the beginning of the third phase. From the Iranian perspective this arrival provided a new opportunity for deepening United States involvement in Iran, both as a means of countering the adverse effects of the wartime presence of the Soviet and British forces on Iranian soil and as a measure of insuring the withdrawal of these forces at the end of the war. By using the unsolicited arrival of the American forces toward this end, Iran first sought to get the United States to adhere to the Tripartite Treaty, as evidenced by its preparedness to change it to a four-power treaty. Having failed to do so, Iran then strove to negotiate a separate agreement with the United States guaranteeing, inter alia, American protection for Iran against not only Germany but "aggression by any government." The major target in all this was the Soviet Union, although fear of British ambitions was seldom laid to rest. Against the backdrop of all these Iranian efforts to secure the support of the United States since August 1941, it can be seen why Iran attached so much significance to the Tehran Declaration. It was the outstanding symbol of United States public support for the independence and territorial integrity of Iran. This was no naive joy over a piece of paper. To Iran, the declaration signaled greater American involvement as a counterweight to Soviet and British power. This goal also directed Iran's search for expanding ties with the United States by other than diplomatic means.

But it may be asked whether Iran really enjoyed sufficient freedom of action in wartime to warrant a discussion of its objectives and courses of action vis-à-vis the United States. The answer to this question should be in the affirmative. All available evidence, including numerous sources cited in this chapter, support such an answer. As was suggested in the previous chapters, Iran did not lose control of its foreign policy even vis-à-vis Great Britain and the Soviet Union, although its margin of choice contracted substantially after the invasion. As we proceed it will become increasingly clear that Iran's foreign policy enjoyed a greater degree of autonomy vis-à-vis the United States. To no small extent this was made possible by the attitude of Great Britain. Whether for Britain's want of resources, or for reasons of general Iranian reluctance to approach the British for aid, or for the British design to counter Soviet influence by encouraging American entrenchment in Iran, or for all or some combination of these reasons, Great Britain encouraged American receptivity to Iranian overtures. Yet Iran itself chiefly took the initiative in expanding a multitude of ties with the United States.

The nondiplomatic means by which Iranian leaders sought to involve the United States in Iran fell into two broad categories: aid and trade. Aid in particular was regarded as important, and it included military, financial, economic, educational, health, and others. My concern here will be those that were particularly significant to Iran during the war and produced far-reaching implications for its postwar policies toward the United States.

Obtaining American Military Aid

As early as January 7, 1942, Iran asked the United States for a specialist who would have the responsibility of entirely reorganizing the Iranian police forces throughout the country. The Department of State believed that Iran was turning to the United States in "its hour of need" because of the serious crisis caused by the Anglo-Russian occupation and at a time when Iran did not wish to invite British and Russian "control of its police forces" in view of the influence already exercised by the British and Russian military authorities.[1] Although the American advisers arrived in Iran in 1942, it was not until late 1943 that the necessary law was enacted. On October 21, 1943, the Majlis passed a law authorizing the Iranian government to sign an agreement covering the employment of Col. H. Norman Schwarzkopf, who was already working in Iran. He was the former director of rural police for the state of New Jersey, popularly known in America for his work in the Lindbergh kidnapping case and recognized in the profession as a "leading American authority on rural police."[2] The law authorized the government to engage the services of no more than eight American army officers, the senior officers to head the

---

[1] See *Foreign Relations of U.S., 1942,* D.P., 4:222-23.

[2] U.S. State Dept. *Bulletin* 11, no. 265 (July 23, 1944): 91.

mission and be advisers to the Ministry of the Interior for the Gendarmerie,[3] or rural police.

On November 27, 1943, Iran signed an agreement with the United States in pursuance of this law. The agreement terminated the preceding period, during which the mission members had been mere advisers with no legal authority to put their reforms into effect. The agreement, effective retroactively as of October 2, 1942, declared that the purpose of the mission was "to advise and assist the Ministry of Interior of Iran in the reorganization of the Imperial Iranian Gendarmeries." The mission was to continue at least for two years from the effective date of the agreement, which could be canceled at the initiative of Iran or the United States. The mission was made responsible solely to the minister of interior through the chief of the mission; was paid by the Iranian government; and was made subject to the disciplinary regulations of the Iranian Gendarmerie except insofar as such regulations were contrary to the regulations of the United States Army. Most of the provisions of the agreement concerned matters of duties, rank, compensation, and the like. The only other major provision was contained in article 20. It stated that the chief of the mission "will have immediate charge of the entire administration and control of the Gendarmerie and he will have the right to recommend to the Ministry of Interior and in accordance with regulations the appointment, promotion, demotion, or dismissal of any employee of the Gendarmerie and to put this into effect with the approval of the Ministry of the Interior and no other authority shall have the right to interfere, and he will have the right with the approval of the Minister of the Interior to transfer and reassign any officer, gendarme, or employee of the Gendarmerie."[4]

The agreement was extended through the exchange of notes on September 6, 1944, and again on September 29, 1945, and subsequently.[5] But the work of the mission was made no easier as the result of the agreement or its extensions. By spring 1944 the principal difficulties encountered by the mission were three. One major problem arose from the traditionally thorny relationship of the Gendarmerie to the army within the Iranian political system. As the head of the mission, Colonel Schwarzkopf became involved in

[3]*Foreign Relations of U.S., 1943,* D.P., 4:550-51.

[4]For the text of the agreement in English and Persian, see U.S., Department of State, *Executive Agreement Series 361* (Washington, D.C.: Government Printing Office, 1944), pp. 1-16.

[5]For the text of the notes exchanged see U.N., Secretariat, *Treaty Series* 31 (1949): 470-73. For details on the Schwarzkopf mission see U.S., Department of State, *Foreign Relations of the United States, 1944,* Diplomatic Papers, vol. 6, *The Near East, South Asia, Africa, the Far East* (Washington, D.C.: Government Printing Office, 1965), pp. 425-35.

a struggle with the Iranian army over the independence of the Gendarmerie in which he appeared to achieve a marked victory against the opposition of the shah and his advisers. The second major difficulty of the mission resembled that of the American missions in general—stiff opposition to the mission's reform programs in spite of the fact that the Americans working with the Gendarmerie enjoyed far more popularity in Iran than any of the other American advisory organizations.[6] And the third problem arose from the colonel's rank, on the one hand, and his extensive actual powers, on the other. In the eyes of the prestige-minded Iranians, a mere colonel was issuing orders usually reserved for generals. To the Iranian officials this was no little matter. And this aspect of Iranian political culture was no small obstacle in the way of the American mission.

Iran also took the initiative in obtaining American aid for its army. On March 20, 1942, Iran advised American authorities of its intention to engage a high-ranking American officer to take charge of "the entire finance and army supply divisions of the Iranian War Department."[7] The Iranian minister in Washington, in pressing this request at the State Department on the same day, claimed that the Iranian force of two- to three-hundred thousand men was rather well equipped and was officered by men nearly 80 percent of whom were European educated. This could be made "a formidable force," and American aid through a specialist could "bring about a large measure of cooperation with the Allied cause by the Iranian army to the benefit of all concerned." On June 16, 1942, Iran accepted Maj. Gen. John N. Greely, designated by the War Department, to undertake work of the Intendant General of the Iranian army in an advisory capacity. Encouraged by this success of its own efforts, Iran then pressed for the acquisition of an American military mission. Premier Qavam told the American minister in Tehran on August 13, 1942, that such a mission would reorganize and train the Iranian army, "which is demoralized, inefficient, depleted in materials and almost disintegrated as a result of the Anglo-Russian invasion, and claimed that the request for a military mission of this kind was not inconsistent with Iran's position because it was strongly pro-American." The American minister, however, in advising the secretary of state of this conversation, wondered whether such a reorganization of the Iranian army could be carried out in time to be of assistance in the war; whether the Iranian guarantees could be relied on in view of pro-German sentiments in Iran; and how the British and the Russians would react to such a mission. The shah tried to impress upon the American minister in Iran, in the same manner that Qavam had spoken to him, of the Iranian need for an American military mission, but as the year 1942 drew to an end Iran

[6]Ibid., pp. 393-95.

[7]*Foreign Relations of U.S., 1942,* D.P., 4:551.

had only the service of an American officer, Maj. Gen. Clarence S. Ridely, who replaced General Greely and who was also responsible to the War Department.[8]

But by the end of 1943 Iran had largely succeeded in its efforts to obtain military aid from the United States. General Ridely was trusted by the shah, Premier Qavam, and the war minister, Field Marshall Amir Ahmadi; Ridely, and subsequently his whole mission as well, enjoyed unusual success in their work, in comparison with the Millspaugh mission, to be discussed presently. In a glowing report to the Department of State about the Ridely mission, the American minister in Tehran stated that it had weathered the storm of disillusionment so apt to overcome foreign advisers in those difficult days and had not succumbed to the feeling of futility prompted by such difficulties. The minister ascribed the success of the Ridely mission at the time to the general's own simplicity, dignity, hard work, good leadership, and ability to win the confidence of the Iranian leaders.[9]

The chief problem confronting Iran regarding the Ridely mission was to obtain the consent of the United States to continue its services in Iran. The original agreement covering the engagement of the mission had been signed on November 3, 1943, and required renewal.[10] In October 1944 Iran requested the Department of State to obtain the consent of the War Department for the continuation of the mission beyond the termination date of March 1, 1945, which had been set by the War Department on the basis of a report by General Ridely "that there exists no military necessity for this mission and that virtually its entire usefulness to Iran has already been accomplished." The acting secretary of state, Edward R. Stettinius, supported the request of Iran in his letter of October 25, 1944, to Secretary of War Henry L. Stimson. He agreed with the War Department that the limited objectives of the mission in advising the Iranian Quartermaster Corps of the army would be accomplished by March 1, 1945, but said that "the ultimate objective of building up the Iranian Army to an efficient and self-reliant organization has only been begun." After a meeting held between the officials of the War and State Departments and attended by General Ridely on December 18, 1944, the secretary of state recommended to the secretary of war the continuation of the mission in Iran for "an indefinite period beyond March 1, 1945." On the basis of this recommendation, the secretary of war decided to continue the mission in Iran indefinitely because "the protection and advancement of our interests in Iran will require the strengthening of the Iranian security forces so that order

[8]Ibid., pp. 230-55.

[9]*Foreign Relations of U.S., 1943*, D.P., 4:527-51.

[10]This information is based on ibid., p. 553. It has not been possible to locate the text of the agreement.

may be maintained in this area, where world security might be threatened, after the withdrawal of Allied troops."[11] But as the war ended and the termination of the declared national emergency became imminent, continuation of the mission required general congressional enactment covering such missions beyond the declared national emergency.[12] We shall return to this matter in the discussion of Iran's postwar foreign policy.

Acquisition of American Financial Aid

As in the acquisition of military assistance, Iran took the initiative in securing financial aid from the United States. Like the military assistance, the financial aid consisted of technical aid. And just as the original request for a few military experts escalated into whole missions, the initial request for a financial expert broadened into the largest American mission in Iran. But several factors distinguished the financial mission from the military missions. This was the third American mission of its kind in the twentieth century; the first had served in Iran in 1910-11, the second in 1922-27. It was headed by Arthur C. Millspaugh, who had already served in Iran in a similar capacity in 1922-27. This mission proved to be the single most important and controversial mission in the relations of Iran and the United States.

Iran's relations with the financial mission constituted one of the most important components of Iran's wartime policy toward the United States. Securing financial aid was another means by which Iran was seeking to achieve its goal of deepening the involvement of the United States. As with the military mission, the British government generally encouraged American involvement in Iran. As early as March 1942 the British government informed the United States of its concern over the deteriorating financial and economic situation in Iran and inquired whether the United States would be prepared to lend its assistance in securing the services of an American financial adviser. On June 3, 1942, Iran formally advised the United States of its desire to engage an American financial expert, one who would have "a broad knowledge and experience in the financial field." On June 8, 1942, the Iranian prime minister told the American minister in Tehran that Millspaugh's name was being mentioned in Iranian circles and that he would be considered if he was available, but added that his powers would be less than on the previous visit (1922-27). Once the United States reached the conclusion that

[11] *Foreign Relations of U.S., 1944,* D.P., 5:412-13, 433-34, 442-44.

[12] See U.S., Department of State, *Foreign Relations of the United States, 1945,* Diplomatic Papers, vol. 8, *The Near East and Africa* (Washington, D.C.: Government Printing Office, 1969), pp. 534-36.

Millspaugh was "the logical choice," the Iranian prime minister, Ahmad Qavam, expressed pleasure but reiterated that Millspaugh would have less broad powers than on the previous mission because of the "democratic form of government" in Iran at the time. Furthermore, he stated that Iran's financial problems were vaster and more difficult than twenty years ago, that a man of the greatest ability was needed, and that Millspaugh's assistants on his last mission to Iran had not been of the "highest type."[13] This matter of the capability of assistants was reiterated by the Iranian foreign minister, 'Ali Sohaily, when he advised the American minister on October 5, 1942, that the cabinet formally approved the employment of Millspaugh.

The Majlis enacted the law necessary for the engagement of Millspaugh. The law, which was enacted on November 12, 1942, authorized the government to employ him as administrator general of the finances of Iran. Article 8 of the sixteen-article law provided for the scope of his powers. Under the supervision of the minister of finance, Millspaugh was given immediate charge of "the entire financial administration"; could reorganize the Ministry of Finance and the related departments; could appoint, promote, demote, transfer, or dismiss any employee of the ministry in consultation with the finance minister; and could attend the meetings of the Council of Ministers and committees of the Majlis when financial questions were being discussed. Millspaugh's contract, signed in pursuance of this law, authorized "substantial powers," to borrow his own words, although final authority rested formally in the Majlis and in the cabinet. In comparing his powers under this contractual arrangement with those of his first visit to Iran, Millspaugh singled out two differences. First, he noted that because of "nationalistic feeling" in Iran in the 1940s, any dispute between him and the Iranian government had to be referred, under the contract, to the Majlis, whereas during his first mission it had to be settled by resort to arbitration. Second, he added, as contrasted with the first mission, he was not consulted in the grant of foreign economic and commercial concessions by the Iranian government.[14]

Before taking up the assignment, Millspaugh insisted upon specific operational authority, not only in the financial, but also in the economic, sphere. He considered Iran's problems to fall into two broad categories, the emergency difficulties caused by the war and the more fundamental problems inherited from the past. In emphasizing the latter, he stated that the mission was called upon to deal, not with temporary "embarrassment caused by war devastation and the dislocation or stoppage of normal procedures, but with a Government

[13]*Foreign Relations of U.S., 1942,* D.P., 4:224-25, 238, 244-45, 253.

[14]For the text of the Law of Engagement of the Administrator General of the Finances, Nov. 12, 1942, see Arthur C. Millspaugh, *Americans in Persia* (Washington, D.C.: Brookings Institution, 1946), pp. 253, 269-72.

and country that have suffered radical alterations and perversions at the very foundation of financial, economic and social life. We are asked, while still in the midst of a war emergency, to pick up where autocracy left off, an autocracy that was as ruthless as it was ignorant and that worked its distracted and wasteful whims for fifteen years with amazing thoroughness on a prostrate and plastic people."[15] In order to cope with both wartime problems and the more basic matter of economic development, he urged a comprehensive program that, inter alia, would require strict governmental regulations of grain collection, prices, transportation, and distribution; he demanded the enactment of a high graduated income tax to combat inflation and other wartime problems.[16] I shall discuss the opposition to the mission's program shortly; suffice it to state here that as early as April 1943 this opposition reached such proportions as to be considered a "campaign against American advisers," especially the Millspaugh mission, whose requests had been hanging fire in the Majlis. In order to implement his comprehensive programs, Millspaugh sought to increase his staff, and the necessary proposal was approved "with lightning speed" by the Council of Ministers,[17] but it was not enacted into law by the Majlis until after the mission threatened resignation. The law was passed by the Majlis on October 24, 1943, authorizing the engagement of sixty Americans for a period of four years.[18]

The lull that followed the passage of this law was short-lived. The greatest opposition to the mission was in the Majlis, although the press played a part as well. During the course of the Majlis debate over the cabinet of Muhammad Sa'id, who had replaced 'Ali Sohaily as prime minister and formed a new government on April 6, 1944, the mission came under violent attack by several deputies, one of whom, Abolqasim Kazimi, criticized what he called the dictatorial attitude of Millspaugh and demanded that he be removed. Vituperation, misstatements, and even personal attacks on individual advisers, launched by Deputy Kazimi, probably did not hurt the mission as much as the oratory of the popular and prestigeous Muhammad Mussadiq. But the mission was defended by Sayid Zia ed-Din Tabatabai, "presumably at the suggestion of Sir Reader Bullard," the British ambassador in Tehran.[19] The frequency and intensity of the attacks against the American advisers in the Majlis and the press prompted American representations to the Iranian government. In the draft of a note for delivery to the Iranian authorities by

[15] Ibid., p. 60n.

[16] See U.S. State Dept. *Bulletin* 11, no. 265 (July 23, 1944): 90-91.

[17] *Foreign Relations of U.S., 1943*, D.P., 4:518-20, 534-35.

[18] For the text of the law see ibid., pp. 557-58.

[19] *Foreign Relations of U.S., 1944*, D.P., 5:395-99.

the American legation, Secretary of State Hull expressed Washington's "especial surprise and concern" to the Iranian authorities for their failure to give the Americans attacked the "support which they have the right to expect" as foreign advisers as well as high officials of the Iranian government.[20]The legation's note, the secretary also suggested, should remind the Iranian government that from the outset the legation had insisted on full support and sympathy of all the Iranian authorities concerned and that on the basis of Prime Minister Qavam's assurance of support for the advisers had the Department of State agreed to lend its assistance. More important, the note said that the Department of State "deprecates any suggestion that American advisers were sent to Iran to act as mere political buffers. They were sent to Iran to assist the Iranian Government to rebuild its financial and economic structure which had suffered so severely because of the war, and for no other purpose." The note was delivered to the prime minister by the American chargé in person on May 27, 1944, and produced a long reply from Iran on June 1. The note claimed that the Iranian government was entirely favorable to the advisers; supported them in the past and intended to do so in the future; and expressed surprise at the idea that the advisers had been hired as political buffers.[21]

The Iranian reply also indicated that Millspaugh's powers should be confined to the financial sphere. On June 20, 1944, the prime minister told the American chargé that it had been decided to introduce a bill in the Majlis to repeal Millspaugh's plenary economic, as distinguished from financial, powers. Millspaugh submitted his resignation to the prime minister on June 23, 1944, to be effective on June 29, accusing the Iranian government of violating its obligation under the law for his engagement and the full powers acts, objecting to the creation of a separate organization to handle economic matters, and concluding that the government's policy made continuance of any useful work in Iran impossible.[22] The prime minister refused to accept Millspaugh's resignation, Secretary of State Hull regretted his decision to resign and asked him to avoid anything in the nature of public recriminations, and the shah and the cabinet joined in the chorus to persuade him to stay on. While Millspaugh was caught in the tangled web of bargaining with Iranian officials, the Majlis Deputies proceeded with the bill to repeal his economic powers, and on December 20, 1944, the Finance Committee of the Majlis approved in

[20]For the text of the proposed draft see ibid., pp. 402-3. Indications are that the note was presented to Iran after only minor changes.

[21]See ibid., pp. 403-8.

[22]Ibid., p. 410. For details on the tangled problem of the Millspaugh resignation, see ibid., especially pp. 412-28.

modified form the prime minister's bill for the repeal of Millspaugh's economic powers.[23] Finally, on January 8, 1945, the Majlis passed the bill canceling as of that date the special economic powers. Millspaugh left Iran on February 28, 1945.[24] After his departure, the American ambassador suggested that the Department of State assist in bringing to Iran from abroad some disinterested and highly qualified man such as James M. Landis, former director of American Economic Operations in the Middle East, to reorganize the Millspaugh mission. But Acting Secretary of State Crew declined to go along with this suggestion in view of what had occurred during the preceding two years. The work of the mission was ended on December 11, 1945.[25]

The failure of the Millspaugh mission was rooted in a complicated and interrelated web of factors. It included the roles of the Soviet Union and the United States on the one hand, and the problems concerning Millspaugh's perception of Iranian society and programs and Iran's political culture, on the other. The overall role of the Soviet Union in Iran did not spare the American advisory missions, particularly the Millspaugh mission. Millspaugh's own account of the Soviet role in undermining his mission's work in Iran may still be read with profit. I shall concentrate here on other relevant factors.

Let us first take up the role of the United States. The record seems to indicate a degree of harmony between Millspaugh and the Department of State that is not borne out by the facts. Although the department was instrumental in the engagement of Millspaugh, Millspaugh himself blamed the failure of his mission on poor organization, defective information, and lack of coordination among various departments in Washington, on the one hand, and on confusion of purpose, delays, compromises, personal jealousies, intrigues, and incapacity or laziness within the Department of State, on the other.[26] But Millspaugh was not a reasonably detached observer, and the department's own published record on the subject must be consulted as well. Although the charge of lack of coordination seems not unfounded, that of laziness is difficult to support. This is evidenced (1) by the fact that on several occasions the department took pains to grapple with the problems of American policy, particularly the advisory programs in Iran; (2) by the sympathetic

[23] Ibid., pp. 443-44.

[24] The exact date of Millspaugh's resignation is difficult to ascertain. In *Americans in Persia* he states that his resignation took effect Feb. 15, 1954 (pp. 151-52). In a telegram to the Department of State, the American ambassador in Iran reported on Feb. 28, 1945, that Dr. Millspaugh left Tehran "this morning." As will be seen in the text, the date of the end of the *mission*'s work was still different. For this information see *Foreign Relations of U.S., 1945*, D.P., 8:550n, 563.

[25] Ibid., pp. 554, 536.

[26] See Millspaugh, p. 208.

cooperation of the American legation, even by Millspaugh's own admission, with his mission; and (3) by the department's decision to make representations on behalf of the mission in spite of the fact that the United States was determined to avoid unpleasant relations with Iran during the critical war years.

Three major problems troubled the American policy in Iran. The first was the problem of the identification of American objectives in general and the relation of the mission to those objectives in particular. At various times the stated American objectives were to assist the Allied war efforts; to fulfill the principles of the Atlantic Charter and to establish the foundations for a lasting peace throughout the world, in part by maintaining Iran's territorial integrity and political independence; to build a prosperous and stable Iran in order to thwart a British or Russian bid for supremacy; and to prevent any great power from establishing itself on the Persian Gulf opposite the important American petroleum development in Saudi Arabia.[27] Although it would appear, for example, that assisting the Allied war effort was a short-range objective as compared with the long-range goal of building a prosperous and stable Iran, it is difficult to ascertain consistency and clarity in American priorities in general and in their relation to the mission in particular in the admittedly difficult times between 1941 and the oil crisis of 1944. As will be seen, it was largely in the course of this crisis, and particularly during the Azeri and Kurdish rebellions in 1945-46, that some degree of clarification in American objectives in Iran was achieved.

A second problem in the American role in Iran related to the nature of the relationship of the United States government to Millspaugh. On the one hand, the mission was *officially* an employee of Iran; but on the other hand, it, like other American advisory missions, was to contribute to American objectives.[28] The euphemism that the mission acted in a "private capacity" points to a basic contradiction in the American position, and this contradiction emboldened the forces of opposition to it. Moreover, a degree of ambivalence in the American attitude toward Great Britain and particularly the Soviet Union seems to have had some effect on the fate of the mission. The United States showed much awareness of the historic rivalry between these two powers in Iran; yet it continued in the belief that not only could they somehow cooperate but that the United States could indeed maintain "Allied solidarity" in Iran. Even as late as August 1945, by which time the Soviet Union had

[27] *Foreign Relations of U.S., 1943,* D.P., 4:378-79.

[28] George V. Allen, chief of the division of Middle Eastern affairs of the Department of State, said that the various "advisory missions in Persia are an important implementation of the American Government's policy of assistance to that country [Iran]" (U.S. State Dept. *Bulletin* 11, no. 265 [July 23, 1944] : 88-93).

repeatedly demonstrated its expansionist designs in Iran and the United States itself had assisted Iran to resist Soviet interference, the United States at least contemplated the replacement of its own advisory program by an Anglo-Soviet-American program dedicated to the reconstruction of Iran.[29] Such a perception not only contradicted American awareness of the traditional ambitions of Great Britain and the Soviet Union but also clashed with the Iranian policy of seeking to intensify the involvement of the United States as a friendly third power capable of checkmating British, and particularly Soviet, ambitions.

Millspaugh's own perception of his role in Iran also clashed with the view of Iranian policymakers. As seen throughout, Iran's primary goal in securing the services of this mission as well as others was to deepen American involvement in its affairs. Although Iran would have officially denied the attribution of this motive to its policy toward the United States (as indeed it did in its response of June 1, 1944, to the American representations discussed before), its statesmen admitted it in their more candid moments. A superb example of this may be found in a long "personal conference" between Muhammad Sa'id and the American chargé on February 21, 1944, during which Foreign Minister Sa'id "repeatedly stressed that he had personally been responsible for bringing American advisers to Iran but that from the beginning he had felt that this country did not need their technical skill so much as for them to act as a cushion between British-Soviet conflicting political interests."[30] Millspaugh, however, perceived the role of his mission quite differently. The mission's task was primarily economic, whether it related to what he termed "emergency economic problems" or "long-range plans." It was particularly the latter that he believed to be his primary concern and contribution to the Allied war effort, though the resolution of emergency economic problems was "in the main incidental" to the task that the Iranian government had assigned to him. He believed he "could not overlook the fact that we had come to Persia, as previous missions had, to help in the development and progress of the country."[31] The incompatibility between this vision and the Iranian political goal has prompted an observer-scholar to characterize Millspaugh as

[29] *Foreign Relations of U.S., 1945,* D.P., 8:343-400, especially p. 399. This same theme of Anglo-Soviet-American cooperation was expressed earlier by George V. Allen in these terms: "The situation in Persia today is in one striking respect better than it has been for many years: close collaboration is maintained among the representatives of the United States, Great Britain and Russia in Tehran. British and Russian policies are similar to the American one in that all three desire to see a strong Persia, capable of maintaining peace and order in the country after the war."

[30] *Foreign Relations of U.S., 1944,* D.P., 5:390-92.

[31] See Millspaugh, pp. 55-71, 221.

one who was "plus catholique que le pape,"[32] or, as a Persian saying goes, *kasih-ye az ash dagh-tar* ("a bowl hotter than the soup").

But this factor, even when added to the Soviet opposition and the troubled American role, would still prove an insufficient explanation for the failure of the Millspaugh mission. It does not suffice because it approaches the problem merely from the angle of the purpose of the political system as a whole. While this approach does assist in identifying the "primary interest" of Iran in engaging the Millspaugh mission, by itself it neglects the problem of "variable interests."[33] These interests as used here refer to both groups and individuals within the Iranian political culture. The Majlis was the single most important *forum* within which these interests found expression, but it was not the only one. In its tumultuous career the Millspaugh mission clashed with diverse interests within the Iranian political structure. Within the bureaucracy, for example, he faced opposition to his programs almost consistently. Most of this opposition represented the interests of the landed aristocracy, merchants, grafters, and others that were also represented in the Majlis. Some of the opposition was rooted in the clash of personalities, exemplified in Millspaugh's public quarrel with the minister of interior. Taddayyun, over the so-called census issue,[34] and his fateful dismissal of the honest and courageous, but ambitious and temperamental, 'Abulhasan Ibtihaj, the director-general of the National Bank.[35] Once, at least, Millspaugh's curtailment of the army budget alarmed the shah who, as a rule, supported the mission.[36] A similar move by Millspaugh in 1927 prompted Riza Shah to deal the final blow to his first mission. In 1944-45, however, the interests that brought down the mission were more complicated.

The Majlis was the main scene of opposition to Millspaugh. Although Sayid Zia supported the government's third-power policy and hence the Millspaugh mission, the overwhelming number of deputies increasingly gravitated toward the two main focuses of opposition to the mission. One of the two major "fractions" within the Fourteenth Majlis represented the Soviet-supported Tudeh party. This was the group characterized appropriately as "small in number, but large in means" (*qalil al'adad valy kassir al-vasai'l*) as contrasted with the other group that formed the nucleus of the majority,

---

[32] See Lenczowski, p. 271.

[33] For somewhat similar usage of these terms, see Thomas W. Robinson, "National Interest," in James N. Rosenau, ed., *International Politics and Foreign Policy* (New York: Free Press, 1969), pp. 182-90.

[34] *Foreign Relations of U.S., 1943*, D.P., 4:536-37.

[35] *Foreign Relations of U.S., 1944*, D.P., 5:430-40.

[36] *Foreign Relations of U.S., 1943*, D.P., 4:521-22.

consisting of a large number of deputies but enjoying few means. The Tudeh group within the Majlis was supported by the best-organized party, the presence of the Red Army in Iran, the propaganda machinery of Moscow, and some fifty newspapers in Tehran and the provinces.[37] It opposed any kind of American buffer between Great Britain and the Soviet Union because it was committed to the elimination of both British and American influence and the expansion of Soviet power. But the Tudeh opposition to the Millspaugh mission was largely overshadowed by a small group of nationalist Deputies led by Musaddiq. As the leading Deputy from Tehran and as one who enjoyed immense popularity within and outside the Majlis, his vociferous attack upon the Millspaugh mission was largely instrumental in the eventual repeal of Millspaugh's economic powers. Strangely enough, Millspaugh's own book makes only scant reference to Musaddiq,[38] whereas the American chargé in Tehran reported the Musaddiq attack on the mission to the Department of State with perceptive concern. Unfortunately, the chargé said, Musaddiq "is a very popular man in Iran, and his words carry a great deal of weight." Furthermore, he indicated that the prestige of Musaddiq "bodes no good for the future of the mission."[39]

Musaddiq's campaign was essentially political. It was a reflection of the nationalist attitudes and tendencies associated with the doctrine of "negative equilibrium" (*muvazinih-ye manfi*) that gained widespread adherence among various new groups in the postwar period. Suffice it to say here that insofar as the mission was concerned, this doctrine coincided with the Tudeh position. The pro-Musaddiq, as well as the Tudeh, deputies were one in their opposition to the mission, the former seeking the elimination of all foreign influences from Iran and the latter wishing the same except for the Soviet Union.

It is doubtful, however, that the coincidence of the interests of these two groups alone could have resulted in the breakup of the Millspaugh mission. There was a third group—the largest and most powerful one—variously labeled "profiteers,"[40] "politico-economic racketeers,"[41] or simply the "Gang."[42] Regardless of the label, this group consisted in the main of large landlords and merchants, who occupied positions of power within the Iranian political structure, including the Majlis.[43] As already seen, Millspaugh's comprehensive

[37] See Kirmani, 2:543.

[38] See Millspaugh, pp. 86, 146, 147.

[39] *Foreign Relations of U.S., 1944,* D.P., 5:397-99.

[40] Ibid.

[41] Millspaugh, p. 139.

[42] Sir Clarmont Skrine, *World War in Iran* (London: Constable & Co., 1962), p. 172.

[43] See Kirmani, 2:548-49.

economic programs, aimed at coping with both the wartime difficulties and the long-range economic development of Iran, faced stiff opposition in the Majlis. The two most important reform measures were the high graduated income tax, enacted into law by the Thirteenth Majlis and bitterly opposed by the Fourteenth Majlis, and the strict governmental regulation of grain collection. The large landowners resented the implementation of the grain collection regulations because the government purchase of grains under the law deprived them of the high profits obtained by selling in the black market. The large commercial interests resented the income tax law because it raised tax rates from 10 percent to 80 percent for high income merchants. They also opposed government monopoly of the import of sugar, tea, and cotton piece goods.[44] It was no coincidence that Millspaugh's leading opponents comprised mainly the deputy-landlords, who represented the landed aristocracy.[45] An interesting study of the professional and social background of the deputies of the Majlis has shown that 57 percent of the deputies of the Fourteenth Majlis were landlords and some 13 percent were merchants.[46] The Tudeh group in the Majlis agreed to leave the campaign against the American advisers to the leading opponents of the Millspaugh mission, who after four sessions of bitter debate succeeded in mustering some 69 votes out of 95 cast for the repeal of Millspaugh's economic powers.[47] It was the interplay of this combination of the extreme nationalist, Tudeh Communist, and large landed and commercial interests with the Soviet opposition, American ambivalence, and Millspaugh's personal shortcomings that seems to have undergirded the failure of his mission. This failure was also a partial defeat for the supporters of the wartime policy of deepening American involvement as a technique of thwarting Anglo-Russian pressures. As such, the failure of the Millspaugh mission foretold the postwar direction of Iranian foreign policy under the impact of both nationalist and Communist groups.

[44] Ibid. and *Foreign Relations of U.S., 1943,* D.P., 4:532-36, 551-54.

[45] Besides Musaddiq the leading opponents of Millspaugh in the Fourteenth Majlis included 'Abduh, Amini (Abolqasim), Amir-taymour (Kalali), Ardalan (Nasirquli), Itibar (Abdolhusain), Farivar (Gholamali), Lankarani (Shaikh Husain), Rahimyan (Gholamhusain), and Muzaffarzadih (Mirsalih). Kirmani, from whom these names are taken, does not give first names; these have been furnished in parentheses here in order to avoid confusion with similar surnames. See Kirmani, 2:566.

[46] This information is based on Zahra Shajia'i, *Namayandigan-i Majlis-i Showra-ye Milli dar Bist va Yek Dowrih-ye Qanungozari* (Tehran: Mu'assihsih-ye Motali'at va Tahqiqat-i Ijtima'i, 1965/66).

[47] See Kirmani, 2:566-67.

Expansion of Trade

Besides seeking American military and financial aid, Iran turned to the United
States for trade after the Anglo-Russian invasion in 1941. American trade,
like American aid, was sought for the overriding objective of intensifying
American involvement. It was also sought as a substitute for German trade.
Iran's geographical pattern of trade had often been dominated by political
considerations. Riza Shah had sought to reduce Iran's dependence on Russian
trade by increasing trade with Germany. Subsequent to the signing of the
Payment and Clearing Agreement with Germany October 30, 1935, Irano-
German trade had increased, particularly because of Russo-Iranian trade
difficulties.[48] Although Iran had hoped to clear these difficulties by means of
a comprehensive treaty of commerce and navigation signed with the Soviet
Union on March 25, 1940, Iranian trade with Germany continued to rise until
the German attack on Russia and the subsequent Anglo-Russian invasion of
Iran. By the time of the invasion Germany had become Iran's leading trade
partner, with imports of 47.87 percent and exports of 42.09 percent of the
totals. The figures for the United States at the same time (1940-41) had
reached merely 13.64 percent and 8.39 percent of the totals, respectively.
After 1942 trade with Germany disappeared, and Iran actively sought a trade
agreement with the United States.

Such an agreement was signed on April 8, 1943, but before I examine its
major features, a few words must be said about Iranian perspectives and
problems revealed in the course of long negotiations preceding its signature.
To be sure, economic considerations were not totally absent but were, in the
Iranian perspective, of secondary importance. In their trade negotiations,
however, the Iranian officials did not parade their real political concerns except in their more candid moments. Trade with the United States was sought
initially in part to enhance Iranian prestige. In resuming conversation with
American officials for a trade agreement, Allahyar Salih, chief of the Iranian
Trade and Economic Commission, stated candidly on January 23, 1944, that
a great many people thought that Iran was no longer an independent country,
and he felt that the conclusion of a trade agreement with the United States
would call attention to the fact that Iran was a going concern.[49] Although at
the time of the release of information on the agreement American officials
stated that it was designed to facilitate trade between the two countries during
the wartime emergency and to provide a basis for expansion of trade between
Iran and the United States after the war,[50] there were indications that the

[48] For details see Ramazani, *Foreign Policy of Iran*, pp. 280-84.

[49] *Foreign Relations of U.S., 1942*, D.P., 4:276-77.

[50] See U.S. State Dept. *Bulletin* 8, no. 198 (Apr. 10, 1943): 299.

United States also considered the conclusion of the trade agreement "politically desirable."[51]

The main problem in concluding the agreement was Iran's difficulty in making changes in its previous trade policy and practices. The United States insisted on assurances that the Iranian government be prepared to consider reductions of duties or supplementary charges on products of interest to the United States.[52] In light of the strict government control of trade inherited from the Riza Shah era, the kind of flexible trade policy the United States Trade Agreement Act required was not easy for Iran to consider, but the eagerness of the Iranian government to conclude a trade agreement with the United States finally prompted Iran to grant the assurances sought by the United States before the signing of the agreement.[53]

Iran's trade Agreement with the United States of April 8, 1943, entered into force thirty days after completion of the necessary formalities, which took place only on May 29, 1944. The Iranian agreement was the twenty-seventh of its kind signed with any country by the United States and the second, after Turkey, in the Middle East. As a developing country Iran was chiefly an importer of manufactured goods and an exporter of raw materials. As such, its major imports from the United States—automobiles and trucks, tires, tubes, and similar products—constituted 70 to 85 percent of total Iranian commercial imports. Iran's major exports to the United States consisted largely of handicraft products and raw materials. Under the agreement, Iran and the United States made reciprocal concessions. The Iranian concessions included removal or reduction of duty and the abolition of the Iranian monopoly tax. Foreign trade monopolies, which formerly played an important part in Iran's foreign trade policy, had either been discontinued or modified in the war years, although the Iranian government continued to maintain control of foreign trade through the remaining monopolies, exchange restrictions, and other means. Of special interest to American trade was the automotive import monopoly, which was discontinued. Another major concession was Iran's grant of nondiscriminatory treatment in the application of all its foreign trade and exchange control measures. This provision removed the disadvantages incurred by American exporters as the result of Iran's clearing agreements with certain other countries.[54]

[51] See *Foreign Relations of U.S., 1942,* D.P., 4:280.

[52] Ibid., p. 282.

[53] Ibid. Only after these assurances were granted did the United States give public notice of the negotiations. See also U.S. State Dept. *Bulletin* 7, no. 162 (Aug. 1, 1942): 664-69.

[54] See U.S. State Dept. *Bulletin* 8, no. 198 (Apr. 10, 1943): 300.

The American concessions to Iran fell under three major categories. The first category included the Iranian products for which the American duty was reduced, especially the duty on rugs, the most important Iranian product in terms of nonoil trade value. Under the United States Tariff Act of 1930, "oriental rugs" were generally dutiable at fifty cents a square foot, but under the trade agreement with Iran the rate was reduced to twenty-five cents a square foot but not less than 22½ percent ad valorem. Other items for which the American duty was reduced were opium, copperware, beautiful articles of inlaid wood, and engraved and inlaid silver. The second category of American concessions included items such as pistachio nuts and sturgeon caviar, the duty rates for which were bound under the agreement. The third category consisted of items such as furs and turquoise, which were bound free for the first time.[55]

The fundamental principle guiding the new reciprocal Irano-American trade was unconditional most-favored-nation treatment. Article 1 of the agreement provided that the two countries "will grant each other unconditional and unrestricted most-favored-nation treatment in all matters concerning customs duties and subsidiary charges of every kind and in the method of levying duties, further, in all matters concerning the rules, formalities and charges imposed in connection with the clearing of goods through the customs and with respect to all laws and regulations affecting the sale, taxation or use of imported goods within the country."[56] This important principle of non-discrimination was made applicable to import quotas, prohibitions, and other forms of restriction on imports in article 3; to exchange control in article 4; and to foreign purchases by either country in article 5. The agreement was to remain in force for three years unless terminated earlier in accordance with its relevant provisions.

The trade agreement with the United States marked one more step in the direction of change in the Iranian prewar international posture. The drastic changes in the international system marked by the outbreak of the Second World War, the German invasion of Russia, and particularly the Anglo-Russian invasion and occupation of Iran lay at the heart of this change in the direction of Iranian foreign policy.

The Allied occupation imposed serious limitations on the autonomy of Iranian foreign policy, particularly vis-à-vis the Soviet Union and Great Britain, but within these limits Iran sought to exercise a degree of independent choice in world affairs. To no small extent the Allied need of Iranian

[55]Ibid., pp. 302-5.

[56]For the text of the agreement and related documents in English and Persian, see U.S. Department of State, *Executive Agreement Series 410* (Washington, D.C.: Government Printing Office, 1944), pp. 1-38.

territory and cooperation in the execution of the war effort contributed to the preservation of a degree of Iranian autonomy in foreign policy. But Iran's own efforts were not without meaningful effects. Insofar as these efforts were directed toward the search for American involvement in Iran, the evidence seems to show a remarkable degree of success from the Iranian standpoint despite formidable odds. The Iranian diplomatic efforts to counteract Anglo-Russian pressures with American influence and to invite American intervention against the subsequent invasion proved ineffective, and, given the configuration of international politics at the time, it could not have been otherwise. But subsequent to the invasion, Iran's repeated appeals to the United States for the support of its independence and territorial integrity were not without effect on the United States demand for British and Soviet assurances of the temporary nature of the occupation. These assurances were eventually included in the Tripartite Treaty, which was regarded with satisfaction by Secretary Hull as a fulfillment of *American* demand for guarantees of Iran's independence and territorial integrity. The ability of the Iranian statesman Prime Minister Muhammad 'Ali Foroughi to overcome the opposition of the pro-German elements within the Majlis finally insured the passage of the treaty, the crucial provisions of which on the evacuation of foreign troops from Iran, as will be seen, provided the main legal basis for legitimization of the Iranian, British, and American demands for the withdrawal of Soviet troops from northern Iran. To be sure, Iran was not involved in efforts that finally produced the Tehran Declaration, but, as seen, Iran was not completely unaware of the activities preceding its formation. More important, Iran's repeated diplomatic appeals to the United States for the support of its independence were not without effect on the United States, whose role proved decisive in the formulation of the declaration and its acceptance by the Soviet Union. At the diplomatic level the declaration signaled the single most important development to that date in the direction of greater American involvement in Iran; the United States had publicly gone on record in supporting Iran's independence and territorial integrity.

Iran's nondiplomatic efforts of 1941-43 seem, in the perspective of Iranian foreign policy, to have proved even more rewarding. To deepen American involvement in Iran by means of obtaining technical, military, and financial aid and of expanding trade proved a formidable task. The opposition of the Soviet Union, the ambivalence of the United States, the variable interests of the nationalists, Communists, and the large landlords and merchants as well as the conflict of Millspaugh's personality with various Iranian officials eventually led to the failure of the economic mission, and as such this failure may be considered a setback for Iranian policy. Yet this obviously dismal experience was somewhat offset by three factors. First was the Irano-American determination to immunize their overall relations from the ill effects of the fate of the financial mission. The second was the spectacular success of the Ridely mission. This mission well fitted the Iranian power structure; it pleased the shah as its reform measures benefitted the army. Third, neither the American nor the Iranian policymakers felt that the end of the Millspaugh mission doomed to failure other types of American technical aid to Iran at the time or in the future.

Finally, the trade agreement with the United States was regarded by Iranians as another successful step in their efforts to intensify American interest in Iran. Like the Tehran Declaration and the acquisition of technical, military, and financial assistance, the trade agreement was regarded as contributing to the emerging Iranian posture and prestige. From a strictly commercial standpoint it signaled a drastic departure from the prewar patterns of Iranian trade policy; it introduced an unprecedented degree of liberalization of government control. But the primary significance of the agreement for Iranians lay in its perceived political effects. The geographical pattern of Iranian trade once again followed the political direction of Iranian foreign policy; the main thrust of that direction at the time was toward friendship with the United States.

IV

Defiance of the Soviet Union

IRAN'S WARTIME FOREIGN policy was, in its basic patterns, a microcosm of the foreign policy of Riza Shah. Riza Shah's favorite third power had been Germany, but he turned to the United States in the fateful days of 1941, and his successors pursued fundamentally the same course of action after his abdication. Riza Shah feared the Soviet Union more than Great Britain, and his successors also distrusted the former more than the latter. Riza Shah's policy toward Germany as the favorite third power was largely a corollary of his policy toward the Soviet Union; similarly Iran's wartime policy toward the United States was influenced chiefly by Iranian apprehensions of the Soviet Union, Iran's traditional bête noire.[1] This chapter on Iran's wartime policy toward the Soviet Union should shed additional light on Iran's wartime policy toward the United States, treated in the preceding chapter.

The inevitable alliance with the Soviet Union wrought no change in the Iranian estimation of Soviet objectives in Iran. How were these objectives perceived? The Soviet notes of June 26, July 19, August 16, and August 25, 1941, expressed Soviet displeasure with activities of German agents in Iran, and the note of August 25, which was delivered on the day of invasion, clearly linked the invasion to the threat of German activities to the Soviet Union. The Soviet Union invoked article 6 of its 1921 treaty with Iran to justify "temporarily sending its troops into Iranian territory in the interests of self-defence." But, as already seen, neither before the invasion nor shortly afterwards did Iran believe that German activities posed such a threat to Russia. Nor did the Iranian statesmen believe that the short-term Allied objective of securing the supply of war materials to the Soviet Union through Iranian territory would prevent the Soviets from seeking to achieve expansionist ends. Iranian skepticism was informed not only by long experience with Russia but also by the Soviet behavior, or better yet, misbehavior, in the wake of the invasion. The sudden revival of the old Soviet demand for the Kavir Khorian oil concession, the refusal to reduce Soviet areas of occupation at Iran's request, and the indiscriminate bombing in the vicinity of Tehran

[1] These parallels are based on research for the present work and *Foreign Policy of Iran*, particularly chapters 9-12.

and the simultaneous dropping of propaganda leaflets glorifying the lot of Soviet peasants and workers as contrasted with the sorry plight of their counterparts in Iran left little doubt in the Iranian mind that Russia's long-term goal continued to be the aggrandizement of its power and, eventually, control in Iran.[2]

Instruments of Soviet Policy

Iranian wartime policy toward the Soviet Union was largely characterized by a determination to resist the Soviet bid for control. This resistance can best be seen in light of the multifaceted means adopted by the Soviet Union. The principal instruments of Soviet policy in Iran included the Red Army, diplomatic methods, and local Communist parties. Iran had experienced all these in the 1920s,[3] but they proved far more effective during the Second World War, and consequently Iranian resistance proved to be a far more formidable task. As contrasted with Raskolnikov's brief incursion into northern Iran in 1920, the Red Army occupation lasted for nearly five years, from August 1941 to May 1946. Soviet wartime diplomacy in Iran was backed by a powerful and stable government as contrasted with the relatively insecure, nascent Soviet government of the early 1920s. And the Iranian Communists of the 1940s far surpassed their counterparts of the 1920s in the nature and extent of social support, organizational strength, and scope and diversity of activities.

The Red Army constituted the most formidable instrument of Soviet policy in Iran from the very outset. For all practical purposes it established its own rule in northern Iran throughout the war and shortly thereafter. As such, it reinforced all other instruments of Soviet policy, including the Iranian Communist parties, be it the Tudeh party or the Azerbaijani and Kurdish democratic parties. (Red Army support of the two provincial parties and the establishment of the Azeri and Kurdish republics will be examined in the next chapter.) First I shall examine the role of the Red Army in the Soviet zone of occupation in 1941-43. The Red Army during this period, I believe, aimed at the separation of northern Iran from the rest of the country, despite the Soviet assurances of Iranian independence and territorial integrity embodied in its diplomatic notes before the Tripartite Treaty, in the treaty itself, and in the Tehran Declaration.

Red Army behavior in northern Iran constituted the single most difficult

[2]For documentary evidence of these acts, see *Foreign Relations of U.S., 1941*, D.P., 3:444. I witnessed these acts as a resident of Tehran.

[3]See Chapter 7 of Ramazani, *Foreign Policy of Iran*.

problem of Russian policy for Iran and caused deep concern also in Great Britain and the United States as early as September 1941. Sir Anthony Eden, on September 23, 1941, informed Ivan Maisky, the Soviet ambassador to Great Britain, that he considered most harmful any undue interference in Iranian affairs or sympathy towards separatist movements by the Russians in northern Iran. The secretary of state, Cordell Hull, instructed the American ambassador to Great Britain to inform Eden that the United States government "views with concern Russian political activities in Iran and is extremely apprehensive of the effect upon Turkey of any display of Russian sympathy toward an Armenian separatist movement in Iran."[4] No matter what beneficial effects the British and American representations may have had on the behavior of Russian forces in late 1941, they were short lived. By the spring of 1942 the Russian forces were interfering with the movement of Iranian forces in Azerbaijan. The Iranian central government was alarmed in May 1942 by the Kurdish attack upon gendarme posts at Rizaiyih, but the Soviet authorities refused to grant permission to Iranian troops to proceed there. The shah complained of the Soviet behavior to the American minister and hoped for assistance from the United States.[5]

By spring 1943 the United States itself, however, had become the object of some most aggressive Soviet behavior in northern Iran. By that time the American presence had become increasingly unpalatable to the Soviets. On the one hand, the American troops had arrived in Iran. The Russians complained bitterly that they had not been informed in advance about the arrival of American troops. On the other hand, the American military missions and the Millspaugh financial mission had begun their extensive activities. By April 1943 the Soviets had launched an anti-American campaign in northern Iran. They expelled Rex Vivian, an American representative of the food and supply adviser, placed obstacles in the way of the operations of General Connolly's force, which was involved in the transportation of supplies to Russia, refused to grant a permit to Colonel Schwarzkopf to visit Rasht officially, and forced, for all practical purposes, the replacement of the American consul at Tabriz.[6]

A second major instrument of Soviet policy in Iran was the Tudeh ("Masses") party. The real question of interest here is whether the party was an instrument of Soviet policy and hence a major problem of foreign policy as well as domestic politics for Iran. The role of the Tudeh party in the oil crisis between the Soviet Union and Iran will be treated later in this chapter;

---

[4]*Foreign Relations of U.S., 1941*, D.P., 3:465-67.

[5]*Foreign Relations of U.S., 1942*, D.P., 4:318-19.

[6]*Foreign Relations of U.S., 1943*, D.P., 4:345, 349, 357, 362.

here my concern is Red Army support of the Tudeh elements in northern Iran.

A few words about the Tudeh party itself may prove helpful (it has been treated elsewhere by others[7]). The party was established after the abdication of Riza Shah, who had jailed the members of a group of fifty-three in 1937 on the charge of Communist persuasion. The leader of the group, Taqi Arani, died in the shah's prison, but his close associates, consisting of four intellectuals—a surgeon, a lawyer, a university professor, and a writer—founded the party after their release. The party aspired to the recruitment of the masses and espoused the principle of democratic centralism; it was organized in terms of a party congress, provincial committees, local committees, and cells. Local branches of the party mushroomed all over the country, most particularly in the north under the protective wing of the Red Army. As we shall see, the Russian forces protected the Tudeh elements even in Tehran during the oil crisis, but before that they did so patently in Mazandaran and Gorgan in northern Iran.

One of the best examples of the Red Army protection of the Tudeh party members and Iran's resistance to it involved the case of a so-called Husain Nouri. He was in fact a Soviet citizen by the name of Julin Elyasof, who was commissioned by the Tudeh party to organize branches in northern Iran. The government of Premier 'Ali Sohaily showed deep concern about him and his activities, and the burden of staving him off fell on the shoulders of the governor of Mazandaran and Gorgan, Muhammad 'Ali Majd. In a series of confidential telegrams to the central government, the governor exposed the activities of Husain Nouri and his associates, complained of the intervention of the local Soviet commander in behalf of the arrested Tudeh members, and requested his government to take up the matter with the Russian ambassador in Tehran. When Husain Nouri was imprisoned in Sari, Riza Radmanish, one of the founders of the Tudeh party, paid him a visit, and supplied him some cash, stating that the money came from Tudeh party funds. A second example of the Red Army intervention in behalf of the Tudeh elements in the north occurred in the wake of a Tudeh-agitated incident involving four thousand workers in Shahi. The local Red Army commander at Sari protested the arrest of the agitators to Governor Majd, demanded the removal of specific Iranian

---

[7]For annotated bibliographical references to the Tudeh party, see Rouhollah K. Ramazani and Oles M. Smolansky, "Iran," in Thomas T. Hammond, ed., *Soviet Foreign Relations and World Communism: A Selected, Annotated Bibliography of 7,000 Books in 30 Languages* (Princeton: Princeton University Press, 1965), pp. 852-60. For an excellent article on the Tudeh and the Azerbaijan Democratic party that has appeared since the publication of this bibliography, see Ervand Abrahamian, "Communism and Communalism in Iran: The Tudah and the Firqah-e Dimukrat," *International Journal of Middle East Studies* 1, no. 4 (1970):291-316.

officials, police, and gendarme officers, and stated on the same occasion that the imprisonment of Husain Nouri was "illegal and contrary to the friendly relations between the Soviet Union and Iran."[8] The Iranian governor refused to succumb to the Soviet pressures, protested the Russian interference in the internal affairs of Iran, and charged that the commander's behavior breached the Soviet-Iranian treaty of 1921.[9]

Third, the Soviet Union used diplomacy both multilaterally and bilaterally to pursue its ends in Iran before the oil crisis of 1944. This was best evidenced by the Soviet attitude at the Foreign Ministers Conference at Moscow. The British suggested the adoption of a declaration in favor of Iran, confirming the guarantee of its independence in return for facilitating Allied war efforts. The United States supported the British proposal, but the Soviet Union held to "a negative attitude" and showed no disposition to compromise or to put forward alternative proposals."[10] The proposed declaration "ran aground," to borrow again Secretary Hull's words, "on the rocks of Soviet opposition."[11]

Bilaterally, however, Soviet diplomacy during 1941-43 proved quite positive and brought Moscow handsome dividends. The Soviet attempts at domination through the Red Army occupation and at subversion through the Tudeh party were paralleled by the exploitation of Iran through a variety of means, including, most importantly, the conclusion of unfavorable agreements made directly with the Iranian government itself.

Before a consideration of these agreements, the major instances of Russian exploitation by other means should be mentioned. The Soviets defaulted on paying Iran outstanding debts incurred in connection with trade; they ran the Russo-Iranian Fisheries Company with a deficit because they had a monopoly on the caviar and fixed prices; they utilized the shoe factories in Azerbaijan for themselves while the Iranians had to obtain shoes from abroad; they made no payments to the Iranian government for the maintenance of roads in the north and for the Caspian Sea ports they used (the Americans and British paid for the upkeep of the Persian Gulf ports they used); they occupied buildings and facilities in northern Iran without payment of rent; and they owed Iran large sums for customs duties.[12]

---

[8] These accounts are based on documentary sources reproduced in Kirmani, 2:460, 462.

[9] For details see ibid., pp. 458-72.

[10] *Foreign Relations of U.S., 1943,* D.P., 4:400-405.

[11] Hull, 2:1506.

[12] This account is based on a report by Millspaugh, who was at the time Iran's administrator general of the finances. See *Foreign Relations of U.S., 1944,* D.P., 5:314-16.

Soviet exploitation by means of imposing unfavorable agreements on Iran resembled more the czarist patterns of behavior in Iran than the letter or the spirit of its 1921 treaty of friendship or its 1942 Tripartite Treaty of alliance with Iran. The main exploitative agreements were three: the arms agreement of January 23, 1943, the financial agreement of March 18, 1943, and the rice and cotton piece-goods deal of November 4, 1943.[13] Briefly stated, under the arms agreement Iran was required by the Soviet Union to manufacture certain small arms and ammunition in Iranian plants for delivery to the Soviet government; was required to finance the preparation and operation of the plants and to provide raw materials; and was to allow Soviet military delegates to be stationed in the plants to observe and stimulate production. The Iranian government accepted this agreement "only because there seemed no other course than to acquiesce in the Russian demands."[14] Iran fared not much better under the financial agreement, which accorded the Iranians substantially less favorable treatment than that given them by the British under their agreement and by the United States in the absence of any agreement. Iran had to advance the rials (Iranian currency) needed by the Soviet Union for its operations in Iran. The rice and cotton piece-goods deal consisted of two contracts calling for sales of Iranian rice to the Russians and of Russian cotton piece goods to the Iranians, but it amounted in the last analysis to the Iranian subsidization of the export of rice to the Soviet Union.

Rejection of the Soviet Bid for Oil Concessions

The oil crisis of 1944, precipitated by the arrival in Tehran of a Soviet delegation headed by Sergey Ivanovich Kavtaradze, vice commissar of foreign affairs, brought into play all the instruments of Soviet policy identified above: the Red Army, Soviet diplomacy, and the Tudeh party. The Soviet move in 1944 represented the boldest Soviet attempt up to that time to block favorable Iranian overtures to the United States. The Iranian determination to grant oil concessions to American interests paralleled Iran's initiative in acquiring two military missions and the Millspaugh financial mission as means of deepening the United States involvement. The Russian interest in Iranian oil was set forth, as seen, in its note of August 30, 1941, but was not taken up seriously until 1944. By this time, quite apart from the overall trend of Iranian foreign policy, which favored the United States as the third power, the specific move that triggered the Iranian overtures to American oil interests

[13] For the basic provisions of these agreements, which are difficult to find elsewhere, see ibid., pp. 311-14.

[14] Ibid., p. 313.

was, it seems, the British search for further oil concessions in Iran. This proposition may be supported by examining the emergence of the quest for oil concessions in Iran before 1944.

As early as February 1943 Iran showed interest in American oil companies. At that time the Iranian commercial attaché in Washington inquired whether the Standard Vacuum Oil Company was interested in a concession and was told that although the company was interested, it would rather wait, given the Iranian political situation. In November 1943, however, the company expressed interest in obtaining an oil concession in Iranian Baluchistan, but by that time two British oil representatives had already been in Iran trying to negotiate for a Baluchistan concession. Premier Sohaily, however, wished to have the "concession go to America." The British representatives pressed him to speed up the negotiations, but he kept urging the United States to send oil company representatives to Iran as quickly as possible during late 1943.[15]

By March 1944 both the Standard Vacuum Oil Company and the British Royal Dutch Shell Company had submitted their proposals, but Premier Sohaily, Foreign Minister Muhammad Sa'id, and Husain 'Ala, the court minister, wished to see American oil interests enter Iran because Iran was particularly opposed to "having entire [*sic*] southern coast of Iran tied up under British concessions." The first indication of Russian interest before the crisis of late 1944 came in a Tass release on the Kavir Khorian oil in northern Iran. Muhammad Sa'id, who was appointed prime minister by the shah on March 19, 1944, told the American chargé in Iran that the Russian claim to exclusive rights in northern Iran was based upon the Khoshtaria Concession, which was never approved by the Majlis, and hence he considered northern Iran definitely open to development by oil interests of any nation.[16] Another new element in the oil concession picture by the spring of 1944 was the entry of the Sinclair Oil Company. The Sinclair group claimed that the Standard group was too closely tied to British Shell to appeal to the Iranians. The Department of State tried to maintain an impartial attitude by supporting both companies and at the same time strove to maintain a distinction between their interests and those of the American government as such. Meanwhile, Iran had hired A. A. Curtice and Herbert Hoover, Jr., two petroleum geologists, who were asked to study the firm proposals of both American companies. By August 1944 the oil concession negotiations had matured to the point that American officials in Tehran believed that it was imperative that the American companies involved send representatives from the highest

---

[15] *Foreign Relations of U.S., 1943,* D.P., 4:627-28.

[16] *Foreign Relations of U.S., 1944,* D.P., 5:445-47. The controversial Khoshtaria Concession was granted to a Russian subject by that name on Mar. 9, 1916, by the Iranian prime minister, Sipahsalar, but was never ratified by the Majlis.

executive level, and the American chargé was "reliably informed that one bid or another will be accepted by [the] Cabinet and presented to [the] Majlis for approval by September 1."[17]

The arrival of the Kavtaradze delegation could not have been timed more perfectly. On September 13 they had an interview with the prime minister and on September 16 were received by the shah. During the month of September it was believed that the purpose of the Kavtaradze mission was to look into the oil fields at Kavirkhourian in Semnan, but the Soviet ambassador and the vice commissar had asked the shah on October 1 for exclusive rights over a five-year period for petroleum exploration by the Russian government in an area of 200,000 square kilometers in northern Iran, stretching from Azerbaijan to Khorasan.[18] Kavtaradze himself told the Tehran press representatives in a conference on October 24 that the Soviet delegation had several purposes in mind, one of which was to obtain information about the northern mines as well as the Kavir Khorian oil and that this purpose had been communicated to the Iranian government in advance of the mission's arrival through Ambassador Ahy. In the same interview, which will be considered again below, Kavtaradze stated that "the Soviet government is considering the acquisition of oil concessions in the areas of northern Azerbaijan, Gilan, Mazandaran, a portion of the Semnan region, and several districts in northern Khorasan [northern Quchan]." He also stated that the Soviet proposals had been submitted to Premier Sa'id on September 26.

The Soviets pressed for an answer until October 8, when the prime minister announced to the Majlis that his cabinet had agreed to postpone all oil concession negotiations until after the war.[19] In the same announcement the prime minister stressed that the decision of his government had *preceded* the arrival of the Kavtaradze mission. He stated that while the oil negotiations with the British and American companies had been proceeding, the Iranian government had learned about an oil conference held in the United States; this prompted the Iranian cabinet to decide on September 2 that the grant of any oil concession was undesirable and unnecessary in light of the economic, financial, and worldwide security problems at the time. The Iranian cabinet, the prime minister added, repeatedly affirmed its decision of September 2 after the arrival of the Kavtaradze mission.[20] In any event, the announcement of the government decision touched off the crisis that led to the resignation

[17]Ibid., p. 452.

[18]Ibid., p. 452-54.

[19]Ibid.

[20]See Kirmani, 2:575-76.

of the Sa'id government on November 9, the enactment of the law on December 2 forbidding the grant of concessions to any foreign oil interests, and finally the departure of Kavtaradze on December 8.[21] In the course of this crisis the Soviet Union boldly employed all three major instruments of its policy in Iran to combat the Iranian decision to defy the Russian demands.

Diplomatically, the Soviet opposition to the Iranian decision was partly reflected in the activities of Kavtaradze himself, with the full support of the Soviet embassy in Iran. On October 12, 1944, Prime Minister Sa'id told the representatives of the American and British companies as well as Kavtaradze of the Iranian decision to postpone the grant of all oil concessions until after the war, but Kavtaradze replied that this decision could have unhappy consequences.[22] Russian opposition reached a peak on October 24, when the Soviet embassy through its extensive contacts with Iranian officials and newspapers placed the blame for Iran's "negative" decision squarely on Prime Minister Sa'id. More important, Kavtaradze himself held a press conference in the Soviet embassy in Tehran, roundly denouncing the Iranian decision. He stated that the Iranian decision to postpone the grant of concessions to the Soviet Union amounted to "the rejection of the Soviet proposals." "I should state," he added, "plainly and clearly that the Sa'id decision has been considered totally negative." Public opinion in the Soviet Union, he continued, felt that the government of Sa'id had contributed to the deterioration of Irano-Soviet relations by adopting such an attitude towards the Soviet proposals. In attempting to undermine the government of Sa'id as effectively as possible, Kavtaradze used the press conference to link the future of Irano-Soviet relations to the fate of the Sa'id government. In reply to a newspaper editor, he stated that "the relations between the government of the Soviet Union and the Iranian people are friendly, nevertheless any contact and cooperation between the Soviet government and the government of Mr. Sa'id is impossible."[23]

Kavtaradze's denunciation of the Iranian government in the Iranian capital city was voiced by the Soviet press just before the vice commissar's press interview and by Radio Moscow afterwards in most violent language. *Trud*, technically the organ of the Soviet trade unions but in reality an organ expressing official Soviet policy, brutally attacked the Sa'id government on October 22 without even mentioning the oil concession question. Instead it accused the Iranian government in general and Premier Sa'id in particular of

---

[21]These dates are based on U.S. Department of State publications cited previously.

[22]*Foreign Relations of U.S., 1944*, D.P., 5:456.

[23]Kavtaradze's press conference was reported in the newspaper *Rahbar*, the organ of the Tudeh party, Oct. 26, 1944.

tolerating and even encouraging acts of sabotage of the flow of supplies to the Soviet Union on the part of "pro-Fascist elements in Iran."[24] As we shall see in connection with the role of the Tudeh party in the crisis, the charge of fascism was picked up and used even more aggressively by the Tudeh press. Radio Moscow accused Premier Sa'id personally of being a "traitor" to Iranian national interests; charged that he wished to restore Riza Shah's dictatorship; cited Kavtaradze's remarks that contact with the Sa'id government was impossible; and asserted that the Red Army had saved not only Stalingrad and the northern Caucasus but also Iran from the "fascist pincers," but beginning in fall 1942 a group of "reactionaries" had intrigued against the Soviet Union and nowadays the government of Sa'id pursued this policy.[25]

The Red Army was also used by the Soviet Union during the oil crisis of 1944, as in the 1941-43 period, to further Soviet ends. The role of the Red Army in the course of the crisis took two major forms: increased obstruction of Iranian troop movements and communications and outright support of the Tudeh-sponsored demonstrations in Tehran and the provinces against the Sa'id government. In October 1944 Red Army troops for the first time paraded through certain sections of Tehran, notably before the parliament building, while a considerable number of soldiers sat in military trucks and were conspicuously armed with tommy guns. In the same months all transport to and from Tehran and various points in the Russian zone of occupation was suspended (with the exception of Soviet military supplies) until November 1. On October 27 the Tudeh party started mass demonstrations in front of the Majlis, demanding the ouster of the Sa'id government while Soviet troops armed with tommy guns protected the demonstrators against the police. Meanwhile, in the north the Russians captured many Iranian troops and police; took their weapons and ammunition; and cut off highways, leaving large segments of the population without water and food.[26]

Aided and abetted by the Red Army and the Soviet embassy propaganda machine, the Tudeh party not only sponsored demonstrations in Tehran and the provinces but also launched a savage press campaign against the Sa'id government. *Rahbar*, the organ of the Tudeh party, criticized the Sa'id government for refusing even to enter into negotiations with the Soviets when it had been negotiating for some six months with the American companies. Its editorial of October 21 charged that Premier Sa'id had injured Iran's relations with its ally, the Soviet Union; had pursued Riza Shah's policy of neglecting Russia; and had followed a "conspiratorial policy" in the oil

[24]*Foreign Relations of U.S., 1944*, D.P., 5:351-52.

[25]*Rahbar*, Nov. 2, 1944.

[26]*Foreign Relations of U.S., 1944*, D.P., 5:458, 460, 467.

question, which was of "vital" significance to Iran and should have been discussed openly rather than clandestinely by Sa'id and some of the Majlis establishmentarians.[27] Kavtaradze's press conference, mentioned before, emboldened the Tudeh party, whose organ gave full display to his interview of October 24 and followed the example of *Trud* of October 22 in labeling the Sa'id government as fascist and doomed to downfall.[28] The Tudeh's violent press campaign continued during the government crisis between the fall of the Sa'id government on November 9 and the introduction of the government of Mortiza Quli Bayat to the Majlis on November 26. *Rahbar* of November 22 declared that it would oppose any government that supported the "traitorous policy of the Sa'id government" or included ministers from the previous cabinet or from the "mummies of the Riza Shah era."

The Tudeh vituperations were reinforced by its puppet front called the "Freedom Front" (*Jibha-ye Azadi*). Formed initially in 1943, the Front in its early phase consisted of fifteen newspaper editors, including several noncommunists, but also a triumvirate of hard-line communists: Ja'afar Pishihvari, Radmanish, and Iraj Iskandari. The last named edited the newspaper *Rahbar*. According to one of the newspaper editors who originally joined the Front but was the first one to withdraw after discovering its "real aims," one of the major purposes of the Front was to discredit Sayid Zia, one of the staunchest opponents of the Tudeh party.[29] The Front's extreme subservience to Moscow was vividly revealed during the oil crisis. On the day after the Kavtaradze press conference, the Front published its first bold declaration (*qat'anamih*), contending that the continuation of the Sa'id regime would produce no results other than domestic and foreign complications threatening the Iranian nation, and called for Sa'id's immediate resignation.[30] Two days before the fall of the Sa'id government, the Front published its second major declaration listing the name of twenty-seven newspapers from Tehran and the provinces as its supporters and hailing the "noble sentiments of patriotic people" shown in the course of demonstrations against the "tactless and incompetent" government of Sa'id. The declaration complained that the post-Shahrivar governments (August-September 1941) had followed the path of Riza Shah's dictatorship; that the Sa'id cabinet had caused misunderstanding between Iran and the Soviet Union; that the cabinet had resorted to "traitorous propaganda" by means of Radio Tehran, which patently reflected

[27] Oct. 21, 1944.

[28] *Rahbar*, Oct. 26, 1944.

[29] This editor was Husain Kuhi Kirmani. He edited the newspaper *Nasim-i Saba*. For his account of the "real aims" of the Front, see Kirmani, 2:472-77.

[30] *Rahbar*, Oct. 25, 1944.

"fascist propaganda"; and that Sa'id had "betrayed" Iran, and hence his cabinet was doomed to fall and must be put on trial.[31]

Iran's resistance to the Soviet bid for an oil concession was also supported by statesmen other than Premier Sa'id and members of his cabinet. Throughout the crisis the shah encouraged resistance to Soviet pressures; his court minister, Husain 'Ala, kept the Americans informed; and the shah himself tried in vain to prevent the downfall of the Sa'id cabinet. But the main resistance emanated from the Deputies of the Fourteenth Majlis. The main actors were the same as those in the Millspaugh case, but the roles were played differently. The Tudeh Deputies, of course, supported the Soviet demand for oil concessions, but effected their support by attacking the "one-sided policy" (*syasat-i yikjanibih*) of the government, meaning primarily disapproval of Iran's expanding ties with the United States. For example, on November 27, 1944, Kishavarz, a Tudeh Deputy, in opposing the new government of Mortiza Quli Bayat in the same speech, pointed out not only the "mistakes" of the former government of Sa'id but also attacked the Millspaugh mission and the American advisory program in Iran.[32]

At the other end of the spectrum was Sayid Zia, who was the staunchest supporter of the Millspaugh mission in the Majlis but fiercest opponent of the Soviet demand for an oil concession. Sayid Zia's opposition to the Tudeh party had been signaled from the time of his return to Iran from exile in 1943. The first issue of his newspaper *Ra'd-i Imruz*, reminiscent of his editorship of a newspaper called simply *Ra'd* some twenty-five years earlier, declared his fundamental goal to be a "New Iran, Free Iran, Independent Iran" (*Iran-i Now, Iran-i Azad, Iran-i Mustaqil*), but his continued opposition to the Tudeh party marked him as a conservative politician who drew support from the clergy, the Bazaari merchants, and the large landlords. Nevertheless, Sayid Zia said or did little openly against the Soviets before the oil crisis in 1944. On the contrary, he tried to modify his anti-Soviet image by capitalizing on his role in the rejection of the 1919 Anglo-Iranian agreement and the conclusion of the 1921 Soviet-Iranian treaty of friendship. But the oil crisis provided the opportunity for an open attack on the Soviets. He published an important declaration on December 21, 1944.[33] The immediate reason for issuing this declaration was the publication of an interview with Kavtaradze in the newspaper *Doost-i Iran* ("Iran's Friend"), an organ of the Soviet embassy in Tehran. In addition to calling the enactment of the Iranian law forbidding the grant of concessions to foreign interests a "mistake," the vice

---

[31] Ibid., Nov. 7, 1944.

[32] Ibid., Nov. 28, 1944.

[33] See Kirmani, 2:604-22, for the full text of the declaration.

commissar claimed that the error of the Iranian Parliament had been the result of pressures by individuals hostile to Soviet-Iranian friendship, such as Sa'id and Sayid Zia. Sayid Zia denounced Kavtaradze's remarks in his declaration, stating in part that Kavtaradze's derogatory remarks about the decision of the Iranian Parliament constituted "a great mistake, an unforgivable insult, and a grave political error." He also stated that whether the decision of the Iranian Parliament was a mistake "is beyond the purview of any foreigner, and the Majlis alone has competence to decide what it pleases." The real significance of the declaration, however, derived from its detailed account of Soviet interference in wartime Iran. The role of the Red Army, the subservience of the Tudeh to the Soviet Union, and the intrigues of the Soviet embassy—in short, all acts of Soviet interference were openly and severely criticized.

The leadership of Iranian resistance to the Soviet demand for an oil concession within the Majlis fell to Muhammad Musaddiq. Although Sayid Zia defended the law that Musaddiq sponsored, the two men entertained old personal and political animosities. For the fiercely nationalistic Musaddiq, the path and policies of Sayid Zia were too closely identified with the British. He vehemently opposed Sayid Zia during the customary parliamentary consideration of the latter's credentials in the Fourteenth Majlis on the ground that Sayid Zia had cosponsored Riza Khan's coup d'etat of 1921, had unjustifiably interned individuals, and had attempted to arrest Musaddiq himself. In several leading articles Sayid Zia's newspaper, *Ra'd-i Imruz*, criticized Musaddiq for engaging in such criticism twenty-two years after the event. In any case Musaddiq's resistance to the Soviet demand for an oil concession was first signaled on October 29, 1944, by a long speech in the Majlis. It was prefaced importantly by a detailed examination of the British oil concession in the south; it regretted the Soviet intention to sever diplomatic relations with Iran in retaliation for the Sa'id government's decision to postpone negotiations; and it urged upon his countrymen the wisdom of a policy of "negative equilibrium" rather than a positive one, which would lead to granting the neighboring great powers what they wanted. He then identified two alternatives for the Soviets: an oil concession in the north or purchase of Iranian oil. He rejected the former by stating sarcastically that the Soviets had arrived too late and wished to depart too quickly and that the grant of the oil concession to the British had occurred at a different time and under different circumstances, the like of which did not obtain at the time.[34]

In the course of a second well-known speech in the Majlis, Musaddiq introduced the proposal that was enacted into law on December 2, 1944. In

[34]For excerpts from Musaddiq's speech, see ibid., pp.577-600.

this speech, as in the one before, he advocated the exploration of Iran's oil by the Iranians themselves. In other words, he went beyond the decision of the Sa'id government merely to postpone the grant of concessions to the postwar period. In fact, in introducing his bill to the Majlis, he accused those who suggested such a policy of playing into the hands of foreigners. He addressed the new government of Mortiza Quli Bayat by stating categorically, "You must attach importance to entrusting the exploration of the Iranian oil to the Iranians, and should organize a special Ministry for this purpose at the earliest possible moment."[35] Musaddiq himself gave credit for the idea of his bill to "one of the Majlis Deputies who wished to remain unmentioned," but others gave considerable credence to the story that the bill was prepared in consultation with Sa'id and 'Ala and that the British had nothing to do with it.[36] The bill was received and enacted during the same session of the Majlis, on December 2, 1944, prohibiting any government official to discuss or sign any oil concessionary agreement with official or unofficial representatives of oil companies or with any person; permitting the government to undertake negotiations aimed at the sale of Iranian oil or its exploitation and administration; and punishing the violators of this law with three to eight years imprisonment and permanent debarment from government service.[37]

The departure of Kavtaradze only after the passage of this law was no coincidence; the law killed any chances of obtaining an oil concession at the time even if the vice commissar had extended his nearly three months stay in Iran. Whatever kind words the Tudeh party had sparingly showered on Musaddiq while Kavtaradze was still in Tehran vanished with his departure. On the same day that he left for the Soviet Union, Musaddiq's bill, already enacted into law, came under heavy attack in the same article of *Rahbar* that regretted the departure of Kavtaradze. It said that Musaddiq's bill had been rushed through with "amazing haste" just as the controlled bills of the Riza Shah era had been; Iran's "one-sided policy" had not changed; the Majlis, Musaddiq, and his partisans had only demonstrated that the ruling class in Iran was incapable of handling such problems and was not allowed to make its own decisions; and Musaddiq and his followers had failed to do anything about the "real problem," which had been simply left to foreign circles.[38]

In resisting Soviet pressures, the Iranian government tried to secure American support in keeping with its third-power policy, but the parallel difficulties in the Millspaugh affairs tended to ruffle Iran's relations with the

[35]Ibid., pp. 601-3.

[36]*Foreign Relations of U.S., 1944,* D.P., 5:480-81.

[37]For the text of the bill see Kirmani, 2:600-601.

[38]Dec. 9, 1944.

United States in spite of nebulous efforts by both sides to regard the Mills-paugh mission as a private undertaking. A second problem that set limits upon what the United States could do to help Iran was the desire to avoid any more Soviet-American friction than was necessary. Nevertheless, with persistent British encouragement the United States supported the Iranian resistance. The first formal sign of American support came from the American message to Iran and particularly United States representations to the Soviet Union on November 1, 1944. The American ambassador advised the Sa'id government that it took note of the Iranian decision to postpone all negotiations concerning the development of oil in Iran; expressed confidence that the Iranian government was acting in good faith while the two American oil firms were conducting negotiations; and expected that Iran would inform the United States when it was ready to consider applications again. More important, the United States told the Soviets that the American "policy in this case is based on the American Government's recognition of the sovereign right of an independent nation such as Iran, acting in a nondiscriminatory manner, to grant or withhold commercial concessions within its territory." [39] The United States expressed concern to the Soviet Union particularly in regard to the strict application of this policy in Iran in view of the Tehran Declaration, signed as recently as December 1, 1943.

As the crisis developed it seemed that further action might become necessary by the United States, and Acting Secretary Stettinius sought President Roosevelt's approval in advance so that the question could be taken up with the Russians swiftly if it became necessary. The president's reply of December 8, 1944, stated that he thought the matter should be taken up by Averell Harriman with Stalin himself, that the Tehran Declaration was "pretty definite," and that he recalled his suggestion to Stalin and Churchill to the effect that three or four trustees build a new port in Iran at the head of the Persian Gulf (free port) and run the whole railroad from there to Russia for "the good of all." However, the Department of State had scotched the notion of the trustees because it might "cause the whole house to fall in on our heads," and the question of Soviet-Iranian relations was not taken up with Stalin because by mid-December the situation in Iran had begun to quiet down. [40]

Whether the American representations to the Soviet Union produced any significant check upon Soviet behavior is difficult to say because the Soviet Union exhausted every means at its disposal to bring down the Sa'id government. [41] It is difficult to believe that Kavtaradze was stopped from scrapping

---

[39] *Foreign Relations of U.S., 1944*, D.P., 5:462-63.

[40] Ibid., pp. 482-85.

[41] The British made their own representation separately on Nov. 2, 1944.

the Musaddiq-sponsored law because of Anglo-American protests. Only the Majlis itself could have theoretically done so. The Tudeh party did not enjoy much support in the Majlis, where for all practical purposes the passage of the law had taken them by surprise. The influence of the Anglo-American stand was more instrumental in bolstering the Iranian position than in checking the Soviet moves. This, then, brings us to the specific decision of the Sa'id government to postpone all oil negotiations until after the war.

Any assessment of this decision must ultimately rest upon some interpretation of the Soviet objective in pressing for an oil concession in northern Iran. The Iranian interpretation is, of course, most relevant. Iran's view of the Soviet objective could reveal whether the Iranian policymakers felt they had succeeded or failed to block the attainment of the Soviet objective by their decision to postpone all oil negotiations. It is possible to suggest in the context of this study that the Iranian government in general considered the Soviet objective as aggressive—that is, the Soviets sought to maximize their power and, eventually, to control Iran. This interpretation was informed not only by Iranian experience with Russia but also by the vivid acts of Soviet interference after the invasion in 1941. To the extent that the position of Sayid Zia overlapped with that of the Iranian government, and this was indeed the case to a large extent, the most graphic description of Iran's perception of Soviet objectives and behavior in Iran was set forth in his famous declaration mentioned above. Sayid Zia was one of the strongest supporters of Iran's third-power strategy with its leaning, here, toward the United States.

Given this interpretation of the Soviet objective in demanding an oil concession, it is easy to see why the decision to postpone all oil negotiations could be regarded, as indeed it was by all groups except, of course, the Tudeh party, as a patriotic act blocking the attainment of Soviet expansionist ambitions in Iran. But if the Soviet objective was preemptive rather than aggressive, then how does one assess the Sa'id decision? This is not a hypothetical question. At the time of the crisis the preemptive interpretation of the Soviet objective came from two entirely different sources. First, the Tudeh party assessed the Soviet objective as follows: "The purpose of the Soviet government in applying for an oil concession is not to secure an imperialistic concession. The existential fact of the Soviet Union, its practice over the past twenty years or so, and its current behavior in other countries confirm our view [of the Soviet objective], and we see no evidence or indication of any departure from this [nonimperialistic] behavior. Conversely, the Soviet government inevitably needs to block imperialistic influences in Iran and regards an oil concession as a means of achieving that end."[42]

A second source also regarded the Soviet objective as basically preemptive,

[42]*Rahbar,* Dec. 9, 1944.

but not for the reasons expounded by the Tudeh party. George F. Kennan, the American chargé in Moscow at the time, advised the State Department of his view of the Soviet objective in characteristically thoughtful terms. He did not believe that the Soviets needed Iranian oil as such but were afraid of potential foreign penetration in northern Iran:

The oil of Northern Iran is important not as something Russia needs, but as something it might be dangerous to permit anyone else to exploit. The territory lies near the vital Caucasian oil centers which so closely escaped complete conquest in the present war. The Kremlin deems it essential to Russian security that no other great power should have even the chance of gaining a footing there. It probably sees no other way to assure this than by seeking greater political and economic control for itself and finds this aim consistent with contemporary Soviet conceptions of prestige. If the methods employed in this connection seem unimaginative and old-fashioned it must be remembered that there is extensive preoccupation in Moscow today with the methods as well as the aims of Tsarist diplomacy.[43]

If this interpretation held true then it might be supposed that the Soviet Union achieved its objective, because Kavtaradze's demand prompted Iran to cancel its oil negotiations with the American companies. This could, therefore, be considered a Soviet gain and an Iranian loss, insofar as the grant of concessions to the United States constituted a component of Iran's third-power policy. In other words the Soviets, and of course the Tudeh party, succeeded in undercutting Iran's wartime policy of favoring the United States as the third power in this instance as in the parallel case of the Millspaugh mission. Such an interpretation, however, assumes that the Soviet demand for an oil concession indeed solely and exclusively *caused* Iran to decide to postpone all oil negotiations until after the war. But one important piece of evidence stands in the way of such an assumption. That is the statement of October 8, 1944, of Prime Minister Sa'id himself. In announcing publicly the decision of his government to the Majlis, he stated clearly that the decision to postpone all oil negotiations had been reached by his cabinet on September 2, about two weeks before the arrival of the Kavtaradze mission in Tehran. In emphasizing this point, he also stated that this previous decision was affirmed by his cabinet several times after the start of negotiations with the Russian vice commissar.

If Sa'id's statement is accepted, it is difficult to see how Iran could have lost because of the Soviet move. The Soviets could not have preempted the grant of oil concessions to the American companies if Iran had indeed reached its decision to postpone all oil negotiations before the arrival of Kavtaradze. The question, therefore, is whether the statement of Prime Minister Sa'id

[43]*Foreign Relations of U.S., 1944*, D.P., 5:470-71.

about the cabinet decision of September 2 can be verified. In explaining this decision, he remarked that it was reached after Iran had learned about an oil conference in the United States. This allusion probably refers to an understanding between the United States and Great Britain "to observe the principle of equal opportunity with respect to new concessions."[44] Given the Iranian fear of the extension of British oil interests that prompted Iran to approach American oil interests in the first place, it is conceivable that when Iran got wind of the Anglo-American understanding and exchange of pledges about the acquisition of new concessions, it indeed reached its decision of September 2. With only the evidence now available further speculation about the timing of this decision can hardly be justified, but the timing of the Sa'id decision was clearly of crucial importance and will require further research.

It should be emphasized, however, that the Sa'id decision was not in fact confirmed by the Musaddiq-sponsored bill enacted into law by the Majlis on December 2, 1944. The bill made no reference to the *postponement* of negotiations for granting oil concessions to foreign interests until after the war. While making any such negotiations a crime, the law entrusted the exploration of oil to *Iranian hands*. The significance of this provision must be seen less in what it accomplished at the time than in what it foretold of Iran's desire to control one day its own oil industry. We shall see the influence of this abiding aspiration on Iranian foreign policy in decades to come.

[44]Ibid., pp. 450-51.

V

Expulsion of the Soviet Union

IRAN'S FOREIGN POLICY most of the time during the Second World War was basically patterned after the foreign policy of Riza Shah in terms of its overriding objective and principal means. During this period, too, Iran sought to preserve its independence and territorial integrity vis-à-vis Great Britain and the Soviet Union principally by involving a third power, with the United States replacing Germany after the Anglo-Russian invasion in 1941. Did this same policy continue in the early postwar period before 1951? If not, what took its place, and how long did that last? Assuming that the same basic patterns continued, did Iran face the same kinds of problems with the USSR, or did these change? And assuming that the United States remained Iran's favorite third power, did Iran continue to pursue the pre-1945 policies? Did it continue to seek economic, technical, and commercial ties with the United States, or did it modify this policy? These questions are explored in the following chapters.

The first major problem in Iran's relations with the Soviet Union in 1945-46 was Soviet interference in Iranian affairs. This problem led to the creation of two separatist regimes in Northern Iran and constituted the basis for Iran's initial complaint to the nascent United Nations. This complaint formed the first case before the Security Council; it was watched universally with concern as the first acid test of great-power cooperation within the newly established world organization. The meticulous documentation of Iranian charges of Soviet interference brought "the Iranian question" into the glaring limelight of the world forum, but the Iranian bill of particulars concentrated chiefly on the Soviet acts of interference, leading to the establishment of the Azeri and Kurdish rebel regimes in 1945.[1] Yet in the perspective of this study, Soviet support of these regimes represented only the boldest and latest Soviet act of open interference. On the basis of this examination of Irano-Soviet relations during 1941-44, I suggest that Soviet interference in Iranian affairs was a cumulative and multifaceted process that in fact began in the wake of the

[1] For details of "Particulars of Interference by Soviet Authorities" and the related documents, see U.N., Security Council, *Official Records,* First Year: First Series, *Supplement* no. 1 (cited hereafter as U.N., Security Council, *OR*).

Anglo-Russian invasion of Iran. The events that underpinned this process, therefore, go back to 1941. As these have already been fully explored in the preceding chapter, it will suffice here to draw them together swiftly as the most appropriate backdrop for examining the Soviet acts of interference during 1945-46.

Soviet Interference

The instances of Soviet interference in Iran's internal affairs followed the Soviet occupation of northern Iran. On September 23, 1941, Sir Anthony Eden, alarmed by Soviet conduct, told Ivan Maisky, the Soviet ambassador to Great Britain, that he considered most harmful any undue interference by the Russians in Iranian affairs or sympathy towards separatist movements in northern Iran, and Secretary of State Cordell Hull also expressed the extreme apprehension of the United States about Soviet behavior. The Soviet solemn obligations under the Tripartite Treaty of January 29, 1942, "to respect the territorial integrity and political independence of Iran"[2] and to understand that "the presence of these forces on Iranian territory does not constitute a military occupation and will disturb as little as possible the administration and the security forces of Iran, the economic life of the country, the normal movements of the population, and the application of Iranian laws and regulations" [3] did not seem to place any serious check upon Soviet behavior. As already seen, the Red Army prevented Iranian troops from quelling the Kurdish attack upon the Gendarmerie post at Rizaiyih in May 1942. This was the earliest instance of outright Soviet interception of Iranian security forces. By the spring of 1943, it may be recalled, Soviet acts of interference in the north had reached such proportions as to affect adversely the performance of Americans in Iran, as evidenced by the expulsion of Rex Vivian, the departure of the American consul in Tabriz under Soviet pressures, the obstruction of General Connolly's forces, and the denial of permission to Colonel Schwarzkopf to visit Rasht on official business. The idea of adopting a declaration confirming the guarantee of Iran's independence in return for facilitating Allied war efforts, which was first proposed by the British and supported by the United States at the Foreign Ministers Conference at Moscow on October 23, 1943, was opposed, as seen, by the Soviets, but its adoption at the Tehran Conference, where it was signed by Stalin as well as Churchill and Roosevelt, seemed to produce no perceptible change in Soviet policy.

[2]Article 1 and article 6(i). For the text of the treaty and annexes, see Goodrich and Caroll, *Documents* 4:681-86.

[3]Article 5. See ibid., p. 684.

As a matter of fact, we may recall, the boldest Soviet acts of interference occurred after the adoption of the Tehran Declaration. The oil crisis of 1944 brought into play all the major instruments of Soviet policy simultaneously. Diplomatically, the Soviet Embassy in Tehran housed vice commissar Kavtar-adze, who publicly denounced Prime Minister Sa'id in Iran's own capital, furnished opportunity for inflammatory press interviews by the vice commissar, who not only criticized the decision of the Iranian cabinet regarding the postponement of all negotiations with foreign oil interests but also denounced the act of the Iranian Parliament forbidding any such negotiations. Militarily, the Red Army launched an unprecedented array of interventionary acts during the oil crisis, ranging from increased obstruction of Iranian troop movements and communications, the disarming of Iranian troops and police in several areas, the cutting of highways, the suspension of transport to and from Tehran and various points to the Russian zone of occupation, and the outright protection of the Communist-sponsored demonstrations. And politically, it may be recalled, the Soviet instrument in Iran, the Tudeh party, and its affiliated Freedom Front outdid the Soviet press and propaganda machinery in denouncing the "fascist" government of Premier Sa'id.

The Soviet failure to gain an oil concession as a means of achieving the Soviet objectives of maximum power in, and control of, Iran in general and the northern provinces in particular was followed by resort to even more aggressive acts. In a most revealing discussion, Averell Harriman learned just after the oil crisis from Maximov, the Soviet ambassador at Tehran, that he "intended to take aggressive measures to attain the Soviet objectives, which appeared to be much more far reaching than simply the oil and mineral concession and to include the upsetting of the Government which he [Maximov] characterized as representing only 5% of the Iranian population. Maximov expounded the extraordinary thesis that, since the Soviets knew what the Iranian people wanted, it was proper for the Soviet Government to see that this opinion found political expression." [4]

True to the interpretation of its ambassador, the Soviet Union did see to it soon afterwards that two insurgent regimes were established in northern Iran. The support of these regimes represented the boldest instances of Soviet interference in Iran. This brings us to the first major problem of Iranian policy toward the Soviet Union in 1945-46. In examining it, we may ask whether Iran encountered the same major instruments of Soviet policy at this time as in the 1941-44 period. The answer must be generally in the affirmative. The Soviet Union used the Red Army, party apparatus, and diplomatic channels to openly aid the Azeri and Kurdish rebellions against the central government. But while the Red Army and diplomatic channels were the same in 1945-46

---

[4] *Foreign Relations of U.S., 1944*, D.P., 5:355.

as in 1941-44, political parties other than the Tudeh were involved in the seizure of power and the establishment of the Azeri and Kurdish republics.

One of these was the Democratic party of Azerbaijan, established in 1945. The leader of this party, Ja'far Pishihvari, was also released from Riza Shah's prison but did not belong to the group that formed the Tudeh party, as mentioned previously. He was a Turkish-speaking Azeri who was born in Tabriz (1893), emigrated to Russian Azerbaijan at the age of twelve, assisted the formation of the first Iranian Communist organization in Baku (1920), and was a member of the Executive Committee of the Soviet Socialist Republic of Gilan (1920-21). Although he had been a member of the Tudeh party for a short while, he published articles in his own newspaper, *Azhir*, criticizing the Tudeh party. He says in his memoirs that at the time of the formation of the Democratic party, no party other than the Tudeh existed in Azerbaijan, and the Tudeh had become "weakened and discredited as the result of years of struggle."[5] As a result of three days of discussions between himself and two other fellow Azeris, they decided to establish their own party, and he instructed one of his colleagues to get the local Tudeh leaders to join his party. It has been argued successfully that the Tudeh and the Azeri parties were not simply two sides of the same coin, as some Western authors had implied. "On the contrary, they were separated from each other by contrasting social bases, conflicting interests, and at times clashing policies. The former was organized by Persian intellectuals who had come to Communism through the Marxism of Western Europe. The latter was formed by Azeri patriots who had reached the same destination through Leninism of the Bolshevik Party in the Caucasus."[6]

The sociological-ideological analysis on which that conclusion is based sheds much light on the separateness of the Tudeh and the Democratic party of Azerbaijan, but more relevant to this study is the greater vulnerability of the latter to Soviet manipulation. In fact, we are here confronted with the Soviet manipulation of not only one but two provincial parties, namely, the Democratic party of Kurdistan as well as of Azerbaijan. Detailed analysis of this problem is beyond the scope of this study, but I submit some general propositions for further investigation. The ease with which the Soviet Union manipulated these local parties was partly a result of the presence of the Red Army, as will be seen; but the susceptibility of these parties to Soviet infiltration (and, it may be argued, even their separateness from the Tudeh party) was to no small extent rooted in the psychopolitical conditions of Iranian society. Granted the linguistic, social, and ideological differences between the

[5] Najafquli Pisyan, *Marg Bood Bazgasht Ham Bood* (Tehran: Shirkat-i Sahami-i Chap, 1948/1949), p. 21.

[6] Abrahamian, p. 315.

Azeris and the Kurds who organized the local parties, on the one hand, and the Farsi-speaking group that organized the Tudeh party, on the other, the conditions that made them all vulnerable to Soviet exploitation were basically the same. The processes of modernization set in motion during the rule of Riza Shah and accompanied by increasing centralization and acts of detribalization had inevitably produced all kinds of psychological dislocations. A profound sense of insecurity in particular affected all groups, including the Azeri and Kurdish minorities. So long as the armed forces of the central government had remained in the provinces, the increasing identity of the Azeris and the Kurds with their own communities as a means of insuring a greater sense of security did not find open political expression, but once these forces were incapacitated after the Anglo-Russian invasion, open defiance of the central government was made possible.[7]

The Azeri and Kurdish alienation and increasing sense of self-consciousness alone did not render them susceptible to Soviet manipulation. The political and psychological legacy of the prewar era played into the hands of the Soviet Union. The factional, cliquish, and personalistic features of pre-Riza Shah party politics, with all their susceptibility to foreign manipulation, re-emerged after the shah's abdication. The removal of his stern rule unleashed unprecedented political activities, including explosive party politics, but the Azeri and Kurdish parties, like all other parties, except the Tudeh, suffered grievously from organizational and other weaknesses. Decades of repression of political participation had provided no real opportunity for experimentation with modern political organizations, including parties.[8]

The other party (also used as the vehicle of rebellion) was the Democratic party of Kurdistan. This party was formed in September 1945 by Qazi Muhammad, hereditary judge and religious leader of Mahabad and a member of its most respected family. He announced the formation of the party shortly after his return from a brief trip to Baku, arranged by the Soviet Union. This Soviet-sponsored party was created at the expense of a Kurdish nationalist party known as *Komala* ("Committee"), which had been in existence, although secretly, since 1943. Although it was organized by Kurdish nationalists and aspired to Western liberal democratic models in party organization and function, its extremely small base of social support and its organizational weaknesses proved conducive to its replacement by the Democratic party, led

---

[7] My conceptualization of the Azeri and Kurdish problems here is influenced by Robert Melson and Howard Wolpe, "Modernization and the Politics of Communalism: A Theoretical Perspective," *American Political Science Review* 64, no. 4 (1970):1112-30.

[8] In this discussion I have been influenced largely by Samuel P. Huntington, *Political Order in Changing Societies* (New Haven: Yale University Press, 1968).

single-handedly by the Qazi, who proved, it seems, far more amenable to Soviet manipulation.

Both the Azeri and Kurdish parties sought to attain autonomy within the Iranian state. They based their claims to autonomy on similar grounds. The Kurdish party's manifesto, signed by the Qazi and other leading Kurds, complained of Riza Shah's denial of their human and constitutional rights; and declared Kurdish as the official language. The Democratic party of Azerbaijan also stressed the distinctive Azeri linguistic and cultural heritage. Of the two parties, however, the great share of Soviet support went to the Azeris from the beginning. Their first manifesto received generous Soviet press coverage on September 14, 1945. In reporting this, George F. Kennan, the American chargé in Moscow, saw parallels between the problem of nationality in Azerbaijan and Eastern Poland, Sinkiang, Turkish Armenia, and other areas, believing that in Azerbaijan, as "in these areas, Soviet fissionist technique seems to be based on racial affinities transcending [the] Soviet border."[9]

Besides the infiltration of the parties, the Soviets employed two other major methods in assisting the seizure of power by the Azeri and Kurdish rebels. These were interception of central government forces and protection of the local rebels. The hands of the Red Army and Soviet consular officers and agents were clearly visible in the use of these methods. The fissionist technique, to borrow Kennan's words, was put into effect in Azerbaijan by the Soviet consul general in Tabriz, who masterminded the rebellion. The military arm of the rebellion was strengthened by the import of a large number of refugees from Soviet Azerbaijan into Iran and by the wholesale distribution of arms to the rebels.[10] The Soviets also nurtured open rebellion among the Kurds; "Soviet agents circulated among the tribes, told them to mobilize for the coming struggle for independence," and armed the "democrats" of Kurdistan, many of whom hailed from Soviet Azerbaijan.[11] Despite all this Soviet aid to the Azeri and Kurdish parties, the rebellions, which were finally launched in mid-November 1945, would have probably fallen short of the establishment of an Autonomous Republic of Azerbaijan (December 12, 1945) and a Kurdish People's Republic (December 15) had it not been for the direct intervention of the Red Army by means of intercepting central government forces sent from Tehran and protecting the rebels against forces of the central government stationed in Azerbaijan.

[9] *Foreign Relations of U.S., 1945*, D.P., 8:400-424.

[10] Robert Rossow, Jr., "The Battle of Azerbaijan," *Middle East Journal* 10, no. 1 (1956):18.

[11] Archie Roosevelt, Jr., "The Kurdish Republic of Mahabad," *Middle East Journal* 1, no. 3 (1947): 247-69.

The Red Army had rehearsed the interception of Iranian forces well before the fateful date of November 20, 1945, when it halted an Iranian relief column at Qazvin on its way to aid the beleaguered garrisons in Azerbaijan.[12] As mentioned before, the earliest instance of outright Soviet interference with Iranian forces occurred in May 1942 when the Red Army prevented Iranian troops from quelling the Kurdish attack on the Gendarmerie post at Rizaiyih. But only a few months before November 20, the Red Army intervened in two other instances. First, Soviet authorities prevented the Iranian commander at Meshed from acting against thirty-seven officer and enlisted deserters, refused to permit reinforcement of gendarmes at Gunabad, and prohibited the landing of Iranian army planes. The second incident took place at Firuzkuh when 200 gendarmes dispatched from Tehran for Shahi were stopped by the Russians and ordered to return to the capital.[13] The Soviet armed interception at Qazvin, however, was the boldest of its kind, and, of course, the one that most directly assisted the Azeri rebels; a Soviet commander threatened to open fire if Iranian forces moved northward any further than Qazvin.[14]

A third kind of Soviet aid to the rebels in the north was their armed protection against the Iranian forces stationed there. Before the fall of Tabriz the rebels seized control of the main Azerbaijan communications arteries by capturing the principal towns on the major routes entering the province. They controlled the main towns by cutting telegraphic communication with Tehran and Tabriz, by occupying post office buildings, by terrorizing the civilian population, and, most of all, by disarming government soldiers, the police force, and the Gendarmerie. The Red Army troops intervened in favor of the rebel forces in most towns and prevented the free movement of government units.[15]

On December 18, 1945, the Iranian prime minister, Ibrahim Hakimi, reported to the Majlis the reasons underlying the decision to strengthen the local troops in the north ("the Third and Fourth Provinces"); the decision to send "security forces" (*qovih-ye ta'minyyih*) there; and the recent return of these forces as the result of their "unexpected obstruction" by the Soviet

[12] For eyewitness accounts by American officials, see *Foreign Relations of U.S., 1945*, D.P., 8:447-48.

[13] See Muhammad Khan Malik (Yazdi), *Ghoghay-i Takhlieh-ye Iran* (Tehran: Shirkat-i Sahami-i Tab'i Kitab, 1947/48), pp. 42-43, and *Foreign Relations of U.S., 1945*, D.P., 8: 447-48.

[14] Rossow, p. 17.

[15] For the texts of reports from government forces to Tehran and related accounts in Persian on the role of the Red Army troops, see Pisyan, *Marg Bood*, pp. 46-61; in English see *Foreign Relations of U.S., 1945*, D.P., 8:480-83, 490-91, and U.N., Security Council, *O.R.*, First Year: First Series, *Supplement* no. 1.

Union.[16] The initial decisions of a government threatened by internal war, Lucian Pye has suggested, "are usually the most fateful and long-lasting of any it will be called upon to make throughout an insurrection."[17] These decisions generally define the issues at stake, the presumed character of the struggle, and the legitimate basis for any eventual termination of the struggle. Premier Hakimi's decision to dispatch troops northward in mid-November 1945 showed that his government viewed the upheaval as illegitimate. His report to the Majlis clearly named the Azeris involved as "aggressors and insurgents" (*mutijavazin va mutajasirin*), condemned their "treasonous plans," (*naqshihay-i kha'inanih*), and placed the blame squarely on the Soviet Union for the interception of Iranian forces at Sharifabad and the protection of the rebels in the northern provinces. As we shall see, this early characterization of the Azeri and Kurdish upheavals as insurrections aided by the Soviet Union was maintained subsequently by Ahmad Qavam, despite differences between his tactics and those of Hakimi.

Soviet Nonevacuation

Iran's other major problem with the Soviet Union in 1945-46 arose from the Soviet attitude toward the evacuation of Russian forces from Iran. The problem of the presence of the Red Army on Iranian soil had been from the outset closely linked with the problem of Russian interference in internal Iranian affairs. But as time went on Iran's concern with the presence of the Soviet troops on its soil deepened significantly. This concern had first figured predominantly, as seen, in the negotiations of Prime Minister Foroughi with the British and the Russians regarding the provisions of the 1942 Tripartite Treaty, particularly its article 5. But in the years after 1942 the problem of Soviet interference constituted Iran's primary concern until the defeat of Germany in May 1945, when the problem of the Soviet attitude toward the evacuation of its forces also began to loom as the other major problem of Iranian foreign policy. The problem of Soviet interference as such constituted the ground for Iran's initial complaint to the United Nations, but the problem of nonevacuation soon formed the basis for another complaint. And when the nonevacuation problem was finally resolved in May 1946, that of interference continued until the collapse of the two rebel governments in December 1946. I shall first trace the problem of nonevacuation to its beginnings before examining Iran's recourse to the Security Council concerning both problems. It will prove helpful to keep the following points in mind. First, in coping

[16]The text of the report is in *Ittila'at*, Dec. 18, 1945.

[17]*Aspects of Political Development* (Boston: Little, Brown & Co., 1966), p. 139.

with the problem of Soviet troops on its soil before or after complaining to the United Nations, Iran relied heavily on the United States. Although Iran was primarily concerned with the withdrawal of the Russian forces, it was by no means unconcerned with those of the British in the south. This point was clearly made to American policymakers before the British withdrawal. Second, by its very nature the problem of the evacuation of Russian forces was of concern to Great Britain and the United States as well as Iran. Although the United States was not a party to the Tripartite Treaty (which obligated the Soviet Union and Great Britain to withdraw), it felt committed to the principle of evacuation by virtue of the Tripartite Declaration of 1943. The declaration as such did not provide specifically for evacuation of any of the Allied troops, but Great Britain and the United States understood that the undertakings embodied therein did cover such an obligation. The Soviet Union, animated by different interests, considered its obligation to emanate solely from the Tripartite Treaty, but even then it chose to interpret its article 5 strictly or invoke its old 1921 treaty with Iran, as will be seen. Third, the two problems of Soviet interference and nonevacuation were closely interwoven with the Soviet hunt for an oil concession from the very beginning, although rhetorically the Allied powers and Iran sought to separate these publicly. One important point to be examined is the way Iran linked agreement to conclude an oil contract with the Soviet Union to the evacuation of Soviet troops. With these points in mind, let us now turn to the development of the problem of evacuation.

As early as February 1, 1945, Foreign Secretary Anthony Eden and Secretary of State Stettinius agreed at Malta on the importance of getting Soviet concurrence on the principle of gradual, pari passu withdrawal. The oil crisis of 1944 was looming large in the minds of the British and Americans at the time. Eden raised the question of Iran in light of this crisis, emphasized the need to maintain its independence, and proposed that the gradual withdrawal of troops should be suggested to the Soviets after "the Governments had agreed that the supply route through Persia was no longer required, which might be about June," but he felt it might be necessary for the British to retain "certain troops for the protection of the vital oil fields in southern Persia." The United States representative recalled the Russian demand for an oil concession in the north when the American and British negotiations for concessions in the south had proceeded quite far. He also stated that the British and the Americans "had a grievance against the Russians" and blamed the "ham-handed procedure of the Russians" for the arrest of the British and American oil negotiations.

At Yalta Eden raised the question of withdrawal of troops from Iran with Molotov on February 11, 1945, but the oil concession problem was not overlooked either. He said that Great Britain "did not dispute the Soviet need for

Iranian oil and that it was not part of British policy to prevent the Soviet Union from obtaining oil from Northern Iran." Indeed, the Soviet Union was a natural market for this oil; Britain did not wish to put any obstacles in the way of the Soviet acquisition of oil concessions "if and when the Iranians were prepared to negotiate," and Eden suggested that the Allies would not press the matter of oil concessions any further until their troops had been withdrawn from Iran. Molotov considered the oil concession and the withdrawal of troops as two different questions and stated that the question of the withdrawal of troops "had never been placed before the Soviet Government until today." He maintained that this was a question of fulfilling the provisions of the treaty signed by Iran. If there was any need to amend this agreement, the question should be studied. This matter would take some time. By contrast, Molotov did not brush aside the oil concession question as briskly as the withdrawal of troops, which was the main subject of discussion. He went into the details of the 1944 oil "controversy," stating that at first the Sa'id government had engaged in negotiations with the Soviets but had then stopped negotiations. He then said suggestively that since the Iranians had changed their minds before, he saw no reason why they should not change them again in order to negotiate now that Kavtaradze had returned "and the strong-armed methods he had used have subsided." Stettinius, like Eden, expressed no opposition to the granting of oil concessions to the Soviet government. The United States, however, was content to leave the question of oil negotiations until the end of the war.[18]

The negative attitude of the Soviet Union with respect to the withdrawal of its troops from Iran became evident at Yalta when a British proposal was discussed. The British draft suggested a declaration to the effect that the Allies had agreed that "a commencement of the withdrawal of forces need not await the termination of hostilities, but should begin pari passu in stages as military considerations, including the use of the Persian supply route, may allow." It also suggested that none of the Allies would favor further demand for oil concessions pending the withdrawal of their forces from Iran. Several times at the conference, Eden inquired whether Molotov had considered the British proposal, but to no avail. Eden then asked whether it would be advisable to issue a communiqué on Iran, and Molotov retorted it would be inadvisable. Stettinius urged that at least some reference be made that the Iranian problem had been discussed and clarified during the Crimean Conference, but Molotov opposed the idea. Finally, Eden suggested

---

[18]U.S., Department of State, *Foreign Relations of the United States,* Diplomatic Papers, *The Conferences at Malta and Yalta, 1945* (Washington, D.C.: Government Printing Office, 1955), pp. 438-500.

that it be stated that the Tripartite Declaration had been reaffirmed and re-examined during the present meeting, but this was also opposed by Molotov. The only point on which the Allies could finally agree was to pursue the matter through diplomatic channels.[19]

Iran's own efforts aimed at the withdrawal of foreign troops from its soil must be dated from May 10, two days after V-E Day. On that date Mustafa 'Adl, chairman of Iran's delegation to the United Nations Conference on International Organization, mentioned to the members of the American delegation (including the secretary of state, at a meeting in San Francisco) the question of the retirement of the Russian and British forces from Iran now that Germany had unconditionally surrendered; explained that an ambiguous phrase of the Tripartite Treaty would allow the British to retain troops in Iran until six months after the termination of hostilities with Japan but that this phrase did not apply to the Russians since they were not at war with Japan; reported that Eden had made it clear to him that the British would not take advantage of that phrase and would like the United States to take initiative in proposing troop withdrawal to the British and the Russians; and felt rather that Iran should take this initiative.[20] On May 18 the shah told the American ambassador in Tehran that the six-month period mentioned in the Tripartite Treaty began on V-E Day since the Russians no longer engaged in hostilities with anyone and Japan had denounced treaties with Germany and had therefore ceased to be a German associate. He also declared that Iran intended to seek Allied departure before the expiration of the six months if possible. Iran's first official note, dated May 19, 1945, was delivered to all three Allied powers in identical terms, however. The note stated in part that because the war had ended in Europe and the presence of the Allied troops on Iranian soil was by no means needed and it was necessary to return to normal conditions, Iran requested that the troops evacuate the country.[21] In a discussion with the American ambassador in Tehran, Anushiravan Sipahbodi, Iran's foreign minister, stated on May 19 that Iran's request for evacuation was not based on a strict reading of article 5 of the Tripartite Treaty, which, he admitted, entitled the Allied forces to remain in Iran until six months after the end of the Japanese war, but on the spirit of the treaty. Iran felt that the treaty called for withdrawal because the Allied troops in Iran could contribute nothing to the war against Japan.[22]

Foreign Minister Sipahbodi told the American ambassador quite frankly

[19] Ibid., 819-982.

[20] *Foreign Relations of U.S., 1945,* D.P., 8:369.

[21] For the text of Iran's note to the USSR, see Malik (Yazdi), p. 240.

[22] *Foreign Relations of U.S., 1945,* D.P., 8:371.

that the delivery of an identical note to the United States was to avoid a British and Russian complaint of discrimination. This and all other Iranian efforts, to be discussed below, would seem to reveal clearly that Iran was concerned with the evacuation of British, and particularly Russian, forces; and that despite occasional notes and representations to the British and the Russians directly, Iran primarily relied upon the United States as the third power to press for evacuation at various stages of Iran's dispute with the Soviet Union. For this important reason most of Iran's policies concerning its major problems with the British and the Russians at the time can be studied profitably in the context of its relations with the United States.

On June 18, 1945, the Iranian minister asked the State Department officials what attitude they would take concerning the withdrawal of foreign troops from Iranian territory when the question was brought up at the next Big Three meeting (the Potsdam Conference). This pointed inquiry marked the beginning of Iran's diplomatic appeals to the United States to press the Iranian case at various international conferences. At this meeting the State Department officials conjectured that the British might desire to remain in southwestern Iran for the protection of the oil fields and the Abadan refinery, which were essential for the war effort. The Iranian minister rejected this conjecture by pointing out the presence of British troops in nearby Iraq and their battleships in the Persian Gulf. A day later, June 19, the Iranian prime minister, Sadr al-Ashraf, expressed strong hopes that the United States would be able to urge the British and the Russians in the forthcoming discussions to leave Iran free to handle its own internal affairs.[23] He was speaking of the Potsdam Conference, which was expected to meet soon. On July 19, both Premier Sadr and Anushiravan Sipahbodi, Iran's foreign minister, made a forceful appeal to the United States to exert influence at the conference to bring about elimination of Anglo-Soviet intervention in Iran and withdrawal of Russian and British troops. Although Premier Sadr spoke of Iran·as being caught in the Anglo-Soviet vise, he emphasized Iran's concern with the Russians; warned that, like Serbia in the First World War and Poland in the second, Iran might well be the spark to set off the third world war; believed that neither Britain nor the Soviet Union would take the initiative to withdraw forces because both were interested parties, each distrustful of the other; and pleaded that the United States as a signatory to the Tripartite Declaration could and should use its "great moral force" to cause the other two powers to act; even token withdrawal would help the situation.[24]

[23]Ibid., pp. 380-81.

[24]U.S., Department of State, *Foreign Relations of the United States,* Diplomatic Papers, *The Conference of Berlin (The Potsdam Conference), 1945,* 2 (Washington, D.C.: Government Printing Office, 1960): 1390-91.

On July 21 the British at the Potsdam Conference recalled, in a proposal, their previous suggestion to the Soviet Union for the withdrawal of the Allied forces pari passu and in stages before the final treaty date was reached, and the lack of response by the Soviet Union. In Britain's view the time had then come for the complete joint withdrawal of the Allied forces in three stages: (1) immediate withdrawal of Soviet and British forces from Tehran; (2) withdrawal from the whole of Iran except for the British troops in Abadan and the southern oil fields and for the Russians in the northeast or northwest; and (3) withdrawal finally from these areas as well. As will be seen, the agreement was reached to withdraw forces merely from the "City of Tehran," but during the conference George V. Allen, the deputy director of the Office of Near Eastern and African Affairs, had hoped that this could be extended to include Tehran and its vicinity because withdrawal from Tehran alone would leave considerable bodies of troops on the outskirts of the city and would do little to help the internal situation in Iran. The agreement reached at the Potsdam Conference was set forth in article 15 of the Protocol of Proceedings of the conference dated August 1, 1945, which stated: "It was agreed that Allied troops should be withdrawn immediately from Tehran, and that further stages of the withdrawal of troops from Iran should be considered at the meeting of the Council of Ministers to be held in London in September, 1945." [25]

Foreign Minister Sipahbodi expressed Iran's deep disappointment after hearing on August 2, 1945, (from the British chargé in Iran) that the Potsdam agreement would probably mean British and Russian withdrawal only as far as Qum, in the south, and Qazvin, in the north, respectively. On August 7 the Iranian minister in Washington expressed disappointment and regret at the action of the Potsdam Conference but was assured by State Department officials that the United States continued to favor the withdrawal of the Allied forces from Iran as soon as possible and would lend its efforts toward that end. Iran, however, went beyond criticism of the Potsdam agreement; it demanded that both Britain and the Soviet Union allow its presence at the forthcoming conference in London because Iran's interest in the question of the withdrawal of foreign troops was obvious, and its request was based on article 6 of the Tripartite Treaty and annex 1, which provided for consultation with Iran at postwar international conferences where its direct interest was discussed. Iran also appealed to Acting Secretary Acheson to see to it that the United States would support actively at the London meeting Iran's claim to be heard on the question of evacuation of troops and any other question of concern to Iran. [26]

[25] Ibid., pp. 1391-97.

[26] See *Foreign Relations of U.S., 1945,* D.P., 8:389-404.

The end of the Japanese war on September 2, 1945, spurred Iranian efforts for the withdrawal of foreign troops. It occasioned Iran's second major note to the Allies, dated September 9, for withdrawal of their troops. A similar note was received on September 12 by the United States ambassador to Iran, asking the American government to expedite the departure of its last soldier from Iranian soil.[27] The Iranian note to the Soviet Union, like those sent to the British and the Americans, reminded the Soviets of Iran's first note of May 19, 1945, which still remained unanswered; pointed out that according to the Tripartite Treaty the six-month period after the armistice during which the Allied forces must leave Iran began on September 2 (the day the war ceased with Japan); and expected that Iranian soil should "be completely evacuated on March 2, 1946, when not even one person attached to the Allied Army, Air and Naval Forces should remain on the Iranian soil and waters. This is the definitive date on which Iran should be evacuated."[28]

The end of the war with Japan also prompted the British to press for a definitive evacuation date from the Russians. The British secretary of state for foreign affairs, Bevin, wrote to Molotov on September 19, 1945, stating that the end of the Japanese war had changed the situation since the Potsdam Conference, when it was agreed to place the further stages of troop withdrawal on the agenda of the London Conference for discussion. The British and the Russian governments would now be completing the withdrawal of their forces from Iran by March 2, 1946, six months after the signing of the Japanese Instrument of Surrender. Bevin, therefore, suggested that when the question came up at the London Conference, the Soviet and British governments agree that by the middle of December, 1945, their forces should be withdrawn from the whole of Iran except Azerbaijan and the southern oil area. The brief and ambiguous Soviet reply of September 20, 1945, stated that the Potsdam agreement about the evacuation of Tehran had already been implemented; that the complete withdrawal of Soviet troops should be effected by the Tripartite Treaty; and that there was no need to discuss this question in London. If necessary, the note intimated, the plan for the final withdrawal of Soviet and British forces from Iran could be discussed between the two governments concerned "towards the end of the said period." This exchange of notes was followed by two undated notes between Bevin and Molotov that left the Soviet position as ambiguous as before. The British were puzzled by the "apparent evasiveness" of the Soviets in these exchanges and hoped that it would not be borne out in the actual implementation of the Tripartite

[27]Ibid., pp. 408-9.

[28]For the text of the letters to the Soviet Union, see Malik (Yazdi), pp. 47-48. See also *Foreign Relations of U.S., 1945*, D.P., 8:408-9.

Treaty.[29] As we shall see, however, subsequent events proved the futility of this hope.

In fact, Soviet evasiveness paralleled the worsening of the situation in Azerbaijan where, as seen before, the process of Soviet interference reached its peak by late November 1945 when the Red Army actually assisted the Azeri insurrection. The problem of Soviet interference overshadowed that of Soviet nonevacuation as such for a short while, and once the rebel regimes were established in December 1945, Iran faced both problems simultaneously and with unprecedented urgency. Furthermore, the Azerbaijan crisis produced the sharpest exchanges regarding Iran between the United States and the Soviet Union to that date. In a long note from Secretary Byrnes delivered to Molotov by Averell Harriman on November 23, 1945, the United States related the uprisings in northern Iran, "where Soviet troops are stationed"; mentioned the Soviet interception of Iranian forces; called attention to Stalin's signing of the Tehran Declaration, which required full freedom of action without Soviet interference; and stated that the Azerbaijan situation had "convinced the American Government that it would be in the common interest for all Soviet, British, and American troops to be withdrawn immediately."[30] Molotov's reply of November 29, 1945, denied that the situation in northern Iran was one of armed uprising against the government of the shah; claimed that the Azeris sought "national autonomy" based on their own particular language and therefore this was a matter of the aspirations of "the democratic rights of the Azerbaijan population of northern Iran"; justified the Soviet opposition to the dispatch of Iranian troops on the ground that it could "cause not the cessation but the increase of the disorders, and likewise bloodshed, which could compel the Soviet Government to introduce into Iran further forces of its own for the purpose of preserving order and of assuring the security of Soviet garrison."[31] In regard to the withdrawal of

[29] See Malik (Yazdi), pp. 37-38. See also *Foreign Relations of U.S., 1945,* D.P., 8: 413-28.

[30] Although the note was delivered on Nov. 23, the official date is Nov. 24. For the text of the note see Raymond Dennett and Robert K. Turner, eds., *Documents on American Foreign Relations* (Princeton: Princeton University Press, 1948), 8:851-52. The proposals concerning the withdrawal of *all* foreign troops contained in this note were simultaneously made to the British government. See U.S. State Dept. *Bulletin* 13, no. 336 (Dec. 2, 1945): 884-89.

[31] For the text of the Soviet note see Dennett and Turner, *Documents,* 8:852-54; see also U.S. State Dept. *Bulletin* 13, no. 337 (Dec. 9, 1945): 934-35. For the text of the British reply to the United States proposals for the evacuation of all foreign troops from Iran by Jan. 1, 1946, see U.S. State Dept. *Bulletin* 13, no. 338 (Dec. 16, 1945):946. The British note stated: "The Soviet Government, having intimated to the United States

troops, the Soviet note dismissed the relevance of the Tehran Declaration to the question of Soviet armed forces in Iran which, the note asserted, fell within the purview of the 1942 Tripartite Treaty and the 1921 treaty between Iran and the Soviet Union; and claimed that the removal of British and Soviet forces from Iran had been decided by the British-Soviet exchange of letters of which note had been taken at the Council of Foreign Ministers (the London Conference) as little as two months ago without any objection from any quarters. The exchange of notes referred to the Bevin-Molotov correspondence, which, as seen, produced no definitive withdrawal date, to Britain's great disappointment. Molotov had only vaguely remarked that the question could be discussed, if necessary, toward the end of the period, presumably ending on March 2, 1946.

Iran's disappointment with the outcome of the London Conference, as with the Potsdam Conference before it, was further aggravated by the results of yet another conference, namely, the Moscow Conference of the American, British, and Soviet Foreign Ministers held December 16-26, 1945. By this time the outlines of Iran's two major problems with the Soviet Union had become graphically clear. The events in Azerbaijan, on the one hand, and the persistent refusal of the Soviet Union to commit itself to any definitive withdrawal date, on the other, prompted Iran to press even more vigorously for the resolution of both problems in anticipation of the Moscow Conference. On December 10, 1945, Husain 'Ala, Iranian ambassador to the United States, conveyed a strong message to the United States aimed at exerting every effort to place the question relating to Iran on the agenda of the conference. The steps that Iran considered "extremely pressing" were: (1) the immediate evacuation of Iran; and (2) pending such rapid withdrawal, "absolute and complete freedom of action" of the Iranian government in restoring order and restraining "mischief-makers, undesirable immigrants and unknown individuals" who had arrived in Azerbaijan from across the border.[32]

Iran's urgent appeal to the United States fell on sympathetic ears, but

---

Government that they are not prepared to accede to the United States Government's proposal, British military authorities are not continuing their plans to examine the details involved in arrangements for withdrawal by January 1, 1946."

[32]The purport of Husain 'Ala's message was contained in a letter dated December 13 to the American government from the Iranian Ministry of Foreign Affairs. This note stated in part, "It is imperative that in this Conference the question should be discussed and a decision taken that the forces of the three Allied and friendly Governments should immediately evacuate the whole country." The note also stated that the "regrettable incidents of Azerbaijan provide the most outstanding example of the sinister effect of the presence of foreign troops in this country." For the full text of the note, see *Foreign Relations of U.S., 1945*, D.P. 8:492-93. For reference to Husain 'Ala's message, see ibid., pp. 487-88.

neither before the Moscow Conference nor at the time of its meeting did the Soviets prove receptive to American pleadings on behalf of Iran. Harriman and Bevin during separate conversations with Stalin on December 19, 1945, raised the question of withdrawal of troops from Iran. The substance of Stalin's remarks to Harriman was: (1) Iran was "hostile to the Soviet Union"; (2) this hostility threatened sabotage of the Baku oil fields, for which reason Russia continued to maintain troops in Iran; (3) Russia had the right to send troops to Iran under the 1921 treaty between Iran and the Soviet Union in light of Iranian hostility; (4) the Soviet Union would consider later whether it would withdraw its troops under the 1942 Tripartite Treaty or keep them there under the 1921 treaty; (5) Soviet forces were not interfering in Azerbaijan; and (6) Iran was trying to stir up trouble between Russia and the Anglo-Saxon powers. The American ambassador in Iran refuted Stalin's remarks about an Iranian threat to the Baku oil fields by stating forcefully that the suggestion was "so patently absurd" that it was difficult to see how the Soviets would expect it be given any serious consideration.[33]

Absurd or not, by such tactics the Soviet Union managed to defy both Britain and the United States at the Moscow Conference. First, the Soviets managed to get the agreement of their Western counterparts to remove Iran from the formal agenda, although Iran could be discussed informally, and then relied on the technical distinction between formal and informal discussion in order to bar any Anglo-American effort to pin down the Soviet Union on the question of evacuation. The British, in desperation, sought to reduce the scope of the Azerbaijan autonomy by suggesting an Anglo-American-Soviet Commission that would assist Iran in its relations with the provinces, and the Americans added to this suggestion the proposal that the commission would also investigate the question of troop withdrawal with a view to its acceleration.[34]

Given the Iranian view of the proposed commission as a device to replace Three-Power interference, Premier Hakimi treated the study of the proposal with utmost secrecy, but the pressure from the Majlis for full information and open discussion proved too great. On January 6, 1946, the Foreign Affairs Committee of the Majlis decided that it could not express its view on the Tripartite Commission without "complete information" about the Moscow Conference and the proposal for the formation of the commission. Apparently irked by the secrecy surrounding the question, Muhammad Musaddiq took the floor of the Majlis on January 9, 1946, to attack the government policy and to demand resignation of Premier Hakimi and formation of a truly neutral

[33] *Foreign Relations of U.S., 1945,* D.P., 8:510-17.
[34] Ibid., pp. 517-19.

government. He pointed out that the foreign minister, Najm, had been so evasive in the Foreign Affairs Committee of the Majlis that he himself had to get Prime Minister Hakimi to arrange for a special briefing session in the Ministry of Foreign Affairs. At that meeting, Musaddiq continued, the foreign minister had produced an eleven-item document without date and signature; he had stated that it possessed no official significance; and he had himself proved irritable when several Majlis Deputies wished to obtain copies of the document. Deeply disturbed by Musaddiq's speech, Hakimi finally broke the silence on January 15, 1946, when he disclosed Iran's rejection of the proposal for a Three-Power Commission. Furthermore, he told the Majlis that after Iran's initial refusal to consider the proposal, the Iranian government had been asked to express its views on the powers and duties of the commission if it agreed in principle with the dispatch of the American, British, and Soviet representatives to Iran. Iran had replied, according to the prime minister, that the Allied representatives could come temporarily (only for a few months), in order to work together with Iran's own representatives toward two ends: (1) expeditious evacuation of foreign troops before March 2, 1946, and (2) restoration of normal conditions in Iranian affairs. Both objectives should be fulfilled in accordance with the Tripartite Treaty of 1942 and the Tripartite Declaration of 1943. Since the government had not received any reply to its counterproposal, the premier concluded, the matter had not been referred to the Majlis.[35]

As we shall see presently, the Iranian policy on the evacuation of foreign troops officially entered a new phase four days after the public statement by Premier Hakimi in the Majlis with the lodging of an Iranian complaint to the United Nations on January 19, 1946. It should be noted that the idea to complain to the United Nations had been entertained by Iran for quite some time and was made known to the Russians by the United States at the Moscow Conference. The idea was rooted in Iran's frustration with Soviet interference and the Soviet attitude toward evacuation. Iran's exclusion from the Allied conferences dealing with Iranian problems spurred Iran to take its disputes with the Soviet Union to the world forum. The probability of Iran's complaining to the United Nations was first brought to the attention of the Soviet Union on December 13, 1945, at the Moscow Conference when Secretary Byrnes expressed fear that the dispute would be raised at the January meeting of the United Nations. Stalin replied that the Soviet Union was not afraid of having the Iranian question raised at the United Nations meeting and "no one need to blush if it should come up."[36]

[35] *Ittila'at,* Jan. 6, 9, 15, 1946.

[36] *Foreign Relations of U.S., 1945,* D.P. 8:517-19.

"The Iranian Question"

Iran's decision to take its case to the United Nations proved difficult to execute at first. The reason for this is to be seen in the British attitude. The Tripartite Commission's proposal was before the Iranian government at the time. Britain and the United States supported it, but the Soviet Union held back, in part because the commission's functions would place a check on unilateral Soviet interference in Iranian affairs. Both the shah and Premier Hakimi favored the proposal for the formation of the commission in principle, but some of the influential Majlis Deputies, including several supporters of the Hakimi government, strenuously opposed it. The British government was at first strongly opposed to the decision of the Hakimi government to complain to the United Nations, and, in fact, the British ambassador to the United States, on January 3, 1946, requested Under Secretary Acheson to instruct the American ambassador in Tehran to join the British in urging the Iranian government not to complain to the United Nations.[37] Apparently the reason for the British opposition was to avoid spoiling the chances of the Soviets' joining the Tripartite Commission by antagonizing them. The American government sternly refused to put pressure on Iran in this matter, probably because it did not believe that the commission would be agreeable to either the Soviets or the Iranians. In response to Acheson's inquiry about the United States attitude toward the British request just mentioned, the secretary of state replied "that we could not possibly urge Iran not bring the matter up if they wished to do so." A day before, January 2, 1946, the secretary of state had instructed the American ambassador to inform the Iranian government that the United States believed that any of the United Nations "should be entirely free to present its case to that organization."[38] This statement had been prompted by the inquiry of Husain 'Ala, Iran's ambassador to the United States, who sought American prior assurance to the effect that the United States would support the Iranian position should Iran file its complaint against the Soviet Union with the United Nations.

Conscious of American support, the Iranian government finally filed its complaint, but still not without difficulty. Premier Hakimi instructed Hasan Taqizadih, the Iranian ambassador to Great Britain, to submit the Iranian dispute with the Soviet Union to the United Nations, but he subsequently

[37] U.S., Department of State, *Foreign Relations of the United States, 1946,* vol. 7, *The Near East and Africa* (Washington, D.C.: Government Printing Office, 1969), p. 293.

[38] Ibid., pp. 292-93.

ordered him to withdraw the request, apparently "under strong British pressure without consultation with other Cabinet Ministers."[39] Hakimi's subsequent instruction to Taqizadih (probably on January 7, 1946) to go ahead with the lodging of the complaint was probably in response to the strenuous objections expressed by the cabinet to that earlier step. As we have seen, Iran faced two related problems with the Soviet Union, interference and non-evacuation. In light of the connection between these problems, how did Iran lodge its complaint with the United Nations?

An answer to this question must be attempted here because the linkage between the problem of interference and nonevacuation proved crucial for the Iranian strategy at the United Nations. Iran's letter of January 19, 1946, which embodied its initial complaint to the world organization, reveals that "interference of the Soviet Union through the medium of its officials and armed forces, in the internal affairs of Iran" constituted the basis of its complaint to the United Nations, namely, the Soviet interference that led to the establishment of the Azerbaijan Republic. This is evidenced not only by the language of the letter of January 19, just cited, but also by the documents submitted to the Security Council on January 28, including Taqizadih's memorandum and a bill of "Particulars of Interference by Soviet Authorities" and two sets of related documents.[40] As a matter of strategy, Iran confined its initial complaint to the problem of Soviet interference as "a situation which may lead to international friction." In fact, Iran's paramount concern stemmed from the Soviet attitude toward evacuation, but the language, if not the spirit, of the 1942 Tripartite Treaty entitled the Soviet Union to keep its troops in Iran until six months after the hostilities, namely, March 2, 1946. Hence, despite its overriding concern over the problem of troop withdrawal, Iran reserved formal complaint about that problem for a more appropriate time.

Nevertheless, Iran made no secret of its deep concern over the negative Soviet attitude toward the evacuation of troops at the time of its first complaint to the United Nations. First, in taking advantage of the opportunity to respond to the Soviet letter of January 24, 1946, Taqizadih wrote the Security Council president on January 26 that the Iranian government in its January 19 note to the Security Council did not raise the question of the withdrawal of Soviet forces, but it should be stated that "the *raison d'etre* for the presence of foreign troops in Iran has disappeared and that it is desirable that all foreign troops should leave Iranian territory immediately, thus following the example set by the United States Government as regards its forces. The Treaty

[39] Ibid., p. 299.

[40] See U.N., Security Council, *OR*, First Year: First Series, *Supplement* no. 1, pp. 16-17, 25-73.

provides that foreign troops *may* remain until six months after the end of the war, but does not require that they shall do so."[41] Second, during the first session of the Security Council meeting on the Iranian question, Taqizadih, in presenting the Iranian case on January 28, 1946, stated that

the request of Iran, therefore, is that Soviet authorities should cease interfering in the internal affairs of Iran, and that Iranian forces and officials should not be prevented from proceeding freely in and through territory in which Soviet forces are stationed or from the full exercise of their duties, and more particularly that no hindrance should be put in the way of the Iranian security forces proceeding to Azerbaijan or to any part of Iran to restore law and order. In addition, the Iranian Government requests that the Soviet Government give the necessary instructions to effect complete withdrawal of all Soviet troops and officials by 2 March 1946.[42]

I shall not reproduce here the official presentation to the Security Council of the problems of interference and nonevacuation because the preceding discussion in this chapter has been concerned with the analysis of these two problems. Instead I shall examine the Iranian strategy and tactics (and the Soviet reactions) in the light of discussions in the Security Council.

To continue with the question of strategy, the Iranian presentation during the first phase of the debate in the Security Council focused on the problem of Soviet interference in Iranian affairs and the inability of Iran to negotiate with the Soviet Union. After two sessions of debate on January 28 and 30, 1946 (the first phase), the Security Council resolved unanimously (on the latter date) to request the parties to inform it of any results achieved through negotiations.[43] We shall see the nature and outcome of these negotiations subsequently, but it must be noted here that the crucial date of March 2, 1946, arrived at the time of these negotiations and hence Iran's other, and more crucial, problem, nonevacuation, could then appropriately constitute the basis for a fresh complaint to the United Nations.

This newer complaint was also aimed at calling worldwide attention to Iran's problems with the Soviet Union and thereby exerting pressures on its giant neighbor. This second phase was signaled by Iran's letter of March 18, 1946, to the Security Council. Husain 'Ala, Iran's representative before the Security Council and ambassador to the United States, brought to the attention of the Security Council (according to article 35, paragraph 1 of the charter) a "dispute between Iran and the Union of Soviet Socialist Republics,

---

[41] For the text of the letter see ibid., pp. 19-24.

[42] Ibid., First Series, no. 1, p. 38.

[43] Ibid., p. 70.

the continuance of which is likely to endanger the maintenance of international peace and security." This dispute had arisen, the letter stated, as a result of new developments since the Security Council Resolution of January 30 relating to "the earlier dispute," and it stemmed from the maintenance of Soviet troops in Iranian territory after March 2, 1946, "contrary to the express provisions of article V of the Tri-Partite Treaty." In another letter (dated March 20, 1946, in response to the Soviet request for postponement of the Security Council meeting), 'Ala wrote the Security Council that the Soviet-Iranian negotiations on the earlier dispute had "failed," and the new dispute that had arisen as the result of Soviet nonevacuation was not "a proper subject for negotiations under the Charter of the United Nations or the constitution of Iran."[44] Just as in the first phase of the United Nations debate, when Iran's strategy focused on the problem of Soviet interference without losing sight of the evacuation problem, in the second phase (March 26 to the last session on Iran, May 22, 1946) that strategy concentrated on the evacuation problem without overlooking the problem of Soviet interference.

Iran's tactics in the Security Council, like its strategy, were designed to bring pressure to bear on the Soviet Union through full discussion in the forum of the United Nations. The first necessary move, of course, was the inclusion of the Iranian question on the agenda of the Security Council. At the suggestion of the president of the council, both Iran and the Soviet Union were given an opportunity to make oral observations concerning their written communications, and in "this way, the Council will be fully seized of the matter under consideration." The initial Soviet agreement to place the question on the agenda was confined only to the session of January 30 and was a procedural move. The Soviet Union strove persistently to remove the question from the agenda. Supported most often by the United States, Great Britain, Egypt, and Mexico, Iran insisted vigorously on keeping the question on the agenda. Even when Iran contemplated negotiations under the Security Council resolution adopted on January 30, Taqizadih stated emphatically that Iran wished to negotiate "provided that the matter in dispute remains before the Council. I can not think that that is a formality. Even if it is a formality, if it is taken off the agenda we have had the experience always that that is to the detriment of [a] small country."[45]

Retention of the Iranian question on the agenda was Iran's most favored tactic throughout the debate. The only seeming exception to this was its request of April 15, 1946. But this can be explained. On April 9 'Ala advised

[44] See ibid., *Supplement* no. 2, pp. 43-45.

[45] Ibid., First Series, no. 1, p. 32.

the Security Council that Iran wished to retain the matters relating to the continued presence of Soviet forces in Iran and the interference in internal affairs of Iran on the agenda, but on April 15 he informed the council that his government "withdraws its complaint from the Security Council." This "sudden reversal," to borrow the words of the United States representative, "by the Iranian Government of the position which it had steadfastly maintained until yesterday occurred while USSR troops were still stationed in Iran."[46] Twenty-three years later the publication of relevant United States documents revealed what was behind this general statement. The Soviet ambassador pressured Ahmad Qavam, the Iranian prime minister, to instruct 'Ala to withdraw Iran's complaint. Sadchikov, the Soviet ambassador in Iran, told Qavam that Iran's insistence on retaining the case before the Security Council was an insult to the USSR and would not be tolerated, and Qavam promised Sadchikov to telegraph 'Ala to withdraw the complaint.[47] During the public debate at the Security Council, 'Ala placed, understandably, a much more generous construction on the behavior of the Soviet ambassador. He told the Council that the Soviet ambassador's "definite and reiterated assurances" in Tehran on the question of evacuation had prompted Premier Qavam to ask the council to withdraw the complaint from the agenda. But 'Ala's generous characterization of Soviet behavior was to assist him in an ingenious interpretation of the withdrawal of the complaint that resulted in its partial retention. He argued that the withdrawal was concerned with the question of evacuation and therefore the council was still seized of the Iranian question on the ground of Soviet interference, which had been the basis of Iran's initial complaint to the Security Council.[48]

The technical question of retention of an item on the agenda after the parties to a dispute have withdrawn it was complicated further by a legal opinion of the secretary-general, which was in effect against the retention of the Iranian question on the agenda. At its meeting of April 16, the Security Council decided to refer the problem to the Committee of Experts. The committee considered whether the Security Council could remain seized of a matter after the interested parties had requested its withdrawal. Eight members of the committee inclined toward a more functional view of the Security Council's role, one that would favor the retention of a matter despite the agreement of the interested parties to withdraw, and three other members opposed this view. Although the Committee of Experts was not able to formulate "a common opinion" on the question put to it by the Security

[46]Ibid., no. 2, p. 146.

[47]*Foreign Relations of U.S., 1946* 7:417.

[48]U.N., Security Council, *OR*, First Year: First Series, no. 2, p. 293.

Council, there was "agreement in principle that when a matter has been submitted to the Security Council by a party, it cannot be withdrawn from the list of matters of which the Security Council is seized without a decision by the Security Council."[49] This agreement was, of course, welcomed by Iran, but was attacked by the Soviet Union.

The Soviet reaction to Iran's strategy and tactics in the Security Council requires examination, but it must first be asked whether the Soviet Union was really concerned over the discussion of these problems in the United Nations. If they were not, little weight could be attached to the Iranian decision to complain, as it could have no significant impact on Soviet policy, including the decision eventually to withdraw Soviet troops from Iran. If the Soviets were concerned, then the Iranian decision to complain was reasonably well calculated in terms of Iran's own basic objectives of bringing about the withdrawal of Soviet troops and the elimination of the two autonomous republics in the north.

Obviously, it is impossible to ascertain Soviet concern over the public debate of its policy in Iran at the United Nations so long as access to Soviet sources is denied, but published documentary sources in the West can shed some light on the subject. It may be recalled that Stalin, in response to Secretary Byrnes's apprehension about the probability of Iran's complaint, stated categorically at the Moscow Conference that the Soviet Union was not afraid of having the Iranian question raised at the United Nations meeting— "no one need to blush if it should come up." This nonchalance of the Soviet leader, however, was more apparent than real. On the morning of January 28, 1946, just before the question was first discussed at the United Nations, Bevin told Stettinius that Vyshinsky "had shown considerable nervousness," and said he was ready to drop the Russian charges regarding Greece and Indonesia if Britain would make satisfactory concessions in the Balkan situations. Bevin had told Vyshinsky "flatly that he would not allow the Iranian situation to be dropped by the Security Council."[50] In addition to this testimony, Soviet concern over the public debate of its activities in Iran at the United Nations (even after the Iranian question was taken up) may be inferred, I submit, from Soviet reaction to the Iranian strategy and tactics.

Whether Vyshinsky battled Taqizadih in the first phase of the United Nations debate or Gromyko struggled with 'Ala in the second phase, the Soviet Union adopted every possible tactic to impair the discussion of the Iranian question. For example, when Iran asked the Security Council to reopen the debate on the Iranian question, the Soviet Union first urged postponement, and then walked out of the Security Council on March 27, 1946,

[49] Ibid., *Supplement* no. 2, pp. 47-50.

[50] *Foreign Relations of U.S., 1946* 7:320.

when Egypt moved to invite the Iranian representative to participate in the discussion.[51] Apart from these particular moves, the Soviet tactics throughout the United Nations debate may be divided into two major categories.

One tactic was to try to scotch the debate by insisting on bilateral negotiations between the Soviet Union and Iran. In response to Iran's initial complaint, the Soviet Union insisted in its letter of January 24, 1946, that the Soviet Union and its neighbor Iran "can and should" settle the questions that affected their relations "by means of bilateral negotiations."[52] And during the oral observations in the Security Council, the Soviet representative insisted, contrary to Iran's contention, that the USSR had negotiated with Iran before; it was prepared to negotiate again; Iran was to blame for non-negotiation; and it would not consider any solution other than negotiation. When the Iranian question was taken up again, the Soviet Union claimed that negotiations were still proceeding according to the council's resolution of January 30, while Iran contended that the negotiations had "failed."[53]

The most favored Soviet tactic, however, was to keep the Iranian question off the agenda. In the first phase of the debate the Soviet Union wished to remove the question from the agenda and leave it to a less definite procedure so that when the negotiations called for by the January 30 resolution failed, any member might bring it up again; and during the second phase, the Soviet representative attempted to remove the question from the agenda once again, but this time by claiming that the withdrawal of Soviet forces had generally begun on March 2, 1946, and was proceeding further since March 24 in accordance with an understanding between the Soviet and Iranian governments.[54] Having failed to persuade the council to drop the Iranian question from the agenda on the basis of yet another argument, namely, Iran's withdrawal of complaint (April 15), the Soviet representative then charged "breach" of the charter by the council for taking up the question.[55]

The Red Army Withdraws

Just as Iran took the initiative in lodging a complaint with the United Nations as a means of achieving its objectives, so too it took the initiative in starting

---

[51]U.N., Security Council, *OR,* First Year: First Series, no. 2, p. 58.

[52]For the text of the note see ibid., *Supplement* no. 1, pp. 17-19.

[53]Ibid., First Series, no. 1, pp. 39-44, and no. 2, pp. 12-13.

[54]For evidence of these two Soviet attempts, see ibid., no. 1, pp. 65-67, and no. 2, p. 11.

[55]Ibid., no. 2, p. 124.

negotiations with the Soviet Union toward the attainment of the same goals. It would be tempting to conclude quite differently; for example, to conclude from the sequence starting with the United Nations Resolution of January 30 calling for negotiations to the actual beginning of discussions in Moscow in February that Iran was merely responding to the Security Council's initiative. Or it would be tempting to infer from Iran's relatively limited freedom of action at the time that it was probably doing what the Americans or the British wanted in order to avoid antagonizing the Soviet Union. The record, however, reveals clearly that Iran was prepared to talk with the Russians as early as December 1945. This fact was well known in Iran and was recalled publicly by Taqizadih in the first session of the United Nations discussion of the Iranian question: "We have sought that negotiation. We went so far in that direction that the Iranian Prime Minister and the Minister of Foreign Affairs offered to go to Moscow to negotiate, not only at the time of the conference of the Three Powers in Moscow, as was said by the Soviet representative, but even before that time and also later in a note sent to the Soviet Embassy, and once again in a speech delivered in the Iranian Parliament on 18 December, a copy of which was sent to the Soviet Embassy with a note on 21 December."[56]

Furthermore, both Premier Hakimi and Foreign Minister Anushiravan Sipahbodi were prepared as late as December 27, 1945, to make direct personal appeal to Stalin in order to resolve the Iranian problems with the Soviet Union.[57] But, it may be recalled, as early as December 19, 1945, Stalin told Harriman that the Iranian government was "hostile to the Soviet Union." The government at the time was led by Premier Hakimi, and subsequently during the Qavam mission to Moscow the Soviet Union put its finger squarely on Hakimi as an example of those who pursued "discriminatory policy" toward the Soviet Union.[58] Hence, Iran had wished to negotiate long before the Security Council's call, but the Soviets had held back because they regarded the Hakimi government as "hostile" to Russia.

By the time the United Nations called on the parties to negotiate, however, Premier Hakimi had resigned and Ahmad Qavam had been appointed prime minister. The Soviets did not view him in the same way they regarded Hakimi. They disfavored Hakimi ostensibly because he had, in 1919, served in the government of Samsam al-Saltanih, which, at the Paris Peace Conference, had

[56]Ibid., no. 1, p. 48.

[57]*Foreign Relations of U.S., 1946* 7:514.

[58]Qasim Masudi, *Jarayan-i Musafirat-i Misyon-i I'zami-i Iran Be-Mosko* (Tehran: Shirkat-i Sahami-i Chap, 1946/47), pp. 73-74.

[59]Ibid. Iran was not allowed participation.

demanded from Soviet Russia the return of certain formerly held Iranian territories.[59] But Qavam al-Saltanah's name was intimately associated with the Soviet-favored 1921 Treaty of Friendship with Iran; he had been Iran's prime minister at the time of its submission to the Majlis for ratification. For Qavam the parallels between the two periods must have been astounding. The actor was the same and the play was remarkably similar. In late January 1946, as in late June 1921, he faced two major problems vis-à-vis Russia, the presence of Russian troops on Iranian soil and the threat of Soviet-supported local insurrection. Instead of the Soviet Republic of Gilan, he now faced the two Republics of Azerbaijan and Kurdistan.

Qavam swiftly decided to keep the Iranian question on the United Nations agenda, to negotiate with the Soviet Union, and at the same time "tame" the rebels. On the day he was formally appointed prime minister, January 27, 1946, he instructed the Iranian ambassador to London to approach Vyshinsky and ascertain whether any opportunity existed for direct settlement of Irano-Soviet problems.[60] He delayed the selection of his cabinet ministers and the formation of his government deliberately in order to emphasize to the Soviets his intention to resign if he felt unable to talk about Iran's problems with them. Finally when he went to the Majlis to introduce his government on February 17 (nearly a month after the Majlis had chosen him prime minister), he broke the news dramatically that in less than twenty hours he would lead a mission to Moscow at Stalin's invitation.[61]

At Moscow he raised Iran's two problems, first with Molotov. "Molotov spread the Iranian map in front of me," Qavam reported to the Majlis subsequently, "and spoke of oil [concession], and charged our [past] policy in this regard as a one-sided and discriminatory policy."[62] Stalin as well as Molotov separately raised the question of oil concession, but the latter in particular insisted on the charge of discrimination, Qavam subsequently told the American ambassador in Tehran confidentially.[63] Qavam, however, pointed out to the Soviets the different circumstances under which the 1901 British oil concession had been granted and refused to discuss the grant of an oil concession to the Russians with Molotov or Stalin. To Qavam, more disturbing than the charge of discrimination was the tough Russian position on the evacuation of forces from Iran; the Soviet troops would begin to leave only certain parts of Iran beginning on March 2, 1946. In great despair Qavam

[60] *Foreign Relations of U.S., 1946* 7:315.

[61] *Ittila'at,* Feb. 17, 1946.

[62] Qavam's speech to the Twenty-Fifth Meeting of the Fifteenth Majlis, Iran, Majlis, Majlis-i Panzdahum, *Ruznamih-ye Rasmi,* pp. 2189-201.

[63] *Foreign Relations of U.S., 1946* 7:351.

decided to submit to the Soviet leaders a memorandum setting forth unequi-vocally the Iranian position. The substance of Iran's first memorandum of February 23, 1946, was as follows: (1) The Iranian Majlis by law had for-bidden any discussion of oil concession with foreign interests (This referred to the Musaddiq-sponsored bill passed December 2, 1944, during the oil crisis.); (2) Azerbaijan had always been an inseparable part of Iranian territory; and (3) the subject of evacuation was governed by the Tripartite Treaty of 1942, and the Allied forces must evacuate *all* Iranian territory *by* March 2, 1946. Therefore there could be no ground for the retention of any Soviet troops beyond that date.[64]

The Soviet response to the Iranian memorandum contained the following proposals: (1) Soviet troops to remain in some parts of Iran for an indefinite period; (2) the Iranian government to recognize the internal autonomy of Azerbaijan; and (3) the Soviet government to abandon its demand for an oil concession; instead, an Iranian-Soviet joint-stock company should be estab-lished in which fifty-one percent of the shares would be owned by the Soviet Union and forty-nine percent by Iran.[65] In attempting to justify orally the retention of troops, Stalin first invoked the 1921 treaty; this Qavam countered by telling the Soviet leader that he personally knew what had been intended by that treaty because he himself had been in office at the time. After going over some other excuses, the Russians ultimately fell back on the bald and unexplained statement that their "interests" required retention of troops in Iran.[66] In his second memorandum to the Soviets, Qavam emphatically reiterated Iran's initial position on the problems of evacuation and Azerbaijan, but subtly yet firmly linked the oil question to the complete evacuation of troops from Iran.[67] The entire game seemed to hinge on this one point. The Soviets tried to use the issue of evacuation of troops to extract from Iran what they had failed to gain in 1944, namely, an oil concession. And Qavam was willing to use oil as bait to get the Soviet troops totally out of Iran. Meanwhile, the magical date of March 2, 1946, arrived while the prime minister was still in Moscow. Iran immediately pursued two courses of action at the same time.

First, Qavam at once lodged Iran's protest with the Soviet government on March 3, 1946. The Iranian protest referred to an official Soviet communiqué published in *Izvestia* on March 2 to the effect that the Soviet troops would evacuate certain designated areas (Khorasan, Shahroud, and Semnan) as of

---

[64] Masudi, p. 66-69.

[65] U.N., Security Council, *OR*, First Year: First Series, no. 2, pp. 64-65.

[66] *Foreign Relations of U.S., 1946* 7:351.

[67] Masudi, p. 71.

March 2 but would remain in other parts of northern Iran until the situation had been clarified. Qavam's protest then stated that according to the Tripartite Treaty of 1942 "the evacuation of Allied forces from Iran is definitely and unconditionally fixed for 2 March 1946"; the British troops had already been withdrawn from the whole of Iran; the Soviet decision to retain some troops in Iran "is absolutely incompatible with the constitutional laws of Iran and with existing treaties between Iran and the Union of Soviet Socialist Republics"; and concluded, "I am compelled to protest on behalf of the Iranian Government against the USSR Government's decision and to insist that orders should be given for the withdrawal of USSR forces as promptly as possible from the whole territory of Iran."[68] On the same day, March 3, 1946, Muhammad Musaddiq delivered a passionate speech on the problem of evacuation in the Majlis, which was received with "an unusual outburst of applause and excitement." He declared that the problem of evacuation would definitely be resolved by the application of the terms of the Tripartite Treaty, which was unequivocal on the subject. The Soviet decision to evacuate only certain parts of Iran was incompatible with this treaty. Musaddiq also believed that Iran was not prepared to discuss this problem in any way with anyone; characterized the problem as "vital" for all Iranians; and expressed hope that "Iran's great neighbor which claims championship of the powerless nations would no longer delay the fulfillment of what is Iran's legitimate right."[69]

Qavam's second course of action was in keeping with Iran's third-power policy, to which he himself had contributed so much as early as the 1920s by inviting American oil interests to Iran. His ambassador to the United States, Husain 'Ala, who had also been an architect of the third-power policy in the 1920s, on the night of March 2, 1946, urged the Department of State to register an immediate protest to the Soviet government for its failure to withdraw troops from Iran during that day according to the Tripartite Treaty. He said he had no instructions from his government to make this request, but knowing Iran's basic policies, he was sure it would have the approval of his government. Qavam himself made a similar request in his talk with George Kennan in Moscow on March 4 and inquired whether the United States would support Iran if the discussions with the Russians failed and Iran wished to reopen the case in the United Nations. On March 6, 1946, 'Ala wrote the secretary of state, advising him of receiving instructions from Qavam urging the United States to protest the failure of the Soviet Union to withdraw its troops from Iran. Meanwhile, Soviet policy in Iran took a turn for the worse;

[68] For the text of this protest see U.N., Security Council, *OR*, First Year: First Series, no. 2, pp. 65-66.

[69] *Ittila'at,* Mar. 3, 1946.

on March 3, 1946, the number of Soviet troops in northern Iran suddenly increased and feverish troop movements ensued. These developments were reported promptly in great detail to Washington from Tabriz by the American vice consul, Rossow, in a number of urgent dispatches. The problem was seriously studied at the Department of State with a great sense of urgency. Secretary Byrnes believed that it was then clear that the USSR was adding military invasion to political subversion in Iran, and he told his colleagues in the department, "Now we'll give it to them with both barrels." Acheson believed that the United States ought to let the Russians know emphatically that it was aware of Soviet moves, but "leave a graceful way out" if it desired to avoid a showdown.[70]

These developments reinforced Iran's attempt to get the United States to protest the Russian decision not only to retain troops but also to bring in fresh troops and heavy equipment after the March 2 deadline. In a letter to Molotov, dated March 6, 1946, the United States expressed earnest hope that the Soviet Union would withdraw "immediately all its forces from the territory of Iran."[71] In a strong message, dated March 8, Secretary Byrnes said the United States wished "to learn whether the Soviet government, instead of withdrawing Soviet troops from Iran . . . is bringing additional forces into Iran. In case Soviet forces in Iran are being increased, this Government would welcome information at once regarding the purpose thereof."[72]

Whether the American diplomatic efforts in behalf of Iran extended beyond these representations is difficult to say—mostly because of President Truman's remarks on two separate occasions. First, he stated in a press and radio conference on April 24, 1952, that at the time he had to send an "ultimatum" to the head of the Soviet Union to get out of Iran. On the same day, however, a White House spokesman told the press that "the President was using the term ultimatum in a nontechnical layman sense"; he was referring to the American leadership in the United Nations in the Spring of 1946, which was the major factor in bringing about Soviet withdrawal from Iran.[73] Second, despite this retraction, President Truman repeated in 1957 even more unequivocally what he had said in 1952; he himself wrote in an article:

From my experience with the Russians, I have learned that they are bound to move where we fail to make clear our intentions.

[70]*Foreign Relations of U.S., 1946* 7:336-347.

[71]For the text see ibid., pp. 340-41, and U.S. State Dept. *Bulletin* 14, no. 350 (Mar. 17, 1946):435-36.

[72]For the text see *Foreign Relations of U.S., 1946* 7:348.

[73]Ibid., pp. 348-49.

For example, shortly after the end of World War II, Stalin and Molotov brazenly refused to keep their agreement to withdraw from Iran. They persisted in keeping their troops in Azerbaijan in northern Iran. Formal steps were taken through diplomatic channels and the United Nations to get the Russians to withdraw. The Soviet Union persisted in its occupation until I personally saw to it that Stalin was informed that I had given orders to our military chiefs to prepare for the movement of our ground, sea and air forces. Stalin then did what I knew he would do. He moved his troops out.[74]

What significance can be attached to this statement? In an editorial note on the president's 1952 statement, the *Foreign Relations of the United States, 1946* states: "No documentation on the sending of an ultimatum to the Soviet Union has been found in the Department files or in the files of the Department of Defense, nor have several highest officers of the Department in 1946 been able to affirm the sending of an ultimatum."[75] Unfortunately, the passage quoted above from the president's 1957 article has apparently gone unnoticed, despite the fact that this source carries the 1969 publication date. Nor do the president's own memoirs or those of Secretary Byrnes make any mention of an ultimatum, although the president does mention his instructions to Secretary Byrnes for sending a "blunt message" to Premier Stalin.[76] But the president provides no date, and it is tempting to surmise that this is what he was talking about in 1952 and again in 1957. The problem certainly requires further research. At present the question whether the United States went beyond its protestations of March 6 and 8 in behalf of Iran in 1946 will remain.

Qavam's trip to Moscow brought no immediate result. 'Ala considered the discussions to have "failed," and for this reason as well as the nonevacuation of the Soviet troops after the March 2 deadline, Iran filed its second complaint to the United Nations on March 18. Gromyko used the communiqué of March 7, issued at the end of Qavam's stay in Moscow, to show that Iran and the Soviet Union "were prepared to continue dealing with the matter through the ordinary channels," and hence requested the Security Council for postponement of the question until April 10. 'Ala did not counter Gromyko's invocation of the communiqué, but I suggest that the reason for Gromyko's

[74] The article was published under the president's name in the *New York Times*, Aug. 25, 1957 (reprinted by permission of North American Newspaper Alliance, Inc.). The article may have gone unnoticed by students of Iran because it was concerned with the Middle East crisis, particularly the Syrian crisis and the role of the United States vis-à-vis the Soviet Union.

[75] *Foreign Relations of U.S., 1946* 7:349.

[76] Harry S. Truman, *Memoirs by Harry S. Truman,* vol. 2, *Years of Trial and Hope, 1946-1952* (Garden City, N.Y.: Doubleday, 1956), p. 94.

inability to make more use of it than he actually did was probably Qavam's extremely careful wording of the communiqué in Moscow. At the end of the talks, the Soviets had proposed the text of a joint communiqué including the statement that "negotiations had been conducted in [a] spirit of friendship and good understanding" and that they "would be continued in Tehran thru [*sic*] the Soviet Ambassador." Fearing that this phraseology was intended to indicate that the negotiations had ended in agreement and so prevent further recourse to the United Nations, Qavam had crossed out the words "good understanding." Likewise, to prevent possible assertion that negotiations were still in progress, he had changed the final sentence to read that the two governments would make every effort through the new Soviet ambassador to consolidate friendly relations.[77] The text of the communiqué was published in Tehran in full on March 10, the same day that Qavam returned to Tehran. Two days later the Fourteenth Majlis completed its term, and the prime minister pursued his policies almost single-handedly. Now the veteran states-man showed up at his best.

Qavam's strategy between the time of his return to Tehran (March 10) and the announcement of the results of the Irano-Soviet negotiations on April 6 had to take note of three major considerations. First, he wanted to keep the Iranian question before the United Nations. Second, he expected the arrival of the new Soviet ambassador. And third, he wished to strike a course that would not unduly antagonize the Soviet Union. He enjoyed British and American support for the revival of the question at the United Nations. He also enjoyed the service of 'Ala, whom he considered an able and patriotic, though somewhat "excitable," statesman. The timing of the complaint was becoming crucial, because on March 14 the Soviet chargé, who had heard about Qavam's plan to reappeal to the United Nations, called on him to state that an Iranian complaint would be regarded as an unfriendly and hostile act that would have unfortunate results for Iran, but the chargé retracted once he encountered the "stout resistance" of the prime minister.[78] Qavam also learned from this meeting that the arrival of the Soviet ambassador might increase the pressure on him. Hence, the complaint was filed only two days before the arrival of Sadchikov, the new Soviet ambassador to Tehran. The ambassador called on Qavam several hours after his arrival on March 20, pro-posing that the Soviets might withdraw if the shah and the prime minister would sign letters to him assuring joint Irano-Soviet exploitation of the northern oil. Once the suggestion became known to the American embassy,

[77] These remarks were made by Qavam himself to the American ambassador. See *Foreign Relations of U.S., 1946* 7:352. For the text of the communiqué see Masudi, p. 200. According to this text Qavam's stay in Moscow is dated Feb. 19 to Mar. 6, 1946.

[78] *Foreign Relations of U.S., 1946* 7:356-57.

its second secretary broached the question of American oil interests, which Qavam was willing to entertain so long as it related to the Baluchistan area. The second secretary's raising the issue, however, was regretted by the Department of State and caused an immediate retraction by the embassy officials. [79]

Qavam broke the long silence in Tehran on April 6 by publishing a "proclamation" (*iblaghiyih*) indicating Irano-Soviet agreement of April 4, 1946. It was agreed that (1) the Red Army had begun evacuation on March 24 and would complete it within one and a half months; (2) an agreement for the establishment of a joint Irano-Soviet oil company would be presented for ratification to the Fifteenth Majlis no later than seven months after March 24; and (3) as Azerbaijan was an internal Iranian matter, conciliatory arrangements would be made for the implementation of reforms in accordance with the existing Iranian laws. The agreement of April 4 consisted in fact of *two sets* of letters exchanged between Qavam and Sadchikov on that date in regard to evacuation and oil operations. In Persian they were published as two agreements (*movafiqatnamih-ha*) on April 8 and contained nothing on the question of Azerbaijan, which was mentioned in the proclamation and in Qavam's press conference.[80]

Ambassador Sadchikov wrote Qavam that "the Soviet Army Command in Iran had taken all preliminary steps for the complete evacuation of Iranian territory by all Soviet Army units within a period of one-and-one half months as from March 24, 1946"; and Qavam took note of the purport of this note. This exchange of notes constituted the agreement on evacuation. Qavam wrote to Sadchikov that "the Imperial Government of Iran agrees that the Iranian and Soviet Governments should establish a joint Irano-Soviet Company to explore and exploit oil producing territories in northern Iran." Qavam's note also included the "fundamental conditions" under which this would be done. The substance of the main conditions was: (1) Iran would hold 49 percent of the shares and the Soviet Union 51 percent during the first twenty-five years of the company's operations, and the proportions would be reversed during the second twenty-five years; (2) the profits of the company would be divided in proportion to the shares; (3) Iran's capital would consist of "the oil bearing lands" delineated on a map, and the USSR's would consist of "any kind of expenditures involved, instruments, equipment, and the salaries of the experts and laborers who may be needed for the extraction and refining of oil"; (4) the Iranian security forces would protect all the related lands; and (5) the agreement to be concluded later for the establishment of the said joint

[79] Ibid., p. 413.

[80] The full texts of these letters are found in *Ittila'at*, Apr. 8, 1946. For background information see *Ittila'at*, Apr. 6, 1946. For relatively complete texts in English, see *Foreign Relations of U.S., 1946* 7:414-15.

Irano-Soviet oil company according to the text of this note will be presented for ratification by the new Iranian Majlis as soon as it has been elected and has begun its legislative activity in any case not later than 7 months after March 24 of the current year."

The nature of Qavam's agreement is clear from this quotation, but the importance of the question requires further analysis. Did Qavam grant an oil concession to the Soviet Union, or did he conclude an agreement, through the exchange of notes, to establish a joint Irano-Soviet company? In a major press interview on April 7, 1946, in Tehran, he declared clearly: "There is no question of a concession; an agreement (*movafiqatnamih*) has been signed at the present time so that subsequently a contract (*qarardad*) would be drafted for submission to, and approval of, the Majlis."[81] Obviously, the power to grant or withhold approval belonged to the Majlis under the Iranian Constitution. But did Qavam have the authority to do what he did under Iranian law? The relevant law had been enacted on December 2, 1944, during the oil crisis with the Soviet Union. It prohibited any government official from discussing or signing "any concessionary agreement" and made a violation of this prohibition a crime punishable by three to eight years imprisonment and permanent debarment from government service. As will be seen, Qavam's agreement was subsequently declared null and void by the Majlis, being viewed not as a "concession" within the terms of the 1944 law. The Majlis's rather charitable view can be explained. As already seen, Qavam himself cited in Moscow the 1944 oil law in refusing the Russian demand for a concession, but he regarded his subsequent promise to conclude a contract for the creation of a joint Irano-Soviet Company as the only way he could observe that law without at the same time jeopardizing Iran's vital national interests. In reporting the nature of his decision to the Majlis in 1974, he stated:

When I decided to sign the agreement I was completely aware of my grave responsibility before the Iranian people, and recognized that its signing was the only way to resolve the problems at the time. I believe now, as I believed then, in the propriety of my judgment because it was after [the signing of] this agreement that the dangerous situation in Iran improved little by little: the foreign forces evacuated the country, the events in Azerbaijan and Kurdistan gradually terminated, the nation witnessed calm and quiet, and briefly, Iran escaped the entangled web of its plight. . . . I was convinced that the signing of the agreement in regard to the oil company was in the best interest of the country, and any other patriot in my place in those days would have inevitably agreed to such a suggestion.[82]

[81]*Ittila'at,* Apr. 7, 1946.

[82]This is my own close translation of Qavam's speech to the Twenty-Fifth Meeting of the Fifteenth Majlis; for the Persian text, see Iran, Majlis-i Panzdahum, *Ruznamih-ye Rasmi,* p. 2191.

In order to insure that the evacuation of Russian forces would proceed within the one and a half months (starting March 24 as stated in the agreement of April 4, 1946), Qavam constituted a fact-finding mission and dispatched it to Azerbaijan. 'Ala reported to the Security Council the status of evacuation as far as it could be factually verified by this mission. In his letter of May 6 he told the council that as of that time the Soviet troops had been "completely evacuated from the provinces of Khorasan, Gorgan, Mazandaran and Gilan." Further reports were filed on May 20 and 21, but neither in these reports nor during the discussions in the Security Council through its last session (May 22) did 'Ala fail to stress the difficulties in the way of acquiring accurate information on the evacuation of Soviet troops because of the inability of the Iranian government to establish control over the north in the face of continued Soviet interference.[83] In effect, he stressed that so long as the Azerbaijan and Kurdish regimes existed, Soviet interference persisted. Iran continued, therefore, to report the Azerbaijan situation even after the Soviet troops had completely evacuated. Insofar as the evacuation of Soviet troops from the entire Iranian territory was concerned, Qavam issued a proclamation on May 25, 1946, indicating that as the result of the investigations of his mission dispatched to Azerbaijan, the evacuation of the Red Army had been verified. Meanwhile, he received a letter from the Soviet ambassador, the text of which was reproduced in Qavam's proclamation, declaring that the evacuation of Soviet forces "had been completed on May 9."[84]

Iran Regains the North

The agreements of April 4, 1946, seem in retrospect to have marked the beginning of earnest efforts by Qavam to deal with the problem of Azerbaijan and Kurdistan in the north. The Soviet commitment to evacuate *all* its troops *completely* within one and a half months from March 24 seemed concrete enough to turn full attention from the problem of Soviet evacuation to that of Soviet interference. Hence, while Qavam kept the matter of evacuation before the Security Council and sent his own mission to ascertain the actual progress of troop withdrawal, he tried to resolve the Azeri and Kurdish problems. The beginning of his serious efforts must be dated from April 22, 1946, when the Council of Ministers reached its decision regarding the "Azerbaijan events" (*havadis-i Azarbaijan*) and published it in a communiqué

---

[83] For the text of the letter and reports, see U.N., Security Council, *OR,* First Year: First Series, *Supplement* no. 2, pp. 50-54.

[84] *Ittila'at,* May 25, 1946.

on the following day. Despite the tactical differences between Hakimi and Qavam, the latter, like the former, basically considered the Azeri and Kurdish upheavals as rebellions aided by the Soviet Union. As will be recalled, this earliest characterization of the Azeri and Kurdish upheavals as rebellious and illegitimate was signaled by the decision of the Hakimi government to dispatch troops northward, a decision that failed to be implemented because of interception by the Red Army at Sharifabad on November 20. The decision of Qavam's Council of Ministers in essence took the same view; it regarded Azerbaijan as an integral part of Iran and hence any discussion with the Azeris had to take place within the framework of Iranian laws. The relevant law was cited as the foundation of the Council's decision. That was the law of 1907 authorizing the election of Provincial Councils. As applied to Azerbaijan, the Council decided this meant (1) that the directors of all major services would be elected by the Provincial Councils and "their official commissions would be issued by the central government in Tehran"; (2) that the central government would appoint the governor-general and the army and Gendarmerie commanders; and (3) that the official language of Azerbaijan, as in all other parts of the country, would be Persian. In order to pursue a course of conciliation without appeasement, the decision also provided for (1) the teaching of the first five grades of the elementary schools in the Azerbaijani language; (2) a promise not to take action against the members of the democratic party for their past behavior; and (3) an increase in the number of deputies from Azerbaijan in the Majlis in proportion to the actual population of the province.[85]

The first phase of Qavam's negotiations with the Azeri leaders was marked by the arrival in Tehran of Pishihvari at the head of a Commission (April 27?) and his return to Tabriz in an "angry mood" on May 13, 1946. At the end of the negotiations, in which the Soviet ambassador had tried to act as mediator in keeping with his assurances to Qavam but in fact tried harder to put pressure on him rather than the Azeri delegation, Qavam issued an announcement about the negotiations.[86] The announcement revealed clearly that Qavam had followed the Council of Ministers decision as the only framework for discussions; that contrary to the terms of that decision, the Azeri delegation had insisted that the appointment of governor-general should be made by the central government *as proposed by the Provincial Council*; that the appointment of the military and Gendarmerie commanders should also be based on the Provincial Council's proposal; and that the central government could not endorse the distribution of public domains and ceded lands among the

[85] For the text see *Ittila'at*, Apr. 23, 1946.

[86] Qavam himself made these remarks to the American ambassador; see *Foreign Relations of U.S., 1946* 7:460-62.

peasants because this had to be confirmed by the Majlis.[87] The most interesting segment of Qavam's announcement was his clear and clever linking of negotiations with the Azeri leaders to the elections of the Majlis in keeping with his agreement with the Soviet ambassador. There were two significant elements in this linkage. One was to indicate to the ambassador that he should exert pressure on the Azeris in these negotiations if he wished an early opening of the Fifteenth Majlis, which was to take up the oil question. The other was to leave no doubt whatever that the central government intended to control the elections in Azerbaijan as in any other Iranian province.

The second phase of Qavam's negotiations with the Azeri leaders was marked by the departure of a delegation from Tehran for Tabriz on June 11, 1946. The delegation was headed by Muzaffar Firuz, the minister of labor and propaganda and the deputy prime minister, who signed an agreement with the Azeri leaders on June 13, 1946. Firuz's delegation included, among others, General Hidayat, deputy minister of war. His so-called agreement was, according to its own terms, subject to the approval of the Council of Ministers and the Azerbaijani Provincial Council. Furthermore, the fifteen-article agreement was signed by Firuz, but opposed by his military associates. Pishihvari signed it for the Azeri side. Firuz boasted, in a radio announcement from Tabriz, that in accordance with the terms of the agreement the "principles of autonomy and national self-government of Azerbaijan would be transformed into those of Provincial Council."[88] His excessive flattering of the prime minister in the same speech betrayed an attempt to compensate for the over generous terms of his agreement with Pishihvari. He left his military associates behind to iron out their disagreement with the Azeri. leaders, but they returned to Tehran without associating themselves with the agreement. The principal source of disagreement was article 7 of the document. Not only would the Communist party (Democrats), in effect, remain in power under the general terms of the agreement, but this particular article would in fact amount to the recognition of the Azerbaijani upheaval as a legitimate movement. This would be contrary to the entire course of Iran's policy since the inception of the Azerbaijan problem. Premier Hakimi had characterized the upheaval as rebellious. Qavam basically viewed it in the same way although he pursued a more conciliatory course as a matter of tactics rather than policy. But his deputy seemed to have missed the point completely; appeasement rather than conciliation characterized his action, despite the lip service paid to the Council of Ministers decision. Firuz's agreement would transform

[87]For the text of the announcement see *Ittila'at,* May 12, 1946.

[88]For the text of his radio speech see *Ittila'at,* June 15, 1946.

the Soviet-supported, Communist-dominated Fada'i forces into the Gendarmerie of Azerbaijan; would amount to disbanding the central government Gendarmerie; and would recognize the Azeri forces "as part of the Iranian Army."[89]

The third phase of Qavam's negotiations with the Azeri leaders proved inconclusive, principally because of the unacceptability of the Azeri demands in regard to the military matter just mentioned. Military leaders were included in the respective delegations of the two sides. General Razmara, the Iranian chief of staff, considered the demands of the Azeri leaders totally unacceptable because they "would amount to a decisive dissolution of the Iranian Army by virtue of the inclusion of notorious deserters amongst its ranks," but Muzaffar Firuz kept pressing upon the central government delegation the merit of the Azeri demands. Najafquli Pisyan, a well-known Iranian writer, stated in 1949 that Qavam also sided with Firuz, but the shah vehemently opposed the Azeri proposals in regard to the army.[90] The shah also repeats Pisyan's statement in his book,[91] but there is no way of ascertaining Qavam's position at the moment. It is certain, however, that even after the Firuz agreement, Qavam considered the Azeri demands exorbitant; denied that he had made any concessions; and claimed that he merely listened to the Azeris at the time in order "to draw them out."[92] In any event, no agreement was reached at Tehran, and this marked the end of Qavam's attempt at negotiating with the Azeri leaders.

While Qavam was pursuing a conciliatory course with the Azeris, he also took a number of other measures principally aimed at placating the Soviets and the Tudeh party. These measures, like the negotiations with the Azeris, followed shortly after the agreements of April 4 with Sadchikov. Some of these measures were clearly designed to project a picture of domestic reform, basically for Soviet consumption. The roots of this must be found not only in Qavam's desire to undermine the so-called progressive posture of the Tudeh party and the Azeri Democrats, at home, but also in persistent Soviet pressures for reform. The subject of reform had been stressed by Stalin during Qavam's visit to Moscow, and the Soviet ambassador never tired of insisting on it ever since his arrival in Tehran on March 20, 1946.[93] The fact that genuine aspirations for reform also existed at the time coincided with Qavam's desire

[89] For the text of the so-called agreement, see ibid.

[90] Pisyan, *Marg Bood,* p. 219.

[91] *Mission for My Country,* p. 117.

[92] Qavam made these remarks to the American ambassador; see *Foreign Relations of U.S., 1946* 7:513.

[93] See Masudi, p. 157.

to maintain a democratic (that is, non-Fascist) posture vis-à-vis the Russians. To mention only a few of these measures, they included creation of the Higher Labor Council, composed of representatives of government, the Tudeh labor organizations, business, university professors, and the mayor of Tehran; creation of the Supreme Economic Council; and introduction of reforms into the Army and the Gendarmerie, the special targets of Communist propaganda.

Qavam's most well-known measure of this kind was the formation of a new political party under his own leadership. His Democratic Party of Iran was so named to steal the thunder of the Democratic Party of Azerbaijan and bring it under the eventual control of the central government. In announcing its creation on June 29 from Radio Tehran, he prefaced his remarks by referring to his success in the evacuation problem and "good understanding" with the Soviet Union, the settlement of the Azerbaijan difficulty, and the overall preparations for extensive reforms. He then stated, "I am determined to strengthen progressive thoughts and democratic principles throughout the country." His party was being created, he declared, with the support of "the lovers of freedom" and for the purpose of systematic advancement of internal reforms.[94] These and similar tactical measures preceded the shah's bestowal (July 24, 1946) of the title of "Highness" (*Jinab-i Ashraf*) on Qavam for his "distinguished services," but Qavam's other conciliatory measures, which began soon thereafter, created serious doubts on the part of the shah about the wisdom of Qavam's policy of conciliation.[95]

These measures mainly concerned the invitation of certain Tudeh members to participate in government posts, including cabinet positions. In introducing his new cabinet to the shah on August 1, 1946, Qavam included three well-known Tudeh leaders. They were Murtiza Yazdi, minister of health; Iraj Iskandari, minister of commerce and industry; and Firaydoun Kishavarz, minister of education. In commenting on the party affiliation of the cabinet members, *Ittila'at* stated on August 1, 1946, that according to political circles "the principal purpose of the Prime Minister in forming such a Cabinet is to make it possible for all parties to participate in implementing reforms." Despite this semiofficial explanation it is more reasonable to suggest that the inclusion of the Tudeh members in the cabinet fitted Qavam's overall strategy to placate the Tudeh party, the Azeri leaders, and the Russians by yet another means. This is evident not only from the train of similar measures preceding the formation of this coalition cabinet, just discussed, but more importantly, from reliable sources revealing Qavam's basic distrust of the Tudeh and its members.

[94] For the text of this radio speech by Qavam, see *Ittila'at,* June 30, 1946.

[95] For the shah's relevant *farman* see *Ittila'at,* July 24, 1946.

This brings us to the momentous cabinet change of October 17-19, 1946, which marked the beginning of a drastic shift in Qavam's policy toward the problem of Azerbaijan and the Soviet Union. The nearly three months between the formation of the coalition cabinet and the dismissal of the Tudeh ministers in October contained a series of far-reaching events that require careful analysis.

The single most crucial question is, What prompted the change? For some thirteen years the explanation of Robert Rossow, Jr., (who was in charge of the United States Consulate in Tabriz in 1945-46, and then chief of the Political Section of the United States Embassy in Tehran until January 1947) was the only reliable source available in English. According to his account the change of government in October 1946 was "dictated by the Shah" who "demanded his [Qavam's] resignation."[96] The 1969 publication of *Foreign Relations of the United States, 1946*, however, reveals clearly that Rossow's explanation is almost entirely based on the shah's version of events, which was related by him to the American ambassador, Allen, in Tehran on October 19, 1946.[97] More importantly, the same Department of State publication includes a dispatch containing an analysis of the government change that was sent by the ambassador to the State Department a day earlier. According to this analysis, the "initiative" for change in the cabinet was Qavam's; the shah's version denied Qavam's initiative.[98] To leave the matter to these two different views is unsatisfactory. An objective analysis should be possible now, a quarter of a century later.

Probably the single most important consideration underlying the cabinet shake-up was Qavam's increasing conviction that his tactics of conciliation were becoming counterproductive. The major factors that contributed to this growing conviction included first and foremost his own basic distrust of the Tudeh party and its members. As early as August 24, about three weeks after the formation of the coalition cabinet, he told the American ambassador that the Tudeh party was clearly directed by the Soviet embassy, and he implied strongly that he was searching for a good excuse to throw the Tudeh members out of the cabinet. A second factor was his ill-fated negotiations with the Azeri representatives, on the one hand, and the tumultuous uprising of the Qashqa'i and Bakhtiari tribes in the south, on the other. The question of British complicity aside, the important fact is that the "Fars problem" (*Ghailih-ye Fars*) forced Qavam to realize that his conciliatory attitude toward Azerbaijan had failed to yield favorable results, and this attitude in turn encouraged

[96] Rossow, p. 28.

[97] *Foreign Relations of U.S., 1946* 7:537-39.

[98] Cf. ibid., at pp. 536-37 and 537-39.

other minority groups to make impossible demands.[99] A third factor was Qavam's disagreement with the Tudeh members of his own cabinet over various issues, including his decision of October 15 to replace the governor of Tehran, a Tudeh sympathizer, by a member of his own Democratic party of Iran. The three Tudeh members of the cabinet strongly objected to this decision and absented themselves from the next cabinet meeting in protest. At the time the cabinet change was announced in Tehran (October 19, 1946) still two other points of Qavam's disagreement with the Tudeh members of his cabinet were revealed. One was the truculent attitude of the Tudeh ministers toward the settlement of the Fars problem, and the other was the elections of the Fifteenth Majlis. The Soviets had kept pressing Qavam to hold the elections in anticipation of the approval of their oil agreement, and after the shah finally decreed (October 6) the start of the elections, the Tudeh ministers objected to the composition of the Supervisory Commission for National Elections. Qavam had so constituted the commission as to preempt their drive to control the forthcoming Majlis.[100] Given Qavam's own attitudes during nearly three months preceding the cabinet shake-up, it is impossible to attribute the change so categorically to the initiative and action of the shah alone.

Yet it also seems unwarranted to conclude that Qavam alone was the author of the cabinet change. Two other sets of considerations also seem to have contributed to the decision to overhaul the cabinet. One stemmed from the attitude of the United States. There is no doubt that the United States was becoming increasingly alarmed at the turn of events in Iran after the establishment of the coalition cabinet.[101] Although the American officials never entertained doubts about Qavam's patriotism, there were times when his courses of action seemed to them too conciliatory and hence ultimately prejudicial to the best interests of Iran as well as the United States. Ambassador Allen went so far as to make representations to Qavam on October 11, 1946, stating unequivocally that Qavam's government had lost its freedom of action and independence and "we might as well recognize the fact and cease pretending."[102]

---

[99]Ibid., pp. 513-18.

[100]*Ittila'at*, Oct. 19, 1946, and *Foreign Relations of U.S., 1946* 7:537.

[101]*Foreign Relations of U.S., 1946,* especially dispatches and conferences relating to the period of August-November 1946.

[102]This representation was occasioned by the circumstances surrounding an Iranian Cabinet meeting, which was discussing an aviation agreement with the Soviet Union. Shortly after the meeting one of the members of the cabinet had been asked by a Soviet

The other major consideration was the attitude of the shah. As already seen, shortly before the formation of the coalition cabinet, he had bestowed upon Qavam the title of "Highness" for the prime minister's "outstanding services," but soon afterwards he, too, began to have doubts about Qavam's conciliatory attitude towards the Azeri leaders and the Tudeh party. Husain 'Ala, Iran's ambassador to the United States, increasingly shared the shah's alarm and insisted on conveying his disagreement with Qavam's tactics to State Department officials. One of the serious causes of their disagreement was the timing of the announcement regarding the Majlis elections. The shah opposed such an announcement while Azerbaijan was still controlled by the Azeri rebels. At last, however, at Qavam's insistence (and Qavam, in turn, was under pressure from the Soviet ambassador), he issued the decree for the start of the elections on October 6. The day before, the shah told the American ambassador that a Majlis elected under the circumstances would "end Iranian independence." He also toyed with the idea of asking Qavam to resign in order to enable the formation of an interim government to conduct elections.[103] Yet the fact remains that the resignation of Qavam did not occur until October 17, and the intervening developments cast doubt on the simple thesis that the shah's attitude was solely responsible for the cabinet change. By that time the representations of the United States and particularly Qavam's own disagreement with the Tudeh ministers over the dismissal of the governor of Tehran, over the Fars revolt, and over the elections of the Fifteenth Majlis seem to have prepared both Qavam and the shah for a drastic change in government and a reversal of the tactical policy of conciliation toward the Azerbaijani rebel government.

The Tudeh ministers were dropped from the new cabinet, and Qavam himself not only headed the cabinet but also filled the posts of minister of interior and foreign affairs. The holding of these two posts foretold attitudinal changes towards Azerbaijan and the Soviet Union. The message was not lost on the Soviets, who first launched a propaganda campaign against Qavam. In his first public speech after the formation of the new government, Qavam took the occasion to complain about the recent broadcasts of Moscow Radio and declared that these "were contrary to the principles of mutual friendship and non-intervention in Iranian affairs." In less than a month after this statement Qavam issued an important circular (*bakhshnamih*), declaring on November 21, 1946, that "for the purpose of maintaining law and order during the elections security forces will be dispatched to all parts of the

---

official why he had opposed the agreement. The leak, which was cited by the American ambassador as an example of Iran's loss of freedom of action, was apparently from a Tudeh member of the cabinet. See *Foreign Relations of U.S., 1946* 7:537.

[103]Ibid., pp. 522-23.

country without exception." Furthermore, the circular stated that "because the government is fully responsible to the Majlis for the good conduct of the elections it must make every effort to maintain order and security and dispatch the necessary armed forces."[104] After the publication of the circular, the governor of Azerbaijan, Javid, cabled Qavam, inquiring whether armed forces would be sent to Azerbaijan as well. On November 27 Qavam cabled the governor of Azerbaijan and Qazi Muhammad, the Kurdish leader, advising them both of the dispatch of armed forces from Tehran. In a long proclamation published on December 9, Qavam vociferously denounced the Azeri leaders for acts of "rebellion" (*tamarrud*) and "separation" (*juda'i*). And on December 10 Qavam sent a cable to the governor of Azerbaijan telling him bluntly: "I have ordered the security forces of the central government to move to Mianeh today and they have my orders to prevent armed personnel from offering resistance."[105] Qavam, like Hakimi a year earlier, was treating the Azerbaijan problem as a rebellion aided by a foreign power. Despite tactical differences they shared the objective of maintaining Iranian integrity.

On the military front, the shah exercised leadership. Before the dispatch of armed forces to Zanjan, he ordered a full-scale study of the military strength of the Azerbaijan government through the elements sympathizing with the central government. The report based on this study and accompanied by a map indicated positions of the Azeri forces; discounted the numerical significance of 10,000 men under arms because of low morale; and warned that the increase in the number of "immigrants" and weapons, if continued, could entail serious consequences, not only for Azerbaijan, but also for the integrity of all of Iran. In a secret session at the shah's palace, which included the shah, the prime minister, the minister of war and the chief of staff, a military plan was adopted. According to an author who claims to have acquired the text of this report with much difficulty, the shah ordered "immediate and basic measures for the freedom of Azerbaijan and the entire northern regions."[106] The bits and pieces of evidence from a documentary source, however, suggest that "the military plan" did not from the outset aim at the freedom of the "entire northern regions," although this was indeed intended by the shah as well as the prime minister. As early as November 8 Qavam told the American ambassador that he was determined to occupy Zanjan within ten days, but he intended to progress "little by little." The military plan originally extended only to the occupation of Mianeh because both the shah and Qavam considered as genuine the strenuous Soviet efforts

[104]*Ittila'at,* Oct. 28, Nov. 2, and Dec. 9, 1946.

[105]For the text of the cable see *Ittila'at,* Dec. 9 and 10, 1946.

[106]See Pisyan, *Marg Bood,* pp. 228-29.

to prevent the Iranian government from sending its troops to Azerbaijan and expected that the USSR would assist the Azerbaijanis much more effectively than they did.[107]

The reoccupation of Zanjan was followed by the shah's personal reconnaissance flight to the town's airport, where he met with Razmara, the chief of staff, and gave instructions to the military commanders for advancement towards Azerbaijan. In concluding a long speech, he told the army officers that if they did not act immediately "and with all their might" to liberate Azerbaijan it would prove most difficult, if not impossible, to do so subsequently. "For this reason," the shah continued, "we order the security forces to advance towards the beloved Azerbaijan, break down every kind of resistance, and liberate fellow-citizens from the clutches of despotism."[108] The Iranian army attacked the Azeri forces defending the Qaflankuh Pass. The shah himself supervised the military operations by aerial reconnaissance. On December 10, 1946, the same day that Qavam cabled the governor of Azerbaijan to surrender, the Azeri forces began to fall back without making any significant resistance. In the afternoon of December 12 Iranian troops entered Mianeh, and then Tabriz the following day. The sudden collapse of Azerbaijan stunned the Kurdish leaders at Mahabad, who traveled to Miandoab on December 14 to surrender to the government forces. Qazi Muhammad himself followed suit on December 15, and the Iranian army entered Mahabad on December 17, marking the end of the Kurdish Republic.[109]

The military decision and operations of Iran, however, were buffeted by the pressures and counterpressures of the United States and the Soviet Union. In anticipation of the outbreak of heavy fighting in Azerbaijan, Qavam contemplated an appeal to the United Nations and asked the American ambassador on November 24 for assurances of United States support in case such an appeal were made. On November 27 in response to a question by the newspaper *Ittila'at* regarding the government decision to send troops to Azerbaijan, the American ambassador answered that the maintenance of Iranian sovereignty and territorial integrity was a principle embodied in the Tripartite Declaration and a well-known policy of the United States. "The announced intention of the Iranian Government," Ambassador Allen continued, "to send its security forces into all parts of Iran, including any areas of Iran where such forces are not at present in control, for the maintenance of order in connection with the

[107] See *Foreign Relations of U.S., 1946* 7:545, 564-65.

[108] For the text see Pisyan, *Marg Bood,* pp. 237-38.

[109] For details in Persian see Najafquli Pisyan, *Az Mahabad-i Khunin ta Karanih-ha-ye Aras* (Tehran: Shirkat-i Sahami-i Chap, 1948/49), pp. 4-7. For the best work in English see William Eagleton, Jr., *The Kurdish Republic of 1946* (London: Oxford University Press, 1963), pp. 112-25; for a more recent firsthand account, see Arfa, *The Kurds.*

elections, seems to me an entirely normal and proper decision." This decision, on the other hand, was received quite differently by the Soviet Union. A day after the American ambassador's public statement, the Soviet ambassador told Qavam that the sending of Iranian troops into Azerbaijan was considered undesirable by the Soviet government because it would create difficulties within Azerbaijan and on the Soviet-Iranian frontier. On December 10, when Qavam cabled the governor of Azerbaijan that security forces were being dispatched to Mianeh, the Soviet ambassador made further representations, threatening in a very angry tone that the Soviet government would not remain passive in the face of disturbances near the Soviet frontier.[110] The shah was also threatened by the Soviet ambassador, who demanded in the name of his government that the shah as the commander-in-chief withdraw his forces.[111] But both Qavam and the shah resisted Soviet threats. A passage in Qavam's impassioned speech to the Fifteenth Majlis in 1947 summed up the patriotic sentiments that had animated both Iranian leaders in the tumultuous days of 1945-46:

In striving to realize my heartfelt desire to liberate my beloved country I endured throughout this period all kinds of malicious accusations, pressures, and difficulties at home and abroad. What sustained me throughout these dark and difficult times was His Imperial Majesty's support and assistance in all important and complicated matters. I witnessed His Majesty's intense anxiety and desire to return Azerbaijan and Kurdistan [to Iran]. For the attainment of this objective he spared no assistance reaching the limits of self-sacrifice.[112]

[110] See *Foreign Relations of U.S., 1946* 7:547-60.

[111] *Mission for My Country*, p. 117.

[112] This is my free translation of Qavam's speech to the Sixteenth Meeting of the Fifteenth Majlis; for the Persian see Iran, Majlis, Majlis-i Panzadahum, *Ruznamih-ye Rasmi*, 2020.

VI

Friendship in Frustration

THE ANALYSIS OF the Iranian policy toward the Soviet Union in the preceding chapter has already shed some light on several basic questions concerning Iran's policy toward the United States. Iran's reliance on the United States in its troubles with the Soviet Union was not confined to diplomatic means; Iran also sought American economic and military support. This search constituted a major element of Iranian foreign policy for two reasons. First, it followed in the wake of Iranian wartime efforts to obtain aid from the United States, as seen in chapter 3, although different kinds of aid were sought after 1945. Second, the search continued well beyond 1945-46; it marked the entire period before oil nationalization in 1951. This chapter examines the Iranian search for American aid during the 1946-51 period.

Meager American Money

One of the major components of Iranian policy toward the United States in 1946-51 was the search for substantial financial aid. This search was quite different from Iran's wartime efforts to acquire American aid. The creation of the Millspaugh Mission, its checkered work, and its demise will be recalled. In 1946, as in 1941, Iran took the initiative in requesting American aid, but this time it looked for American dollars as well as advisers. The request for American financial aid was launched by Ahmad Qavam at the height of the Azerbaijan crisis. His ambassador to the United States wrote the acting secretary of state on September 9, 1946, requesting a loan of $45 to $50 million. The request was based on the estimated need for $85 million in implementing four projects enumerated in the note.[1] In the same month Qavam himself told Ambassador Allen that Iran needed substantial financial credits immediately in order to "reestablish Iran as [a] nation." He also indicated determination to institute "far-reaching economic reforms which Iran needed so urgently." The American ambassador understood that Iranian requests for credits totaled some $250 million; told Qavam that the United

[1] *Foreign Relations of U.S., 1946* 7:520n.

States could be moved to help Iran only to the extent its aid was regarded by the American people as being given to support the United Nations; and that $10 million was the "most Iran could expect in credit from [the] Export-Import Bank." In a secret and urgent message to the secretary of state, Under Secretary Acheson expressed apprehension about the domination of Iran by a "single power" (the Soviet Union) or its division "into spheres of influence" (between the Soviet Union and Great Britain); complained of the American ambassador's inability to give assurances of economic aid to Qavam, who had pleaded for aid repeatedly; and blamed this inability on "our hitherto narrow concept of economic aspects [of] our Iranian policy." Although on October 3, 1946, Secretary Byrnes replied to Acheson that the United States should extend economic aid to Iran through sales of noncombat surplus property and an Export-Import Bank credit,[2] the Iranian request for American credit was not met until years later, when it seemed both too little and too late to the Iranian government.

Along with its urgent request for American economic aid in the fall of 1946, Iran instituted economic planning by engaging the services of American consultants. Ahmad Qavam called a conference of about fifty Iranian notables and experts and presented to them the shah's desire to have a Seven Year Development Plan drafted. On December 17, 1946, Iran signed a contract with the American firm Morrison-Knodson International Company for purposes of studying Iran's capabilities and problems with a view to economic development. After the company submitted its report on August 2, 1947, the matter seemed to require further study. On February 1, 1949, Iran renewed a former contract it had signed (on October 7, 1948) with Overseas Consultants Incorporated (OCI), an American group, for the purpose of a more thorough study of Iranian economic needs and capabilities. On February 15, 1949, the Majlis enacted into law its support of the study for a wide variety of economic development purposes ranging from increasing production, expanding exports, and developing agriculture to improving public health and education "within a period of seven years from the date of the approval of this law"; hence the designation Seven year Development Plan.[3]

As noted above, as early as 1946 the American ambassador understood that the Iranians expected a $250 million loan from the United States. This, in fact, became the magic figure that the Iranian government still repeated to American Ambassador Henry F. Grady as late as 1951. In the intervening years between Qavam's first approach to the United States for substantial

[2] Ibid., pp. 518-21.

[3] S. Rezazadeh Shafaq, "The Iranian Seven Year Development Plan: Background and Organization," *Middle East Journal* 4, no. 1 (1950):100-105.

credits in September 1946 and the eventual announcement of a small Export-Import Bank loan in October 1950, Iran's active search for aid produced no results. In the hope of acquiring substantial American aid, the shah himself accepted President Truman's invitation to visit the United States. His visit to the United States in fall 1949 proved deeply disappointing because it produced no positive results insofar as Iranian expectations for economic aid were concerned. The Iranian ambassador, Husain 'Ala, revealed on May 1, 1950, that in his visit to President Truman he requested "urgent American assistance" for his country. When finally the Export-Import Bank proposed to extend a $25 million loan to Iran, the shah expressed his conviction in a press interview on September 23, 1950, that the proposed loan was only the *beginning* of American aid to his country. We now know from a subsequent first-hand account by the American ambassador in Iran that the shah's conviction was in fact based on the ambassador's statements to the Iranian government. Ambassador Grady told the new Iranian prime minister in June 1950 when he first arrived in Tehran, and on a number of later occasions, that a "$25,000,000 credit, if promptly and successfully implemented, would be the beginning of a line of credit which would make possible the rebuilding of his country's economy."[4] But the ambassador added that the loan agreement was not ready for signing with the Iranian government until January of 1951, by which time Prime Minister 'Ali Razmara was discouraged and believed that the offer was too little and too late. The American ambassador tried, according to his own account, to persuade Washington to indicate that the $25 million should be regarded as an opening credit and that the bank was prepared to go up to $100 million, but Washington refused on the grounds that this would be interpreted as a definite promise of that amount.

A few words about Point Four aid in Iran are in order at this point. Although the Memorandum of Understanding of October 19, 1950, which set the foundation of the program in Iran, stated in its preamble the request of Iran for the exchange of technical knowledge, it is quite clear that the program was initiated by the United States government in keeping with the worldwide effort permitted under the Act of International Development.[5] For this reason the Point Four program in Iran was quite different in inception from Iran's employment of the O. C. I. experts or the Millspaugh Mission. Insofar as the program aimed at improvement of the living conditions in rural areas and extended the services of American technicians in the fields of

[4]Henry F. Grady, "What Went Wrong in Iran?" *Saturday Evening Post,* Jan. 5, 1952, p. 30.

[5]For the text of the Memorandum of Understanding, see U.S., Department of State, *United States Treaties and Other International Agreements* 1, TIAS no. 2139 (Oct. 19, 1950):721-31.

education, agriculture, and health, it was in principle acceptable to Iran. The program, however, was viewed by the Iranians against their own long-standing initiative to obtain considerable financial assistance from the United States government. Iran would receive only $500,000 under the Point Four program at the time. Although one Iranian author and official speculates about a jumble of motives for Iran's acceptance of the program,[6] this study makes it clear that the Point Four program was received in Iran primarily in keeping with its long-standing objective of deepening American involvement in Iran for ultimately political ends.

Gaining American Military Assistance

The second major component of Iran's policy toward the United States in 1946-51 was the acquisition of military assistance. The term *military assistance* as used here refers to both the purchase of military equipment and continuation of the acquisition of technical military aid. This was a notable change from the 1942-1945 period, when Iran's acquisition of American military aid involved no purchase of military equipment. I shall first take up the origin and the development of Iran's purchase of military equipment from the United States and then examine its acquisition of technical military aid.

Military Equipment

The presence of American forces in Iran since late 1942 had become one of the problems of Iranian foreign policy in 1943, when Iran and the United States tried without success to conclude an agreement governing the status of American forces in Iran. Toward the end of the war considerable amounts of American fixed and movable property in excess of military needs became available in Iran. The notion of disposing of American surplus property at a time when Iran was having difficulties acquiring needed supplies from abroad appealed to Iranian government circles, but the news of the purchase of such surplus property stirred up a great deal of discussion in the public and was misrepresented by the Tudeh papers. In response the American embassy issued a statement on September 29, 1945, to the Iranian press in order to clear up "misunderstanding" about American policy in disposing of surplus property in Iran. The statement told of the arrival of United States forces in Iran "with the express agreement of the then Prime Minister of Iran, His

[6]See Jahangir Amuzegar, *Technical Assistance in Theory and Practice* (New York: Frederick A. Praeger, 1966), pp. 119-27.

Excellency Qavam-es Saltanah"; claimed that Iran had suddenly suspended negotiations for an agreement on the status of United States forces in Iran in December 1943 and had told the United States in 1945 that no longer was an agreement necessary; hence the absence of such an agreement was "entirely the responsibility of the Iranian Government itself." Details of the sale of the surplus nonmilitary property are of no interest in this study, but the question has been mentioned in order to point out that in many quarters, and not just in Tudeh circles, the disposal of surplus American property was received with varying degrees of concern for its possible adverse effect on Iran's overall request for American assistance. In an attempt to dispel such concerns the secretary of state instructed the American ambassador on October 11, 1945, to assure Iranian authorities that the United States had not altered "its traditional policy of friendship for Iran or its pledges of assistance as contained in Declaration on Iran" but that such assistance must necessarily be considered separately from the technical question of surplus disposal.[7]

As noted before, Iran's initiative to acquire financial credit from the United States was launched by Prime Minister Ahmad Qavam on September 9, 1946. On September 30 Iran also requested military equipment from the United States. But the United States at the time did not believe it wise "to supply combat material."[8] As it turned out, however, Iran's request for American military equipment did not face the delays that its request for financial credits did. As the result of discussions that began in October 1946, an agreement was signed on June 20, 1947, for the extension of credit to Iran for the purchase of surplus war equipment through the Office of the Foreign Liquidation Commissioner. Before signing the agreement, Iran dispatched a purchasing mission, under Maj. Gen. A. Hidayat, to Washington to review its essential needs for the army and the Gendarmerie. The agreement provided for the sale of mainly noncombat equipment with some light combat material on the basis of $25 million credit extended to Iran and made repayable in 15 years.[9] The agreement was subject to ratification by the Majlis, which instead approved on February 17, 1948, the purchase of surplus military equipment from the United States up to the amount of $10 million. But because of the shortage of dollar exchange, it requested the Iranian government to obtain credit to cover the cost of repairing, packaging, and shipping the equipment as well as the cost of the equipment itself. The United States government proved sympathetic to the Iranian request and initiated a request to Congress for a $19,155,000 appropriation, of which $15,675,000 was designed to cover the

[7]*Foreign Relations of U.S., 1945*, D. P., 8:575-77.

[8]*Foreign Relations of U.S., 1946* 7:521.

[9]U.S. State Dept. *Bulletin* 17, no. 418 (July 6, 1947):47.

cost of repairing, packaging, and shipping.[10] Finally, an agreement was signed on July 29, 1948, extending a credit to Iran for the purchase of $10 million worth of surplus military equipment and a credit not to exceed $16 million to cover the relevant costs. This agreement replaced the June 20, 1947, agreement.[11]

Military Advisers

The third and last major component of Iran's policy toward the United States in 1946-51 was the acquisition of technical military assistance. Iran took the initiative as early as 1942 to acquire American aid for modernization of its army and police forces, including the rural police, or Gendarmerie. To take up the Gendarmerie first, on January 6, 1942, it may be recalled, Iran approached the United States for a single specialist for "entirely reorganizing the Iranian police forces throughout the country." On October 21, 1943, the Majlis passed the law authorizing the Iranian government to sign an agreement covering the employment of the Col. H. Norman Schwarzkopf mission. The agreement was signed on November 27, 1943, and was extended subsequently on September 5, 1944, and again on September 29, 1945. This recapitulation brings us to the status of the Schwarzkopf mission during the early postwar period. The basic agreement of November 27, 1943, which had been renewed twice before, was renewed again in 1946 as the result of an Iranian note of July 25 and an American note on August 8.[12] The renewal was for another two-year period that extended it into 1948, when Iran took time to decide whether it wished to renegotiate the basic agreement or terminate it. The American embassy made it clear to the Iranian press that the note of August 8 was not a protest as it was up to Iran to decide the fate of the contract.[13] In September 1948 the basic contract was extended and entered into force on September 13, but this time the basic agreement of November 27, 1943, was *not* merely renewed. It was also amended. The amendment was, from the Iranian perspective, significant because it limited the powers of the chief of the mission. It may be recalled the basic agreement had provided in its article 20 that the chief of the mission "will have immediate charge of the entire administration and control of the Gendarmerie," but the amendment stated that the "Minister of Interior will appoint the Chief of the Mission as Advisor

[10]U.S. State Dept. *Bulletin* 18, no. 467 (June 13, 1948):780-81.

[11]U.S. State Dept. *Bulletin* 19, no. 476 (Aug. 15, 1948):210-11.

[12]For the texts of these notes see U.N., Secretariat, *Treaty Series* 31 (1949):424-25.

[13]U.S. State Dept. *Bulletin* 18, no. 453 (Mar. 7, 1948): 307.

to the Ministry of Interior for affairs relative to the Imperial Gendarmerie for the period of this contract, *and his services shall be purely of an advisory nature."* 14

Iran's acquisition of military aid from the United States extended to the army as well. In a sense the postwar effort of Iran was a continuation of the wartime policies, as in the case of the Gendarmerie, but again with some significant changes. To recapitulate the wartime developments quickly, it may be recalled that Iran's initiative of March 20, 1942, led to the employment of Maj. Gen. John N. Greely and then Gen. Clarence S. Ridely and his mission, which was the single most popular American mission in Iran during the war. Since the basic agreement of November 3, 1943, governing the mission was to expire by March 1, 1945, Iran requested the United States to extend it. The mission was extended for "an indefinite period beyond March 1, 1945," because the United States recognized that "the protection and advancement of [United States] interests in Iran will require the strengthening of the Iranian security forces so that order may be maintained in this area, where world security might be threatened, after the withdrawal of Allied troops." But termination of the declared national emergency in the United States required general congressional enactment covering such missions beyond the declared national emergency.

After the war Iran persisted in acquiring American assistance for the army and finally signed a new agreement with the United States on October 6, 1947. This important agreement governed the status and operations of the American military mission in Iran throughout the period under discussion with only minor modifications before the nationalization of the oil industry. The major provisions of its twenty-five articles may be categorized and summarized as follows: 15

1. *Duration*: The agreement was to continue in force until March 20, 1949, but it could be extended by means of Iranian proposal and American agreement on certain specified dates. It could also be terminated before the stipulated date by a variety of means including written notice by either party at any time "if that government considers it necessary due to domestic disturbances or foreign hostilities."

2. *Organization*: The mission consisted of personnel of the United States Army as determined by the minister of war of Iran and the War Department

---

[14] For the text see U.S., Department of State, *United States Treaties and Other International Acts Series 1941,* "United States Military Mission with Imperial Iranian Gendarmerie," amending and further extending Agreement of Nov. 27, 1943.

[15] For the text of this agreement, see U.N., Secretariat, *Treaty Series* 11 (1947):304-10. See also U.S., Department of State, *United States Treaties and Other International Acts Series 1666.*

of the United States, and its members were assigned to the Advisory Department of the Iranian Ministry of War.

3. *Duties*: The duties of the mission were to advise and assist the Iranian Ministry of War as well as subordinate sections of the Iranian General Staff about plans, organizational problems, and administrative principles and training methods for the purpose of "enhancing the efficiency of the Iranian Army." Tactical and strategic plans or operations against a foreign enemy were excepted from the advisory duties of the mission. Furthermore, it was stipulated that members of the "Mission will assume neither command nor staff responsibility in the Iranian Army." In the normal execution of their duties, the chief of the mission and other members could "visit and inspect any part of the Iranian military establishment, and officers in authority shall facilitate such inspections and make available plans, records, reports, and correspondence as required." If essential to their duties, members of the mission could also concern themselves with secret matters.

4. *Foreign Advisers*: The significance of this provision requires full quotations: "So long as this agreement, or any extension thereof, is in effect, the Government of Iran shall not engage the services of any personnel of any other foreign government for duties of any nature connected with the Iranian Army, except by mutual agreement between the Government of the United States of American and the Government of Iran."

With slight modification in phraseology the agreement was extended for a year from March 20, 1949, through the exchange of notes by Iran and the United States on December 29, 1948, and January 5, 1949.[16] Further exchange of notes on November 28, 1949, and January 10, 1950, extended the agreement for another year to March 20, 1951.[17] As will be seen, this agreement and the agreement of 1943 constituted the fundamental bases of American military assistance to Iran during the decades thereafter.

Meanwhile, the United States foreign aid policy underwent a major change. In 1950 American aid significantly shifted to military assistance through the inauguration of the Mutual Defense Assistance Program. Under the program eight NATO countries would receive about $1 billion, Turkey and Greece more than $210 million. Finally, a third category of recipients included Iran, Korea, and the Philippines, which were granted over $27 million collectively.[18] In a sense Iran's search for American aid was just beginning to be met by circumstances beyond its control. As will be seen, the oil nationalization crisis

[16]For the text of these notes, see U.S., Department of State, *United States Treaties and Other International Acts Series 1924*, "Agreement between the United States and Iran," amending and extending agreement of Oct. 6, 1947.

[17]For the texts of these notes, see ibid., no. 2068.

[18]See U.S. State Dept. *Bulletin* 22, no. 554 (Feb. 13, 1950): 227.

was soon upon Iran, and although the United States placed serious limitations upon its aid to Iran, military aid was continued even during the regime of Musaddiq. The basis of this aid was, however, worked out before. Iran adhered to the Mutual Defense Assistance Program by means of an agreement effected through the exchange of notes between Iran and the United States on May 23, 1950.[19] Under the agreement Iran was to receive from the United States on a grant basis such "equipment, materials, and services as the Government of the United States of America may authorize." The agreement specifically confirmed the basic agreements governing the American missions to the Iranian Gendarmerie and the army, discussed before, but there was little doubt that Iran's adherence to this program was quite different from its previous efforts since 1942, when Iran initiated all requests for American economic and military assistance. In 1950 it was clearly the United States that was launching another program of foreign aid in pursuance of its own worldwide security objectives.

Clashing Perspectives

The futility of the Iranian search for American credits before nationalization of the oil industry and Iran's unhappy relation with American consultants (OCI) are too closely related and too important to conclude this chapter without an attempt at explanation. These are related because they shared certain common problems. And this linkage was important for two reasons: the employment of American consultants and the search for United States credits constituted a major component of Iranian foreign policy before the nationalization of the oil industry; and the ill fate of American economic assistance to Iran became one of a complex of factors that led to the nationalization of the oil industry in 1951.

Any serious attempt at explanation, however, must also take note of Irano-Soviet and Irano-British relations. Since these will be treated in subsequent chapters, it will suffice to note that insofar as the explanation attempted here touches on these other relations, the supporting evidence can be found in those chapters. Furthermore, no explanation will suffice unless it takes into account the relevant domestic conditions.

Iran's basic difficulty in forging satisfactory relations with American consultants and in acquiring substantial and prompt American financial aid derived from the essential incompatability of Iranian and American perspectives, interests, and priorities. Iran's interest in the United States from the

---

[19]For the texts of the exchanged letters, see U.S., Department of State, *United States Treaties and Other International Agreements* 1, TIAS no. 2071 (May 23, 1950):420-24.

inception was first and foremost *political*, even when the means were economic. The truth of this proposition was borne out by Iran's own admissions in more candid moments when it was seeking the employment of American advisers or the expansion of commercial relations with the United States. This fundamental interest was significantly reinforced by the Azerbaijan crisis, at which point Iran launched its postwar search for American financial credits and economic advisers. When Qavam first approached the American ambassador for American economic aid, it may be recalled, he requested credits immediately in order to "reestablish Iran as a nation." Although Qavam did admit Iran's need for far-reaching "economic reforms," there was little doubt that the aid was sought mainly for political purposes. Just as he created his Democratic party overnight in order to steal the thunder from the Azeri Democratic party, his economic "reforms" were aimed primarily at easing Tudeh and Soviet pressures. His call for the conference that led to the establishment of the Seven Year Plan was no less animated by the same political considerations. Qavam was not alone in his view of the purpose of economic development in Iran; his view was shared by other members of the elite. In writing on the Iranian Seven Year Plan, for example, Rizazadih Shafaq, a long-standing member of the elite and a staunch supporter of the plan, stated, "What is important is that the mere conception of the Plan and the determination of the Government to carry it out indicate the awareness of the Government of world conditions and of the necessity for any *nation which wishes to retain its independence and way of life to raise the standard of living of its people.*"[20] In the Iranian perspective the welfare of the individual citizen was subordinate to the overriding goal of national independence.

The evacuation of Soviet troops and the collapse of the Azeri and Kurdish rebel regimes by no means resolved the problem of maintaining national independence. As a matter of fact, the Soviet cold war with Iran only began, as will be seen, in the wake of these events. Incessant Soviet pressures simply reinforced Iranian thinking that Iran's independence must be preserved by every possible means, including massive American economic aid. Every other Iranian goal, including socioeconomic betterment for its own sake, was to be subordinated to Iran's primary concern. Furthermore, the threat to Iran's independence was perceived in the early postwar years not only in terms of direct Soviet diplomatic pressures and the activities of the Tudeh party but also in light of the growing nationalistic dissatisfaction with the Anglo-Iranian Oil Company. The era of Iranian disenchantment with American economic aid was paralleled by the cold war with the Soviet Union, on the one hand, and, on the other, a growing nationalistic crusade against the British.

[20]Shafaq, p. 105. Italics are mine.

Iran's interest in American financial aid and advisers was motivated by internal as well as external political considerations. As in 1941-44 Iran's interest in seeking American aid in 1946-51 was not only to counterbalance adverse relations with the Russians and the British but also to bolster the shaky position of the ruling elite in the face of surging explosive forces of nationalism from the left and the right. As we shall see in the discussion of the oil nationalization movement, these pressures increasingly limited the choice of the ruling elite. As anti-British feelings became widespread, the government's freedom of choice contracted to the point that it finally could find no alternative but to play the nationalist fiddle willy-nilly. There is little doubt that the shah perceived a direct relationship between his ability to withstand an eventual nationalist attack on his regime and the success of his policy to acquire substantial American aid.

Despite all appearances of compatability, American perspectives and priorities clashed with those of the Iranians. Let us first take up briefly the OCI. Given the political nature of Iran's interest in United States economic assistance from the beginning, the clash with any American aid that emphasized economic considerations was probably inevitable, and the OCI advisory aid was no exception. The real question then is whether the OCI experts, as contrasted with Iranian officials, did place such emphasis on their advice. There is little doubt that they perceived their role primarily in economic advisory terms. They were mainly concerned with economic criteria and problems, and they formulated priorities in these terms. At the time of the collapse of their work in Iran, OCI's vice president, Max Thornburg, singled out Iran's "political interference" as the reason for the "doom" of the Seven Year Plan. The Iranian officials, on the other hand, blamed the termination of the OCI work in Iran on "disagreement on priorities," presumably in order to reduce the basic political-economic divergence to mere differences of economic priorities. But the nature of disagreement on priorities still revealed the more fundamental divergence in perspectives. The Iranians preferred industrial development over the agricultural, educational, and health improvement projects that were regarded essential by the OCI experts; industrialization in Iran, as in many developing nations, was viewed as the main road to, and the symbol of, national prestige and power. As noted above, Shafaq clearly revealed that the raising of the standard of living through the Seven Year Development Plan was favored for its contribution to Iran's national independence.

The same political-economic divergence partly lay behind the Iranian difficulty of obtaining substantial financial credit from the United States government. This divergence was perceptible from the very beginning in 1946. At that time, it may be recalled, Under Secretary of State Acheson complained to Secretary of State Byrnes about "our hitherto narrow concept of economic aspects of Iranian policy." It was clear at the time that he feared the Iranian political situation would lead to Soviet domination or the division of Iran into spheres of influence. But as already noted, no credit was extended to Iran until 1950-51, when it amounted to only $25 million from the Export-Import Bank, which refused, according to Ambassador Grady, to regard it as the beginning of $100 million credit to Iran. In 1950 Grady was deeply concerned about Iran's political situation as had been Under Secretary of State Acheson in 1946, but economic considerations during both the Azerbaijan crisis and the nationalist upsurge in 1950-51 apparently dominated the thinking in Washington. About a year after the nationalization of the oil industry, the American ambassador wrote: "The weakness of our effort was on the side of adequate financial assistance. If we had come in quickly and with adequate amounts, the whole situation in Iran might very well be different today."[21]

It would be tempting to see parallels between Kuomintang China and Iran during the shah's visit to the United States in 1949 and his empty-handed return to Tehran in order to explain the failure of the United States to come through with substantial financial credit at the time and even subsequently. But this parallel by itself can hardly explain the attitude of the United States in 1949, let alone during the whole 1946-51 period. It is true that in Tehran as well as in Washington the expression "pouring money down a rat hole" was perfectly familiar. The corruption of the ruling elite, the nationalist reformist urge of the post-Riza Shah era, and pressures from the extreme left and the right all seemed to call for the Iranians' putting their house in order before receiving substantial financial credit from the United States. But from the record in 1946, 1947, and 1948 as well as 1949 and 1950, it would be difficult to imagine the relevance of the Kuomintang analogy. As indicated above, all evidence seems to point to the proposition that during the entire period under study the Iranian problem was viewed in Washington more as a problem in lending economics than as a political problem. Dean Acheson's complaint in 1946 about the narrowness of American economic policy in Iran was as applicable in 1950-51.

Yet the crucial failure of the United States to provide prompt and adequate credits in spite of Iran's repeated requests may be explained only in part by the predominance of economic analysts over political analysts in Washington. Although it is true that many political analysts were convinced that the protection of the security of Iran was an important interest of the United States because of its strategic location and its oil resources, few would place Iran on

---

[21]Grady, p. 57.

the same scale of importance to the United States as the countries of Western Europe. In other words, the problem of inadequate economic aid for Iran was not only a manifestation of clashing perceptions but also of competing priorities in American foreign policy. During the period under discussion American time, effort, *and* money were primarily being concentrated in Western Europe. This was the era of the Truman Doctrine, Marshall Plan, and North Atlantic Treaty Organization. Iran had to await the mid-1950s when the American concept of security was broadened to include the Middle East and when the United States was prepared to pay economically, as well as militarily, for maintaining a Middle Eastern alliance including Iran. By that time the era of buying a cheap buffer had ended, but even an expensive one like Iran posed numerous other problems.

VII

Cold War with a Superpower

NEITHER THE EVACUATION of Soviet forces from Iran nor the collapse of the Soviet-supported Azeri and Kurdish rebel regimes ushered in normal relations between Iran and the Soviet Union. On the contrary, between 1946, when these problems were eventually settled, and 1951, when the Anglo-Iranian Oil Company was nationalized, the relations of the two countries were characterized by mutual antagonism. A close examination of Irano-Soviet relations in 1946-50 reveals that three major problems contributed to the cold war between Tehran and Moscow. These were the Majlis's rejection of Prime Minister Ahmad Qavam's promise for an oil agreement with the Soviet Union, the outlawing of the Tudeh party, and Iran's economic and military ties with the United States.

Rejection of the Soviet Oil Agreement

Soviet interest in Iranian oil of the northern provinces as a means of expanding Soviet influence and preventing a Western foothold in areas south of the Soviet border has already been examined. It is enough to recall here Qavam's note of April 4, 1946, to the Soviet ambassador, which stated in part that "the Imperial Government of Iran agrees that the Iranian and Soviet Governments should establish a joint Irano-Soviet Company to explore and exploit oil producing territories in northern Iran."[1] His note also contained several "fundamental conditions," including a provision that the "agreement to be concluded for the establishment of the said joint Irano-Soviet oil company according to the text of this note will be presented for ratification by the new Iranian Majlis as soon as it has been elected and has begun its legislative activity in any case not later than seven months after March 24 of the current year."

The new Iranian Majlis to which Qavam's note referred was the Fifteenth Majlis. The elections for this Majlis began on January 12, 1947, and the Majlis

---

[1]This letter together with a letter from the Soviet ambassador to Qavam on the same date constituted the "Agreement." See chapter 5.

convened on July 17, but it was not until August 26 that it began its legislative activity because it was engaged in the customary examination of credentials of deputies. On August 27 the government of Qavam resigned as required by law. On August 30 the new Majlis voted Qavam prime minister and he was appointed by the shah on the same day. On September 11 Qavam presented his government to the shah and on September 14 to the Majlis. October 1947 was the earliest Qavam was able to go to the Majlis for an oil agreement with the Soviet Union, but from the Soviet standpoint the Iranian government had been engaged for a year in deliberate dilatory acts.

Soviet displeasure with Qavam was first revealed after the historic cabinet shake-up of October 19, 1946, discussed previously. The dismissal of the Tudeh cabinet members was received with hostility in the Soviet Union, which launched a campaign of vilification through Radio Moscow.[2] Subsequently a cabinet reshuffling (June 19, 1947) further antagonized the Soviets as it included several members who were described as "very friendly towards the Western Governments." Amid increasing Soviet intemperance and the slow establishment of a new Majlis, the Soviet ambassador handed to Qavam a draft treaty along the lines of his promise of April 4, 1946, for an oil agreement. Six days later Qavam reportedly told the ambassador he disliked the terms of the draft treaty and could not force the Majlis to ratify it, whereupon the Soviet ambassador handed him a note (August 28) charging the Qavam government with "a return to the policy of hostility and discrimination against the Soviet Union."[3]

Soviet vituperation escalated into intimidation before Qavam went before the Majlis regarding his promise for an oil agreement. Associates of Qavam stated on September 10, 1947, that the Soviet ambassador had warned him that Russia would consider Iran a "bitter blood-enemy" if the Majlis did not ratify the agreement. At this point the British and the Americans diverged in their reaction to Qavam's position vis-à-vis the Soviet demand for an oil agreement. The British feared that if the Iranian government was encouraged to reject the Soviet demand for a northern oil agreement, "their latent nationalism might be tempted to challenge the Anglo-Iranian concession in the south," and they cautioned the Qavam government not to give a "blank refusal" to the Soviets but to leave the door open for terms better than those included in the Soviet draft treaty mentioned above. The United States, which had no direct oil interest in Iran at the time and which had been animated by a long record of support for Iranian independence, took up Iran's cause. On September 11, 1947, the American ambassador told the Irano-American

[2]For Qavam's complaint of this early Soviet propaganda campaign, see *Ittila'at,* Oct. 28, 1946.

[3]Royal Inst. Intl. Affairs, *Survey, 1939-46,* p. 86.

Cultural Society that the United States respected Iranian sovereignty, that "Iran's resources belonged to Iran," and that patriotic Iranians may rest assured that "the American people will support fully their freedom to make their own choice."[4]

On October 22, 1947, Qavam made a long presentation to the Majlis regarding the circumstances surrounding his agreement of April 4, 1946. Since this has already been discussed, it will suffice to recall here his concluding remark. He was convinced that the signing of the agreement in regard to the oil company "was in the best interest of the country, and any other patriot in [his] place in those days would have inevitably agreed to such a suggestion." As noted previously, the law of December 2, 1944, prohibited any government official from discussing or signing "any concessionary agreement" and made a violation of this prohibition a punishable crime. After Qavam's presentation a resolution was adopted 102 to 2, providing that Qavam's negotiations for an oil agreement with the Soviet Union were "null and void," but he was exempted from the penalties of the law, three to eight years imprisonment and permanent debarment from government service. This important resolution contained other provisions regarding the exploration and exploitation of Iranian oil in general and southern oil in particular, which will be discussed in the next chapter. I shall here examine the impact of this resolution on Iran's relations with the Soviet Union.

On November 5, 1947, Qavam wrote the Soviet ambassador about the decision of the Majlis, stating that his agreement had been found contrary to the law of December 2, 1944. On November 20 the Soviet ambassador replied that the agreement of April 4, 1946, had been in regard to the establishment of a joint-stock company, had not been a concession, and had been approved by the shah on April 8, 1946. He then charged Iran with three kinds of violation: Iran had breached its agreement with the Soviet Union by refusing to conclude the instrument necessary for the establishment of a joint-stock oil company as envisaged by the agreement. It had also violated the agreement by submitting the question of the joint-stock oil company to the Majlis a year after the period designated by the agreement and intriguing within the Majlis against the conclusion of an agreement. The Soviet note also stated that the Soviet Union could not fail to mention that the nullification of the agreement for northern oil in the face of the existence of the Anglo-Iranian oil concession in the south was a "patent discrimination against the Soviet Union," and in light of these points the government of the Soviet Union protested Iran's "hostile actions" and warned it against their "consequences." Qavam replied that the law of December 2, 1944, prohibited the signing of concessionary agreements, but his government had believed that it was allowed under that

[4]Ibid., p. 87-88.

law to enter into negotiations for establishing companies and selling oil and to report the results of discussions to the Majlis. This view of his government, he pleaded, was found contrary to that law by the Majlis, which is solely responsible for the interpretation of laws. Furthermore, he continued, it was obvious that his agreement for the establishment of an Irano-Soviet joint-stock company was contingent on the ratification of the Majlis because under the Iranian constitution no agreement could have legal effect without that ratification and the signing of the shah. In regard to the charge of delay in opening the Majlis, he stated that it had been beyond his power to control, and with respect to his failure to sign an oil agreement for submission to the Majlis, he claimed he was prevented by the law of December 2, 1944. In response to the Soviet charges of discrimination, he found himself "duty-bound to reject the charges strongly and emphatically" and denounced in the same breath the threats, vituperation, and abuse hurled by Radio Moscow and the Soviet press.[5]

Soviet Concern over the Tudeh Party

The servility of the Tudeh party as an instrument of Soviet policy in Iran during the war in general and at the time of the 1944 oil crisis in particular was shown in previous chapters. The decision of the Iranian government to send forces to Azerbaijan and Kurdistan not only led to the destruction of the Democratic parties of Azerbaijan and Kurdistan but also was regarded as an ominous threat to the survival of the Tudeh party as the mouthpiece of the Communist movement in Iran. Throughout the Azerbaijan crisis the Tudeh party followed the relations between the Azeri regime and the central government with keen interest, championed the cause of the Azeri negotiators in Tehran, and criticized Qavam's policies. To the Tudeh party the Azeri regime was simultaneously a symbol of the success of Soviet policy, which the Tudeh wholeheartedly supported, and an example of a Communist regime in Iran, regardless of the differences that separated the Tudeh from the Azeri Democratic party. The nervous concern of the Tudeh leaders with the fate of the Azeri regime reached a new peak once the forces of the central government were dispatched northward. About four days before the actual restoration of government control in Azerbaijan, a *Rahbar* editorial vociferously attacked the government policy, drew a parallel between the hand of "British imperialism" in Riza Khan's coup d'etat of 1921 and "the American imperialism today which has risen to strangle the Azeri national movement and colonize the Iranian government" and charged that Qavam's policies would result in

[5]For the text see *Ittila'at,* Nov. 25, 1947.

the destruction of the nationalist movement, in the reestablishment of dictatorship throughout Iran, in the exploitation of Iranian resources, and in the transformation of Iranian territory "to an imperialist base for the battle against Soviet socialism." A day later *Rahbar* intensified its attack on the central government and the United States, predicting an Iranian submission to American economic and military imperialism similar to the Chinese subservience to the United States.[6]

The collapse of the Azeri and Kurdish rebel regimes in addition to the evacuation of the Red Army dealt the Tudeh party a severe blow. The ideological, factional, and organizational problems the party faced in the wake of these serious setbacks of Soviet diplomacy have been discussed elsewhere and are beyond the scope of this study.[7] Suffice it to say that within a year after the collapse of Azerbaijan, the Tudeh party began to show signs of revival. "If anything, the party manifested every indication of increased militancy and a marked shift toward the leftist radicalism from which it had previously shied away."[8] By early 1949 the party's renewed strength was indicated by the participation of some thirty thousand members and sympathizers at a rally on February 4. On that day an attempt was made against the life of the shah at the University of Tehran. This marked the beginning of a relentless effort by the government against the Tudeh party, which has been outlawed ever since.

It is often assumed that since the Red Army had departed from the scene and the Azeri and Kurdish republics had been destroyed, the Soviet Union was, in the post-Azerbaijan years, perhaps losing interest in the Tudeh party or was at least more restrained in its support of the party. I suggest, however, that the value of the party increased in Soviet eyes since the Soviet Union enjoyed neither military presence in Iran nor normal relations with the Iranian government. The cold war between Tehran and Moscow was well underway before 1949, and the ill fate of the Tudeh party (then the only Soviet ray of hope in Iran) contributed further to the rapidly deteriorating relations between the two countries.

The intensity and seriousness of Soviet concern with the fate of the Tudeh party can be gleaned from the Soviet press. Four days after the attempt against the shah, *Pravda* reported "repressive action against the People's Party in Iran," claiming that 500 members of the party, including party leaders and the editor of *Mardom*, had been arrested.[9] *Pravda* of February 10 charged

---

[6]Dec. 8, 9, 1946.

[7]See Sepehr Zabih, *The Communist Movement in Iran* (Berkeley and Los Angeles: University of California Press, 1966), pp. 123-65.

[8]Ibid.

"terror against democratic organizations in Iran," reporting the arrest of "thousands" as the result of the military's attack, "encouraged by American advisors," on the Tudeh party and its ban. The same issue also noted that the acting minister for home affairs, "well-known for his connections with the Anglo-Americans," had stated in the Majlis that notes were discovered showing that the would-be assassin of the shah was a member of the Tudeh party, and found it particularly interesting to notice that the recent events in Tehran had taken place after a wave of protests against a secret agreement with "the Anglo-American Oil Company."[10] On February 14, however, *Pravda* reported that this statement of the Iranian minister, Abbas Iqbal, caused Soviet diplomatic protest to the Iranian government. The minister's "excerpts" from the notebook taken from the would-be assassin contained "references to alleged support of the People's Party of Iran [the Tudeh] by the Russians." The Soviet ambassador in Iran, Sadchikov, visited the Iranian foreign minister, Hikmat, and declared that the Soviet embassy regarded "the publicizing in the Majlis of these materials of dubious origin, containing slanderous inventions, as an act of provocation directed against the Soviet Union and aimed at worsening Soviet-Iranian relations to favor certain foreign circles."[11]

Deterioration of relations between the two countries continued in the following months. The Soviet press pursued two favorite themes: militarism and United States advisers. The real concern, however, was the fate of the Tudeh party. During most of April and May 1949 the Soviet press watched the trial of the Tudeh leaders with interest and reported its development and finally the sentences meted out to them.[12] Of the two themes, the attack upon Iran's relations with the United States proved the more persistent and intensive.

Early Superpowers' Squeeze on Iran

Iran's Seven Year Plan, discussed in the previous chapter, was the first postwar target of Soviet criticism of American economic advice to Iran. The plan was viewed in Moscow as a pseudoreform and reorganization project for the country "devised by American counsellors and experts." It was seen as a

[9] *Current Digest of the Soviet Press* 1, no. 6 (Mar. 8, 1949):37 (hereafter cited as *CDSP.*

[10] Ibid.

[11] Ibid., no. 7 (Mar. 15, 1949):30.

[12] See, for example, ibid., nos. 7, 9, 10, 14, 16, 18, 19, and 21 at pp. 30, 31, 35, 45, 48, 45, 39, and 35, respectively.

question that occasioned an "embittered struggle between the Americans and the British." By means of granting a loan to Iran, "American monopolists" would be able to monopolize supplies of materials and capital equipment, "establish direct control over the utilization of this equipment," and thereby "squeeze the British rival into the background."[13]

The shah's visit to the United States, discussed in the previous chapter, was followed with particular interest in the Soviet Union. In a long article *Pravda* finally broke silence some twelve days after the shah's arrival in the United States. It found "strange irony" in the name of the Truman plane, *Independence*, which brought the shah to the United States, reported the shah's discussions with not only President Truman but also General Bradley, cited the shah to the effect that he had discussed United States military aid to Iran in order to avert "the infiltration of communism into the Middle East," and charged that "the American monopolies are more and more taking over the country's economy." In regard to the last point *Pravda* stated that the "fate of the Bahrain Islands is a characteristic example. The archipelago was severed from Iran when Britain, in the 19th century, declared herself 'protector' of the local princes. Now the American monopolies have completely taken over production of oil in the Bahrain Islands. This is the position: the islands are Iranian, the 'protectorate' is British and the Americans extract oil!"[14] After the shah's disappointing visit to the United States, *Izvestia* carried an article entitled "Promises and Reality," elaborating the high hopes for *economic* aid the Iranian public had attached to the shah's visit; claimed that just in order to appease the Iranian public the shah had stated in New York that the conclusion of an agreement in the Near East similar to the NATO pact would be premature; and concluded from the text of the Shah-Truman statement and also from American aid practices in other countries that "Iran is being drawn more and more into the sphere of influence of American monopolists, who, as is known, are striving for world domination and giving no small attention to the countries of the Near East in their aggressive plans. The statement fully confirms the fears the Iranian public expressed before the Shah's visit to the United States and testifies to the fact that talks on what was allegedly only economic aid by the U.S.A. were needed in order to try to hide reality."[15]

The reality that *Izvestia* charged the United States with trying to hide was American technical military aid, which, interestingly enough, was hardly discussed in the Soviet press but was in fact the single most important Irano-

[13]Ibid., no. 34 (Sept. 20, 1949):18.

[14]Ibid., no. 49 (Jan. 3, 1950):21.

[15]*CDSP* 2, no. 3 (Mar. 4, 1950):30-31.

American kind of cooperation threatening Soviet-Iranian relations. The specific occasion was Iran's signing of the October 6, 1947, agreement discussed previously. The Soviet attack on Iran took direct diplomatic form. On January 31, 1948, the Soviet embassy delivered a note to the Iranian government, setting forth the terms of Iran's agreement with the United States and interpreting these to mean the following: All training of the Iranian army was entrusted to the United States military mission; the United States acquired a monopoly of sensitive military positions; and to the extent that the agreement subjected the Iranian military establishment to United States influence, it ceased to be the army of a sovereign independent nation. The note also went into great detail about the activities of the American military mission in Iran and claimed that these operations were aimed at transforming Iranian territory into an American military base. Furthermore, the note expressed concern over the creation of military establishments under American supervision near the Soviet borders, claimed that the signing of the agreement was incompatible with the Irano-Soviet treaty of 1921, and hence stated that "the Soviet government expects Iran to take necessary measures immediately in order to remove this abnormal situation."[16]

Iran rejected the Soviet assertions in a note of February 4, 1948. The note stated that all Soviet information was "unfounded and untrue." Although the Soviet complaints of activities concerning Iranian domestic affairs were unacceptable to Iran, the note stated, the government of Iran undertook to explain its position in order to clear "misunderstanding" and show the "untrue" nature of Soviet charges. The Iranian explanation then followed along these lines: (1) the agreement of October 6, 1947, was concluded for the purpose of employing a number of American military advisers for Iran; (2) members of the mission were not allowed to assume either command or staff responsibility in the Iranian army, nor were they permitted to concern themselves with tactical and strategic plans or operations; and (3) they did not have a monopoly of Iran's sensitive military positions. The note then explained Iran's need for military equipment as the result of damages incurred during the war and reminded the Soviet Union of Iran's previous approach to the Soviets for arms, which were unacceptable to Iran because of their high price. In regard to operations near Soviet borders, Iran claimed that it "did not allow any foreign national to visit the prohibited area let alone permitting foreign nationals in the employ of the Iranian government to fly over it for purposes of photography." The Iranian note, however, went far beyond what was called for by the Soviet note. It took this opportunity to complain about past Soviet behavior in the border area·in Azerbaijan. It charged that the Soviet Union had made no effort whatsoever to prevent "adventurers and

[16]For the text of the note, see *Ittila'at,* Feb. 5, 1948.

traitors who were supported by the Soviet government" from insurrection against the central government. On the contrary, the Soviet Union had given them moral and material support until they were quelled, and even then it had opened its borders and given them refuge. Today, the note claimed, according to "irrefutable and correct information," the Soviet Union still took the side of these elements as evidenced by the broadcast of Radio Moscow and Radio Baku and a secret radio by the name of the Democratic party of Azerbaijan, located in the Caucasus. The note then concluded that the favorable Soviet treatment of Pishihvari and his supporters as well as the Barazani Kurds in the Soviet Union had helped protect these groups that entertained "aggressive designs on Iranian territory."[17]

The Soviet Union responded to the Iranian note on March 24, 1948. Since this response largely repeated the contents of the January 31, 1948, note already discussed, the Soviet arguments need no recapitulation. The Soviet Union tersely rejected Iran's charges in regard to the Soviet role in Azerbaijan as "malicious tales."[18] The Iranian response of April 1, 1948, however, contained several new points that require at least a brief mention. First, Iran rejected the Soviet charge that, as in 1941, Iran had denied that foreign elements (Germans) were active in its territory and expressed surprise over the Soviet attempt to draw parallels between 1948 and 1941 as even in the latter year no foreign force planned an attack on the Soviet Union from Iranian territory. Second, in an attempt to support further its statement about the role of the Soviet Union in Azerbaijan, Iran simply mentioned the Red Army interception of the Iranian forces in November 1945, the Soviet refusal to withdraw forces from Iran according to the Tripartite Treaty of 1942, and numerous instances of Soviet interference in the internal affairs of Iran.[19]

The Soviet attack on Iran's employment of American military advisers under the October 6, 1947, agreement extended beyond diplomatic and propaganda means. Following the employment of these methods, border incidents between the two countries reached unusual proportions. When the Soviet forces withdrew from Iran in spring 1946, they chose to disregard the boundary line between the two countries in the district of Gorgan, where it follows the course of the Atrak River. Actually the river had silted up over the years and shifted its course to a more northerly, or Russian, route. The Soviet Union not only did not use this obviously more disadvantageous line as the boundary but failed to withdraw to the accepted boundary line. Instead it decided to withdraw only to the Atrak River's most southerly course,

[17] Ibid.

[18] Ibid., Mar. 28, 1948.

[19] Ibid., Apr. 3, 1948.

which had never been accepted as a boundary line. The Soviets established frontier posts there and forbade the Iranian guards to proceed to the former line.[20] This potential source of irritation between Iran and the Soviet Union became an active arena of armed skirmishes at the height of the Soviet-Iranian cold war. On March 22, 1949, a detachment of fifty Soviet troops killed an Iranian soldier and wounded and captured two others in the Gorgan district, and on March 28 the Iranian Foreign Ministry protested the Soviet attack on Iranian troops. On April 4 a Russian regiment supported by tanks and armored cars reportedly made a foray into Azerbaijan, attacking an Iranian army post. Border incidents like this continued intermittently until summer 1950, when the overall Irano-Soviet relations began to change somewhat for the better during the premiership of General 'Ali Razmara. The Soviets then gradually began to release the soldiers captured in border incidents in 1949. Finally, on October 3, 1950, the Iranian government announced that it was setting up a joint commission with the Soviet Union to settle eight border disputes of long standing. The actual settlement of boundary problems with the Soviet Union, however, remained to be worked out.

Finally, another development in Iran's relations with the United States that severely strained Irano-Soviet relations during the 1946-50 period concerned the establishment of the Iranian Joint-Stock Oil Company. Although the company was established under Iranian law, the areas of its planned activities, the assistance of the United States, and perhaps above all the still fresh memory of Iran's rejection of the Soviet-Iranian Joint-Stock Oil Company all combined to prompt the Soviet Union to launch a severe diplomatic attack on Iran. The Soviet attitude was first signaled by *Pravda* and *Izvestia* of May 5, 1950, when they printed an article entitled "Intrigues of American Military Personnel in Iran." It noted a particular intensification of activity of American officers in the regions adjacent to the Soviet-Iranian frontier; named chiefly the border region of Iranian Azerbaijan and the provinces of Khorasan and Gorgan; and claimed that American officers were making topographic surveys, studying road conditions, inspecting ports and coastal islands, and measuring the depth of the sea. The article asserted that the trips of the American personnel to the north were connected with the inspection and training of Iranian army units stationed on the frontier.[21]

On May 14, 1950, the Soviet embassy in Tehran delivered a note of protest to the Iranian government. The note cited two sources to indicate the nature of the activities objectionable to the Soviet Union. It referred to the Iranian Seven Year Plan Organization's notification to the Soviet embassy in March 1950 to the effect that bids would be accepted for aerial photography to be

[20] See *Middle East Journal* 3, no. 2 (1949):189-190.

[21] *CDSP* 2, no. 19 (Jan. 24, 1950):40-41.

carried out and maps to be prepared of certain areas in Gorgan, Mazandaran, and Gilan, which border on the Soviet Union, and claimed that the aerial photography was for military as well as industrial and geological purposes. The other source of information to which the note referred was a report published in the Iranian newspaper *Keyhan*, April 25, 1950, to the effect that the Iranian Joint-Stock Company was at the time concluding contracts with foreign enterprises for topographical work, a geological survey, and aerial photography, also in the areas bordering on the Soviet Union. The Soviet government then called Iran's attention to its note of January 31, 1948, mentioned previously, alleging that the works of foreign representatives in Iran might "create a danger to the frontiers of the Soviet Union" and claimed that the measures that were carried out in connection with the company's work show that "the Iranian government pursues aims in these areas which are incompatible with good neighborly relations between the USSR and Iran provided for by the clauses of the Soviet-Iranian Treaty dated February 26, 1921."[22] Iran replied on May 18, 1950, first expressing astonishment at the Soviet note of May 14, which dealt with the establishment of an Iranian company and aerial photography, matters "completely within the domestic jurisdiction of Iran," and then stating that the company in question was established under Iranian laws and had so far not undertaken any photography in the north or the south. Furthermore, Iran claimed that it had employed a number of Swiss nationals and bought certain equipment from the United States. Nevertheless the Iranian government had instructed the Plan organization to refrain from land photography in order to obviate Soviet concern.[23]

Once again, however, the Soviets protested Iranian activities in the north on June 20, 1950. The second Soviet note repeated most of the contents of the first one, and as further evidence of Iranian cooperation with the United States in the north, it cited a representative of the United States Department of State who had, on May 16, commented on the Iranian note of May 14 to the Soviet Union, stating that "in carrying out the seven-year plan, the Iranian government has signed a contract with an American company for exploratory drilling of oil wells in the northern part of Iran." This note, like the previous one, referred to the Soviet note of January 31, 1948, alleging that the work of the American "military and other representatives in Iran is turning Iranian territory into a U.S. strategic base." It again drew Iranian attention to the "fact that the measures of the Iranian authorities in the areas bordering on the Soviet Union, which they admit to have military significance and which are being carried out with the participation of foreign and, in

[22]Ibid., no. 20 (July 1, 1950):26.

[23]For the text see *Ittila'at,* May 20, 1950.

particular, American representatives, may create a danger to the USSR frontiers." The Soviet Union not only claimed incompatability of Iranian aims with the 1921 Soviet-Iranian treaty but also called upon Iran "to adopt measures to rectify the abnormal situation which has arisen." [24] On July 15, 1950, Iran once again expressed surprise at Soviet objections to "matters essentially within the domestic jurisdiction of Iran"; stated that Iran had purchased drilling equipment from the United States (where the Soviet Union itself purchased such equipment) because it was the best of its type for deep drilling; and had contracted the services of an American contractor for test drilling and considered both actions as "natural and logical." [25]

[24] For the full text see *CDSP* 2, no. 25 (Aug. 5, 1950):36-37.

[25] For the full text see *Ittila'at,* July 15, 1950.

Part Two

Negative Equilibrium

VIII

Oil Nationalization
From Conception to Decision

NATIONALIZATION OF THE Anglo-Iranian Oil Company in 1951 marked the beginning of a new phase in modern Iranian foreign policy that terminated with the downfall of the government of Muhammad Musaddiq in 1953. No comparable decision in modern Iranian foreign policy before 1951 produced such far-reaching international and domestic repercussions. Unanimous invalidation of the Russian Khoshtaria oil concession by the Fourth Majlis in 1921, Riza Shah's cancellation of the British D'Arcy oil concession in 1932, Sa'id's rejection of the Russian demand for an oil concession in 1944, and the Majlis's nullification of the Qavam-Sadchikov oil agreement in 1947 were major policy decisions,[1] but none reflected such profound and complex underlying causes or produced such multifaceted and diverse effects. For these reasons I shall attempt to explore a variety of related questions in detail in this and the following two chapters.

This chapter is concerned with preliminary questions. How did the decision to nationalize the oil industry come about? What was its primary objective? What was its nature? Was it principally a political or an economic decision? Who were the makers of the decision?

The Conception of Oil Nationalization

When the Fifteenth Majlis nullified Qavam's oil agreement with the Soviet Union on October 22, 1947, it simultaneously called upon the Iranian government to enter into negotiations with the Anglo-Iranian Oil Company (AIOC) and to take the necessary steps with a view to "securing Iran's national rights" (*istifa-ye hoquq-i milli*).[2] Given the long-standing grievances of the Iranian government against the AIOC, it would be tempting to infer that the Majlis merely meant that the government should seek satisfaction of its outstanding claims against the company, but the evidence makes it difficult to support

---

[1] For comparable decisions in Iranian foreign policy, see Ramazani, *Foreign Policy of Iran.*

[2] For the text in Persian see *Ittila'at,* Oct. 23, 1947.

such an inference. To explore that intent, we must examine other ideas both in the Majlis and the government. In analyzing the decision of the Sa'id government to reject the Soviet bid for an oil concession in 1944, I noted an important distinction between his cabinet's decision to *postpone* oil-concession negotiations until after the war and the Musaddiq-sponsored bill that was enacted by the Majlis into law December 2, 1944. This law prohibited oil-concession negotiations without any time limit and allowed discussions for only the sale of oil and "the way the government of Iran exploits and administers its own oil resources." The author of the law envisaged that the ideal way the Iranian government should do so was to do it itself. He made this more than clear in his two speeches at the time, and in the second speech he went so far as to state bluntly to the prime minister that he must "attach importance to entrusting the exploration for the Iranian oil to the Iranians, and should organize a special Ministry for this purpose at the earliest possible moment."[3] The idea of the exploration for Iranian oil by Iranians was advocated with a view not only to block the Russian bid for an oil concession in the north but also to vindicate Iran's historic claims against the British oil operations in the south. To Musaddiq such a national oil policy was dictated by the doctrine of "negative equilibrium" (*movazinih-ye manfi*) vis-à-vis Iran's neighbors to the south as well as the north, the British as well as the Soviets.

The notion of Iran's playing its own role in developing its oil resources was voiced inside the Fifteenth Majlis by individuals from quite diverse political standpoints before the enactment of the law of October 22, 1947. In a long speech in the Majlis Deputy Masudi criticized the program of the Qavam government on September 28, 1947. He stated that in "vital matters" there was no majority-minority division and objected to the government's failure to include in its program provisions for the exploitation of oil by Iranian hands. He went on to state that the only effective means for greater productivity and increase of employment opportunity in Iran was utilization of its own oil resources, and in the face of fierce international competition for oil Iran must not allow intervention by foreigners. Iran, however, should sell its oil to those who offer better conditions. At the end he proposed the following item for inclusion in the government's program: "The Government shall take immediate steps for the exploration of natural resources of Iran, particularly oil; and shall entrust the exploitation of those resources exclusively to Iranian domestic capital and companies which shall have the right to conclude agreements for the sale of oil to foreign interests upon prior authorization by the Cabinet."[4]

[3]See chapter 5.

[4]*Ittila'at,* Sept. 28, 1947.

Deputy Masudi's proposal shrewdly sidestepped the question of the only *existing* oil resource, at the time under the British concession, but it was brought up to show that *quite apart from the fate of the AIOC*, the notion of the utilization of Iranian oil resources by the Iranians themselves existed early, side by side with the attack in the Majlis upon the British oil concession. Deputy Abbas Iskandari launched such an attack before the adoption of the October 22, 1947, law. In expressing disapproval of the government's program, he denounced the oil concession of 1933 and the British oil operations in the south and demanded that the Qavam government include in its program a statement to the effect that the extension of the 1933 oil agreement was contrary to the wishes of the Iranian people because it was harmful to Iranian national interests.[5] In a major speech from Radio Tehran after the enactment of the law of October 22, 1947, Qavam himself declared that given Iran's strategic position, the country must follow a "policy of equilibrium" (*syasat-i tavazun*), and after referring to the unfavorable change in Soviet policy toward Iran as the result of the Majlis's nullification of the Soviet oil agreement with him, he stated that from the "very moment" he advised the Soviet ambassador of the Majlis's decision, he pursued the question of the Anglo-Iranian oil concession and "will persist in this effort until I secure satisfaction for the Iranian people."[6]

It took months, however, before that inchoate notion of national control of the oil industry crystallized into the demand for nationalization. Open advocacy of nationalization was first voiced in various speeches by Deputy 'Abbas Iskandari, a relative of a Tudeh party leader, but not himself a member. For example, in an interpellation of the government on January 23, 1949, he found an opportunity to demand nationalization of the oil industry. In his introductory remarks he generally thanked those who had congratulated him for his previous speeches on oil, but singled out Musaddiq specifically for mention because of his "great service to the nation in the Fourteenth Majlis." In advocating nationalization of Iranian oil, he cited Burmese nationalization as a precedent, stating that by means of nationalization the Burmese had eradicated British control over their resources and cited Bevin's statement in the House of Commons to the effect that Burmese resources belonged to the Burmese and the British could not interfere in their internal affairs. Iskandari also envisaged compensation for the British upon nationalization.[7]

More important than Iskandari's speeches, the solemn, careful, and scholarly statement of Deputy Taqizadih in regard to the 1933 oil concession gave

[5]Ibid., Oct. 2, 1947.

[6]Ibid., Dec. 2, 1947.

[7]Ibid., Jan. 25, 1949.

heart to the advocates of nationalization at the time and for years to come. After much hesitation about the wisdom of revealing the circumstances surrounding the cancellation of the D'Arcy concession in 1932 and the conclusion of the 1933 agreement (which carried his signature as minister of finance), he stated that he was impelled to disclose the matter in "the interest of the country." He remarked that most events of the past thirty years or even the past century or two had occurred in Iran in the shadow of strong personalities, and then, without specifically mentioning the name of Riza Shah at first, he attributed good deeds to him, called him a "true patriot" who valued the welfare of his country highly but who also made mistakes. The late shah, he stated, was determined to annul all harmful treaties and agreements with foreign nations and succeeded in doing so until it was the turn of the D'Arcy concession. In this case, however, one day he suddenly decided to act. All his decrees were implemented within the hour, and in this particular instance it was done almost immediately because the concession irked the shah so deeply. "No one would dare say a word," and this sudden cancellation without any study caused difficulties that were subsequently reflected in the "undesirable terms" of the new agreement (1933). Deputy Taqizadih also explained his own role. "I must confess that I had no part whatsoever in this matter, except that my signature is appended to that instrument and whether it is my signature or someone else's it would not have made an iota of difference in what actually happened." He then concluded his remarks in these words:

I personally never consented to the extension of the concession, nor did the other statesmen involved; and if there were any fault or mistake in this matter, it should be blamed not on the instrument of the action, but on the actor, who unfortunately made a mistake and could not go back on it. He himself did not wish to extend the concession, and in the first instance of its mention by the British he exclaimed abusively right in front of them: "Really such an action is quite out of the question! Do you expect us, who for thirty years have been cursing our predecessors because of this matter, to allow ourselves to be cursed for another fifty years by our successors?"[8]

But in the end, Taqizadih added, the shah "submitted to their insistence."

While the demand for nationalization of the oil industry or the annulment of the D'Arcy concession was being voiced in the Fifteenth Majlis in one way or another, the government was engaged in secret negotiations with the AIOC in pursuance of the law of 1947. The efforts of Qavam were cut short by the fall of his government soon after the law was passed, but negotiations with the company were pursued by the government of Hakimi and subsequently Hazhir, Sa'id, and Razmara. The government of Hazhir invited the AIOC to

---

[8]For the full text of the statement, see ibid., Jan. 27, 1949

send a delegation to Tehran to pursue negotiations in 1948. Meanwhile an Iranian group consisting of Varastih, the minister of finance, Shadman, the minister of agriculture, and Pirnia, the general-director of the ministry of finance prepared a long memorandum including twenty-five items for discussion. According to its preamble the document aimed to show that in the past fifteen years the 1933 agreement had not been fulfilled in accordance with the intentions of the parties concerned; in certain instances the agreement had not been fulfilled at all; and therefore the consequent damages must be paid to the Iranian government. Furthermore, the memorandum stated, even if the agreement were implemented in the way the parties had actually intended fifteen years ago, it would not nowadays secure Iranian national interests because of changes that had occurred during that period of time. The AIOC delegation, consisting of N. A. Gass and several others, stayed in Tehran nearly three weeks for discussions and finally departed for London, requesting three months during which time they would take up the matter for discussion with the AIOC board of directors.[9]

Further negotiations took place under the Sa'id government. The cabinet was presented to the Majlis on November 16, 1948, and included among its members 'Abbasquli Gulsha'iyan as minister of finance. It was during this government that 'Abbas Iskandari and Sayid Hasan Taqizadih addressed the Majlis Deputies on nationalization and the circumstances surrounding the conclusion of the 1933 agreement discussed above. On June 8, 1949, Gulsha-'iyan read a detailed report on the government negotiations to that date to cabinet ministers and a group of Deputies in the Iranian Ministry of Foreign Affairs, and a day later he repeated the report to the whole Majlis, some of whose members, particularly Deputy Rahimian, had been complaining about the secrecy surrounding the government negotiations. The report outlined previous discussions with the AIOC and detailed Gulsha'iyan's own negotiations with the company representatives in Tehran. He reported that he had confronted them at the outset with his general view about the need for revising the agreement of 1933 in order to bring it more into line with the changed conditions in Iran and elsewhere in the world, but the company representatives seemed unprepared to discuss revision and even "threatened to break up negotiations." Once they agreed to continue discussions, he reported, "I told them that the two most important principles which should be considered were: (1) the amount of royalties and taxes, and (2) duration of the concession." In regard to the first point he had insisted that there should be a

[9] These accounts are based on a documentary record prepared for the Majlis and the Senate by Husain Makki as the rapporteur of the Majlis special oil commission and published subsequently under the title *Kitab-i Siyah* (Tehran: Muhammad 'Ali 'Almi [1951/1952]), pp. 267-68 (cited hereafter as Makki).

fifty-fifty division of all the company's profits, as in Venezuela and other countries where this principle was then being accepted. And with respect to the second point he had proposed that any future agreement should be reviewed every fifteen years. In setting forth these principles, the Iranian government had in advance acquired the advice of Max Thornburg, an adviser to the Seven Year Plan, A. A. Curtice, an adviser to the government in 1944, and C. S. Gulbenkian, the well-known Armenian oil magnate. The government had also been advised by Gidel, an expert in international law, and Jean Rousseau, a financial expert. Negotiations, however, proved unproductive and broke down. On June 11, 1949, the same report was examined by the Iranian Council of Ministers, which decided not to submit the case to arbitration under the circumstances and recommended continuing negotiations with the company.[10]

Subsequent discussions finally produced the mysterious Gass-Gulsha'iyan, or Supplemental Agreement. This agreement between the Iranian government and the AIOC was signed July 17, 1949, and submitted to the Fifteenth Majlis on July 19. The mystery of the agreement derives from the fact that not much is known about what went on behind the scenes before its sudden appearance. A sympathetic British scholar reports that the advisory committee to the minister of finance, which had vigorously opposed the new agreement, was dissolved, and Gulsha'iyan and Sa'id invited a number of Majlis Deputies simply to tell them that the government was trying to get better terms than those offered by the company.[11] On the other hand, a subsequent report of a special oil commission of the Sixteenth Majlis states that "as the result of political visits, which are exactly reflected in the files, the Government of Mr. Sa'id had no other alternative but to place the exact proposals of the company before the Majlis." [12]

The Demand for Oil Nationalization

The timing of the submission of the agreement to the Majlis irked the Deputies as much as its mysterious origins. The Fifteenth Majlis was coming to the end of its term on July 28, 1949, only five days after the debate on the agreement could begin. The government might have wished to rush the matter through, but the Majlis had awaited the results of the government negotiations in keeping with the law of 1947 for nearly two years, and it was in no mood to

[10]Ibid., p. 274.

[11]See L. P. Elwell-Sutton, *Persian Oil: A Study in Power Politics* (London: Lawrence and Wishart, 1955), p. 174.

[12]Makki, p. 275.

examine overnight a cumbersome and complex agreement on such a vital question. As will be seen, the Majlis did not act on the agreement before its term expired, but the intense debate of those few days contributed to favorable publicity for a handful of Deputies who styled themselves "the fighting minority" (*aqalliyat-i mohariz*). In criticizing the government of Sa'id for his signing the agreement and its submission to the Majlis, this minority group launched simultaneously an interpellation against the government in order to insure that no outside force might intervene to muster the necessary majority for the agreement. The interpellation was launched on the grounds of (1) failure of the government to secure Iranian national rights, and (2) government interference in legislative functions. No majority could pass the government bill on the agreement while the government itself was under the fire of interpellation.[13]

Whatever theory one may favor about the reasons for the government's haste and timing in placing the bill before the Majlis, the action had a profound effect on Iranian politics and foreign policy. The government may well have done what it did primarily because it expected that the approval of the agreement by the Majlis would immediately increase oil revenues, much of which were to finance the new Seven Year Plan in the absence of any substantial financial credit from the United States. But instead the bill acted as a major catalyst in crystallizing more vehement opposition to the AIOC as well as the government. It provided the opportunity for a handful of deputies of the "National Front Fraction" (*feraxcion-i jibhe-ye milli*), including Makki and Baqa'i, to consolidate their ranks. And it proved to legitimize and spread the demand for nationalization of the oil industry. Makki, Baqa'i, Ha'erizadih, and 'Abdulqadir Azad signed the interpellation just mentioned, and Makki was the first to speak for the Opposition. His filibustering tactics, oratory, and long expositions and queries occupied much of the remaining time of the Majlis before its term expired, but the voices of other opponents of the bill, added to his, served to stir and spread national sentiments against the AIOC and the British.

The adverse implications of hasty action on the agreement for "Iranian national independence" were first pointed out not by Makki but by 'Abdullah Mo'azzami, a Tehran University professor. The occasion was offered by the attempt of the Majlis Speaker to place strict limits on Makki's initial speech according to the rules of procedure. Mo'azzami protested excitedly: "Mr. Speaker! Iran's national rights are at stake." He then addressed the Majlis spontaneously, counseling caution, deliberation, and preparation of an Iranian counterproposal for submission to the AIOC rather than rash action by the

[13] See Abulfazl Lissani, *Talay-i Siyah ya Balay-i Iran* (Tehran: Chap-i Mihr, 1950/ 1951), p. 541.

Majlis.[14] The fundamental objections of the Opposition were three: First, the Supplemental Agreement for all practical purposes would wipe out Iran's outstanding financial claims to AIOC. These claims were rooted partly in the AIOC's failure to pay taxes and duties to the Iranian government and in selling Iranian oil to the British navy at cut-rate prices for fifteen years. Second, the proposed agreement envisaged only a meager increase in taxes and duties to be paid to Iran. These would still fall quite short of revenues that would accrue to Iran if the principle of fifty-fifty profit sharing were applied. As a *minimum*, Iran should enjoy the kind of financial arrangements that obtained in Venezuela. Third, and most important of all, the agreement would both explicitly (by means of article 10) and implicitly confirm the "invalid" 1933 agreement that would expire, according to its terms, only in 1993. The proposed agreement, furthermore, made no provisions for either periodic revision or for a shorter duration.[15]

Technically, the Fifteenth Majlis did not reject the proposed agreement, but the sentiment of the body was probably against it. The minority group was, of course, clearly against the agreement, but since there was not enough time for all concerned to express their views it was not possible to ascertain the position of the Majlis as a whole. Nevertheless, it seemed safe enough for a nonminority deputy to voice the sentiment of the Majlis on its floor without any adverse comments from other deputies; in fact the record would indicate that approval of his remarks was voiced at least by some deputies. Amirtaymoor Kalali stated that the sentiment of the deputies was to reject the agreement, but they did not have the opportunity to do so. He also stated that the discussion of the last days of the Majlis showed that the agreement "did not secure fully Iran's national rights. Thank God, this term of the Majlis expires propitiously; it did not favor the Agreement."[16]

It thus fell to the Sixteenth Majlis to decide the fate of the Supplemental Agreement. The new Majlis opened on February 9, 1950, and Premier Sa'id was forced to resign on March 19 because he could not get a vote of confidence from the Majlis. The new premier, 'Ali Mansur, Iran's former premier during the Anglo-Russian invasion in 1941, literally ignored the agreement in his program presented to the Majlis which, he believed, had to decide the oil matter. The government's nonchalant attitude toward the agreement was not shared by the new Majlis. Reaping the benefit of its vigorous opposition to the agreement in the Fifteenth Majlis, the National Front was able to send to the Sixteenth Majlis Muhammad Musaddiq and eight of his supporters. These

[14]Ibid., pp. 509-10.
[15]Ibid., pp. 510-15.
[16]Ibid., p. 542.

men were determined to bring about the rejection of the agreement, but beyond that it is difficult to say whether there was any concerted plan for nationalization at this time. The idea, as seen, was there as was also the idea of cancellation of the 1933 oil concession.

On June 20, 1950, the Majlis entrusted the fate of the agreement to a special oil commission. The elected commission first met on June 26, the day that coincided with the dismissal of Premier Mansur and the appointment of Gen. 'Ali Razmara, a favorite of the shah, a hero of the Azerbaijan return to central government control, and a "strong man" favored by the United States for pushing social and economic reforms. The eighteen-member commission consisted of Musaddiq, Makki, Shaygan, Ha'erizadih, Allahyar Salih of the National Front, and thirteen other deputies, including Jamal Imami, majority leader of the Majlis. It met twenty-five times until November 25, 1950, when it wrote its report to the Majlis. At its first meeting by secret ballot it elected Musaddiq chairman by a vote of 14 to 1.

At the first session of the commission, Musaddiq emphasized the need for a great deal of time and for access to government documents because the questions involved were extremely complicated and required thorough study.[17] This question of access to government files on the AIOC turned out to be a thorny issue between the government and the commission. The commission also invited several government experts to appear before it, including Pirnia. The government, however, while agreeable to the presence of Pirnia in the meetings, seemed to drag its feet in complying with the commission request. As the result the commission decided during its third meeting to write the government to send the necessary documents without further delay, otherwise it would have to resort to interpellation.[18] Once the government finally decided to furnish the requested files, the commission decided, on the basis of a motion introduced by Jamal Imami during its sixth session, to study first the memorandum prepared during the government of Hazhir, mentioned previously. Examination of this lengthy memorandum and the discussion of its twenty-five items engaged the commission until its fourteenth session, when Forouhir, the minister of finance, appeared before the commission, and the ensuing debate between him and Musaddiq spurred open discussion on major substantive questions. The minister's provocative question about the nature of the commission's jurisdiction during this meeting antagonized Musaddiq and other members of the commission, such as Ganjih'i and Hidayati, who seldom spoke out during the meetings. Musaddiq, however, confined his remarks to a statement about the election of the commission by the Majlis

[17] These accounts on the discussion of the oil commission are based on Makki, p. 33.

[18] For the text see ibid., p. 276.

which, he explained, had "charged the commission to express its views on the Supplemental Agreement," and emphasized that the government must appear before the commission in order to express its position on the matter. As the result of this exchange it was clearly admitted for the first time by a government representative in the Sixteenth Majlis that the Supplemental Agreement had not been taken back by the government, and that the government was standing behind it.[19] During this same meeting Ha'erizadih, in addressing Forouhir, counseled courage on the part of the government in securing Iranian national rights, praised Riza Shah's patriotic sentiment in canceling the D'Arcy concession, and excused him for the conclusion of the 1933 concession agreement because of duress and the overwhelming power of Great Britain, and expressed the belief that it might not be such a bad idea if fire were set to Iran's oil because "whatever corruption took place in Iran was the result of the AIOC operations."[20]

Premier Razmara appeared before the commission during its fifteenth meeting. Jamal Imami told Razmara that he had extended the invitation to him because he thought Forouhir might not be well informed about the progress of government negotiations with the AIOC. Imami rushed into summarizing the sentiments of the commission up to that time, stating that the commission was against the Supplemental Agreement; Ha'erizadih, or perhaps all the members of the National Front, insisted on the cancellation of the 1933 agreement (Musaddiq interrupted to say that the agreement was void and did not need nullification) whereas the rest of the commission members did not find it in the national interest to do so; and wished to see the government bring a "more equitable" agreement (*yek qarardad-i monsifanih-tari*) to the Majlis. Hidayati made it clear that the views expressed by Imami only amounted to his own understanding of the sentiments within the commission and did not necessarily reflect those of the commission members.

Razmara advised the commission that since the beginning of his premiership some four months ago, he had been engaged in negotiations with the AIOC. He refused to divulge the nature of the negotiations, but counseled cooperation between the legislative and the executive branches of the government instead of acrimony and suspicion because he, too, believed with the commission that oil was an "extremely sensitive" problem for the nation; expressed serious doubts that the law of October 22, 1947, had intended to call for cancellation of the 1933 concession agreement; and, most important of all, squarely repeated what he had told the Senate about his government's support of the Supplemental Agreement.[21]

[19] Ibid., p. 144.

[20] Ibid., p. 152.

[21] For the text of Razmara's remarks, see ibid., pp. 158-60.

Makki responded to Razmara's remarks, charging procrastination by the government and voicing the demand for nationalization for the first time in the commission. He denied Razmara's insinuation about the want of study in the commission; objected to Razmara's indication that the government negotiations might take four more months: charged procrastination in such a "vital" matter; and went on to explain why financially the Supplemental Agreement was objectionable. Furthermore, he recalled Taqizadih's statement in the Fifteenth Majlis and his own private conversation with him in order to stress the nullity of the 1933 agreement. At the end he stated that the National Front "had decided" that the 1933 agreement was null and void and "we believe that it must be nationalized. Whether this is to be done now or later I have expressed my view that it must eventually be nationalized."[22]

Musaddiq undertook to respond to Razmara's seeming uncertainty about the status of the 1933 agreement at first. He outlined certain principles of law governing validity of agreements, including the requirement of consent of the parties, and then invoked the statement of Taqizadih made in the Fifteenth Majlis, in order to indicate that Iran as one of the parties to the 1933 agreement had lacked consent and hence the agreement was null and void. He also addressed himself to the intent of the law of October 22, 1947, and expressed the view that the Fifteenth Majlis believed that the 1933 agreement was void but chose not to state so in that law. He then told Razmara pointedly that the government of Sa'id had failed to secure Iranian national rights, and "you who are charged with the responsibility of securing those rights did not do so either because if the government had told the company that it did not accept the Supplemental Agreement; if you had any conscience and were not under foreign influence you would not have said here the things you did for the sake of satisfying personal ambitions."[23] Razmara was thus impelled to speak once again. He pleaded for trust and understanding. His views on the oil matter were not what they were, he stated, in order to hold on to the premiership. "I swear," he added, "my holding this job is for the purpose of serving my country; believe me if you look upon me with suspicion today you will judge in a future day that I did not aspire to this position in order to harm the interest of my country." While admitting Musaddiq's knowledge of the law, he refused to believe as a nonexpert that reliance on the statement of Taqizadih would make any difference in the way "the law-abiding countries" would invoke the 1933 agreement as a valid instrument.[24] Ha'erizadih, like Musaddiq, spoke of the invalidity of the 1933 agreement, but despite what Makki had said about the decision of the National Front for eventual

[22] Ibid., pp. 162-64.

[23] Ibid., pp. 146-66.

[24] Ibid., pp. 169-72.

nationalization, he urged the government to set the case before English courts if it had to in order to show its nullity. He trusted such courts would declare that the 1933 agreement had been null and void, and then Iran could revert to the 1901 D'Arcy concession, which had only twelve more years to run.[25]

As further meetings were held, however, the members of the commission, including Jamal Imami, expressed the view that the oil problem was primarily a *political* question. Makki held to the view that the British in 1950 could not do what they did in the 1930s. They could not force Iran to act as they wished because, on the one hand, the Iranian people then clearly showed a greater degree of national consciousness, and, on the other hand, the world conditions had changed and small nations enjoyed the support of the United Nations.[26] Ha'erizadih also emphasized the political aspects of the problem, and shared Makki's view about the limitations of great-power ability to coerce small nations; he cited the example of Soviet behavior to show that limitation, namely, Soviet reluctance to resort to force when the Fifteenth Majlis rejected their oil agreement with Qavam. Imami, however, proved far more skeptical about great-power behavior. He did not believe for a moment that the British were any less capable of action then than before. He chided Ha'erizadih for declaring preparedness to die for his country over the fate of the Supplemental Agreement, and stated that if he were convinced that the rejection of this agreement threatened Iran's independence, he would not reject it.[27]

As the National Front members of the commission got deeper into the government files and as the discussions with Forouhir and Razmara clarified the vast difference between their position and that of the government on so many issues, they talked themselves into presenting nationalization for adoption by the commission. In reading his letter to Forouhir during the twenty-second meeting of the commission, Musaddiq set before the commission the National Front statement of November 6, 1950, demanding "that the oil industry of Iran be declared as nationalized throughout all parts of the country without exception, namely, all operations for exploration, extraction and exploitation shall be in the hands of the government."[28] He then addressed the commission:

I believe more in the moral than economic aspect of nationalization of the oil industry. Assuming that we could not extract and sell as much oil as the company we should be able under any circumstances to satisfy domestic

[25] Ibid., p. 168.

[26] Ibid., pp. 199, 204.

[27] Ibid., p. 205.

[28] For the text see ibid., p. 245, and *Ittila'at,* Nov. 25, 1950.

consumption and secure the equivalent of the current revenues received from the company; the remaining oil should stay in the ground until the future generation could better benefit from it. The Iranian people have not so far benefitted from the efficient management of the company; the oil revenues have been expended in a way that has profitted either foreigners or those [Iranians] who have been the stooges of the company and the enemy of Iran. Should the oil industry be nationalized no longer a company would exist which would, for the advancement of its own interest, interfere in our internal affairs and assign [jobs to] corrupt individuals instead of patriotic and honest individuals.[29]

The National Front proposal for nationalization, and some others were discussed during the twenty-third meeting, which was declared secret, but it became apparent in the twenty-fourth meeting that rejection of the Supplemental Agreement was the only proposal on which the commission unanimously had agreed. Nevertheless, some felt that the report of the commission to the Majlis should go beyond the rejection of the agreement. The debate of the twenty-fourth and the twenty-fifth meetings, therefore, revolved around the search for a formula acceptable to all the members of the commission if possible. Of the National Frontists, Ha'erizadih, who had voted for both the Front's proposal for nationalization and the rejection of the agreement, proposed that the commission's report to the Majlis should call for Majlis's confirmation of the commission's rejection of the Supplemental Agreement, and, in addition, should instruct the government to take the necessary measures for securing Iran's full national rights with a view to the discussions of the commission particularly in regard to the problems of duration of the 1933 agreement and financial matters. He did not see any contradiction between this formula and the proposal for nationalization because nationalization would still remain one of the options of the government in addition to some others such as cancellation of the 1933 agreement or reduction of its duration.[30] Musaddiq objected to this proposal on the ground that the government in power, like the previous governments, could not be trusted.[31]

Meanwhile, these discussions provided the opportunity for airing two diametrically opposed views on the proposal for nationalization. Jamal Imami clearly opposed the nationalization proposal on the ground that its implementation "is not that easy" (*bih-in asani nihmishavad*), while Allahyar Salih made his frankest and fullest statement in favor of nationalization at this time. He attempted to refute Imami's view about the impracticability of nationalization, pointing out the inability of Great Britain to impose its will

[29] Makki, pp. 245-46.

[30] Ibid., pp. 254-55.

[31] Ibid., pp. 255-56.

on Iran because it itself was a founder of the United Nations, and, further-more, Iran could hire foreign experts from Britain or other countries or allow the existing British experts to continue. The main thrust of Salih's position, however, was the same as that of other National Frontists, namely, the *political* necessity of nationalization. He, like Musaddiq, did not mind seeing Iranian oil stay in the ground if it had to as the result of nationalization because "no nation could overlook its sovereign right." He then cited the example of Egypt's defiance of Great Britain, urging the commission to act favorably on the nationalization proposal and assuring them "that such an act will enhance Iran's honor."[32]

Finally the commission reported to the Majlis on November 25, 1950. During the twenty-fifth and the last meeting Javad Amiri set a proposal before the commission for inclusion in its report to the Majlis. The proposal stated that since the responsibility of the commission was to express its view on the Supplemental Agreement, and this had been done unanimously, consideration of other proposals was outside its jurisdiction and it was for the Majlis to decide on these. This proposal was approved 10 to 6. The five National Front members voted against it and two members abstained. The final report of the commission to the Majlis, which was adopted unanimously, stated simply that the commission "after study and discussion has reached the conclusion that the Sa'id-Gass Supplemental Agreement does not secure the rights of Iran and therefore expresses its opposition to it."[33]

The commission's report was subsequently placed before the Majlis. Musaddiq made a long speech, first examining the economic, social, political, and legal aspects of the oil problem for the Majlis deputies. He then told them categorically, "If you consider yourselves the representatives of the people there is no other option for you except securing fully the rights of the Iranian people by means of nationalization of the oil industry throughout the country."[34] In a surprise move Forouhir told the Majlis that the government would withdraw the agreement and resume negotiations with the company for more royalties. The Majlis immediately set up a new committee. The oil problem thus entered a new and final phase.

The Oil Nationalization Decision

The withdrawal of the Supplemental Agreement further consolidated the ranks of the National Frontists and legitimized their demand for nationaliza-

[32]Ibid., pp. 259-62.

[33]For the text see ibid., p. 294, and *Ittila'at,* Nov. 26 and Dec. 10, 1950.

[34]Makki's reading of the text of the speech to the Majlis was due to Musaddiq's "illness." See Makki, pp. 437-51, and *Ittila'at,* Dec. 17, 1950.

tion of the oil industry. The decision to take back the bill on the agreement was undoubtedly made by Razmara himself, probably in the presence of the shah, and a few cabinet members, including the ministers of foreign affairs, interior, and finance, and took even other cabinet members by surprise.[35] Although the unfavorable decision of the Majlis oil commission was unanimous, there was little doubt within and outside the Majlis that the strongest opposition to the agreement had come as early as July 28, 1949, from the National Front when the government of Sa'id placed the bill before the Fifteenth Majlis. Furthermore, since the National Front opposition to the agreement had been associated, in the Sixteenth Majlis, with the demand for nationalization, the government's withdrawal of the agreement was regarded by many as an implied endorsement of the demand for nationalization.

Yet except for the National Front, even as late as the end of 1950, there was no indication that the decision to nationalize the oil industry was a foregone conclusion. In fact, as late as January 1951 some sixty proposals were circulating in Majlis circles, but the momentous events that occurred between the withdrawal of the agreement and the adoption of the principle of nationalization by the new oil commission must be outlined for deeper understanding of the final decision of the entire Majlis and the Senate to nationalize the oil industry.

To begin with, the act of withdrawal of the bill occasioned extremely emotional outbursts both from the Majlis deputies and the audience watching. Forouhir faced unfriendly demonstrations from the crowd during the course of his ill-fated speech of December 26, 1950, when the withdrawal took place.[36] The atmosphere of the Majlis was no less charged with emotion on December 30 when Razmara himself appeared before the Majlis in order to explain the withdrawal decision. The prime minister's speech was preceded by those of Mo'azzami, Shaygan, and 'Abbas Islami and was delivered amid an atmosphere charged with a deep sense of indignation against his minister of finance, Forouhir. Razmara described the course of the discussions of the oil question in the commission and remarked that "since confusion had occurred" the government had decided to withdraw the bill in order to go ahead with securing Iran's rights according to the law of October 22, 1947. His speech was repeatedly interrupted by unfavorable remarks from the floor, particularly by Makki, and at times by the entire minority group. At the end of this unusually tumultuous session, some forty deputies proposed a bill refuting the remarks of the finance minister during the previous session; the Majlis,

[35] See 'Abdulhusain Bihnia, *Pardihha-ye Siyasat: Naft, Nihzat, Musaddiq, Zahidi* (Tehran: Shirkat Chap-i Rangin, n.d.), p. 35.

[36] See *Ittila'at,* Dec. 26, 1950.

however, lost its quorum before it could act. On January 11 the Majlis confirmed and approved the commission's report about the inadequacy of the Supplemental Agreement and charged the new oil committee, also headed by Musaddiq, to consider proposals suggested by deputies within two weeks and to prepare and submit to the Majlis a report within two months setting forth a policy for the government.[37]

As told, numerous proposals were prepared by the deputies; these fell into three major categories. These were, in essence, proposals for (1) cancellation of the 1933 agreement, (2) profit sharing on a fifty-fifty basis, and (3) nationalization of the oil industry throughout the country. The proposal for nationalization was signed by Musaddiq, Allahyar Salih, Shaygan, Ha'erizadih, 'Abbas Islami, 'Abdulqadir Azad, Baqa'i and a few others. It was set forth before the new commission on February 19, 1951. Since this meeting had been held in secret, Musaddiq claimed in the meeting of February 21 that he found it advisable to divulge some of the discussions of the secret session in view of the distortions committed by several newspapers. He remarked that now that the question of oil was before the Majlis, some of Iran's "Western friends" believed that the cure for the Iranian situation lay in land distribution. This suggestion, he said, would harm the interests of the Iranian people, if implemented, for two reasons: first, without judicial security the peasants would not benefit from land distribution and judicial security could not exist so long as governments in Iran were corrupt and the instrument of foreigners. Second, general poverty and unemployment could not be helped by land reform; "the chief cause of all these miseries is the oil situation." He then turned to the oil question, rejecting the fifty-fifty profit-sharing proposal on the ground that it would affirm the 1933 agreement and asking why the Iranian people should share in oil revenues when they could be owners themselves. In favor of the nationalization proposal specifically, he stated:

In proposing nationalization of the oil industry throughout the country, the National Front Deputies have attached greater significance to its political than financial aspects, and the reason for this has been sure knowledge of the Iranian people, and especially the Majlis Deputies and the oil commission that the source of all the misfortunes of this tortured nation is only the oil company. The telling evidence for this is to be found in the events and miseries of this nation during the last fifty years and particularly the events of the recent two years, including numerous attempts on life and assassinations.[38]

The significance of this secret meeting of the commission derives not only from what Musaddiq's remarks revealed about his thinking on the nature of the Iranian problem shortly before nationalization of the oil industry and his

[37]Ibid., Jan. 11, 1951.
[38]Ibid., Feb. 22, 1951.

subsequent premiership but also from the fact that the outlines of the subsequent controversial nine-article law were also suggested to the oil commission even before the decision for nationalization in principle was reached. Since this nine-article implementing law will be discussed later, it suffices to state here that Musaddiq's proposal at this time envisaged a parliamentary supervisory joint committee, which would perform implementing functions very similar to those subsequently entrusted to a joint committee of the Majlis and the Senate.[39]

Concern with the details of implementation as early as February 19, 1951, revealed that the chances of acceptance of the principle of nationalization were considered quite good at the time. This inference is confirmed by the fact that the commission "indicated its general approval of the principle of nationalization, and a sub-committee of four was formed to draft a resolution summing up the committee's conclusions" on March 6 when Musaddiq reportedly burst into tears for the first time.[40] A day later an assassin's bullet struck down Premier Razmara. Khalil Tahmasibi, the assassin, was a member of the Fada'iyan-i Islam, an extremist religious group that had emerged as a political force openly supporting nationalization. On March 8, 1951, the oil commission unanimously adopted the nationalization of the oil industry. A day later Fada'iyan-i Islam threatened to kill the shah and other government officials if Tahmasibi was not freed in three days. The terrorist activities of the right were matched by extreme leftist demonstrations in front of the United States Embassy. On March 11 Husain 'Ala was approved unanimously by the Senate as prime minister, and a day later he was confirmed in the Majlis by a vote of 70 to 27. The National Front deputies walked out in protest. On March 15 the Majlis as a whole approved the oil commission's recommendation for nationalization. The principle of nationalization was also approved unanimously by the Senate on March 20.

One more step remained to complete the decision to nationalize the oil industry throughout Iran. The law of March 15 and 20, 1951, embodied, as seen, only the *principle* of nationalization, whereas the *decision* to nationalize includes not only that law but also the nine-article law of implementation. This law, too, was prepared by the oil commission and resembled significantly the proposals that Musaddiq had set before the commission as early as February 19, 1951. The Majlis approved it unanimously on April 28, and then recommended to the shah the appointment of Musaddiq as the prime minister. On April 30 the Senate also unanimously approved this law. The shah promulgated it as the law of the land on May 1, 1951.

---

[39]For details see ibid.

[40]See Ellwell-Sutton, p. 207.

IX

Iran Takes Over the Anglo-Iranian Oil Company

IRAN'S DECISION TO nationalize the oil industry was based upon the single-article law of March 15 and 20, 1951, and the nine-article law of May 1. The single-article law simply provided: "For the Happiness and Prosperity of the Iranian nation and for the purpose of securing world peace, it is hereby resolved that the oil industry throughout all parts of the country, without exception, be nationalized; that is to say, all operations of exploration, extraction and exploitation shall be carried out by the Government." The nine-article law charged the Council of Ministers with the enforcement of this law, but the same law entrusted the actual implementation of the law to a mixed board composed of five senators and five deputies elected by the two houses and of the minister of finance or his deputy. The decision to nationalize was, as seen, actually the act of the National Front Deputies of the Majlis in defiance of the policies of the Razmara and previous governments, who had all been considered untrustworthy by Musaddiq and his followers. For that very reason the nine-article law of implementation gave much greater weight to legislative representation on the mixed board, but the unexpected appointment of Musaddiq as prime minister in fact placed the implementation of the nationalization decision in the hands of the National Front deputies in general and Musaddiq in particular. The outs were now in, and hence the policy of nationalization was actually first and foremost the policy of Musaddiq.

The conduct of the nationalization policy falls into two discernible periods. The first period began with the enactment of the nine-article law of implementation of May 1, 1951; it ended October 19, 1951, when the United Nations Security Council postponed its discussion of the complaint by the British government, and, more important, by which time the British personnel had withdrawn from Abadan after some half a century of service with the company in Iran. The second period began with Security Council decision and ended with the downfall of the Musaddiq government on August 19, 1953.

This chapter will examine Iran's nationalization policy during the first period, or the "take-over phase" (*marhalih-ye khal'a yad*). In this phase Iranian policy concerned relations with the Anglo-Iranian Oil Company, the British government, the International Court of Justice, the Security Council, and indirectly the United States. During the take-over phase the United States acted primarily as a neutral party, attempting mainly to bring the disputants together for negotiations toward the settlement of their problems, but in the second phase its approach to Iran drew increasingly closer to the British approach, as will be seen in the following chapter.

Given the overriding influence of Musaddiq on the conduct of the Iranian policy of nationalization, we shall pay close attention to his perceptions as well as policy, both in this and the following chapter. The best place to start is Musaddiq's own conception of the fundamental objectives of oil nationalization policy and the style with which he intended to carry out dispossession of the AIOC. In his first speech to the nation as prime minister, he indicated that the primary objectives of the National Front from the beginning had been "the extension of democracy and establishment of freedom" and the welfare of the Iranian people, and toward these ends "economic independence and control of industrial resources of the nation" were the necessary means.[1] In briefly outlining the program of his government before the Majlis he confined himself to two points: (1) implementation of the nine-article law, and (2) reforms in electoral laws of the Majlis and the municipalities.[2] Also, in his speech to the nation he concentrated on calling upon the public to strenuously avoid divisions and disturbances, and to maintain calm and order so that "the enemy would be deprived of excuses."[3] Musaddiq repeated this plea for order throughout the take-over phase of nationalization.

The British government's concern with the fate of the AIOC was made known to the Iranian government even before the adoption of the law of nationalization. On the eve of the approval of the principle of nationalization by the Majlis the British ambassador delivered a note, dated March 14, 1951, to Husain 'Ala, Iran's prime minister at the time, stating that the British government "cannot be indifferent to the affairs of the Anglo-Iranian Oil Company, an important British, and, indeed, international interest. It is, therefore, with much concern that His Imperial Majesty's Government learn that the Majlis Oil Commission have indicated that they are contemplating the 'nationalization' of that interest before the expiry of the Company's concession agreement."[4] This early note also asserted that the 1933 agreement, which had been "regularly" negotiated and on the basis of which enormous

---

[1] Iran, Idarih-ye Kull-i Intisharat va Tablighat, *Asnad-i Naft* (Tehran: n.p., 1951/1952), pp. 66-67 (hereafter cited as *Asnad-i Naft*).

[2] Ibid., p. 72.

[3] Ibid., p. 67.

[4] Royal Institute of International Affairs, *Documents on International Affairs, 1951* (London: Oxford University Press, 1954), pp. 475-77 (hereafter cited as Royal Inst. Intl. Affairs, *Documents*).

sums of money had been invested, was valid until 1993 and could not be legally terminated; that recourse to arbitration and good offices of the International Court of Justice was possible under that agreement; and that the AIOC was prepared to discuss a new agreement with Iran on the basis of "an equal sharing of profits." Iran replied on April 8 that the company had paid no attention to "the justified claims of Iran" and had declared the Supplemental Agreement "to be their maximum possible limit of concession." The note concluded by stating that the present position of Iran was that both Houses of the Parliament had "unanimously accepted the principle of nationalization of the oil industry," and the oil commission was studying "how to put that principle into practice."[5]

The first reaction of the British government after the adoption of both the single-article and the nine-article law and the shah's promulgation of the latter was voiced in the House of Commons. Herbert Morrison, the secretary of state for foreign affairs, stated on May 1, 1951, that before the resignation of the 'Ala government the British government, with the consent of the AIOC, had proposed to him a new agreement for the creation of a new British company on the board of which the Iranian government would be represented; for a progressive increase of Iranian employees in the company's operations; and for an equal sharing of profits. He concluded emphatically, "We do not, of course, dispute the right of a Government to acquire property in their own country, but we cannot accept that the Company's whole position in Persia should be radically altered by unilateral action, when the Agreement into which the Persian Government freely entered with the Company itself provided against such action."[6] On the following day Morrison sent a telegram to Francis Shepherd, British ambassador in Iran, in which he stated he had told the Iranian ambassador in London that he took "a very serious view" of the situation in Iran, and indeed, he had added that "the democratic free world" was interested in the outcome of the situation. He also claimed to have told the Iranian ambassador that the subject of nationalization "had been handled in Persia in a very irresponsible fashion and no well-thought-out scheme had been produced."[7] How much of this was in fact communicated to Musaddiq is not known, but the British government's message through the Iranian ambassador brought a polite but firm answer on May 8, 1951. Musaddiq wrote Morrison that Iran had no other object in nationalization than to exercise its sovereign rights and to undertake the exploitation of its own oil resources through the implementation of the relevant law under which Iran was ready to consider "the claims of the former Oil company—an

[5]Ibid., p. 478.
[6]Ibid., p. 480.
[7]Ibid., p. 482.

act which in no way bears comparison with the Communist way of conducting affairs"; and that Iran was prepared under that law to "sell petroleum to its former buyers at fair international rates." Insofar as the 1933 agreement was concerned, without mentioning it by name, Musaddiq stated: "It is the sovereign right of every nation to nationalize its industries. Assuming that agreements or concessions have been concluded with persons or private companies in respect of these industries and assuming that from a judicial aspect these agreements and concessions are considered to be valid, the fact remains that they cannot form a barrier against the exercising of national sovereign rights nor is any international office competent to consider such cases."[8]

On the same day that Musaddiq replied to Morrison's letter he received a letter from the representative of the AIOC in Tehran, demanding arbitration under the 1933 agreement, advising the prime minister of the company's appointment of Lord Radcliffe as its arbitrator, and requesting Iran to appoint its own arbitrator. Musaddiq asked his finance minister, Muhammad 'Ali Varastih, to reply to that letter. Varastih rejected the request for an arbitrator on May 20, 1951, stating that nationalization was a sovereign act of every nation and in the present case "the sovereignty of the Iranian Nation is not referable to arbitration, no international authority has the competence to deal with this matter," and invited the company to nominate immediately its representative with a view to carrying out the implementation law of nationalization.[9] Meanwhile, Morrison sent Musaddiq an *aide-mémoire*, dated May 19, stating that the British government neither desired nor intended to question the exercise by Iran of any sovereign rights, but the action proposed then against the company was "not a legitimate exercise of those rights"; repeated the British view of the validity of the 1933 agreement; claimed that the position of the company "should never be altered" by even the action of the Iranian legislation as foreseen in the 1933 agreement; repeated the provisions of the agreement regarding arbitration, but added that this was the only remedy open to the company and if it were made illusory by the action of Iran the British Government, which had majority share in the British-registered company, "would have an unanswereable [sic] right under international law to take up the case, and, if they deemed it expedient, to bring their complaint" before the International Court of Justice. The interests of the British government and the company were "identical," the aide-mémoire stated, and Great Britain was prepared to send a mission to Iran immediately "to discuss the terms of a further agreement." This offer to negotiate, however, was combined with a vague threat if Iran proceeded with its plan to take over

[8]Ibid., p. 484.

[9]Ibid., p. 486.

the company. Morrison concluded: "I should, however, be less than frank if I did not say that a refusal on the part of the Imperial Government to negotiate, or any attempt on their part to proceed by unilateral action to the implementation of recent legislation, could not fail gravely to impair those friendly relations which we both wish to exist, and to have the most serious consequences."[10]

This veiled threat and its accompanying offer to discuss a new agreement made no impression on Iran; they were simply ignored. The government proceeded to take preliminary steps for taking over the company, and since Varastih had not heard from the company about his request for nomination of a representative in connection with the take-over procedures he sent the company a terse note on May 24 telling N. R. Seddon, the company representative, that he awaited a company delegation at his office every day and would proceed in accordance with the implementation law if the company failed to nominate its representatives by May 30.[11] Three days after this ultimatum, the company wrote to the Iranian government that N. R. Seddon would attend meetings of the oil committee as an observer. When Seddon did so on May 30, Varastih handed him a memorandum.

This memorandum included regulations that had been prepared in pursuance of the nine-article implementation law. That law required the government (article 2) to dispossess the company at once under the supervision of the mixed board, mentioned before. In pursuance of this function these regulations created a provisional three-man board of directors for the adminstration of the "National Iranian Oil Company" (*Shirkat-i Milli Naft-i Iran*) with "all the necessary powers for managing the company's affairs, including exploration, production, refining, distribution, sale and exploitation." Another important regulation provided: "Foreign and Iranian experts, staff, and workers of the former oil company shall remain in their service as before and shall be considered employees of the National Iranian Oil Company from this date on." Equally important was the provision that upon arrival in Khuzistan, the board should issue in Iran and abroad a declaration to the effect that "oil products will be supplied to former purchasers against receipt for a period of one month, according to the existing program of the former oil company" in order to ascertain fair international rates, and at the same time "prevent any difficulties or stoppage in the export of oil abroad."[12]

Iran believed that its position had been made amply clear before the company made any kind of response subsequent to the memorandum of

[10]Ibid., p. 486-88.

[11]For the text of the note see *Asnad-i Naft*, p. 89.

[12]For the text see ibid., pp. 104-6.

May 30. The memorandum itself left no doubt about the government's determination to take over all operations of the AIOC if this had not already become clear from not only the text of the nationalization law but the whole history of its inception before, during, and after the Majlis's consideration and rejection of the Supplemental Agreement of 1949. The only other major point that was made in this memorandum was that nationalization "shall not in any way cause damage to previous purchasers and consumers," and if any damage were proved as the result of nationalization, the government had agreed to compensate the company. The nine-article law (article 2) provided that up to 25 percent of "current revenues," after deduction of exploitation expenses, could be set aside in order to meet the "probable claims of the Company." The memorandum's reference to Iran's interest in the "experience and knowledge" of the company, which was invited to make recommendations "not contrary to the principle of nationalization,"[13] was, in the Iranian perspective, a conciliatory and polite gesture certainly not to be interpreted as an invitation to change the nationalization law!

The company responded on June 3, 1951, to the Iranian memorandum of May 30. Seddon said that the British government and the company had been ready "from the outset to attempt to solve all ... difficulties by negotiations"; took note of Iran's expression of interest in the company's knowledge and experience; and declared that "the company, while reserving its legal rights, will send representatives from London to Tehran as soon as possible in order to hold full and frank discussions" with Iran.[14] Given the clarity of its position, Iran believed the company's singling out of Iran's interest in its experience and recommendations and its leaving out the important proviso "not contrary to the principle of nationalization" did not appear to be a good omen for a "full and frank" discussion.

To further clarify its intention in inviting the company's recommendations, Iran dispatched the provisional board of directors of the National Iranian Oil Company (NIOC) to Abadan for discussions with company officials before the arrival of the company delegation to Tehran from London. The message was again clear to the Iranians that the government was determined to take over all the AIOC operations, and the negotiations with company officials from London could only be concerned with the implementation, rather than modification, of the nationalization law. The Iranian representatives held their first meeting with the AIOC delegation in Tehran on June 14, stating at the outset that the opening of discussions was conditional upon the issuance of immediate instructions by the delegation that the AIOC's income as of March 20 (the date of the Majlis's approval of the principle of nationalization)

[13]Ibid., p. 106.
[14]Ibid., pp. 110-11.

be handed over to the Iranian government, after 25 percent had been deducted for probable claims of the company. After postponement and finally breakdown of negotiations, each side set forth its own version of the difficulties involved.

Before a discussion of these, the principal points of the proposal of the company delegation should be mentioned. It was proposed that the Iranian assets of the company be vested in the NIOC in return for which the *use* of its assets would be granted to a new company to be established by the AIOC. This new company would in fact operate in behalf of the NIOC and would have a number of Iranian directors on its board. Another entirely owned and operated AIOC company would be established for distribution purposes in Iran.[15]

Morrison reported to the House of Commons the proposals of the AIOC delegation, as did Musaddiq to the public and the Majlis. Morrison repeated the proposals of the company, mentioned above; emphasized the offer of the company to pay certain sums of money for Iranian necessities; claimed that the proposals envisaged acceptance of "the principle of nationalization" as well as beneficial partnership; and reiterated that the British government would not hesitate to act if the lives of British subjects were endangered.[16] Musaddiq addressed the public by radio on June 21, 1951, stating that the company, after being advised about the take-over procedures, expressed interest in making proposals "in regard to the implementation of the nationalization law" and in sending a delegation toward that end. The Iranian government, he continued, welcomed the delegation and complied with their request for the extension of time "in good faith," but "discovered last night that they did not wish to understand our language." Once again he urged the people to "watch the situation with vigilance and greater foresight which are in keeping with the status of the historic Iranian nation"; and expressed trust that the task [of take-over] would be accomplished with admirable "calm and dignity."[17] On the same day Musaddiq reported to the Majlis on negotiations, stating at the outset that Iran's basic purpose in entering these negotiations was to "insure that the implementation of the nationalization law and the take-over process would be accomplished as far as possible with the co-operation of the former oil company in order to avoid any possible harm to the oil operations." More specifically he referred to articles 2 and 7 of the nine-article law of implementation to indicate exactly that negotiations with the company had been welcomed only in regard to probable company claims, and

[15] The Brookings Institution, *Current Developments in United States Foreign Policy* 4, no. 10 (1951):34-41.

[16] *Asnad-i Naft*, pp. 138-41.

[17] Ibid., pp. 149-51.

the sale of oil to England.[18] He then read the text of the AIOC proposals to show their fundamental incompatability with the nationalization law.

Musaddiq's report to the Majlis indicated at the end that the government was then proceeding with the take-over operations without delay. A day earlier, June 20, new directives were announced for the take-over operations: The AIOC orders must be countersigned by the NIOC provisional board of directors to be effective; Iranian officials would be sent to take over the Naftishah and Kermanshah oil fields and the refinery supplying domestic consumption; Iranian officials would take over other AIOC departments; and revenues from oil sales were to be deposited in the National Bank of Iran in the account of the NIOC. A day later the Iranian take-over mission demanded that the AIOC general manager, Eric C. Drake, inform all British staff members that they would have one week to decide whether they would work for the NIOC and inform them whether he himself would serve the NIOC.

The AIOC's reaction to Iran's swift measures in the south was negative. It would obstruct the take-over operations at any cost, and this for the company could mean individual or mass resignation of the British employees, cutback in oil production, shutdown of oil operations, and stoppage of Iranian oil to world markets. Musaddiq made a personal appeal to foreign experts, staff, and workers on June 26, 1951, to continue their services as before with the same pay and fringe benefits, and promised greater encouragement. He also told them that the talk of mass resignation was most unfortunate and would cause enormous damage to not only Iran but also the consumer countries as well.[19] The company, however, ordered its staff to get ready to leave, and on the day following the Musaddiq appeal the British staff began evacuation. At the same time the general manager of the company ordered tanker masters not to sign the kind of receipts furnished by the Iranian government without a statement to the effect that their signatures did not constitute recognition of nationalization and did not prejudice the legal rights of the AIOC. The controversy between the provisional board and the company led to the departure of tankers without oil, and left Iran without oil exports. By the end of July 1951 the gigantic Abadan refinery was closed down.

The company's resistance to the Iranian takeover was paralleled by military preparations by the British government, perhaps for the purpose of protecting British lives, but more probably as a show of force. These preparations consisted of both naval and land forces. In March 1951 the frigates *Flamingo* and *Wild Goose* arrived off Bahrain, and the cruiser *Gambia* left Malta for the Red Sea. In June and July more ships arrived in the Persian Gulf area, the tank-loading ship *Messina* arriving off Basra and four destroyers arriving from

[18]Ibid., pp. 144-48.

[19]For the text see ibid., pp. 168-69.

Malta.[20] Meanwhile troop movements were underway. On May 25 the British minister of defense announced that the sixteenth Independent Parachute Brigade Group would soon be going to the Mediterranean, and on June 4 some three thousand British paratroopers left for duty on Cyprus, purportedly in readiness for possible action in Iran.

Musaddiq Welcomes American "Neutrality"

All these moves were watched with great anxiety not only in Tehran but also in Washington, but American concern with the Iranian situation had deeper roots. The United States had always championed the cause of Iranian territorial integrity and political independence; had been a firm friend of Iran's despite Iranian frustration with its aid policy, discussed previously; feared that the Anglo-Iranian dispute might lead to the stoppage of oil to Western European allies of the United States; worried that the Iranian act of nationalization might set a bad example for other oil-producing states of the Middle East where the United States oil interests were involved; and was alarmed by the increasing strength of the Tudeh party and the possibility of a "Communist coup d'etat," to borrow Acheson's words.[21] At the same time Great Britain was the staunchest American ally, their historical, cultural, and economic ties far exceeding the American ones with Iran. This was the essence of the American dilemma at the beginning of the nationalization crisis when the American and British approaches to Iran diverged significantly. In view of its predicament, the United States tried at first to adopt an attitude of neutrality in the hope of defusing the tense emotions involved toward a possible future settlement through negotiations.

On May 18, 1951, the United States government for the first time made its "position on [the] Iranian oil situation" public. It expressed deep concern over the dispute; wished amicable settlement as the firm friend of both countries; and reported what it had already told both countries. The British government had been told by the United States that, in the American opinion, arrangements should be worked out with Iranians that gave "recognition to Iran's expressed desire for greater control over and benefits from the development of its petroleum resources." The Iranian government had been told of the strong opposition of the United States to any unilateral cancellation of contractual relationships. The statement also declared that American oil companies had indicated to the United States government "That they would

---

[20]Royal Inst. Intl. Affairs, *Survey, 1951*, pp. 311-12.

[21]Dean Acheson, *Present at the Creation* (New York: W. W. Norton & Co., 1969), p. 506.

not in the face of unilateral action by Iran against the British company be willing to undertake operations in that country."[22]

Musaddiq interpreted the above statement as unjustifiable intervention in the internal affairs of Iran, and his minister of foreign affairs handed an *aide-mémoire* to that effect to the American ambassador in Tehran on May 21. The United States responded to this on May 26, reiterating its opposition to unilateral "cancellation of contractual relationships"; regretting Iran's "misconstruing" the American statement as intervention; and emphatically pointing out that it had no intention of interfering in the internal affairs of Iran, and did not wish to oppose Iran's sovereign rights to control Iranian resources.[23]

This preliminary skirmish between Iran and the United States was quite unprecedented; the charge of intervention had hardly been leveled at the United States by any Iranian government before. Yet it was in keeping with Musaddiq's general policy of negative equilibrium and the particular determination of his government to carry out the take-over operations without foreign intervention. Nevertheless, because of the mediations of the American ambassador, Henry F. Grady, Musaddiq heeded the request of the AIOC delegation for extension of the time limit originally fixed for negotiations in Tehran, which, it may be recalled, broke down in June, 1951. On June 3 President Truman himself had sent Musaddiq a personal message, and after the breakdown of negotiations with the AIOC Musaddiq wrote the president a long letter on June 28, reporting the course of the negotiations and declaring that there was no doubt that "Iran will make every effort with all the means at its disposal to prevent any stoppage, even temporarily, in the flow of oil, but it would be the cause of great regret if any stoppage occurred as the result of the resignation en masse of the British employees, or any delaying tactics in loading and shipping of the oil products because of the refusal on their part to give the receipts required. In such an eventuality the responsibility for the grave consequences which might follow will naturally lie upon the shoulders of the former oil company authorities."[24]

With the breakdown of negotiations and the departure of the AIOC delegation from Tehran, it may be recalled, take-over measures were pushed with unprecedented determination until July 31, when the refinery was shut down. Meanwhile, the United States became increasingly alarmed about the situation in Iran and decided to bring the British and the Iranians to the discussion table if at all possible. Former Secretary of State Acheson suggested to Averell Harriman on July 4, 1951, that he should go to Tehran, and the

[22] U.S. State Dept. *Bulletin* 24, no. 621 (May 28, 1951):851.
[23] Ibid., no. 622 (June 4, 1951):891-92.
[24] Ibid., 25, no. 628 (July 9, 1951):72-73.

following day President Truman, when he heard of the idea from Acheson, "warmly welcomed it and immediately sent a cable to Mosadeq."[25]

The idea of more negotiations through American mediation occurred to Acheson after he came to the conclusion that armed intervention by the British would not pay off. He, Harriman, Paul Nitze, Doc Matthews, George McGhee, and Ambassador Oliver Franks discussed the Iranian situation. The British ambassador told them how seriously and angrily the British government and public viewed "what they regarded as the insolent defiance of decency, legality, and reason by a group of wild men in Iran who proposed to despoil Britain." However, Sir Oliver doubted that Musaddiq's "despoilation" should or could be met with greater force. The group was unanimous in the opinion that armed intervention by Britain at Abadan would, in all probability, lead to armed intervention by the Soviet Union in Azerbaijan in support of their rejected oil concession (the Qavam-Sadchikov agreement). Furthermore, such an action would both fail to gain control of the oil fields for Britain and create "an uproar in the United Nations." "In this battle," Acheson wrote later, "it seemed inevitable that Washington, in view of its leadership of the 1946 fight to get Russian troops out of Iran, would end up at loggerheads with London. Finally, if Mosadeq or an even more extreme government invited Russian intervention in the hope of forcing withdrawal of both foreign forces, we might end up with the British out and the Russians in."[26]

President Truman sent a message to Musaddiq on July 8, 1951. The president told him that he hoped that "ways could be found to recognize the principle of nationalization and British interests to the benefit of both"; that he had watched "with concern" the breakdown of negotiations and the drift toward the collapse of oil operations with all the attendant losses to Iran and the world; and believed that surely "this is a disaster which statesmanship can find a way to avoid." At the end he suggested that if Musaddiq were willing, he would be happy to have Averell Harriman go to Tehran as his "personal representative" to talk over the situation with him.[27]

Musaddiq responded to the president's message on July 11, welcoming Harriman's visit, and hoping to take "full advantage of consultations with a man of such high standing." He, in particular, was "extremely glad" to see the president's reference to the principle of nationalization because "Iran has had and is having no aim other than the acceptance of this principle by virtue of the laws ratified by the two Houses of Parliament, and has always been

---

[25] Acheson, pp. 505-6.

[26] Ibid., p. 507.

[27] For the text see U.S. State Dept. *Bulletin* 25, no. 630 (July 23, 1951):129-30.

ready, within the terms of these laws to take any measures for the removal of the present dispute."[28]

Harriman's departure for Iran on July 13 was viewed with great hope and confidence in Washington. The president, Secretary Acheson, and General Marshall were all on hand to wish him "good luck." The president told him that he had undertaken "a very important job," and hoped that he would tell the Iranian government that the United States interest was world peace and the welfare of Iran and the rest of the world, and concluded, "We have no selfish interest in the matter whatever." Harriman expressed the view that there was great mutuality of interest between Iran, Britain, and the rest of the world, and Europe and the Far East were dependent on Iranian oil.[29] There was no mention in these remarks of the American oil interest in the neighboring countries of the Middle East. Nor was there any mention of the serious American concern with the Soviet and Communist attitudes toward Iran. On the same day, however, George C. McGhee, assistant secretary of state for Near Eastern Affairs, minced no words about this side of the United States interest. In a television program he stated: "We can be sure that the Kremlin is losing no opportunity to fish in the troubled oil of Iran, for Iran would be a great and strategic prize quite apart from oil."[30]

Harriman's arrival in Tehran was followed by extensive discussions with the Iranian government and the British officials in Tehran and subsequently in London. Technically the president had not offered Harriman's "mediation" and Musaddiq had not accepted anything but "consultations" with the president's personal representative. The first important task before Harriman, therefore, was to see if he could get the Iranian and British governments to agree to negotiate with each other because Iran had taken the position that the party to the dispute was the company and not the British government. Finally, at a meeting of the Council of Ministers at Musaddiq's house on July 23, 1951, the "Harriman formula" was approved. The formula included the following:

1. The Iranian government would be prepared to enter into negotiations with the British government in behalf of the company in case the British government recognized the principle of nationalization of the oil industry in Iran on behalf of the company.

2. Before the departure of the British delegation for Tehran, the British government would make public its agreement to the principle of nationalization of the oil industry in behalf of the company.

[28]Ibid., p. 130.
[29]Ibid.
[30]Ibid.

3. The "principle of nationalization" meant the proposal that was approved by the special oil commission of the Majlis and was confirmed by the Majlis on March 20, 1951.

4. The government of Iran would be prepared to enter into negotiations in regard to "the manner of implementing the law" (*tariqih-ye ijra'-i qanun*) insofar as it concerned British interests.[31]

Afterwards, Harriman personally took his formula to London where he faced the British demand for assurances by Iran for relieving tensions in the oil fields as well. Upon Harriman's further communications with, and before the arrival of, the British mission in Tehran, through an exchange of notes between the Iranian Ministry of Foreign Affairs and the British embassy on August 3 the British agreed to the formula, and Iran acknowledged "the importance of creating the best possible atmosphere by both governments with a view to the success of negotiations" and assured Britain that it would enter discussions with "the same good will that is expressed by the British government."[32]

Iran believed that by specifying in the formula exactly what it meant by the principle of nationalization, on the one hand, and by including in it the provision that it would enter negotiations in regard to "the manner of implementation of the law" insofar as it affected the British interest, on the other, it had removed the principal obstacles to successful settlement of the dispute, but it soon was disabused. The British delegation, headed by the lord privy seal, Richard Stokes, handed Iran a proposal, reiterating the fifty-fifty principle of profit sharing, and suggesting creation of purchasing and operating organizations, the former exclusively and the latter largely controlled by the AIOC. To Iran this was a far cry from accepting the principle of nationalization because that principle required that "all operations of exploration, extraction, and exploitation" be carried out "by the Government." A British scholar sympathetic to the Iranian viewpoint subsequently described the Stokes proposals in these terms: "Put very succinctly, the British attitude was that, in return for their recognizing the principle of nationalization, the Persian government should forego its insistence on that principle."[33]

This difficult start spelled trouble for the Harriman mission, but his strenuous efforts did a great deal to solicit concessions from both sides. Stokes proposed a British general manager under the direction of the Iranian government (the NIOC) instead of an operating organization of the kind he had

---

[31]This is my own verbatim translation from the Persian. For the text see *Asnad-i Naft,* pp. 366-67.

[32]Ibid., pp. 374-75.

[33]Ellwell-Sutton, p. 252.

originally suggested. Musaddiq suggested two general managers, British and Iranian, instead of Iranian management solely. This was not agreeable to Stokes, and therefore Musaddiq proposed a board of management composed of outstanding experts "from countries with no special political interest in Iran," but Stokes insisted on his previous demand for a British general manager, refusing to consider Iran's new proposal before he left Iran. After the Stokes departure and the rupture of negotiations, Iran proposed a director "of foreign nationality" for both refinery and extraction organizations, but the British rejected it on the ground that the relevant document had not been dated and signed.[34]

Musaddiq, who had, as seen, strenuously emphasized his determination to retain foreign personnel up to this time, proposed to the Senate on September 5, 1951, to give the British government a fortnight to resume negotiations, or submit counterproposals, or alternatively, face the cancellation of the residence permits of the British technicians. A week later, however, he himself wrote a proposal to Harriman to be submitted to the British. In regard to management, the principal point on which the previous negotiations had broken down, he suggested the setting up of "a mixed board," consisting of "foreign technicians from neutral countries and the Iranian specialists," to jointly manage the administrative and technical affairs of the NIOC. He concluded, Iran "regrets to state its compulsion to cancel the residence permits" of the British staff and experts if in fifteen days from the date of submission of his new proposal to the British government no satisfactory conclusion were achieved.[35] Harriman replied that Musaddiq's proposals were generally the same as those made by Iran during the course of negotiations and in "some respects the proposals in fact present a retrogression from the positions taken during the discussions." In regard to the principal point on management, he pointed out, as he had in Tehran, "the impracticability of attempting to operate a large and complex industry" the way Musaddiq suggested, and "effective operations" of a refinery such as that in Abadan required an integrated organization rather than the employment of individual foreign specialists. In conclusion Harriman regretted that it was not possible for him to submit Musaddiq's proposals to the British government.[36]

On September 25 Musaddiq instructed the oil board to inform British experts that "since they have not agreed to serve with the National Iranian Oil Company their presence in Iran is redundant and there is no need for their staying in Khuzistan." Each British technician was to be told to leave Iran

[34]Ibid., pp. 252-57.

[35]For the text see U.S. State Dept. *Bulletin* 25, no. 640 (Oct. 1, 1951): 547-48.

[36]Ibid., pp. 448-50.

one week from the morning of September 27. "I must emphasize to the Oil Board," he concluded, "the necessity for punctilious execution of the above decision, and further insist that until the last moment, British technicians should benefit from traditional Persian hospitality."[37]

Fortuitous Legitimization of Nationalization?

In implementing the takeover of the AIOC, Iran faced two other moves by the British in addition to those discussed thus far. Both of these moves represented the British attempt to utilize international organizations to achieve British ends in the face of the Iranian policy of nationalization. One was the International Court of Justice. Shortly before Varastih presented the AIOC representative with the implementation regulations of the take-over operations, mentioned before, the British government instituted proceedings on May 26, 1951, in the Court against the government of Iran, which rejected the Court's jurisdiction on May 28. This application asked the Court to take jurisdiction in the merits of Britain's case against Iran in behalf of the AIOC. But after the breakdown of negotiations between Iran and the AIOC, mentioned before, the British government sought to stop Iran from proceeding with its take-over operations by means of seeking a Court injunction against Iran. The application for this was filed on June 22,[38] pending the final judgment of the Court on the merits of the case. The Court granted the British request for what is technically called "interim measures of protection" on July 5, 1951. It "ordered" Iran and Britain to take no action that might (1) prejudice the carrying out of a subsequent decision by the Court on the merits, (2) "aggravate or extend the dispute," (3) hinder the operations of the AIOC, which should continue under its management as constituted before May 1, 1951. It also ordered them to establish by agreement a Board of Supervision to insure that the AIOC's operations were carried out according to the order of the Court just stated.[39] The Court's dissenting opinion was delivered by the Egyptian and Polish judges, Winaiarski and Badawi Pasha, who found the Court's jurisdiciton in regard to the merits and such measures of protection interlinked and therefore did not see how the Court could indicate such measures without considering its competence "reasonably probable." "If there is no jurisdiction as to the merits, there can be no jurisdiction to indicate interim measures of protection." Measures of this kind

---

[37] Royal Inst. Int. Affairs, *Documents, 1951*, p. 519.

[38] International Court of Justice, *Order of July 5th, 1951*.

[39] Ibid.

in international law were exceptional; "they may easily be considered a scarcely tolerable interference in the affairs of a sovereign State."[40]

Iran rejected the Court's order principally on the same ground that it had stated as early as May 28, namely, the Court's lack of jurisdiction. Nor did Iran participate in the hearings before the Court leading to the order, largely for the same reason, but in the six short hours before the Court delivered its interim decision, Shaygan, a leading jurist of Iran and the regime's "brain," met with the president of the Court, his own former professor, presented the Iranian views on the matter, and made the most of the opportunity then and later to give the Iranian nationalization decision as much favorable publicity as possible.[41] The minister of foreign affairs expressed Iran's outrage before the Majlis at what he called "the Court's strange and peculiar decision," without precedent and totally "unjust and uncharitable."[42] On July 9 Iran advised the secretary-general of the United Nations that it rejected the Court's order and simultaneously withdrew its declaration accepting the Court's compulsory jurisdiction. Just as Britain resorted to the Court and accepted its order for the purpose of blocking Iran's take-over operations, Iran disputed the Court's jurisdiction, rejected its order, and used the opportunity to publicize its views in order to proceed uninterruptedly with its take-over action.

The second attempt of Britain to use an international organization was launched on September 28, 1951, when it wrote the president of the Security Council and the secretary-general to place on the agenda of the council "Complaint of failure by the Iranian Government to comply with provisional measures indicated by the International Court of Justice in the Anglo-Iranian Oil Company case." As just seen, the Court's order had been issued as early as July 5 and this was quite a tardy complaint if Iran's noncompliance were the real reason for the British complaint. Nor could it have really been an attempt by Britain to prevent the withdrawal of British personnel by October 4 according to Musaddiq's order of September 25, mentioned before, despite the fact that the British letter did give Iran's "expulsion" as the other reason for the complaint.

Not unlike other states, Britain aimed at using the world forum for publicizing its position, but as it turned out Iran used that forum to give its policy of nationalization international legitimacy with unusual skill and success. Before the Security Council could hear Iran on the British complaint on October 15, the deadline for the withdrawal of the British personnel had

[40]Ibid., pp. 96-98.

[41]See Shaygan's own statement to the Majlis in *Asnad-i Naft,* pp. 346-52.

[42]For the text see ibid., pp. 282-84.

expired, forcing Britain to revise its original complaint of October 12 which had to be revised and watered down once again on October 17.

The original draft resolution, which complained against Iran's noncompliance with the Court order and the threat to peace as the result of Iran's withdrawal order to the AIOC personnel, requested the council to call upon Iran to act according to the interim measures of protection of the Court in all respects. Sir Gladwyn Jebb told the Security Council during its first meeting on October 1, 1951, that resort to the council was the only recourse open to Britain at the time; complained about Iran's withdrawal order; condemned Iran's "flouting" of the Court's decision, and urged the council to promptly check the Iranian take-over action that would make, if not stopped, "the whole of the free world," including the "deluded people of Iran," much poorer and weaker.[43] Ardalan, the Iranian representative, told the council about Iran's rejection of both the Court's jurisdiction and its order; expressed surprise at the British complaint because of the British recognition of the principle of nationalization (the Harriman formula); declared if the council decided to examine the British complaint Iran was determined to appear before it "to show cause why the complaint should be rejected," and requested the council to adjourn for at least ten days so that the Iranian representatives could reach New York from Tehran.[44]

Musaddiq first appeared in person before the Security Council when it met on October 15th. In Tehran and abroad his trip was dramatically publicized. Here was his chance to tell the world what he had so often told the Fourteenth Majlis during the oil crisis of 1944, and the Sixteenth Majlis during the turbulent months of his chairmanship of the oil commission. Pleading ill-health or fatigue when suitable, he rose to the occasion with unusual skill praised by both his detractors and admirers and matched only by his trusted colleague Allahyar Salih, who did most of the talking in presenting the Iranian case in the limelight of the world forum.

The British changed their first draft resolution on October 12 and set it before the council meeting on the 15th, requesting the council to call for the "resumption of negotiations at the earliest practicable moment" between the parties. Although this draft also mentioned the Court's order as the basis of efforts by the parties to resolve their differences, it did not request the council to call upon Iran to act in accordance with the Court's order as had the previous draft resolution. Furthermore, this draft was further watered down by adding the alternative that the parties could also make arrangements consistent with the "Purposes and Principles of the United Nations Charter." Nevertheless, the British case had little chance of success. The attack upon

[43]U.N., Security Council, *OR*, 6th Year, 559th Meeting: Oct. 1, 1951, p. 11.

[44]Ibid., p. 26.

the British resolution was launched first by Musaddiq himself, who told the council that he had come to tell the answer of Iran to the "baseless complaint" of Britain to the council and "the whole world." Although rejecting the jurisdiction of the council at the very outset, he touched a note which appealed to the small states in the council. The United Nations, he said, "is the ultimate refuge of weak and oppressed nations, the last champion of their rights. I appear here today after a long journey and in failing health to express my country's respect for this illustrious institution." He then added:

It is gratifying to see that the European Powers have respected the legitimate aspirations of the peoples of India, Pakistan, Indonesia and others who had struggled for the right to enter the family of nations on terms of freedom and complete equality. It is encouraging to know that the United Nations has spared no pains to help to bring such aspirations to fruition. Iran demands just that right. It expects this exalted international tribunal and the great Powers to help it, too, to recover its economic independence, to achieve the social prosperity of its people, and thus to affirm its political independence.[45]

The theme of Iran's nationalization ultimately aiming at affirmation of its political independence was not merely an appeal for support from the Asian members of the council, it was a long-held conviction that Musaddiq often emphasized within and outside the Majlis. This conviction was that the political aspects of the oil nationalization were more significant than the economic ones. Salih as well as Musaddiq could not get away from this theme even when he tried to address himself to the legal side of the complaint before the council. International law and organization, stated Salih, in rejecting the council's jurisdiction, might be one day perfected to afford protection to the rights of small and large nations alike, but "this is still a vision of the future. International law is presently weak and deficient. The great and powerful still lord it over the world, and even in the international organizations of the family of nations. In this condition of affairs, the protection of the fundamental rights of the weak requires them to be most jealous of their independence and sovereign rights and to insist on the most scrupulous respect for them from others."[46]

In refuting the British claim that the dispute between Iran and Britain threatened international peace and security and hence was within the jurisdiction of the Security Council, Iran carefully avoided getting entangled in sterile legal argumentation at the expense of the opportunity to publicize internationally the British behavior in the past and during the nationalization crisis. Salih not only took much of the council's time to expound his view of

[45] Ibid., 560th Meeting: Oct. 15, 1951, pp. 3-4.

[46] Ibid., p. 26.

the history of Iran's international relations in general and the British oil operations in particular, but also attacked the British show of force and their resistance to Iranian proposals. Whatever danger to peace there might be, he told the council, lay in the British actions, which "by overt display of force" had sought to keep Iran from exercising sovereignty over its natural resources. The British government, he added, "made ominous gestures such as the dispatch of paratroops to nearby places and of vessels of war to the vicinity of our coastal waters. The irresponsible threats to land forces in Iran might have had the most disastrous consequences by lighting the flames of another world war. . . . Iran had stationed no gunboats in the Thames."[47]

The British representative contested that the right to nationalize was "absolute," went into great detail to show that Iran had benefited from the operations of the AIOC in Iran, and refuted Iranian charges of the company's interference in Iran's internal affairs. Furthermore, while he did not doubt the sincerity of Musaddiq in championing the national aspirations of the Iranian people, he warned Iran of the dire economic consequences of their course of action; appealed to Musaddiq "to face the practical facts of the situation"; and emphasized: "We must consider the whole broad question of the free world's increasing needs for raw materials and the inter-dependence, not the independence—of all free countries. I appeal with all the earnestness at my command to the Prime Minister of Iran to look beyond the narrow bounds of nationalism to the wider common interests of the world community."[48]

This British reference to "narrow bounds of nationalism" stung the Iranian representatives most, but we must first examine Sir Gladwyn Jebb's portrayal of the economic benefits of the AIOC to Iran. This is no place to repeat his detailed statistics, but the gist of his argument was captured in the statement that the AIOC "has for many years provided four-fifths of the foreign exchange which the Iranian Government needs for its essential imports. It was on the basis of the substantial revenues provided by the activities of the Company that the Iranian Government was able to launch its seven-year plan for economic reform, which at the time was generally acclaimed as a far-sighted measure of good government. It is a fact that the steadily increasing wealth which the Anglo-Iranian Oil Company has been able to contribute in Iran has been and is today the basis of that country's economic viability."[49] With regard to his remarks on nationalism, Salih responded vigorously: "I should not like to plead guilty to a charge of national selfishness, although I do not pretend that my people are more virtuous than any

[47]Ibid.

[48]Ibid., 561st Meeting: Oct. 16, 1951, p. 14.

[49]Ibid., pp. 9-10.

other in that regard. I may, perhaps, meet the point by observing that, in the condition in which my people find themselves, there would be some virtue in our acting on the view that charity begins at home."[50]

The British representative's cutting remark was hurled at Tsarapkin, the Soviet representative, who had objected to the inclusion of the British complaint on the agenda. Tsarapkin stated that the consideration of the complaint by the council constituted "intervention in Iran's domestic affairs and a flagrant violation of the sovereignty of the Iranian people." Later on he added, whatever "verbal smoke-screen, whatever verbal camouflage is used in these amendments and proposals, the gist of the matter remains the same: under one pretext or another and in a more or less stringent form, to force Iran to conduct negotiations."[51] Sir Gladwyn Jebb addressing the Soviet representative stated: "Of course one recognizes his motives in rushing so powerfully to the assistance of the neighbour on his right. I can only wonder what his attitude would be if, for instance, the free and independent Government of Romania repudiated the existing contractual obligations whereby the USSR exploits Romanian oil. We can only wonder what his attitude would be as regards domestic jurisdiction in that regrettable event."[52]

Noting the rough going of even his revised draft resolution of October 12, the British representative further "watered-down," to borrow his words, the resolution on October 17.[53] This resolution merely requested the Security Council to call upon the parties to resume negotiations without any mention of the interim decision of the Court. The long and tedious presentation of the United States representative in favor of the British resolution did not help the situation. Nor did the initial French support, but the subsequent French suggestion that the Security Council had better adjourn its debate on the draft resolution until the "International Court of Justice has ruled on its own competence in the matter" at least put a nice face on the matter for the British because even the watered-down resolution of October 17 did not have a chance to pass. So, after six meetings the Security Council, on October 19, 1951, postponed the discussion of the question, an action that in fact meant that no substantive decision was reached. As the representative of China pointed out, the jurisdiction of the Court and the council was not the same. This, however, was the best way to spare the British embarrassment.

Musaddiq and his colleagues at least felt that they had had "their day in court." Obviously his success in New York, at least at the time, helped to blunt the growing opposition to his policies in Tehran. Moreover, it remained

[50]Ibid., 563d Meeting: Oct. 17, 1951, pp. 20-21.

[51]Ibid., 561st Meeting: Oct. 16, 1951, pp. 21-22.

[52]Ibid., p. 23.

[53]Ibid., 565th Meeting: Oct. 19, 1951, p. 3.

to be seen whether logic and eloquence so skillfully displayed at the United Nations would be matched by statesmanlike realization of the limits as well as possibilities of Iranian determination to control its own oil industry "completely" in the face of formidable domestic and international obstacles.

X

Oil Nationalization and
Iranian Foreign Policy

WITH THE TAKEOVER of the Anglo-Iranian Oil Company (AIOC), Iran's policy of nationalization entered a new phase. This phase lasted from the departure of the British personnel in October, 1951, to the downfall of the government of Musaddiq in August 1953. The principal factors that distinguished this phase from the take-over phase, discussed in the preceding chapter, are two. First, during the first phase Iran's immediate goal was to *gain control* of the AIOC; in the second phase the primary objective was to *maintain* that control. In a physical sense Iran was now in possession of the AIOC installations, but many legal, technical, economic, administrative, financial, political, and diplomatic problems faced the government of Musaddiq. The array of questions was staggering. For example, what was the nature of Iran's willingness and capacity to pay compensation, what was the acceptable compensation for the British, and who was to determine the amount and method of payment of compensation? Could Iran refine, sell, and market the oil? What would the British do next, what kind of role would the United States play? How would the Soviets behave? Above all, how long could the government of Musaddiq continue in power without oil revenues and in the face of increasing domestic political opposition and Tudeh agitation? All these and similar questions had significant bearing on the ability of the government of Musaddiq to achieve its goal of maintaining the control of the oil industry now that it had gained physical control of the installations.

The second factor that distinguished the new phase of oil nationalization policy from the take-over phase was the impact of that policy on Iran's overall foreign policy. What was the effect of Musaddiq's nationalization on his general diplomatic relations with Britain, the United States, and the Soviet Union? To take Iran's policy toward the Soviet Union, for example, the cold war between Tehran and Moscow had characterized Soviet-Iranian relations during most of the 1946-50 period; how did the policy of nationalization affect those relations? The Tudeh party had played the double role of internal political force and external instrument of Soviet policy; how did it behave during the nationalization crisis in regard to foreign as well as domestic political issues confronting Iran? To cite another example, despite Iran's frustration with the United States financial aid in the 1946-50 period, Iran had continued its traditional wartime reliance on the United States, diplomatically, militarily, and economically; how did American-Iranian relations fare during the nationalization crisis, not only concerning the oil issue, but also in regard to other aspects of their relations?

Although these and similar questions will be borne in mind in the examination of the second phase of the Iranian oil nationalization policy in this chapter, we shall in particular be concerned with one fundamental question that undergirds all others. The evidence examined in the two preceding chapters suggested that nationalization of the oil industry was motivated primarily by *political* considerations. The important question in this chapter is whether this same perspective continued to dominate Iranian foreign policy until the fall of the government of Musaddiq.

Musaddiq Responds to the World Bank and the World Court

The initiative for the bank's involvement in the nationalization dispute was attributed to the government of Pakistan through the intermediary of its ambassador to the United States when Musaddiq was visiting Washington after his appearance before the United Nations in October, 1951. But the real initiative came from the bank and international finance, a fact that was known in Iran, and hence the cover of Pakistan as Iran's fellow-Muslim and neighboring country did more to intensify Iranian suspicion than to help the favorable start of discussions, as evidenced by the adverse statements of Shaygan and Hasibi to the Iranian newspaper *Kayhan* before the opening of negotiations.[1] Despite this unpromising start, the discussions between the bank officials and the British and American officials with the Iranian government led to the arrival of a bank mission in Iran in December 1951 and the submission of its views to Musaddiq in a letter dated December 28, 1951. In order to avoid subsequent "misunderstanding," the bank first defined the limits of its ability to help the operations of the oil industry. The bank did not expect to enter into the oil industry permanently or commercially and did not expect to provide for definite settlement of the problems involved. It would merely propose to make temporary arrangements in order to resume oil operations in Iran. The bank would, the letter continued, try its best to run the oil industry in the interest of all concerned; the industry would be run by a neutral board of management selected by the bank and responsible to it; the temporary services of the bank would not in any way prejudice the rights of

---

[1] See Mustafa Fatih, *Panjah Sal Naft-i Iran* (Tehran: Shirkat Sahami-i Chap, 1957/58), p. 587.

the parties concerned; the bank would make a bulk export contract for the sale of oil and the profits would be divided into three parts, one part for Iran, one for the foreign bulk buyer, and one to be held in reserve by the bank. Musaddiq's letter of January 3, 1952, first disputed the bank's suggestion that the views it had expressed were based on discussions with him in Washington because, he claimed, those oral discussions had revolved around general principles whereas the bank's letter entered into details that had not been previously discussed. He then picked various major points of the bank's letter for comments and queries. What did the bank mean by a "neutral board"? Did it mean individual persons from neutral countries? What did the bank mean by "full powers" that it would enjoy? Did these powers concern only technical operations or include economic ones as well? Most important of all, Musaddiq's reply emphasized at the end that the bank must not overlook the fact that its involvement in the Iranian oil industry "would be in behalf of the Iranian government."[2] These and similar questions and critical comments foreshadowed the eventual failure of the bank's subsequent discussions with Iran. In the course of these it became abundantly clear that the powers of the bank could not be defined to Iran's satisfaction, nor could the composition of personnel. Iran was determined to control the oil industry itself, and the return of the AIOC technicians was not welcome at this time. Even if British technicians were excluded the problems of price setting, profit sharing and, above all, management of the industry would prove insurmountable.[3]

Not long after the breakdown of negotiations with the bank the Iranian question came up before the International Court of Justice for public hearing. It may be recalled that the British had instituted proceedings as early as May 26, 1951, but the Court, on July 5, 1951, had ordered interim measures or protection as the result of a subsequent British request. This did not, however, remove the case from the Court, which was yet to deliver a final judgment. Detailed discussion of the legal position of the parties, the judgment of the Court, the concurring opinion of President McNair, and dissenting opinions of several judges are obviously beyond the scope of this study. The Court's own single volume of 890 pages, the *Anglo-Iranian Oil Company Case*, is rich in legal and relevant diplomatic materials. We shall here confine ourselves to the

---

[2]For the text of these notes see A. Danishpoor, *Nairangbazan-i Naft ya 'Allal-i Shikast-i Misyon-i Garner* (Tehran: Chapkhanihye Musavi, 1953/54), pp. 37-42. The author claims that throughout the bank mission's negotiations with Iranian officials, he was involved in the procedures, but his "first-hand" accounts must be taken with care. Some of the materials reproduced are quite useful, however.

[3]For a detailed and reliable discussion of these problems, see Ellwell-Sutton, pp. 277-78. For reasons for the mission's failure as seen by Musaddiq, see his report to the Majlis, in Fatih, pp. 590-91.

gist of the principal issue on the basis of which the Court found itself without jurisdiction in the case, and note Iran's primary concern in the case before the Court.

Public hearings before the Court were held in June 1952. Iran was represented by Husain Navab, as agent, and Musaddiq, who were assisted by Nasrollah Intizam, Henri Rolin, professor of international law at Brussels University and former president of the Belgian Senate, as advocate, and by Allahyar Salih, Shaygan, Baqa'i, Hasibi, 'Aliabadi, and Marcel Sluszny of the Brussels bar, as counsel. Great Britain was represented by Sir Eric Beckett, legal advisor of the Foreign Office and a group of assistants including Professor Waldock. H. A. P. Fisher, member of the British bar, and D. H. M. Johnson, assistant adviser of the Foreign Office, acted as counsel. Because the Court included on the bench President Lord McNair of British nationality, Iran, under the Court's statute, appointed Karim Sanjabi, professor and former dean of the law faculty of the University of Tehran, to sit as a judge ad hoc, and since the president of the court was British, he transferred the presidency for the case to the vice president under the rules of the Court.

The principal issue to which the Court addressed itself was its jurisdiction. Iran objected to the Court's jurisdiction on the ground of its declaration of October 2, 1930. Iran recognized the jurisdiction of the Permanent Court of International Justice, and hence the present Court, by virtue of this declaration, which was ratified on September 19, 1932. It recognized that jurisdiction in "all disputes arising after ratification with regard to situations or facts relating directly or indirectly to the application of treaties accepted by Iran and subsequent to the ratification." Iran contended that this declaration covered only treaties and conventions concluded subsequent to its ratification. Great Britain, on the other hand, contended that the word "subsequent" referred to "situations or facts" and not to "treaties or conventions." In other words, the Court had jurisdiction in disputes arising directly or indirectly from the "application of treaties or conventions accepted by Iran *at any time.*" If the British interpretation of the Iranian declaration were upheld, then it would mean, according to the British argument, that the Court had jurisdiction in the present dispute arising out of the application of treaties or conventions between Iran and Great Britain concluded at any time. The Iranian law of nationalization, the British reasoned, violated Iran's obligations toward Great Britain resulting from (1) Iran's treaties of 1857 and 1903 in conjunction with Iran's treaties with third states, (2) the exchange of notes between Iran and Great Britain in 1928, and (3) the "Treaty stipulation" arising out of the settlement of the dispute between Iran and Britain in 1933. If, on the other hand, the British interpretation of the Iranian declaration were not upheld by the Court, namely, if the Court held that the declaration referred to disputes arising out of the application of treaties and conventions after the ratification of the declaration in 1932 then, the British would argue, the Court still had jurisdiction because Britain was entitled to rely upon the Iranian treaty with Denmark (1934), and the "Treaty stipulation" of 1933 mentioned above.

The Court rejected the British arguments for reliance on the 1857 and 1903 treaties and the "Treaty stipulation" of 1933. In regard to the first two treaties, while it admitted that Iran was bound by its obligations under these treaties as long as they were in force, Britain "is not entitled to rely upon them for the purpose of establishing the jurisdiction of the Court since they are excluded by the terms of the Declaration." In regard to the 1933 "Treaty stipulation" the Court rejected the British contention that the 1933 agreement between the Iranian government and the Anglo-Iranian Oil company had a "double character," (a concessionary contract between Iran and the company, on the one hand, and a treaty between the two governments, on the other). The Court declared that Britain was not a party to the 1933 agreement; there was no "privity of contract" between Iran and Britain despite the fact that the concessionary contract was negotiated through the good offices of the Council of the League of Nations, acting through its rapporteur.[4]

The crucial point on the basis of which the Court declared its lack of jurisdiction, therefore, concerned the intention of the Iranian Declaration. The Court upheld Iran's contention that its declaration applied to treaties and conventions accepted by Iran after the ratification of the declaration. The Court stated that if the declaration were considered from a purely grammatical point of view, both contentions of Iran and Britain might be regarded as compatible with the text, but the Court could not base itself on such a point. It upheld the Iranian contention because it was compatible with Iran's intention. Iran intended to exclude the earlier treaties from the Court's jurisdiction because at the time of signing the declaration it had unilaterally abolished capitulatory treaties and was uncertain about the legal effect of its unilateral denunciation.[5] In such circumstances, the Court reasoned, it was unlikely that Iran should have been willing, on its own initiative, to agree that disputes relating to such treaties might be submitted for adjudication by virtue of a general clause in its declaration. Furthermore, the Iranian intention to exclude earlier treaties was confirmed, the Court continued, by an Iranian law of June 14, 1931, by which the Majlis approved the declaration. This was passed some months after the declaration was signed and some months before it was ratified. It was stated in that law that one of the conditions of the

---

[4] International Court of Justice, *Anglo-Iranian Oil Co. Case (United Kingdom v. Iran)*, Judgment, July 22, 1952, pp. 109-12 (hereafter cited as ICJ, *Anglo-Iranian Oil Co. Case*).

[5] For a discussion of the abolition of capitulations in the context of Iranian foreign policy, see Ramazani, *Foreign Policy of Iran*, pp. 243-47.

Iranian government's acceptance of the compulsory jurisdiction of the Court was that this acceptance was in respect of all disputes arising out of the execution of treaties and conventions "which the Government will have accepted after the ratification of the Declaration."[6]

The Court declared itself without jurisdiction in the case on July 22, 1952, and simultaneously stated that its order of July 5, 1951, indicating interim measures of protection ceased to be operative. By a vote of 9 to 5 the Court's judgment favored Iran, including the separate but concurring opinion of Judge McNair of Great Britain.

Obviously the decision was hailed by Musaddiq in Iran, but this success, as the success scored in the Security Council before, was viewed mainly as a vindication of the Iranian bid for complete national independence. The fact that the issues raised before the Court, as contrasted with the Security Council, were legal and technical did not deter Musaddiq from perceiving the entire matter before the Court essentially as another stage in his struggle for political independence. The most eloquent evidence of this is found in his decision to appear before the Court in person and in his address during its first session on June 9, 1952. He not only repeated the charges of the Anglo-Iranian Oil Company's interference in Iran's internal affairs, which he had enumerated before the Security Council, but also tried to place the relationship of Iran and the company in the broader context of Iran's past experiences with imperial rivalries between Britain and Russia who, in 1907, divided his country into spheres of influence. He also noted the British attempt at exclusive domination of Iran by means of a treaty in 1919, which Iranian patriots opposed. Then Britain favored the establishment of a "despotic government" that insured British influence in. Iran for twenty years. What inspired the British politics during this period, he added, was evidently their determination to control Iranian oil exclusively. More important, in explaining his motive for appearing in person before the Court, he stressed not only Iran's "extreme respect" for international organizations, but also his desire to get the Court to understand, in addition to the legal reasons for the Court's lack of jurisdiction, "the moral and political impossibility" in which Iran found itself to allow the question of oil nationalization to be raised before the Court again.[7]

[6]ICJ, *Anglo-Iranian Oil Co. Case*, p. 106.

[7]For the text of Musaddiq's statement to the Court in French, see ibid., Pleadings, Oral Arguments, Documents, pp. 437-42.

Anglo-American Proposals and Musaddiq's Rupture
of Diplomatic Relations with Britain

There is little doubt that Iran's success at the Court lay at the heart of the Iranian initiative to seek direct negotiations with Britain in August 1952 for the first time since the breakdown of Anglo-Iranian discussions during the Harriman mission. But the deteriorating relations between the two countries, particularly since the announcement of the Iranian decision in regard to the withdrawal of the British personnel on September 5, 1951, proved to be a far more compelling reason. This decision, it may be recalled, had prompted the British government to break off negotiations altogether, to send four destroyers to join the ten warships in the Persian Gulf, and to lodge a complaint against Iran in the Security Council. These measures had then been followed by the British ban imposed on the export of sugar, iron, steel and other goods to Iran. These steps, in turn, invited reprisals by Iran. On September 17, 1951, Iran ordered that the British Bank of Iran and the Middle East be denied the privilege of buying and selling foreign currencies, which would henceforth be exclusively vested with the Bank Melli-i Iran. A day later Musaddiq ordered all government departments to withdraw their deposits with the British bank and transfer them to other banks. On January 9, 1952, the Iranian Ministry of Foreign Affairs presented a note to the British ambassador in Tehran, protesting strongly the "intensification of open interference of British officials" in Iran's internal affairs and threatening "more serious decisions" (*tasmimat-i jiddi-tari*) for putting a stop to this undesirable situation if the British authorities did not change their behavior.[8] On January 12, 1952, the Ministry of Foreign Affairs wrote the British embassy that all British consulates must be closed by January 21. And on February 5, 1952, all foreign cultural institutions, including the British Council, were ordered to close down.

Hence, by the time the Court's decision was announced, Iran not only was feeling increasingly the adverse effects of its loss of oil revenues (and the denial of financial aid by the United States) but also daily irritations of its unhappy diplomatic relations with Britain. Iran's initiative to resume discussions with Britain was, therefore, at the same time a sign of confidence in the propriety of its cause as the result of the Court's favorable decision and the consequence of its failing economic conditions and deteriorating diplomatic relations with Britain.

Musaddiq's letter of August 7, 1952, to the British government signaled the Iranian initiative for the resumption of negotiations. The letter declared Iran's readiness to start negotiations of the AIOC in order "to find a solution for the problem of the rightful claims of the Company within the provisions

[8]Fatih, p. 584.

of the law of May 1, 1951" (the nine-article law of nationalization), and, in case no agreement was reached through direct negotiations, the company was invited to submit its case to competent Iranian courts. The letter, however, began with the statement that nationalization was "the incontestible right of every nation"; complained of the company's measures, such as the seizure of the tanker *Rose Marie*, to debar the sale of Iranian oil abroad; and listed the financial damages and economic difficulties caused by the actions of both the company and the British government, such as the AIOC's nonpayment of its debts, the nonpayment of funds belonging to the Iranian government deposited in British banks, and the prevention of the sale of Iranian oil by "means of intimidations, threats and intrigues practiced by" the company with the aid of the British government.[9] According to a joint Anglo-American note to be discussed below, on August 14 the British chargé d'affaires at Tehran sought clarification of Musaddiq's note, and during this discussion the prime minister stated that if the British wished to submit the question of compensation to arbitration, he was prepared on his part to agree that the International Court of Justice should be asked by both parties to settle the question of compensation, though the Court could not be asked to adjudicate on "the question of the 1933 agreement or on the validity of the nationalization laws."[10] In a statement to the Majlis on September 16, Musaddiq stated that after getting no reply to his note of August 7, he had to ask for an explanation from the British representative by telephone. Finally, he continued, the United States ambassador and the British chargé paid him a visit during which they delivered a message signed by President Truman and Mr. Churchill.

The Anglo-American proposals, which this message included, were delivered to Iran on August 30, 1952. The very fact of these joint proposals signaled a degree of harmony between the United States and Britain with respect to the Iranian situation that had not existed before. Dean Acheson testified later in his book that as early as March or April 1951 "a distinct cleavage appeared between the British and American approach to the Iranian threat of nationalizing the oil industry." The United States had taken the view that the AIOC's predicament had been caused by "their own folly,"[11] to borrow his words, because they had not followed the example of Aramco, which granted to Saudi Arabia what it could no longer withhold. The United States feared the adverse effect of the Iranian nationalization on everyone's interest including, of course, those of the United States and the West as a whole because "it

[9]The text of the note is included in Musaddiq's report to the 17th Majlis on Sept. 16, 1952. See Iran, *Prime Minister's Reports* (Tehran: Bank Melli Iran Press, 1952), pp. 2-4.

[10]Royal Inst. Intl Affairs, *Documents, 1952.* p. 338.

[11]Acheson, p. 506.

upset relations with the oil-producing states and opened rare opportunities for Communist propaganda." This concern with communism in particular had prompted Acheson, as seen, to suggest to President Truman the Harriman mission to Iran at a time when the British foreign secretary, Morrison, wanted to wait longer, "thinking that Mosadeq was weakening," whereas Acheson was convinced that both Iran and Britain "were pressing their luck to the point of suicide in this game of Russian roulette." The Anglo-American divergency of approach to Iran must have continued into the early days of the Conservative government as well, if we judge from Acheson's criticism of the British policy toward Iran. He complained that Eden continued to take advice from the same sources that Acheson thought "had poisoned the judgment of the Labour Party—the bureaucracy of the Anglo-Iranian Oil Company , the Ministry of Fuel and Power, and the Treasury, where Sir Leslie Rowan played the part of St. Michael, the avenging angel. Rowan decreed that Mosadeq, leading the attack on British foreign investments, had to fail, to be crushed and punished."[12]

The gap between the American and British approach to Iran narrowed as the American hope for an early settlement dimmed, as the Iranian economy increasingly deteriorated, and as the threat of the Tudeh increased by leaps and bounds. But the reappointment of Musaddiq as prime minister after the crisis of July 1952 during the brief premiership of Qavam must have also convinced the two Western powers that they still had to deal with Musaddiq. The Truman-Churchill message declared that the United States and Britain were determined not to neglect the opportunity that Musaddiq's proposals appeared to present, and therefore made the following proposals:

1. The question of compensation for the nationalization of the "enterprise" of the AIOC in Iran should be submitted to the International Court of Justice.

2. Representatives should be appointed to represent the Iranian government and the AIOC.

3. If Iran agreed to these two points, it would be understood that (*a*) representatives of the AIOC would seek arrangements for the movement of oil already stored in Iran, (*b*) Britain would "relax restrictions on exports to Iran and on Iran's use of sterling," and (*c*) the United States would make an immediate grant of $10 million to Iran to assist in their budgetary problem.[13] In a press conference, Secretary Acheson stated on September 3, 1952, that the proposals "were fair and reasonable and had no strings attached"; the proposals "accept the nationalization of the oil industry in Iran as a fact"; the proposals did not propose that "the AIOC should be the sole purchaser of Iranian oil"; and the purpose of the $10 million grant would be to provide

[12]Ibid., p. 511.

[13]U.S. State Dept. *Bulletin* 17, no. 689 (Sept. 8, 1952): 360.

Iran with funds for a short term to "assist that nation financially until flow of Iranian oil to world markets could be resumed."[14]

Musaddiq replied to the Anglo-American proposals on September 24, 1952, and made a counterproposal to be valid for ten days from the date of the delivery of the proposals, none of whose provisions could be invoked separately. The reply first criticized the Anglo-American proposals because Iran feared that it was "desired to legalize the invalid 1933 agreement"; it then declared that Iran had always been prepared to sell its oil, but if the Anglo-American proposals were intended "that a purchaser monopoly be given to a specific company and interference in the management of the oil industry be renewed, this will never be approved by the Iranian nation." Iran proposed four points:

1. The amount of compensation to be paid for "The property" of the AIOC and the arrangement for its payment be based "on any law carried out by any country for nationalizing its industries in similar instances which may be agreed to" by the AIOC.

2. Examination of claims and counterclaims by methods considered "fair and just" by the International Court of Justice.

3. Examination and determination of damages to Iran caused by the AIOC's direct or indirect obstruction of the sale of Iranian oil and by the delay in payment of funds owed by the company.

4. Payment of forty-nine million pounds in advance due to Iran, provided that Iran would pay back the AIOC in oil if the International Court of Justice did not consider Iran entitled to part or all of this amount.[15]

Secretary Acheson and Eden both sent almost identical replies to Musaddiq on October 5, 1952. They were both disappointed to learn that the Anglo-American proposals had been unacceptable to Iran; stated that the proposals clearly "recognized the fact of nationalization and did not seek to revive the 1933 concession or any concession"; and disclaimed any condition or suggestion of a foreign management or any intention to propose any monopoly of the purchase of the Iranian oil.[16]

Musaddiq replied to Acheson and Eden in separate letters on October 7, 1952. The temper and tone of both letters reflected Iran's increasing impatience with Britain. Even the United States was not spared expressions of both annoyance and warning. Musaddiq wrote that Acheson's remarks that the president was "disappointed" to learn that the Anglo-American proposals were unacceptable to Iran might possibly have been the result of the president's failure to remember that nineteen months had elapsed from the date of the

[14]Ibid., no. 690 (Sept. 15, 1952): 405-6.

[15]Ibid., no. 693 (Oct. 6, 1952): 532-35.

[16]Ibid., no. 694 (Oct. 13, 1952):569. For Eden's reply see Royal Inst. Intl. Affairs, *Documents, 1952*, p. 347.

Iranian nationalization while in the meantime nothing useful had been accomplished and the question of compensation had been "entirely left to correspondence and procrastination." He again complained of the British "economic blockade" of Iran; stressed Iran's "huge losses" as the result of procrastination; and warned against "any sinister consequences and unfortunate development which may result from the maintenance of this policy." Musaddiq's reply to Eden showed greater irritability and contained a new invitation to the AIOC for negotiations and a warning to Britain. In order that "the dispute may be definitely and clearly disposed of as soon as possible "representatives of the AIOC were invited to leave for Tehran within a week from October 7. Before their departure, however, he demanded the AIOC should put at Iran's disposal £20 million out of the £49 million that in his letter of September 24 he had claimed were due to Iran. At the end he particularly called Eden's attention to the point that Iran had always indicated "the serious consequences of procrastination and delay" and once again reminded Eden of "the impossibility of the continuation of this state of affairs and warned that any eventuality arising from pursuit of this policy is not the responsibility of the Iranian government."[17]

No reply was made by the United States, whose attitude toward Iran before the downfall of the Musaddiq government will be treated later in this chapter, but Britain replied to Musaddiq for the last time before Iran broke diplomatic relations. Britain's response of October 14, 1952, addressed itself in detail to the points raised in Musaddiq's letters of September 24 and October 7, attempting to show why this counterproposal was "unreasonable and unacceptable." The real points of difference between the two countries emerged more clearly in this correspondence. The position of the two countries on the questions of British recognition of the principle of nationalization and the proper forum for the settlement of claims and counterclaims and compensation seemed to have grown closer, but the problems of claims and counterclaims and compensation as such were still serious obstacles. Britain accepted the principle of nationalization but in return claimed just compensation. Since Iran had never disclaimed compensation there was no problem in principle, but the really tough question in this, as in many other nationalization cases, was what constituted just compensation. Although Britain agreed that the question of compensation should be referred to the International Court of Justice, it claimed compensation for the "unilateral termination" of the 1933 agreement as well as the AIOC's property. In presenting claims on behalf of the company to the International Court of Justice the British government would ask the Court, stated the British note, "not for the mere loss of the Company's installations in Persia, but for the unilateral termination of the

[17] U.S. State Dept. *Bulletin* 27, no. 695 (Oct. 20, 1952):624-25.

1933 Concession Agreement contrary to the explicit undertaking in the Agreement that it would not be so terminated." Yet the note said that neither the British government nor the company sought to revive the 1933 agreement in any other respect.[18]

Musaddiq did not reply to the latest British note, but his views on it were broadcast October 16, 1952. He singled out for comments the British position on the question of compensation.

None of the countries, who have nationalized their industries, have given indemnification for the annulment of private agreements even though these agreements have been in full force and effect. But the British Government intends to demand compensation for the annulment of the agreement from the suffering Iranian nation. That is, not only the British Government claim that the Iranian Government are to take into account the price of the former company's properties in Iran but they also claim indemnification for *dommages et intérêts*. Whereas not only the 1933 Agreement is annulled and lacks any legal effect but even if it were in force now that the nationalization of the oil industry is realized that Agreement is null and void having no legal bearing.

He then drew attention to his interpretation of the origins of the 1933 agreement, calling it "the offspring of Riza Khan's coup d'etat."[19]

Musaddiq broke off Iran's diplomatic relations with Britain on October 22, 1952. Why? Without specifically attempting to give reasons for Iran's decision, the notification of the Ministry of Foreign Affairs included three points: (1) Had the British government paid proper attention to the aims of Iran, which had been seeking, and was still seeking, to secure its rights, the relations between the two countries "would have never reached such a stage." (2) Britain not only refrained from helping to solve the dispute in nationalization, "which is vital for our nation," but also prevented an agreement by "unlawfully supporting" the AIOC. And (3) some of the British official representatives created difficulties aimed at disturbing Iran's "order and security" through "intrigues and improper interference."[20]

Musaddiq's announcement of his intention to break off diplomatic relations with Britain could give rise to any number of interpretations about the reasons for his decision. At one point he clearly pointed out that Iran's "interest required termination of increasing intrigues and pretexts by means of rupture of [diplomatic] relations." At another point he left the impression that such a rupture would put a stop to "fruitless correspondence" (*mukatibat-i bihasil*) that aimed at preventing Iran from pursuing alternative and useful

[18] Royal Inst. Intl Affairs, *Documents, 1952*, pp. 350-51.

[19] *Prime Minister's Reports*, pp. 34-35.

[20] Royal Inst. Intl. Affairs, *Documents 1952*, pp. 351-52.

courses of economic action. Such specific examples could be multiplied, but the overall thrust of his remarks and the diplomatic correspondence preceding the decision seem to indicate that in his view Iran had compromised as far as possible and had reached a point that further correspondence could not bring about any settlement.[21] He had always believed that the British government was bent on destroying his government, a belief not completely unjustified, as evidenced by Acheson's accounts quoted previously. Musaddiq stated this belief after his return from the United States in 1951. In the course of reporting to the Majlis, he declared, "I must clearly state here that the British policy has from the very beginning aimed at undermining the Iranian people and government by playing with time."[22] He had, as seen, taken the initiative on August 7, 1952, to approach the British government for the resumption of negotiations with the AIOC. The Anglo-American proposals, which were partly in response to his initiative, proved disappointing to him as he had tried without avail to get the British and American representatives to take them back for modification before they were made public. All the difficulties in the way of reaching agreement with Britain seemed to him confirmation of his earlier belief in the British determination to destroy his government by prolonged diplomatic correspondence and "procrastination" as well as by "economic blockade and pressures and political intrigues and interference."

But Musaddiq's determination to stay in power and his perception of a British threat to his regime, important as they are, are not sufficient to explain his breaking diplomatic relations with Britain. Fuller comprehension requires examination of the influence of other factors as well. The remaining sections of this chapter will examine these other factors, but it is clear so far that Musaddiq's long-standing and intense dislike of the British primarily lay at the heart of his decision.

Musaddiq, the Tudeh Party, and the Soviet Union

Oil nationalization policy primarily concerned Iran's relations with Britain and to a lesser extent with the United States. The rupture of diplomatic relations with Britain for all practical purposes ended relations with that country until after the downfall of the Musaddiq regime, but concern with the United States attitude toward his government continued, as will be seen. This dominant concern with these two Western powers was paralleled throughout the nationalization crisis by problems posed by the attitudes of the Soviet Union and the Tudeh party toward Musaddiq's policy of nationalization. For

[21]Fatih, pp. 629-37.

[22]For the text see ibid., p. 572.

purposes of clarity I have so far reserved these problems for separate discussion here.

Musaddiq favored the doctrine of negative equilibrium at least as early as 1944 when he first advocated it in connection with his leading opposition to the Soviet demand for an oil concession. In the course of his speeches in the Fourteenth Majlis against the grant of oil concessions to foreign powers, he demanded the creation of a special ministry for the exploitation of Iranian oil by the Iranians themselves. Musaddiq proposed his bill against negotiating or granting foreign aid concessions, which was enacted into the law of December 2, 1944, amid the open and vociferous Tudeh support of the Soviet demand for concession. It may also be recalled that *Rahbar*, the organ of the Tudeh party, attacked Musaddiq's bill, charging that Musaddiq and his "partisans" had only demonstrated that the ruling elite in Iran was incapable of making its own decisions and had done nothing, *Rahbar* continued, about "real problem."[23] Since Musaddiq was not a deputy in the Fifteenth Majlis his direct influence on the law of 1947, which annulled the Qavam-Sadchikov oil agreement, cannot be ascertained, but his influence on the National Front group, who were staunch supporters of that law, is universally admitted.

This basically suspicious attitude of Musaddiq toward the Tudeh and the Soviet Union was seldom, if ever, called into question before his assumption of power as prime minister. It paralleled his anti-British attitude, and both of these attitudes were deeply grounded in his fundamental belief that past governments in Iran had always been the instruments of one foreign power or another primarily the instrument of British or Russian policies until the Bolshevik Revolution and particularly of the British ever since the coup d'etat of Riza Khan in 1921.[24] The reasons for doubts about his opposition to the Soviet and Communist bid for power in Iran after his appointment as prime minister were manifold. The fact that nationalization of the oil industry was actually directed only against the British interest (because the Soviets did not operate oil concessions) despite the general and nondiscriminatory nature of the law that nationalized the oil industry "throughout" Iran was one contributing factor. The undeniable British propaganda was another.[25] Still a

---

[23] See chapter 4 of this study.

[24] My research does not confirm Musaddiq's thesis. See Ramazani, *Foreign Policy of Iran*, pp. 171-330. Conversely, Riza Shah was so successful in gaining an unprecedented degree of freedom of action in world politics that I have characterized him as "the architect of Iran's independence."

[25] For example, as early as April 16, 1951, the Iranian ambassador was impelled to issue a statement in London to explain the nature of the Iranian act of nationalization. He said that to ascribe "to Communist intrigue and agitation the nationalist movement

third factor was Musaddiq's expedient utilization of the Tudeh support for both foreign and domestic political purposes.

Yet the evidence does not support the notion that Musaddiq's use of the Tudeh party or his policy toward the Soviet Union was actually anything more than correct. Tolerance of the Tudeh party and friendly gestures toward the USSR for tactical purposes were significantly related to his relations with Britain and the United States. So long as the United States seemed to diverge from Britain in its approach to Iran, the use of the Tudeh party was underplayed; but as the gap between the two Western powers seemed to narrow and his domestic problems multiplied, his reliance on the Tudeh increased. Insofar as his relations with the Soviet Union were concerned, he continued to deal with it cautiously, always mindful of the dangers of twisting the tail of the British lion while in the hug of the Russian bear. His essentially nationalistic outlook made all foreign powers suspect, including the United States. Before we proceed to examine Musaddiq's Soviet-Communist dilemma, let us examine briefly the Soviet-Tudeh perceptions of the Musaddiq regime.

From the time Qavam dropped the Tudeh members of his cabinet in 1946, and particularly from the moment the Majlis rejected his oil agreement with the Soviet Union in 1947, until the nationalization of the oil industry in 1951, a cold war existed between Moscow and Tehran, except for a very brief period during the premiership of Razmara, before he fell to an assassin's bullet. The enactment of the nationalization laws and the unexpected premiership of Musaddiq marked a dramatic change in the 1946-51 pattern of Soviet hostility toward the Iranian government. In fact, until Musaddiq's acceptance of the Harriman mission during the summer of 1951, the Tudeh party as well as the Soviet Union showed outward sympathy toward his government, but from that time until the downfall of his regime, the Tudeh adopted an increasingly hostile attitude toward Musaddiq while the Soviet Union continued its outwardly friendly posture. A fundamental factor underlying the break of the Tudeh with the National Front was the Communist intolerance of Musaddiq's willingness to continue to negotiate with the British until the rupture of diplomatic relations with London, his hopeful attitude toward the United States, and the continued presence of American economic and military advisers in Iran. These aspects of the Musaddiq policy toward the United States were not only severely attacked by the Tudeh but were also criticized by some of the nationalists, who considered those aspects evidence of Musaddiqist deviation from the tenets of the doctrine of negative equilibrium. This doctrine, they argued, was the same as "neutralism" (*bitarafi*) in the

in Persia is blinking at hard facts and trying to find scapegoats for a purely nationalistic sequence of social evolution." For the text see Royal Inst. Intl. Affairs, *Documents, 1952,* pp. 478-79.

cold war, and Musaddiq's flirtation with the United States not only was contrary to its principles but also was the main reason for the failure of his foreign policy; they hence advocated "absolute neutralism" (*bitarafi-i muttlaq*).[26]

Just as Musaddiq found it expedient at times to try to use the Tudeh and the Soviet Union for achieving political independence from the British through control of the oil industry, the Iranian Communists and Moscow tried to exploit the opportunity provided by the nationalization crisis toward several ends simultaneously. These ends were: (1) elimination of the British oil interest in the south and British influence in Iran and the Persian Gulf area; (2) projection of the Iranian nationalist uprising as a basically anti-imperialist movement spreading throughout the Middle East; and (3) substitution of the nationalist regime by a Communist one when the opportunity was ripe.

Major illustrations supporting the propositions of the foregoing analysis must start with the example of the Harriman mission, which, as mentioned before, marked the break between the Tudeh and the National Front. Before the Harriman mission, the Tudeh advocated "strong and unhesitating action" (*'amali shadid va bidon-i tazalzol*) by the Musaddiq government against the "usurping company" (*compani-i ghasib*).[27] But the tone and temper of Tudeh criticism changed dramatically with the Harriman mission. Musaddiq was then urged to adopt a stronger and less hesitant course of action against the AIOC, and the Tudeh condemned the "interference" of President Truman and Ambassador Grady in oil affairs. In a frontal attack upon Musaddiq *Bisoy-i Ayandih*, the Tudeh organ, demanded, before the mission's arrival in Tehran, that he adopt a stronger policy toward the United States so that "American imperialism would be no longer encouraged to interfere in the country's internal affairs. The Government of Dr. Musaddiq must know that any kind of acquiescence in Truman's impositions, such as his proposal for mediation, will prove one hundred per cent harmful to the Iranian people; and therefore it is necessary to declare clearly right now that his government will not accept such mediation."[28] A few days later the Tudeh demanded categorically that "Harriman must not come to Iran. We condemn any kind of interference by American imperialists in Iran's internal affairs with all severity."[29] After the arrival of the Harriman mission, Tudeh belligerency escalated to the point of outright condemnation of Musaddiq and his government. In an editorial

---

[26] See for example, Rahim Gudarzi-i-Tabrizi, *Lozum-i Hifz-i Bitarafi* (Tehran: Chap-khanih-ye Musavi, 1955/56), p. 48. For a more radical and leftist view, see Doktor Mehdi Bahar, *Miras-khar-i Ist'amar* (Tehran: n.p., 1966/67), pp. 602-29.

[27] *Bisoy-i Ayandih*, Khordad 21, 1330.

[28] Ibid., Tir 12, 1330.

[29] Ibid., Tir 20, 21, 1330.

Bisoy-i Ayandih wrote in bold letters that the "government of Dr. Musaddiq has retreated before the pressures of the British and American imperialists; has accepted various proposals made by Acheson, Truman, and Harriman; and has openly committed treason against the Iranian nation by neglecting to implement the take-over, by submitting to imposed negotiations in Tehran, and by breaching the rights of the Iranian nation."[30]

The Soviet attitude paralleled the Tudeh attack upon the Harriman mission. Ever since the beginning of nationalization, the Soviet press advanced several major themes, most often emphasizing "the Anglo-American struggle for oil in the Near East."[31] The Harriman mission gave the Soviets favorable opportunity to claim vindication of their interpretation. But it also brought out vividly the way Moscow perceived the broader significance of the Iranian nationalist movement. The Soviets viewed the nationalization movement as part of a broader "obscure and hidden struggle" between the United States and Britain around scores of raw materials and export markets. In this atmosphere of "increasingly acute contradictions" the Iranian nationalization "has acted like a can of gasoline poured on a bonfire." At the beginning of the crisis the American oil monopolies, the Rockefeller Company in particular, tried actively to seize Iran's oil from the British and made secret proposals to the Iranian government. But the mass movement in Iran against the British oil monopoly is acquiring ever-growing dimensions and is turning into a movement against imperialism as a whole."

Against such a backdrop the first Soviet reaction to the Harriman mission was revealed on July 26, 1951, when he was called "Wall Street's emissary" whose trip to London in connection with the ongoing negotiations "was met with great mistrust. . . . It is well-known in London that when the United States intervenes between two parties, it unfailingly has in mind the interest of a third party itself! . . . Enough evidence already exists to show that Harriman is exerting the most unceremonious pressure on the Iranian government and is trying to strengthen the position and influence of American monopolies in Iran."[32] This theme was repeated by the Soviet press during the Harriman mission, and finally *Pravda* of October 22, 1951, charged that the main purpose of American mediation was "to ensure the American oil monopolies a share in the Iranian oil at any rate." It then cited *U.S. News and World Report* that "Harriman's real task was to report to Washington as to the scale and form of American power needed to fill the 'vacuum,' formed by the

[30] Ibid., Mordad 17, 1330.

[31] *CDSP* 3, no. 24 (July 28, 1951): 20, no. 25 (Aug. 4, 1951): 17, and no. 26 (Aug. 11, 1951): 15.

[32] Ibid., no. 30 (Sept. 8, 1951):19. For similar themes see ibid., no. 36 (Oct. 20, 1951):19-20.

decline of Britain's military and political power. In any case Britain will no longer play the leading role in the Near East, but she can become a junior partner of the United States."[33]

Direct Soviet attack on the Musaddiq government was occasioned by the extension of American military aid to Iran. Musaddiq's acceptance of this aid on April 24, 1952, invited the Soviet protest of May 21, 1952; the Soviet note stated that through the exchange of notes on military aid with the United States, the government of Iran "undertook definite commitments of a military and political nature"; that exchange resulted in the resumption of the work of the American military mission that had come to an end in January 1952; that the agreement of May 23, 1950, between Iran and the United States was thus renewed; and, as the result, both American military aid to, and the mission in, Iran were continued. Thus, the note continued, "the Iranian Government places the Iranian army under the control of the United States Government. Thereby the Iranian army loses its character as the national army of an independent, sovereign state." The Soviet Union then called to Iran's attention that by its acceptance of the United States military aid, "the Iranian government is in fact setting out on the path of helping the United States Government to carry out its aggressive plans directed against the Soviet Union" and charged that Iran's action was "incompatible with the principles of good neighbourly relations, the maintenance and consolidation of which is the duty of the parties who signed the Soviet-Iranian Agreement of February 26, 1921."[34]

These developments in Tudeh and Soviet attitudes toward the government of Musaddiq reveal the nature of his differences with them on foreign policy questions. Even more direct evidence of his basic opposition to the Tudeh and the Soviet Union was furnished by the course of his actions toward them both. Generally the outlawed Tudeh party enjoyed much freedom of action in protesting Musaddiq's foreign policy or in attacking Britain and the United States, but the Tudeh was also subjected repeatedly to severe action by the police. On June 29, 1951, for example, the Tudeh staged a demonstration against the United States and Britain; they repeated this in July of the same year at the time of Harriman's arrival. Musaddiq declared martial law and between one hundred and fifty and two hundred Tudeh demonstrators were arrested and held.[35] Between September 30 and October 16 a series of incidents led to severe police measures against Soviet "espionage," the Tudeh plot

[33]Ibid., no. 40 (Nov. 17, 1951):9-10.

[34]For the text of the Soviet note, see Royal Inst. Intl. Affairs, *Documents, 1952*, pp. 334-35. For Soviet Press reports on it see *CDSP* 4, no. 21 (July 5, 1952):14-15.

[35]See *New York Times,* July 7, 15, 17, 1951.

against the life of police officials, and the Tudeh propaganda activities. The London *Times* of October 15, 1951, reported that the chief of police called newspaper correspondents to inform them of recent discovery of documents that, he said, "proved that the Persian Communist Party is backed and financed by a foreign Government." On November 1, 1951, the police reportedly captured Tudeh documents showing that the Soviet Union would have intervened in Iran militarily had Britain landed troops in Abadan. The police charged additionally that the Tudeh was involved in a plot with the Soviet Union to take over northern Iran if Britain were to capture Abadan.[36] When the occasion offered itself Musaddiq also revealed his basically negative attitude toward the Soviet Union in action as well.

Musaddiq decided against the renewal of the Soviet fisheries concession of October 1, 1927. This concession in connection with Iran's policy toward the Soviet Union during the rule of Riza Shah has been discussed elsewhere, and it need not be repeated here.[37] The factors underlying the decision to allow the concession to expire twenty-five years after it had gone into effect, namely, on January 31, 1953, were manifold, but the major considerations in the Iranian perspective are not difficult to detect. First, the Soviet fisheries concession was the only remnant of the detested czarist era because it had been first granted to Russia by Nasir ed-Din Shah in 1876 and renewed thereafter. Second, it was a remnant of Riza Shah's rule, which, in Musaddiq's view, represented a period of Iran's modern history when its government had no freedom of action in foreign affairs. The fisheries concessions was the only czarist concession that survived the Soviet denunciation of former Russian concessions in Iran. Iran undertook by article 14 of the Soviet-Iranian treaty of 1921, which denounced all czarist concessions, to reissue the Caspian Sea fisheries concession to the Soviets. Third, the Soviets acquired, under the inadequate terms of the concession, not only monopoly of the sales of the fishing industry, but also most of the profits. Fourth, the Musaddiq government had always advocated the principle of negative equilibrium, which required adopting an even-handed policy toward the Russians and the British. Oil nationalization policy, in effect, adversely affected only the British interest in the south, and any extension of the Soviet fisheries concession in the north would have made a mockery of Musaddiq's claim to "negative equilibrium." Finally, it would appear from various sources that Musaddiq discussed with Sadchikov the future of the fisheries concession in January 1953 in anticipation of its expiry on January 31 and found the Russian proposals unacceptable. According to both *Pravda* and *Izvestia* "the Soviet government proposed that the work of the company be prolonged for a further

---

[36] See ibid., Nov. 1, 4, 5, 1951.

[37] See Ramazani, *Foreign Policy of Iran*, pp. 225-28.

period,"[38] but the details of the Soviet proposals were not made known in Soviet sources. It is generally clear, however, that the prolongation of the existing arrangements would have meant continuing Soviet monopoly for at least another ten years. It is also clear that the Soviet proposals were viewed in Tehran as politically motivated and contrary to the interests of Iran.[39]

Soviet reaction to Musaddiq's decision was shrewd. The Iranian decision, coming at the peak of Musaddiq's difficulties with Western powers, provided Moscow with an opportunity to show how calmly and understandingly it reacted to this adverse Iranian decision and to emphasize to the Iranian government that the Soviet Union expected Iran to comply with its obligations under the fisheries agreement in regard to other foreign states and their nationals. The Soviet note of February 2, 1953, to Musaddiq stated that in not renewing the fisheries concession, the Iranian government had "exercised its legal right" in accordance with the fisheries agreement that had been concluded "on the basis of complete equality of the parties and the State sovereignty of Iran and from the national interest of the Iranian people." The Soviet note also "deemed it necessary to mention the great importance of fulfilment by the Iranian Government" of the article of the agreement which provided that the Iranian government undertook in the event of nonrenewal of the concession "not to grant a concession on these fisheries for the next 25 years to third States and their subjects. It undertakes to exploit them solely through the appropriate organs of the Persian Government and not to invite for its part specialists other than Persian subjects for the exploitation of these fisheries."[40]

We have so far confined the examination of the Musaddiq-Tudeh-Soviet interactions to foreign policy questions, but domestic issues are also important. Obviously, the Tudeh-Musaddiq interactions on domestic political questions are more important in a study of Iranian domestic politics as such, and since these interactions have already been treated by others in discussions of both Iranian nationalism and communism, they need not be repeated here.[41] We shall instead be concerned primarily with the Soviet attitude toward major domestic political issues of the Musaddiq era that have not received attention so far.

The advent of Musaddiq to power occurred in the wake of the 1946-50 cold war between the various Iranian governments and Moscow. To Moscow, all these governments during that period, ranging from Qavam to Mansur and

[38] *CDSP* 5, no. 5 (Mar. 14, 1953):19-20.

[39] See *Times* (London), Jan. 9, 21, 28, 30 and Feb. 2, 3, 4.

[40] For the text see Royal Inst. Intl. Affairs, *Documents, 1953,* pp. 348-49.

[41] See Richard W. Cottam, *Nationalism in Iran* (Pittsburgh: University of Pittsburgh Press, 1964) and Zabih, *The Communist Movement in Iran.*

and even Razmara, were made of the same cloth, but the nationalist government of Musaddiq represented a new breed. Moscow hoped that the nationalist movement led by these men could be made to serve two ends: the transformation of an anti-British crusade into an antiimperialist movement in Iran and ultimately the rest of the Middle East and, in time, its turning against the monarchy and thus paving the way for the creation of a people's democracy in Iran. Given this perspective, it is no surprise that on only two occasions did the Soviet press express any serious interest in Iran's internal affairs throughout the Musaddiq regime. Once during the July crisis of 1952 when he was briefly replaced by Qavam and the other during the August 1953 crisis, which led to the downfall of the Musaddiq regime. Both crises were viewed by the Tudeh as well as Moscow as favorable instances of nationalist toleration to be exploited for Communist ends; and both crises were rooted in the domestic struggle between the shah and Musaddiq.

Both *Pravda* and *Izvestia* of July 25, 1952, three days after Musaddiq's return to power, cited the Communist publication *Dej*, published in place of *Bisoy-i Ayandih* in Iran, for its attack on the shah. The Tudeh declared, and the Soviets published approvingly, that "the Iranian Court must be absolutely forbidden to interfere in large and small affairs of the State."[42] The family of the shah, his brothers, sisters, and relatives, like ordinary people, must be subordinated to the same principle. *Trud*, August 7, 1952, claimed that American intrigue had brought Qavam to power, but indicated that the British had not expressed "enthusiasm concerning [his] appearance on the scene in the role of the Iranian Premier."[43] The fullest account of the Soviet attitude toward the July crisis, however, appeared in *Trud*'s August 17, 1952, issue, which went into the details of the role of Loy Henderson, United States ambassador to Iran, in regard to Qavam's "sudden" accession to power. The American ambassador had repeatedly recommended that Musaddiq be replaced by a person "capable of controlling the domestic situation," and he told the shah that Qavam enjoyed the reputation of a "strong man" in the United States and that his advent to power could create an atmosphere conducive to American financial assistance to Iran. For the implementation of the American "plan," the services of the head of the American military mission in Tehran were enlisted, but he "took a number of rash steps which exposed and compromised all the State Department political activity." The head of the mission (Zimmerman) was told, according to *Trud*, to prepare, with the aid of the Americans attached to the Iranian army and police, a number of emergency measures to support the political steps by Qavam.[44]

[42] *CDSP* 4, no. 30 (Sept. 6, 1952):13.

[43] Ibid., no. 31 (Sept. 13, 1952):23.

[44] Ibid., no. 33 (Sept. 27, 1952):19-20.

The Tudeh and Soviet attitudes toward the internal political situation of Iran during the Musaddiq era began to appear most vividly and aggressively with the weakening of the government in January 1953 as the result of the disintegration of Musaddiq's support. His demand for the extension of his powers was opposed not only by Mullah Kashani but also by his most ardent supporter of the oil-commission and take-over days—Husain Makki. Musaddiq did get his powers extended, but the weakening of the National Front, on the one hand, and the widening rift with the shah, on the other, whetted the Tudeh appetite for a new bid for power. In the wake of the late February 1953 crisis over the shah's proposed travel abroad, a bold editorial entitled "Invitation for the Formation of a United National Front against Imperialism," *Bisoy-i Ayandih* invited Musaddiq, his colleagues, and "all the democratic organizations, individuals and groups," on behalf of the "National Group for the Struggle against Exploitation" (*jam'yat-i milli mobarizih ba isti'mar*), to create a united front subscribing to the following: (1) Destruction of the present "imperialist plot," which is supported by the court, the punishment of all the "treacherous participants in the present and the July 1952 [30th of Tir] conspiracy, and termination of anti-nationalistic activities of the Court." (2) Rupture of oil negotiations with "the British and American imperialists, and eradication of their, and their stooges', interference in Iran's internal affairs." (3) Maintenance of "democratic freedoms throughout the country, and abolition of martial law," and (4) "expulsion of American spies and destruction of their espionage organizations throughout the country." At the end Musaddiq was personally reminded that he had been invited in an open letter to undertake these "obligations" during the July 1952 crisis, which would not have led to the present crisis if he had chosen to act differently.[45]

Two days later the Tudeh party attacked the supporters of the government for their slogan "Both the Shah and Musaddiq" (*ham Shah ham Musaddiq*) and for their support of "constitutional monarchy" (*saltanat-i mashrotih*), once again criticizing Musaddiq personally for having failed to follow the Tudeh demand for destroying the Court—"this nest of espionage and corruption" (*in lanih-ye jasousi va fisad*).[46] On March 3, 1953, the Tudeh attacked both Musaddiq and the shah even more abusively because of the government's police action against the Tudeh demonstrators and for cooperation between the two. On this day *Bisoy-i Ayandih* went so far as to declare boldly, "We are a nation awakened; we don't want the Shah; and down with this monarchy" (*Ma millat-i bidarim; ma Shah nimikhahim; barchidih bad in saltanat*).[47]

---

[45]*Bisoy-i Ayandih,* Feb. 29, 1953.

[46]Ibid., Mar. 2, 1953.

[47]Ibid., Mar. 3, 1953.

The Soviet Union watched the internal crisis in Iran closely between January and August 1953, always seeing the American hand in the events but looking with great favor upon the Tudeh-sponsored demonstrations and disturbances as manifestations of "the national liberation movement in Iran." In January 1953 the situation in Iran was viewed in a broader perspective of "the national struggle in the Near and Middle East." As a backdrop to this portrayal the nationalization of the oil industry in Iran was viewed as a watershed insofar as it was an attack upon the British who controlled what little industry existed in Iran, as in Egypt and Iraq; Musaddiq's reform measures favoring the peasants were viewed as insignificant insofar as four-fifths of peasant income would still go to the landowners. Nevertheless, "reactionary circles in the Middle East were trying to suppress the liberation movement of peoples. This was particularly true in Iran—where the antiimperialist liberation movement has made the most headway in recent years." The liberation movement in Iran was supported by the workers and peasants, but "artisans and craftsmen, small and middle merchants and entrepreneurs are also participating in the movement. The Iranian working class is marching in the vanguard of the Iranian people's liberation struggle. The working class has formed a revolutionary bloc with the petty bourgeoisie to liberate the country from the imperialist yoke." As viewed from Moscow, the Iranian liberation movement, like similar movements in the Middle East, relied "on the sympathy and constant support of the camp of peace and democracy, headed by the Soviet Union, which invariably stands as a consistent champion of the interests of peoples in colonial and independent countries."[48]

As the events leading to the crisis of August 1953 and the downfall of the Musaddiq regime were unfolding, the Soviet Union watched the scene with even greater interest. It noted frequent meetings of the American ambassador, Loy Henderson, right up to the time of his departure, with Iranian political and military leaders known for their anti-Musaddiq attitude, including particularly Mullah Kashani, Mozaffar Baqa'i, Ha'erizadih, Qanatabadi, and also Generals Baharmast and Hidayat. In his meeting with them, *Pravda* of August 9, 1953, reported, Henderson gave them to understand that "more coordinated and vigorous actions by the group in opposition to Mossadegh would meet with no objections from the State Department." *Pravda* cited a representative of a Western country in Tehran to report that General McClure [*sic*], head of a group of American military advisers in Tehran, "has established secret contact with retired General Zahedi, Generals Shahbakhti, Ahmadi and others, who were given the tasks of persuading the Tehran garrison, through several trusted officers, to start fighting Mossadegh."[49]

[48]*CDSP* 5, no. 16 (May 30, 1953):4-6.

[49]Ibid., no. 32 (Sept. 19, 1953):20.

In retrospect, the Soviet Union rejoiced in the crisis of August 13-19, 1953, rather prematurely. *Pravda* recounted the attempted coup d'etat of August 15, when the shah dismissed Musaddiq through the delivery of a "letter" (*dastkhat*) and appointed Gen. Fazlollah Zahidi in his place, but Musaddiq defied the order and had the messenger arrested. Ironically, *Pravda*'s joyous article was published on August 19 when the tide was turned against Musaddiq as the result of the success of the monarchist army officers in a tank battle. Taking heart in the frustration of the shah's attempt of August 15 and his flight from the country, *Pravda* clearly attributed the plot to "reactionary United States forces through the Shah's court and certain statesmen who are agents for foreign powers." The real purpose of the plot, according to *Pravda*, was to replace the Musaddiq government with one that would join the Middle East defense scheme of the United States. At the end *Pravda* quoted the anti-American as well as antimonarchist slogans of the Tudeh Party, including "Yankees Go Home."[50]

Musaddiq and the United States: Bilateral Relations

Obviously the policy of nationalization primarily concerned Iran's relations with Britain, but from the very outset the United States was deeply concerned about the consequences of this policy. The principal considerations underpinning this concern were: (1) that the Anglo-Iranian controversy might lead to the stoppage of the flow of oil to Western European allies of the United States; (2) that the example of Iranian nationalization might have an adverse effect upon the United States oil interests in the Persian Gulf area; (3) that the British departure from the south would mean dimunition of Western influence in the area; and (4) that a breakdown of the Iranian economy in the face of turbulent domestic politics, particularly resulting from increasing Tudeh influence, might drive Iran to a "Communist coup d'etat." This last consideration was probably the single most important factor underlying the United States concern in Iran at the time. It was a particular reflection of the general American interest in the containment of the Soviet Union and Communism. While the statements of the president and the secretary of state never directly mentioned this American interest in Iran and preferred to go even so far as to claim that the United States had "no selfish interest," to borrow President Truman's words, in the oil dispute, George C. McGhee, assistant secretary for Near Eastern, South Asian and African affairs, spoke more than once about the real nature of the United States concern in Iran.

---

[50]Ibid., no. 34 (Oct. 3, 1953):4-5.

The "issues at stake," McGhee stated on July 13, 1951, "in Iran go far beyond the question of oil." Although he spoke about "law and justice" in connection with these stakes, the more specific stake was revealed in the course of the same statement. He declared: "We can be sure that the Kremlin is losing no opportunity to fish in the troubled oil of Iran, for Iran would be a great and strategic prize quite apart from oil. Control of Iran, an area approximately as large as the United States east of the Mississippi River, would put the Soviet Union astride the communication routes connecting the free nations of Asia and Europe."[51] In an address at the University of Virginia's Institute of Public Affairs on July 10, 1951, McGhee discussed the American policy toward the Middle East in terms of not only the area's indigenous problems but also the Soviet pressures particularly on Iran and other neighbors of the Soviet Union and declared that a solution to the oil nationalization problem was not only very important to the countries directly involved but "to the entire free world."[52]

During the oil nationalization crisis the United States policy toward Iran underwent a significant change. From the beginning of the oil dispute the United States tried to play the role of disinterested and impartial observer in the hope of bringing the contestants together. But the Anglo-American proposal revealed, as discussed before, a closing of the gap between the divergent approaches of the United States and Great Britain, which had been noted by Secretary Acheson at the outset of the crisis. There is little doubt that the American view of the rapidly deteriorating internal political and economic situations in Iran, following the Abadan shutdown and the cessation of Iranian oil exports, exerted a major influence on the closer American cooperation with Great Britain. The British ability to persuade the United States finally to close ranks with London against Musaddiq was, however, achieved by the Conservative government.

The harsh and unremitting Conservative criticism of the Labour government's policy toward Iran foreshadowed the policy of the new government, as evidenced by Churchill's attacks on the Labour government in the House of Commons. Prior to the evacuation of the British personnel, for example, the Conservative party leader urged the government: "Every effort should be made to rally this nucleus of British personnel to the high opportunity they have of rendering distinguished service to their country. They must stay, and we must never agree to their being withdrawn. If violence is offered to them, we must not hesitate to intervene, if necessary by force, and give all the necessary

[51] See U.S. State Dept. *Bulletin* 25, no. 630 (July 23, 1951): 130-31.

[52] Ibid., no. 631 (July 30, 1951):174-78.

protection to our fellow subjects."[53] In a devastating attack upon the government after the withdrawal of the British personnel, Churchill remarked that Britain had fled the field, and Dr. Musaddiq, he added sarcastically, could "hardly follow us here." Dr. Musaddiq, Churchill continued,

has won a triumph at a heavy cost to his own people. He has penetrated the minds and measured accurately the will power of the men he had to deal with in Whitehall. He knew that with all their cruisers, frigates, destroyers, tank-landing craft, troops and paratroops sent at such great expense, and all their bold, confident statements, they were only bluffing. They were only doing what the Prime Minister calls "rattling the sabre." Dr. Moussadek shrewdly chose the moment of the election, knowing what they would be thinking about them. And so this chapter is finished.[54]

The Conservative party's victory marked the opening of a new chapter in Anglo-American relations concerning Iran. Upon taking control of the Foreign Office, Eden resented that the British were out of Iran; that the British "had lost Abadan" and that British "authority throughout the Middle East had been violently shaken."[55] He first and foremost set himself the task of seeking "common ground" on which the British and American governments could stand in regard to Iran, but in discussions with Secretary Acheson, he found "sharply differing views on the future of Iran." The United States, according to Eden, considered it a "reckless policy to allow the situation to deteriorate," if Musaddiq should be left without any help, but Eden did not accept the American argument that "the only alternative to Musaddiq was Communist rule."[56] He thought that if Musaddiq fell, his place "might well be taken by a more reasonable Government." In trying to convince the United States that the two countries should stand on common ground vis-à-vis Iran, he told the American officials that throughout the nationalization crisis Musaddiq "played off the United States against the United Kingdom. This must be stopped." From Eden's accounts it appears that the United States position drew ever-closer to the British even before the Eisenhower administration took over in Washington. He singles out the appointment of Loy Henderson as a factor in the closer relations between Washington and London on the Iranian question; Henderson, Eden states, "never allowed himself to be played off against us by Musaddiq."[57] But it was during the Eisenhower administration that

[53] Royal Inst. Intl. Affairs, *Documents, 1951,* pp. 514-18.

[54] Ibid., pp. 520-21.

[55] Anthony Eden, *Full Circle* (Boston: Houghton Mifflin Co., 1960), p. 217.

[56] Ibid., p. 222.

[57] Ibid., p. 226.

Washington agreed with Eden's thought that "we should be better occupied looking for alternatives to Musaddiq rather than trying to buy him off."[58]

Before an examination of the development of Iran's bilateral relations with the United States during the nationalization crisis, we may look briefly at Musaddiq's perception of the United States. Better understanding of his view can be achieved by first examining the traditional policy of Iran toward the United States by drawing upon the materials presented throughout this study. We have seen the persistent Iranian efforts to involve the United States in Iran as its favorite third power. But we have also noted the origins of the idea of negative equilibrium along with the idea, the demand, and finally the decision to nationalize the oil industry. The idea of negative equilibrium, it may be recalled, was long advocated by Musaddiq and his National Front group. Strictly speaking, its fundamental assumptions clashed with those of the third-power policy. It assumed that Iranian resistance to Soviet and British pressures and influence must be equal and that this was both possible and desirable *without* Iran's dependence on a third power such as the United States. Musaddiq's severe protest of May 26, 1951, against the United States first public statement on nationalization in Iran, mentioned before, might be taken as the earliest indicator of his attitude toward the United States, that he would not tolerate American interference in Iran's internal affairs in keeping with the tenets of his negative equilibrium policy. His critics, however, found his ties with the United States, such as Point Four and American military aid, incompatible with the requirements of negative equilibrium. This is why his attitude toward the United States was attacked by not only the Tudeh and the extreme right, but also by some of the ardent nationalists who, as mentioned before, advocated "absolute neutralism."

In fact, Musaddiq's strategy of negative equilibrium ran into complicated difficulties in the practical conduct of foreign policy. On the one hand, the increasing community of approaches between the United States and Great Britain to the Iranian situation made it difficult for him to play off the United States against Britain and both Western powers against the Soviet Union (and the Tudeh party). On the other hand, the divergence of approaches between the two Western powers seemed to offer an opportunity to play one against the other, while still offering resistance to the Soviet Union (and the Tudeh party). Musaddiq's predecessors did not face such a dilemma for two major reasons. First, their third-power strategy basically assumed reliance on the power of the United States so long as the American posture differed from those of both the Soviet Union and Britain. Second, as the East-West cold war developed and the resultant bipolar international system did not allow much divergence of approach between the United States and Britain on matters of

[58]Ibid., p. 236.

common concern, the proponents of third-power strategy found it more palatable to side with the United States than with the Soviet Union. This was partly the reason why Iran's foreign policy during the 1946-50 period was characterized, as seen, by cold war with Moscow and friendship with the United States, despite disenchantment with American aid policy. Doctrinally, Musaddiq found it difficult to rely on the United States; yet practically he wished to do what the proponents of third-power strategy would do. This is why, in the early stage of the nationalization crisis, he did not hesitate to rely on the United States despite the charges of deviation from the path of negative equilibrium by his critics. But as the American approach to the Iranian situation drew closer to that of the British later on, the appeal of playing off the Soviet Union (and the Tudeh party) against both Britain and the United States proved irresistible.

In light of the above analysis, Iran's bilateral relations with the United States during the Musaddiq period may be traced from where we left them just before the inauguration of the nationalization policy.[59] Musaddiq continued the Point Four Program after his appointment as prime minister and reached an understanding with the United States on January 19, 1952, for the expansion of the Point Four Program in Iran. It was announced at the time that the United States might contribute as much as $23,450,000 toward the program of technical cooperation and economic development. The program, it may be recalled, began as the result of a memorandum of understanding between the two countries on October 19, 1950. By the time of Musaddiq's extension of this understanding some 62 American technicians and administrative personnel were working in Iran under the Technical Cooperation Administration of the Department of State. It was expected at the time that the number of American personnel would increase to 150 within a year, and the majority of these would be technicians in the fields of agriculture, public health, sanitation, and education.[60]

The closing of ranks between the Americans and the British on the nationalization problem soon affected the United States aid policy toward Iran. In February 1952, Eden stated subsequently, the British and American policies toward Iran were "more closely aligned." In reply to a request for financial aid, the Iranian government was told that "they would receive no help from the United States unless and until they reached agreement with us. This was straight talking."[61] On March 20, 1952, the Department of State announced that several written and oral requests for aid had been received from the gov-

---

[59] See chapter 6 of this study for Iran's earlier relations with the United States.

[60] U.S. State Dept. *Bulletin* 26, no. 659 (Feb. 11, 1952):217-18.

[61] Eden, p. 226.

ernment of Musaddiq in order to "ease the acute situation" resulting from the loss of oil revenues. The United States position in regard to these requests was that "it could not justify aid of the type requested at a time when Iran has the opportunity of receiving adequate revenues from its oil industry without prejudice to its national aspirations." The statement claimed that the United States had not stipulated as condition for granting financial aid to Iran that it should accept any particular proposals.[62]

The effect of the British influence on the United States aid policy toward Iran was not total; the United States not only continued technical aid under the Point Four Program, just mentioned, but also continued the long-established military aid program as well. As seen, Iran had adhered to the Mutual Defense Assistance Program on May 23, 1950, and the relevant agreement had confirmed also the basic agreements governing the American missions to the Iranian Gendarmerie and the army. The extension of these arrangements under the requirements of the Mutual Security Act seemed difficult in light of Musaddiq's general posture favoring neutralism in the cold war but at the same time wishing to keep American aid flowing into Iran for both political and economic purposes at a time of increasing financial difficulties. The formula to satisfy the requirements of the act, ostensibly without compromising his position, was found in the statement that "Iran supports and defends the principles of the United Nations to the extent that its resources and general conditions permit." At the outset of his letter of April 24, 1952, which contained this formula and which produced Soviet protest, as seen before, he stated that "in view of its financial and economic situation," Iran welcomed the assistance of the United States.[63]

This selectivity of American aid, however, did not cover up the fact that Iran's most pressing need was direct financial aid rather than technical or military aid as such. And it was the denial of this kind of aid that proved most critical during the turbulent days preceding the downfall of the Musaddiq government. President Eisenhower flatly told Musaddiq in his letter of June 29, 1953, that the United States was "in no position to extend more aid to Iran or to purchase Iranian oil." In justifying this position, the president wrote: "There is a strong feeling in the United States, even among American citizens most sympathetic to Iran and friendly to the Iranian people, that it would not be fair to the American taxpayers for the United States Government to extend any considerable amount of economic aid to Iran so long as Iran could have access to funds derived from the sale of its oil and oil products if a reasonable agreement were reached with regard to compensation whereby

[62] U.S. State Dept. *Bulletin* 26, no. 666 (Mar. 31, 1952):494.

[63] Royal Inst. Intl. Affairs, *Documents 1952*, pp. 333-34.

the large-scale marketing of Iranian oil would be resumed. Similarly, many American citizens would be deeply opposed to the purchase by the United States Government of Iranian oil in the absence of an oil settlement."[64]

Eisenhower's letter to Musaddiq was subsequent to Washington's agreement with London that they should look for alternatives to him, and hence it may be inferred that the letter was in keeping with that general agreement, if Eden's remark about the agreement is accurate. Regardless of the specific considerations underlying the Eisenhower letter, the fact is inescapable that the American attitude toward Musaddiq had come full-circle from a position of sympathetic impartiality to one of near identity with the British hostile attitude toward him. This letter marked the end of the divergence in Anglo-American approaches to the oil crisis. Acheson, who had been critical of the British earlier, was himself coming around to the British position later on, if Eden's account of the nature and success of his discussions with Acheson are taken seriously.

Eden reported that the Eisenhower letter encouraged the opposition to Musaddiq in the Majlis.[65] This opposition preceded the critical events of July and August and the downfall of the Musaddiq government on August 19, 1953. Examination of these events as such is beyond the scope of this study, but we may identify three major views in regard to the nature of his overthrow. One view considers the downfall of the Musaddiq regime simply the result of the internal political struggle between the shah and Musaddiq. This view basically denies any foreign interference in the crisis. The fullest account of this view is to be found in the shah's own book and needs no repetition here. Suffice it to state that the shah's account amounts to the claim that no foreign power had any hand whatever in the matter and that the shah himself was in full control of events, including his departure from Iran during the crisis and his return to Iran on August 22, three days after General Zahidi had assumed control of the situation. He justifies his dismissal of Musaddiq on the grounds that he "tried his best to weaken my constitutional position"; had the ambition to become "an absolute dictator unless he found means to overthrow the Shah"; and "wanted to destroy my dynasty."[66]

A second view attributes the overthrow of the Musaddiq regime to the British government. The best exponent of this view was Musaddiq himself. After his overthrow and during the course of his trial, he repeatedly addressed himself to the events of the crisis. He admitted that there had been serious divergence of viewpoints between himself and the shah concerning the latter's

[64]U.S. State Dept. *Bulletin* 29, no. 734 (July 29, 1953):74-75.

[65]Eden, pp. 236-37.

[66]*Mission for My Country,* pp. 96-97.

constitutional prerogatives as the commander-in-chief, but avoided, throughout the trial, to directly attribute his overthrow to the shah.[67] Instead he claimed that "it was the foreign view" (*nazar-i khariji in bood*) to destroy his government by whatever means. In describing what means had been adopted to bring about the "elimination" of his regime, it became clear that he held the British responsible for his ill fate. He claimed that after Britain failed at the Security Council and the International Court of Justice, it then turned to the internal situation in Iran. He held the British responsible for accusations hurled at him in the Majlis, for creating dissensions among the National Front deputies, and for all the major events leading to his overthrow.

A third and final view amounts to the claim that the United States brought down the government of Musaddiq. Ever since the publication of an article in the *Saturday Evening Post* in 1954 in a series entitled "The Mysterious Doings of CIA," the American role in the overthrow of the Musaddiq regime has been discussed in a number of sources. The *Post* article itself painted a black picture of Musaddiq's deals with the Communists and the Russians and then described a cloak and dagger story of the role played by the Americans and Iranians together in order to rescue the strategic little nation of Iran from the "closing clutch of Moscow." The article reports with satisfaction, however, that "the physical overthrow" of Musaddiq was accomplished by the Iranians themselves, but this statement is followed by this remark: "It is the guiding premise of CIA's third force that one must develop and nurture indigenous freedom legions among captive or threatened people who stand ready to take personal risks for their own liberty."[68] In *CIA: The Inside Story* Andrew Tully argues that the overthrow of Musaddiq was a "coup necessary to the security of the United States, and probably to that of the Western World." He regrets that the United States did not, in return for its support of those who gained from overthrowing Musaddiq, require "tough enough terms," and adds, "it is senseless, as some observers have written, to say that the Iranians overthrew Mossadegh all by themselves. It was an American operation from beginning to end."[69] In 1968 Richard J. Barnet argued, in *Intervention and Revolution*, that Musaddiq was vehemently against the Communists, an opposite view of his predecessors, just mentioned. But he, too, claims that the United States was involved in Musaddiq's overthrow. A certain CIA agent, whom he mentions by name, arrived in Iran at the time of the crisis to "direct a coup against

---

[67]*Matn-i Difa'a-i Doktor Muhammad Musaddiq* (Tehran: Bongah Sarsar, n.d.), pp. 23-29.

[68]Richard and Gladys Harkness, "America's Secret Agents: The Mysterious Doings of CIA." *Saturday Evening Post,* Nov. 6, 1954, p. 34.

[69]Andrew Tully, *CIA: The Inside Story* (New York: William Morrow, 1962), p. 96.

Mossadeq. His mission was to replace him with General Zahedi."[70] A year later Miles Copeland stated in *The Game of Nations* that the same agent carried a number of missions in the Middle East in the "tradition of Lanny Budd of the Upton Sinclair novels—the last of which was Operation Ajax in August 1953, when he almost single-handedly called pro-Shah forces on to the streets of Tehran and supervised their riots so as to oust Mossadeq and restore the Shah, who had fled to Rome."[71]

[70]Richard J. Barnet, *Intervention and Revolution* (New York: World Publishing Co., 1969), pp. 226-27.

[71]Miles Copeland, *The Game of Nations* (London: Weidenfeld and Nicolson, 1969), p. 51.

Part Three

Positive Nationalism

XI

The Quest for Security
Alliance with the United States

THE OVERTHROW OF the Musaddiq government on August 19, 1953, by the loyalist army and the return of the shah to Iran placed the decision-making power squarely in the hands of the monarch. This marked a break with the immediate past when the prime minister was for all practical purposes the main decision maker in Iranian foreign policy. It also signaled a return to the traditional patterns of decision making. The shah began to perform the principal role in Iran's foreign policy decisions; most often Iranian monarchs had done the same throughout modern Iranian history. My general examination of the foreign policy of Iran from the rise of the Safavi dynasty to the abdication of Riza Shah suggested the existence of a long pattern of control of Iranian foreign policy by the king.[1] This was significantly true even after the Constitutional Revolution. Although prime ministers such as Mushir al-Dolih, Mostofi al-Mamalik, and Vosuq al-Dolih, or deputies of the First, Second, Third, and Fourth Majlis at times made major foreign policy decisions, the monarch, on the whole, made the largest number of major decisions most of the time until 1941.

Although the accession of Muhammad Riza Shah Pahlavi to the throne in 1941 meant the continuation of the institution of monarchy, it did not necessarily mean that royal control of foreign policy ensued. The evidence in support of this proposition is found throughout the preceding chapters. The paramount role of various prime ministers such as Muhammad 'Ali Foroughi, Sa'id, Hakimi, Qavam, Razmara and Musaddiq, or the Fourteenth, Fifteenth, and Sixteenth Majlis in a wide variety of foreign policy decisions was quite evident.

Yet it would be an oversimplification to suggest that between 1941 and the downfall of the Musaddiq government in 1953, the shah's role in the making of foreign policy decisions was uniformly overshadowed by the more prominent part played by prime ministers and Majlis deputies. On the contrary, the record indicates his pervasive influence both directly and indirectly on not a few major foreign policy decisions. Materials already presented in this study provide the evidence. To begin with, we have seen the continuous

---

[1] Ramazani, *Foreign Policy of Iran.*

attraction of third-power policy for Iranian decision makers from 1941 to 1951. Every Iranian prime minister, and most of the time Majlis deputies as well, *initiated* courses of action fostering involvement of the United States in Iran often as a counterweight to both the Soviet Union and Great Britain. After the arrival of the United States forces in Iran, the shah as well as Premier Qavam actively sought United States adherence to the Tripartite Treaty of 1942. Although this effort did not succeed, it foreshadowed the shah's consistent support of subsequent decisions to acquire American military and financial advisers beginning in 1942. The shah's great interest in utilizing the interests of a third power such as the United States was clearly revealed not only in his actual support of decisions to invite American advisers but also in his foreign policy statements at the time. For example, he told American officials in Tehran on November 6, 1943, that he would like "to see American interests in Iran continue and grow, as he believed it in his country's interest to have three Great Powers, rather than two, concerned with Iranian developments. Two or three times he spoke of his conviction that the United States was completely disinterested, having no contiguous frontiers and no selfish ends to serve in Iran."[2]

The shah's interest in the United States as the favored third power, like his father's interest in Germany, was, of course, motivated by the tactical advantages of counterbalancing the Soviet-British pressures with the American presence in Iran for the purposes of maximizing Iranian national interests. At the same time this strategy would strengthen domestic conditions favorable to the consolidation of royal power as well. In the shah's perspective, as in his father's, the two interests were inseparable. The only instances of his major disagreement with American advisers, including Millspaugh and Schwarzkopf, concerned the size, the organization, and the budget of the army.[3] Yet of American missions working in Iran, military missions enjoyed the greatest success and protection. This was to a large extent because of the support of the shah. Given the demonstrable impact of Irano-American relations on every major Iranian foreign policy decision, the shah's favorable attitude toward the United States made his influence consistently felt in the decision-making process through the acts of loyal and, most often, obedient prime ministers.

It should not be assumed that during the tenure of all "strong" prime ministers the shah's influence on Iranian foreign policy necessarily diminished. In fact, during the tenure of reputedly strong Premier Ahmad Qavam at the height of the Azerbaijan crisis, the shah played a crucial role in several

[2]*Foreign Relations of U.S., 1943*, D.P., 4:410.

[3]On the shah's disagreement with Millspaugh see, Millspaugh, pp. 104-5. And for his disagreement with Schwarzkopf, see *Foreign Relations of U.S., 1944*, D.P.,5:393-95.

decisions. It may be recalled, for example, that Muzaffar Firuz's agreement with the Azeri leaders would have made the Soviet-supported and Communist-dominated Fada'i forces "part of the Iranian Army." The shah, as seen, vehemently opposed and defeated this agreement.[4] To cite another example, it may be recalled that Qavam's cabinet shake-up of October 17-19, 1946, had far-reaching foreign as well as domestic policy implications. The shah's influence on this decision was unquestionably substantial. Finally, there is no doubt that he played a decisive role in both the making of, and implementing, the decision to destroy the Soviet-supported Azeri and Kurdish rebel regimes by resort to force. Despite all his differences with the shah, Qavam was not amiss to acknowledge the shah's significant role in the Azerbaijan crisis: "I witnessed His Majesty's intense anxiety and desire to return Azerbaijan and Kurdistan to Iran. For the attainment of this objective he spared no assistance reaching the limits of self-sacrifice."

In light of the foregoing, Musaddiq's premiership stands out as one that was marked by the fullest concentration of decision-making power in the hands of a postwar prime minister. The idea to nationalize the oil industry had its origins among the deputies of the Majlis, was transformed into a demand for action against the wishes of the government, and was finally formulated as a legislative decision primarily as the result of vociferous agitation by National Front deputies under Musaddiq's leadership inside and outside the Majlis. It was not a cabinet decision enacted into law. The shah supported the decision; he did not actually make it. Nor was he satisfied with all subsequent decisions of Musaddiq during the course of the takeover, and negotiations with the British, the World Bank, and American officials.

Obviously, the shah's consolidation of power within Iran was not accomplished by the sheer overthrow of the Musaddiq government. The events of August 19, 1953, marked only the beginning of a relatively long process of the increasing strength of forces loyal to the shah at the center of political activity. Examination of this process as such is beyond the scope of this study, as is the so-called mystique of the longevity of his regime. This involves analysis of the interplay of his "style of rule with the attitudes and expectations of the political elite, those whose relations to the political process allow them to execute, thwart, or alter his wishes."[5] However, given the theoretical necessity and empirical demonstrability of domestic-foreign policy interaction as well, analysis of the shah's foreign policy should further assist understanding his domestic policies as well. Consideration of his foreign policy could all the more assist understanding his domestic politics because foreign policy

[4] See chapter 5 of this study.

[5] Marvin Zonis, *The Political Elite of Iran* (Princeton: Princeton University Press, 1971), pp. 22-23.

decisions in Iran were frequently designed to serve both external goals and also domestic ends of crucial utility to the longevity of the regime. The most obvious example of this technique was the strengthening of the armed forces for consolidation of control at home as well as defense abroad. In fact, the rising international capabilities of Iran economically and diplomatically as well as militarily not only contributed significantly to its more effective response to international pressures, but international prestige was also utilized as a substitute for negligible response to domestic pressures for political freedom. I shall examine Iran's increasing military capability in a later chapter. This and the next chapter examine the shah's foreign policy from the downfall of the Musaddiq government to 1962. Essential to an analysis of that foreign policy is an examination of his perception of Iran's international position at the time.

The Shah's Perception of Iran's Foreign Policy during the 1950s

The shah's most fundamental assumption about Iran's foreign policy during the 1950s, like Musaddiq's before him, has not so far been clearly articulated. His basic assumption must be extracted from his perception of Iranian experience in international politics. In the last analysis, the shah, like Musaddiq, viewed Anglo-Russian imperial rivalries as the most fundamental problem of Iranian foreign policy before the defeat of the British-sponsored 1919 agreement. But, interestingly enough, the real difference between the perceptions of the two lay in their interpretation of the subsequent period. In Musaddiq's view the British failure to effectuate the 1919 agreement as the result of patriotic opposition by the Majlis led to the British establishment of the "despotic government" of Riza Shah, which insured British influence in Iran for twenty years when Britain exclusively controlled Iranian oil fields, and when the 1933 oil concession agreement was "imposed" on Iran. In contrast, the shah viewed the advent of Riza Shah to power and his policies detrimental to British interests and definitely favorable to Iran's greater attainment of independence. As the shah perceived the events, after the rejection of the 1919 agreement Britain and other powers for a time continued to operate under the capitulations system and enjoyed various commercial concessions; "but eventually my father abolished the capitulations and either eliminated the concessions or placed them under the firm control of the Iranian government." He admitted that after the abolition of capitulations the British economic and political influence in Iran revolved mainly around their control of the oil fields, but he believed that his father in 1933 "negotiated a new agreement with the former Anglo-Iranian Oil Company under which the Iranian Government gained larger revenues and fuller control."[6]

[6]*Mission for My Country*, pp. 111-12.

In Musaddiq's perception, Great Britain emerged as the principal menace to Iranian political independence, but the shah viewed the Soviet Union as the main threat to Iranian independence and territorial integrity. The shah believed that the advent of the Bolshevik Revolution inspired the hope in Iran that it meant "the end of Russian imperialism," but the hope was "doomed to disappointment." The shah drew upon Iran's experience with the Soviet Union for his continuing skepticism about Soviet intentions in Iran. The Soviet support of the Gilan Republic under Kuchik Khan, the rebel Azeri and Kurdish Republics, and the Soviet reluctance to withdraw the Red Army were cited as the cases in point. The shah also vehemently resented the activities of the Tudeh party in Iran since 1941 and most particularly during the Musaddiq regime, in part because at that time the army was grievously infiltrated by the Communists; "even the commander of the most trusted battalion of my Imperial Guard was a hard-core Communist. The testimony of these men revealed their plan to kill Mossadeq as soon as he had overthrown the Pahlavi dynasty, then to establish their own Communist regime following the pattern in other countries."[7]

Within this general framework of the shah's perception of Iranian international experience, what basic assumption did the shah seem to make about the nature of the Iranian problem in world politics, and what did he assume would aid its solution? Musaddiq and his National Front colleagues assumed that the Anglo-Iranian Oil Company in Iran lay at the heart of the Iranian malaise. In analyzing the motives behind the act of nationalization of the oil industry, he wrote President Truman, for example, that during "the half century of the former company's domination it has never been possible for the Iranian Government to make a free decision in its internal affairs and its foreign policy."[8] As we have already seen, this was not an idle and isolated statement; it was paralleled by Musaddiq's words and deeds, based on the same assumption, on other occasions.[9]

What can be said about the shah's most basic assumption regarding the nature of the Iranian problem? There is little doubt that the shah, like Musaddiq, regarded Iran's political independence and territorial integrity as his overriding external goal. The patriotic sentiment underlying this goal was reinforced not only by his bitter memory of the invasion of Iran by Britain and the Soviet Union and the departure of his father. He also resented their dictations about his own accession to the throne. The two great powers, in

[7]Ibid., pp. 105-15.

[8]
For the text of the letter, see U.S. State Dept. *Bulletin* 27, no. 693 (Oct. 6, 1952): 532-35.

[9]See chapters 8, 9, and 10 of this study.

recognizing the Iranian wishes for his succession, made their recognition contingent upon his "good behavior." The British and Soviet ambassadors told the American minister in Iran in September 1941 that they agreed with the shah's succession to his father's throne, but their "approval is contingent in both cases on the Shah's future good behavior." [10] Furthermore, Eden informed Secretary Hull that "the new Shah had given assurances that the Iranian Constitution would be observed, that the properties taken by his father would be restored to the nation and that he would undertake the carrying out of all of the reforms considered necessary by the British Government." [11] The Allied occupation of Iran left the shah little choice, but he showed both in words and deeds that he tried consistently to counterbalance the Anglo-Russian pressures on Iran by fostering United States involvement. Furthermore, the assurances that the British and Soviets were able to extract in 1941 about his "future good behavior" did not prevent him from defying both powers within the limits of possibility. For example, when in 1945 the British demanded on one occasion that he close the Majlis he refused to accede, and subsequently told the American ambassador in Iran that he had told the British minister at the time "that if the Majlis were ever closed it would be because the Iranians desired it and never on foreign demand." [12]

Unlike Musaddiq, who assumed that the root cause of Iranian malaise was the pernicious influence of the British, the shah might appear to have assumed that the social and economic backwardness of Iran was the most fundamental reason. This impression may be gleaned from the mass of his speeches, interviews, and statements in the first decade of his accession to the throne. For example, he left that same impression on the American ambassador in Iran. The ambassador reported to the State Department in 1945 about his favorable impressions of the shah and marveled at his "maturity" at the age of twenty-five. The shah, he reported, believed that if Iranian patriotism were to be revitalized in order to stem the tide and appeal of Communism, "drastic and urgent steps must be taken to relieve the misery in his country." [13] The same impression may be reinforced by the shah's verbal emphasis on the need for social and economic reforms before the 1960s, but careful examination of his deeds as well as words in the 1940s and 1950s reveals that his most basic assumption about the nature of the Iranian problem was quite something else.

Before the 1960s the shah did not believe that either the British influence in Iran or social and economic backwardness lay at the heart of the Iranian

[10]*Foreign Relations of U.S., 1941*, D.P., 3:461.

[11]Ibid., p. 462.

[12]*Foreign Relations of U.S., 1945*, D.P., 8:384-85.

[13]Ibid.

problem. He instead assumed that the root cause of Iran's inadequate freedom of action in world politics as well as its domestic social, economic, and political problems was *insecurity*. Regardless of the psychological, political, or other factors that might have underpinned this assumption, the shah's actions and words over a decade or so before the early 1950s support this inference. As already noted the shah, like his father, placed the highest value on retivalization and strengthening of the Iranian armed forces as the sine qua non of Iranian security. He unreservedly supported the initiative of Iranian statesmen from 1942 in requesting American military know-how for the Iranian Army and the Gendarmerie. In fact, his overriding concern with Iran's military strength in the 1950s was partly at the bottom of his pursuing an alliance policy with the United States.

The attainment of social, economic and political development as well as true independence, all hinged, in the last analysis, on the achievement of security. Although the shah's concept of security underwent significant changes in the early 1960s, as we shall see, during the 1950s security was perceived primarily in military terms, and, as such, it was clearly accorded the highest priority. In the shah's perception Western Europe and the Middle East countries, including Iran, despite all differences in levels of social, economic, and technical development aspired fundamentally to the achievement of progress in these fields, and the peoples of both areas needed "adequate security" in order to do so. Countries like Iran, he believed, "must strive for the security which is *their first essential for advancement. Freedom-loving peoples forget—but the Communist powers never forget—that most of the world's economically underdeveloped countries are also militarily underdeveloped.*"[14]

Given the shah's basic assumption that the achievement of true national security, or independence, as well as domestic social, political, and economic development rested on the establishment of military security first, what strategy did he envisage for this purpose? As noted previously, the shah favored a third-power policy in the 1940s. But by the early 1950s he no longer perceived it possible to pursue a third-power strategy. The emergence of the United States and the Soviet Union as superpowers and the concomitant decline of the British changed the character of the international system. There was no longer a "third and disinterested" great power in the world on which Iran could rely as it had on the United States in the 1940s and on Germany during most of Riza Shah's rule. As seen, Musaddiq's perception called for the policy of negative equilibrium, which theoretically would apply to Iran's relations with the Soviet Union and Great Britain, and also to the United States as the substitute for Great Britain.

[14]*Mission for My Country,* pp. 290-96. The italics are mine.

In contrast, the shah did not see how Iran could pursue a neutralist course in world affairs. He did not deny the evils of British or Western imperialism, but the larger question for him was where "the greater danger lies" for Iran. "In our experience," he said, "it is the new imperialism—the new totalitarian imperialism—that the world's less-developed countries today have most to fear. . . . It concentrates on negative, destructive nationalism and thrives on the chaos that follows. . . . We all saw this happening in our country, right under our noses, in Mossadeq's time." Musaddiq, according to the shah, cried out against the imperialist British, but during the later part of his regime forgot to mention "another even more lethal kind of imperialism."[15] This more lethal kind of imperialism, in the shah's view during the 1950s, was Soviet imperialism, and to protect Iran's interests against its menace Iran had to discard negative equilibrium for the adoption of the shah's policy of "positive nationalism." This basically meant alignment with the West in the cold war, as we shall see. I have already tried to articulate the shah's perspective of modern Iranian history in order to get at his basic diagnostic assumption about the malaise of Iran and his prescription for its resolution. The nature, problems, and implications of his policy of positive nationalism will emerge as we follow the course of Iranian foreign policy developments from the downfall of the Musaddiq government to the early 1960s.

Resumption of Diplomatic Relations with Britain

Only four days after the shah's return to Iran the first public manifestation of a drastic change in Iran's foreign policy of the Musaddiq era was signaled in a letter from Gen. Fazlollah Zahidi, the shah's new prime minister. He wrote President Eisenhower on August 26, 1953, that it was the intention of his government to improve Iran's international position. Although he did not specifically mention Iran's relations with Britain, it was perfectly obvious that he intended to assure the United States that Iran would sooner or later resume diplomatic relations with Britain. He stated that his government "desires to maintain friendly relations with the other members of the family of nations on a basis of mutual respect. It will pursue a policy of eliminating such differences as may exist or which may develop between other countries and itself in a spirit of friendliness and in accordance with accepted principles of international intercourse."[16] The important hint was not lost on the president, who replied that he was pleased to have General Zahidi's assurances about Iran's relations with other countries mentioned in his letter.

[15] Ibid., pp. 127-31.

[16] U.S. State Dept. *Bulletin* 29, no. 742 (Sept. 14, 1953):349.

The main purpose of Zahidi's letter, however, was to acquire desperately needed financial aid from the United States. He told the president that the "treasury is empty; foreign exchange resources are exhausted; the national economy is deteriorated. Iran needs immediate financial aid to enable it to emerge from a state of economic and financial chaos."[17] This was, of course, no news to the president. Musaddiq had written him as early as January 1953, before the Republican administration had taken over in Washington, hoping that the new president would prove more sympathetic toward Iran at the time.[18] He had also written to the president in his letter of May 28, 1953, complaining of no change in the position of the American government despite the change in administration, and adding that Iran "is now facing great economic and political difficulties. There can be serious consequences, from an international viewpoint as well, if this situation is permitted to continue. If prompt and effective aid is not given this country now, any steps that might be taken tomorrow to compensate for the negligence of today might well be too late." [19]

This was Musaddiq's desperate message that brought the crucial negative reply of the president, as seen before; but General Zahidi's urgent aid request was answered favorably and immediately. He told the prime minister that his "request will receive our sympathetic consideration" and informed him that he authorized the American ambassador to consult with him about Iran's immediate needs.[20] The first sign of the implementation of the president's favorable response appeared on September 3, 1953, when the United States agreed to continue technical assistance to Iran at the level of $23 million annually—the largest expenditure in any country. Two days later the president granted $45 million to Iran because the United States "was satisfied that the new government would not be immovable in the matter of reaching an understanding with Britain over the nationalization of British-owned oil industry in Iran." The White House statement pointed out great need for immediate assistance in order to "restore a measure of stability and establish a foundation for greater economic development."[21]

In accepting the aid, Premier Zahidi similarly sounded the note of economic development, but it was not seriously believed in either Tehran or Washington

[17]Ibid.

[18]Dwight D. Eisenhower, *Mandate for Change, 1953-56* (Garden City, N.Y.: Doubleday & Co., 1963), pp. 160-61.

[19]U.S., President, *Public Papers of the Presidents of the United States,* Dwight D. Eisenhower, 1953 (Washington, D.C., Government Printing Office, 1960), pp. 484-86 (Hereafter cited as U.S., *Public Papers of Presidents of U.S.*).

[20]U.S., State Dept. *Bulletin* 29, no. 742 (Sept. 14, 1953):349.

[21]*New York Times,* Sept. 6, 1953.

that the immediate objective of Iran's request was really economic development. Although continuation of the technical assistance aid generally contributed to that end, emergency aid was clearly viewed in both capitals as the kind of aid then needed for internal political stability. It provided funds for the two major pillars of the regime's support, the army and the bureaucracy. It was believed in Iran and the United States that financial aid was at the time needed first and foremost to bolster the Zahidi regime politically until oil revenues could make their contribution. The political strength of the regime was considered essential in combatting the Tudeh party at home and resisting Soviet pressures as well. The nationalization policy of Musaddiq had been viewed with alarm from Washington primarily for its adverse effects on the strategic position of Iran in the cold war and the conciliatory attitude of the Zahidi government toward the United States was regarded as the West's best opportunity in Iran in years.

The Zahidi government sought more aid from the United States. So long as the flow of Iranian oil could not be resumed without lengthy negotiations this was a good enough reason to cash in on the favorable situation. His finance minister, 'Ali Amini, stated on September 10, 1953, that the prime minister had told the American ambassador that the $45 million emergency aid was insufficient and that Iran expected "at least $300,000,000 to cope with the economic chaos left by the former government of Dr. Musaddeq." The United States, on the other hand, was not eager to rush into extending much more aid than was provided by the funds because it did not wish to forfeit its leverage too quickly insofar as it considered the oil dispute settlement essential to any real immediate amelioration of the Iranian situation. What further grants were made subsequently and before the signing of an oil agreement were relatively small and far apart. Only on March 6, 1954, another grant of $6 million was made to the Zahidi government bringing the total emergency grants to $51 million, and the third grant of $9 million was not made until May 10 of the same year. On October 26, 1954, the United States officials stated clearly that the amount of American aid to Iran in 1954-55 would not be finally determined until after the Iranian parliament had ratified the oil agreement which, as will be seen, had been initialed in August of that year. And the Foreign Operations Administration announced the offer of $127,300,000 in loans and grants to Iran only two days after the first tanker load of Iranian oil actually moved out of Abadan.[22]

The Zahidi government hoped that the American emergency grants, coupled with armed suppression of opposition to his unpopular regime, would insure longevity for his government, but the Musaddiq legacy was not confined to financial distress. Premier Zahidi faced two other urgent problems.

[22]Ibid., Sept. 11, 1953; Oct. 27, Nov. 3, 1954.

These were settlement of the oil dispute and resumption of diplomatic relations with Britain. Obviously, these two problems were closely interlinked; nevertheless, the question was, Which one should be tackled first? His assurances to the United States of resumption of diplomatic relations with Britain had helped bring in rapid American aid; his promise of resumption of diplomatic relations, he hoped, would result in a prior settlement of the oil dispute. The main reason for wanting to settle the oil dispute first was the explosive internal situation marked by heightened anti-British sentiments. Immediate resumption of diplomatic relations with Britain would arouse greater domestic public wrath than the slower pace and secrecy of negotiations for an oil settlement. Great Britain, however, preferred resumption of diplomatic relations first because it would facilitate direct oil discussions. Tehran in the end accepted London's preference for according resumption of diplomatic relations first priority. The Iranian government announced on October 11, 1953, its preparedness to arrange for the return of Iranian oil to world markets, hinting at its readiness to resume diplomatic relations with Britain as well as to settle the oil dispute. The Iranian foreign minister, 'Abdollah Intizam, showed interest on October 26 in Eden's proposal, announced in the House of Commons on October 20, for resuming diplomatic relations as a first step toward the settlement of the oil dispute.[23] Iran, however, moved cautiously toward the resumption of diplomatic relations, hoping to see at least some signs of a more favorable British attitude toward Iran. It may be recalled that long before Musaddiq's rupture of diplomatic relations with Britain, and, in fact, as early as September 1951, the British had imposed increasing economic restrictions against Iran. Iran would at least wish to see some of these removed before it went any further in resuming new relations with Britain. The British made at least two conciliatory gestures toward the new government in Iran. They withdrew the proceedings instituted in Tokyo against Japanese purchases of Iranian oil, and offered to release the export of British-built locomotives for the Iranian railways, long held up by the commercial blockade.[24]

The positions of Iran and Britain drew closer together toward the end of 1953. Foreign Minister Intizam stated on November 24 that Iran was willing to reestablish diplomatic relations with Britain "if Britain agreed to reconcile Iran's position in the oil question and treat the matter in a spirit of justice and mutual respect."[25] The effort, echoed in a section of the British press, to represent the collaboration of Britain with Iran as a "sterile battle" to regain

[23] Royal Inst. Intl. Affairs, *Documents, 1953*, p. 56.
[24] *New York Times,* Oct. 29, 1953.
[25] Ibid., Nov. 25, 1954.

the dominant position it had had for half a century did not make the slightest dent in the determination of Iran to welcome resumption of diplomatic relations. Iran and Britain issued a communiqué on December 5, 1953, announcing their decision to do so and to "exchange Ambassadors without delay." The same statement revealed that they had also agreed to negotiate a settlement of the oil dispute.[26] Ironically, the arrival of the British diplomatic mission in Iran on December 21, 1953, coincided with the conviction of Musaddiq by a military court. The British mission was headed by a chargé d'affaires to pave the way for exchanges at the ambassadorial level. Iran's chargé, Amir Khusrow Afshar-Qasimlu, arrived in London on January 14, 1954, and on January 26 it was announced that London had agreed to the appointment of 'Ali Sohaily as the Iranian ambassador to Britain; he had been Musaddiq's ambassador until the rupture of diplomatic relations in October 1952.

The Oil Dispute Settlement
Economics of Security

Substantial American financial aid and resumption of diplomatic relations with Britain paved the way for settlement of the oil dispute. This was Iran's most important objective from the beginning, but it had to await a "better atmosphere." The real point, of course, was what kind of a settlement would be acceptable to Iran and Britain. The protracted dispute between the two countries, as seen, had involved numerous points of disagreement, such as management and control, the amount of compensation, the method of payment, the level of production, marketing, price-setting and profit sharing. To be sure, the new government sought a rapid settlement of the dispute, but nationalization of the oil industry had been associated with the Iranian national struggle against British influence, had involved great powers, had been decided by means of solemn acts of the Majlis and the Senate, and continued to enjoy widespread popular support within the country. In order to insure that Iranian national aspirations would not be totally disregarded, Iran had insisted on, and the British had accepted, including in the communiqué regarding the resumption of diplomatic relations, mentioned before, a statement to the effect that "a solution can be reached which will take account of the national aspirations of the Persian people regarding the natural resources of their country and which, on the basis of justice and equity, will safeguard the honour and interests of both parties."

On the other hand, the fact remained that the new government believed that its destiny was tied to the West. Iranian interests and those of the West

---

[26] For the text see Royal Inst. Intl. Affairs, *Documents, 1953*, p. 356.

were basically compatible insofar as both Iran and the West thought real threats to those interests were posed fundamentally by Soviet ambitions and Communist subversion. However, beyond these considerations of broader interests lay the limits imposed upon the Iranian situation by the realities of the international oil industry. Generally speaking, Iran needed foreign technicians, a fact never denied by Musaddiq, and lacked the necessary marketing facilities. But the more crucial practical consideration at the time, it was claimed, was the problem of absorbing Iranian oil into the structure of the international oil industry. The shutdown in Iran had been followed by stepping up production in other Middle Eastern oil fields and the building of new refineries in Germany, Britain, Australia, and Aden. To cut back production in other Middle Eastern countries in order to make a market for Iranian oil would have entailed for the oil companies the risk of arousing resentment in the oil-producing countries involved. On the other hand, world consumption of petroleum was rising by about 5 to 6 percent a year, so that, provided the rate of expansion in other fields could be controlled, Iranian oil could be reabsorbed into the market over a period of a few years. This, however, required the cooperation of the seven big oil companies that, with the AIOC, were interested in all the operations of the world supply of petroleum (production, transportation, refining, and marketing) and were estimated to control 88 percent of the industry outside the Soviet bloc.[27]

This difficulty meant that quite apart from negotiations with Iran, the oil companies concerned had to negotiate among themselves. These negotiations in turn raised two major questions: (1) susceptibility to antitrust prosecution in the United States, and (2) resentment of smaller American companies. The role of the United States government, therefore, proved important if the giant companies were to participate in a consortium arrangement in Iran, and some allowance had to be made for the American independents. Through a decision of the National Security Council the Americans were given the assurance that their participation would not subject them to prosecution under the antitrust laws. The Justice Department advised the president that this would hold only for the consortium, not for any existing or new system of transportation and distribution.[28] Furthermore, a number of smaller companies were allowed to share among themselves 5 percent of the American allotment.

This latter question had another side that really concerned Iran. What would be the share of the American companies in general as contrasted with the unwanted AIOC? It may be recalled that the oil dispute dragged on in part as the result of the Iranian insistence that the AIOC not return. Those

[27] Royal Inst. Intl. Affairs, *Survey, 1954*, p. 221.

[28] See Robert Engler, *The Politics of Oil* (New York: Macmillan Co., 1961), p. 207.

days were obviously gone with the overthrow of Musaddiq, but the question was still of serious concern to Iran. The negotiations among the giants, therefore, had to take note of this problem as well. This question was one of the reasons for the relatively slow pace of intercompany negotiations. The oil companies agreed tentatively on the marketing of Iranian oil, once the settlement was reached, as early as December 19, 1953, after a week of discussions, but the issue of Britain's share held up the negotiations. The British government was understood to be asking 44 percent for the British in the consortium, and the United States government had suggested 40 percent because it expected objections in Iran, where the Anglo-Iranian Oil Company was the symbol of foreign domination. [29] Even worse, from the Iranian perspective, was the AIOC's initial reluctance to settle for less than a 50 percent interest in the consortium, but the possibility of Iran's rejection of the consortium, if the AIOC held a dominant position, finally resulted in a smaller share. AIOC eventually accepted "a minority share," though it was the largest single one because it was alloted 40 percent in the consortium, while the American 40 percent was divided among Gulf Oil, Socony-Vacuum Oil (Mobil), Standard Oil of New Jersey, and Texaco. Still the AIOC fared better than its 40 percent share if its interest in Royal Dutch Shell was also taken into account. In any event, the other 20 percent was divided between Royal Dutch (14 percent) and Companie Francaise des Petroles (6 percent).

The Iranian government and the consortium initiated an agreement in principle on August 5, 1954. What were the main features of this agreement once it was drafted insofar as Iran's primary concerns were involved? As seen, throughout the nationalization dispute the problem of management persisted in one form or another. How did this agreement deal with that overriding problem? The actual management of the oil industry in the consortium's concession area was entrusted to two foreign-owned operating companies, one in charge of exploration and production, and the other of refining operations. From subsequent statements of the Iranian foreign minister and the minister of finance, it seems clear that they both had wished to see the "ultimate control" of the oil fields and Adaban refinery resting in Iranian hands and that they had pressed hard for majority representation on the board of these two operating companies. The agreement, however, alloted only two seats on the Board of Directors, out of seven, to Iranians (nominated by the NIOC). Furthermore although the board was to act "on behalf of Iran and NIOC," the operating companies would determine and have "full and effective management and control of all their operations."

This was why the critics of the agreement, as we shall see, considered it as an act of "denationalization." Its defendants argued that the agreement did

[29]*New York Times,* Mar. 1, 1954.

accept "the principle of nationalization." The legal title to ownership remained with Iran, but effective control of both the Abadan refinery and the main oil fields passed to the consortium. To the critics of the agreement this was nothing more than a legal fiction.

Another question of primary concern to Iran, it may be recalled, had been revenues from the oil industry. The effect of the agreement proved controversial. Did the arrangements amount to a fifty-fifty profit sharing or less? Supporters of the agreement generally believed that Iran would obtain a 50 percent share of profits as was the case with other Middle Eastern countries. As contrasted with the position taken by the Musaddiq government, and also the 'Ala government before him, this was, to say the least, nearly four years too late, but to the Iranian leaders in August 1954 this was the best they could do in a bad situation. The same could be said about the duration of the agreement, which was to last for twenty-five years with provisions for three five-year extensions. If the fifteen year extension was added to the twenty-five year duration, it would exceed the duration of the 1933 concessionary agreement, which was to expire in 1993, by one year.

A fourth major concern of Iran during the nationalization crisis, was, as seen, the problem of compensation, often coupled with the related question of claims and counterclaims. The agreement indicated that claims and counterclaims of the parties were taken into account in determining the amount of compensation. These claims included Iran's view that in equity it should receive additional sums that would have accrued to it under the Supplemental Agreement of 1949 had it come into force. Article 2 of part II of the agreement provided that the sum of £25 million paid by Iran to the AIOC would constitute "full and final settlement" of all claims and counterclaims of Iran and the AIOC. This was Iran's share of compensation to the AIOC because the latter transferred its rights in Iran to the consortium for $600 million. Iran undertook under the agreement to pay its share in ten annual equal installments. On October 25, 1954, Britain and Iran concluded a general agreement through the exchange of notes, establishing arrangements for payment relations between the two countries. This agreement provided that payment arrangements would apply for an initial period of twelve months from the date of the ratification of the consortium agreement. The principal purpose of the payment agreement was to give Iran transferable account facilities "only when necessary for goods and services which are essential to the Iranian economy and which cannot otherwise be obtained on equivalent terms."[30]

The Western governments most directly concerned and the representative of the consortium showered Iran with compliments for initialing the agreement. Howard Page, chairman of the group representing the companies, on

[30]U.N., Secretariat, *Treaty Series* 204, no. 2754 (1955): 131-35.

the day of initialing the accord, expressed his great happiness; declared that the arrangement was "unique"; confessed that there had been particularly difficult questions to settle; and paid his particular respect to Amini who, he said, was a "brilliant, capable, and tough negotiator." He and his Iranian colleagues, he added, "squeezed the maximum benefit for Iran out of every point," while they had been fair at all times. [31] Secretary of State Dulles sent a message on the day the agreement was initialed (August 5, 1954) to Premier Zahidi, expressing his "heartiest congratulations" and his conviction that it represented a "satisfactory and entirely equitable arrangement." He also sent a message on the same day to Foreign Secretary Eden, expressing his "deep appreciation" for the part played by the British government and calling the agreement a "milestone" from which point the British and American governments together with the government of Iran would be able to take further constructive steps to advance mutual interests in the area. [32]

Eden responded in the same vein, and the American ambassador expressed similar views on the matter. President Eisenhower's messages to the shah and to Ambassador Henderson and Herbert Hoover, who had been most active during the negotiations from the beginning, pointed out the larger interests in stability and security, that the settlement would enhance. In his message to the shah, he expressed satisfaction for the success of the negotiations to which "you personally have made valuable contribution," and confidence that implementation of the agreement, under the shah's leadership, would mark the beginning of a new era of economic progress and stability for Iran. In his message to Hoover, the president expressed appreciation for his contribution to the solution of the dispute "which has so long been a threat to the stability of the Middle East." The political significance that the president attached to the settlement of the dispute emerged even more vividly in his message to the United States ambassador to Iran. He stated that the solution of the dispute, for which the Ambassador deserved "such a large share of the credit, is a major achievement which will not only further our objectives in the Middle East but also contribute to our good relations with our European allies and our friends in other parts of the world as well." [33]

The shah's response to the president was *not* merely a message of thanks; it contained, in a few words, the essence of the Iranian predicament. He said he was satisfied that his government had been able to arrive, in principle, at a

---

[31] U.S., Congress, House, Committee on the Judiciary, *Hearings before Antitrust Subcommittee* (Subcommittee No. 5) of the Committee on the Judiciary, House of Representatives, pt. 1, 84th Cong., 1st sess., 1955, pt. 1, p. 724.

[32] U.S. State Dept. *Bulletin* 31, no. 790 (Aug. 16, 1954):231.

[33] *Public Papers of Presidents of U.S.,* Dwight D. Eisenhower, 1954, pp. 688-89, 690.

settlement of the dispute, which, *"in the light of present world conditions, appears to be as equitable a solution of a difficult problem as could have been reached."* [34] In presenting the agreement to the Iranian Parliament for ratification on August 10, 1954, the shah had asked the legislative body "not to waste a minute" in ratifying it, and said it was "honorable and equitable," but he deliberately repeated the caveat implied in his message to the president, emphasizing that Iran considered the settlement as favorable under "present world conditions." [35] The Majlis ratified the agreement on October 21, 1954, 113 to 5 with 1 abstention; nine deputies were absent; and the Senate ratified it on October 28, 41 to 4, with 4 abstentions.

What the shah himself did not wish to say specifically about his reservations at the time was stated for him publicly by others. During the consideration of the agreement by the Majlis and the Senate, the shah's government allowed devastating criticism of the terms of the agreement within both legislative bodies. The government's permissiveness at a time when freedom of expression in Iran was extremely curtailed should not cast doubt on the sincerity of the critics in the Parliament. Nevertheless, the fact remains that its reluctance to curtail criticism served to make public its own lack of satisfaction with the agreement.

The most outspoken critic of the agreement within the Majlis was Deputy Muhammad Darakhshish, an early supporter of Musaddiq who broke with him later and sided with the shah. As a professional teacher and an able speaker, he showed none of the passionate outbursts so frequently associated with the supporters of nationalization; instead he set himself the task of dissecting the Iranian situation by making at the outset two fundamental assumptions. First, he argued that the international oil cartel was fundamentally motivated by profit making. This meant that interests of the oil companies were basically incompatible with those of the oil-producing countries. These countries were, in the last analysis, concerned with the social and economic welfare of their peoples. For example, in an oil-producing country like Iran this would mean that the oil companies by the very nature of their interest would be inclined to keep Iran backward. Second, he argued, Iran, by virtue of its geographic position, was strategically important to Western governments, and the interests of these governments in the cold war would require keeping a country like Iran strong. From juxtaposing these two propositions, he concluded that the government of Iran in negotiating the oil dispute settlement had failed to take

---

[34] Ibid., p. 689. Italics are mine.

[35] *New York Times*, Aug. 11, 1954. In presenting the agreement to the Majlis, Amini clearly admitted that it fell short of the Iranian "national ideal" but stated that it was necessary because of the "realities" of the situation (*Khandaniha,* 15th Year, no. 1, p. 17).

advantage of this basic conflict between the interests of the giant oil companies and their governments. [36]

On the basis of the above argument, Deputy Darakhshish attacked the settlement with a view to its specific features. First and foremost he argued that the agreement was contrary to the letter as well as the spirit of nationalization laws because it squarely placed in the hands of foreign companies all exploration, production, and refining operations. Nationalization of the oil industry throughout Iran had meant, according to the letter of the law, that "all operations of exploration, extraction and exploitation shall be carried out by the Government." The agreement, in fact, entrusted all these operations to foreign companies despite the euphemism that they worked in "behalf of Iran and NIOC." He regarded these arrangements not only contrary to the "principle of nationalization," but also to the nine-article law of implementation which, he told Amini, was still the law of the land. Furthermore, he argued, the settlement really amounted to the grant of an oil concession that was forbidden by the laws of 1944 and 1947.

He also attacked the settlement with respect to the matter of compensation. It may be recalled that the British government had insisted in the Musaddiq days that compensation should include not only the property of the AIOC but also its "future profits" as determined under the 1933 concessionary agreement, which was to expire in 1993. Musaddiq, on the other hand, had been prepared to pay for only the physical facilities of the company. Deputy Darakhshish argued that the fact that the settlement did not seem to include future profits of the AIOC should not be considered as a great gain for at least two major reasons. First, Iran's refusal to pay compensation for future profits had been based in part on the basic assumption that Iran itself would control all operations of the oil industry. Now that this settlement was introducing AIOC participation through the back door, there was no loss of future profits to begin with. Second, Iran's refusal to pay compensation for future profits had also been based upon the assumption that no new *concession* would be granted. Now that a concession for the next forty years was indeed going to be granted, it would be absurd to speak of future profits. In fact, the very absence of provisions relating to the payment of compensation for future profits vividly showed, he argued, that this settlement amounted to granting a new concession contrary to Iranian laws. [37]

At the end of his critique, Deputy Darakhshish repeated his plea for "realism" (*vaq'a-biny*); denied that he was totally against any settlement with

[36]For the full text of Deputy Darakhshish's speech, see Iran, Majlis, *Nutq-i Aqa-ye Muhammad Darakhshish dar Mukhalifat-i ba Qarardad-i Naft-i Amini-Page keh dar Majlis-i Shora-ye Melli-Iirad Shodeh* (Tehran: Chapkhanih-ye Majlis, 1954), pp. 2-120.

[37]Ibid., pp. 50-51.

the consortium; requested the government to take back its bill regarding the agreement; and made his own proposal. He challenged General Zahidi to take back the government bill if he had "courage in politics" as he did in the battlefield. Such a courageous act, he argued, would constitute "the greatest blow" (*bozorg-tarin zarbih*) to the Tudeh party; would make it unnecessary to maintain martial law; and would create support for the government by the majority of the people who were currently discontented. In making his own proposal, he declared that he would accept the principle of fifty-fifty profit sharing; and the provisions regarding the settlement of compensation. But he (1) would entrust all oil operations to Iranian hands; (2) would accept a foreign manager only under the supervision of the Iranian government; and (3) would allow employment of foreign technicians so far as necessary. In conclusion he drew a parallel between the act of Taqizadih who had signed the 1933 concessionary agreement during Riza Shah's rule and the approval of the new agreement by the Majlis in 1954. He saw no difference between Taqizadih's signing under duress, and "compulsory approval" (*tasvib-i ijbary*) of the 1954 agreement by some hundred deputies of the Majlis. [38]

Very similar objections were raised in the Senate. Senator Riza-'ali Divanbaigy also attacked the agreement for its failure to entrust the oil operations to Iranian hands, and its provisions regarding the duration and compensation as well. He also showed analytical rigor and clarity, but his caustic and humorous remarks turned his critique into a sophisticated ridiculing of the settlement. He first and foremost attacked the euphemism of Iranian control of operations under complicated arrangements that "fooled no one." The fact was that all oil operations were entrusted to foreign hands for another forty years. This arrangement was not only contrary to nationalization laws of Iran but also previous recognition of the principle of nationalization by the Western governments and the oil companies themselves. For these reasons Iran would have the right to refuse later to fulfill its so-called obligations under the agreement. When an "appropriate time and free environment" (*zamani musa'id va muhity azad*) could be found. In conclusion, Senator Divanbaigy, like Deputy Darakhshish, complained of the ratification of the agreement without regard to Iranian laws and "under force and pressure" (*ba zor va fishar*); wondered how long it would last because the British and American companies, instead of erecting such a large petroleum edifice for the next forty years on solid ground, had built on quicksand; and urged his fellow Senators *not* to approve the agreement. To consent to *this* settlement after *that* dispute would amount to falling from the frying pan into the fire![39]

[38] Ibid., pp. 97, 89, 119.

[39] For the text of Senator Divanbaigy's speeches, see Iran, Majlis, *Bakhshi az Parvandih-ye Naft-i Iran, Matn-i Nutqha-ye Senator Divanbaigy dar Majlis-i Sina* (Tehran: Chapkhanih-ye Majlis, n.d.), pp. 1-88.

Whatever reservation the shah himself might have had about the terms of the oil dispute settlement, he did not view it in such a pessimistic light. According to Foreign Secretary Eden, "the Shah played a decisive part by preventing the endless delays in ratification which could have killed the agreement."[40] And the shah himself, looking back on the settlement years later, considered the 1954 agreement a milestone in Iran's relations with Britain. The agreement as such, he believed, greatly increased the payments to Iran, "but its most important result was the termination, once and for all, of the British monopolistic hold over Iran's oil industry. No longer could a giant private corporation, or the Government behind it, dominate a large sector of our economy. The agreement symbolized the fact that Persia and Britain now dealt with each other on the basis of full equality, and paved the way for the neighbourly relations"[41] which developed between the two countries subsequently. Indeed, as we shall see below, within the framework of the Baghdad Pact and subsequently the Central Treaty Organization (CENTO) the two countries cooperated as allies for many years to come. Even outside the alliance system, bilateral relations between the two countries improved on an unprecedented basis during the rest of the 1950s and into the 1960s. The only major issue that sometimes ruffled the relations of Iran with Britain was the ancient dispute over Bahrain, which will be taken up later in this study.

Improvement in the bilateral relations of the two countries was crowned on May 6, 1959, by the conclusion of a "Cultural Convention" for an initial period of five years after ratification with option for renewal. The basic purpose of the convention was to promote "the fullest possible understanding" between the two countries in intellectual, artistic, and scientific activities as well as in their history and ways of life. Toward this general end, Iran and Britain undertook to (1) encourage creation of universities and other educational institutions, teaching posts, Chairs, and cultural institutes; (2) facilitate importation of books, films, and other educational materials; (3) exchange university staff, students, research scholars, and school teachers; (4) and insure to scholars access to collections, archives, and libraries.[42]

This put a happy end to the tumultuous and acrimonious relations between Iran and Britain. But what cemented the relations between the two countries after the downfall of the Musaddiq regime was the fact that the government of the shah found it helpful to the durability of his regime and the interests of Iran, as he saw them, to befriend Britain as part of his drive for an alliance with the West in the 1950s.

[40]Eden, p. 242.

[41]*Mission for My Country,* p. 112.

[42]U.N., Secretariat *Treaty Series* 398, no. 5717 (1961): 51-69.

The Shah's Favorite Ally

The shah favored the United States as Iran's principal ally. As we have already noted, ever since his accession to the throne in 1941, he had favored the growth of American interests and involvement in Iran, largely as a means of insuring domestic and external ends. And as we have also noted, there was a major difference between the interest of the shah in the United States during the 1950s as contrasted with the 1940s. In the wartime in particular, he favored the United States as the third great power on which Iran could rely in withstanding the pressures of Anglo-Russian diplomacy, but with the bipolarization of international politics and the emergence of the cold war between the Soviet Union and the United States, the choice became increasingly clear for the shah—Iran had to side with the United States.

Washington's support for the shah had been clear long before the 1950s. Before the premiership of Musaddiq the United States had favored the shah during the government of able prime ministers such as Ahmad Qavam and General Razmara. In the course of the nationalization crisis, President Eisenhower wrote, "The United States had done everything it possibly could to back up the Shah. I conferred daily with officials of the State and Defense departments and the Central Intelligence Agency and saw reports from our representatives on the spot who were working actively with the Shah's supporters."[43] To Eisenhower the fall of Musaddiq, a "semi-invalid" who carried on a "fanatical campaign,"[44] and the emergence of the shah as the supreme policy maker was an auspicious opportunity for the United States to work with the shah. An informant, whom President Eisenhower quotes, but cannot identify, told him after Musaddiq's overthrow that the shah "recognizes now his debt to us, and hopes that we have a realistic understanding of the importance of Iran to us." The same source told the president that the shah was fully aware of the importance of the army to the "security of his country and is also convinced that with the proper help Iran can become a significant link in the Free World's defense." Following this passage the president then quotes from his own diary on October 8, 1953, to the effect that if the shah and his new premier would be only "a little bit flexible," and the United States would stand by to help both financially and with wise

---

[43] Eisenhower, *Mandate*, p. 164.

[44] Ibid., p. 159. Eisenhower's view of the shah was, in contrast with his view of Musaddiq, quite favorable, as evidenced in still another of his writings: "The Shah had always impressed me as a man of good intent, concerned for the welfare of his people. Though far from being a dictator he possessed much more authority than any constitutional monarch of Europe" (*Waging Peace, 1956-1961* [Garden City, N.Y.: Doubleday & Co., 1965], p. 505).

counsel, "we may really give a serious defeat to Russian intentions in that area."[45]

This was a remarkable coincidence of American and Iranian perceptions of the Soviet threat at the highest level before the oil settlement. The shah and the president were both animated by vigorous opposition to Soviet ambitions in Iran and the Middle East. There was no doubt in Washington and Tehran that the significance of the oil dispute settlement for both transcended the confines of oil revenues and the interests of the international oil industry. For reasons of broader strategic and political interests, Iran and the United States did not wish to see the details of the agreement among the oil companies divulged. Secretary of State Dulles, in refusing repeatedly to release these details, stated that he did not wish to do so because "the foreign relations of the United States are involved." "There is danger that the exposure of these issues could again be used by irresponsible elements contrary to the interests of the United States and its allies." The secretary also stated that Iran as well as several other countries expressed "strong objection" to the disclosure of certain documents related to the oil dispute settlement.[46]

In the same way that American emergency financial aid and resumption of diplomatic relations with Britain had paved the way for the settlement of the oil dispute, this settlement prepared the way for the shah's government to cast its lot clearly with the West in the cold war. This was the fullest expression of his positive nationalism. To him, however, the West at the time meant primarily the United States. And the relations with the United States dominated Iranian foreign policy during the rest of the 1950s and well into the early 1960s. These relations fell into two major categories: Iran's general alliance policy and its bilateral relations with the United States

Iran Joins the Baghdad Pact

On October 11, 1955, Iran declared publicly its intention to join the Pact of Mutual Cooperation between Iraq and Turkey, commonly known as the Baghdad Pact, which had been signed at Baghdad on February 24, 1955. It is believed traditionally that Iran's decision to do so was a departure from its long-standing policy of neutrality. This is a myth, and like all myths it has had a tenacious hold. First, it is important to distinguish between *neutrality*

---

[45] See Eisenhower, *Mandate,* p. 165-66.

[46]
    U.S., Congress, House, Committee on the Judiciary, *Hearings* before Antitrust Subcommittee no. 5) of the Committee on the Judiciary, House of Representatives, 84th Cong., 1st sess., 1955, pt. 1, p. 724.

and *neutralism*. The former is a concept used primarily to denote a non-belligerent position on the part of a state in an armed conflict situation of a local or global nature. The latter is a concept primarily used with reference to peacetime conflict situations that might or might not lead to actual armed conflict. Neutralism was a concept most often used during the 1950s in connection with the cold war and was often used interchangeably with "non-alignment." It comprised all kinds of variations of neutralism, including the well-known concept of positive neutralism adopted by Gamal 'Abd al-Nasir of Egypt. With this distinction in mind, it is clear that Iran's adherence to the Baghdad Pact was certainly incompatible with neutralism. But it could be considered as a departure from Iran's traditional neutralism only if it could be shown that neutralism in fact had characterized the Iranian position for any considerable length of time. We have seen in this study that from the Anglo-Russian invasion of Iran in 1941 until 1951, every Iranian government pursued a third-power policy. Only during the government of Musaddiq did Iran attempt to pursue a neutralist course in foreign affairs. As we have already seen, his negative equilibrium was theoretically akin to neutralism, but in practice Musaddiq faced serious problems in adhering strictly to this doctrine—a fact that opened his policy to criticism from many quarters. Some nationalist critics advocated "absolute neutralism" (*bitarafi-i mutlaq*) as a corrective of negative equilibrium as practiced by Musaddiq. Even assuming that Musaddiq's aborted policy could be indeed considered neutralist, the brief duration of its existence would certainly disqualify it as an established tradition in Iranian foreign policy. And in such case Iran's adherence to the Baghdad Pact could not justifiably be considered a break with tradition.

On the other hand, if Iran's adherence to the Baghdad Pact is regarded as a break with Iran's declared policies of neutrality during the world wars, the proposition about the break with past policies is still subject to qualification. In the first place, such a proposition totally disregards the distinction between peacetime neutralism and wartime neutrality. In the second place, it assumes that Iran's policy in the First and Second World Wars was neutralist. As I have tried to show elsewhere, unless legal rhetoric is taken for actual policy, no such claim could be made in view of the fact that in neither world war was Iran capable or willing to pursue consistently a neutralist foreign policy.[47]

What, then, was so different about Iran's adherence to the Baghdad Pact? If it did not make a break with a tradition of neutralism or neutrality in Iranian foreign policy, what did it signify? As I have tried to suggest throughout this study, the prewar tradition of third-power policy continued without a break until 1951, and only during the brief period of Musaddiq's government

---

[47] See Ramazani, *Foreign Policy of Iran,* pp. 114-37, 277-300.

was any attempt made to pursue a neutralist policy. In this light, Iran's adherence to the Baghdad Pact signified that Iran clearly abandoned its tradition of third-power policy and refused to experiment with a neutralist foreign policy of the Musaddiqist or any other variety. Instead it chose to ally itself with the West. As seen, Iran's foreign policy became clearly the shah's foreign policy after the overthrow of the Musaddiq regime. As such, it primarily reflected his perception of the Iranian position in world politics, his assumptions about the nature of the Iranian problem, and his projected solution for that problem.

The most fundamental assumption of the shah in the 1950s, as shown, concerned security. To him, Iran's national security was inseparable from domestic security, and domestic security was in turn intertwined with the security of his regime and the Pahlavi dynasty. The single most important outside threat to national security was posed by "totalitarian imperialism," or Soviet imperialism, and from within by subversive Communism. This latter meant the Tudeh party. The first essential instrument of resisting both these related internal and external threats in the 1950s, the shah believed, was the armed forces, and the single most powerful state that could, and was willing to, help Iran preserve its national security was the United States. As we have already noted, at least during the Eisenhower administration, the shah's diagnosis of, and prescription for, Iranian problems significantly paralleled those of the president and particularly Secretary of State Dulles. The secretary's proverbial hostility toward the Soviet Union and communism was paralleled by his equally proverbial antagonism toward neutralism, which he considered both "immoral and obsolete."

The attraction of the Baghdad Pact for Iran stemmed primarily from the fact that it originated as the result of American initiative. Secretary Dulles himself introduced the concept of a northern tier in his report of June 1, 1953, to the nation over radio and television after his historic trip to the Middle East. Iran had not been included in the trip because, to borrow the secretary's words, it "is now preoccupied with its oil dispute with Britain. But still the people and the Government do not want this quarrel to expose them to Communist subversion."[48] The secretary of state despaired of a Middle East Defense Organization including the Arab states but seemed to be hopeful about the countries closer to the Soviet Union. He stated: "There is more concern where the Soviet Union is near. In general, the northern tier of nations shows awareness of the danger." Contrary to the secretary's assumption, however, what would prevent Iran at the time from joining any such Western-sponsored alliance system was not merely Iran's preoccupation with the oil dispute but the neutralist thrust of Musaddiqist foreign policy.

[48] U.S. State Dept. *Bulletin* 28, no. 729 (July 15, 1953):833.

President Eisenhower had been told that the shah believed (in the wake of the fall of the Musaddiq government) that Iran could "become a significant link in the Free World's defense."[49] But no public statement of this kind could be made before the Zahidi government was able to establish itself firmly in power. Furthermore, despite Secretary Dulles's northern tier concept and the shah's desire to join the Western defense system, no real sign of realization of the concept became visible before April 2, 1954. Then Turkey and Pakistan signed a treaty of friendship for security. Although this was not a military alliance it was a helpful sign to Iran. The treaty's open invitation to other states for accession was joyfully noted in Tehran. On July 26, 1954, Premier Zahidi made the most candid statement of his government about Iran's desire to move closer to the West. Addressing a group of Iranian editors, he stated that "we have witnessed how aggressors have wantonly occupied neutral countries in defiance of international law and their own undertakings. Therefore, it is certain in this turbulent world that a government can preserve itself only if it has the power of resistance against an aggressor."[50] The signing of the Baghdad Pact between Iraq and Turkey on February 24, 1955, further encouraged Iran to defy the Soviet Union and identify itself publicly with the United States. The Iranian representative to the Bandung Conference, for example, attacked "aggressors" who reinvented "colonialism" under such forms as subversion and economic or political interference, and praised the United States aid to Iran "as a fruitful way of reaching real economic and political independence, and of combatting colonialism under all its forms."[51]

Iran's intention to join the Baghdad Pact was thus publicly known before October 1955, but the announcement of its decision was being delayed as long as possible partly in view of Soviet opposition. However, the situation began to change rapidly in September. Late in that month, Egypt's arms deal with Czechoslovakia was announced for the first time. The Soviet Union was probably involved under the Czech cloak. Iran was already quite uncomfortable with the development of the Soviet position in Afghanistan, and the Soviet thrust into the Arab Middle East would further flank Iran with unfriendly powers. Another consideration that affected the timing of the Iranian decision was the anticipated meeting of the Big Four foreign ministers in Geneva on October 27. The three Western foreign ministers did not wish to face the Soviet protest at the time as the Soviet Union had encountered theirs when the Czech arms deal had been announced in September. At that time they asked Molotov how his government reconciled solicitude for the "Geneva

---

[49]*Mandate*, p. 165.

[50]*New York Times*, July 28, 1954.

[51]Ibid., Apr. 19, 1955.

Spirit" with the opening of a new front in the Middle East.[52] Could not the Soviet Union ask the same kind of question if Iran announced its accession to the pact at the time of the foreign ministers meeting? Iran announced its decision on October 11, 1955, and it was then anticipated that the Majlis and the Senate would ratify it quickly before the Geneva meeting on October 27. Both houses strongly favored Iran's adherence to the Baghdad Pact,[53] which was open to "any state actively concerned with the security and peace in this region." [54]

As we shall see in the next chapter, the Soviet Union vigorously opposed Iran's adherence to the pact, but both the United States and Great Britain welcomed it warmly. The State Department, with an eye to the Soviet Union, declared that "in no respect can this natural association be deemed hostile or threatening or directed against any other nation." The British Foreign Office hailed Iran's decision on October 13, 1955, as a step that would "increase security and help the cause of peace in the area." In anticipation of the expiration of its treaty with Iraq, which had in the past provided for British bases, Britain itself had joined the Baghdad Pact on April 5, 1955, and signed, at the same time, with Iraq a new bilateral treaty. Pakistan, for its own reasons, including concern with India, had also adhered to the pact on September 23, 1955. Thus Iran's adherence completed the Middle Eastern alliance across the northern tier linking it with the Western alliance system through Turkish membership in NATO and Pakistan's in SEATO.

The formalities of Iran's accession to the Baghdad Pact followed rapidly thereafter. The Senate's approval was granted on October 19, 1955, 39 to 5, and the following day the Foreign Affairs Committee of the Majlis approved the cabinet decision for accession unanimously. Finally, on November 3, 1955, Iran deposited the instrument of accession with the Ministry of Foreign Affairs of Iraq according to article 5 of the pact.

Endorsement of the Eisenhower Doctrine

Following Iran's accession to the Baghdad Pact, the five members set up the formal organization, but to Iran's great disappointment the United States chose to stay out of the organization. The United States did not want to provoke any new Soviet move into the Middle East and wished to keep

[52]*Times* (London), Oct. 3, 1955.

[53]*New York Times,* Oct. 12, 1955.

[54]See article 5 of the pact. The text is in U.N., Secretariat, *Treaty Series* 233, no. 3264 (1956): 211-17.

whatever chance still remained of working with Saudi Arabia and Egypt.[55] The Iranian disappointment was rooted in the fear of the shah's regime that (1) the organization might fail to provide for effective defense against the Soviet Union; (2) American nonparticipation might place serious limitation on economic and particularly military aid; and (3) the decline of the British power in the Arab Middle East without adequate American presence might create conditions favorable to the Soviet Union and Arab revolutionary regimes and hence eventually undermine the position of Iran's friendly Arab neighbors in the Persian Gulf area.

The United States reappraisal of its policy after the Suez crisis of 1956 raised Iran's hopes once again that the chances of American membership in the Baghdad Pact might improve. The Eisenhower administration, however, decided to seek a congressional resolution in support of American policy instead of membership in the Baghdad Pact organization. The president's proposals in a special message to Congress on January 5, 1957, led to the joint resolution, commonly known as the Eisenhower Doctrine, authorizing the president to employ, as he deemed necessary, American armed forces to protect the integrity and independence of any nation or group of nations in the general area of the Middle East requesting such aid against "overt armed aggression from any nation controlled by international communism." To Iran, this was not as desirable as United States membership in the alliance, but it was an improvement over the previous American position insofar as it declared unequivocally the American intentions vis-à-vis the Soviet Union. The other feature of the doctrine that appealed to Iran was the greater freedom the president would enjoy in extending already appropriated funds for military and economic aid in the Middle East.

Iran, as well as Turkey, Pakistan, and Iraq, announced jointly on January 21, 1957, their support of the president's proposals as "best designed to maintain peace" in the Middle East and to "advance the economic well-being of the people."[56] Premier Husain 'Ala and members of his cabinet met with Ambassador James P. Richards, special representative of the president, to discuss the doctrine on March 27, 1957. During these discussions, Prime Minister 'Ala reaffirmed Iran's endorsement of the purposes of the "new American policy." During the same discussions it was stated that because of Iran's own "increasing capabilities" it was anticipated that American aid would "accelerate progress in Iran's economic development program and toward the Government's goal of a better standard of living, with full

[55] See John C. Campbell, *Defense of the Middle East* (New York: Frederick A. Praeger, 1960), p. 60.

[56] *New York Times,* Jan. 22, 1957.

national security, for its people." [57] What interested Iran most was Ambassador Richards's remarks about the military assistance aspect of the American policy. He said that the United States was willing to join the Military Committee of the pact; agreed that the United States would provide increased financing for an already planned large military construction program to meet the needs of the Iranian forces; and would also provide certain additional items of military equipment.

Despite its endorsement of the Eisenhower Doctrine, Iran continued to complain about nonmembership of the United States in the pact and the inadequacy of American military and economic aid through the organization. For example, after Manuchihr Iqbal was appointed prime minister, he welcomed the United States decision to join the pact's Military Committee but stated that "full participation" by the United States was needed to give the alliance "moral and military strength." [58] Insofar as the military aid as such was concerned, Iran kept insisting on its need for "more modern defensive weapons," although it did not refrain from requesting more rapid economic aid as well. For example, Jamshid Amuzigar, chairman of the Iranian delegation to the Economic Committee, stated on January 17, 1958, that the "prosperity and contentment of the people" were the only stabilizing elements that would permanently assure prosperity and peace. "Military strength," he declared, "is a necessary evil, but we all realize that we can do everything with a bayonet except sit on it." [59]

Iran, like the other Middle Eastern members of the pact, however, continued to support the Eisenhower Doctrine. The Lebanese crisis is the case in point. The Middle Eastern members of the pact, except for Iraq, which was then plunged in its own revolution, sent a message of support to the president on July 16, 1958. They declared that this "bold and appropriate decision of the United States will not only ensure the protection of the independence of Lebanon . . . but will at the same time strengthen the determined position of Iran, Pakistan and Turkey." [60]

The Quest for Greater Security
The Defense Agreement of 1959 with the United States

No single event between 1953 and 1958 exerted a more profound effect upon Iranian foreign policy than the Iraqi revolution, the destruction of the

[57] U.S. State Dept. *Bulletin* 36, no. 932 (May 6, 1957):724-31.

[58] *New York Times,* May 28, 1957.

[59] Ibid., Jan. 18, 1958.

[60] U.S. State Dept. *Bulletin* 39, no. 997 (Aug. 4, 1958):183.

monarchy and the emergence of the military regime of 'Abd al-Karim Qasim. We shall examine later the impact of the revolution on Iran's Persian Gulf policy; but we should note here that it also affected Iran's alliance policy. The shah had watched revolutionary political developments of the Arab Middle East with concern because they accompanied the rise of Soviet influence in the Arab Middle East and open Arab hostility to monarchical regimes. Any threat to the shah's regime was regarded as a threat to Iran's national security. The threat of the Iraqi example seemed both "clear and imminent." Unlike Egypt and Syria, Iraq was Iran's next door neighbor, and the example of its antimonarchical revolution was too close to be ignored by the antiroyal elements both within and outside Iran. It was also feared that the example of Iraq might expose other Arab states in the Persian Gulf area to military coup d'etats, Arab radicalism, and Soviet penetration and hence reduce the number of regimes friendly to Iran. At first sight it looked as if Iran would get caught in a pincer of Soviet threat from the north and antimonarchical Arab threat from the south, but with increasing Soviet influence in Iraq after the revolution and Qasim's flirtation with the Iraqi Communists, it appeared in Tehran that eventually Iran might get caught in a pincer with Soviets at both ends.

The Iraqi revolution entailed reappraisal of Iran's relations with a number of states. Quite apart from a drastic change in Iran's policy toward Iraq, the revolution also marked the beginning of reassessment of Iran's policy toward the Soviet Union as evidenced by its negotiations with the Soviet Union for a nonaggression pact, as we shall see in the following chapter. It also affected Iran's attitude toward Israel partly because of the absence of Iraq from the Baghdad Pact after the revolution when not only Iran but also Turkey and Pakistan began to admit that they had in fact some community of interests with Israel. [61] This led to the controversial pronouncement on the state of Iranian recognition of Israel which, in turn, prompted the rupture of diplomatic relations between Iran and Egypt in 1960. And finally, the Iraqi revolution turned Iran's attention dramatically to the entire Persian Gulf, as we shall see later.

The immediate effect of the Iraqi revolution on Iran's foreign policy, however, concerned its relations with the United States through the Baghdad Pact organization, which was renamed the Central Treaty Organization (CENTO) after the withdrawal of Iraq. Few events had taken Iran or other countries within or outside the region by greater surprise. It was seriously asked whether the pact itself could survive the crisis. Such questions alarmed the shah's regime more than any other member of the organization. At their ministerial meeting in London, the pact members, in the presence of the

[61] See *New York Times,* July 28, 1958.

United States, "reexamined their position," to borrow the language of the declaration of July 28, 1958, issued at the end of the meeting, "in the light of recent events and conclude that the need which called the Pact into being is greater than ever. These members declare their determination to maintain their collective security and to resist aggression, direct or indirect." More important, the declaration stated that "the United States in the interest of world peace, and pursuant to existing Congressional authórization, agrees to cooperate with the nations making this Declaration for their security and defense, and will promptly enter into agreements designed to give effect to this cooperation."[62]

Iran's negotiations with the United States on the basis of this declaration for a defense agreement proved disappointing. The United States proposed to conclude an executive agreement with Iran, rather than a treaty, under the authority already contained in the Eisenhower Doctrine and the mutual security legislation. Iran, on the other hand, urged a commitment by the United States to come to Iran's assistance in case of armed attack, but this would go beyond the authority in the joint congressional resolution. The shah's government asked that the United States increase its military and economic aid commitments, but the State Department objected that these required long and detailed study.[63]

Nevertheless, Iran signed an executive agreement with the United States on March 5, 1959, as the best possible alternative under the circumstances. A major aspect of the circumstances at the time was, as we shall see, the Soviet offer of a fifty-year nonaggression pact with Iran, which the shah decided to reject, choosing to stand with his allies after the direct appeal to him by the leaders of Britain, Turkey, and Pakistan.[64] In its agreement with Iran, the United States regarded as "vital to its national interest" Iran's independence and integrity and undertook (1) to continue to furnish Iran military and economic assistance, and, more importantly, (2) to come to Iran's assistance in case of aggression. Article 1 of the agreement stated: "In case of aggression against Iran, the Government of the United States of America, in accordance with the Constitution of the United States of America, will take such appropriate action, including the use of armed forces, as may be mutually agreed upon and as is envisaged in the Joint Resolution to Promote Peace and Stability in the Middle East, in order to assist the Government of Iran at its

---

[62]For the text of the declaration see U.N., Secretariat, *Treaty Series* 335, no. 4788 (1959): 206-9. For the United States position on these agreements, see U.S. State Dept. *Bulletin* 40, no. 1030 (Mar. 23, 1959): 416-17.

[63]*New York Times,* Feb. 12, 1959. For the United States position see U.S. State Dept. *Bulletin* 40, no. 1025 (Feb. 16, 1959):223-30.

[64]*New York Times,* Feb. 12, 1959.

request." [65] In return, Iran undertook to utilize the aid for the purpose of "effectively promoting economic development."

The deaths of the Iraqi monarch and the reputedly pro-Western Premier Nur al-Sa'id and the sudden disappearance of a charter member of the Baghdad Pact were also viewed with great alarm elsewhere. But neither Iran nor any other like-minded regional or Western power could do much else. The examples of the landing of United States Marines in Lebanon, at the invitation of the Chamoun government, or the British dispatch of paratroopers to Jordan could not be imitated in Iraq without further aggravation of the already explosive Middle Eastern situation. Nor could Iranian-Turkish-Pakistani intervention turn back the tide of events. The avoidance of military intervention by Western powers was followed by conciliatory action. The United States and Britain recognized the new regime in Iraq. Iran and Pakistan extended recognition to that regime on July 30, 1958, before the two Western powers.

With an eye to placating violent Soviet protests and propaganda, Iran emphasized the "defensive aspect" (*janbih-ye defa'i*) of the agreement, but the Iranian reaction contained other elements as well. After all, this was the first direct and efficient American commitment to Iran's national security despite the fact that the United States did not undertake any new major commitments beyond the existing ones. Foreign Minister Hikmat objected to a deputy's drawing a comparison between the agreement and the Eisenhower Doctrine. He argued that the doctrine was a unilateral and general act of the United States, whereas the agreement signified specific and bilateral commitment of the United States toward Iran. The semiofficial *Ittila'at* editorialized on a similar theme, putting an even more favorable face on the agreement. The agreement, it stated, recognized Iran as a "significant force in the preservation of international peace" as the 1943 declaration had recognized the role of Iran as the "Bridge to Victory" (*pol-i pirouzy*) in the common struggle against fascism. [66] Some Iranian statesmen, however, were irked by implied conditions attached to the agreement. This was revealed by the remarks voiced by Deputy Arsalan Khal'atbary, who, with four other deputies abstained from voting, on March 8, 1959, when the agreement was adopted by the Majlis. He resented the implication of Iran's commitment regarding effective utilization of aid for economic development. He thought the United States was too exacting in dispensing aid. He charged that Washington was more generous with its funds in dealing with neutralist and Communist states than with its allies. His mention of neutralism prompted the foreign minister

[65] For the text of the agreement see U.N., Secretariat, *Treaty Series* 327, no. 4725 (1959):277-83. "Joint Resolution" referred to the Eisenhower Doctrine.

[66] *Ittila'at Hava'i*, Mar. 7, 1959.

to counsel caution and point out the wisdom of the continuation of the present alliance policy in the light of Iran's geostrategic location. The foreign minister hinted at the advisability of neutralism, however, only from a position of strength rather than weakness.[67]

There was little doubt that the Iranian quest for security was not fully satisfied with this agreement, but for the time being it at least contained a promise of more economic and military aid. What the shah had really looked for was American commitment to support Iran against *any kind of aggression,* not just one controlled by international communism. Iraq was the specific case in point, but the United States was not prepared to go any further than restating existing commitments in a bilateral form. This Iranian expectation of aid against any aggression lay back of the shah's receptivity before the 1959 agreement to the idea of creating a confederation composed of Iran, Turkey, Pakistan, and Afghanistan. He stated at a news conference on September 27, 1958, without giving any details about the negotiations in which he was then engaged, that "I am proud that for the first time Persian-speaking nations are forming such a unity, which is aimed at defending their own territories against *any aggression."* [68] In retrospect, what is also interesting about the impact of the Iraqi revolution on Iran's foreign policy was the birth of the idea of regional powers helping themselves that finally led to the formation of the Regional Cooperation for Development (RCD) between Iran, Turkey, and Pakistan in 1964.

Finally, mention must be made that despite the fact that Turkey and Pakistan also signed similar agreements with the United States, Iran alone was subjected to severe diplomatic and propaganda attacks by the Soviet Union. We shall examine this problem in the following chapter. Suffice it to state here that Pakistan and Turkey as well as the United States denounced the Soviets for their violently anti-Iranian campaign. During its Seventh Session, the Ministerial Council of CENTO (October 7-9, 1959) issued a declaration condemning the propaganda campaign waged against Iran by the "communist bloc." The declaration stated that communist broadcasts in Persian against the Iranian government totaled some seventy-four hours weekly, and were supplemented by a clandestine station—calling itself "the National Voice of Iran"—purportedly operating from within Iran, but "in fact located within Soviet territory in the Causacus." This station in particular broadcast "abusive and violent" programs, not only encouraging the Iranian people to overthrow their government, but also making personal attacks on "the Head of the

---

[67]Ibid., Mar. 8, 1959.

[68]*New York Times,* Sept. 28, 1958. Italics are mine.

State." [69] This last point referred to Khrushchev's personal attacks on the shah, as we shall see in the next chapter.

From the Iranian perspective the single most important gesture of support in the face of Soviet attacks came from the United States. President Eisenhower visited Iran in the wake of the 1958-59 crisis while Soviet propaganda attacks on Iran were being continued. Some believed that the president's visit was prompted by Iran's concern over his discussions with Premier Khrushchev. Iran feared, it was speculated, that Soviet-American discussions might lead to agreement between the superpowers at its expense. [70] The circumstances surrounding the visit, the president's remarks on arrival in Tehran, his speech to the Iranian Parliament, and similar indications, however, indicate that the visit was primarily intended to stiffen the Iranian resolution to continue to stand with its allies in defiance of Soviet attacks. On his arrival on December 14, 1959, in Tehran, the president stated to the shah that he was returning His Majesty's visit to the United States, and spoke of Iran's "vital role in the defense of the free world, and the golden future that is assured Iran and its people in a world of peace with Justice." [71] In his speech to the members of the Parliament, the president stated: "Without flinching, you have borne the force of a powerful propaganda assault, at the same time that you have been working at improving the living standards in your nation." Elsewhere in the same speech, he stated, "We cannot abandon our mutual effort to build barriers, such as the peaceful barrier of our Central Treaty Organization, against the persistent dangers of aggression and subversion." In his joint statement with the shah, he revealed that the two leaders discussed the CENTO alliance; emphasized its "importance in preserving stability and security in the area"; and recognized the "usefulness of their bilateral agreement." [72]

Forging New Bilateral Ties with the United States

Iran's policy toward the United States after the downfall of the Musaddiq regime until the early 1960s extended beyond the confines of its alliance policy. It comprised the continuous search for, and an unprecedented acquisition of, American military and economic aid outside the CENTO framework.

---

[69] U.S. State Dept. *Bulletin* 41, no. 1061 (Oct. 26, 1959):586.

[70] *New York Times,* Oct. 13, 1954.

[71] *Public Papers of Presidents of U.S.,* Dwight D. Eisenhower, 1959, p. 850.

[72] Ibid., p. 54.

It may be recalled that the basic agreements for American aid to Iran had been concluded in 1943 and 1947, which were confirmed by Iran's agreement with regard to the Mutual Defense Assistance Program in 1950.[73] The pre-Musaddiq military aid to Iran, it may be recalled, was continued by Musaddiq, who agreed to extend the 1950 agreement on April 24, 1952. Basically these arrangements constituted the foundation of Iran's acquisition of American military aid during the rest of the 1950s except for changes required because of the Mutual Security Act of 1954.[74]

What distinguished the wartime military aid from the early postwar aid was, it may be recalled, the type of aid Iran had been able to acquire. Before 1947 all American military aid had been of a technical and advisory nature, whereas only beginning in 1947 did Iran finally succeed in acquiring American military equipment as well. What distinguished the military aid in the post-Mussadiq 1950s from the 1947-52 period was the amount. In the 1949-52 period, total military assistance from the United States amounted to only $16.7 million, whereas in 1953-61 it totalled $436 million. The enormous rise in the value of American military aid to Iran was surpassed by the amount of economic aid during the same period. Total economic aid in 1949-52 was $16.5 million; in the 1953-61 period it rose to $611 million; $345 million was grant, and the rest was loan. The fall of the Musaddiq government marked only the beginning of an unprecedented flow of American funds to Iran.

Quite apart from the magnitude of the aid, the post-Musaddiq 1950s witnessed unprecedented changes in the general pattern of economic and commercial relations of Iran with the United States. For the first time in the history of modern Iran, American interests became heavily involved in Iranian oil. This was largely the result of substantial American share in the consortium. Also American interests in Iranian oil were expanded through partnership agreements with the NIOC. Furthermore, American investment in a multitude of fields expanded significantly during that period. We shall examine these developments in a later chapter.

These developments qualified Iran to become the thirteenth country in the world since the Second World War to conclude a Treaty of Amity and Economic Relations and Consular Rights with the United States.[75] This treaty constituted the most comprehensive treaty of its kind between Iran and the United States. It was signed on August 15, 1955, at Tehran; was "ratified" by the United States Senate on July 11, 1956; was ratified by Iran on April 30, 1957; and entered into force on June 16, 1957. It was to remain

[73] See chapters 3 and 6 of this study.

[74] See U.N., *Treaty Series* 303, no. 1057 (1958):320-21.

[75] U.S. State Dept. *Bulletin* 33, no. 844 (Aug. 29, 1955): 367-68.

in force for an initial period of ten years and to continue in force thereafter unless terminated at the end of that period or subsequently by Iran or the United States after giving one year's written notice. It replaced Iran's "provisional" agreement relating to commercial relations with the United States concluded on May 14, 1928, and its "provisional" agreement relating to personal status and family law of July 11, 1928, and confirmed Iran's trade agreement of April 18, 1943, discussed previously.[76] We shall examine the major terms of the treaty presently, but, it should be noted that the trade agreement of 1943 was terminated by mutual agreement between the two countries in 1960.[77] The reason for this termination was the Iranian economic crisis. That agreement had been concluded under the United States Trade Agreement Act in order to free Iranian trade from the strict government control of the Riza Shah era and provide for reduction of duties for products of interest to the United States.[78] This termination was to assist Iran in 1960 with its economic stabilization program because it would in effect increase the Iranian tariff on American products and hence increase the badly needed revenues for Iran.[79]

The Amity and Economic Relations Treaty covered a wide range of subject matters. Its twenty-three articles contained provisions relating to basic personal freedoms, the protection of persons and property, taxation, exchange regulations, the treatment of exports and imports, navigation, and other matters affecting the status and activities of citizens and enterprises of one country within the territories of the other. It also contained provisions setting forth in general terms the treatment to be accorded to diplomatic and consular officers. The real significance of the treaty derived from Iran's readiness to undertake to avoid many of the policies and practices ordinarily associated with developing countries regarding foreign investments and enterprises. It signaled Iran's recognition of the need to encourage American investments in Iran by providing for their protection.

The most important provisions of the treaty may be categorized as follows:[80]

1. *Treatment of Nationals and Companies*: Iran and the United States undertook to accord fair and equitable treatment to each other's nationals and companies and to their property and enterprises; to refrain from "unreasonable or discriminatory measures" that would impair their legally acquired

---

[76] See chapter 3 of this study.

[77] U.N., Secretariat, *Treaty Series* 393, no. 5288 (1961):338-41.

[78] See chapter 3 of this study.

[79] See *Middle East Economic Digest* 4, no. 32 (1960):378.

[80] For the full text see U.S., Department of State, *Treaties and Other International Agreements* 8, TIAS no. 3853 (1955): 899-932.

rights and interests; and to insure effective means of enforcement for their contractual rights. They also undertook to accord "the most constant protection and security" within their territories to each other's nationals and companies, "in no case less than that required by international law"; not to take property except for public purpose, nor take it "without prompt payment of just compensation," which must be effective and adequate.

2. *Taxation*: Iran and the United States undertook to apply most-favored-nation treatment in levying taxes on the nationals and companies of each country within the territory of the other.

3. *Immunity*: No enterprise owned or controlled by either Iran or the United States would claim or enjoy in its business activities immunity from taxation, suit, execution of judgment or other liability to which privately owned and controlled enterprises were subject.

4. *Dispute*: Any dispute between Iran and the United States about the interpretation or application of the treaty, if not adjusted by diplomacy, would be submitted to the International Court of Justice, unless they agreed to settle it by some other pacific means.

In view of the recency of nationalization of the oil industry, Iran's acceptance of obligations regarding expropriation and nationalization of American property in a solemn international treaty revealed quite a change in policy. Equally, the acceptance of the well-known American position regarding the payment of "prompt, effective and adequate" compensation was quite novel in Iran's international economic relations. Few developing countries, in fact, would consent to such qualifications for the payment of compensation, as was revealed in the well-known Mexican expropriations dispute before the Second World War and the attitude of numerous other developing countries in the postwar era. It appeared that in throwing its lot with the West in the post-Musaddiq 1950s, the shah government was prepared to go quite far in encouraging American capital investment.

Iran also took advantage of the surplus agricultural commodities program of the United States during that period. On February 20, 1956, it signed an agreement for this purpose. The United States undertook to finance the sale for Iranian rials of certain agricultural commodities determined to be surplus. Both countries agreed that the Iranian rials accruing to the United States as a consequence of such sales would be used (1) to help develop new markets for the United States agricultural commodities and to finance international educational exchange activities in Iran; (2) to procure military equipment, materials, facilities, and services "for the common defense"; and (3) to extend loans to Iran to prompt its economic development.[81]

_____

[81] For the text, see U.N., Secretariat, *Treaty Series* 272, no. 3934 (1957): 136-43, 390-93. For related exchange of notes and amendments see ibid., pp. 354-57.

One of the most beneficial effects of this agreement was the activation of the Fulbright Program in Iran on November 25, 1957. Iran had signed an agreement for the establishment of this program as early as September 1, 1949, but it had become inactive several years later when funds earmarked for its use were exhausted. The new agreement provided for the expenditure during the first year of the program of the equivalent of $250 thousand in rials for the exchange of students, teachers, lecturers, research scholars, and specialists between Iran and the United States. The program would be administered by a renewed United States Commission for Cultural Exchange, consisting of eight members, with equal representation of Iranian and American nationals. All recipients of awards under the program authorized by the Fulbright Act were selected by the Board of Foreign Scholarships, whose members were appointed by the president of the United States.[82]

Finally, in the post-Musaddiq 1950s Iran entered into an unprecedented field of activity with the United States. On March 5, 1957, it signed an agreement for cooperation in civil uses of atomic energy for an initial period of five years.[83] Quite apart from the merits of the agreement, its prestige utility was not overlooked in Iran. The shah himself announced the signing of the agreement at the opening ceremony of the United States atoms-for-peace exhibit at Tehran on March 6. The agreement, however, did not come into force until April 27, 1959, when all the necessary requirements were fulfilled. Iran would receive information as to the design, construction, and operation of research reactors and their use as research development and engineering tools. The United States Atomic Energy Commission would lease to Iran uranium enriched in the isotope U-235, and Iran would assume responsibility for using and safeguarding the fissionable material. The agreement would, it was hoped, enable the Iranians to enhance their own country's training and experience in nuclear science and engineering for the development of peaceful uses of atomic energy within the framework of the atoms-for-peace program. Iranian students had already enrolled in reactor technology courses at the International School for Nuclear Science and Engineering. More important, the agreement expressed the "hope and expectation" of Iran and the United States that this initial agreement would lead "to consideration of further cooperation at some future date in an agreement in the field of nuclear power."[84]

[82] U.S. State Dept. *Bulletin* 37, no. 964 (Dec. 16, 1957):979.

[83] For the full text see U.N., Secretariat, *Treaty Series* 342, no. 4898 (1959):29-41.

[84] U.S. State Dept. *Bulletin* 36, no. 924 (Apr. 15, 1957):629-30.

XII

Resistance and Reconciliation
Reactions to the Soviet Union

IRAN'S INCREASING RAPPROCHEMENT with the West, marked by the resumption of diplomatic relations with Britain, the oil dispute settlement, accession to the Baghdad Pact, and the bilateral defense agreement with the United States, was paralleled by (1) resistance to Soviet pressures, (2) suppression of the Tudeh party, and (3) sporadic acts of reconciliation with Moscow. Resistance and reconciliation, which characterized Iran's policy toward the Soviet Union in the post-Musaddiq 1950s, largely reflected the response of the shah's regime to the twofold characteristic of Soviet policy toward Iran during that period. On the one hand, Soviet policy returned to the 1946-50 pattern of pressures and intimidation, discussed previously.[1] The only major difference was the fact that the 1946-50 cold war between Iran and the Soviet Union was only in part a reflection of the Soviet-American antagonism. It may be recalled that Iran's own rejection of the Soviet oil agreement marked the beginning of deterioration of their postwar relations. Otherwise, in the post-Musaddiq 1950s, as in the 1946-50 period, the Soviet policy toward Iran related to the nature and development of Irano-American relations. During the earlier period, for example, the presence of American advisers in, and the extension of American aid to, Iran constituted a major ground for Soviet pressures against Iran. If anything, Iran's rapprochement with the West later in the 1950s intensified American activities there to an unprecedented degree. Correspondingly, Soviet hostility toward Iran surpassed antagonism of the earlier period. As we saw in the previous chapter, the shah's regime regarded rapprochement with the West in general and the United States in particular to be in Iran's national interest. As viewed from Moscow, however, every Iranian move to increase American involvement in Iran was somehow regarded as an act directed against the security and interest of the Soviet Union.

The other characteristic of Iranian policy toward the Soviet Union in the post-Musaddiq 1950s was also a reflection of its actions in response to Soviet policy. Iranian attempts at reconciliation, in the last analysis, reflected response to the Soviet new look of the post-Stalin era. Iran's conciliatory

---

[1]Chapter 7 of this study.

moves corresponded with the "peaceful coexistence" overtures of the Soviet Union. As seen from Tehran the Soviet Union was pursuing simultaneously a "policy of intimidation and ingratiation" (*syasat-i tahdid va tahbib*). [2] Given the hostility between the two countries from the rise of the Zahidi government into the early 1960s, the settlement of a number of major and long-standing disputes in this same period and the creation of several new areas of cooperation should not be attributed merely to the success of a Soviet peace offensive. Iran's own ability to reach agreement with the Soviet Union also revealed the pragmatic thrust of the shah's foreign policy. Despite opposition to most Soviet policies and attitudes, Iran did not easily overlook the opportunities for accommodation afforded by Soviet overtures. In this respect Iran's policy at the time seemed to resemble its policy during the early 1920s. That was, as I have shown elsewhere, a policy of "reconciliation without appeasement." [3] Positive nationalism was not merely anti-Soviet and pro-Western. It favored the Soviets when it paid off.

This chapter will illustrate these twofold characteristics of Iranian policy toward the Soviet Union. Resistance if necessary and reconciliation if possible. I hope this will dispel the simplistic pro-Western and anti-Soviet characterization of Iran's foreign policy during the post-Musaddiq 1950s.

Resistance to Soviet Pressures against Alignment with the West

Iran's efforts to reach an oil settlement with Britain were viewed from Moscow basically as a struggle between the American and British "oil monopolies" and as part of a larger effort by the United States to replace Britain in the Middle East. The Soviet government as such did not protest the oil settlement, but the Soviet press revived its favorite theme of the Musaddiq era, American-British rivalry for Iranian oil. More important, the efforts at settling the oil dispute were seen by the Soviet Union as part of the American effort to draw Iran into a Western-sponsored alliance system in the Middle East. For example, *Izvestia* of March 3, 1954, stated that the plan for establishing the oil consortium "is a definite result of the struggle to redistribute Iran's oil resources to the American monopolies' advantage and to the British monopolies' detriment." [4] After the oil settlement was initialed in Tehran on August 5, 1954, *Pravda* claimed that the consortium arrangements represented an attempt to place the Iranian oil industry under the control of

[2] See *Khandaniha*, 16th Year, no. 45, p. 7.

[3] See Ramazani, *Foreign Policy of Iran,* pp. 152-67.

[4] *CDSP* 6, no. 9 (Apr. 14, 1954):26-27.

the Western oil companies. It also represented an attempt to control Iran's "entire economy." The Soviet press attempted to portray the activities of the American advisers, the settlement of the oil dispute, and the formation of a Western-sponsored alliance system in the Middle East all as part of the same "aggressive" and "adventurous" military-political plans of the United States in the area.

More than a year before Iran announced its decision to adhere to the Baghdad Pact, the Soviet Union began its diplomatic and propaganda attacks on the shah's policy. Soon after the Turkish-Pakistani treaty was signed, the Soviet Union tried to discourage Iran from deciding to adhere to the treaty by offering three concessions within a week. Attempts at enticement having failed, the Soviet Union launched a diplomatic offensive. On July 8, 1954, the Soviet government sent a note to Iran, stating that it had learned about American efforts to draw Iran into "the aggressive military bloc" that was being created in the Middle East on the basis of the Turkish-Pakistani agreement; called Iran's attention to its "obligations" under the Soviet-Iranian treaty of October 1, 1927; and requested explanations.[5] Iran replied on July 18, 1954, that it would participate "publicly and in good faith" in regional groupings and denied that it was being drawn into aggressive military blocs directed against the Soviet Union. The Soviet press repeated the contents of the Soviet note, but also added its long-standing attack on the presence of American advisers in Iran.[6]

Iran's announcement of its accession to the Baghdad Pact on October 11, 1955, was protested vigorously by the Soviet government and the press. The Soviet note of October 12 complained that the Soviet government had not heard about Iran's decision directly. It had learned from press reports that the Iranian government intended to join the pact and could not "fail to attach serious importance" to such reports. It then went on to state that the Baghdad Pact was a military alignment "which is the tool of certain aggressive circles" and that Iran's accession to this pact was "incompatible with the interests of strengthening peace and security in the area of the Near and Middle East and is in contradiction with Iran's good-neighborly relations with

[5] Royal Inst. Intl. Affairs, *Documents, 1954*, pp. 189-190. Article 3 of the 1927 treaty, to which the Soviet notes repeatedly referred for pointing out Iran's "obligations," states in part: "Each of the Contracting Parties agrees to take no part, whether *de facto* or *de jure*, in political alliances or agreements directed against the safety of the territory or territorial waters of the other Contracting Party or against its integrity, independence or sovereignty." For a discussion of the Oct. 1, 1927, treaty in the broader context of Irano-Soviet relations in the interwar period, see Ramazani, *Foreign Policy of Iran*, pp. 217-41.

[6] *CDSP* 6, no. 32 (Sept. 22, 1954):3 for *Pravda* of Aug. 9, 1954.

the Soviet Union and the known treaty obligations of Iran."[7] The Iranian reply of October 16 refuted the Soviet interpretation of the Baghdad Pact and stated that its action in joining the pact, which was established within the framework of the United Nations Charter, had "no objective other than that of ensuring peace and security in the Middle East."[8] The Soviet press was far more vehement in its denunciation of both Iran and the United States. Iran's accession to the pact was blamed on "certain powers which advocate the 'Spirit of Geneva' in words, but are really forging aggressive military blocs." The statement of the shah to the Senate about the harmfulness of a policy of neutrality, given Iran's experience in the two world wars, was attacked, charging that Iran had joined "the Hitlerite bloc" in the Second World War and that by joining the Baghdad Pact it was "going downhill. This one-sided position, which contradicts the interests of the Iranian people and the interests of peace, bodes no good for Iran."[9]

Extreme Soviet annoyance with Iran's resistance occasioned a second note on November 26, 1955. This long note vigorously disputed Iran's claim that the pact was only defensive in nature, charged again that Iran's accession was contrary to its obligations under the 1927 treaty with the Soviet Union, and rejected the Iranian suggestion that its act was in keeping with the Charter of the United Nations. The note then asserted that the creation of the pact and Iran's accession to it were not necessitated by defense requirements

but serve the purposes of certain powers which are seeking to turn the countries of the Near and Middle East, Iran included, into their military *place d'armes*, and to ensure thereby the presence of foreign armed forces and the organization of their military bases on the territories of those countries. It is well known, at the same time, that no one has threatened or threatens Iran, and if there is a danger to Iran's security and independence, it comes primarily from the powers that are setting up aggressive blocs directed against other states.

The Soviet Union warned that Iran's accession to the pact "seriously injures Soviet-Iranian relations, and this at a time when the efforts of the Soviet Union and some other states have led to definite successes in easing international tension and in establishing confidence between nations, and when the Soviet Union has taken a series of steps towards strengthening and developing good relations with Iran." At the end the Soviet Union placed on the Iranian government "the entire responsibility for the probable conse-

---

[7] Royal Inst. Intl. Affairs, *Documents, 1955*, p. 305.

[8] Ibid., pp. 305-6.

[9] *CDSP* 7, no. 41 (Nov. 23, 1955):17-18.

quences of its decision to join the Baghdad Pact military bloc."[10] Iran rejected the contents of the Soviet note on December 10, 1955, along, more or less, the same lines as its previous note, and the Soviet Union once again protested Iran's accession to the pact on February 4, 1956, reiterating the contents of its note of November 26, 1955, just quoted.[11]

Defying Soviet Threats and Testing Soviet Peaceful Coexistence

Iran's signing of a defense agreement with the United States on March 5, 1959, produced the most violent and durable Soviet reaction against Iran. It may be recalled that the agreement was concluded in keeping with the United States undertaking to enter into agreements with Iran, Turkey, and Pakistan on July 28, 1958, when the CENTO powers met in London to "reexamine" their position in light of the Iraqi revolution.[12] The declaration of this meeting produced no immediate reaction from the Soviet Union. Nor did the subsequent discussions between Iran and the United States until October 1958, when a draft agreement was being considered by the two countries. On October 31, 1958, the Soviet Union protested Iran's intention to conclude an agreement with the United States in one of its most strongly worded notes to Iran. The note stated that Iran's further extension of its military cooperation with the United States "directly promotes the aggressive plans of certain foreign circles against the USSR and other peace-loving states"; made Iran both politically and militarily more dependent on the United States; and contradicted Iran's obligations under its treaty with the Soviet Union on security and neutrality of October 1, 1927. More important, the Soviet Union denounced Iran's attempt to link itself with the United States by "a military agreement of a character plainly unfriendly, and more than that directly hostile to the Soviet Union." Furthermore, the Soviet Union warned that it would remain even less indifferent when "faced with the situation now developing through Iran's conclusion of a new military treaty with the USA, which exposes the southern frontiers of the Soviet Union to immediate danger."[13]

[10]For the text see Royal Inst. Intl. Affairs, *Documents, 1955,* pp. 309-10. See also *CDSP* 7, no. 48 (Jan. 11, 1956):22-23.

[11]*CDSP* 8, no. 6 (March 21, 1956):29-30.

[12]See chapter 11 of this study.

[13]*CDSP* 10, no. 44 (Dec. 10, 1958):17.

This basic theme of Soviet concern with the security of its southern frontiers was further emphasized through both diplomatic channels and the Soviet press. The Soviet aide-mémoire of December 28, 1958, to the Iranian government stressed that the conclusion of a military agreement between the United States and Iran would make a sharp turn in Iran's foreign policy and would place Iran among the enemies of the USSR. These enemies or third powers "do not conceal their desire to use Iran and Iranian soil against the Soviet Union."[14] The Soviet press denounced the projected Irano-American agreement, alleging that it would "increase the danger of an American attack on the southern areas of the USSR" and that Iran was allying itself with "a country that makes no secret of its insane plans to wipe the Soviet Union off the face of the earth."[15] Iran's reply to the Soviet aide-mémoire was delayed until April 30, 1959, when it had already signed an agreement with the United States.[16] Meanwhile, the two countries suddenly entered into negotiations with a view to concluding an agreement, called a "Treaty of Friendship, Non-aggression," by the Soviet Union.

The secrecy surrounding the discussions for such an agreement at the time and conflicting Iranian and Soviet versions of these discussions published subsequently make it difficult to pin down with certainty what, in fact, took place between the two countries. Nevertheless, these discussions and their failure are too crucial to remain unexplored. The Soviet statement of February 10, 1959, claimed that the Iranian government did not want to sign the treaty that it "proposed itself"; attributed the initiative for the negotiations to Iran; claimed that Iran forwarded a "proposal" for the conclusion of a treaty to the Soviet government; and Iran invited the Soviet Union to send a mission to Tehran for discussions.[17] According to this statement, also, the Soviet Union submitted its own draft treaty, which included the principles propounded at the Bandung Conference and which also contained an undertaking by each of the parties "not to grant third states the right to build military bases and aerodromes on its territory or to use the existing ones, and not to allow the stationing of armed forces of any third state on it." The Soviet draft treaty, according to the same statement, expressed willingness of the Soviet Union to give assistance to Iran in a variety of agricultural, technical, industrial, social, and cultural fields. The Soviet statement also mentioned that during the negotiations Iran "attached special importance to the annulment of Articles 5 and 6 of the Soviet-Iranian Treaty of 1921"; and

[14] *CDSP* 11, no. 3 (Feb. 25, 1959):25-26.

[15] *Mizan Newsletter* 1, no. 3 (Feb. 1959):9.

[16] Royal Inst. Intl. Affairs, *Documents, 1959,* pp. 352-56.

[17] For the text see ibid., pp. 327-36.

claimed that Iran had stated that it would not conclude with the United States or any third countries military agreements directed against the Soviet Union, if such a treaty was concluded with the Soviet Union. The Soviet statement also revealed that the Soviet Union had expressed the opinion that it would be a good thing if, while concluding a treaty, Iran withdrew from the Baghdad Pact, but the Soviet government "did not insist on Iran's withdrawal." However, the statement did reveal that it accepted "the full text" of the Iranian draft treaty but expected at the same time that Iran "and the Shah personally would take corresponding actions." From the context it seems clear that the Soviet Union expected that Iran in turn would undertake (1) "not to conclude with any third states bilateral agreements directed against the Soviet Union"; and (2) "not to make its territory available for the setting up of foreign military bases and the stationing of foreign troops on any pretext."

The statement of the Iranian foreign minister on February 14, 1959, to the Senate, on the other hand, revealed certain differences from the Soviet version.[18] The statement, without saying specifically that the Soviets took the initiative in starting the negotiations, definitely left the impression that they did do so. The Iranian foreign minister emphasized the "friendly tone" of the Soviet aide-mémoire and the Soviet readiness to enter into "friendly negotiations." The Iranian statement was far more clear, however, in placing the blame for the breakdown of negotiations squarely on the Soviet Union. Furthermore, the Iranian statement claimed that at the outset of discussions between the Soviet mission and Iran, it was made clear to the Soviets that "we would remain constant and loyal to the defensive Baghdad Pact;" and added that "we are at liberty to conclude any agreement with any country we desire." But Iran was willing to insert in its agreement with the Soviet Union a provision to the effect that any agreement it signed with any other state would "contain no threat of aggression against the Soviet Union" and that Iran "would grant no military base" on its territory to any state; so long as it was not attacked, it would not permit the entry of the armed forces of any country "into its territory to the prejudice of any other country." The Iranian statement also revealed that Iran would insist on the clarification of the term "military bases" by a group of military and legal experts so that no room would be left for future ambiguity and misunderstanding.

The contradictory Soviet-Iranian versions of the secret negotiations were more amplified than clarified by what was published subsequently. In his book the shah left at least the impression that the Soviet Union took the initiative. He said the Soviets "made overtures and through intermediaries

---

[18] For the text see ibid., pp. 336-40.

held out promises of a long-term non-aggression pact and tremendous economic help." He also stated that one of the mistakes the Russians made after their arrival was their demand that "[we] get out of the Baghdad Pact. Although they dropped this demand when they saw our violent reaction, they insisted upon our not signing the proposed bilateral agreement with the United States." [19] The shah also indicated that the proposed Soviet pact contained clauses "that would have weakened our ties with our friends." The shah's version, however, was purportedly repudiated by a long article published in the Soviet Union under the pseudonym "Irandust," meaning "Iran's friend." [20] This article gave a day-by-day account of the Soviet version of the discussions, but at the outset attempted to refute categorically three statements made by the shah regarding the question of initiative, the Soviet position on Iran's withdrawal from the Baghdad Pact, and the Soviet position on the signing of a new agreement with the United States. Despite the categoric assertions of this article at its outset, however, it became clear in the rest of its text that, as the shah stated, the Soviet Union had first tried to get Iran out of the Baghdad Pact but subsequently seemed to drop that demand for a pledge by Iran not to go through with its bilateral agreement with the United States. The article's assertion that Iran rather than the Soviet Union had, at the start of negotiations, declared that it would sign no military agreement with the United States seems incomplete in view of the fact that the Soviet statement of February 10, 1959, discussed above, clearly showed that the Iranian willingness to do so was contingent upon the signing of a treaty with the Soviet Union.

From all these accounts it appears that what lay at the heart of the breakdown of negotiations was in part the fate of articles 5 and particularly 6 of the Soviet-Iranian treaty of 1921.[21] Elsewhere I have tried to show how presistently the Soviet and Iranian interpretations of this treaty diverged.[22] In the 1958-59 negotiations Iran aimed at mutual renunciation of these articles because they had outlived their usefulness. The Iranian draft treaty had proposed their renunciation, according to both Iranian and Soviet

---

[19]*Mission for My Country*, p. 122.

[20]See *Mizan Newsletter* 3, no. 3 (Mar. 1961):10-15.

[21]Iran's interest in the cancellation of these articles in the 1950s was mentioned in public as early as 1956, before the shah's trip to Moscow. See *Khandaniha*, 15th Year, no. 96, p. 38.

[22]For a full discussion of the problem of articles 5 and 6 from the inception of the 1921 treaty to the early 1960s, see Rouhollah K. Ramazani, "Treaty Relations: An Iranian-Soviet Case Study," in Albert Lepawsky, Edward H. Buehrig, and Harold Lasswell, eds., *The Search for World Order* (New York: Appleton-Century-Crofts, 1971), pp. 298-311.

accounts, but Iran also insisted that the term "military bases" should be defined so that in the new agreement, as contrasted with the old 1921 treaty, the Soviet Union would not in future invoke such a term at its own discretion for intervening in Iran militarily as it had done in 1941. The Soviet reluctance to do so at least precipitated the breakdown of negotiations. For Iran to have left the interpretation of that term completely to the discretion of the Soviets after nearly fifty years of bitter experience with the Russians would have been unimaginable, particularly if Iran were to limit its freedom of action in world politics by undertaking obligations principally in favor of the Soviet Union.

As for the Iranian position, the following seem warranted: (1) Iran was prepared to undertake in its pact with the Soviet Union not to sign an agreement, with the United States or any other third state, that posed a threat of "aggression to the Soviet Union." (2) Iran was prepared to undertake not to grant military bases to the United States or any other third state on its territory, provided that the term "military bases" was defined by mutual agreement in advance. And (3) Iran would not allow the entry of the armed forces of the United States or any other third state into its territory if that entry was prejudicial to the Soviet Union, unless Iran was attacked first. In return for these undertakings, Iran would expect that the Soviet Union would renounce articles 5 and 6 of the 1921 treaty and extend substantial economic and technical aid to Iran in addition to the inclusion of provisions compatible with the principles adopted at the Bandung Conference. [23]

From these points, can it be explained why Iran entered into negotiations with the Soviet Union to begin with? Definite answers are not possible now and probably for quite some time to come, in view of the unavailability of relevant archival materials in Iran and the Soviet Union. Two propositions seem feasible, however. First, Iran entered into negotiations in order to pressure the United States to come through with a more comprehensive and solemn commitment to Iranian defense and more generous economic and sophisticated military aid. Iran's long-standing unhappiness with United States nonmembership in the Baghdad Pact, its undeniable concern over the Iraqi revolutionary developments, and its chronic dissatisfaction with American economic and particularly military aid would support this proposition. Second, Iran's entry into negotiations with the Soviet Union aimed to secure Soviet commitment to nonaggression and extensive Soviet economic-technical aid *without* abandoning its past or future ties with the United States. This

[23]The Soviet draft included provisions regarding the principles of respect for territorial integrity and sovereignty, nonaggression, noninterference in internal affairs, and equality and mutual benefit. It is interesting to note that the Irano-Soviet treaties of 1921 and 1927 embodied many of the principles adopted at the Bandung Conference many years later.

proposition is not necessarily tantamount to having the cake and eating it. Iran, as well as its allies, was, in the late 1950s, experiencing Soviet blandishments and enticements. At the time it was by no means unusual to think that alliance with the West and coexistence with the Soviet Union would be possible. Iranian thinking on this score is, I submit, amply evident from the extent and nature of its discussions with the Soviet Union. Its entry into negotiations was neither the sign of weakening determination to resist the Soviet Union, as it was universally assumed in the West at the time, nor a reflection of "double-dealing," as was charged by the Soviet Union. It was probably an attempt to test the potential and the limits of the Soviet policy of peaceful coexistence. At the time the limits seemed too stringent to Iran, and hence the signing of a long-term treaty of that kind with the USSR was regarded unwise.

After the breakdown of negotiations on February 10, 1959, and before Iran actually signed an agreement with the United States on March 5 of that year, Premier Nikita Khrushchev personally attacked the shah's regime. In a speech on February 17 he repeated the Soviet version of the negotiations briefly, stating that the shah offered to conclude a treaty and then rejected his own proposals under pressure from the United States, Britain, and Turkey. The treaty with the United States, he stated, "will entail the transformation of Iran into an American military base"; and in doing so the shah spoke as if a threat to Iran existed from the Soviet Union. Khrushchev then made a personal attack on the shah, which signaled the beginning of unprecedented hostility in Iran's postwar relations with the Soviet Union. He asked: "Whom then, in actual fact, does the Shah of Iran fear? He does not fear us, but fears his own people. He, it is clear to see, is not assured of the stability of his throne, and for that reason keeps his personal money invested not in Iran but in England. He is seriously disturbed by what has taken place in Iraq. The Shah of Iran fears, above all, his own people and, by the signing of a bilateral military treaty with the USA, wants to ensure that American troops shall protect his throne."[24] On February 24 Khrushchev in a speech on the relations of Iraq, the United Arab Republic, and Iran with the Soviet Union once again denounced Iran's intention to conclude an agreement with the United States; adumbrated Soviet offers of aid and cooperation with Iran in the past; again expounded his favorite thesis that the shah's fear of the Iranian people or internal "subversion" lay at the root of his decision to conclude a bilateral military agreement with the United States; and declared that no "external forces will save anybody from his own people"![25]

[24]*Mizan Newsletter* 1, no. 3 (Mar. 1959), Appendix B, pp. 1-2.

[25]Ibid., pp. 2-4.

Khrushchev's repeated verbal attacks on the shah made it all the easier for Iran to do what it had refrained from doing over the decades; it renounced articles 5 and 6 of the 1921 treaty. Once in 1935 and again during the 1958-59 negotiations with the Soviet Union, just discussed, Iran had tried to renounce articles 5 and 6 by mutual agreement. In 1935 the Soviet Union proposed a protocol that would, in effect, retain the substance of section 3 of article 5 but would explicitly cancel article 6 because of fundamental changes of circumstance. Article 5 was the more equitable article in that it committed *both* Iran and the Soviet Union to prevent the stationing of troops by a third power in their territory, if the presence of such forces was likely to threaten either's frontiers and interest or security. But article 6 gave solely to the Soviet Union the right to intervene in Iran militarily if a third party should attempt to carry out armed intervention in Iran, or if such power should desire to use Iranian territory as a base of operations against Russia, or if a foreign power should threaten the frontiers of Russia or those of its allies. But the Soviet Union alone was the sole judge of what constituted "a base of operations against Russia" and whether a foreign power was in fact threatening the Russian frontiers at a given time. Iran's 1935 attempt to get the Soviet Union to agree to the renunciation of article 6 finally failed, as did its efforts during the 1958-59 negotiations, which broke down in part because of disagreement on the meaning of the term "military bases." On both occasions Iran maintained that these articles had been drafted solely with a view to preventing possible threats to Soviet Russia from czarist counter-revolutionary forces that might have wished, in the 1920s, to use Iranian territory as their base of operations.

In any event, at a press conference on March 2, 1959, only three days before the actual signing of Iran's agreement with the United States, the Iranian deputy foreign minister stated that articles 5 and 6 of the 1921 treaty were "obsolete because they are no longer applicable." This statement was apparently made to allay the impressions created by press reports that the 1921 treaty in toto had been denounced by Iran. Iran made clear that it denounced only those two articles and the rest of the treaty remained "valid."[26] *Pravda*, March 15, 1959, cited the Iranian action disapprovingly and declared that *all* the provisions of the treaty were "unalterable." The official Soviet disapproval of the Iranian denunciation could be inferred from the Soviet statement of May 14, 1960, to the Iranian chargé d'affaires in the Soviet Union. The statement was primarily a protest against the alleged permission given by Iran to the United States, Britain, Turkey, and Pakistan

---

[26]See the statement of the Iranian deputy foreign minister in *Ittila'at Hava'i*, Mar. 3, 1959. See relevant remarks by various Majlis deputies in *Ittila'at Hava'i*, Mar. 4, 1959. See also *New York Times*, Mar. 3, 1959.

to use Iran's air space for air force maneuvers for a few days, but the statement specifically cited the contents of article 5 of the 1921 treaty in order to call Iran's attention to its "obligations" under that treaty.[27]

Khrushchev's personal attack on the shah was followed by intensification of the Soviet propaganda campaign against Iran. The war of nerves dominated Soviet-Iranian relations most of the time until 1962. Iran's reaction was not confined to counterpropaganda activities, such as the installation of loudspeakers at the frontier town of Julfa to offset the Soviet broadcasts, which could be heard on the Iranian side of the border. Insofar as Khrushchev's own attack on the shah was concerned, the shah personally ignored it. In a major press conference on February 22, 1959, after Khrushchev's violent speech at Tula, mentioned before, the shah refused to make any reference to Khrushchev's remarks. Looking at the Soviet radio propaganda in the wake of the breakdown of negotiations, the shah underplayed the importance of the breakdown by stating that it was quite normal for states to negotiate without definite results, and declared that lack of success in negotiations should not cause annoyance. More important, he stated firmly that there would be no change in Iran's foreign policy, and on the basis of the general principle of that policy "we are prepared to reiterate that no country has asked us for bases; nor do we intend to permit any nation to establish on our soil offensive bases, particularly rocket bases." [28]

Although the shah himself ignored Khrushchev's remarks, the Iranian Senate and the Majlis took up the matter frankly and defiantly. On February 25, 1959, Senator Jamal Imami gave a historical sketch of Soviet-Iranian relations and denounced the unprecedented remarks of Khrushchev: "Please turn the pages of history and see there could not be found an instance in which the head of one state insulted the leader of another nation. What is this? Is it fitting for a great nation like the Soviet Union to insult the Iranian people, the Iranian government, and the Iranian verities?" [29] On the same day, Deputy Hishmati denounced Khrushchev's remarks by emphasizing the longevity, durability, and sacredness of the institution of monarchy in Iranian history over millennia. He also charged that the Soviet misbehavior constituted an interference in Iran's internal affairs. Khrushchev, he concluded, preached "peaceful coexistence" but in practice intensified the cold war.[30]

A well-known technique in Iranian political culture was also employed in response to Soviet attacks on the shah and Moscow's continuous propaganda

[27] *CDSP* 12, no. 21 (June 22, 1960):17-18.

[28] *Ittila'at Hava'i*, Feb. 23, 1959.

[29] Ibid., Feb. 25, 1959.

[30] Ibid., Feb. 26, 1959.

warfare. Suddenly rumors spread throughout Tehran that the shah was leaving Iran. Demonstrations followed, and a variety of groups joined the Bazaaris, who closed their shops, left their jobs, and marched toward the palace in order to persuade the shah to stay on. It was also reported that the crowds pleaded with Ayatullah Bihbihani to accompany them to the palace in order to plead with the shah to remain in Iran.[31] The other demonstration of support for the shah was produced by means of instant creation of an "Association for National Defense" (*jam'iat-i difa'a-i milli*) for the avowed and specific purpose of resisting Soviet propaganda attacks upon the shah and Iran. The association held its first meeting on September 8, 1959, in the Shah Mosque in Tehran; denounced the Soviet campaign against Iran; announced the display of a great show of support for Iran's independence and integrity by peoples from all corners of the country; and declared Iran's steadfastness, courage, and dignity in the face of insult by the Soviet Union. The speakers at the meeting were selected from various groups to show the solidarity of the nation, including the Iranian Chamber of Commerce and the Tehran and Bazaar guilds.[32]

The only major instance between 1958 and 1962 that seemed to hold some hope of improvement in Irano-Soviet relations was occasioned by the fall of the government of Iqbal on August 29, 1960, and the appointment of Sharif-Imami as the prime minister. The Soviets first viewed the resignation of Iqbal's government as "a blow to the Shah's regime" and as proof of the scandalous nature of the elections that had preceded it. The Soviet ambassador returned to Tehran on September 14, 1960, after nine months of absence from the capital. This was followed by discussions for finding ways of improving Irano-Soviet relations. Finally, on February 15, 1961, the Iranian Ministry of Foreign Affairs announced the decision of the Iranian government to send a goodwill mission to Moscow headed by Premier Sharif-Imami himself for talks with Khrushchev.[33] The Soviet Ministry of Foreign Affairs in turn made an announcement on February 28, stating that as early as November 1960 Soviet officials had agreed to the desire of the Iranian government to send a delegation to the Soviet Union "to discuss the normalization of Soviet-Iranian relations" and other questions of mutual interest.[34] Iran, however, advised that the mission would not travel to Moscow until after the Majlis elections. As it turned out, however, the government of Sharif-Imami resigned

[31] Ibid., Feb. 28, 1959.

[32] Ibid., Sept. 8, 1959.

[33] Ibid., Feb. 16, 1961.

[34] *CDSP* 13, no. 9 (Mar. 29, 1961):20.

on May 6, 1961, and he did not get a chance to make the trip to the Soviet Union.

The premiership of Amini, in principle, did not bode well for the improvement of Iran's relations with the Soviet Union. Unlike Sharif-Imami, a former supporter of Musaddiq, Amini was well-known in Soviet circles for his leading role in the oil consortium agreement, which the Soviets regarded as a cloak for "American imperialism" in Iran, and his strong statements against possibilities for Iran's adoption of a policy of neutrality. Nevertheless, the Soviet press and government continued to pay close attention to internal developments in Iran. The resurgence of the National Front with its dedication to the policy of non-alignment was watched with interest, although the Soviets never fully and unreservedly endorsed either Musaddiq or his supporters. The Soviet handbook *Modern Persia*, for example, viewed the government of Musaddiq as one that looked to the oil nationalization law to promote the interests of the Iranian landlords and bourgeoisie and resisted an expansion of the "democratic and worker and peasant movement," which was "the only firm basis of the struggle against imperialism." The Musaddiq government had also been criticized for its use of armed force against "democratic demonstrations" and for compelling the Tudeh party and "democratic trade unions" to work underground.[35]

The National Front's bold call for a mass meeting on July 21, 1961, in commemoration of Musaddiq's return to power on that day in 1952 touched off a new wave of controversy between Iran and the Soviet Union. First, the Iranian press charged Soviet incitement to revolt and disturbances within Iran. The Soviet press retaliated by violently attacking the Amini government. On July 23, 1961, the Iranian foreign minister called in the Soviet ambassador and handed him a strongly worded protest against "direct Soviet interference in Iran's internal affairs." [36] Despite some later signs of improvement in Iran's relations with the Soviet Union toward the end of the Amini government, no major development occurred until the premiership of Assadullah 'Alam.

Earliest Efforts for Conciliation with the Soviet Union

Obviously, Iran felt disappointed in finding out that the element of coexistence in Soviet policy was overshadowed by cold war considerations, as evidenced by the breakdown of its negotiations with the Soviet Union for a

[35] For the fullest account of the Soviet attitude toward Mussadiq in English translation, see *Mizan Newsletter* 3, no. 8 (Sept. 1969):7-11.

[36] *Ittila'at Hava'i*, July 23 and 27, 1961.

nonaggression pact. Iran's favorable response to the Soviet offer, as I have already proposed, was an attempt to test the limits of the Soviet peaceful coexistence policy. The failure of negotiations revealed that at the time neither the Soviet Union nor Iran was quite prepared to cooperate in matters bearing on their security; no agreement was reached on the definition of "military bases." The possibilities for cooperation in other fields, however, seemed more promising from the very beginning. The downfall of the Musaddiq government was preceded by the death of Stalin. The rise of the Zahidi government therefore coincided with the early signs of Soviet policy of peaceful coexistence. The timing of the earliest Soviet conciliatory gestures toward Iran in matters other than military security was, nevertheless, designed to serve Soviet security interests. It was no coincidence that these gestures occurred in the wake of the signing of the Turkey-Pakistan treaty and the increasing signs of Iran's attraction to accession to a Western-sponsored alliance system in the Middle East. Only a few months after that treaty was signed, the Soviet Union offered Iran three concessions within a single week. It offered, in the last week of June and the first day of July 1954, to release some three hundred Iranian citizens long detained in the Soviet Union; to turn over to Iran the inactive installations of an oil company at Pahlavi and other northern cities; to negotiate ancient boundary problems; and to turn over to Iran some eleven tons of long-overdue gold and goods worth $8 million. [37]

The first major response of Iran to these aspects of Soviet peaceful coexistence was manifested in its determined effort to come to a basic agreement with Russia on perennial boundary disputes. Iranian boundary problems with the Soviet Union were a legacy of the nineteenth century, when czarist treaties with Iran purportedly established new boundaries between Russia and Iran on both sides of the Caspian Sea. The Irano-Russian boundary began at the junction of the Aras River and the Kara Su, followed the thalweg of the Aras, trended across the Moghan Steppe, and finally followed the crest of the Talish Range and the thalweg of the Astara River; on the west side of the Caspian Sea the boundary left the seacoast, reached the Atrek River, and finally connected with the Hari Rud River. All this meant that Iran shared over a thousand miles of boundary with Russia across rugged mountain areas, desert plains, various rivers, and the seacoasts, but these were not clearly defined, despite various attempts in the nineteenth century. Nor did Riza Shah ever get to the actual settlement of boundary problems with the Soviet Union despite the fact that he signed an agreement in 1928 for the establishment of a "simple system" governing the age-old problem of crossing the common frontiers by Iranian and Russian nationals. He also established

[37] *Khandaniha*, 14th Year, no. 84, pp. 8, 39: *New York Times,* July 2, 1954.

boundary commissions with the Soviet Union, according to the Soviet-Iranian treaty of 1921, but the commissioners did not have the power to settle boundary or territorial questions.[38]

Discussions for the settlement of the boundary problems began at least as early as January 1954, but an agreement was not signed until December 2, 1954. The shah ratified it on March 2, 1955, the Presidium of the Supreme Soviet on April 25, 1955, and the exchange of ratifications took place on May 20, 1955. It was registered with the United Nations under the title Agreement between Iran and the Union of Soviet Socialist Republics concerning the Settlement of Frontier and Financial Questions.[39] No useful purpose would be served by summarizing the technical details of the agreement and the relevent protocols here. Suffice it to state that this was an unprecedented agreement in the history of Iran's boundary relations with Russia. The fact that it was signed in the early phase of Soviet peaceful coexistence policy is significant from the standpoint of Soviet foreign policy. It was equally significant from the Iranian standpoint, not only because it removed satisfactorily an ancient irritant in Iran's relations with Russia, but also because its terms were probably of greater advantage to Iran. Insofar as the financial settlement was concerned, it occurred at a time of great financial difficulty for Iran in the wake of the Musaddiq downfall. The fact that the Soviets owed Iran $8 million and eleven tons of gold from the Second World War and that the Soviet timing was for political ends did not detract from the usefulness of the settlement. According to the testimony of Marshall Amanullah Jahanbani, who headed the Iranian boundary delegation for several years after the signing of the agreement, although the village of Firuzeh was retained in Soviet territory, Iran gained some hundred square kilometers in the Moghan Steppe, about twenty square kilometers in the Dayman area, the controversial area of Yedi Evlar near the Astara River, and some twenty square kilometers in the Sarakhs district.[40]

Although the boundary agreement of 1954 settled the basic problems of boundary definition, much work had to take place before the written words could be translated into actual demarcation of boundaries. Furthermore, the lack of precise definition and demarcation had always been intertwined with

[38] See Ramazani, *Foreign Policy of Iran*, pp. 231-33. See also Rouhollah K. Ramazani, *The Northern Tier* (Princeton: Van Nostrand), pp. 9-19, 42-63.

[39] For the text and a related protocol, see U.N., Secretariat, *Treaty Series* 451, no. 6497 (1963):265-67.

[40] The fullest and most authoritative account on the Soviet-Iranian boundary settlement in Persian is written by Sipahbud Amanullah Jahanbani, *Marzha-ye Iran va Showravy* (Tehran: Chapkhaneh-ye Majlis, 1958/59).

numerous related problems, including boundary crossing, utilization of boundary river waters, and river navigation. For this reason the mere delimitation and marking of boundaries according to the 1954 agreement would not suffice, and diligent work by Iranian and Soviet boundary delegations over several years after the signing of that agreement was needed. Their work finally led to the most comprehensive treaty in the history of Irano-Soviet relations on the entire boundary regime and the settlement of frontier disputes and incidents that had always plagued the relations of the two countries. This treaty was signed on May 14, 1957, and was registered with the United Nations as the treaty concerning the Regime of the Soviet-Iranian Frontier and the Procedure for the Settlement of Frontier Disputes and Incidents. [41]

This treaty covered in great detail a wide variety of questions of significant concern to Iran. It provided for the maintenance of frontier marks and clearings; for the use of frontier waters and railways and main roads intersecting the frontier line; for regulating hunting, forestry, agriculture, and mining in the frontier areas; for the settlement of frontier disputes; and for the regulation of crossing the frontier. These functions were entrusted to Iranian and Soviet frontier commissioners, and they, their deputies, and assistants were to be stationed in specified frontier areas. The broad powers of the commissioners seemed to bode well for the settlement of numerous problems. In regard to the settlement of disputes, for example, the decisions taken jointly by frontier commissioners would be final. If the commissioners could not agree on the settlement of certain disputes or incidents, these would be referred to diplomatic channels, but resort to such a procedure would not preclude reference back to the commissioners of a matter discussed through diplomatic channels.

Definition of exact boundaries between Iran and the Soviet Union in 1954 thus paved the way for the actual demarcation of the boundaries and the establishment of a comprehensive boundary system and dispute settlement procedure in 1957. These basic achievements in turn led to Iran's first major postwar attempt at economic-technical cooperation with the Soviet Union. In the same year that the treaty on the boundary regime and dispute settlement was signed, Iran and the Soviet Union reached a new agreement on joint utilization, for irrigation and power, of the frontier sections of the Aras and Atrek rivers. As early as February 20, 1926, Iran had concluded an agreement regarding the division of waters of various rivers in different proportions.[42] The Irano-Soviet Agreement of August 11, 1957, provided for "equal rights

---

[41]For the full text and related documents, see U.N., Secretariat, *Treaty Series* 457, no. 6586 (1963):212-61.

[42]See Ramazani, *Foreign Policy of Iran*, p. 232.

of fifty per cent of all water and power resources of the frontier parts of the rivers Aras and Atrek for irrigation, power generation and domestic use." And to this end the two countries agreed to establish joint enterprises. In preparation for these enterprises they also agreed to establish composite groups of experts three months from the signing of the agreement for the purpose of exploratory work, to be followed by the establishment of survey teams on matters of topography, geology, hydrology, and economics.[43]

Iran also responded favorably to gestures of peaceful coexistence at the level of exchange of visits. At the invitation of the Supreme Soviet, a group of Iranian parliamentarians visited the Soviet Union for three weeks in 1956. More important, at the personal invitation of the chairman of the Presidium of the Supreme Soviet, the shah of Iran and Queen Soraya paid a state visit to the Soviet Union beginning on June 25, 1956. The shah exchanged views on political and security matters with Bulganin, Mikoyan, Shepilov, and particularly Nikita Khrushchev. He has reported these himself in detail, and they need no repetition here.[44] From his account it is quite clear that the primary concern of the Soviet leaders at the time was Iran's membership in the Baghdad Pact. More important, the shah then made his earliest personal pledge to Soviet leaders about the defensive nature of Iran's membership in the Baghdad Pact. He stated, "I gave Khrushchev my pledge as a soldier that as long as I reigned Iran would not in any way countenance or take part in any aggressive schemes against his country." Another important observation of the shah is that his visit to the Soviet Union had a catalytic effect upon improvement in Soviet-Iranian relations regarding boundary problems, frontier river water utilization, and similar matters.

This is generally true, but Iran's agreements with the Soviet Union during the post-Musaddiq 1950s suffered from the adverse effects of the bitter relations of the two countries over political and security matters. Cold war considerations adversely affected these major agreements in various ways. For example, the 1954 boundary agreement took years to finalize, not only because it involved time-consuming technical problems, but also because of the adverse Irano-Soviet political relations. Amanullah Jahanbani, the head of the Iranian boundary delegation, indicates, for example, how Iran's eventual accession to the Baghdad Pact had an adverse effect momentarily on the discussion of even technical questions.[45] Political difficulties with the Soviet Union also delayed the finalization of the boundary treaty as evidenced by

[43]For an English translation of the text, see *Middle East Journal* 13, no. 2 (1959): 193-94.

[44]*Mission for My Country*, pp. 118-21.

[45]See Jahanbani, *Marzha-ye Iran*, p. 61.

the fact that although it was signed in 1957 it did not enter into force until December 20, 1962. The same is true of the water utilization agreement. Although it was also signed in 1957, no significant effort got underway until the early 1960s. Finally, the same must be said about the crucial trade and transit relations between the two countries. A transit agreement between Iran and the Soviet Union was also reached in 1957 after the shah's visit to the Soviet Union, but its significance was overshadowed by the fact that no major and durable trade agreement between Iran and the Soviet Union was signed until the mid-1960s, as we shall see.[46] Iran's trade with the Soviet Union had always been a major concern to Iran. Riza Shah tried persistently to resolve Iran's commercial problems with the Soviet Union, but his latest and most comprehensive treaty with the Soviet Union, signed on March 25, 1940, had provided only a general framework for trade relations between the two countries. In the 1950s and early 1960s Iran drew up a list of commodities to be exchanged each year with the Soviet commercial agency according to the 1940 treaty. Exchange of these lists constituted annual "agreements" (*mova-fiqatnamih-ha*) that did not amount to full-fledged new trade "treaties" (*qarardad-ha*) between the two countries.[47] Hence, despite Iran's conciliatory response to Soviet peaceful coexistence overtures in the 1950s, no serious breach in the generally unhappy relations between the two countries occurred until the 1960s. The following chapter will explore the factors underlying the change in Iran's policy toward the Soviet Union in the early 1960s. Later we shall examine the development of Iran's relations with the Soviet Union from the early 1960s until the early 1970s.

[46]The 1957 transit agreement as such was not, of course, without significance. For a good discussion of it see *Middle East Economic Digest* 1, no. 14 (1957):4.

[47]The best example of the annual nature of these trade agreements was the trade agreement (*movafiqatnamih-ye Bazargani*) of May 4, 1961. For details see *Ittila'at Hava'i,* May 4, 1961.

Part Four

Independent National Policy

XIII

The Genesis of Iran's "Independent National Policy" and "Normalization" of Relations with the Soviet Union

EVER SINCE THE early 1960s the shah has characterized Iran's foreign policy as an "independent national policy" (*siyasat-i mustaqill-i melli*). This new designation replaced the name of the shah's foreign policy of the 1950s, namely, the policy of positive nationalism. Was this merely a change of labels, or did it in fact signify a major change in Iranian foreign policy? The answer to this question must await an account of the development of Iran's foreign policy after the early 1960s. It is enough to state here briefly that the new designation was generally associated in Iran and abroad with "normalization" of Iran's relations with the Soviet Union and "dealignment" with the United States. But this characterization is not supported by the facts. As we shall see, normalization of relations with the Soviet Union meant in part commerical, economic, and technical cooperation, but insofar as political relations were concerned, reduced tensions between the two countries lasted only between 1962 and 1967 and were replaced by heightened tensions subsequently. As we shall also see, dealignment with the United States never occurred, either in fact or in law, despite a brief spell of disenchantment with the United States in the early 1960s. As a matter of fact Iranian alignment with the United States was intensified beginning in 1968. Furthermore, Iran's independent national policy had another major component, its policy in the Persian Gulf, which was not confined to relations with the superpowers.

This chapter will explore the basic factors underlying that policy as a backdrop to the examination of its various components in subsequent chapters. Since new relationships with the Soviet Union signaled the very birth of that policy, examination of those factors will also aid in understanding the beginnings of Iran's new attitudes toward the Soviet Union in the early 1960s. These emerging attitudes were signaled by Iran's pledge to the Soviet Union in 1962 that it would not allow the use of its territory for foreign missile bases. Hence, this chapter should provide better general understanding of the basic factors underlying Iran's foreign policy in the early 1960s and should also contribute to a fuller comprehension of the earliest Iranian attempt at normalization of relations with the Soviet Union.

But it must first be asked whether there was any change in the structure of decision making in foreign policy in the early 1960s as compared with the post-Musaddiq 1950s. The answer must simply be in the negative. The shah continued to act as the supreme decision maker. We may recall from the detailed treatment of Iran's foreign policy during the post-Musaddiq 1950s that the shah played the decisive role in that policy, as evidenced, for example, by his part in the settlement of the oil nationalization dispute and in negotiations with the Soviet Union for a nonaggression pact in 1958-59. In the oil settlement it may be recalled his important role was hailed by President Eisenhower and Foreign Secretary Eden. The shah's injunction to the Majlis "not to waste a minute" in ratifying the oil agreement of 1954 was regarded by Eden as "decisive" in preventing endless delay in its ratification. The shah's personal insistence on the definition of the term "military bases" in the Soviet-Iranian negotiations was equally decisive in pressing on the Soviet Union the Iranian definition, which was then rejected by the Soviets but, as we shall see shortly, was accepted in 1962. The shah's paramount role in making foreign policy is often inferred from the fact that his return to Iran after the downfall of the Musaddiq regime was followed by an unprecedented rise in his domestic power. The problem with this approach is twofold. First, as I have already shown, the proposition that the shah played little or no significant role throughout the period before the downfall of Musaddiq is not wholly true.[1] Second, the decisive role of the shah in foreign policy decisions during the post-Musaddiq 1950s is empirically demonstrable and need not simply be inferred from the nature of his domestic control.

The shah has continued to play the dominant role in decision making since the early 1960s, as we shall see from the actual development of Iranian foreign policy. If anything, his role expanded in the 1960s and 1970s, partly because his new foreign policy was marked by an unprecedented growth, complexity, and diversity of ties with an ever-widening circle of nations in Africa, the Far East, South and Southeast Asia, Latin America, and Eastern Europe as well as regional and universal organizations. I have broached the question of decision making as a whole at this point simply to indicate that the shah continued to be the supreme decision maker, and prior examination of *his* perception of international politics and Iranian foreign policy may prove helpful to a better understanding of Iranian foreign policy in the early 1960s.

The Shah's Perception of Iran in World Politics
in the Early 1960s

In attempting to discover the shah's basic assumption about Iranian foreign policy in the 1950s, we examined his conception of Iran's modern history. He viewed Anglo-Russian imperial rivalries as a fundamental problem of Iranian

---

[1] See chapter 11 of this work.

foreign policy; and of the two imperialisms that of the Soviet Union appeared to him as the "more lethal kind of imperialism." In looking back on Iranian history in the early 1960s, the shah seemed least concerned with foreign imperialism and most perturbed by the behavior of some Iranian "statesmen" (*rejal-i siyasi*) who, in effect, acted as the agents of foreign powers.[2] This represented a departure from the shah's view in the 1950s in that his criticism focused primarily on domestic conditions. The best evidence for the shah's conscious inward look for sources of Iranian malaise is his book on the White Revolution.

The shah wrote that his new foreign policy, or "independent national policy," was, in the last analysis, rooted in the "principles and ideas" that guided his domestic reform policies, that is, his White Revolution. He regarded Iran's new foreign policy as a product of that revolution. He seemed to argue that his drastic social and economic reform measures removed from the power structure those elements in Iranian society who served foreign interests. Furthermore, he argued, his land reform and the abolition of "the worst type of feudalism" helped narrow oppressive differences between the poor and the rich and hence contributed to national unity. Thus, Iran was able to adopt a new foreign policy that was truly "independent" and "national" in nature.[3]

A closer examination of the shah's perception, however, reveals a more intimate association between his notion of an independent national foreign policy and his assumption about international politics. His assumption was clearly more optimistic in the early 1960s. In the 1950s he seemed preoccupied with the defense of Iran against the threat of totalitarian imperialism in general and Russian imperialism in particular. He seemed pessimistic about international peace and security and hence emphasized national security, which, in his view, was the essential prerequisite for social and economic development. In the early 1960s the shah expanded his concept of security to include not only military strength but social and economic progress as well. As we have already noted, the shah, since his accession to the throne, showed a keen interest in socioeconomic reform, but it was only in the early 1960s that he gave these his highest priority.[4]

This more optimistic assumption about international politics lay at the heart of the shah's emphasis on international understanding, international cooperation, and international interdependence before 1968. He decried

[2]*Mission for My Country,* pp. 8-9.

[3]Ibid., pp. 10-12.

[4]I have discussed this at length in "Iran's 'White Revolution': A Study in Political Development," *International Journal of Middle East Studies,* 5, no. 2 (1974):124-39.

ideological rigidity and denounced resort to force in international politics.[5] In a rare admission of the overriding role of force as an instrument of foreign policy in the past, the shah's Ministry of Foreign Affairs acknowledged the fact that Iran, like other imperial powers, had sought royal grandeur and strength in the expansion or the defense of its domain by means of "war."[6] Iran's new foreign policy, the shah reasoned, was based on the principles of the pursuit of peace; on peaceful coexistence with all nations and societies irrespective of different ideologies and systems of government; on support of every effort to establish and assure social justice on national or international scales and of every attempt to bridge the gap between the rich and the poor; and on international cooperation in the struggle against illiteracy, starvation, disease, and other contemporary social ills.[7]

The shah's optimistic assumption about international politics and consequently his greater emphasis on socioeconomic reforms in the early 1960s was undergoing change, however, by the end of the 1960s. The factors contributing to this change will emerge in the course of our examination of the substance and development of Iranian foreign policy since the early 1960s. The shah's emphasis began to swing, in the later 1960s, from social and economic development back to military strength. Once again a more pessimistic assumption about international politics began to emerge and Iran's independent national policy began to emphasize the value of military security, as had the positive nationalism of the 1950s. In his inaugural address to the Parliament in 1969, the shah stated: "The international situation, we must confess, is turbulent and chaotic. In the light of these conditions and so long as man's quest for general disarmament, a desire which we have always advocated and endeavored to realize, has not been effectively achieved, we have no alternative but to strengthen and bolster our defenses. This policy has now assumed greater significance in view of the unforeseen responsibilities which may confront us when British forces withdraw from east of the Suez in 1971."[8]

Although the shah's perception of the role of Iran in world politics sheds some light on Iranian foreign policy, his view is more helpful to the understanding of that policy *after* it had already been launched. When the shah spelled out the principles of his new foreign policy in the mid-1960s for the

[5]*Mission for My Country*, p. 25.

[6]Iran, Ministry of Foreign Affairs, *Ravabit-i Khariji-i Iran dar Sal-i 1346* (Tehran: Chap-i Matbua'ti-ye Iran, 1968/69), p. 12.

[7]Iran Ministry of Foreign Affairs, *Iran's Foreign Policy: A Compendium of the Writings and Statements of His Imperial Majesty Shahanshah Aryamehr* (Tehran: Iranchap, n.d.) p. 13.

[8]Ibid., pp. 94-96.

first time in his book on the White Revolution, much water had already gone under the bridge of the new independent national policy. For this important reason, his brief account of Iran's new foreign policy was more a rationale for, than a theory of, that policy. Even from a chronological perspective it would be difficult to ascribe the change in Iran's foreign policy or the adoption of the independent national policy to the effects of the White Revolution, which did not really begin to move until after January 1963 when Iran had already begun the conduct of its new foreign policy. More importantly, in the early 1960s it was more the new foreign policy that helped the launching of the White Revolution. Only after Iran was able to normalize its relations with the Soviet Union could it seriously consider a "White" revolution without aggravating its already poisoned relations with the Soviet Union and exacerbating the "Red" or "Black" or any other kind of opposition at home. As we shall see, the adoption of a more relaxed policy toward the Soviet Union paved the way so well for launching the White Revolution in January 1963 that when the storm of opposition to it broke in June of that year, the opponents of the shah's regime who had been consistently supported by the Soviet Union were for the first time condemned by Moscow!

Hence, it was not really the principles of the White Revolution that guided independent national policy; it was, in the last analysis, the shah's reappraisal of both domestic and international conditions at the time that led to the launching of both socioeconomic reforms at home and a more independent course abroad. The rest of this study will bear out the truth of this proposition. The shah's ability to perceive without any doctrinal or ideological hindrance the dictates of the new international and national situations lay at the heart of his new domestic and foreign policies. This same pragmatic quality lay at the heart of his much misunderstood foreign policy of positive nationalism. As we have already seen, both domestic and external circumstances dictated the adoption of an alliance with the West; yet despite the shah's own basic preference for collaboration with the West, he proved receptive to Soviet overtures of peaceful coexistence as early as 1954, as evidenced, it may be recalled, by efforts to settle a variety of disputes with the Soviet Union regarding financial, boundary, transit, and other matters.[9] These problems were, however, easier of resolution in the 1960s, when domestic and international circumstances favored their settlement.

The Pledge of No Missile Bases

The change in Iran's policy toward the Soviet Union was signaled by a pledge to the Soviet Union on September 15, 1962. By means of a note from the

[9]See chapter 12 of this study.

Iranian Ministry of Foreign Affairs to the Soviet embassy in Tehran, the Iranian government "assured the Soviet Government that it will not grant any foreign nation the right of possessing any kind of rocket bases on Iranian soil."[10] This pledge was accompanied by an official statement promising that Iran would not become a party to any aggression against the Soviet Union. Moscow hailed this pledge as a "vivid example of a patient, reasonable approach to the solution of disputed questions affecting the vitally important interests of two neighbouring countries"; claimed that this pledge "substantially narrows the opportunities for external aggressive forces to operate from the territory of Iran against the Soviet Union"; and stated that the exchange of notes constituted an "important factor in the improvement of relations between the two countries" and signaled an end to the "existing tension in Iranian-Soviet relations."[11]

Why did Iran decide to make this pledge in the first place? And why did the Soviet Union accept it? The latter question is no less important than the former. It may be recalled that the Soviet Union had refused in its 1958-59 negotiations with Iran to accept Iran's restriction of bases to "rocket or missile bases," and yet in 1962 it was, in effect, accepting the Iranian definition. Iran had opposed in those negotiations a broader definition of "military bases" because it would provide a basis for a Soviet claim to dismantling the whole American military aid and advisory programs in Iran within and outside the framework of CENTO.

Détente and Strategic Changes

We shall consider below the strategic changes that may shed light on the missile bases agreement, but we should first note the more general change in the international system that significantly improved the climate of Soviet-Iranian relations. The atmosphere of the international system in the 1960s was marked by a perceptible relaxation of tensions between the superpowers. In both the 1950s and the 1960s the movement toward détente was discernible with, however, significant differences. In 1955 the realization that invulnerability to nuclear attack was virtually impossible and that the curbing of nuclear production was desirable supported the views in Moscow and Washington that a nuclear holocaust had to be avoided. But the fear that nuclear production could escape inspection, combined with time-honored ideological,

---

[10]This is my verbatim translation from the text. For the texts of the notes exchanged between Iran and the Soviet Union, see *Ittila'at Hava'i,* Sept. 15, 1962.

[11]*CDSP* 14, no. 37 (Oct. 10, 1962):16.

historical, and political antagonisms and suspicions, dealt the blow to whatever optimism might have been generated by the "spirit of Geneva."

In contrast, in the 1960s the Soviet's conciliatory attitude toward the West boded well for the détente movement. Shortly before the Cuban missile crisis erupted, the Soviet's conciliatory posture was reflected in two important issues: "the necessity for an inspected moratorium to accompany a limited nuclear test ban, and the retention of Soviet and American deterrents during the disarmament process."[12] This greater flexibility in the Soviet attitude toward the West lay at the heart of its more conciliatory attitude toward Iran. The breakdown of Soviet negotiations with Iran in 1959 was in full keeping with the evaporation of the "spirit of Geneva." The friendly Soviet attitude toward Iran in 1962, on the other hand, corresponded with a greater progress toward détente with the West. At the broadest level of analysis this was why in 1962 the Soviet Union accepted Iran's 1959 definition of missile bases. And by the same token this general thaw in the East-West cold war was conducive to a more relaxed attitude on the part of Iran toward the Soviet Union.

Just as the amelioration of general East-West relations had a salutary effect upon Soviet-Iranian relations as a whole, specific changes in the strategic thinking and policies of the Soviet Union and the United States proved helpful to Soviet-Iranian agreement on the bases problem. To take the Soviet Union first, traditional Stalinist strategic thought had emphasized the significance of conventional forces and weapons in Soviet security policies. In keeping with this emphasis the presence of Western troops, military advisers, and bases in countries bordering on the Soviet Union was the prime target of Soviet opposition. But once the traditional doctrine came under attack and more particularly when the obsolescence of conventional military bases was recognized in Moscow, the presence of American military advisers in Iran did not seem to concern the Soviets as much. Khrushchev's address of January 14, 1960, to the Supreme Soviet provided the guidelines for a comprehensive military strategy that placed the nation's defense on the principle of nuclear deterrence.[13] As a result of this shift in Soviet strategic thought, what then became important to Soviet security was twofold. First, it was important to eliminate all missile bases in the neighborhood of the Soviet Union. Second, it was important to keep such missile bases in the neighborhood of the United States. Thus, the Soviet Union in 1962 extracted the pledge of no missile bases from Iran and asked the United States to withdraw its missiles from Turkey, while it itself had to be forced to withdraw its missiles from Cuba.

[12]For a discussion of major changes in Soviet strategic policy, see Michael P. Gehlen, *The Politics of Coexistence* (Bloomington: Indiana University Press, 1967), pp. 67-108.

[13]Ibid., p. 73.

The important point here is that as the result of changes in Soviet strategic thought and policy, Moscow was prepared at the time to accept the kind of pledge that Iran was willing to make.

The Iranian preparedness to make such a pledge was reinforced, by 1962, by changes in American strategic thought and policy. It may be recalled that as early as February 1959, when the Irano-Soviet crisis over the breakdown of negotiations erupted, the shah reiterated Iran's determination not to allow the establishment of "rocket bases" on Iranian soil.[14] Yet the changes in American strategic policy between that time and 1962 made Iran all the more willing to make such a pledge to the Soviet Union. The increase in American capability during that time gave heart to American allies. Iran witnessed the emergence of the American ballistic missile submarine and the increases in range and payload of the Polaris. The Polaris A1, which became operational in 1961, deployed from sea areas, could bring Moscow and Leningrad under counterattack, and the Polaris A2, which became operational in June 1962, could reach the major industrial centers of the Ukraine, and Baku oil fields, and parts of Soviet Central Asia from submarines deployed in the Eastern Mediterranean.[15] More important, as an ally of Turkey as well as the United States, Iran was relieved to learn that the American withdrawal of Jupiters from neighboring Turkey was underway. As early as fall 1960 the Joint Committee on Atomic Energy made on-site inspection in Turkey and other NATO bases, and as the result of its study recommended that construction on Jupiter sites in Turkey should not be permitted, and instead "an alternative system such as a Polaris submarine with 16 IRBM'S . . . could be assigned to NATO." This system would be therefore "a much better retaliatory force."[16] It is doubtful that Iran's own territory had ever been seriously considered for missile sites. This can be seen from the reaction of the Western press to the Iranian pledge to the Soviet Union. It was considered in London, for example, that the pledge did not signify "a fundamental military change," probably because no American rocket bases had been visualized for Iran.[17]

American Refusal of Budgetary Support

Quite apart from these general political and strategic changes in the international system, specific external considerations contributed to the Iranian

[14]*Ittila'at Hava'i*, Feb. 23, 1959.

[15]See Geoffrey Jukes, *The Indian Ocean in Soviet Naval Policy* (London: The International Institute for Strategic Studies, May 1972).

[16]U.S., Congress, House, Committee on Armed Services, *Hearings on Military Posture,* 88th Cong., 1st sess., 1963, pp. 276-84.

[17]*Times* (London), Sept. 17, 1962.

decision to make the missile bases pledge and to begin to normalize its overall relations with the Soviet Union. One of these considerations was the very unpalatable nature of Soviet relations with Iran. As noted in detail in the previous chapter, the breakdown of the Irano-Soviet negotiations for a non-aggression pact in 1959 was followed by a violent and relentless Soviet propaganda campaign, against not only the Iranian government but even the person of the shah. To be sure, Iran made every effort to retaliate in kind without ever breaking international diplomatic ettiquette,[18] but the pressure of the Soviet Union at the time seemed excessive in view of mounting internal problems and other external concerns, as we shall see presently.

Far more crucial than Soviet hostility was the emerging attitude of the United States toward Iran. I shall deal with this attitude in connection with Irano-American relations later. Suffice it to state here that by the early 1960s the United States began to entertain increasing doubts about the utility or the wisdom of continuing American budgetary aid to Iran. Such aid, it may be recalled, had begun on a large scale with the rise of the Zahidi government in view of the fact that the Iranian economy had suffered grievously as the result of the interruption of flow of oil abroad during the nationalization crisis. Yet by the late 1950s, when oil revenues were pouring in, Iran was caught in a serious economic crisis. American disenchantment with the Iranian situation was serious enough to give rise to a major report in the *Christian Science Monitor*, January 15, 1960, to the effect that the United States government had made "a crucially important decision to cultivate the opposition parties there [Iran] in the hope of taking out diplomatic insurance in case of an overthrow of the present regime." It was also reported in the *Monitor* that a National Front representative then in the United States assured Washington officials and executives of American oil companies that should "the National Front take power United States oil interests would not be affected or the country's pro-Western orientation altered." On January 22, 1960, the Department of State "categorically denied that there is any substance whatsoever to the report" and went on to state that the United States had the "closest and most cordial relations with the present Government of Iran, which under the able leadership of the Shah, is striving effectively to maintain Iran's independence and to improve conditions within the country."[19]

Regardless of the validity of the report about Washington's clandestine flirtation with National Frontists, the important fact remains that the United States was not at the time satisfied with Iran's domestic social and economic conditions. The gist of the dissatisfaction was that despite increasing oil revenues, on the one hand, and millions of dollars of American aid, on the

[18]See chapter 12 of this study.

[19]U.S., State Dept. *Bulletin* 42, no. 1076 (Feb. 8, 1960):201.

other, the Iranian economy was still unable to stand on its own feet because of the lack of basic and long-overdue social and economic reforms. As early as 1956 some of this dissatisfaction was expressed in great detail in the voluminous report of the International Operations Subcommittee of the Committee on Government Operations of the House of Representatives, which held hearings in June and July of that year.[20] However, congressional criticism of the way the aid to Iran was used was at the time overshadowed by a political consideration, namely, the greater concern of the administration with the maintenance of Iran's independence in the cold war. By the early 1960s, however, dissatisfaction with budgetary support of Iran in the face of inadequate social and economic reforms was spreading in Washington, and the "reform government" of Amini was initially welcomed in the hope that this old friend of the United States might be able to put the Iranian house in order through serious reforms.

Despite some $30 million in American aid to the Amini government and his vociferous anti-corruption and social and economic reform measures, his inability to handle the legacy of some $70 million budgetary deficit contributed in part to the downfall of his government. Amini himself blamed the fall of his regime squarely on the United States, claiming that "tardy economic aid" and the cutting off of military assistance had made it impossible for him to carry on.[21] The *New York Times* acknowledged that the aid that Amini had expected for his 1962 budget from the United States had not been forthcoming, and "the United States' refusal to give further budgetary support was a factor in Dr. Amini's resignation."[22] There is little doubt that the American refusal to provide further budgetary support, the insistence, during the Kennedy administration, on the need for basic social and economic reforms, and coolness toward further demands for military aid contributed in part to the historic land reform decision that signaled the beginning of the White Revolution. Equally important, there is little doubt that the missile bases decision and the subsequent amelioration of Iran's relations with the Soviet Union were also triggered in part by the American attitude at the time. As already mentioned, the Soviet demand was accompanied by offers of "enormous economic aid," to borrow the shah's words. This offer proved difficult to resist in the face of the United States' more discriminating economic and military aid policies.

[20]U.S., Congress, House, Subcommittee of the Committee on Government Operations, *Hearings,* 84th Cong., 2d sess., 1956.

[21]*New York Times,* July 19, 1962.

[22]Ibid., July 26, 1962.

Threat from the Persian Gulf

Another external consideration that influenced Iran's pledge to the Soviet Union in 1962 was Iran's increasing concern over the situation in the Persian Gulf. As noted previously, no single event in the 1953-58 period exerted a greater impact on Iran's foreign policy than the Iraqi revolution. The destruction of the monarchy in Iraq and the possibility of other antimonarchical and revolutionary developments in the gulf area seemed to make the situation in the south as menacing as the one in the north. As also noted, the concern of the shah's regime with the Iraqi-Persian Gulf situation was influential in Iran's simultaneous negotiations with the United States and the Soviet Union for bilateral agreements. In negotiating with the United States, Iran sought to insure its security against the hostility of such local powers as Iraq; the Baghdad Pact provided no such insurance as it aimed against Soviet aggression. In negotiations with the Soviet Union for a nonaggression pact, Iran sought to escape the pincer of the Soviet threat from the north and revolutionary Arab hostility from the south. A nonaggression pact with the Soviet Union would enable Iran to concentrate attention on the south. The breakdown of these negotiations and the reluctance of the United States to commit itself to the defense of Iran beyond the mandate of the Eisenhower Doctrine resulted, as seen, in the hostility of the Soviet Union and a bilateral agreement with the United States in which Iran fared no better than previously insofar as protection against the situation in the Persian Gulf was concerned.

Meanwhile, the concern of the shah's regime over the situation in the Persian Gulf was increased in the early 1960s. We shall trace this development more fully in the chapter on Iran's policy in the Persian Gulf. Suffice it to state here that Egypt suddenly broke diplomatic relations with Iran in 1960. The Egyptian action was prompted by Iran's alleged recognition of Israel, but the shah's regime regarded the Egyptian move primarily as an indication of Egyptian ambitions in the gulf in the face of Iran's expanding ties with the Arab sheikhdoms of the area. Hence, Tehran began to perceive the Arab revolutionary threat as emanating not only from Baghdad but even more particularly from Cairo. When Iran made its pledge of no bases to the Soviet Union in 1962, it appeared to the shah's regime that any step in the direction of normalization of relations with the Soviet Union in the north could pay off in Iran's greater ability to handle the situation in the south. As it turned out, however, Iraq's increasing rapprochement with the Soviet Union and its flirtation with internal Communists made the Soviets appear as the principal and indirect source of threat in the south as well.

Identity of Views with Turkey

The pledge to the Soviet Union was dictated by yet another consideration. The Turkish-American negotiations regarding the obsolescence of the Jupiter as early as April 1962 must have been known to the Iranian leaders, who worked closely with Turkish leaders both within and outside the framework of CENTO. In their communiqué of July 22, 1962, the Turkish and Iranian foreign ministers announced the *identity* of their viewpoints on "the assessment of the international situation," and the Turkish and Iranian missions found their negotiations in Tehran "extremely friendly and fruitful."[23] There is every reason to believe that the assessment of the international situation at the time concerned particularly the Soviet's friendly overtures to both Iran and Turkey and their implications for CENTO and NATO alliances. Iran had watched with great interest the news of the scheduled visit of Premier Menderes to Moscow before the Turkish revolution of May 27, 1960. On April 19, 1960, the Iranian foreign minister, 'Abbas Aram, was called upon to provide information in the Majlis in regard to the "close relations developing between Turkey and the Soviet Union." The foreign minister assured the deputies that the planned visit of the Turkish leader to the Soviet Union had been discussed with Iran in advance.[24]

The Turkish revolution, which temporarily resulted in the closing of the Irano-Turkish border, caused some apprehension in Tehran regarding its implications for CENTO and Turkish-Soviet relations as well as Iranian domestic policies. In his letter of June 28, 1960, Premier Khruschev wrote Prime Minister Gürsel "directly that it is our deep conviction that the relations developed between our two neighboring countries would be most cordial should Turkey take the path of neutrality." The invitation to neutrality was categorically rejected in Gürsel's reply of July 8, 1960, which stated in part that "Turkey will abide by its international commitments, in particular those that stem from the fact of the existence of such alliances as NATO and CENTO."[25] This Turkish determination to stand by its Western alliances resembled Iran's position during the 1958-59 negotiations with the Soviet Union. Both countries suspected Moscow's overtures but at the same time felt the need for testing the Soviet declarations of good neighborliness and peaceful coexistence. The fact that Turkey was also unopposed to exploring the chances for improving relations with the Soviet Union probably encouraged Iran to go ahead with its pledge of no missile bases to the Soviet Union.

[23] *Ittila'at Hava'i,* July 22, 1962.

[24] Ibid., Apr. 19, 1960.

[25] *CDSP* 12, no. 35 (Sept. 28, 1960):16-18.

Domestic Political Turmoil and Economic Chaos

To suggest, however, that Iran's improved relations with the Soviet Union were influenced by the general political and strategic climate of the international system and the specific external factors discussed above is by no means to imply that domestic considerations were not important. To take up relevant domestic *political* conditions, it may be recalled from the previous chapter that the downfall of the government of Iqbal on August 29, 1960, and the appointment of Sharif-Imami as the new prime minister were accompanied by the first signs of normalization of Soviet-Iranian relations after the breakdown of the 1958-59 negotiations; but the downfall of his government and the appointment of Amini as prime minister destroyed any immediate chances for improvement in the relations of the two countries. Yet insofar as domestic politics were concerned, the pressure for improving Iran's relations with the Soviet Union was building up rapidly at the time. The resurgence of the National Front during the Amini government has been noted by scholars almost exclusively for its domestic political implications. Yet the demand for liberalization of the political system in general and free elections in particular was accompanied by attacks upon the shah's policy of positive nationalism and the urge for the adoption of a neutralist foreign policy.

From the standpoint of the National Front leaders, "liberty and democracy" at home were to be matched by an "independent Iranian policy" abroad. The demand for liberty and democracy was voiced publicly on the seventh day of the teachers' strike by Javad Tabataba'i in a meeting held at the Mihran Club on May 8, 1961, and was reiterated subsequently. Five days earlier the strike had acquired a more ardent political overtone with the killing of 'Abdul Husain Khan'ali, a teachers' leader. In the presence of Amini, who attended a second meeting at the Mihran Club on May 9, Darakhshish threatened continuation of the strike unless the killer of Khan'ali was brought to trial by the government. Meanwhile, the National Front leaders such as Baqir Kazimi, Kazim Hasibi, Allahyar Salih, Karim Sanjabi, and others continued to issue statements supporting the teachers' strike and pressing their demands for political liberalization and an independent foreign policy. The clearest expression of these demands was made public at the Maidan Jalaliah on May 20, 1961, at a meeting of the National Front, held for the first time since the appointment of Amini. The National Front leaders declared that "the aim of the National Front in foreign policy is the establishment of an independent Iranian policy based on mutual respect for real national sovereignty and friendship with all nations, particularly [our] neighbors."[26]

[26] For details see *Ittila'at Hava'i,* May 20, 1961.

The shah's regime was willing at the time to allow attacks on its dependence on the United States and the call for a nonaligned foreign policy. This tolerant attitude was evidenced, for example, by the inclusion, in the Amini cabinet, of Qholam'ali Farivar, the minister of industry. He headed the Executive Committee of the Iranian Organization for Co-operation with Asian and African Nations. This organization published a declaration urging a non-alignment for Iran. In a "private capacity" Farivar himself favored Iran's adoption of a neutralist foreign policy such as that of Nehru of India and believed that such a policy would be acceptable to his colleagues in the cabinet.[27]

The suppression of the National Front that had begun with the rise of the Zahidi government in 1953 ultimately spelled the doom of any chance for political liberalization that might have appeared on the horizon in the turbulent 1960-63 period, but the utility of a more neutralist foreign policy did not escape the shah's attention. It is seldom realized that even in label the new independent national policy adopted by the shah's regime in the early 1960s corresponded in effect with the National Front's demand for an Iranian independent policy. A major feature of this National Front demand was the call for normalization of relations with the Soviet Union. Hence, the shah's pledge of 1962 to the Soviet Union was in keeping not only with his own desire to test the Soviet claim to peaceful coexistence but also with the aspirations of the articulate elements of the National Front.

The shah's pledge and normalization of relations with the Soviet Union would, it was hoped, not only deprive the National Front of one of its most important platforms and thereby assist the domestic political situation but would aid the struggle against domestic economic crisis as well. The Soviet interest in a nonaggression pact with Iran and the demand for the Iranian pledge regarding bases was from the very outset accompanied by economic enticement. According to the shah the Soviets "held out promises of a long-term non-aggression pact and tremendous economic help" during the 1958-59 negotiations.[28] By this time the Iranian economic crisis was well underway. Following the example of the Plan organization's high expenditures on development, the rest of the government plunged into an unprecedentedly high level of expenditures, and this high government spending, "combined with liberal bank credit and easy access to foreign exchanges, quickly generated a major economic boom in private investment, mainly in urban housing and industry, both heavily concentrated in Tehran. The boom also generated ex-

[27] Ibid., May 27, 1961.

[28] *Mission for My Country*, p. 122.

cesses that took the form of rising prices and falling exchange reserves."[29] According to the Higher Economic Council's report at the time, despite the considerable increase of government revenue from oil royalties, the proportion spent on development under the Seven Year Plan fell from the scheduled 80 percent to 55 percent.[30] One of the basic reasons for this was the use of oil revenues for huge budgetary support. Moreover, by the time of the Amini government it was openly acknowledged in Tehran that a very substantial proportion of the financial aid from abroad was lost to the economy through sheer waste, inefficiency, and acknowledged corruption. Amini himself launched his reforms by what he termed "a vigorous campaign to rout corruption and oust corrupted and treacherous agents." He stated in a broadcast in May 1961 that it is "not concealed from anyone that misuse of governmental positions, and conspiracies among opportunists and swindlers, have now become a plague. . . . We are facing great economic and financial difficulties, a great deal of capital has been wasted, the balance of the budget has been upset, and the financial regulations ignored. We are facing a rise of prices, lack of money, and economic poverty."[31]

Amini's inability to balance the budget contributed to the fall of his government, but, as we saw before, the reluctance of the United States to bail out its friend was also a major factor. What is of interest to us here, however, is the fact that the Soviet promise of economic credits in conjunction with normalization of relations with Iran fell on far more sympathetic ears in Tehran in 1962 than in 1959. The continuing economic crisis, the inability of the reform government of Amini to cope with it effectively, and the reluctance of the United States to come to Iran's aid through further budgetary support combined to underpin Iran's greater receptiveness to Soviet promises of economic cooperation. Under the circumstances the Soviet Union was seen more clearly as a serious prospective donor of much economic credit. The Soviet Union had already extended billions of dollars to developing countries, including some $400 million to Iran's neighbor, Afghanistan, by 1962. A pledge from Iran to the Soviet Union could test the economic as well as political aspect of Soviet peaceful coexistence. It could not only pave the way toward normalization of political relations with Moscow at a time of increasing domestic political trouble, but it could also open up an important new source of economic and technical gains at a time of deteriorating domestic economic conditions and drying up of long-standing American support for the Iranian budget.

[29] For details see George B. Baldwin, *Planning and Development in Iran* (Baltimore: Johns Hopkins University Press, 1967).

[30] *Middle East Economic Digest* 3, no. 43 (1959):514-15.

[31] Ibid., 5, no. 18 (1961):207

Foreign Policy, the White Revolution
and Consolidation of Royal Power

The preceding analysis has tried to show the complex of factors that underpinned the very birth of the new Iranian foreign policy, but its immediate impact on Iran's domestic policy deserves attention. The two most important components of the shah's domestic policy were the launching of the White Revolution and consolidation of royal power. The shah's alliance with the West and struggle with the Soviet Union during the 1950s had produced no significant change in Iran's socioeconomic structure, which, in the last analysis, lay at the heart of the economic crises of the late 1950s and early 1960s and of the disenchantment of the United States, already discussed in this chapter. As the shah himself looked back in the early 1960s, he admitted, in his book on the White Revolution, that during the earlier years of his rule the "worst type of feudalism" had prevailed in Iran.

During the 1950s every effort had been made to consolidate the royal power primarily in the face of challenges emanating principally from Communists and the National Front followers of Musaddiq. The suppression of the Tudeh in the 1950s was evidenced, for example, by the arrest of some ninety-one persons in 1953; the destruction of the Tudeh network in the army in 1954; the execution of Khusrow Ruzbih (the so-called Lenin of Iran) in 1957; and the dispersion in 1961 of a vast and secret Tudeh organization in Isfahan led by Kianury from exile in Austria. A similar fate befell the National Frontists in the 1950s, as evidenced by the execution of Husain Fatimi and the smashing of all National Front activities, such as the street riots sponsored by the National Resistance Movement in 1953 and the arrest of some seventy pro-Musaddiq activists in 1957. The death sentence of the popular Musaddiq himself, however, was prudently reduced to confinement by the shah.

Despite all this, by the early 1960s neither the problem of an oppressive socioeconomic structure nor that of political upheaval had been sufficiently overcome. In fact, as already seen, the early 1960s witnessed the resurgence of the National Front. What is of interest to us here is the fact that before Iran's pledge to, and start of normalization of relations with, the Soviet Union, Moscow continued to condemn the shah's regime and its socioeconomic reform measures and to openly support the opponents of the Iranian government. For example, *Izvestiya*, July 27, 1961, published a long article describing the suppression of the National Front demonstrations of July 21 in Tehran and indignantly denying the Iranian charges that Soviet incitement was partly to blame for the demonstrations. Instead of calling for revolt, declared the article, the Moscow broadcast of July 21 "gave the truth about Persia, the truth about the pillaging of the Persian people by foreign plunderers who are given free hand, with Amini's blessing. . . . No, Mr. Amini, your cheap tricks will not deceive even the most gullible Tehran bazaar-dweller."[32]

All the shah's reform efforts prior to the Iranian pledge were condemned. For example, an article published in *Trud* sought to prove that the government's declarations about plans for economic improvements and the eradication of corruption were meaningless and that the people were aware "whence blew the wind which was turning their country into uninhabited desert." "The wretched position of the Persian workers is felt particularly sharply against the background of the prosperity of the Transcaucasian and Central Asian republics."[33] Even land reform measures were denounced before the pledge. As late as June 1962 Amini's agrarian reform law was regarded by Moscow as "being carried out in the interests of the landlord and feudal circles themselves and of the small kulak layer. According to the intentions of its framers, it is intended to distract the popular masses from struggle for their rights and, what is no less important, to strengthen the rotten monarchical regime."[34]

Against this background of Soviet support for opponents of the shah's regime and condemnation of the monarchy and its land reform measures, the dramatic change in Soviet attitude toward all this after the Iranian pledge was simply remarkable. Arsanjani, the minister of agriculture, who had been denounced only in June 1962, was hailed in January 1963 for his service to the peasants, and the "rotten monarchical regime" of a few months ago was now presented in the person of the shah as a "pioneer in land distribution." Peasant reform, while not fully solving the problem, was "definitely a step forward." It would release millions of peasants from feudal bondage, assist the modernization of agriculture, improve living standards, and "help Persia to break out of feudalism and foreign dependence."[35] What the Soviets were then mildly praising was ironically labeled by the Iranians themselves the "White Revolution" as an antidote to a "Red" one! More ironically, although the Soviets never used the Iranian label in their discussions of the land reform program or other reforms of the shah, they, in fact, came to be one of the important sources of support for Iran's socioeconomic developments of the 1960s, as we shall see in the next chapter. There is little doubt that land reform was in part designed to strengthen the shah's regime in Iran, but it is seldom noted that it was launched seriously only after Iran made its pledge to the Soviet Union. The Soviet Union not only abandoned its attack on the

[32]*Mizan Newsletter* 3, no. 7 (1961):11-13.

[33]Ibid., 4, no. 1 (1962):26.

[34]Ibid., 6, no. 7 (1964):11.

[35]Ibid., p. 12.

shah's regime after that pledge but also abandoned support of all opponents of the shah when they suffered their gravest reversal in June 1963. The riots then were led by the clergy, but the shah's vehement response led to the arrest of the National Frontists and the Tudeh members as well.[36] It would be easy to imagine with what fury the Soviets would have attacked the shah's government if this bloody mass suppression had taken place before the missile pledge, but since it occurred afterwards, the Soviet condemnation fell on the opponents of the shah. The Soviet press vigorously condemned the antigovernment riots, blamed the mullahs for them, and charged that they were "acting in close concert with all the reactionary elements, notably the big feudal lords."[37]

In light of the above analysis there is no escaping the proposition that the adoption of a new look toward the Soviet Union contributed both to the launching of the White Revolution and the ultimate consolidation of royal power. The shah's independent national policy removed for the moment the single most destabilizing external element directed against the shah's regime. For the first time in Iran's modern history the Soviet Union reversed its role and became a supporter of the shah's regime.

[36] See Rouhollah K. Ramazani, "'Church' and State in Modernizing Society: The Case of Iran." *American Behavioral Scientist* 7, no. 5 (1964):26-28.

[37] *Mizan Newsletter* 6, no. 7 (1964):11.

XIV

Troubled Cooperation
with the Soviet Union

THE PRINCIPAL COMPONENT of Iran's "independent national policy"(*syasat-i mustaqill-i melli*) at inception was normalization of relations with the Soviet Union. The pledge of no missile bases to the Soviet Union signaled the beginning of improved relations between the two countries, but as shown in the previous chapter deeper considerations undergirded Iran's initial decision to forge new ties with the Soviet Union. To recapitulate swiftly, these considerations included intensification of the détente movement; favorable changes in Soviet and American strategic policy; American differences with Iran over assistance; Soviet preparedness to undertake economic cooperation with Iran; mounting concern of the shah's regime with the Iraqi, Egyptian, and Syrian policy in the Persian Gulf; and the shah's determination to consolidate royal power, to launch basic socioeconomic reforms, and to pursue a more independent course in world politics.

Most of these factors continued to persist in 1963-73, when Iran's new policy toward the Soviet Union developed. Constancy and change in these factors are observable. For example, the détente movement, Soviet preparedness to assist Iran economically, and the shah's determination to consolidate royal power and implement basic social and economic reforms persisted throughout the decade in spite of considerable changes. But dramatic changes also took place. The concern with Iraqi policy in the Persian Gulf intensified after the announcement of the British decision in 1968 to withdraw forces from the Persian Gulf by the end of 1971; the American-Iranian debate over economic assistance largely disappeared with the termination of the American economic aid program in Iran; and, most important of all, beginning in 1968-69 the United States began to reappraise its military support of Iran as the result, primarily, of a combination of factors—the United States' increasing need of Iranian oil and the British decision to withdraw from the Persian Gulf, and increasing Soviet interest and activities in the area. This last change, as we shall see in the following chapter, intensified Iranian alignment with the United States. Simultaneously, the increasing rapprochement between the Soviet Union and Iraq, the Soviet naval build-up in the Indian Ocean and visits of Soviet vessels to the Persian Gulf, and Soviet support of the "national liberation" movement in Oman began to contribute to Irano-Soviet tensions.

The Irano-Soviet political calm of the 1962-67 period began to show increasing signs of strain during the late 1960s and, particularly, early 1970s, while commercial, technical, and economic cooperation between the two countries continued.

This chapter will examine the development of Iran's policy toward the Soviet Union in the 1963-73 period. It is one of the three chapters that will examine Iran's foreign policy during that decade. The others will take up two other major components of Iran's foreign policy during that period. One will examine Iran's policy toward the United States, the other its policy in the Persian Gulf. This division of the subject matter is, of course, only an analytical device; Iran's policy toward the Soviet Union, the United States, and in the Persian Gulf in 1963-73 should be studied together for a more comprehensive understanding of each.

Stabilization of Trade and Transit

One major aspect of Iran's policy toward the Soviet Union in 1963-73 was the establishment of stable trade and advantageous transit relations with the USSR. Iran's trade relations with the Soviet Union from 1921 to 1964 often suffered from grievous fluctuations and ad hoc measures, as evidenced by the problems surrounding the arrangements of 1927, 1931, and 1935. Even the general treaty of 1940, which in part formed the basis of all postwar Irano-Soviet commercial transactions, proved unsatisfactory as the two countries could only draw up lists of exchangeable goods annually.[1] Such provisional lists often were subjected to the vicissitudes of turbulent Irano-Soviet political relations, and as a result Iranian merchants were unable to foresee any significant degree of predictability in Soviet commercial behavior. Against such a background, Iran's trade relations with the Soviet Union were revolutionized in the sense that for the first time in the history of commercial relations between the two nations, stable trade relations were established during the decade of the 1960s.

The earliest breach in the pattern of Iran's traditionally unstable trade with the Soviet Union was made in 1964, but the two most important stabilizing steps were taken in 1967 and 1970. The first trade agreement, signed on June 20, 1964, regulated Iran's commerce with the Soviet Union for a period of three years. The duration of this agreement, given Iran's past short-term arrangements and difficulties with the Soviet Union, seemed significant enough for the shah to emphasize it on his arrival in Moscow in June 1965. This agreement paved the way for the signing of the first five-year trade agreement with the Soviet Union on March 2, 1967. And, in turn, the

---

[1] For details see Ramazani, *Foreign Policy of Iran,* pp. 224-25.

success of the two countries in introducing a degree of stability in their commercial relations after this agreement proved conducive to the signing of Iran's "greatest agreement" (*bozorgtarin movafiqatnamih*) of its kind for another five years on July 30, 1970. [2]

Traditionally, the major economic attraction of Russian trade for Iran lay largely in the close proximity of its markets and the relatively cheap water transportation. But during 1963-73 Soviet trade appealed to Iran for other economic reasons as well. The principal economic reason was the significance of trade with the Soviet Union for Iran's overall socioeconomic development. The decade of rapid increase in Irano-Soviet trade coincided with an unparalleled rate of growth in Iran's modern economic history. One of the major features of the development strategy was the objective of diversification of industry, partly to reduce dependence on the oil industry. To put it simply, Iran felt need for capital goods imports, on the one hand, and, on the other hand, greater markets for not only the export of its traditional commodities but also the manufactured goods of its emerging industry. The trade agreement of 1967 increased the value of Iran's exports to the USSR from $20 million annually to $70 million. More important, out of the $350 million exports to the Soviet Union over a period of five years, $100 million consisted of Iranian manufactured goods, such as foot wear, oil stoves, and refrigerators. The increased value of Iranian exports to the Soviet Union at the time did not include gas, which subsequently became a major export item. Furthermore, as the result of the 1967 trade agreement, Iran was able to save some $13 million annually by importing vegetable oils on a barter basis from the Soviet Union.

The export of Iranian manufactured goods to the Soviet Union was further augmented by the trade agreement signed on July 30, 1970, for another period of five years. On the basis of this agreement the value of trade between the two countries over the following five years was estimated to increase over one billion dollars, including $720 million of Iranian and $318 million Russian exports. As viewed from Tehran, under this agreement Soviet markets would constitute the largest single market for Iranian manufactured goods. The Soviet Union would supply Iran with industrial equipment, ferrous metals, timber, cement, and other products necessary for Iran's economic development; Iran would supply the Soviet Union with an increasing number of consumer goods, such as knitted wear, woolens, textiles, and substantial amounts of petrochemicals, carbon black, and some new items, including aluminum and processed metals.[3] On the day of the signing of the trade agreement Iran also signed a protocol with the Soviet Union for the creation

[2] *Ittila'at Hava'i*, no. 7211, Aug. 1, 1970.

[3] *Kayhan* (Weekly, English), Aug. 8, 1970.

of a mixed Irano-Soviet transport company in which each country would hold 50 percent of the shares. The establishment of the company would facilitate Iran's transit trade through Russia and at the same time offer the Russians transit facilities through Iranian territory. Before leaving Moscow, after the signing of the trade agreement and the protocol, the Iranian minister of economy, Hushang Ansari, held a press conference with Soviet journalists. In reply to a question about Iran's assessment of the barter-type trade with the Soviet Union, he stated: "We in Iran believe that trade relations on a barter basis are interesting from various aspects. Considering our relations with our friendly neighboring country, the existing arrangement for the exchange of goods is beneficial to both countries. In this way you will be in a position to supply our needs within the framework of a relatively balanced plan and, in return, Iran will be able to furnish the USSR with the needed consumer and industrial goods so that an excessive imbalance will not be created."[4]

The creation of a mixed Irano-Soviet company in 1970 was for the purpose of facilitating transit trade. Although in the late 1950s Iran had been able to reach some general understanding with the Soviet Union regarding transit trade, no definite agreement was reached until the 1960s. On November 27, 1963, Iran reached a transit agreement with the Soviet Union that was to come into force immediately. Although every major trade agreement between Iran and the Soviet Union from 1921 to 1963 had provided for transit rights, no concrete and stable pattern had developed. Transit trade, like trade between the two countries, had often been used as a Soviet instrument of economic pressure, and Iran preferred ad hoc arrangements to durable trade and transit relations, largely because of traditional suspicion of Russia.[5] Against such a background, the concrete terms of the 1963 transit agreement were significant. It provided for reciprocal transit rights between the two nations. Iranian exports to and from Europe over Soviet territory would averagely enjoy 25 percent reduction in transportation costs, and Soviet exports to and from Iran's southern ports of Khoramshahr, Shahpoor, and Khosravi would benefit from some 22.5 percent reduction in rail transportation rates. The difference in reduction rates probably stemmed from the fact that rail transportation is generally more costly than transportation by water. The prospects for effective implementation of this agreement were significantly enhanced subsequently when in June 1964 the new Soviet Volga-Baltic route was opened. As a result Iranian goods to and from Europe over Russian territory could be transported by water to the Caspian Sea. Traditionally,

---

[4]From a broadcast by Moscow in Persian, in U.S., Foreign Broadcast Information Service, *USSR International Affairs* 2, No. 149 (Aug. 3, 1970) (hereafter cited as U.S., FBIS, *USSR Intl. Affairs*).

[5]See Ramazani, *Foreign Policy of Iran*, pp. 217-18.

Iranian goods had to be exported over Soviet territory to and from Baku by rail, but now they could be handled all the way by water transportation to and from the Iranian ports of Pahlavi and Nowshahr. The first shipment of Iranian goods from Nowshar to a southern port in Poland by means of this new route took place on December 20, 1964. Quite apart from the relative inexpensiveness of this northern route, as opposed to the southern route through the Persian Gulf, Iranian goods to and from Europe could reach their destination in a shorter period of time.

The prospects for facilitation of Iranian transit trade over Soviet territory were further improved in 1971 when a regular shipping line was established between the two countries. The relevant agreement was "the first shipping agreement between Iran and the Soviet Union in the last fifty years."[6] Soviet ships loaded with Iranian cargos from Europe frequented the Caspian ports of Iran and carried Iranian exports to Baku for Soviet and European destinations. Although the Caspian route never rivaled the Persian Gulf route, the increase in Irano-Soviet trade and the greater facilitation of their transit trade accorded the northern route a new place in Iran's commercial life in modern times. For example, Iran's total imports and exports by way of the northern ports in 1964-65 amounted to only 158,700 tons; in 1970-71 it reached 443,000 tons. Quite apart from the establishment of this regular shipping line between Baku and Iranian ports, developments in the Soviet Union's own merchant marine assisted Iran's transit trade through Russia. For example, in 1972 a Soviet ship specially equipped to sail both on the high seas and in intricate river channels delivered "cargo consisting of steel from Spain, mixed feed from France, various chemicals from Italy and soda ash from Rumania" to Pahlavi on the Caspian Sea at the end of its route through the Mediterranean, Aegean, Marmara, and Black Seas and the Sea of Azov, and the Don and Volga river systems.[7]

Establishment of Economic and Technical Ties

The other major aspect of Iran's policy toward the Soviet Union in 1963-73 was the establishment of economic and technical relations with its northern neighbor. As early as 1921 the two countries had expressed the desire to forge economic and technical ties, but no significant development had materialized. The only major area of activity other than trade had been fisheries. As seen, once the relevant fisheries concession expired in 1953, the government of Musaddiq refused to establish any new arrangement with the Soviet Union. In fact, Irano-Soviet technical and economic ties during the decade under

[6]*Kayhan* (Weekly English), July 31, 1971.

[7]*CDSP* 24, no. 23 (July 5, 1972):22.

examination surpassed, in their importance to Iran, the rapidly expanding commercial transactions. As will be noted, however, the economic-technical relations of Iran were closely tied to its trade and transit with the Soviet Union. Activities in the economic and technical fields were numerous, complicated, and highly technical, ranging from the construction of Iran's first steel mill at Isfahan to machine tool plants at Arak, the hydroelectric dam over the Aras border river, and expansion and improvement of the Caspian Sea ports and fisheries.

The single most important agreement in the economic-technical field was signed on January 13, 1966, for the construction of a steel mill, a gas pipeline, and a mechanical engineering plant. The agreement came into force provisionally on the same date, and definitely on June 29, 1966, by the exchange of the instruments of ratification at Tehran. On March 19, 1968, the Soviet Union registered it with the United Nations.[8] Under the agreement, the Soviet Union undertook to execute the necessary planning and exploratory work; deliver any equipment, machinery, and materials unobtainable in Iran; send Soviet experts to Iran to collect initial data; furnish supervision and advise in the construction of the projects; give technical industrial training to Iranian citizens; assist in the assembly, installation, and initial operation of equipment; and receive Iranian citizens for technical-industrial training in the USSR. Furthermore, the Soviet Union undertook to grant Iran a loan of 260 million rubles at 2.5 percent interest per year to pay for the technical assistance to be provided in the construction of the projects. The annexes to the agreement spelled out more fully each of the three projects. Briefly stated, the agreement envisaged a steel mill with a complete metallurgical cycle and an annual capacity of 500,000 to 600,000 tons of steel, which might be increased to 1 to 1.2 million tons. It also envisaged a gas pipeline for the delivery of gas from Iran to the USSR. The Saveh-Astara section of the gasline was to be constructed by the Soviet Union, and the section from the oil and gas fields in the south of Iran to Saveh was to be constructed by Iran. The agreement also envisaged the construction of a mechanical engineering plant with the annual output of 25,000 to 30,000 tons of metal products.

At the time of the signing of these agreements, Soviet sources predicted that the gas pipeline would go into operation in 1970, the steel mill in 1971.[9] The gas pipeline was estimated to be more than one thousand kilometers long; it would carry up to ten billion cubic meters of gas annually to the Soviet Union. In payment for the gas the Soviet Union would deliver to Iran increasing amounts of equipment for heavy and light industry, road building, and

---

[8]For the text of the agreement and annexes see U.N., Secretariat, *Treaty Series* 633, no. 9037 (1968):123-63.

[9]*CDSP* 8, no. 2 (Feb. 2, 1966):26-27.

the like. In payment for the expenses of the Soviet role in building the plants and a section of the gas pipeline, Iran would deliver to the Soviet Union—in addition to gas—cotton, wool, and nonferrous metal.

The opening of the Trans-Iranian Gas Pipeline took place on October 28, 1970. The project was thus completed on schedule. The shah and President Podgorny took part in the ceremony. During the ceremony the shah stated that "our border has become a border of peace, friendship and cooperation. Our trade has grown fivefold in the past few years. The most important thing is that the leaders of our countries understand the necessity of developing cooperation and have worked out a plan for its development over the next fifteen years." He added further that the "importance of the plan that we are implementing today lies in the fact that it marks the beginning of our economic cooperation over a long period; we shall avail ourselves of the fruits of this cooperation." President Podgorny remarked, "A significant event in the history of the cooperation between our two neighbor countries has just occurred." He considered the completion of the project not only a Soviet-Iranian technical achievement but also "a concrete embodiment of the ever growing and mutually advantageous cooperation between the Soviet Union and Iran."[10]

The steel mill project was not completed in 1971, as predicted by the Soviets. Instead, on August 10, 1972, a new agreement was signed between Iran and the Soviet Union for the expansion of output of the Aryamihr steel mill, as the Iranians now called the mill. The Soviet Union undertook to place credit facilities in the sum of 260 million rubles ($300 million) to cover the cost of machinery and equipment needed to expand output at the steel mill by 1.9 million tons annually over a five-year period.[11] In the same year (1972), however, the Arak machine tools plant was completed. At the time of the opening, the Iranian minister of economy reported that the present production capacity of the machine tools plant was 8,000 tons, but it would reach 30,000 tons after two expansion phases. Moreover, at the time the plant employed nearly 2,000 workers, engineers, and others, but during the later stages its work force would rise to 3,000. The plant was completed in three years.[12]

The long-awaited steel mill was finally completed in 1973. Ruffled political relations between Iran and the Soviet Union pushed the news of the Aryamihr steel mill off the front pages of Iranian newspapers. Nevertheless, economically speaking, the completion of the steel mill was a belated realization of an

[10]*CDSP* 22, no. 43 (Nov. 24, 1970):11-12.

[11]*Kayhan* (Weekly English), Aug. 19, 1972.

[12]Ibid., Sept. 23, 1972.

old dream; Iran had tried to construct a steel mill in 1937, 1955, and 1959 with other foreign assistance but without success. Now it had been accomplished with the cooperation of the Soviet Union. The mill took five years to build, its construction required over ten thousand workers and engineers, and represented an investment of $750 million. According to Iranians, the mill's completion marked the end of the first stage of "Iran's ambitious plans to produce an annual total of 15 million tons of iron and steel by 1983."[13] As already noted, by the agreement of August 10, 1972, Iran and the Soviet Union agreed to expand output of the steel mill by 1.9 million tons annually, but in a communiqué issued at the end of the shah's visit to the Soviet Union of October 12-21, 1972, they agreed to increase the steel mill's capacity to 4 million tons of steel a year.

In addition to the three major projects of Irano-Soviet economic-technical cooperation just discussed, a fourth major project was also completed in 1963-73. This was the construction of the hydraulic engineering installations on the Aras River, forming part of the frontier between the two neighboring countries. As noted, an agreement for joint utilization of the boundary river had been signed as early as 1957, but definitive agreement and actual construction work had to await improvement in the political climate between the two countries after the pledge of 1962. The actual construction began under the terms of the July 27, 1963, agreement on economic and technical cooperation and was completed on June 28, 1971. As seen from Tehran, the project had a twofold purpose.[14] First, it was to provide for the irrigation of the plains of Moghan and Mill in Iran and the Soviet Union, enabling them to become major farming centers. Second, it was to provide electricity for both sides. On the Iranian side the dam would provide electricity for a vast part of Azerbaijan, including Tabriz, Rezaieh, Marand, Khoy, and two dozen other smaller cities and villages. The Aras is fed by numerous streams running eastward from the mountains of Erzerum in Turkey and the foothills of Armenia in the Soviet Union. Only 12.5 percent of the Aras's water is provided from sources in Iran. The dam was constructed jointly and the benefits derived from it were to be equally divided. This meant that the 44,000 kilowatts of electricity produced would be shared equally by Iran and the Soviet Union. Accordingly, the Iranian hydroelectric power station, located on the right bank, and the Soviet station, on the left bank, each had a capacity of 22,000 kilowatts.[15] This, Iran's first earthfill dam, 34 meters high and 1,000 meters long, took five years of joint work to complete. As the result of the construction of the dam a new boundary line between Iran and

[13]Ibid., Mar. 24, 1973.

[14]Ibid., Dec. 5, 1970.

[15] *CDSP* 23, no. 26 (July 27, 1971):20.

the Soviet Union through the newly created reservoirs became necessary. The relevant protocol was drawn up and signed in Moscow on May 7, 1970, before the actual completion of the entire project, and was attached to the border and financial question agreement of December 2, 1954, discussed previously.[16]

Finally, just over a decade after the missile bases pledge of September 1962, Iran and the Soviet Union concluded on October 12, 1972, a treaty on economic and technical cooperation for a period of fifteen years. Despite the importance of political considerations prompting the conclusion of this treaty by Iran, which will be discussed later, the fact still remained that the notion of expanding Iran's economic and technical relations with the Soviet Union had been under consideration before the conclusion of the Iraqi treaty (April 9, 1972) with the Soviet Union. Iran's treaty with the Soviet Union was concluded during the shah's visit to the Soviet Union in October 1972. It was concluded, to borrow the language of the treaty, "for the purpose of the development and deepening of comprehensive and mutually advantageous economic and technical cooperation and trade between the two countries on a balanced and long-term basis."[17] Two major provisions of the treaty formally introduced novel ideas into the relations of Iran and the Soviet Union. First, they committed themselves to the promotion of regional, in addition to bilateral, cooperation in the economic and trade fields as well as transit shipments. Second, they declared that the provisions of their earlier treaty commitments with third countries "are not and shall not be in contradiction with the provisions of this treaty." While the treaty was to remain in effect for an initial period of fifteen years from the day it entered into force, it could be extended for each subsequent five-year period. In regard to the trade and economic-technical relations between the two countries, the communiqué issued on October 21, 1972, declared that the trade had increased more than 400 percent during the past five years[18] and that the two nations agreed, as mentioned before, to expand the capacity of the steel mill at Isfahan to 4 million tons of steel a year. Moreover, the communiqué noted with satisfaction the progress made in the cultural and scientific exchanges between the two countries and announced a new plan for further cultural exchanges in 1972-76. The agreement for these exchanges was also signed at the time of the shah's visit. The earliest major cultural relations agreement was signed August 22, 1966, and entered into force March 31, 1966.[19] The Soviet Union registered it with the United Nations August 20, 1968, and

[16]Ibid., no. 10 (Apr. 6, 1971):29.

[17]*CDSP* 24, no. 42 (Nov. 15, 1972):6-7.

[18]For the text of the communiqué see *Kayhan* (weekly English) Oct. 28, 1972.

[19]For the full text see U.N., Secretariat, *Treaty Series* 643, no. 9192 (1968):203-15.

exchanges between Iranian and Soviet scientists, artists, educators, and the like, paralleled the more important fields of economic and technical cooperation between the two countries during 1963-73.

Old and New Political Problems

Stabilization and expansion of trade and transit relations and inauguration of new technical and economic ties constituted the essence of Iran's policy of "cooperation" (*hamkary*) toward Moscow. In contrast to the post-Musaddiq 1950s, when Iran made its earliest attempts to test the Soviet claim to peaceful coexistence, its cooperation policy of the 1963-73 period revealed a definite commitment to place economic relations with the Soviet Union on a new basis. But what about political relations? Did Iran also forge new political ties with the Soviet Union? If so, in what way, and, if not, what then characterized its policy toward Moscow? An answer to these questions will be the concern of the following pages.

It must be recalled that from the post-Musaddiq 1950s until 1962, as in the 1946-50 period, Iran's policy at the political level was characterized primarily by dogged resistance to Soviet "intimidation" (*tahdid*). With the breakdown of Irano-Soviet negotiations for a nonaggression pact in 1958-59, the Soviet Union not only supported the shah's opponents but twice attacked the person of the shah.[20] It may also be recalled that in the wake of Iran's pledge of September 1962 Soviet policy dramatically changed, as evidenced by Moscow's sudden abandonment of the shah's opponents and relatively generous praise of his land reform program.

This dramatic change in Soviet policy toward Iran in 1962 bore a striking resemblance to the shift of Russian policy in 1921. Just as the 1921 treaty of friendship marked a new period in the relations of the two nations, in 1962 the pledge signaled the dawn of a new era. Just as in 1921 the Soviet Union abandoned the Communist-supported rebel regime of Mirza Kuchik Khan in favor of establishing new ties with a "strong government" in Tehran, in 1962 it withdrew support from the opponents of the shah within Iran in favor of normalizing relations with the shah's regime. And, just as after the signing of the 1921 treaty Soviet Russia claimed to pursue a "hands-off" policy, in the post-1962 period it claimed to follow a similar line. This hands-off posture was the political expression of the Soviet Union's policy of peaceful coexistence toward Iran. As we shall see, it meant pursuing basically traditional aims toward Iran by new means. In the wake of Iran's pledge in 1962 all methods

[20]Chapter 12 of this study.

of Soviet pressure and intimidation of the 1940s and 1950s were significantly abandoned. Consequently, Iran's defiance of the earlier period was significantly replaced by deference in the 1963-73 period.

Taking the period of 1963-73 as a whole, Iran's policy toward the Soviet Union was marked by cooperation economically and continued resistence politically. Iran's noneconomic policy toward the Soviet Union consisted of three major components: resistance (1) to the Soviet bid for Iranian dealignment, (2) to a prejudicial break with Western oil interests in Iran, and (3) to the extension of Soviet power and influence to the Persian Gulf. To be sure, Iran also resisted Soviet attempts at aligning the Iranian position with that of the Soviet Union on such issues as the war in Vietnam and the Arab-Israeli conflict, but these matters had little influence on Iran's relations with the Soviet Union and need not detain us here.[21]

The Refusal to Dealign

The nature of Iran's alliance with the United States in 1963-73 will receive separate treatment in the following chapter. Suffice it to state here that the course of this alliance was not uniformly smooth. But, it survived the vicissitudes of Irano-American relations and, as will be seen, began to show a new vigor in 1968 that led to unprecedentedly close relations by 1973.

The first question of importance concerning the Soviet effort to disengage Iran from the alliance is whether Iran's pledge of 1962 signified any subsequent erosion of its alignment with the United States. As shown, Iran's decision to make that pledge was inextricably tied in with an overall shift in its foreign policy, and as such it was prompted by a complex of domestic, regional, and international political and economic factors. These obviously require no repetition here, but insofar as the Irano-American alliance was concerned, it may be recalled that the Iranian pledge was made in full conformity with changes in American strategic thought and policy. Missile bases, which were the main subject of the pledge, were considered obsolete in 1962 in light of the greater military capability of the United States to retaliate by means of an alternative system of Polaris submarines. As shown before, as early as 1959 Iran, on its own, made it clear to the Soviet Union that it had no intention to allow the use of its territory for missile sites against

---

[21] Iran's resistance in these matters is clearly evidenced in a variety of statements and joint communiqués. See, for example, the communiqué issued at the end of the shah's visit to the Soviet Union in 1965, *CDSP* 17, no. 27 (July 28, 1965):24-25. the communiqué issued at the end of Premier Hoveyday's visit to Moscow in 1967, *CDSP* 19, no. 30 (Aug. 16, 1967): 17-18; and the communiqué issued at the end of Premier Kosygin's visit to Tehran in 1968, *CDSP* 20, no. 14 (Apr. 24, 1968):26-27.

the Soviet Union, and the change in the United States attitude toward missile bases reinforced, if it did not simply coincide with, Iran's own predilection. Furthermore, careful examination of the Iranian pledge reveals that it did not contradict the requirements of Iran's alliance with the United States but actually enhanced Iran's position in the alliance. It may be recalled that one of the basic reasons for the breakdown of Irano-Soviet negotiations for a nonaggression pact in 1958-59 was the Soviet refusal to accept the Iranian definition of bases. The Soviet Union would prefer "military bases" while Iran insisted on prohibition only of "missile bases." Obviously the Soviet definition could have provided a basis for a subsequent Soviet claim that prohibition of military bases would require dismantling of all American military operations in Iran. But the Soviet acceptance in 1962 of the narrower Iranian definition left all American military operations in Iran intact.

The first major instance of Iran's determination to remain aligned with the United States, despite its pledge to the Soviet Union, was its launching of joint military maneuvers with some "7,000 American officers and men" in April 1964. The maneuvers were given the Persian name *Delavar*, or "coura-geous," and were denounced by the Soviets. As contrasted with the vituperation of the 1940s and 1950s, the Russian restraint was remarkable. Nevertheless, Moscow alleged that the maneuvers were to take place under the direction of Gen. Paul Adams, who headed the forces set up to wage the so-called dirty wars. In criticism of Iran and in view of the fact that their consent was required for "the provocational idea to be carried out," the Soviet press cited an alleged Persian proverb to the effect that "if you want peace, don't knock at the doors of war" and asked: "Is the holding of American-Iranian maneuvers on Iran's territory in accord with the recent statements of Iranian officials concerning their intention to improve Soviet-Iranian relations and to promote a strengthening of mutual confidence and genuine good neighbor relations between our neighboring countries"? [22]

With the establishment of the Regional Cooperation for Development (RCD) by the three regional members of CENTO (Iran, Turkey, and Pakistan), the Soviet Union sounded for the first time in 1963-73 one of its favorite themes of attack upon CENTO: the inevitable disintegration of CENTO, which, according to the Soviets, was marked first by the Iraqi defection from the Baghdad Pact and was accelerated later by the "isolation" and "complete subordination" of Iran as well as Turkey and Pakistan to the United States because these countries failed to follow the "noncapitalist path toward socialism, and to pursue a policy of nonalignment." The Soviets portrayed the RCD as not only the expression of dissatisfaction of its Middle Eastern

[22] *CDSP* 16, no. 13 (Apr. 22, 1964):24-25.

members with the West but also as an organization that "in effect was taken outside the framework of the pact [CENTO] *and was aimed against it.* "[23] Iran, like Turkey and Pakistan, however, made every effort from the start to indicate that RCD was *not* directed against CENTO. On July 5, 1964, for example, a CENTO official stated that although the organization was not taking part in the tripartite talks (that led to the establishment of RCD), it had been "kept informed on points of interest to the Alliance," and official spokesmen for the three countries emphasized that the talks had been "parallel to, but not against, the Central Treaty Organization." [24]

Another favorite theme of the Soviet Union in encouraging the withdrawal of Iran and other regional members from CENTO was the claim that "the myth" of a Soviet threat to Iran was upset as the result of the Soviet "policy of peace." This myth had been invented in Washington in order to create CENTO, but as the result of "friendly help" from the north it had been upset. Thousands of Iranians were aware of that because, together with Soviet experts, they were building factories and power stations and laying gas pipelines. Moscow repeatedly stated that Iran, like other regional members of CENTO, was seeking to limit its participation in the organization. [25]

The favorite Soviet theme in encouraging the withdrawal of Iran from its alliance with the United States was the portrayal of deep divisions between the "Asian members" of CENTO and the United States and Britain. For example, the reaction of Iran to the American invasion of Cambodia, together with that of Turkey and Pakistan within the RCD framework, was used in May 1970 to indicate the deepening rift between Iran and the United States and Britain. "The United States is escalating the aggression in Southeast Asia. Britain supports America; while Turkey, Iran and Pakistan express their profound concern in this connection." [26] The same broadcast claimed that the interests of Iran and the United States and Britain were also "contradictory" on questions concerning internal development; Iran's determination to free itself from "economic backwardness" was meeting "strong resistance" from these Western nations that were driving it "to the path of stepping up war preparations." The same theme was sounded more vehemently at the time of CENTO's ministerial council's eighteenth annual session held in April 1971 in Ankara. Bearing in mind that Iran's participation in CENTO "threatened involvement in the imperialist war," the Soviets claimed that "social

[23] Ibid., no. 46 (Dec. 9, 1964):16.

[24] "Regional Cooperation Group Formed by Pakistan, Persia and Turkey," *Keesings Contemporary Archives* 14 (1963-64):20, 438-39.

[25] From a broadcast by Moscow in English, in U.S., FBIS, *USSR Int. Affairs* 3, no. 69 (Apr. 9, 1970).

[26] From a broadcast by Moscow in Turkish, in ibid., no. 92 (May 12, 1970).

circles in Iran" continued ever-increasing opposition to CENTO, demanding "the withdrawal" of their country from it.[27]

A decade after Iran's pledge to the Soviet Union and its unprecedented economic cooperation with Moscow, despite all the troubles of the alliance, Iran seemed as firmly committed to it as ever. With an eye to the forthcoming summit conference in Washington between the Soviet Union and the United States and the progress of the détente movement in Europe and with Iran's increasing concern with the Soviet-supported "subversion" in the Persian Gulf area, the Iranian prime minister addressed the CENTO ministerial meeting in Tehran in June 1973. While praising the détente movement, he fervently hoped that it would not be geographically confined to specific areas alone. "Détente is a commodity," he stated, "as much in demand in Europe and the Far East, as it is in Asia and the Middle East. For we believe that peace can only prove durable when it's indivisible. Accord and accommodation in one part of the world should not be achieved at the cost of a free hand for disruption and subversion in other parts." [28] In its editorial comment *Kayhan* stated that "Iran has made it clear that its membership of CENTO will in no way prevent it from pursuing the wise and far-sighted policy it defined in the early '60's and has been pursuing ever since with much success"—meaning that its membership in that organization would be no impediment to its cooperation with the Soviet Union as in the past. While the editorial, too, praised détente and disparaged speaking of CENTO in the same tone as in the days of the cold war, it left little doubt that Soviet-supported subversion was a "serious problem" in the area of concern to CENTO. "There are," the editorial stated, "fanatics who wish to impose their own styles of politics on others. Often they are encouraged, inspired and even armed and financed by various countries still interested in expanding their influence or hegemony through devious adventures." [29] The *Washington Post*, reporting from Tehran on the CENTO meeting, more clearly detected Iran's concern with Russia. It stated generally: "Public statements by the ministers and a joint communique clearly indicated that Iran, Pakistan and Turkey had expressed strong concern about a continuing Russian menace while the United States pushed for a softer public stance." [30]

The most severe Soviet attempt to detach Iran from its alliance with the West in the 1960s stemmed, it seemed in Washington, from the Soviet arms sale to the shah's regime. The first report of Iran's consideration of purchasing

[27] From a Broadcast by Moscow in English, in ibid., no. 85 (May 3, 1971).

[28] *Kayhan* (Weekly English), June 16, 1973, and *Ittila'at Hava'i,* June 10, 1973.

[29] *Kayhan* (Weekly English), June 16, 1973.

[30] *Washington Post,* June 12, 1973.

arms from the Soviet Union appeared on July 14, 1966, but the actual transaction did not take place until later and was not announced to the Parliament by Premier Amir 'Abbas Hoveyda until February 19, 1967. The time lag between the two events was important partly because Iran's move aroused great concern in Washington, which tried to dissuade the shah from going through with the deal. According to the *New York Times*, American officials interpreted the Soviet arms sale to the shah as part of the Soviet Union's "patient but determined campaign to undermine the links to Western defense alliance of the countries along its southern border."[31] This was the first time that a "member of a Western alliance had agreed to buy Soviet arms," it was remarked by officials in Washington, and Iran's move was regarded as merely further, though dramatic, evidence "that the eight-year-old Central Treaty Organization of the Middle East had long since outlived its military role of providing defense against Soviet attack."[32]

From the perspective of the 1970s Western reports of the Iranian arms purchase from the Soviet Union may appear sensational, but from the standpoint of the Irano-American military relations until that time, the surprise with which the news was received in the United States seems warranted. It may be recalled that the foundations of Iran's military relations with the United States were erected in 1943 and 1947, when the earliest agreements were signed. As was shown before, American military aid to Iran before 1947 had been primarily of an advisory nature. But ever since 1947 the United States alone had been the single most important supplier of Iranian military equipment, and hence the Soviet arms sale appeared to jeopardize Iran's alliance with the United States, which had always been based on more than Iran's membership in CENTO.

As it turned out, however, Iran's purchase of Soviet arms in the amount of $110 million created no lasting breach in Iran's alignment with the United States. In the first place, Iran's primary motivation was to acquire more sophisticated weapons for defense in the Persian Gulf in anticipation of the imminent withdrawal of British troops from Aden; Iran's primary concern was with the perceived revolutionary Arab challenge to its interests in the gulf area. There was no intention to wreck the alliance with the United States but rather to use the Soviet deal as a lever to acquire more modern weapons from the United States. In the second place, the Soviet Union itself seemed reluctant to sell surface-to-air missiles to Iran. The reported Soviet explanation was that it would be potentially embarrassing to the Soviet Union among

[31]*New York Times,* Feb. 8, 1967.
[32]Ibid., Feb. 11, 1967.

"revolutionary" Arab states to supply arms to a "reactionary" state, particularly since Iran wanted the surface-to-air missiles as a defense against Soviet planes supplied to the United Arab Republic.[33] The Soviet arms sale to Iran as a result amounted to a small fraction of the billion dollars the United States had provided Iran since the establishment of the alliance, and the Soviet equipment consisted primarily of trucks, antiaircraft guns, and other equipment. If the Soviet motive was to weaken the alliance by arms sales to Iran, it accomplished the opposite result; Iran succeeded at the time in getting the long-sought offer of modern weapons from the United States.

The acid test of Iran's alignment with the United States was the long-standing tradition of acquiring military assistance from the United States. At the same time Iran's membership in CENTO and its bilateral defense agreement of 1959 with the United States represented Iran's de jure alignment with the United States. Nothing was done by Iran to terminate this relationship. And as we shall see in the following chapter, the alliance survived in the 1960s, as in the 1950s, despite all the strains of Irano-American relations. More important, Iran's de facto alignment with the United States was actually intensified in 1968, primarily as the result of its ability to purchase long-sought modern weapons from the United States. And as we shall also see in the following chapter, this intensification of alignment reached a new peak in 1972, when Iran contracted in the United States for $2.5 billion of military hardware, and in 1973 Washington hoped to add the United States Navy's new fighter, the F-14 Tomcat.[34]

Resistance to Total Break with the Western Oil Companies

Continued Soviet pressures against Iran's alignment with the West in general and the United States in particular during 1963-73 were accompanied by consistent Soviet encouragement of the expulsion of Western oil interests from Iran. The Soviet perspective on the oil issue in Iran was significantly similar to their assessment of the oil situation in the 1950s. It may be recalled that Iran's efforts to reach an oil settlement with Britain in 1954 were viewed by Moscow basically as a struggle between the American and British "oil monopolies," and the agreement between Iran and the Western oil consortium was regarded as a Western attempt to place the Iranian oil industry under the control of the Western oil companies and to control Iran's "entire economy." Throughout the 1960s and the early 1970s Moscow continued to view Iran's 1954 agreement with the oil consortium and its operations in Iran as

[33]Ibid., Sept. 19, 1966.

[34]*Washington Post*, July 24, 1973.

"enslaving and imposed" by the "capitalist monopolies." The struggle between the British and American "oil monopolies" of the 1950s, however, was viewed somewhat differently in the 1960s and 1970s. First, the rapid growth or demand for oil against "the background of the mounting anti-imperialist struggle and the continued shift in the world balance in favour of socialism strengthened the positions of the oil exporting countries" vis-à-vis the Western oil companies. Second, the growing dependence of "the developed capitalist countries on an uninterrupted supply of oil from the Third World tends to intensify inter-imperialist rivalry. Western Europe, for instance, is evincing concern over the fact that the United States oil monopolies and Administration are out to ensure a steady flow of Middle East oil primarily to the American market and to secure the most advantageous terms for themselves." [35]

Iran's relations with the oil consortium, directly or through the Organization of Petroleum Exporting Countries (OPEC), were viewed in 1963-73 by the Soviets from the perspective of the "anti-imperialist" struggle of Iran against "Western oil monopolies." It may be recalled that Iran's aspiration to control its own oil industry through nationalization was not fully realized in its 1954 agreement with the consortium, and for this important reason the shah considered the agreement at the time as beneficial "under the circumstances." As we shall see in the following chapter, the post-1954 settlement was marked by increasing attempts by Iran to realize its national economic aspirations more fully, and thus the relations with the consortium were subjected to repeated assessment through negotiations either directly or through the OPEC, of which Iran was a member. The most significant developments in Iran's relations with the consortium, however, took place in 1971-73, and the Soviet attitudes during these years require closer scrutiny.

The OPEC, led by Iran, achieved a spectacular success in reaching a new agreement with Western oil companies in 1971. The talks in Tehran between the OPEC and the Western oil companies were viewed by Moscow as the scene of "a decisive clash between the interests in the largest Western oil monopolies and the six oil exporting countries, OPEC members in the Persian Gulf area"; the Western oil companies tried every means to hold on to their old position, while the six oil-producing nations of the Gulf "wanted to rid themselves from the predatory exploitation of their national wealth." However, Western oil companies "were forced to sign an agreement under which they would have to pay the treasuries of these countries a thousand million dollars more already in this year." [36]

[35] See Ruben Andreasyan, "The Energy Crisis and Mid-East Oil," *New Times,* no. 16, Apr. 1973, pp. 23-25.

[36] From a broadcast by Moscow in English, in U.S., FBIS, *USSR Intl. Affairs* 3, no. 31 (Feb. 16, 1971), and from a broadcast by Moscow in English, ibid., no. 32 (Feb. 17, 1971).

Moscow's encouragement of Iran to break ties completely with Western oil interests was intensified in 1972 after the Iraqi nationalization of the Iraq Petroleum Company (IPC). The Soviet Union hailed "radical actions" of Algeria and Libya in nationalizing their oil industry in 1971, but the greatest praise was reserved for Iraqi nationalization. In the language of *New Times*: "The heaviest blow at oil imperialism was dealt by Iraq on June 1, 1972, when it nationalized the property of the Iraq Petroleum Company operating in the Kirkuk field with an extraction rate of 50 million tons annually. In challenging oil imperialism, the Iraqi government drew, and still draws, on the unity of the masses and the progressive political organizations of the country, on the strong support of the Soviet Union and other socialist countries, and on the solidarity of the OPEC countries."[37] The Soviets drew parallels between the "plundering activities" of IPC in Iraq and the oil consortium in Iran; foresaw that the Iraqi nationalization "will weaken the position of imperialist oil monopolies in other countries"; and left no room for doubt that the example of Iraq should be followed by Iran.[38]

Encouragement of Iran to follow the Iraqi example was stepped up during Iran's protracted negotiations with the international consortium in fall 1972. In a commentary on these negotiations Moscow suggestively entitled its discussion "Nationalization of Oil Would Hasten Iran's Development," and categorically asserted, "It goes without saying that the nationalization of the Iraqi oil industry enjoys full support from all OPEC members, including Iran."[39] It also claimed that the "attitude of the USSR and the rest of the socialist countries facilitates the struggle of the oil-extracting countries, including that of Iran, against the imperialist oil monopolies."

Iran's decision of January 1973 not to renew its 1954 agreement with the international oil consortium after 1979 was hailed by Moscow. The Iranian decision, in the Soviet view, "exploded like a bomb at the consortium's headquarters in London"; the consortium would no longer operate Iran's oil but it would become "a simple purchaser of Iranian oil," and consequently Iran would take full control of its oil resources." The commentator reminded Iranian listeners pointedly: "As you know, Iran was deprived of this control immediately after the nationalization of the oil industry by the Mossadiq government in 1951." Moscow claimed that "the oil magnates" were trying to "intimidate Iran" and possibly force it to change its decision, but this was "unfair and useless" as similar attempts in the past had failed. Iran was the "natural and rightful owner of the oil and other natural resources within its

[37]Andreasyan, "'Energy Crisis," p. 24.

[38]From a broadcast by Moscow in English, in U.S., FBIS, *USSR Intl. Affairs* 3, no. 110 (June 6, 1972).

[39]From a broadcast by Moscow in Persian, ibid., no. 223 (Nov. 16, 1972).

territory, and no other person was entitled to such rights; the United Nations Charter and international law gave parties to contracts and agreements "the right to settle unilaterally, in certain circumstances, questions concerning the duration and validity of agreement"; and being "true friends of Iran, the Soviet people wish great success to the independent expansion of Iran's oil industry and its maximum use of the country's natural resources for national progress and revival."[40]

Soviet jubilation over the Iranian nonrenewal of the 1954 agreement was meant to encourage further Iraqi-type nationalization by Iran, but Iran's refusal to follow the path of Baghdad was clearly a source of disappointment to Moscow. The best evidence of this was the Soviet reaction to Iran's subsequent decision to forge a new agreement with Western oil companies. Iran's new agreement with the consortium was regarded by the Soviets as a "revision" of the 1954 agreement because the consortium would become a long-term purchaser of Iranian oil under its terms. Hinting at the superiority of the Iraqi example, the Soviets cited Iraq's agreement of March 1, 1973, with the representatives of IPC according to which "the monopolies will relinquish all their demands on that country," and as a result Iraq will win "an important victory" in its struggle against the "imperialist monopolies."[41]

Soviet disappointment with Iran's determination to continue long-term oil sales to the Western oil companies was most clearly revealed in June 1973. In an "unattributed commentary" Radio Moscow beamed to Tehran in Persian a long discussion of Iranian oil. Assessing Iran's new agreement with the international oil consortium, Moscow found it

noteworthy that only an insignificant portion of the oil extracted in Iran will be placed at the disposal of the Iranian Government to meet internal requirements and for exports abroad. The monopolists within the international oil consortium, as previously, will play the role of intermediary between Iran and the consumers of Iranian oil in the international market and will export crude oil from Iran and amass stupendous profits from refining and treating it. It is axiomatic that in the future Iran will have to continue struggling tirelessly for the oil to become the real master of the "black gold." [42]

Sounding out the same theme, the *New Times* observed: "Iran has gained an undisputed victory. It is *becoming* master of its own oil resources—though perhaps *not full master*, considering its commitment to deliver oil to the Consortium."[43]

[40]From a broadcast by Moscow in Persian, ibid., no. 25 (Feb. 6, 1973).

[41]From a broadcast by Moscow in Persian, ibid., no. 46 (Mar. 8, 1973).

[42]From a broadcast by Moscow in Persian, ibid., no. 121 (June 22, 1973).

[43]Andreasyan, "New Developments on the Oil Front," *New Times,* no. 25, June 1973, pp. 23-25. Emphasis added.

Opposition to the USSR in the Persian Gulf

The single most difficult problem facing Iran in its policy toward the Soviet Union in the 1960s and early 1970s was a basic and growing conflict with the USSR in the Persian Gulf. The development of Iran's Persian Gulf policy will be taken up in a separate chapter. What should be noted here is the fact that the rhetoric of Soviet policy in the gulf seemed to correspond with that of Iran's; the Soviet Union, like Iran, proposed that the Persian Gulf should be kept out of great-power hegemony and conflict and that its security should be the responsibility of the littoral states. But it was increasingly apparent to Iran that Soviet policies both directly and indirectly diverged from Soviet statements.

Britain's initial decision of 1968 to withdraw its forces from the Persian Gulf completed the process of the emergence of Iran's "vital interests" in the gulf. Toward the protection of these interests, Iran declared from the outset that the power vacuum that would be left by the British withdrawal must not be filled by any power outside the Persian Gulf area. For example, the shah told Premier Indira Gandhi on January 4, 1969, that Iran would not brook outsiders in the Persian Gulf when Britain withdrew its troops in 1971 and stressed that the defense responsibilities of the region should be left to the littoral states. [44] A similar statement was made by the shah on January 20, 1969. In an interview with *U. S. News and World Report*, when asked how big a role he felt the Russians would play in the Persian Gulf, he stated: "This question must be settled by the countries surrounding the Persian Gulf. We do not want any big powers trying to replace Britain."[45] In a major interview in January 1972, soon after the British withdrawal, the shah was asked what he thought about the American presence in Bahrain. In reply, he stated that "we should not like to see a foreign power in the Persian Gulf. Whether that power be Britain, the United States, the Soviet Union or China our policy has not changed." In reply to a question, in the same interview, about Soviet ships and the Iraqi base there (Um Qasr), the shah stated: "If you are referring to creation of bases, then that would create new problems. But if we are talking about visits, then one cannot prevent military vessels of another country from paying visits anywhere in international waters. But if there should be a question of bases, it is obvious that this would create an entirely new situation."[46]

[44] *Kayhan* (Daily English), Jan. 5, 1969.

[45] Ibid., Jan. 21, 1969.

[46] For an unofficial text of the shah's press interview, see *Kayhan* (Weekly English), Jan. 29, 1972.

Soviet policy statements corresponded with the Iranian ones; the Soviet Union claimed that it, too, believed that all outside powers should stay out of the Persian Gulf, and the affairs of the gulf, including its problem of security, should be resolved by the littoral states. This principle was endorsed in the joint Soviet-Iranian communiqué issued at the end of the shah's visit to the Soviet Union in October 1972, when, as seen, a fifteen-year economic and technical treaty was concluded between the two countries. The communiqué stated in part: "The Soviet Union and Iran expressed the firm conviction that questions relating to the Persian Gulf zone should be resolved, in accordance with the principles of the U. N. Charter, by the states of this region themselves without outside interference."[47] An identical statement was included in the joint Irano-Soviet communiqué issued at the end of Premier Kosygin's visit to Iran for participation in the opening ceremony of the steel mill.[48]

But there were serious indications of real differences between Iran and the Soviet Union in the Persian Gulf. As we shall see, Iran watched with alarm both the development of close Soviet ties with Iraq and the appearance of Soviet vessels, arms, and support for "subversive" activities in the area. The 1972 treaty marked the peak of the Soviet political, economic, and technical alignment with Iraq. In contrast to the subsequent Soviet treaty with Iran, mentioned above, it was primarily a political treaty, and one with definite anti-Western overtones. At the time of the ratification of the treaty with Iraq, V. V. Kuznetsov, Soviet first deputy minister of foreign affairs, stated on June 9, 1972, that along with the Soviet Union's treaty with Egypt the previous year, "the Soviet-Iraqi Treaty is a weighty new contribution to the strengthening and development of Soviet-Arab relations as a whole, and it strengthens the front of the progressive forces opposing imperialism."[49] Furthermore, the Soviet treaty with Iraq provided a long-term basis for political and possibly military cooperation between the two countries. Article 8 of the treaty stated: "In the event of the development of situations that threaten the peace of either side or create a threat to peace or violation of peace, the High Contracting Parties will immediately contact one another for the purpose of coordinating their positions in the interest of removing the threat that has arisen or restoring peace."[50] More important, the Soviet communiqué with Iraq, as contrasted with the ones with Iran, clearly cast the Soviet Union in the role of champion of the Arab revolutionary cause in the Persian Gulf area. There was no reference to the charter of the United Nations

[47] *CDSP* 24, no. 42 (Nov. 15, 1972):6-7.

[48] *CDSP* 26, no. 11 (Apr. 11, 1973):25-26.

[49] *CDSP* 24, no. 24 (July 12, 1972):11.

[50] For the text of the treaty see ibid., no. 14 (May 3, 1972):12.

or to the principle that gulf affairs were to be handled by the gulf states themselves. Instead the communiqué stated: "The two sides expressed full support for the struggle of the Arab states and peoples of the Persian Gulf area for the right to determine their own destiny, for the elimination of imperialist domination and the dismantling of all foreign military bases and against colonialism, and they condemned the intrigues and plots of imperialism in this area."[51]

Stripped of all the antiimperialist rhetoric, the Soviet Union, on balance, clearly cast its lot in 1972 with Iraq. The Soviet move was regarded with deep anxiety in Tehran, and no effort was made to hide Iran's great disturbance over the projected Soviet military and political cooperation with the Ba'thist regime. In a long editorial entitled "Discussions with a Soviet Diplomat," the editor of the semiofficial *Ittila'at* told of the inability of an unnamed Soviet diplomat to convince him that the Soviet military aid to Iraq would not encourage the Baghdad regime to assist "subversive" activities in the Persian Gulf and that the Soviet treaty with Iraq might not prompt the revolutionary government of Iraq to commit acts of "aggression."[52] The same article expressed surprise over the Soviet treaty with Iraq despite extensive ties developed over the years between Tehran and Moscow. Whatever assurances the Soviet Union tried to give Iran, the Iranian dismay was not assuaged; Russia had sided with Iran's number one "enemy" in the Persian Gulf.

The extent of deterioration of Iran's relations with the Soviet Union was well marked by the time the Aryamihr steel mill was dedicated in March 1973. Tehran was originally expecting President Podgorny, who had been present during the opening of the Trans-Iranian Gas Pipeline, to participate in the ceremony, but instead Premier Kosygin showed up. He tried in his meeting with the shah to reassure Iran about his government's friendship and good-will.[53] His speech repeatedly expressed the "hope for continuation of Soviet-Iranian co-operation." None of this apparently did much to erase the bitterness felt over the Soviet-Iraqi Treaty. In his interview with Arnaud de Borchgrave, the shah called the treaty an "alarm bell" in regard to Iran's reasons for its continued military build-up; preferred not to say that the Soviet Union was behind the activities and smuggling of arms by Iraqi agents into Iran and Pakistan, but if it was, then these were "the actions of very irresponsible people"; and stated, "If Moscow wants real détente with Europe, it will have to play the game here too. European security is sheer mockery without stability and security in the Persian Gulf."[54]

[51] For the communiqué see ibid., no. 7 (Mar. 15, 1972):8, 32.

[52] *Ittila'at Hava'i*, Áug. 2, 1972.

[53] *Kayhan* (Weekly English), Mar. 24, 1973.

[54] Cf. *Kayhan* (Weekly English), May 19, 1973, and *Newsweek,* May 21, 1973.

Iran's opposition to Soviet gulf policy was manifest by 1973 also regarding Soviet encouragement of the "Popular Front for the Liberation of the Occupied Arab Gulf" (PFLOAG). The Front's aim of creating a revolutionary Arab state and then spreading the revolution to include Iran was not, to say the least, welcomed by the shah's regime.[55] The overthrow of the sultan of Oman by his son in 1970 and the subsequent reforms launched by the new sultan did not appear to impress the Soviets, who regarded the new Omani regime as the product of a British maneuver and a "new imperialist plot against the Arab liberation movement in the area." *Pravda*'s special correspondent in a major article about the Dhofari rebellion observed that fighters and commanders of the liberation army read the works of Lenin in Arabic, and the merit of these men was that they went over from revolutionary phrases to revolutionary organizations and from revolutionary organizations to actions in their native land, in Dhofar, where the conditions required that they should take up arms.[56] Soviet encouragement of the Front was by no means confined to the labors of Russian writers and radio commentators. The Soviet Communist party fully endorsed the rebellion and received delegations from the Front in Moscow. For example, TASS reported on September 13, 1971, that the secretary of the Central Committee of the CPSU received a delegation of the popular Front led by a member of its executive committee, Ahmad 'Abd al-Samad. The delegation members reportedly conveyed gratitude to the Soviet Union for supporting their struggle, and noted "the Soviet Union's great contribution to the struggle of the peoples of Asia, Africa and Latin America, against colonialism and neocolonialism, against the aggressive course of American imperialism, and for national independence."[57] The sultan's army fought against the "courageous Dhofar patriots" with the support of not only "British and U. S. imperialists" but also Saudi Arabian "reactionaries."[58]

Iran's opposition to Soviet-supported subversive activities finally brought Iranian arms to the aid of the sultan of Oman. On May 14, 1973, in the interview mentioned above, the shah publicly acknowledged Iranian aid to Oman against the Dhofari rebels. In reply to a question concerning the dangers posed to the flow of oil to the outside world through the Strait of Hormuz, the Shah stated that if the Dhofari rebellion in Oman ever succeeded, "just try to imagine what we would be faced with in Muscat. The capital right

[55]See Stephen Page, "Moscow and the Persian Gulf Countries, 1967-1970," *Mizan* 13, no. 2 (1971):72-88.

[56]From a broadcast by Moscow in English, in U.S., FBIS, *USSR Intl. Affairs* 3, no. 149 (Aug. 3, 1971).

[57]From a broadcast by Moscow in English, in ibid., no. 178 (Sept. 14, 1971).

[58]See *CDSP* 25, no. 2, Feb. 7, 1973):20.

in front of the Strait of Hormuz. At first a few rifles and then naval guns and missiles. It's a familiar pattern. I cannot tolerate subversive activities—and by that I mean anything that is imposed from the outside." When asked if that was why Iran was helping Oman, the shah stated that the Omanis asked for assistance and Iran sent it. He was then asked, "Are you saying you cannot tolerate radical regimes taking over any of the Arab sheikhdoms?" He replied, "Yes." [59] By the time these words were uttered, Iran had become one of the world's leading buyers of American arms. In the same interview the shah stated that what arms Iran was buying were "a deterrent that will be credible to all our neighbors. . . . The Nixon doctrine says the United States will help those who help themselves. That is what we are doing."

[59]*Kayhan* (Weekly English), May 19, 1973.

XV

Continuation and Expansion
of Alignment with the United States

ANOTHER COMPONENT OF Iran's "independent national policy" (*syasat-i mustaqill-i milli*) consisted of its relations with the United States. As we have already seen, this policy had its roots in international, regional, and domestic conditions of the late 1950s and early 1960s and was marked at inception by Iran's determination to normalize relations with the Soviet Union. Examination of Iran's policy in 1963-73 toward the United States will involve primarily (1) the nature of Iran's continued alliance in CENTO, (2) the build-up of a "credible deterrent" in the Persian Gulf and beyond with bilateral American support, and (3) nationalization of its oil industry without prejudice to Western oil needs. In addition to these, our examination of Irano-American relations during 1963-73 will concern continuity and change in bilateral and nonmilitary relations of the two countries.

The Muted Alliance: A Brief Phase

Iran's alliance policy toward the United States in the early 1960s was one of continued disappointment inherited from the 1950s. This is no place to repeat the factual basis of this proposition. Suffice it to recall from previous discussions that from the time of its accession to the Baghdad Pact, Iran was disappointed in the American nonparticipation, for it feared that the organization might fail to provide adequate deterrence against Soviet aggression; might limit American military and economic aid to Iran; and might encourage indirect Soviet and Soviet-supported Arab subversive moves in the Persian Gulf area. The last consideration in particular lay behind Iran's simultaneous discussions of a defense agreement with the United States and a nonaggression pact with the Soviet Union. The revolution in Iraq was the principal reason for Iran's move because it intensified Iran's concern over the revolutionary developments in the Arab Middle East, which originated with the rise of Gamal 'Abd al-Nasir in Egypt.

The American defense agreement of 1959 with Iran, it may be recalled, did little to assuage Iranian dissatisfaction. Although it formally and bilaterally committed the United States to the defense of Iran, it failed to go beyond the already existing American commitment under the Eisenhower Doctrine, which Iran had endorsed. The agreement, in keeping with the doctrine, provided for consultation on defense against Soviet and other aggression if controlled by "international communism." Iran was concerned at the time more with the Iraqi and Arab revolutionary threat to its interests in the Persian Gulf. The move for a nonaggression pact with the Soviet Union was motivated in part by the desire to escape any future pincer of Soviet Communism from the north and radical Arab subversion from the south. As we have already seen, Iran's subsequent missile bases pledge to, and improved relations with, the Soviet Union represented a positive move by Iran partly in order to foster Soviet stakes in Iran as a counter against Moscow's expanding relations with Baghdad.

Iran, together with Turkey and Pakistan, created the Regional Cooperation Development Organization (RCD) in 1964, not only out of their disenchantment with CENTO's inadequate activities, but also as a consequence of their dissatisfaction with its inherent unresponsiveness to any conflict other than one with the Soviet Union. Turkey was dissatisfied with it over the Cyprus problem, Pakistan over the Kashmir dispute, and Iran over the conflict with Iraq. The United States and Britain resisted getting caught within CENTO, in regional conflicts of Turkey with Greece, of Pakistan with India, and of Iran with Iraq.

The paralysis of CENTO in the Indo-Pakistan wars of 1965 and 1971 further aggravated Iran's dissatisfaction with the organization. Iran openly characterized India's action in 1965 as "aggression" (*tajavoz*),[1] engaged in fervent discussions with Turkey for a cease-fire between India and Pakistan, and provided whatever nonmilitary assistance it could. But the United States placement of an embargo on the shipment of arms to Pakistan despite its political and military ties was not welcome news in Tehran. The American explanation might have been that it could take no other position in view of the general East-West rapprochement,[2] but to Iran this would only confirm the decreasing military utility of the organization. The 1971 war between India and Pakistan was an even more drastic indication of CENTO's limited capability in the face of a regional conflict. Two years after the war it was revealed that Iran had given protection to Pakistani civilian planes in its own territory during the war, but it was obvious that the CENTO mechanism had been of no particular help to Pakistan during its second war with India.[3]

[1] *Ittila'at Hava'i,* Sept. 9, 1965.

[2] *New York Times,* Dec. 5, 1968.

[3] *Ittila'at Hava'i,* May 10, 1973.

Subsequently *Kayhan* echoed the official Iranian view: "Pakistan, an ally of the United States through two multilateral and one bilateral treaty, has been attacked and dismembered without as a ripple of serious protest. There is no reason why Pakistan's plight should be treated as an isolated case that could not be repeated elsewhere in the region." Citing Premier Amir 'Abbas Hoveyda, the *New York Times* wrote, "It is apparent now that one has to rely on one's own strength for defense." He dismissed CENTO as merely a nice "club," useful in developing economic projects and communications, and a practical forum to discuss ideas, but not "an effective alliance."[4] We must add, however, that the premier was regarding the organization as ineffective primarily in terms of American inability to aid its allies in a regional conflict.

CENTO Revived?

With the British decision to withdraw forces from the area "east of Suez," including the Persian Gulf, by the end of 1971, the concern of CENTO began to shift gradually. Before that decision the organization, in response to the wishes of its regional members and because of the general reduction of tensions between the East and the West, placed noticeable emphasis on economic cooperation.[5] The British decision gave rise to a new question. What was to be the role of the organization? The United States believed that the British decision "will change the pattern of regional security," but it agreed with the Iranian position that "the states of the region should exercise primary responsibility for security in the gulf." Iran's position was reiterated to other members of the organization during the Eighteenth Session of its Council of Ministers held in Ankara on April 30 and May 1, 1971, when they discussed the future security of the Persian Gulf.[6]

[4]*New York Times,* Feb. 9, 1972.

[5]See, for example, Turkey, Central Treaty Organization, *CENTO Conference on National and Regional Agricultural Development Policy* (Ankara: Office of U.S. Economic Coordinator for CENTO Affairs, 1968; Turkey, Central Treaty Organization, *Progress Through CENTO: Communications* (Ankara: CENTO Public Relations Division, n.d.). See also U.S. State Dept. *Bulletin* 45, no. 1164 (Oct. 16, 1961):642. The United States' as well as CENTO members' emphasis on the economic activities of the organization before 1968 may be seen also from a conference held by Secretary Rusk with Turkish journalists in 1966. See U.S. State Dept. *Bulletin* 54, no. 1403 (May 16, 1966): 776-780. On CENTO's own economic concerns see the accounts of the 15th meeting of its Economic Committee in U.S. State Dept. *Bulletin* 56, no. 1452 (Apr. 24, 1967): 668-71.

[6]U.S. State Dept. *Bulletin* 44, no. 1666 (May 31, 1971):692.

After the British withdrawal, CENTO began to show concern even publicly over the problem of subversion in the Persian Gulf area. In their communiqué of June 2, 1972, at the end of their Nineteenth Session, the CENTO Council of Ministers revealed that they had reviewed the international developments since they met a year before, "with special reference to Iran, Pakistan, and Turkey and the neighboring areas"; and discussed other problems of peace and security in the area, "including subversive activities." In this, as in the previous session of the Council of Ministers, the United States agreed with Iran's position that the security and stability of the Persian Gulf was of "vital importance to the littoral states" and that they bore the "primary responsibility for the security of the Persian Gulf." In fact, the American statement at this session was based on the joint communiqué of President Nixon and the shah of Iran issued the day before at the end of the president's visit to Iran after his trip to Moscow for a summit meeting with Soviet leaders.[7]

During the Nineteenth Session of the Council of Ministers the Soviet-Iraqi "alliance" of April 9, 1972, was uppermost in the mind of Iran. The council's reference to subversive activities in its communiqué was most probably included at the insistence of Iran. The United States concern with detente must have been disconcerting insofar as the Soviet rapprochement with Iraq was not welcomed in Tehran, where it was considered out of tune with the Soviet Union's own expanding economic ties and "good neighborly" relations with Iran.

When the Twentieth Session of the CENTO Council of Ministers met in Tehran in June 1973, Iran called for a reappraisal of the organization in light of the changing regional, as well as world, conditions. Iran's concern with the threat of subversion was aggravated in February 1973, when, as will be seen in the next chapter, Pakistani police raided the Iraqi embassy and seized machine guns and ammunition smuggled in as diplomatic baggage from Baghdad with Iran as the target. Iran and Pakistan were worried about Soviet intentions, because the creation of an independent Baluchi state with the aid of Iraqi arms "might provide the Soviet Union with access to the Persian Gulf." Before the CENTO meeting Iranian forces were already aiding the Omani government against the Dhofari rebellion. Premier Hoveyda revealed in a meeting of diplomatic correspondents in England in April 1973 that the government of "Oman has asked for Iranian assistance in fighting subversive insurgents and Iran has lent its help." He told the correspondents that the Persian Gulf and the Strait of Hormuz were Iran's "economic lifeline," the rebels aimed at controlling the strait, and "we cannot allow our economic lifeline to be in the hands of such subversive elements."[8]

[7]Ibid., 67, no. 1723 (July 3, 1972):23-26.

[8]*Kayhan* (Weekly English), Apr. 21, 1973.

With these developments in mind, the shah in his inaugural message to the Twentieth Session of the CENTO Council of Ministers at Tehran in June 1973 called for the reappraisal of the organization. He stated that the "basic philosophy and objectives of our alliance remain unaltered. However, in view of the changes that have taken place in the pattern of international relations since the alliance came into being some eighteen years ago, it is necessary for us to reappraise the role of CENTO and our cooperation within the alliance in order to see how best it can meet new challenges and adapt itself to new conditions." His message spoke of "significant progress" toward "accommodation and détente between East and West," adding that Iran welcomed measures aimed at reducing the dangers of the arms race. "At the same time," his message went on, "we have witnessed with profound shock and dismay how easily international boundaries are violated, and sovereign states dismembered. It has also been demonstrated how quickly local conflicts can turn into major world crises, leaving weaker elements at the mercy of their stronger adversaries." As noted in the previous chapter, Premier Hoveyda echoed a similar theme with an eye to the forthcoming summit conference in Washington between Soviet and American leaders, but he more specifically stated that détente in one part of the world "should not be achieved at the cost of a free hand for disruption and subversion in other parts."[9]

No matter how hard the United States might have privately tried to soften the anti-Soviet stance of the conference in view of the forthcoming summit meeting in Washington, the communiqué and the subsequent news conference of Secretary Rogers in Tehran revealed that Iran succeeded in impressing upon the United States the challenge that foreign-supported "subversive activities posed to the alliance. The text of the communiqué was unparalleled by any before it during the 1960s in its overriding concern with security matters. During that time most CENTO communiqués reflected the economic concern of the regional members; problems of threat of subversion and the like, at least publicly, were overshadowed by the increasing détente with the Soviet Union. The communiqué of June 11, 1973, in contrast, indicated "the need to maintain vigilance in the region," affirmed "the vital importance" attached "to the preservation of the independence and territorial integrity of each of the member states in this region," and, considering "the continuing subversive threats in the region, the Ministers expressed the determination of their Governments to meet such efforts with all the means at their disposal."[10]

Secretary Rogers's important press conference at the end of the CENTO meeting shed a great deal of light on what was decided at the meeting in

[9]Ibid., June 16, 1973.

[10]For the text of the communiqué see U.S. State Dept. *Bulletin* 49, no.1777 (July 16, 1973):83-84.

regard to subversion in the gulf. In response to questions from the press, the secretary stated that while the world was moving toward détente, "we also recognized that as the world moves away from active conflict and nuclear confrontation, and hopefully away from any major conflicts among nations, there are other concerns that occur, dangers of subversion, things of that kind." [11] In response to another question he declared: "As the threat of nuclear war diminishes—and I believe it has—and the threat of war between the major powers is lessened, subversion is a natural way to spread ideology. It is not unexpected, and I think it is important for nations in the region to consider it, to guard against it, and to be sure it does not cause instability." Again out of deference to the progress with the Soviet Union toward détente, he stated that the United States was "very pleased about that. We are going to do everything we can to move in that direction. But that does not suggest that they have changed their ideology. It does not suggest that they are not going to extend their influence in other parts of the world And it does not suggest that military strength is no longer necessary." [12]

What did Iran get out of the CENTO meeting? As has been pointed out repeatedly in this study, to Iran subversion in the Persian Gulf was a two-headed monster: subversion engineered by radical Arab states, such as Iraq and South Yemen, or by extremist groups like Dhofari rebels in Oman. Careful examination of the communiqué reveals Iran's success in getting the United States and Britain to declare that they, along with their regional allies, were determined to meet the "subversive threats" in the region with "all the means at their disposal." But Secretary of State Rogers's news conference clearly shows that the United States recognized publicly only the subversive threat as posed by the Soviet Union. To that extent this was a gain for Iran insofar as the United States' overriding concern with détente made it reluctant to antagonize the Soviet Union. The "anti-Soviet stance" of the regional members might have been softened, as seen by Americans, [13] but there was no escaping the conclusion that recognition of the dangers of Soviet-supported subversion by the United States at a time that it was deeply concerned with the success of the imminent meeting of Soviet and American leaders in Washington was a clear success on the part of Iran. Such a stance by the United States and CENTO in the 1950s cold war was the norm, but not in the 1970s.

Yet Iran's success seems less important when viewed against its conception of the nature of the danger of subversion. Iran's conception of the danger of

[11] For the text of the interview see ibid.

[12] Ibid.

[13] *Washington Post,* June 12, 1973.

subversion in the Persian Gulf after the Iraqi revolution involved as much, if not more, concern with Arab revolutionary efforts as Soviet-supported activities. And from this standpoint the American position in the 1970s was as far from that of Iran as in the 1950s. The same considerations of broader American interests in the Middle East that had kept the United States technically out of CENTO membership and prompted American refusal to broaden the scope of its commitment to include the defense of Iran against any aggression (including Iraqi) in 1959 lay back of the United States resistance in 1973 to go beyond acknowledging Soviet-supported subversive efforts. CENTO's established opposition to Soviet and Communist-supported subversion was reaffirmed in 1973, but it was not extended to include any and every "leftist" Arab activity. According to the Beirut *Arab World* "CENTO's future role, therefore, would be as much to check so-called 'Soviet-led subversive activity' as making sure that the oil of the Gulf could continue to flow to the West and the United States and would not be interfered with by the leftists in the region."[14] This is too generous an interpretation of what was actually decided by CENTO.

Building a Credible Deterrent with United States Support

The 1963-73 decade witnessed Iran's continued struggle to acquire military aid from the United States. In order to appreciate the decade's development more fully, we may recall from previous discussions that by the late 1950s Iranian acquisition of American military assistance had become almost a tradition. The foundation was set by Iran's agreements of 1943 and 1947, which, as seen, were confirmed by Iran's acceptance of the American Mutual Assistance Program in 1950 and its extension by the Musaddiq government on April 24, 1952. Basically these agreements constituted the foundations of Iran's acquisition of American military aid in the post-Musaddiq 1950s and throughout the 1960s. What distinguished the wartime military aid from the post-1947 period, it may be recalled, was the type of military aid Iran was able to acquire. Before 1947 all American military assistance had been primarily of a technical type, later Iran succeeded in obtaining American military equipment as well. What distinguished the pre-and-post-Musaddiq periods, however, was the amount of military aid Iran received from the United States. In the period between 1949 and the rise of Musaddiq to

[14]*Middle East Monitor* 3, no. 13 (July 1, 1973):1.

power, Iran received only some $16 million whereas in 1953-61 it acquired over $430 million.

The period between the late 1950s and 1964 proved a difficult time for Iran to continue to receive the same sympathetic consideration from the United States in regard to arms acquisition. As we have already seen, this was the period that the United States was reluctant to continue budgetary support of the Iranian government. The United States placed its emphasis with respect to countries like Iran on the need for basic socioeconomic development, a posture that had finally much to contribute to Iran's launching almost simultaneously both its land reform program and its more independent course in world politics through its independent national policy. President Kennedy invited the shah to the United States to explain to him the new American foreign aid policy. The president received the shah on April 11, 1962, acknowledging the shah's leadership in bringing his country out of conditions that would have aided Soviet aims. He stated that were it not for his leadership, "we are quite aware that this vital area of the world, which has been as Mr. Molotov made clear, a vital matter of concern to the Soviet Union, for many, many years, would long ago have collapsed." But besides confirming the United States bilateral defense agreement of 1959 with Iran, the joint statement following the discussion with the shah had nothing to say about American military aid to Iran. Instead it stated: "The President and His Imperial Majesty agreed on the necessity for further acceleration of economic development in Iran, and on the need for continued external assistance to Iran to enable that country to pursue the goals of its economic development plans."[15]

The attitude of the Kennedy administration toward Iran's request for military aid was stated by one of the president's close associates: "In Iran, the Shah insisted on our supporting an expensive army too large for border incidents and internal security and of no use in an all-out war. His army, said one government adviser, resembled the proverbial man who was too heavy to do any light work and too light to do any heavy work."[16] In July 1962 the United States ended its annual payments of $30 million budgetary support, and in August Vice President Lyndon B. Johnson paid a two-day "good-will visit" to Iran. The shah accepted the end of the budgetary support and the American emphasis on long-term loans to revive Iran's economic development. Furthermore, he reportedly made no requests for new military equipment, such as F-104 jet fighters, for which he had pressed before and after his visit

[15]For the text see U.S., President, *Public Papers of the Presidents of the United States*, John F. Kennedy, 1962 (Washington, D.C.: Government Printing Office, 1963), pp. 315, 323; for the text of the joint statement see p. 327.

[16]Theodore Sorenson, *Kennedy* (New York: Harper & Row, 1965), p. 628n.

to Washington. [17] The *New York Times* stated at the time, "The Washington view, which we believe is the correct one, is that Iran's military forces are bigger than they need to be and that they absorb funds that would be better spent on desperately needed economic development." [18]

A curious American change of heart occurred in 1964, however, when for all practical purposes the Johnson administration reversed this attitude. It endorsed a new program enabling Iran to purchase $200 million of American military equipment. How this change came about is difficult to say. Yet it is evident that by 1964 much had happened to dampen the American suspicion that no basic socioeconomic reforms would be launched in Iran. This suspicion pervaded the American attitude as late as 1962, when Vice President Johnson visited Iran. But the shah's determined land reform program was launched in January 1963, and President Kennedy lost no time in availing himself of the opportunity to show the American happiness with the shah's reforms. On January 26, 1963, millions of voters went to the polls to vote on the shah's reform program, and on January 29 the president congratulated the shah on the "historic referendum" and declared that this "demonstration of support should renew your confidence in the rightness of your course and strengthen your resolve to lead Iran to further achievements in the struggle to better the lot of your people." [19] Since the American reluctance to grant Iran further military aid stemmed from the absence of basic socioeconomic reforms, it may be assumed that American satisfaction with the shah's land reform program played a role in Iran's later successful requests for arms.

Yet the record also indicates a close connection between the favorable decision of Washington and a Pentagon victory at Iran's expense. The cost to Iran might have been its acceptance of the Defense Department's demand for a Status of Forces Agreement. In 1962 the two basic military agreements of November 27, 1943, and October 6, 1947, were up, once again, for renewal, as in previous years. In its note of March 19, 1962, the American embassy, having stated its consent to the extension of these agreements governing the services of the advisory missions in Iran, went on to recall, at the same time, the "frequent discussions" that it had with Iran regarding the problem of the status of the personnel of the missions, and suggested "simply that such personnel shall have the privileges and immunities specified for 'Members of the Administrative and Technical Staff' in the Convention annexed to the final act of the United Nations Conference on Diplomatic Intercourse and Immunities signed at Vienna, April 18, 1961, it being understood, of course,

[17] *New York Times*, Aug. 27, 1962.

[18] Ibid., Aug. 20, 1962.

[19] For the texts of messages exchanged between the president and the shah, see U.S., *Public Papers of Presidents of U.S.*, John F. Kennedy, 1963, pp. 160-61.

that certain Senior Personnel may by agreement between the two governments be accorded the status specified in the aforesaid instrument for 'diplomatic Agents.' "[20] Iran bided its time in reply to the note, and when it finally responded on March 11, 1963, it made a distinction between the high-ranking members of the advisory mission and the rest of the staff of the mission. Since the first group held diplomatic passports, Iran agreed to give them diplomatic status until they could enjoy, after the approval of Parliament, the relevant immunities and advantages, but in regard to other members of the mission Iran merely advised that the matter was under study.

Iran delayed a reply for another six months before it wrote the American embassy again, on November 17, 1963. It advised the embassy that upon study it was decided that diplomatic immunities and privileges "shall not apply the members [sic] of the Military Advisory Missions of the United States Government in Iran"[21] under the approval of the Vienna convention by the Iranian Parliament and that a "necessary statement be attached" to the Vienna convention at the time of its presentation to the Iranian Parliament "so that the chief and members of the Military Advisory Missions in Iran may enjoy the privileges, immunities, and exemptions which are provided for 'the administrative and technical employees.' " This reflected a change in Iran's initial position. Iran would not accord *"diplomatic* immunities and privileges" to high-ranking members of the mission either. The Council of Ministers decided that those privileges and immunities would apply that were provided in the Vienna convention for "the administrative and technical employees." This distinction was intended to subject all members of the mission to the civil and administrative jurisdiction of Iran for "acts performed outside the course of their duties," to borrow the relevant language of article 37, paragraph 2 of the Vienna convention.

The United States accepted Iran's decision to extend only immunities and privileges of "administrative and technical employees," but it understood, in its reply of December 18, 1963, that the phrase in Iran's note referring to "the members of the United States military advisory missions in Iran" applied to the military personnel or civilian employees of the Department of Defense and their families." In two separate notes on December 9, 1964, Iran advised the American embassy of the law passed by the Iranian Parliament empowering "the government to allow the chief and members of military advisory missions of the United States of America in Iran, whose services are engaged by the Imperial Government, in accordance with the appropriate agreements,

[20]For the text of the U.S. note see U.S., Department of State, *United States Treaties and Other International Agreements* 19, pt. 6, TIAS no. 6594 (1968): 7525-26; for the text of Iran's reply see p. 7528.

[21]For the text of Iran's note see ibid., pp. 7531-32.

to enjoy the privileges and immunities specified by the Vienna Convention on diplomatic relations of 1961, for members of the administrative and technical staff described in Article 1 of the Convention."[22] The other note more specifically referred to article 37, paragraph 2, in order to leave no doubt about Iran's intention *not* to extend immunities from Iranian civil and administrative jurisdiction to members of the mission for acts performed outside the course of their duties. The United States promised in its reply of December 9, 1964, that it "will give sympathetic consideration to a request" from Iran for waiver of immunity in cases where Iran considered such waiver of "particular importance," namely, cases "involving heinous crimes and other criminally reprehensive acts." The American note did not raise the problem of dependents, but in practice the American view prevailed.[23]

The whole demand of the Defense Department was received with resentment in Iran. Even more than half a decade later I was told repeatedly by the politically aware in Iran that ordinary American citizens (referring to American dependents of military personnel) were enjoying *haq-i tavahosh* in their country, namely, privileges enjoyed by civilized men for living among "savages"! For a complacent Parliament it was remarkable that sixty-one votes were cast against the measure, in spite of the assurances of the government that immunities applied only to the acts of the members of the military missions in the performance of their duties. For a nation that still despised the memories of "capitulations" first imposed by czarist Russia after its humiliating defeat of Iran in the war of 1826-28 and abolished by Riza Shah a century later, the legal niceties of diplomatic notes meant little insofar as the American Defense Department's insensitivity to Iranian sensibilities was concerned. Such practical problems as the application of criminal jurisdiction to traffic offenses under Iranian laws were overcome, but at the time and for quite sometime later, this kind of solution fostered much ill will.

In any event, the debate between Iran and the Pentagon over the kind of weapons Iran wished to acquire continued unabated even after the 1964 decision in favor of Iran. Iran's unprecedented move in 1967-68 to obtain military equipment from the Soviet Union, discussed in the previous chapter, was made as much to declare Iran's independence from the United States as it was to wrest more modern weapons from the United States. In the course of the Iranian arms purchase from the Soviet Union, the United States promised to provide Iran with more modern weapons, and in November 1967 it was

[22]For the text of the Iranian note and the relevant law, see ibid., p. 7535; see also p. 7537.

[23]My statement about the practice is based on Richard Pfau's manuscript published subsequently as "The Legal Status of American Forces in Iran," *Middle East Journal* 28, no. 2 (1974):141-53.

reported that the United States had promised to furnish two squadrons of F-4 Phantom jet fighters, used extensively by American forces in Vietnam. These planes and other military equipment were being financed by roughly $250 million in easy credit loans, primarily those arranged by the Defense Department through the Export-Import Bank.[24]

In 1967 it was stated that the American military aid to Iran would be determined by the end of June 1969, but the British decision of January 1968 to withdraw from the Persian Gulf injected an entirely new factor into American calculations. The arms Iran had purchased in 1964-68 amounted to some $300 million but had not been delivered when the news of the British projected withdrawal was released. The shah now pressed for the purchase of modern weapons from the United States. It was reported in May 1968 that he sought to buy $600 million of "sophisticated weapons" ranging from supersonic fighter-bombers and modern tanks to automatic small arms over a six-year period, with the United States offering favorable credit terms to assist the purchase. In support of his request to purchase such American arms the shah reportedly pointed out the modernization requirements of his armed forces, the prospective power vacuum created by the British decision to withdraw from the Persian Gulf, the potential threat posed by increased Soviet activity in the gulf area, and the need to build up moderate, pro-Western regimes in the area to offset the radical Arab regimes, such as those in Iraq, Syria, and the United Arab Republic. All of these "arguments have been received with some sympathy by the Administration. The Defense Department is said to have found the modernization requests to be reasonable. On political grounds, the State Department believes the sales would be justified to maintain American influence in Iran." [25]

In order to obtain the United States agreement in principle, the shah arrived in Washington in June 1968 for a "private" visit. It was believed at the time that he offered to buy, with Iranian funds, over the next five years jet fighrers and naval vessels and other equipment necessary to give Iran "a balanced and significant defense force of her own." It was also realized, however, that Congress, which must authorize such sales, steadfastly resisted agreements on more than a year-to-year basis. In spite of the war in Vietnam, as an indication of the high priority the United States attached to helping Iran build up its defenses, the United States facilitated the delivery of the yet undelivered Phantoms through the American navy.[26] Furthermore, the shah obtained the United States' promise of more support. The joint statement issued on June 12, 1968, declared that the shah "reaffirmed Iran's determina-

[24] See *New York Times,* Nov. 30, 1967.

[25] Ibid., May 22, 1968.

[26] Ibid., June 12, 1968.

tion to sustain an adequate modern defense force to ensure Iran's national security, and the President expressed the desire of the United States to continue cooperating with Iran to this end." [27]

This American promise was reiterated in identical terms to Premier Hoveyda at the end of his visit to the United States in a joint statement with the president, released December 5, 1968. The premier left no doubt in his statement to the president that Iran's request for American support went beyond the requirements of simply defending Iranian territory; he spoke firmly of Iran's greater responsibilities in the Persian Gulf area. "In the troubled seas of the Middle East, Mr. President, Iran stands on an island of stability and progress. We must progress to sustain our stability, and we must have stability to achieve progress. So if changing circumstances in the world impose upon us today added responsibility in working for the preservation of peace in the world at large, and especially in our own immediate area, we accept our share of these obligations willingly in the firm conviction that we possess the indubitable right, the economic capacity, and the political stability to do so." [28] When these firm and far-reaching words were being uttered, the long-awaited squadrons of F-4 Phantom jets had just gone into service for the Iranian air force. [29]

The theme of Iran's "added responsibility," especially in the Persian Gulf area, meant added requests for arms. The change in the White House was welcome in Tehran at this particular time, and to no small extent because "an old friend" of the shah, Richard M. Nixon, was elected president. Their friendship dated back to the early 1950s, when Nixon had been vice president. No single postwar American administration had been as friendly to the shah as the Eisenhower administration, whose perceptions of the Soviet threat coincided significantly with those of the shah's regime, which enjoyed the full support of the United States government in establishing itself in power in 1953-54.

The shah made an official visit to Washington October 21-23, 1969, knowing full well of the sympathetic attitude of President Nixon toward himself and Iranian requests. The meeting between the two leaders was interspersed with expressions of warm feelings and even some reminiscences of the earlier days of their association. The president told the shah: "I believe that the relations between Iran and the United States have never been better. That is due to your leadership. It is due also to the fact that we have a special relationship not only to your country but to you, a relationship which, in my

[27] U.S. State Dept. *Bulletin* 59, no. 1514 (July 1, 1968):15. See also *New York Times*, June 13, 1968.

[28] U.S. State Dept. *Bulletin* 59, no. 1539 (Dec. 13, 1968): 659-62.

[29] *New York Times*, Sept. 19, 1968. They went into service Sept. 18.

case, goes back many years." The shah told the president: "Today more than ever we need the friendship of America as a friend and the leadership of America in the world." He took the opportunity to impress upon the president the greater role of Iran and its need for American support and assistance. Referring to the president's remarks, the shah stated: "As you mentioned, Mr. President, my country is a crossroad between various civilizations and various interests. It will be our duty to be able to honor this task faithfully, with dignity, and, I hope, also in a constructive way. We will be more able to do it always when we have the moral support, assistance, of our friends, the greatest of them being this great country of yours, and your personal friendship, Mr. President, which I personally, and I am sure my people, value to the greatest possible extent."[30]

There was little doubt in Washington that the shah was seeking more sophisticated arms from the United States, but in Tehran the matter was played down. For example, *Kayhan* went out of its way to editorialize that "the main item on the agenda" of talks between the shah and the president would be "greater economic cooperation" between the two countries.[31] But after the American public learned about the shah's proposal regarding Iranian oil for American arms and capital goods on "Meet the Press," *Kayhan* published the text of the shah's interview without editorial comment. Asked if he was proposing that the United States enlarge its quotas to permit more Iranian oil to come into the United States and if he was interested in "more American combat planes," the shah replied, "Exactly." But he went on to point out that besides military hardware Iran would buy capital goods in return for its greater oil sale in the United States for economic development purposes, and this in turn would help the balance of payment problem in the United States. In explaining Iran's determination to build up its own military strength, the shah argued that it was "unfair" and was becoming "unpractical that every nation when in trouble, will just send a wire to Washington: 'Please come to our help.' " First of all, he did not believe that the United States "could do it anymore," secondly "it could become very embarrassing," and third, "that could lead to a confrontation with another big power. So, we want to avoid that. To avoid it, we have got to be able to take care of the situation ourselves."[32]

Sources close to the shah indicated that he hoped to buy up to $100 million worth of American jet aircraft annually with proceeds from vastly increased sales of Iranian oil in the United States—if the import quota of

[30]U.S. State Dept. *Bulletin* 61, no. 1585 (Nov. 10, 1969):399-400.

[31]*Kayhan* (Weekly English), Oct. 25, 1969.

[32]Ibid., Nov. 1, 1969.

Iranian oil could be enlarged.[33] Iran applied to the United States for an "allocation" to sell 250,000 barrels of crude oil a day in the American market. The application was in line with the "discussions held in October 1969 in Washington, D. C. between His Imperial Majesty and the President of the United States, with a view towards implementing the pronouncements made by the Shahanshah to the press and television on October 26, 1969."[34] In November 1969 the Iranian government submitted a bill to the Majlis that would authorize it to secure $400 million in credits "to strengthen the nation's defense forces." This bill would give the government the authority to decide whether to borrow the sums from one or several sources.[35]

After the shah's visit to the United States in 1969 Britain and the United States quickly backed Iran's military buildup. It was finally made public that a billion-dollar Iranian defense program was underwritten by the two Western powers in preparation for the British withdrawal from the Persian Gulf in 1971. The principal American contributions to the program were squadrons of the late-model Phantom jet fighter-bombers, and Britain was providing hundreds of tanks and naval units. Reportedly, "American and British sales of modern equipment to Iran since 1969 have raised her military strength to a relatively advanced stage from what was an obsolete armed establishment."[36] But this effort was being "significantly accelerated" in 1971. The Iranian air force, for example, was to be expanded to a total of 135 Phantoms by 1975 to serve alongside the F-3 and F-86 squadrons already in its possession. Secret deliveries of weapons in 1969-70 were matched by unpublicized sources of financing huge Iranian purchases. In two years Washington reportedly provided credits for $220 million of Iranian aircraft purchases financed under the foreign military sales program ($100 million), and the Export-Import Bank ($120 million), a "rare participation." Believing that a high degree of military mobility was necessary for insuring Persian Gulf security, the shah was also purchasing "the most modern supersonic aircraft, new hovercraft and helicopters, as well as hundreds of tanks suited to the mountain and desert terrain of Iran and adjoining countries." A base for the hovercraft was built on the island of Kharg off the Iranian coast in the northern section of the Persian Gulf. Iran was also expanding the port of Bander Abbas, with its new naval base and airfield, as a measure of protecting the strategic Strait of Hormuz, which connects the Persian Gulf with the Gulf of Oman. New airfields were also being built at Jask, on the northern coast of Oman, and at

[33]*New York Times,* Oct. 24, 1969.

[34]*Kayhan* (Weekly English), Nov. 29, 1969.

[35]Ibid., Nov. 15, 1969.

[36]*New York Times,* July 25, 1971.

Bushire, nearly opposite Kharg. Between 1965 and 1970 Iranian arms purchases on credit totalled $1.6 billion, and it was estimated that purchases in the United States, Britain, and Italy added another billion dollars more to Iranian debt obligations in 1971 and 1972.

Iran's arms buildup in anticipation of Britain's withdrawal from the gulf was even further accelerated as a result of formalization of Iraqi alignment with the Soviet Union. As noted in the previous chapter, the Soviet-Iraqi treaty of April 9, 1972, greatly annoyed, if not alarmed, Iran. The Iranian ambassador in the United States, Amir Khosrow Afshar, subsequently stated in Washington that the arms Iran purchased from the United States are "not much more" than what the Soviet Union supplied neighboring Iraq. The Iranian foreign minister, 'Abbas A. Khala'tbary, told the *Washington Post*'s Jim Hoagland in Tehran that Iran had reluctantly entered what was turning into a major arms race in the Persian Gulf because of a sharp increase in Soviet arms deliveries to Iraq.[37] As shown in this study, however, Iran's concern with the Arab threat to Persian Gulf security went back to the early 1950s, when for years Egypt and Syria were considered the real menace. The impact of the Soviet-Iraqi treaty of 1972 on Iran's military buildup derived much less from Iran's aggravated concern with Iraq's military buildup as such than from the alarm over the development of a Soviet-Iraqi pincer that to Iran looked more and more like a pincer with the Russians at both ends. For this important reason by 1973 Iran was closer to the United States and further from the Soviet Union than at any other time since its missile bases pledge of 1962.

For eighteen months before the release of the news of massive arms purchases from the United States, Iran placed orders for some $2.5 billion of American military equipment.[38] It was reported on February 25, 1973, that Iran was paying cash for eight squadrons of F-4 Phantom fighter-bombers, roughly 144 planes, for delivery over the next three or four years in addition to some 141 new F-5 fighter-bombers, some 489 helicopters and other equipment. It was also reported that Iran insisted on acquiring the services of several hundred more American personnel in Iran. Washington viewed Iran as especially important because of its potential stability and "generally progressive attitudes, because of increased Soviet activity and arms sent into Syria and Iraq, and because of the withdrawal of the British military presence from the Persian Gulf. At a time of increasing energy problems in the United States, Iran also is the world's second largest exporter of petroleum after Saudi Arabia, and its known, or proven, oil reserves are rated as about equal to Saudi Arabia." Aside from the coincidence of Iranian and American

[37] *Washington Post,* Feb. 25, Apr. 23, 1973.

[38] Ibid., Feb. 25, 1973.

interests, Iran's arms purchases in the United States were considered in Washington as "a boost to the sagging United States balance of payments." Senator J. W. Fulbright, chairman of the Foreign Relations Committee, was quoted as saying that the United States had become an "arms salesman" in order to stop Communism but was now continuing in that role in order to enhance its balance of payments. Not so, retorted a top State Department official, Curtis W. Tarr. The purpose of arms sales was to "deal with the valid security requirements" of individual countries; the "business opportunities" are just a "by-product."[39] Iranians, of course, had their own views of the massive arms purchases. These were regarded in Tehran "as part of Iran's long-term plans for modernizing and reinforcing its defense forces in accordance with its national interests." Iran was determined, it was reported in Tehran, "to build up its defenses in a way that would discourage any potential aggressor while also serving as a factor of peace and stability in the Persian Gulf and the Indian Ocean."[40]

Premier Hoveyda unveiled a dramatic budget leap in the Majlis on March 4, 1973, with significant implications for Iran's persistent efforts to build up a "credible deterrent." The record $10.1 billion budget was based "on an expansionist economic policy providing for more guns and more butter." Insofar as guns were concerned the budget foresaw "a very substantial rise of 47 percent in defense expenditures and increases of nearly 38 percent respectively for social affairs and in the field of industry and agriculture." The prime minister promised the Majlis that Iran would build up its defense forces into "one of the most formidable in the world." He said the disturbed world situation made it imperative that Iran strengthen its navy, air force, and ground forces, equipping them with the most advanced weapons and systems.[41]

Iran's military buildup with the help of the United States paralleled momentous developments in great-power relations. President Nixon's visits to China and the Soviet Union in 1972 were watched with great interest in Iran. The increasing rapprochement between Moscow and Washington, in particular, could have implications for a number of interrelated questions of vital interest to Iran. Could this rapprochement entail superpower agreement about the division of the world into spheres of influence? Bitter Iranian memories of the Anglo-Russian convention of 1907 was a powerful influence. What could be the effect of this growing cooperation between the superpowers on Iran's alliance with the United States? What about its impact on American military sales to Iran? And finally, how would Soviet-American détente affect Iran's

[39] *New York Times,* Feb. 25, 1973.

[40] *Kayhan* (Weekly English), Mar. 3, 1973.

[41] Ibid., Mar. 10, Mar. 17, 1973.

role in the Persian Gulf? Iranian concern with these questions must have influenced, in part, the president's decision to visit Iran in the wake of his summit visit to Moscow in May 1972. More than a month before the president's visit to Moscow, it was made public in Washington that he would visit Iran on his way home; no other stop was decided upon at the time. According to the *New York Times* the "Presidential decision to visit Iran underscores United States interest in fostering continued good relations with the strategically situated nation of 30 million people, which borders the Soviet Union and is a major power in the Middle East."[42]

During his visit to Iran May 30-31, 1972, President Nixon went out of his way to address himself to all those questions, mentioned above, which concerned Iran. In assuaging Iran's fear of superpower agreement at the expense of Iran, the president explained the meaning of his visit to the Soviet Union by stating to the shah that "I think it is important for us to bear in mind that while we have been at what is called the summit, that there has been no intention on the part of the two governments represented at that summit conference, no intention to divide the world into two spheres of influence, no intention to set up a condominium." He also told the shah that in talking with the Soviet Union, "we have not overlooked a very fundamental fact of international life, and that is that it is vital that we build our policy on the alliances and the friendships that we have had in the past, that we have now, and that we hope to have in the future." This and similar remarks were clearly intended to assure Iran that détente would not entail American abandonment of the alliance with Iran vis-à-vis the Soviet Union, although the Soviets were not specifically mentioned.

The president also addressed himself to the Iranian concerns about the implications of Soviet-American summitry for the United States assistance to Iran's military buildup and for the Iranian policy in the Persian Gulf. These questions were taken up in the joint communiqué of the president and the shah issued May 31, 1972. Regarding the military buildup, the shah "stressed once again Iran's determination to strengthen its defensive capability to ensure the nation's security," and the president "confirmed that the United States would, as in the past, continue to cooperate with Iran in strengthening its defenses."[43] The two leaders also agreed that the security and stability of the Persian Gulf was of "vital importance to the littoral states" and took the view that "the littoral states bore the primary responsibility for the security of the Persian Gulf." In his own separate statement to the president, the shah reviewed Iran's old ties with the United States before and after the establishment of diplomatic relations between the two countries; singled out the

[42] *New York Times,* Apr. 7, 1972.

[43] U.S. State Dept. *Bulletin* 66, no. 1722 (June 26, 1972):903-9.

services of such individual Americans to Iran as Samuel Jordan, the "noble American" who ran the American College of Tehran, and Morgan Shuster, another "American friend"; recalled American championship of Iran's "sovereign rights" in 1919; and concluded his remarks by stating that "we shall not tolerate any inequality from any quarter in our relations with other countries. Certainly under no circumstances will we allow any violation of our land or our rights." [44]

While the shah was underscoring Iran's resistance to any superpower understanding or agreement prejudicial to Iranian sovereignty, three bombs prematurely exploded in Tehran, underlining the continuing domestic political problems in the country. Ronald Ziegler, the White House press secretary, attributed the incidents to "terrorist activities" of a very small group and claimed that there was "no indication whatever" that the explosions were aimed at the president. The Tehrani sources believed that the bombing might have been the work of an "urban terrorist movement that is bitterly opposed to what it regards as the Shah's autocratic domestic policies, his friendship with Israel and his pro-Western foreign policy."[45]

Iran's military buildup was paralleled not only by the great power summitry, just mentioned, but also by the emergence of the energy crisis in the West and the increasing indications that the Arab states might use the "oil weapon" in order to bring about changes in American policy toward the Arab-Israeli conflict. When the shah visited the United States July 23-27, 1973, the concern with the oil problem was reportedly the "No. 1 topic to be discussed between him and the President." [46] The exchange of statements between the two leaders, however, contained nothing publicly to indicate discussions of the subject matter. Once again the security of the Persian Gulf, which was inseparable from the oil problem, was stressed by both the shah and the president, who on this occasion characterized the shah as "a world statesman of the first rank."[47] On July 25, 1973, while still in Washington, however, the shah announced that Iran had signed a breakthrough contract with Ashland Oil, an American firm, to share fifty-fifty in producing, refining, and marketing oil from the wells to the gasoline pumps. In return for acquiring a 50 percent interest in Ashland's refineries and related operations in New York, Ashland would receive a long-term crude-oil supply contract.

[44] Ibid., pp. 903-7.

[45] *New York Times,* June 1, 1972.

[46] *Washington Post,* July 24, 1973.

[47] U.S. State Dept. *Bulletin* 49, no. 1782 (Aug. 20, 1973): 275-80.

The initial purchase agreement called for Ashland to acquire 60,000 barrels of Iranian oil a day, which would grow to 100,000 barrels a day in 1975.[48]

The shah dissociated himself from joining in the use of oil as a political weapon against the United States, and after the outbreak of the Arab-Israeli war on October 6, 1973, Iran did not participate in the decision of the oil-producing states to use oil as a weapon against the countries friendly to Israel. As we shall see presently, by the time of his visit to the United States in July 1973 the shah had already reached a new agreement with the oil consortium operating in Iran for the sale of Iranian oil to the West for twenty years. It may be recalled that the shah had suggested the enlarging of the American quota for the sale of Iranian oil during his 1969 visit to the United States. It may also be recalled that he then admitted at the same time that he wished to acquire more military equipment and capital goods as the result. At the time the shah's suggestion was not adopted by Washington, but in 1973 the United States was more than receptive to such suggestions.

The Continuing Struggle for Control of the Oil Industry

Iran's policy toward the United States in 1963-73 involved more than its role within CENTO and the building up of a credible deterrent. It also inevitably involved Iran's oil policy. As seen, American oil companies emerged from the 1954 settlement of the oil nationalization dispute with about as much interest as the British in the establishment of the newly formed international oil consortium. The French and Dutch interests were relatively negligible; it was the entry of large American interests that really upset the traditionally exclusive British interest in Iran's oil industry. It is true that these represented private American interests, but it would be folly to believe that this made them of any less concern to the foreign policy interests of the United States. The entire oil dispute, as shown, was intimately interlocked with important strategic and political interests of the United States in the cold war. Its turbulent course was complicated by these considerations that clearly marked the dispute with interstate relations and international politics. The settlement of the dispute, it may be recalled, was equally marked by the strategic interests of the United States government, as evidenced by the crucial roles that President Eisenhower, Secretary of State Dulles, Herbert Hoover, and Ambassador Henderson played in it. Even before the actual

---

[48]*Kayhan* (Weekly English), Aug. 4, 1973, and *Washington Post*, July 26, 1973. Subsequently it was reported that the contract fell through. See *New York Times*, November 27, 1974.

settlement, the overriding interest of the United States in combating the Soviet Union's extension of power and influence both directly and through the Tudeh party in Iran marked American displeasure with the government of Musaddiq.

Iran's interest in oil was always a state concern. What distinguished this concern in the postwar period was its transformation into a nationwide concern under National Front leadership. As shown in detail in this study, the idea of nationalization was imbued, from inception to legislative decision, with highly political aspirations, despite the rhetoric of economics. Given the fact that the British held exclusive interests in the oil industry, naturally the nationalization movement appeared as a crusade against Britain; but as the proponents of the movement repeatedly pointed out, before and after the decision to nationalize Iran's oil industry, it was fundamentally a struggle for national self-determination and independence. The acceptance of the 1954 settlement by the Iranian government was by no means a rejection of the profound national sentiments that underpinned the entire movement. As shown, the Iranian foreign minister and finance minister "pressed hard" during the negotiations in 1954 for majority representation on the board of directors of the new operating companies of the consortium but did not succeed; the 1954 agreement allotted finally only two seats out of seven on the board to Iranians. As shown, the shah himself, in his reply to President Eisenhower's congratulatory message on the occasion of the settlement as well as in his message to the Majlis, made it clear that "under the circumstances" or "in the light of present world conditions" the settlement was satisfactory to him. And as seen, the violent attacks of Deputy Darakhshish and Senator Divanbaigy on the 1954 agreement were genuine; the fact that they were allowed in the repressive atmosphere of the time said a great deal about the government's own reservations. Senator Divanbaigy echoed the sentiment of the shah's government when he said that Iran had the right to reconsider the fulfillment of its obligations under the 1954 agreement in a more "appropriate time" (*zaman-i musa'id*). Until that time, however, Iran approached the fulfillment of its national aspiration on two separate but related fronts.

The Rise of the National Iranian Oil Company

One of these fronts was opened by Iran's decision to transform the National Iranian Oil Company (NIOC) into an "integrated international oil company" over time, or, as the shah expressed it, make the NIOC "the largest of its kind in the world." As seen, the NIOC had its roots in the nationalization laws of 1951, which entrusted it with the control of all operations of exploration and exploitation connected with the oil industry. This meant that before the 1954 agreement it was given the tremendous responsibility of managing the oil industry, including eight oil fields, two refineries, and two other plants, providing for the fast-growing internal demand for oil, and supporting fifty thousand staff and labor.[49] Under the 1954 agreement, however, the NIOC was to provide for the administration of all activities in the southern area not directly connected with the exploration, production, refining, and export of oil. Even "non-basic" activities such as medical and health services were not entrusted to the NIOC at the time of the signing of the agreement but were to be managed by it when it was ready to take over such duties. This was done in 1956, but the fact still remained that the stigma of "non-basic" responsibilities of the NIOC within the "Agreement area" was a constant reminder of the fact that the 1954 agreement placed the decision-making power in the hands of foreign-owned operating companies. The basic Iranian goal of control of its oil industry was far from realized.

Yet there was a great deal else the NIOC could do. Its transformation into an integrated international oil company was a distant goal, but it had to be accomplished patiently over time. First, any serious measure toward that end would psychologically take the sting out of the inferior role of the NIOC vis-à-vis the consortium. Iran would, on its own, show vitality in oil operations as a participant rather than a mere bystander. Second, the consortium had a limited life under the agreement; the oil industry would be ultimately taken over by the NIOC. Hence, the twenty-five year duration could provide ample opportunity for preparing NIOC for the occasion. With these basic considerations in mind, as early as 1957 it was decided to provide a new legal framework of NIOC's own independent activities outside the consortium's agreement area. The inspiration for this came from the turbulent 1944 and 1947 crises. As seen, as early as 1944 the attack on the 1933 British oil concession was accompanied with the notion of entrusting oil operations outside the concession area to Iranian hands. The law of December 2, 1944, as seen, not only prohibited the grant of foreign oil concessions but also called for discussions on "the way the government of Iran exploits and administers its own oil resources." And the government was called upon in the Majlis to "organize a special Ministry" for the specific purpose of entrusting the exploration of Iranian oil to Iranian hands. It may also be recalled that the law of October 22, 1947, went even so far as to authorize the government to propose measures to realize the utilization of Iranian oil by Iranians outside the 1933 concession area. In the circumstances of 1957 two considerations were taken into account in entrusting the exploration of Iranian oil resources to Iranians. First, the notion of Iranian resources could be expanded to include "areas"

[49]*Mid-East Commerce,* Apr. 1964, p. 50.

beyond the Iranian landmass in light of the post-Truman declaration on the continental shelf. Second, Iran's capital and technical limitations as well as lack of marketing facilities demanded that Iran's participation in its oil operations outside the agreement area begin in partnership with foreign oil concerns. Hence, the Petroleum Law of 1957 empowered NIOC to divide its territory of the country outside the agreement area, including the continental shelf in the Persian Gulf, into petroleum districts for the exploration and exploitation of Iranian oil resources in conjunction with reputable foreign concerns.

In the same year the Petroleum Law was passed the NIOC entered its first partnership with Agip Mineraria, a subsidiary of the Italian state oil organization, ENI. The resulting Iranian-Italian joint-stock company, SIRIP, was entrusted under the relevant agreement with exploration, production, and sale of oil. A year later the NIOC entered into an even more favorable partnership with Pan American Petroleum Company, forming IPAC for similar operations. The American company offered Iran a $25 million cash bonus; undertook to spend $82 million, as contrasted with Agip's $22 million, on exploration within twelve years; and more important, for the first time a leading American oil company recognized NIOC as being technically competent on an equal footing with itself and offered to sell Iranian oil abroad under the Iranian flag whenever possible.[50] A similar partnership was struck in the early phase of NIOC's independent operations with a Canadian company but without similar success.

Iran's determination to increase such efforts led to a spectacular undertaking that marked a new phase in NIOC's ventures outside the consortium's agreement area. On September 15, 1963, Iran undertook a marine seismic survey for the purpose of inducing a greater number of foreign oil companies to enter into partnership with the NIOC by means of providing for them basic data on Iran's District No. 1, which was offered for bidding. Interested oil companies provided proportionate capital, and as a result an area larger than Switzerland was successfully surveyed. The availability of reliable information to foreign oil companies' had a marked effect on the number of bids Iran received after the survey as contrasted with the year 1958 when the same district was opened to bids for the first time. Thirty-one oil companies submitted tenders, as contrasted with only seven in 1958.[51] These thirty-one companies represented five groups and one individual company, and as a result early in 1965 six new joint structures were formed with NIOC's participation, representing American, British, Dutch, Italian, French, Spanish, Indian, and German interests. NIOC's partnership with these interests created such

[50]*Middle East Economic Digest* 2, no. 5 (May 9, 1958):50-51.

[51]*Mid-East Commerce*, Sept. 15, 1965, pp. 53-56.

new companies as Iranian Marine International Oil Company, the Lavan Petroleum Offshore Petroleum Company, the Dashtestan Offshore Petroleum Company, and others. One of the most important features of the new partnership agreements, according to the director of NIOC, was the acceptance of the principle of seventy-five-twenty-five profit sharing, as contrasted with the fifty-fifty principle in the 1957-58 partnership, representing a substantial revenue gain for Iran. Even more beneficial partnership agreements were concluded subsequently. For example, three agreements were concluded in 1971. NIOC and a group of four Japanese companies created INESPCO for operations in Luristan in addition to the creation of Bushire Oil Company (NIOC and American Hess), and Hormuz Oil Company (NIOC and Mobil Oil), operating respectively in 3,715 and 3,200 square kilometers in the Persian Gulf.

Iran's efforts to expand its role in the exploration and exploitation of its oil resources outside the consortium's agreement area made another innovative contribution in 1963-73. NIOC signed an agreement with the French State Group ERAP in 1966, under which the Iranian company would act as employer and the ERAP group as contractor with responsibility for exploration, drilling, production, and transportation as well as making the necessary investments for these operations. The notion of contract in this type of agreement was important because NIOC as employer enjoyed the general decision-making power and was the only owner of petroleum thus produced. A year later two other contract-type agreements were signed with a group of European firms and an American oil company for the areas relinquished by the consortium. Finally, in 1971 NIOC signed three new agreements with American and Japanese companies, all representing greater financial gains for Iran. [52]

NIOC's efforts to approximate the ultimate goal of becoming an integrated international oil company far exceeded the new roles that it undertook under the partnership and contract arrangements outlined above. These efforts encompassed a variety of functions both within and outside Iran, some of which interlocked with the consortium's activities and some of which did not. Examination of all NIOC functions is beyond the scope of this study, but several other major activities will be examined here briefly in order to indicate the range and nature of its preparation for playing an effective role when the time comes to control Iran's oil industry.

Iran's rapid economic growth during the period under study here was accompanied with the beginning of a steady rise in the consumption of petroleum products. In 1965, for example, internal demand amounted to 33,809,000 barrels (not including bunker fuel) with consumption heavily

[52]*Iran Oil Journal*, Feb. 1972, pp. 2-4.

concentrated in the northern part of the country, which took 67 percent of the national total. Tehran district alone consumed 48 percent.[53] To take an earlier year for comparison, total internal consumption of liquid oil products amounted to 4.4 million cubic meters in 1962, but by 1967 it rose to 7.6 million, and in 1972 it amounted to 13 million cubic meters; in ten years the consumption of oil domestically increased nearly threefold.[54] The distance between the southern oil fields and refinery and the main centers of consumption posed formidable problems for NIOC at the beginning. NIOC's Trans-Iranian Pipeline took products from Abadan to Tehran for the central and northern parts of the country, with branches to Meshed to serve the northeast and to Resht for the northwest.[55] Toward meeting Iran's rapidly expanding internal consumption, NIOC completed a new refinery at Tehran in 1965, but the pressure of demand required the expansion of the Kermanshah refinery; finally a new refinery was constructed in Tehran in 1973 while other refineries were being constructed in Shiraz and on Lavan Island, and another was planned for Tabriz. NIOC's own technical know-how and Iranian capital played major parts in performing this important domestic function.

More important indications of NIOC's expanding role were to be found in its international activities. One of these involved Iranian oil sales abroad. In 1965, for example, NIOC arranged to sell Argentina 22 million barrels of oil in return for wheat. It also made an agreement with Rumania to furnish crude oil worth $100 million over ten years. Rumania was to pay in industrial goods, including drilling and refining equipment, port installations and machinery, further enhancing NIOC's expanding role. These and similar semibarter agreements, however, did not quite please the NIOC, which strove to get into international marketing on its own account even if this meant accepting prices offering lower profit than Iran obtained from oil sold by the consortium. [56] This kind of approach showed all the more that Iran attached great value to the goal of transforming NIOC into an integrated international oil company. The best example of this approach was, as seen, the sale of billions of cubic meters of gas annually to the Soviet Union through the Trans-Iranian Gas Pipeline, which was opened on October 28, 1970.

During the 1963-73 decade NIOC also entered a new sphere of international activity, namely, "downstream" operations abroad. The Indian government was known in the early 1960s to plan to implement its refinery building program. NIOC and its American partner, Pan American Petroleum

[53]*Mid-East Commerce,* June 1966, p. 52.

[54]*Iran Oil Journal,* Apr. 1973, p. 3.

[55]*Mid-East Commerce,* Mar. 1966, pp. 24-26.

[56]Ibid.

Company, made a joint proposal to India that led to the completion of Iran's first foreign project with a capacity of 2.5 million tons per year. Up to the end of 1972 a total of 5.3 million tons of crude oil from the Darius field of NIOC-Pan American operations in the Persian Gulf was processed in the refinery at Madras. The second refinery of this type started operations in 1971 in South Africa with a capacity of 2.5 million tons per year as the result of a joint venture between NIOC, South African Coal, Oil and Gas Corporation, and Compagnie Française des Pétroles. In 1972 NIOC was boldly seeking to enter into the field of refining and distribution activities in Western Europe.[57]

From Negotiation to Nationalization

The goal of transforming NIOC into an integrated international oil company was in part related to the eventual preparation of NIOC for taking over the consortium's oil operations. Iran's relations with the consortium were marked by sporadic efforts to improve Iran's enjoyment of its single most important national asset, particularly during 1963-73, the first decade of the White Revolution. Ever since the establishment of Iran's development plans in the postwar period, revenues from oil were considered essential for financing the country's economic development. Oil revenue was expected to provide 37 percent of the total funds for implementation of the First Seven-Year Plan (1948-55), but the nationalization crisis caused a near stoppage in oil income. In the Second Seven-Year Plan (1955-62) over 50 percent of the total oil revenues went to the Plan organization in the first two years and over 70 percent in the remaining years. By 1966 about 75 percent of the total oil revenues went to the Plan organization, which was to receive 80 percent of the oil revenues during the five-year duration of the Fourth Development Plan (1968-73). The objective of increasing Iran's share of income from oil in the 1960s was fully compatible with the long-term goal of ultimately controlling the oil operations within the consortium area. The fact that Iran was unprepared to run the oil industry itself in the early 1960s meant that it would make every effort to improve its income from the operations of the consortium whenever the opportunity presented itself.

The first major opportunity arose in the early 1960s. Oil companies, for their own reasons, reduced posted prices for Middle East crude in August 1960. The Organization of Petroleum Exporting Countries (OPEC) was set up by Iran as well as Venezuela, Iraq, Kuwait and Saudi Arabia (with Qatar joining a few months later) in protest against the reduction. The fifty-fifty

[57]*Iran Oil Journal,* Mar. 1972, pp. 11-12.

profit-sharing arrangements of the 1950s between oil companies and producing countries, including Iran were in the last analysis to increase the producing nations' income from oil, but the cuts in the posted prices on which the calculation of profits was based seemed to these nations to threaten the per-barrel revenues. The overriding objective of the OPEC nations at the time was to safeguard, and if possible improve, their per-barrel income. Specific claims, however, were not formulated until the fourth conference of OPEC, held in Geneva in April and June 1962, demanding the end of marketing allowances, the "expensing of royalties," and the restoration of posted prices in the Middle East to the levels prevailing before August 1960.[58] OPEC also recommended "that each Member Country affected should approach the Company or Companies concerned with a view to working out a formula whereunder royalty payments shall be fixed at a uniform rate which Members consider equitable and shall not be treated as a credit against income tax liability."[59] Out of the tough negotiations on the "expensing of royalties," namely, treating royalty payments not as deductible from tax but as an allowable item of expense, a compromise emerged: the companies agreed to pay royalties as an addition to the taxes on income, counting the royalty as an expense in calculating the profits that were to be shared with the host government.

Iran's negotiations with the consortium in 1964-65 resulted in a "supplementary agreement" but did not end the bargaining pattern that was emerging in the relations of the country and the consortium. Iran repeatedly expressed to the consortium the shah's expectations for a higher increase in Iranian crude oil exports. The NIOC director told the consortium representatives in 1966, for example, that in spite of the addition of newly proven reserves such as the Karun-Marun field, it was "disheartening" to discover that the consortium envisaged a mere 9 to 10 percent increase in offtake from Iran. He told the consortium that this percentage compared

very unfavorably with the plans being carried out in another producing country of the Gulf area with oil of very similar characteristics, marketability, and production costs, where the export of crudes have [*sic*] been steadily increasing at a rate substantially higher than that from Iran. The restriction that is being imposed upon the normal growth of production in Iran in order to enable the fulfillment of other plans elsewhere is most deplorable and I feel it my duty to remind you, Gentlemen, that overlooking Iran's vital interest in this regard is causing grave concern in my country.[60]

[58]*Mid-East Commerce,* Feb. 1966, p. 17.

[59]Muhamad A. Mughraby, *Permanent Sovereignty over Oil Resources* (Beirut: Middle East Research and Publishing Center, 1966), p. 140.

[60]For the text see *Mid-East Commerce,* Nov. 1966, p. 36.

Iran's pressure on the consortium for increased oil production intensified in 1968-69. The Fourth Development Plan (1968-73) called for an unprecedented investment of $11 billion, as compared with any other previous plan, including the Third Plan, which had required only $3 billion. The new plan alloted an unprecedented 80 percent of the oil revenues during the next five years of its duration to the Plan organization, emphasizing development of basic industries—iron and steel, aluminum, and petrochemicals. In light of this requirement, Iran told the consortium representatives in Tehran that it needed $5.9 million from oil revenues for the development plan. On February 26, 1968, the director of NIOC, Iqbal, stated that "anything less than 100 percent increase in production would be disappointing."[61] Behind this joking remark lay Iran's demand for a sharp increase in production, for which it was then entering its fifth round of negotiations with the consortium in six months. Iran simply demanded a 20 percent increase in production every year during the next five years, the life of the new development plan. If accepted, such an increase would have meant that by 1972 the consortium would be providing roughly two and a half times the amount of oil produced in the previous year and that consequently Iran's revenues would rise to $1.58 billion and to $5.676 billion in five years.

The consortium's resistance to Iranian demands was influenced by several considerations. The consortium apparently believed it could not find markets for such a vast increase in Iranian oil output. It did not welcome the suggestion that any excess oil would be marketed by NIOC because it would cause greater competition for markets. More important perhaps, the consortium's opposition to Iran's demand for a sharp increase in production was based on the belief that it would "trigger demands for similar increases in Arab oil countries, where the same companies operate, and that the petroleum market could be glutted because world consumption is increasing at only 8 percent a year." The consortium's failure to meet Iran's demand at the time brought down upon the companies the wrath of Premier Hoveyda, who charged them with "intrigues," stated that the time was past "when they could put their friends in power" (a reference to Amini, who was the principal negotiator of the 1954 agreement), and contended that development capital was vitally needed at this stage of Iran's economic growth and that consequently "we cannot permit our wealth to remain below ground." The failure of the consortium to meet Iran's demands, he said, jeopardizes "the whole five-year development plan." [62]

The demands for increased production and revenues from oil continued in 1969 with an eye to the second year of the Fourth Development Plan. With

[61] *New York Times,* Feb. 27, 1968.

[62] Ibid., Mar. 9, 1968.

the arrival of a four-man consortium team in Tehran for negotiations on May 9, 1969, the Iranian authorities made public their standing demand for an increase in oil revenue to one billion dollars from March 21, 1969, to March 21, 1970. The consortium had been given a two-month breathing spell in order to act on Iran's demands. Iran made it emphatically clear that it would not accept "a penny less than the $1 billion" revenue demanded during the previous negotiations, and the shah added his own voice this time by stating that he would accept nothing less than $1 billion in oil revenue from the consortium in that year.[63] He declared that Iran was no longer prepared to accept simply a consortium offer to do its best to reach that amount, adding: "I can not build the future of my country on promises. What I say is absolutely clear. I say this is our oil—pump it. If not, we pump it ourselves."[64] The demand for $1 billion revenue in one year was accompanied by pressure for an increase of about 16 percent in oil production. The consortium replied to Iran's demands with a "compromise formula" that, it was believed, met Iran's demands in a "circuitous fashion," providing for an increase far below the 16 percent demanded by Iran, but granting low-interest loans or interest-free credits to tide over Iran's need of a billion dollars. Iran, however, was not interested in loans, favoring instead the return of not-fully-exploited fields, such as the Marun reserves, which NIOC could develop in partnership with either independents or Demitex, the new West German state group. The Marun field was considered as the "longest continuous oil deposit in the world," and its possible return to the NIOC would not create a precedent. The consortium had already relinquished one-fourth of the agreement area in 1966, consisting of three parcels near Naft-i Shah, Bushire, and Bandar Abbas totalling some 25,000 square miles.[65]

The communiqué issued at the end of the negotiations did not specify what kind of settlement was finally reached between Iran and the consortium. The shah himself, however, cleared up some of the questions in an interview. He stated that Iran would receive $1.01 billion from the consortium during one year, and this total was made up of an increase in production of 10 percent, an increase of income from production of 12 percent, and an advance of funds sufficient to fill the remaining gap. The advance would be repaid by Iran "when we have the money available," and it would be repeated "the next year and the next year as long as we really need it to implement our development plans." Despite Iran's success in getting the consortium to meet its demands, the shah expressed only "qualified satisfaction" with the

[63]*Kayhan* (Daily English), Mar. 10, 1969.

[64]Ibid., May 11, 1969.

[65]Ibid., May 12, 1969.

agreement. He stated that the oil companies still had given no specific commitments on output and earnings beyond the coming year, and what Iran wanted was long-range assurances that would enable the country to proceed in a planned way with its economic development.[66]

The shah's reservations about the 1969 settlement were increased in 1970. Quite apart from the fact that the 1969 compromise did not meet Iran's demands satisfactorily, a number of developments in the world's oil industry spurred Iran's pressures for a better deal in 1970. These developments consisted of (1) an increase of 10 percent in oil consumption during the first six months of the year, (2) supply cuts to Western Europe as the result of the adverse Syrian action regarding the Tapline carrying Saudi Arabian oil to the Mediterranean, and (3) reduced attraction of the Libyan oil supplies as the result of increase in production cost and decrease in oil production.[67] In one of the "sternest warnings" yet to be given the oil companies, the shah emphasized that oil was Iran's natural wealth, and the country had the right to take whatever steps it found necessary to insure that its resources were properly utilized for the nation's progress. He stated to the two houses of Parliament that Iran would like to see oil production increased through "agreement and understanding" with the oil consortium. "But if this view is not achieved," he continued, "we will take measures through the enactment of laws to secure our interests."[68] The shah's October 1970 message to the Parliament was echoed in the Senate when, for example, Senator Muhammad Sa'idi told the senators that Iran could no longer accept the present situation under which "our oil resources remain untapped." He warned the consortium that Iran would take independent action on the basis of the United Nations resolutions considering the consortium's failure to commit its full resources to the exploitation of Iranian oil. "The unjustified low price of Iranian oil at a time when the price of Libyan oil has been increased is tantamount to a double standard," he stated.[69] In anticipation of the opening of negotiations between NIOC and the consortium in London, the shah stated to Aryamihr University students in early November 1970 that it was Iran's "permanent policy to fight for the full right of Iran in the exploitation of her natural resources" and that "we shall hold firm talks of destiny; we shall once again be fighting for the legitimate rights of Iran which are recognized by international law and principles."[70]

[66]*New York Times,* May 16, 1969.

[67]*Ittila'at Hava'i,* Sept. 27, 1970.

[68]*Kayhan* (Weekly English), Oct. 10, 1970.

[69]Ibid., Oct. 24, 1970.

[70]Ibid., Nov. 7, 1970.

Iran's firm stand and the consortium's recognition of the changed international oil scene in 1970 finally resulted in an agreement between the parties. They issued a communiqué on November 16, 1970, containing the essentials of their agreement after eight days of hard and secret bargaining.[71] In the previous year the consortium had failed to achieve the revenue target of the Fourth Plan but made up the difference through an interest-free loan to Iran. Iran's insistence on the inadequacy of this type of arrangement forced the search for other ways of meeting the Iranian needs. The solution was twofold. First, the tax structure was to be revised from 50 to 55 percent as of November 14, 1970. Second, the price of heavy crude oil was raised from 163 to 172 cents per barrel as of the same date. The twin measures were regarded as "one of the biggest victories for Iranian oil policy in the past sixteen years," and the Iranian success was attributed in part to the fact that finally the oil companies had "seen the light." But the settlement was still regarded as meeting the "minimum needed revenue." [72]

The year 1971 witnessed an even greater victory for Iran in its incessant struggle with the international oil consortium. Its bilateral negotiations and settlement in 1970 in part involved changes in the tax structure, an innovation that was bound to set the example for other oil-producing nations of the Persian Gulf area. An OPEC resolution adopted in Caracas after the Iranian settlement called for an increase from 50 to 55 percent, as in the Iranian case, in taxes paid by oil companies to producers. More important, it called for an increase in the prices of Persian Gulf crude oil. OPEC's secretary-general asked Iran (Finance Minister Jamshid Amuzigar), Saudi Arabia (Petroleum Minister Zaki Yamani) and Iraq (Petroleum Minister Sa'dun Hammadi) to conduct the talks on behalf of the organization. With an eye to the ensuing negotiations held between the OPEC representatives and those of Western international oil companies in Tehran, the shah took advantage of a press conference, his first in 12 years. He devoted his opening remarks to the wide-ranging issues between the Persian Gulf oil producers and Western oil companies, going back to the late 1950s and the beginning of the problem of posted prices. Their unilateral decisions in regard to the price of oil and oil products brought about a situation "which cannot continue." He combined sweet reasonableness and logic with a declaration to the effect that Iran would not try to dissuade other oil-producing nations of the gulf area to stop the flow of oil to the West simply because Iran was in "daily need of her oil revenues." It would be a "mistake to make such an assumption." It must be remembered, the shah stated, "that some of the oil-producing countries have enough

[71] For the text see *Ittila'at Hava'i,* Nov. 16, 1970.

[72] *Kayhan* (Weekly English), Nov. 21, 1970.

deposits saved in banks to enable them—maybe for four years—to live and introduce no change in their spending without the need for even one dollar of their oil revenues."[73]

The shah's carrot-and-stick approach and his finance minister's tough negotiating tactics provided the leadership that led to the historic settlement between OPEC Persian Gulf members and twenty-two major Western oil concerns, represented by Lord Strathalmond of British Petroleum. It was reported in Tehran on February 14, 1971, that barely twenty-four hours before the deadline set by OPEC, the oil companies agreed to meet the terms put forward by Iran and five other Persian Gulf oil-producing nations the week before. Iranian, Iraqi, and Saudi Arabian representatives signed the agreement on behalf of their own countries and of Kuwait, Qatar, and Abu Dhabi. According to the agreement the price of the Persian Gulf crude oil would increase an average of forty-six cents per barrel, representing thirty-three cents "straight increase," two cents for transport costs, seven cents as the result of the abolition of discounts previously granted to the oil companies, and four cents from increases based on "specific gravity." No less important than the average increase in the crude oil price as such was the provision for a 2.5 percent increase per year for the purpose of offsetting inflation in the Western world. Moreover, if transport costs were reduced in future, for example as a result of the reopening of the Suez Canal, the difference would be payable to Iran and the other Persian Gulf nations involved. It was estimated at the time that the new agreement would yield an additional $415 million revenue per annum for Iran immediately.[74] President Nixon's decision of August 15, 1971, however, gave this five-year settlement its first major jolt—the United States devaluation of the dollar. While admitting that the de facto devaluation of the dollar meant loss of revenues to the oil-producing countries, the consortium took the attitude toward Iran that the Tehran agreement's provision for 2.5 percent increase in posted prices to offset inflationary trends in Western countries would automatically compensate for the loss. Iran argued, however, that the 2.5 percent increase dealt with "inflationary trends only and not in changes in the parity of currencies against the dollar." Clearly, the Tehran agreement had not foreseen any turmoil in the international monetary system.[75]

Overriding these and similar disagreements between Iran and the international oil consortium was Iran's ever-present dissatisfaction with the 1954 agreement and its aspiration for fulfilling the age-old goal of controlling its own oil industry. The first major public indication of this was echoed in the

[73]Ibid., June 30, 1971.

[74]Ibid., Feb. 20, 1971.

[75]Ibid., Nov. 13, 1971.

shah's interview during the 1971 negotiations. In response to a correspondent's question regarding his statement of December 29, 1970, about the expulsion of the oil companies, the shah replied that "we will respect the agreements we have signed, unless we are forced to move otherwise. Everybody knows that our patience lasts a long time. But I was remarking that in my opinion the best thing is for us oil-exporting countries to produce and refine our own oil for export when present agreements are over. Then the present oil companies, either those which exist today or others which I do not know, since it is a matter for the other party to decide, will be the sole buyers, to import our products to any place and distribute them anywhere they wish."[76]

At long last, on the occasion of the tenth anniversary of the White Revolution, in 1973, the boom was lowered.[77] The shah declared that Iran would terminate the 1954 agreement. He told a record five thousand representatives of a wide variety of groups in Iranian society: "When we signed the 1954 agreement perhaps it was the best deal we could make at the time. One of the terms of the agreement was that the operating companies would protect Iran's interests in the best possible way. We have evidence that this has not been the case." After enumerating some of Iran's complaints, particularly the problem of production, he outlined two alternative courses of action. One was to let the consortium continue until 1979, when the agreement would, according to its terms, expire unless extended for three additional five-year periods by the consent of the parties. This option would be offered "provided that the total earnings from each barrel of oil are not less than those earned by other regional countries, provided our exporting capacity is increased to 8 million barrels of oil per day." If the consortium accepted this alternative it would mean that in 1979 it "will have to stand in a long queue to buy Iran's oil, without any privileges over the other customers." The second alternative was for the consortium to sign a new agreement with Iran "which would return to Iran all the responsibilities and other things which are not at present in Iran's hands." In such a case the present operating companies could then become "our long-term customers and we would sell them oil over a long term, in consideration for which we would give them good prices and the kind of discounts which are always given to a good customer."[78]

Western displeasure with the shah's decision not to renew the 1954 agreement was swiftly made public. The *New York Times* reported that the "United States and Britain expressed diplomatic concern to the Shah of Iran over his abrupt announcement that Iran will take over full control of Western

[76] Ibid., Jan. 30, 1971.

[77] *New York Times,* Jan. 24, 1973.

[78] For the text see *Kayhan* (Weekly English), Feb. 3, 1973.

oil company operations there by 1979. This is a new blow to Western oil companies which have already suffered nationalization on concessions in Libya and Iraq and have been forced to give Persian Gulf producers the right to acquire majority control of existing private operations by 1983." Iran's nationalization of 1951 had set the example for other countries, and its action in 1973 was particularly viewed with alarm for its effect on other oil-producing nations of the Persian Gulf that had reached agreements on "participation" instead of Iraqi-type nationalization with Western oil companies. The "Shah's move to obtain 100 percent control over the output of the Western consortium is seen as a threat to the recently negotiated participation accords."[79]

The shah personally guided subsequent negotiations with the consortium, and five weeks after his declaration about the nonrenewal of the 1954 agreement, it was announced in London, on February 26, 1973, that a general understanding was reached between the shah and the oil companies in St. Moritz, Switzerland.[80] Subsequently it was revealed by Premier Hoveyda in the Majlis that "the historic St. Moritz document annulled the 1954 agreement, and the relationship between Iran and the companies became that of seller and buyer. The basis of the new agreement was laid down, and fresh efforts to make an agreement with the companies began."[81] St. Moritz's "general understanding" was worked into a preliminary agreement that was signed on May 24, 1973, and was regarded in Tehran as an accord that would give Iran "full sovereignty" (*hakimiat-i mutlaq*) over the oil industry in the southwest, the agreement area of the consortium. Finally, a bill embodying the new agreement was signed into law by the shah on July 31, 1973.[82]

Premier Hoveyda's presentation of the new agreement between Iran and the consortium to the Majlis was accompanied by the dignified jubilation of many spectators. Although disclaiming any central role in the conclusion of the new agreement, the premier drew upon his own experience and observation to illuminate the Iranian perspective on the subject matter. Having traced the earlier stages of Iranian oil difficulties, he regarded Iran's nationalization of 1951 as the "first breach" in the company's "absolute authority, at least in this part of the world," and characterized the new agreement as "the turning point in the seventy-year-old history of concessions in our oil industry."

[79]*New York Times,* Jan. 30, 1973.

[80]Ibid., Feb. 27, 1973.

[81]*Kayhan* (Weekly English), July 28, 1973.

[82]For the text of the agreement and related documents, see Iran, National Iranian Oil Company, *Sale and Purchase Agreement,* July 31, 1973, pp. 1-59. For a relevant account, see *Kayhan* (Weekly English), June 22, 1973.

Despite all the adjustments that were made after the 1954 agreement, the "unpalatable reality" persisted that "the right of management and policy-making" remained outside Iran. With the new agreement, he added, that "state of affairs no longer exists and, in fact, we may say that the Nationalization Act has been implemented in its fullest sense after a lapse of twenty-three years, thus realizing our long-cherished national objective."[83] His remark that from "now on, the fate of our oil will be in our own hands" historically echoed the statements made within and outside the Majlis during the 1944 and 1947 crises.

In pointing out the differences between Iran's new agreement with those of "participation" agreements of other Persian Gulf states and with the old 1954 agreement, Premier Hoveyda was both lucid and persuasive. Saudi Arabia, Kuwait, Qatar, and Abu Dhabi concluded agreements with oil companies that entitled those countries, from January 1, 1973, to 25 percent participation in their oil operations, and their participation was to rise to 51 percent by 1982. "However, in the case of Iran, which had already nationalized its oil, participation was meaningless. The Shahanshah's view was always that in the pursuit of our national goals, whatever we were unable to obtain in 1951, should be obtained in the more favorable conditions of today." The more important part of the premier's address outlined the advantages of the new agreement in comparison with the 1954 agreement. Briefly stated, the new agreement enabled NIOC to "manage and control all oil operations." It would immediately take over the direct management of the Abadan refinery, the Mahshahr refinery, and all related establishments. For a part of the operations that required a sufficient number of experts, a "contractor company" would be formed according to Iranian laws, with Iranian nationality for a period of five years.[84] Under the 1954 agreement, of course, all exploration and exploitation matters had been the responsibility of the two consortium-owned companies with their headquarters in London. In his statement to the Iranian Senate during the budget debate in March, 1973, Premier Hoveyda told the senators that a new Iranian company would be established to assume all the present functions of the consortium, and as such the new company would employ the experts needed regardless of their nationality. The consortium members would become purchasers of Iranian crude oil for a period of twenty years at prices that will secure net revenues for Iran that are no less than those enjoyed by other oil-exporting nations in the region.[85] The pricing policy that Iran would adopt toward the consortium

---

[83] For the text see *Kayhan* (Weekly English), July 28, 1973.

[84] Ibid.

[85] Ibid., Mar. 24, 1973.

members would be in accordance with the decisions of OPEC and would eventually be based on the "international basket" concept of the shah, who proposed in the past that a direct link should be established between a "basket" of commodities that oil-exporting nations buy from industrial countries, on the one hand, and the price of their exported crude oil, on the other, so that the constant "export of Western European inflation into oil-producing countries" could be prevented. In summing up the features of the new agreement, *Kayhan's* "oil correspondent" stated that "the term 'real or complete nationalization' can describe the new agreement because it means no foreign company or groups of companies will have any more say in deciding any aspect of Iran's oil policy."[86]

Continuity and Change in Nonmilitary Relations

Iran's policy toward the United States in 1963-73 involved a variety of nonmilitary bilateral and direct ties, as in the 1950s. In fact, most of these ties represented the continuation of those already in existence in the 1950s or even earlier, and others were newly established.

Termination of American Economic Aid

The single most important change in the nonmilitary bilateral and direct relations between Iran and the United States in the 1963-73 period was the termination of the United States long-standing economic aid. On November 29, 1967, Secretary of State Dean Rusk announced that on the following day "direct economic aid" to Iran would end. It may be recalled that American economic assistance began under the Point Four Program, and it may be added here that the relevant agreement that had been effected by the exchange of notes between the two countries on January 19 and 20, 1952, was superseded by the General Agreement for Economic Co-operation signed on December 21, 1961.[87] Between 1953 and 1961 the total United States economic and technical aid to Iran rose, it may be recalled, to $611 million, consisting of grants as well as loans. This amount was increased by another $301.6 million by 1968. Hence, by the time of the termination of the aid program in 1967 the shah's regime had received nearly one billion dollars of American economic assistance since 1953.

---

[86]Ibid.

[87]For the text of this agreement see U.N., Secretariat, *Treaty Series* 433, no. 6249 (1962):276-85.

President Johnson's message to a varied group of businessmen attending the occasion of the termination of the aid program in Iran stated that "we are celebrating an achievement—not an ending. This is a milestone in Iran's continuing progress and in our increasingly close relations."[88] Secretary Rusk on the same occasion surveyed Iran's rapid economic growth and the American contribution to it. He noted, for example, that in ten years Iran's industrial production had increased 88 percent, its exports by more than a third; its Gross National Product increased 11.8 percent in 1965 and 9.5 percent in 1966. The *New York Times* reported that Iran had "reached the 'take-off' point where it can support its own development—a position already reached by Taiwan and one which is being rapidly approached by Korea and Turkey."[89] Not many years ago, the *Times* commented, the American military and economic aid program in Iran was generally regarded both in the United States and Iran as one of the "more inefficient and corrupted of American overseas aid efforts." Now, however, aid officials in Washington were pointing to Iran as "one of their more notable success stories."

This brings us to the more fundamental question: how could this change in Iran's economic position by 1968 be explained? One explanation was the rapid rise in Iran's oil revenues, which amounted to $600 million in 1966 and was expected to increase to $800 million in 1967. During the fifteen years of American economic aid since 1952, Iran itself invested, according to Secretary Rusk's remarks, mentioned above, more than $3 billion in public programs. Another explanation was the shah's land reform program. According to Secretary Rusk land reform had given fourteen million Iranians a direct stake in agricultural progress. A third explanation was that Iran's "prolonged political stability" lay at the base of its rapid economic development.[90] A fourth explanation emphasized the rise of the middle class in Iranian society and its enterprising endeavors. Still a fifth explanation attributed favorable changes in Iran's economic life to what we may call the "cumulative effect of reforms"; although a "developing nation" Iran's modernization experience was considerable as contrasted with most other Third-World countries.

Probably all these factors could help explain Iran's rapid economic growth and hence the termination of direct American aid, but one other possible explanation may be proposed here. Generally the relationship between foreign policy and domestic conditions is easily underestimated. Even when the importance of this relationship is emphasized theoretically, it somehow escapes attention in the course of empirical examination. With Iran this relationship has been particularly important, as I have tried to show elsewhere

[88] U.S. State Dept. *Bulletin* 57, no. 1486 (Dec. 18, 1967):825-27.

[89] *New York Times,* Nov. 24, 1967.

[90] Ibid.. Dec. 9. 1968, for this and other explanations mentioned.

and throughout this study. Insofar as the specific explanation of Iran's rapid economic growth by 1968 is concerned, we only need to draw upon preceding discussions. It may be recalled that both the serious launching of the land reform program by the shah in 1963 and a more effective consolidation of royal power at the same time followed Iran's missile bases pledge to the Soviet Union in late 1962. The pledge signaled the beginning of normalization of relations with the Soviet Union, which in turn was accompanied by a dramatic change in Soviet attitudes toward the shah's regime. The pledge as such had no particular military significance, but its importance derived from the fact that it signaled the shah's determination to end Tehran's bitter and protracted cold war with Moscow, which had only been accentuated by the 1958-59 crisis over the breakdown of Irano-Soviet negotiations for a non-aggression pact; it had in fact begun in wartime, as we have seen. This sudden end of tensions between the two countries was accompanied by a remarkable about-face by Moscow. Khruschev's attacks on the shah, Soviet vituperation against the shah's regime, and Moscow's support of the shah's domestic opponents suddenly ended. In a matter of only a few months after the pledge, the "rotten monarchical regime" of the shah was considered by Moscow to be a "pioneer in land distribution," the shah's opponents were abandoned, and for the first time in Iran's modern history the Soviet Union reversed its role and became an avowed supporter of the shah's regime.

The reduction of tensions with the Soviet Union in 1962-67 made it possible for the shah's regime, with some early prodding by the United States during the Kennedy administration, to accord in 1963 an unprecedented priority to the goal of social and economic development. The economic crisis of the late 1950s was to no small extent one of the side effects of Iran's emphasis on military security. The crisis represented significantly the social and economic costs paid for according military security top priority throughout most of the 1950s. The early 1960s witnessed a significant and short-lived shift in Iran's priorities.[91] Social and economic development was accorded the highest priority, at least until the British decision to withdraw forces from the Persian Gulf. The spectacular economic growth of the mid-1960s was to a large extent the result of reduced tensions with the Soviet Union. This reduction helped Iran to concentrate attention at home on social and economic reforms, on increasing political stability by the consolidation of royal power, and on forging more beneficial ties with both the United States and the Soviet Union. Just as preoccupation with external security in the 1950s contributed to economic chaos eventually, a more balanced concern with external security in the early 1960s assisted economic growth by 1968.

[91] See Ramazani, "Iran's 'White Revolution.'"

Continuation of Old Ties

Iran's trade with the United States continued to hold its significant position in 1963-73 despite the termination of the old 1943 trade agreement in 1960. It may be recalled that the 1943 agreement had been concluded to free Iranian trade from the strict government control of Riza Shah's era and thereby increase American exports to Iran. Excessive imports were one of the reasons underlying Iran's economic crisis of the late 1950s, and the 1960 abrogation of the 1943 agreement was designed to assist Iran with its economic stabilization program because it would, in effect, increase the Iranian tariff on American products. Nevertheless, as the crisis eased, Irano-American trade improved. For example, American exports to Iran rose 7 percent in 1967, from $230.4 million in 1966 to $246.1 million. By 1968 for the fourth consecutive year total Iranian imports reached $1,126 million in 1967. In other words the United States maintained its position as Iran's second leading supplier, next to West Germany.

Iran not only continued to rely significantly upon the import of American capital goods for industrial development but also encouraged more private investment in 1963-73. Iran ratified in 1957 a Treaty of Amity and Economic Relations and Consular Rights with the United States for a period of ten years. The real significance of this treaty derived from the protection it accorded American investments in Iran, particularly insofar as Iran, contrary to many developing nations, accepted solemnly the obligation to compensate American interests with "prompt, effective and adequate" payments in case of expropriation and nationalization. This is obviously no place to catalog the wide and varied range of investments that Iran received from the United States during the decade under consideration. A 1969 survey by the United States embassy in Tehran showed that some one hundred American business firms had sent about 740 heads of families to Iran to work for them in the expanding Iranian market, and many more were expected to arrive in Iran during the early 1970s. Some thirty firms (excluding oil companies) made sizable capital investments in Iran, and nonoil investment could surpass $120 million by the end of 1970. Total United States private direct investment was estimated in 1969 at $300 million. To cite one example, IBM's case was noteworthy. Most of the IBM computers installed in Iran were completely bilingual and printed either in Farsi or English, French, Italian, or such other language as the application required. The principal users of IBM were a variety of Iranian organizations and companies, such as the Statistical Center of Iran, the Ministry of Finance, the Tehran Water Authority, the University of Tehran, and the Melli Shoe Company.[92] Iran further encouraged private

[92]See U.S., Department of Commerce, *International Commerce,* Mar. 31, 1969 pp. 15-19.

American investment after the adoption of the Fourth Plan, which required some $11 billion investment. About 45 percent was to be provided by private investors, including foreign firms. In January 1972 an Iranian economic mission together with four government ministers arrived in New York for a major investment conference with some forty-three American companies.

Another area of Iran's relations with the United States that was continued was the Fulbright Program. The establishment of the program dated back, it may be recalled, to 1949, but it became inactive because of lack of funds. It may also be recalled that a new agreement for the revival of the program was concluded in 1957, providing for the expenditure of the equivalent of $250,000 in rials for the exchange of students and teachers between the two countries during the first year. A new agreement for cultural exchange was concluded on October 24, 1963, placing the program on firmer ground. This agreement superseded the previous agreements (article 12) and came into force on the date of signature. The two countries declared their intention at the outset to "promote further mutual understanding" by means of "a wider exchange of knowledge and professional talents through educational contacts." The United States Commission for Cultural Exchange under this agreement consisted of eight members, four from each country. The commission was to facilitate the administration of an educational program to be financed by funds made available to it by the United States.[93] The revival and expansion of the Fulbright program in Iran, despite its relatively modest means, was welcomed in Iran by many intellectuals for its effective contribution to the cultural and educational life of the country. Perhaps more than any other single program it was a generator of good will between Iran and the United States. I observed how the news of a radical cutback in its funds in the late 1960s was received with deep concern in not a few educational circles in Iran.

Another major field of Irano-American relations that had been established only in the 1950s was continued with significant modifications in 1963-73. Iran and the United States signed, it may be recalled, the first agreement for cooperation in civil uses of atomic energy on March 5, 1957, which went into force subsequently on April 27, 1959. This basic agreement was amended twice during the 1960s. Technical details need no discussion here. But the continued emphasis on the civil uses of atomic energy and the extension of duration of cooperation between the two countries must be briefly noted. The first amending agreement was signed on June 8, 1964, which went into force on January 26, 1967. The original agreement was amended to read that

[93] For the text of the agreement see U.S., Department of State, *United States Treaties and Other International Agreements* 14, pt. 2, TIAS no. 5451 (Oct. 24, 1963): 1510-22.

the two governments "emphasize their common interest in ensuring that any material, equipment, or device made available to the Government of Iran pursuant to this Agreement shall be used solely for civil purposes."[94] The two countries also agreed to amend the original agreement, which had been concluded for an initial period of five years to ten years. The second amending agreement was signed on March 18, 1969, and came into force on August 1, 1969. This agreement, more than the previous ones, emphasized that any material, equipment, or devices made available to Iran "shall be used solely for civil purposes." It added more specifically that no material, equipment, and devices and, additionally, no special nuclear material produced through these by Iran "shall be used for atomic weapons, or for research on or development of atomic weapons, or for any other military purposes."[95] Insofar as duration was concerned, the 1969 amending agreement envisaged that it would remain in force for a period of twenty years.

New Fields of Cooperation

Iran also entered into three major new fields of cooperation with the United States in 1963-73. On March 19, 1968, it signed an agreement with the United States for studies leading to increased development of the water resources of Iran.[96] The first public indication of Iran's interest in this new field appeared in the joint statement issued at the end of the shah's visit to the United States in 1967. The agreement called for a joint Irano-American study of Iran's water resources for increasing the country's water supply for agricultural, industrial, and domestic uses through such actions as prevention of salinization of sweet water resources along the northern shores of the Persian Gulf and the "Oman sea," cloud breeding, and other methods. The two-year agreement also provided for an Iranian and an American team to undertake the joint studies. The Iranian team was drawn from the Ministry of Water and Power.[97]

Another new field of cooperation between Iran and the United States was opened in 1968. The American ambassador in Tehran, Armin Meyer, wrote Premier Hoveyda on May 23, 1968, to propose "a new medium by which the ties which bind our countries can be strengthened, and by which a vital area of interest to both countries individually can be served." This was the area of

[94] For the text see ibid., 18, pt. 1, TIAS no. 6219 (June 8, 1964):205-10.

[95] Ibid., 20, pt. 2, TIAS no. 6726 (Mar. 18, 1969):2677-83.

[96] For the text see ibid., 19, pt. 4, TIAS no. 6487 (Mar. 19, 1968): 4841-44.

[97] U.S. State Dept. *Bulletin* 58, no. 1502 (Apr. 8, 1968):472.

scientific cooperation. The American ambassador proposed also that each country designate an executive agency for the implementation of scientific cooperation and advised that the Smithsonian Institution of Washington had expressed willingness to act as the American agency. The aim of the program would be to "intensify co-operation between the scientists" of the two countries, including scientists from academic communities, governmental agencies, and other institutions of the two nations. This agreement through the exchange of notes was to last for three years initially, unless it was modified or extended by mutual consent. Premier Hoveyda received the American proposal with "interest" and "pleasure," declared that the Iranian government "warmly welcomes this new field of collaboration between our two countries,"[98] and designated the Ministry of Science and Higher Education to act as the Executive Agency for the Iranian government.

Finally, Iran and the United States signed a new Air Transport Agreement on February 20, 1973. It was scheduled to take effect in two years. This agreement was to establish bilateral civil aviation relations between the two countries on a more regular basis. Iran had terminated its previous Air Transport Agreement in 1971, and the new agreement was designed to be more beneficial to Iran. Under the new agreement Iran Air obtained "for the first time rights to operate scheduled services to the United States."[99] Iran was granted a route via several intermediate points to New York or Detroit with rights at Los Angeles to be added in 1975. In Iran the civil aviation authorities considered the agreement a significant achievement after a year of "complicated" negotiations. The success in reaching an agreement with the United States was expected to have a salutary effect on Iran's similar negotiations with Japan, India, Italy, and England, which were still underway at the time.

[98] For the texts of the notes exchanged between the U.S. ambassador and the Iranian prime minister, see U.S., Department of State, *United States Treaties and Other International Agreements*, 20, pt. 1, TIAS no. 6694 (May 23 and 27, 1968): 811-12.

[99] U.S. State Dept. *Bulletin* 68, no. 1757 (Feb. 26, 1973): 245-46.

XVI

The Persian Gulf and Beyond

ANOTHER COMPONENT OF Iran's "independent national policy"(*syasat-i mustaqill-i melli*) was its policy in the Persian Gulf. This was such a major component that it profoundly affected Iran's policy toward the Soviet Union and the United States. Despite the reduction of tensions between Iran and the Soviet Union and unprecedented developments in their economic and technical relations, the policies, objectives, and interests of the two countries showed increasing signs of conflict by the end of the 1960s, particularly after the Soviet-Iraqi treaty of 1972. Despite a long tradition of friendship between the shah's regime and Washington, the debate between the two over arms acquisition had often troubled their relations. The British decision to withdraw from the Persian Gulf and the American reluctance to pick up the British role directly made Washington more receptive to Iran's pressures for building up a "credible deterrent" with American help. These ideas must be kept in mind for a better understanding of Iran's Persian Gulf policy.

Balancing Power in the Middle East
before the Iraqi Revolution

Iran's Persian Gulf policy was primarily a development following the British withdrawal from Aden and the announcement of the British decision to withdraw also from the Persian Gulf, but its roots can be found in Iranian history. On the basis of a historical survey of Iran's position in the Persian Gulf from ancient times to the abdication of Riza Shah in 1941, I proposed elsewhere the following points: (1) able rulers of Iran aspired to playing the leading role in the Persian Gulf since ancient times; (2) Iran's capability to play a more active role in the gulf depended largely on the leadership qualities of its rulers; (3) the army constituted a crucial ingredient of the capability of rulers to maintain tranquility and to assert Iran's interest in the gulf; and (4) Iran's ability to play an active role in the gulf depended in part on the external circumstances, such as the attitudes and relative power, of other states.[1] We

---

[1] See Rouhollah K. Ramazani, *The Persian Gulf: Iran's Role* (Charlottesville: University Press of Virginia, 1972), pp. 1-27.

shall first examine the patterns of Iran's relations in the Middle East before we take up in detail the development of Iran's Persian Gulf policy after the British withdrawal from Aden in 1967.

As this study has shown, Iran's foreign policy between the Second World War and the downfall of Muhammad Musaddiq's government in 1953 was dominated by concern with great powers. During the war, it may be recalled, relations with the Soviet Union, Britain, and the United States were of primary interest, and the same was true of the postwar era until the downfall of the Musaddiq government. The preponderance of British military power in the Persian Gulf during this period, as in the century before, confined Iran's concern in the gulf area primarily to the problems of Shatt al-Arab and Bahrain. There was no serious problem of gulf security so long as Pax Britannica continued. Between the Second World War and the downfall of the Musaddiq government, Iran quarreled once with the British over Bahrain and once with Iraq over the ancient Shatt al-Arab problem.[2] Iran demanded during the oil nationalization crisis that nationalizations laws be applied to the Bahrain Petroleum Company, but reassertion of Iran's ancient claim to Bahrain on this occasion did not involve any major dispute between Iran and Britain. In the same way the ancient problem of the Shatt al-Arab quietly troubled Iran's relations with Iraq at this time, but again it did not acquire the dimensions of a crisis or a move toward settlement. My examination of the Iranian Foreign Ministry's files revealed that in 1948/49 (Iranian year 1327) the Iranian Council of Ministers approved the draft of a convention for the administration of the Shatt al-Arab for submission to the Iraqi government. Administration of the Shatt had always been one of the major issues in this dispute. Briefly, the 1937 treaty and its relevant protocol committed Iran and Iraq to conclude subsequently a convention for the maintenance and improvement of the navigable channel, and for dredging, pilotage, collection of dues, and the like. No convention was ever concluded. Iraq was made responsible by the treaty for all questions related to navigation, such as collection of duties and pilotage until a convention was concluded within a year or extension thereof by "common accord." Since such an accord was not attained, Iraq simply continued to administer the Shatt, and Iran charged that Iraq was responsible for the inability of the parties to conclude the necessary convention. In any event, despite the Iranian embassy's persistent requests for an Iraqi reply to Iran's draft convention, Baghdad delayed an answer for thirteen months, and when its brief response was delivered in 1950, it was regarded as unacceptable by Iran, principally because it rejected Iran's suggestion to establish under the convention a joint Irano-Iraqi Commission for the ad-

---

[2]For Iran's concern with the Bahrain and Shatt al-Arab problems before the Second World War, see Ramazani, *Foreign Policy of Iran,* especially pp. 247-50, 261-66.

ministration of the river. Iraq demanded that any commission be merely a "consultative" rather than an "executive" agency.

Iran's concern with the rest of the Middle East during the period between the Second World War and the return of the shah's regime to power in 1953 was even more limited than in the Persian Gulf. The best indication of this was the nature of Irano-Egyptian relations. Although diplomatic relations had been established as early as 1923, and particularly 1928, when the first major agreement between the two countries was signed, Egypt was of no particular political interest to Iran. In fact, before 1953, quite apart from the shah's prewar marriage to a sister of King Faruk, there was little else in Egypt that interested the public in Iran. But the shah's earliest postwar efforts at land distribution caught the attention of the Egyptians, including the well-known Egyptian writer Husain Haikal, who, after his travel to Iran, tried to suggest the need for a similar course of action by King Faruk in Egypt. Another isolated event in Iran that spurred Egyptian interest was the oil nationalization decision and particularly Musaddiq's nationalist struggle against the British. Nahas Pasha found it expedient to invite Musaddiq to Egypt during the course of his anti-British struggle in Egypt.

After the downfall of the Musaddiq government and the shah's rise to power, Iran's attention began to turn increasingly toward the Middle East and the Persian Gulf area. The rise of the shah's regime coincided with the beginning of the Egyptian revolution. The rise of Gamal 'Abd al-Nasir not only as the leader of the new Republic of Egypt but also as the symbol of Arab nationalism and unity, was watched with interest, if not concern, in Iran. The shah's decision to join the Baghdad Pact ran counter to the declared Egyptian crusade against the pact as a "Zionist plot," and Nasir's policy of positive neutralism was countered by the shah's positive nationalism. The Suez Canal crisis revealed another divergence of Iranian and Egyptian interests. In November 1956 Iran joined the United States and the Soviet Union in the Security Council over the protests of France and Great Britain to call upon the General Assembly for an emergency session for making recommendations against the invasion of Egypt. The Iranian opposition to the British and the French action, however, was motivated primarily by the concern that hostilities might injure Iran's important interest in transportation through the Suez Canal rather than by the simple desire to support Egypt as a victim of aggression. This great concern of Iran with the implications of Egyptian nationalism for the freedom of navigation through the canal had been expressed immediately after the Egyptian nationalization of the Suez Canal Company on July 26, 1956. On August 9, 1956, the Iranian foreign minister first publicly voiced this concern, and Iran's subsequent statements and actions confirmed it.[3]

[3]*New York Times,* Aug. 10, 1956.

This concern lay back of Iran's decision to attend the first London conference, August 16-23, 1956, to join the Suez Canal Users' Association and to agree to serve on its executive committee. At all times, while Iran sympathized with Egypt's nationalization of the Suez Canal Company as a sovereign act and cautioned against the use of force against Egypt, it held the view that Egypt was responsible under the Constantinople convention of 1888 to maintain freedom of navigation through the canal. In his statement to the London conference, the Iranian foreign minister, 'Aliquli Ardalan, not only invoked that convention but also the Security Council's resolution of September 1, 1951, which called upon Egypt to terminate restrictions on the passage of ships through the canal. He told the conference that "free and uninterrupted navigation of the canal" was of "vital importance to Iran." In support of this he stated that in 1955, 73 percent of Iranian imports and 76 percent of its exports were transported through the Suez Canal. And in the same year no less than five thousand tons of Iranian oil were transported to the Western world through the canal.[4]

Iran's foreign policy in 1953-57 was not only in basic conflict with Egypt's but also with that of another revolutionary Arab state, Syria. It may be recalled that Iran passed a new petroleum Law in 1957 that encompassed not only Iranian oil resources on land but also offshore resources in the Persian Gulf. Subsequently, on November 12, 1957, the Iranian Council of Ministers, in the presence of the shah, approved for submission to the Majlis a bill that clearly designated Bahrain as the fourteenth Iranian province. Officially, this simply detached Bahrain from the province of Fars and set it up as a separate province, but in fact this was a reassertion of Iran's old claim to Bahrain. Iran's action this time, however, not only brought on the usual British protest but also drew out the interest of Arab nationalism in the archipelago. On November 16, 1957, Syria denounced the Iranian move, and a Syrian Foreign Ministry spokesman stated categorically that Syria considered Bahrain part of the "Arab Nation"—a view held by the Arab League since 1954. The Iranian foreign minister stated on December 8, 1957, that Iran would "take all relevant steps" to convert oil-rich Bahrain into an Iranian province.[5]

While the shah's positive nationalism and the Arab nationalism of Egypt and Syria clashed in 1953-57, he tried to balance this with friendship with other Arab states. The shah invited King Saud to visit Iran in 1955. This was the occasion for the shah's first meeting with the king, and paved the way for his own visit to Saudi Arabia later. The shah's visit in March 1957 was viewed

[4]U.S., Department of State, *The Suez Canal Problem, July 26-September 22, 1956: A Documentary Publication* (Washington, D.C.: Government Printing Office 1956), pp. 127-30.

[5]*New York Times,* Nov. 17, Dec. 9, 1957.

as an opportunity for him to press for the formation of a bloc of moderate, pro-Western states. The meeting came at a time when King Saud was reportedly concerned over the "communist penetration" in Syria and Egypt.[6] The shah's government, it may be recalled, had endorsed the Eisenhower Doctrine in 1957, and it was believed that King Saud was "favorably impressed" by the president's policy in the Middle East. Although it was not likely that the shah would press the king to join Iran in the Baghdad Pact, it was expected that he would point out the advantages of association with Iran and Western powers in the area.

Another Arab state the shah tried to befriend in the pursuit of a balance of power in the Middle East in 1953-57 was Lebanon. The shah's visit to Lebanon in December 1957 and his "amity talks" with President Chamoun were regarded by "anti-Western elements" in the Arab world as part of a series of moves to draw Arab countries toward the Baghdad Pact.[7] But given Iran's own frustrations with the pact, as shown previously, the more important consideration underlying Iran's attempt at befriending Lebanon was the shah's own desire to balance Lebanon as well as Saudi Arabia against Egypt and Syria. His interest in the pact and his own balance-of-power strategy in the Middle East were compatible but not identical. For example, when the Lebanese crisis broke out in July, Iran joined its allies in the Baghdad Pact in supporting the Chamoun government. This was fully compatible with the shah's bilateral friendship with Chamoun insofar as the Lebanese president was considered to be under attack by the United Arab Republic as well as Nasirists within Lebanon.

Focusing on the Gulf after the Iraqi Revolution

The single most important event in the 1950s that focused Iran's attention on the Persian Gulf was the Iraqi revolution of 1958. The repercussions of this event in Iran's relations with the West and with the Soviet Union have already been discussed. Suffice it to recall here that it was as a result of this revolution that the shah's regime sought American commitment to Iran against not only Soviet "aggression" but also any other, including that of Iraq. It was also as a result of Iran's inability to obtain such a commitment that it finally resigned itself to a bilateral defense agreement with the United States that, in fact, did not go beyond the Eisenhower Doctrine in committing the United States to the defense of Iran. Suffice it to recall here also that it was

[6]Ibid., Mar. 13, 1957.
[7]Ibid., Dec. 24, 1957.

in part as a result of the Iraqi revolution that Iran sought to negotiate a non-aggression pact with the Soviet Union in 1958-59 in order to escape the development of a pincer of Soviet pressures from the north and Iraqi hostility from the south.

Iran's concern with the implications of the Iraqi revolution, however, was complicated by a variety of other factors as well. It seemed that Iraq was now added to Egypt and Syria in the struggle for power in the Middle East. The former Iraqi regime, despite all the difficulties between Baghdad and Tehran, had been an ally of Iran in the Baghdad Pact, but the defection of Iraq was now only a matter of time. The balance of power seemed to be tilting in favor of anti-Western Arab states. Another fact that intensified Iran's concern with developments in Iraq soon after the revolution was the toleration of Communist elements by the Qasim regime. It may be recalled that the shah's regime had been subjected to the threat of Communist subversion in 1953 and ever since had been engaged in concerted efforts to suppress the Tudeh elements in Iran. Furthermore, it may be recalled, the cold war between Tehran and Moscow reached an unprecedented height by 1959 after the breakdown of Soviet-Iranian negotiations for a nonaggression pact. The appearance of Soviet vessels at this time, reportedly carrying arms to Iraq through the Shatt al-Arab, was an entirely new and unwelcome development in the Persian Gulf. All these considerations were compounded by still other factors. The Shatt al-Arab dispute was still unresolved because the last, and perhaps the greatest, hope for its solution was aborted by the revolution in Iraq. Moreover, the revolution could produce, Iran believed, still other adverse effects. The very fact of the bloody destruction of the monarchy in neighboring Iraq could provide an example for Iranian opponents of the shah's regime within Iran, and the ancient problem of the Kurds could combine with other tribal discontents and erupt into a general tribal rebellion.

All these elements, in one way or another, impinged on the outbreak of the Shatt al-Arab crisis in late 1959. The Kurdish problem took the lead. Insofar as formal diplomatic relations were concerned, on July 30, 1958, Iran recognized the new regime in Iraq, but on July 25 Iran's deputy premier and director of internal security, Taimur Bakhtiar, had reportedly stated in an interview that if the Kurds of Iraq and Syria requested union with Iran, "such a request would be considered with great interest."[8] He warned also that President Nasir might attempt to create a Kurdish satellite state that would provide a land bridge between the UAR and the Soviet Union. At the same time he stated that all Iranian Kurds were completely loyal to the shah. A similar statement made on October 25, 1958, once again revealed Iran's own concern with the Kurdish situation, but such statements were interpreted in

[8] Ibid., July 26, 1958

the Arab world as an Iranian effort to stir up the Kurds against the Iraqi regime. S. C. Sulzberger of the *New York Times,* however, wrote that indications were that there was a Russian plan to upset the shah's regime by "indirect proxies." Outside Iran the "conspiracy would be hatched in Iraq among the Barazani Kurds, who had ties with the Kurdish minority within Iran. Inside Iran another proxy would be employed with no connection with the Soviet Union but whose desires to overthrow the shah coincided with the Kremlin's aims. This second and ad hoc proxy would be the powerful Qashqa'i tribe. Their leaders, Sulzberger continued, recently met in Munich to decide whether to declare war against the shah while they were trying to work out an alliance with the Bakhtiari tribe.[9] The fact of such reports, accurate or not, showed that Iran's concern with the tribal problem was not simply a figment of imagination or a fabrication of Tehran. In fact, in May 1959 the Kurdish problem in Iraq began to have serious repercussions in Iran. According to *Ittila'at,* some ten thousand Iraqi Kurds crossed the Iranian frontier into Iran and sought asylum after fighting in Iraq.[10]

The immediate cause of the Shatt al-Arab crisis is difficult to ascertain. The view in Iran was that the Qasim regime stirred up the ancient problem in order to divert attention from internal problems. In commenting on Iraq's foreign policy during the Qasim regime, Professor Majid Khadduri states generally that he "often resorted to foreign ventures in order to divert the attention of a divided nation from internal to foreign affairs."[11]Although Professor Khadduri cites "a case" in this connection, namely, the Iraqi claim to the sovereignty of Kuwait, his general statement could be equally applied to the Shatt al-Arab crisis in 1959. The other point of view was that Qasim's claim regarding the Shatt al-Arab was precipitated by the shah's reference to Iran's dissatisfaction with the terms of the 1937 treaty with Iraq as "intolerable and unprecedented" in a news conference held on November 28, 1959.[12] The problem with this suggestion is that as early as April 1959 a similar statement by the shah to *Figaro*'s correspondent was widely known[13] and yet produced no known reaction from Qasim.

In any event, President Qasim's claim touched off the crisis in early December 1959. In a news conference he remarked that in 1937 Iraq "was subjected to severe pressure" and because the government of Iraq was caught

[9]Ibid., Apr. 27, 1959.

[10]*Ittila'at Hava'i,* May 17, 1959, and *New York Times,* May 13, 1959.

[11]See Majid Khadduri, *Republican 'Iraq: A Study in 'Iraqi Politics since the Revolution of 1958* (London: Oxford University Press, 1969), p. 187.

[12]*New York Times,* Dec. 24, 1959.

[13]*Ittila'at Hava'i,* Apr. 10, 1959.

in a complicated situation, it granted a strip of five kilometers of the Shatt al-Arab to Iran, and this was a "grant" not an "acquired right." "If the boundary problems are not resolved in the future we shall not be bound by the grant of those five kilometers and will restore them to our motherland."[14] In a long rebuttal of this statement, the Iranian foreign minister told the Majlis that Qasim's claim was totally unfounded, repeated the well-known Iranian position that according to the principles of international law, the boundary between Iran and Iraq in the entire length of Shatt al-Arab, and not just opposite Abadan, should have followed the thalweg and declared that ever since the establishment of the military regime in Iraq, new difficulties were created in the Shatt al-Arab side by side other "unfriendly actions against Iran."[15]

On January 3, 1960, the Iranian government made public a major statement on the crisis.[16] It reiterated the main Iranian complaints concerning the Iraqi failure to conclude a convention for the joint administration of the Shatt al-Arab river, charged that Iraq arbitrarily and contrary to the terms of the 1937 treaty had collected revenues for purposes other than maintenance of the river, and noted that the boundary line designated by the treaty should have followed the thalweg all along the river. More important, it was revealed for the first time that just before the downfall of the monarchical regime in Iraq, an agreement in principle had finally been reached between the two countries on two major points. First, they had agreed to appoint a joint commission for the administration of the Shatt al-Arab. Second, they had agreed to the appointment of a Swedish arbitrator who would settle the boundary demarcation problem in consultation with the joint Irano-Iraqi commission. Preliminary steps had also been taken to implement these agreements when the old regime was overthrown in Iraq. The new Iraqi government declared upon coming into power that it would honor Iraq's international obligations but in practice refused to respond to Iranian representations on the subject.

While exchanges at the political level were pushing the relations of the two countries to the breaking point, they were both engaged in military preparations. Given the vulnerable position of the gigantic Abadan refinery near the Iraqi frontier on the Shatt al-Arab, the Iranian military build-up was largely concentrated around the area. Date plantations lining the river were reportedly bristling with antiaircraft weapons, machine guns, and tanks covered by camouflage netting. Iranian fighter planes from airports throughout Khuzistan could reach the area within eight minutes of an alarm. Iranian warships were stationed at the head of the Persian Gulf, near the town of Fao,

[14]Translated from the Persian text as it appeared in *Ittila'at Hava'i,* Apr. 10, 1959.

[15]Ibid.

[16]For the text of the statement in Persian, see ibid., Jan. 3, 1960.

commanding the entrance to the Shatt al-Arab, scrutinizing all incoming vessels.[17] Except for a few skirmishes, however, no major hostilities occurred. Both the United States and Britain cautioned restraint, and Iran declared itself willing to discuss the case either directly with Iraq or in any suitable international forum. By July 1960 tempers cooled to the point that new ambassadors were exchanged, and Iran assigned one of its most distinguished career diplomats, Yadullah 'Azudi, as its ambassador to Iraq.

Despite the return of relative calm in the relations of the two countries, between July 1960 and the announcement of the British decision in 1968 to withdraw forces from the Persian Gulf, the chances for settlement of outstanding issues were slim. No visible progress toward a settlement was made during the rest of Qasim's rule in Iraq. The rise to power of 'Abd al-Salam 'Arif on February 8, 1963, was accompanied by some hope in Tehran that the change might produce a new approach to Iranian questions in Baghdad. Although about a year later, on February 24, 1964, a high-ranking delegation was sent to Tehran for negotiations for the first time since the beginning of the Iraqi revolution, and although a vigorous exchange of notes took place between Premier Hoveyda and the prime minister of Iraq, 'Abd al-Rahman al-Bazzaz, in December 1965, no sign of progress toward a settlement was in sight. The election of 'Abd al-Rahman 'Arif to the presidency on April 17, 1966, after the plane crash in which his brother died, was accompanied by hopeful developments in Iran's relations with republican Iraq. At the invitation of the shah President 'Arif and his wife visited Iran for six days beginning on March 14, 1967. The discussions between the two leaders were regarded as "fruitful" (*samarbakhsh*) and even "successful" in Tehran. The two countries agreed before their summit meeting to consider six "basic issues" (*mozo'-i asasi*) in Tehran. These were (1) boundary incidents, (2) exploration and exploitation of boundary oil resources, (3) status of Iranian subjects in Iraq and the future position of Iranian schools in Iraq, (4) delimitation of Irano-Iraqi continental shelves in the Persian Gulf, (5) facilitation of Iranian pilgrimage to holy Shi'i shrines in Iraq, and (6) treatment of Iranian residents in Iraq and Iraqi residents in Iran.[18] The absence of any reference to the Shatt al-Arab dispute was conspicuous, but it might well have been intentional in order to avoid stirring up at the outset the emotion-ridden issue.

The text of the joint communiqué issued at the end of the first Iraqi-Iranian summit meeting since the Iraqi revolution revealed that hard bargaining had taken place. For its part Iran joined Iraq in declaring that the Palestinian problem was not only an Arab concern but a question of concern to all Muslim

[17] *New York Times*, Dec. 29, 1959.

[18] *Ittila'at Hava'i*, Mar. 16, 1967.

nations. For its part Iraq joined Iran in announcing its decision that negotiations in regard to the delimitation of the continental shelves of the two countries, cooperation for exploration of oil resources (*Khanih Naft*, and *Naft-i Shah*), and the manner of utilization of common boundary rivers proceed "according to the principles of international law."[19] Although the communiqué stated that the two heads of state did endorse the decisions of their foreign ministers made in December 1966, the general language of the communiqué itself left some doubts about the extent of agreement reached between Iran and Iraq on the basic issues of the Shatt al-Arab. These issues had always involved not only the problem of water utilization but also those of the boundary line in the river, the administration of the river, and the problem of freedom of navigation. For this reason it is difficult to assess the extent of agreement between the two countries at this time; nevertheless there was every sign that some agreement between the two neighboring nations had been reached. Whether they would survive the turbulence of Iraqi domestic politics remained to be seen.

The Egyptian and Syrian conflict with the shah's regime intensified after the Iraqi revolution. The first serious sign of this was the sudden rupture of diplomatic relations between Egypt and Iran in 1960. In July of that year the shah, in reply to a question by a foreign correspondent about whether Iran had decided to recognize Israel, stated that "Iran had recognized Israel long ago." Apparently in reaction to this statement, President Nasir denounced the shah in a speech at Alexandria, labeled the Iranian leaders "colleagues of colonialists," boasted of Egypt's ability to "abolish them," and charged that the shah had acted against Egypt in the Suez crisis. Iran attempted to show the "unfoundedness" of Nasir's assertion by pointing out to Egypt as well as other Arab nations that Iran had recognized Israel in 1950, that the recognitions had been de facto and had not been withdrawn by Musaddiq, and that no new decision had been taken to extend de jure recognition to Israel.[20]

The rupture of diplomatic relations between Iran and Egypt was followed by increasing acrimony not only between the two countries but also with Syria as well. Egypt chose the Arab League as the instrument of its policy in the Persian Gulf in 1964-65. The Persian Gulf Sheikhdoms of Bahrain, Qatar, Dubai, Abu Dhabi, Sharja, Oman, and others were solicited by the secretary-general of the league for cooperation with Egypt for the "general welfare of the area and the Arab Nation," and on July 13-14, 1964, the commission of the Arab League to the Emirates of the Arab Gulf decided to launch its plan of work in the gulf area. Subsequently, on July 5, 1965, the Permanent Committee of the Arab Gulf met in Cairo at the league's headquarters and decided

[19]Ibid., Mar. 20, 1967.

[20]For details see Ramazani, *Persian Gulf*, pp. 36-38.

to recommend to the states of the leagues (1) to reject the British proposal that the Arab League should channel their aid to the Arab sheikhdoms through the British-sponsored Development Fund for the Trucial Coast (DFTC); (2) to remind the British of the "dangerous consequences" of their course of actions; (3) to authorize the secretary-general to strengthen joint Arab efforts in regard to the gulf; and (4) to present to the Committee of the Personal Representatives of Arab Kings and Presidents a draft for submission to the Third Summit Meeting.[21]

Arab aspirations in the Persian Gulf at the time went beyond the Arab interest in the Trucial States of the gulf; they affected Iran's own territory as well. Iran's richest province of Khuzistan was called "Arabistan" to emphasize the view that it was part of the Arab Nation and that it had been lost to the Arab peoples as the result of British manipulation of Riza Shah. On December 11, 1964, a conference of Arab jurists declared Khuzistan "an integral part of the Arab Homeland," and on November 10, 1965, the Ba'thist regime in Syria supported this claim.[22]

Iran's reaction to all this was bitter. The semiofficial newspaper *Ittila'at* in a sensational editorial claimed that 'Abd al-Khaliq Hassounah, the secretary-general of the Arab League, had told the Persian Gulf Arab rulers that Iran wished to colonize the Arab sheikhdoms; that Iran's influence in the gulf was detrimental to the "Arab Nation"; that Iran had armed its agents in the gulf sheikhdoms for the opportune moment to rise against the Arabs; and that the fresh and dried fruits that Iran sold to the sheikhdoms were the products of Israel. In dramatizing the "danger" of the Egyptian role in the gulf area, the editorial concluded: "These are real accounts indicative of the fire that the enemy is building for the destruction of part of our national heritage. These are examples of the intrigues against the Iranians and Iranianism. These form a prelude to the destruction of Iran's influence in the Persian Gulf sheikdoms, for the expulsion of the Iranian residents from the Gulf islands and for the extension of Egyptian control over the entire Persian Gulf.[23]

In a statement to the deputies of the Majlis, the shah himself minced no words in placing the blame on Egypt for the situation in the Persian Gulf. He stated in part: "We are informed that there are committees engaged in conspiracy and planning of subversive plans, and we think that so long as this aggressive and imperialistic policy of the present government of Egypt and the personal head of that government continues you must expect such ventures and conspiracies because a government that is incapable of accomplishing

[21]Ibid., pp. 39-40.

[22]Ibid., p. 41

[23]Ibid., p. 40.

really beneficial tasks for its people perforce must divert their attention to foreign affairs."[24] In referring to President Nasir, the shah also stated that "these policies that he is pursuing today are unfortunately contrary to Iran's basic interests in the Persian Gulf and parts of southern Iran." He then described the vital importance of the wealth of Khuzistan for Iran in terms of its oil resources and industries in order to indicate why some Arab leaders coveted Khuzistan.

To counter the power as well as the perceived ambitions of the revolutionary Arab leaders in the Persian Gulf, Iran began an unprecedented campaign of befriending the gulf states in the early 1960s. The pre-Iraqi revolution attempts at befriending Saudi Arabia in the gulf area were now expanded to include others in the gulf region, but the existence of special British treaty relationships with the Trucial States, the British presence in Bahrain, and in Kuwait before independence, placed serious limits on Iranian means. The chosen instrument of policy therefore varied from one part of the gulf to another. Insofar as the Trucial States were concerned Iran tried to discuss with the British the problem of delimitation of the continental shelf in the Persian Gulf. But the most important instrument of Iranian policy at the time was commercial. Iran recognized the potential of its own industrial growth and ability to export goods of interest to the Persian Gulf sheikhdoms. It therefore resorted to a variety of trade-promotion measures, including sponsorship of trade conferences with smaller Persian Gulf states, abolition of exchange restrictions on the export of fruits and vegetables, substantial reduction of air charges for these items, centralization of export activities, and exchange of merchants and visits of rulers and top officials. The salutary effect of these and similar measures on Iran's growing commercial ties with the gulf states began to show by the mid-1960s. For example, Iran's exports to Kuwait amounted to only $7 million in 1962-63 but reached $24.4 million in 1965-66.[25] Nevertheless, greater expansion of commercial and economic ties with the gulf states had to await their independence, as in the case of Kuwait, which gained its independence from Britain some ten years before the Trucial States. Iran anxiously awaited the attainment of independence by Kuwait; denounced Iraq's claim to Kuwait in June 1961; and dispatched a goodwill mission to Kuwait, with a congratulatory message from the shah on its independence, in preparation for the establishment of an Iranian Embassy in Kuwait and for the promotion of Irano-Kuwaiti economic and cultural relations.[26]

[24] For the text see *Ittila'at Hava'i,* Dec. 6, 1964. My translation from the Persian text.

[25] For details see Ramazani, *Persian Gulf,* pp. 84-86.

[26] *Ittila'at Hava'i,* July 8, 1961.

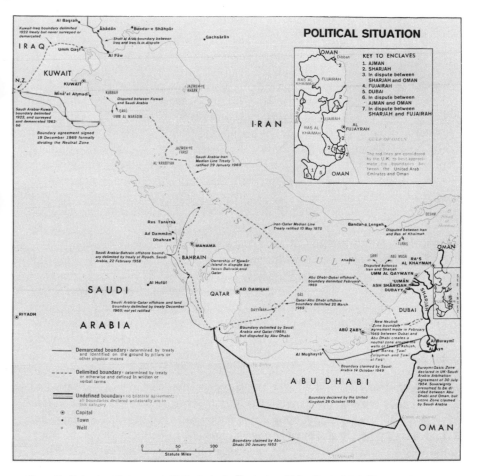

Kuwait, Bahrain, Qatar, and United Arab Emirates. U.S., Central Intelligence Agency, Washington, D.C.: Government Printing Office, April 1972.

Diplomatic Maneuvers before Britain's Departure

The anticipation of British withdrawal from Aden in 1967 and the subsequent British decision in 1968 to withdraw military forces also from the area east of Suez had a profound effect upon Iran's foreign policy in general and its Persian Gulf policy in particular. By 1967 Iran's experience in the Middle East had helped to clarify somewhat its objectives in the Persian Gulf. The patterns of conflict with Egypt, Syria, and Iraq and the growing friendship of the Soviet Union with Iraq had left no doubt in Tehran that Iran's primary objectives in the Persian Gulf were (1) to protect the safety of the shah's regime against internal subversion sponsored indirectly either by radical Arab regimes or the Soviet Union, (2) to protect Iranian oil resources and the vast oil installations concentrated in the gulf area against deliberate or accidental disruption from any quarter, and (3) to preserve freedom of navigation in the Shatt al-Arab, the Persian Gulf, and, particularly, the Strait of Hormuz.

The anticipated British withdrawal from Aden and eventually from the Persian Gulf, however, called for new strategies vis-à-vis the superpowers and the Middle Eastern states, including the Persian Gulf powers. We have already seen how the anticipated British withdrawal injected new elements into Iran's policy toward the superpowers. The tradition of acquiring military equipment from the United States proved helpful in the new circumstances to press successfully for modern American military equipment toward the building up of a credible deterrent. The reduced tensions and the commerical, technical, and economic cooperation with the Soviet Union after 1962 were used to counter the growing Soviet ties with Iraq by giving the Soviets a stake in Iran as well and by impressing upon the Soviet Union in a friendly manner that Iran was opposed to any outside powers, including the Soviet Union, attempting to fill the prospective power vacuum in the Persian Gulf after the British departure. Since we have already examined Iran's policies toward the superpowers after, as well as before, the announcement of the British decision to withdraw, the rest of this chapter will attempt to examine the development of Iran's Persian Gulf policy with particular reference to other powers. The parallel developments in Iran's policy toward the superpowers, previously discussed, should, of course, be kept in mind throughout the following discussions.

As early as November 1967 Britain, in anticipation of its imminent withdrawal from Aden and possibly later from the Persian Gulf, approached Iran for discussions. The British minister of state, Goronwy Roberts, arrived in Iran on November 9, held a meeting with the shah, and began his earliest discussions with Iranian officials on November 11. Despite the great secrecy surrounding the discussions, there was no doubt in Tehran that they concerned the future of the Persian Gulf. The communiqué issued at the end of negotia-

tions spoke generally about British-Iranian "close relations," the atmosphere
of frankness and friendship in which the discussions had been conducted, and
the community of views between the two countries in regard to "the aims
which must be pursued for the maintenance of peace and stability" in the area.
In a subsequent press interview the British minister expressed the view that
the future of the Persian Gulf would depend on the understanding and
cooperation of Iran, Iraq, Kuwait, and Saudi Arabia. He also revealed that
"most of his discussions" with the shah in Tehran concerned the future of the
Persian Gulf.[27]

The British minister of state paid another visit to Iran and other gulf
states before the announcement of the British decision in January 1968 to
withdraw British forces from the Persian Gulf in 1971. The semiofficial
Ittila'at as well as other Iranian newspapers reported on January 8, 1968,
that "political observers" (*nazirin-i syasi*) believed that the British minister
had made a proposal to Iran and other interested states for the establishment
of a joint defense force for the Persian Gulf or for an agreement to that effect,
"but it seems unlikely that this proposal will be acceptable to Iran." On the
following day a spokesman of the Iranian Ministry of Foreign Affairs denied
the news report about Iran's attitude; he stated that "the Iranian government has always been agreeable to any kind of regional co-operation and it
also agrees with regional co-operation in the Persian Gulf as well." A few days
later it was reported that according to high-ranking Foreign Ministry officials,
Iran was taking the initiative to interest Iraq as well as Saudi Arabia and
Kuwait in a regional agreement.[28]

On January 13 the *New York Times* stated that "in spite of objections
said to have been raised by Secretary of State Dean Rusk in his talks
in Washington with Foreign Secretary George Brown—they will pass on
to Iran and Saudi Arabia responsibility for the complex political and military domain that Britain has built up and controlled for centuries."[29]
The reluctance of the United States, implied in this report, to wish to fill
directly the vacuum to be left by the British became more evident by the
statement of Under Secretary of State Eugene Rostow. He stated that the
United States did not expect "to have to rush in to fill a power vacuum" and
believed that Iran, Turkey, Pakistan, Saudi Arabia, and Kuwait were interested
in forming a regional security arrangement in the Persian Gulf area.[30] *Al-Ahram*
reported on January 27, 1969, that the foreign minister of Kuwait stated that

[27]Ibid.,Nov. 14, 15, 1967.

[28]Ibid., Jan. 8, 9, 13, 1968.

[29]*New York Times,* Jan. 14, 1969.

[30]*Daily Star* (Beirut), Jan. 21, 1968.

such arrangements, as suggested by Rostow, could not be "imposed on peoples." The London *Times* also criticized Rostow's statement because it "provided fuel for Egypt's constant charge of an American conspiracy to fill the gulf 'vacuum' by his talk of security arrangements drawing in not only Saudi Arabia and Iran but Turkey and Pakistan too."[31]

Iran's basic objectives, despite this confused and kaleidoscopic pattern of affairs that emerged immediately after the British announcement, were as clear as they were before. Its studied silence was designed to maximize its interests cautiously in this unprecedented opportunity created by the British intention to withdraw from the Persian Gulf after a century and a half. The strategies to be followed had to be flexible in order to accommodate the complications of the situation. The pre-1968 friendship with Saudi Arabia could become the basis for an Islamic entente; or previous friendly relations with Kuwait could also provide the basis for even a tripartite coalition, or even Iraq could be finally won over in view of the fact that at the time of the British announcement Iran's relations with Baghdad were exceptionally calm; or eventually even the Trucial States, which were then being encouraged by the British to form a federation, could join other like-minded Arabs and Iran. With these in mind Iran had declared from the outset its preparedness to cooperate with other gulf states in maintaining security of the Persian Gulf. But at the same time Iran believed that the prospects for any serious formal alliance in the area were poor while its own power position was preponderant. With this in mind, too, Iran intensified, as seen previously, its military build-up as the most certain guarantee of not only its own security but also that of other like-minded gulf states. Iran's Persian Gulf diplomacy therefore paralleled its security policy of creating unilaterally a credible deterrent with the assistance of the United States.

The silence was first broken by Premier Hoveyda on January 27, 1968, in a news conference. He stated that as "the most powerful" (*muqtadirtarin*) state in the entire Persian Gulf, "naturally" Iran was greatly interested in the stability and security of the gulf area, and to that end Iran was prepared to cooperate with any littoral state that desired cooperation. But it must be made clear, the prime minister declared, that this matter did not concern non-Persian Gulf powers, and the idea of such cooperation was not to allow the British departure from one door and American or British entry, in a different form, from another. He emphasized that "there is no doubt" that Iran could protect its own interests and "rights" in the Persian Gulf with all its might and would not allow any outside power to interfere in the Persian Gulf.[32] The prime minister's hands-off warning to great powers, as we shall

[31]*Times* (London), Feb. 10, 1969.

[32]*Ittila'at Hava'i,* Jan. 28, 1968.

see, was meant for the Soviet Union as well. His reference to not only Iranian interests but also Iranian "rights" was meant for the British with a view to the status of Bahrain after the British withdrawal from the Persian Gulf. As we shall see, however, the historical claim to Bahrain was used from the outset to bargain with the British for the establishment of Iranian forces on three other islands in the gulf, which Iran also claimed. The shah himself finally broke the silence on March 13, 1968, in the timely presence of the Soviet premier for the ground-breaking ceremony of a new steel mill at Isfahan. With an obvious reference to Iran's claim to Bahrain, he stated, "We expect other countries to respond with more than mere smiles when we extend the hand of friendship."[33] It meant that Iran would react favorably to the British plan for an Arab federation if Iran's interests in Bahrain and also other islands in the gulf were recognized. He also implied diplomatic retaliation against the British when he stated that "if our present friends do not respect Iran's legitimate rights in the Persian Gulf, they must expect Iran to show the same attitude toward them."[34]

The shah's strategy of withholding approval from a British-sponsored Arab federation as a bargaining point for Bahrain and other islands claimed by Iran in the Persian Gulf surfaced more clearly in a statement by the Iranian under secretary for foreign affairs. Timing it appropriately, on the same day that the shah spoke at Isfahan, he asked what validity the proposed federation might have with its foreign and defense policies in the hands of the British. From the point of view of Iran, he continued, the British government could not relinquish or give away land (that is, Bahrain) that had been seized from Iran by force. Again with obvious reference to Bahrain he stated that Iran reserved all its "rights" in the Persian Gulf and would not "in any shape" tolerate this "historic inequity." The most perceptive remark about Iran's real intention in reviving the Bahrain question at this time was made by the London *Times*, but it was cast in terms of "suspicion" entertained abroad. The suspicion abroad was that "Iranians' real concerns are, first, the Straits of Hormuz, the entry to the Gulf which a hostile power could block to Iranian shipping as the Straits of Tiran were blocked to Israel, and, secondly, that a nationalistic and revolutionary regime, or series of regimes, might soon be installed along the southern shore of the Gulf. Iran wants no second South Yemen on her door."[35]

Iran's strategy vis-à-vis the major gulf states was to seek as much cooperation with them as the situation allowed. The first choice was Saudi Arabia, the gulf's largest Arab state, with which Iran, as seen, had established some

[33]*Times* (London), Mar. 14, 1968.

[34]*Christian Science Monitor,* Mar. 18, 1968.

[35]*Times* (London), Apr. 2, 3, 1968.

rudimentary ties. King Saud first visited Iran in 1955, and the shah returned his visit in 1957. The shah wished to build upon these visits to protect Iran's interests in anticipation of British withdrawal. He was scheduled to visit King Faisal in February 1968, but a few days before he was due to make his trip, the ruler of Bahrain was "royally received" in Saudi Arabia when the king declared full support for the sheik of Bahrain and when there was allegedly some talk about the building of a causeway to link Bahrain to Saudi Arabia. This was interpreted in Iran as a rebuff to its long-standing claim to Bahrain. Iran's under secretary for foreign affairs, 'Abbas 'Ali Khal'atbary, stated in an interview that it "was apparently hoped in Riyadh that His Majesty the Shah's visit would be tacit approval of this." And for this reason Iran had to call off the visit.[36] Egypt paraded the cancellation of the visit as the result of Saudi Arabia's stand against "Iran's ambitions in Bahrain" and claimed that Kuwaiti sources had announced that an agreement had been reached between Saudi Arabia and Bahrain for the construction of a twelve-mile bridge aimed at "thwarting any attempt by Iran against Bahrain." Egypt itself moved quickly to use the momentary rift between Iran and Saudi Arabia by informing the Saudis that they completely supported "any step taken by the King for preservation of Arabism and the independence of Emirates of the Arab Gulf."[37]

Before the relations with Saudi Arabia could be patched up, Iran turned to Iraq by drawing upon the momentary good will that had been created as the result of President 'Abd al-Rahman 'Arif's visit to Iran, mentioned previously. Prime Minister Hoveyda welcomed the Iraqi prime minister, Tahir Yahia, to Tehran on June 24, 1968, and discussed a wide range of outstanding questions between the two countries, including the future security of the Persian Gulf. On June 27 the Iraqi prime minister told newsmen that Iraq was willing to cooperate with Iran, Saudi Arabia, and Kuwait in maintaining the security of the gulf region then and after the British withdrawal. Insofar as the bilateral relations of Iran and Iraq were concerned, in referring to the Shatt al-Arab dispute, he reportedly stated that he saw "no reason why Iran and Iraq should not use this waterway jointly."[38] This optimistic outlook, however, was seriously called into question soon thereafter as a result of the fall of 'Abd al-Rahman'Arif's regime on July 17, 1968.

The shah's important state visits to Saudi Arabia and Kuwait finally began on November 9, 1968. The visit to Saudi Arabia was long in the making, after the cancellation of the shah's scheduled visit in February. Realizing the overriding significance of gulf security, the shah subordinated the ruffled

[36]*Christian Science Monitor,* Mar. 16, 1968.

[37]*Al-Ahram,* Feb. 3, 1968.

[38]*Daily Star* (Beirut), June 25, 26, 1968.

feelings over Bahrain to greater interests. Other factors also assisted in paving the way toward the shah's visit. Opposition to the extension of Soviet influence in the Persian Gulf, it may be recalled, dated back to the 1950s in connection with Iran's membership in the Baghdad Pact, particularly after the Iraqi revolution. Soviet naval visits to ports in Iran, Iraq, the Indian Ocean, and the Arabian Sea had since 1968 dramatically demonstrated growing Soviet interest in the area, and the appearance of two Russian vessels at an Iraqi port as early as May 1968 added to the urgency of patching up differences with Saudi Arabia in view of the imminent British departure.[39] It was also believed that as the result of mediation efforts of King Hasan II of Morocco, the shah stopped in Jedda on June 3, 1968, on the way to Ethiopia. The shah and the king held brief talks and then "embraced warmly," it was announced in Jedda.[40] In any event, before the visit to Ethiopia could take place, the outstanding dispute between Iran and Saudi Arabia over the continental shelf boundaries was finally resolved. The first significant step toward this end was taken August 21, 1968, when the two countries finally initiated an agreement and signed it October 24, 1968. As early as 1965 Iran and Saudi Arabia had initialed an agreement, but it was not ratified by either country. The importance of the new agreement derived not only from the success of the two nations in settling their differences over the continental shelf in the Persian Gulf but also from their ability to compromise on their conflicting claims of sovereignty over the islands of Farsi and al-'Arabi; Iran acquired title over the former and Saudi Arabia over the latter.[41]

The October 24 agreement removed a persistent irritant in Iran's relations with Saudi Arabia. Its speedy settlement was expedient. It had to be removed in light of the imminent British departure as a means of achieving greater Saudi Arabian support at the time for Iranian policies at a later date. The shah's five-day visit to Saudi Arabia was the most important step toward the attainment of that support. Throughout the visit no serious and specific mention of the Persian Gulf situation was made in public; even the joint communiqué issued at the end of the visit on November 14, 1968, did not refer to the Persian Gulf. Instead, the shah chose to speak publicly on two major themes, Islam and, when necessary, and by indirection, Israel. At a dinner he asked, "If we believe that division, separation, machinations and particular designs have acted to the detriment of Muslim nations and of Islam, has not the time arrived for us to re-assess our approach?"[42] In

[39] *Christian Science Monitor,* Oct. 21, 1968.

[40] *Daily Star* (Beirut), July 4, 1968.

[41] For the most comprehensive report of this agreement, see *Kayhan* (Daily English), Oct. 31, 1968. See also Ramazani, *Persian Gulf,* pp. 49-50.

[42] *Kayhan* (Daily English), Nov. 10, 1968.

acknowledging King Faisal's thanks for Iran's helpful attitude during "unto-ward events" that had befallen certain Arab states—a reference to the June 1967 war—the shah said Iran acted "first because we too are Muslims, and secondly because Iran always upholds justice." The shah's statements in support of Islam and his performing an "Umra" (off-season) Haj pilgrimage to Mecca, were not, of course, expected to indicate any real change in his determined modernization efforts in Iran, which had alienated some of the clergy. Nor was his support for the Arab position on Palestine and the with-drawal of Israeli forces from occupied territories expected to introduce any change in Iran's de facto recognition of Israel or the flow of its oil through Western oil companies to Israel. The real issue was the security of the Persian Gulf. These two like-minded monarchs perceived "security" in light of their own ancient claims, such as Bahrain and Burami, and the "threats" of sub-version to their respective regimes. According to sources close to the Saudi throne, the upshot of the shah's visit to Saudi Arabia was that the two leaders agreed not to do anything in the Persian Gulf area that would be detrimental to each other and to work together to exclude revolutionary forces.[43]

No single decision the shah could make would elicit as much support for his Persian Gulf policy from Arab states as the abandonment of Iran's ancient territorial claim to Bahrain, the rallying point of revolutionary as well as conservative Arab states within and outside the Persian Gulf. The shah's state visit to Saudi Arabia and after that to Kuwait must have convinced him of the handsome rewards such a dramatic move would bring. Furthermore, such a move would simultaneously strengthen Iran's bargaining position with Britain for acquisition of other islands in the Persian Gulf before the end of 1971.

As already noted, as soon as Iran broke its silence on the British decision to withdraw from the Persian Gulf, it tied its recognition of the British-sponsored Arab federation to the settlement of Iran's claim to Bahrain and other islands. Before the shah's visit to Saudi Arabia and Kuwait, this diplomatic bargain was made even clearer. In the wake of the creation of a temporary Federal Council representing seven Trucial States and Qatar and Bahrain, the Iranian government strongly denounced the federation on July 8, 1968. The Foreign Ministry's communiqué stated that the Iranian government had "consistently expressed its opposition to imperialism and pseudo-imperialism and any mani-festation thereof. The creation of a so-called confederation of Persian Gulf emirates embracing the Bahrain islands is absolutely unacceptable to Iran. At the same time, however, the Iranian foreign minister, Ardishir Zahidi, told a correspondent of a Viennese weekly that Iran's objection to the federation was based not only on the claim to Bahrain but also on a claim to a number of

[43]*New York Times*, Nov. 17, 1968.

other gulf islands as well.[44] Although the islands were not mentioned by name at this time, they were the two Tumbs and Abu Musa, also claimed by Ras al-Khaima and Sharja, respectively, a claim that had apparently been recognized by Britain.

To reconcile the like-minded Arab states, on the one hand, and bait the British toward a better bargain in regard to the three islands, on the other, the shah dramatically declared his decision to abandon Iran's ancient claim to Bahrain. On January 4, 1969, he declared in a press conference in New Delhi that "if the people of Bahrain do not want to join my country," Iran would withdraw its territorial claims to the Persian Gulf island. He said Iran would accept the will of the people in Bahrain if this was recognized internationally.[45] He insisted that Iran opposed the use of force to achieve that end (he specifically mentioned the United Nations machinery some months later), but his intention to keep the British involved for further bargaining was made quite clear by his insistence that even if the British granted independence to Bahrain on their own, it would be unacceptable to Iran. He warned that if Bahrain became a member of the proposed Arab federation, Iran would refuse to recognize it, and if "Bahrain becomes an independent State, we shall not recognize it, and if it is admitted to the United Nations we shall leave. The U.N. could choose whether to have us or Bahrain."[46] This was driving a hard bargain, but the shah knew the British did not have much choice.

Both the time and place of the announcement of the shah's calculated decision and the choice of the method of the settlement of the status of Bahrain were designed to prove beneficial. To take the method first, for a century and a half Iran had insisted on its "incontestable sovereign right" over Bahrain, a territorial claim hallowed by historical legitimacy. The decision to settle the Bahrain dispute with Britain through the United Nations amid appeals to the charter principles of self-determination and peaceful settlement of disputes made it easier in Iran for the shah's regime to abandon the age-old claim to Bahrain by substituting a legal or moral legitimacy for the old historical one.[47] In its request of March 9, 1970, to the United Nations secretary-general for good offices, Iran stipulated that it would accept the results of his findings "after and subject to their endorsement by the Security Council of the United Nations," and on April 30, 1970, the Security Council

[44]*Kayhan* (Daily English), July 9, Aug. 28, 1968.

[45]Ibid., Jan. 6, 1969.

[46]*Kayhan* (Weekly English), Sept. 20, 1969.

[47]For details see Rouhollah K. Ramazani, "The Settlement of the Bahrain Dispute," *Indian Journal of International Law* 12, no. 1 (1972):1-14. See also *Persian Gulf,* pp. 50-54.

endorsed the report of a mission that was sent to Bahrain from March 29 to April 18. The report stated that "the overwhelming majority of the people of Bahrain wished to gain recognition of their identity in a fully independent and sovereign State free to decide for itself its relations with other States." A resolution, identical to the Security Council's resolution, was introduced to the Majlis and the Senate; on May 14 the former approved the action of the government 184 to 4; all sixty members of the Senate voted in its favor on May 18.

India was chosen as the place for the announcement of the shah's decision on Bahrain in order to gain Indian support as well. During a ten-day visit to that country he made his policy statement dramatically. The visit to India represented the shah's first major attempt to link his concern with the Persian Gulf situation to that of South Asia. He told Premier Indira Gandhi that Iran would not brook outsiders in the Persian Gulf when Britain withdrew its troops in 1971. More important, the shah received endorsement of his gulf policy toward great powers. The communiqué issued at the end of January 2-13, 1969, visit stated in part, "The two leaders affirmed that the preservation of peace and stability in the Persian Gulf is the exclusive responsibility of the littoral states and there should be no interference by outside powers."[48]

While the shah's diplomacy concerning Bahrain was making steady progress between the announcement of the British decision in January 1968 and the actual withdrawal of British forces in 1971, the prospects for accommodation with Iraq worsened more than ever before. As noted previously, the 'Arif-Shah summit meeting seemed to produce some agreement between the two countries in 1967, and even as late as June 1968 Premier Tahir Yahia's visit to Iran seemed to be accompanied by hopeful signs of accommodation. But the fall of 'Abd al-Rahman 'Arif's regime on July 17, 1968, faced Iran with still a new regime in Iraq—the regime of Col. Ahmad Hasan al-Bakr. In the hope of salvaging what agreements had been previously reached, Iran extended immediate recognition to the new regime, and the Iraqi ambassador in Tehran conveyed to the Iranian government his country's appreciation for Iran's rapid move and the new regime's intention to expand relations with Iran. Asked what would happen to the agreements recently concluded between Iran and Iraq before the recent coup, the Iraqi ambassador said the new regime had already declared that it would abide by all international agreements concluded by Iraq before the "change."[49] On July 24 the new Iraqi premier stated in Baghdad that many ties bound his country with Iran, and "we will do everything in our power to further strengthen these ties." And finally on February 1, 1969, talks on the settlement of outstanding disputes between Iran and

[48]*Kayhan* (Daily English), Jan. 3, 14, 1969.

[49]Ibid., July 23, 1968.

Iraq began in Baghdad after a series of meetings between senior officials from the two countries, including the latest visit to Iran by Iraqi Deputy Premier and Defense Minister Takriti and Foreign Minister Shaikhli.

These developments, however, marked the lull before the storm. The lull might have been desired by Iraq while it was considering troop commitments to the creation of the "Eastern Front" in cooperation with Jordan and Syria vis-à-vis Israel. And the storm might have been welcomed by Iran in the knowledge that some six thousand Iraqi troops were engaged elsewhere. The over-zealous Ba'thist regime tried to check the papers of ships moving up the Shatt al-Arab, a right that Iraq had not previously exercised. Its effort to do so sparked the crisis on April 15, 1969.[50] The Iraqi deputy foreign minister told the Iranian ambassador in Baghdad that the government of Iraq "considers the Shatt al-Arab as an integral part of Iraqi territory." He demanded that vessels carrying the Iranian flag lower their flags before entering the river and that no Iranian navy personnel be aboard ships entering the Shatt. He further warned that if these demands were not met, Iraq would use force and in the future would not allow vessels destined for Iranian ports to use the river. In response, the Iranian government declared on April 19 that the relevant 1937 treaty between Iran and Iraq was "valueless, ineffective, and non-valid" legally because of Iraq's alleged nonadherence to the treaty for thirty-two years and because of "change of circumstances" (*Rebus Sic Stantibus*). At the same time Iran declared its "inclination" and preparedness to "start immediate negotiations, even tomorrow, with the Government of Iraq for the consolidation of the frontiers in Arvand Rud [the Iranian designation for Shatt al-Arab] on the basis of [the] thalweg line, which is the accepted international principle, and to sign a new treaty." Insofar as the Iraqi threat of force was concerned, the Iranian statement declared that if at any time "there should be any attempt to insult the imperial Flag of Iran or any prevention is made against the free passage of ships in Arvand Rud any of such actions will be met with a severe reaction," and Iraq would be responsible for any grave consequences" that might result from their "aggressive policy."[51]

The crisis reached a new height when Iran tried to test the Iraqi determination to interfere with the passage of ships flying Iranian flags. On April 22, 1969, and again on April 25 the Iranian freighters *Ibn-i Sina*, and *Arya Far* negotiated without incident the Shatt al-Arab while escorted by elements of the Iranian navy and covered by an umbrella of jet fighters. Iraq took the position that it would not "be drawn into a war with Iran." The Iraqi ambassador in Tehran did not deny the news that Arab states pressured Iraq to focus its attention on the struggle with Israel and not to seek a quarrel

[50]*New York Times*, May 25, 1969.

[51]For the text of the Iranian statement see *Kayhan* (Daily English), Apr. 28, 1969.

with Iran; he disclaimed knowledge of the details but stated that he was sure all Arab countries wished a peaceful and speedy settlement of the Shatt dispute. No such prospects were in sight, however. At the diplomatic level Iran's offer of negotiations would be accepted, Iraq replied, only if Iran retracted its decision to abrogate the 1937 treaty. Iran took the position, on May 3, 1969, that the treaty was "worthless" and that "no power can reimpose it on Iran." At other levels the cold war between Iran and Iraq was resumed with greater intensity than during the Qasim regime through propaganda, deportation of Iranian nationals in Iraq, expulsion of thousands of Iranian residents and pilgrims from Iraq, detention of diplomatic personnel by Iraq, and similar acts.[52]

The eruption of this ancient problem in 1969, however, went far beyond the issues long associated with the Shatt al-Arab dispute. The basic power conflict between Iraq and Iran intensified after the announcement of the British decision in 1968 despite attempts at negotiating differences over the Shatt al-Arab, the status of Iranian residents, and similar issues. The crisis all the more brought out the conflicting ambitions of the two neighboring nations in the Persian Gulf. President Ahmad Hasan al-Bakr linked Iran's action in the Shatt al-Arab to the Arab conflict with Israel and the Iraqi regime's conflict with the Barazani Kurds. He denounced Iran's "illegal ambitions in Iraqi territory and waters as well as in the Arabian Gulf," and said that Iran's moves as well as "Barazani guerrilla movements in the north" were attempts to force Iraq to withdraw troops from the Israeli front.[53] At the same time the Iraqi radio went all out in psychological warfare, alleging popular uprisings in Khuzistan. Quite apart from the Iraqi agitations regarding Khuzistan, at the time of the crisis Iranian military personnel were also concerned with Russian activities in Iraq. They believed that Soviet personnel in civilian clothes were serving with Iraqi forces, that Russian minesweepers, flying Soviet colors, were training Iraqi naval crews in Basra, and that Soviet naval vessels had called at Fao and Basra.[54]

The shah's troubles with the al-Bakr regime did not stop Iran from taking a firm stand against Iraq after the crisis and at the same time offering peaceful accommodation with Baghdad. In countering allegations of imperialism and domination, the shah declared in early June 1969 that Iran had "no colonial designs" in the Persian Gulf, that it was prepared to sign a defensive alliance with all the states of the region to insure its stability after the British military withdrawal in 1971, and at the same time he had been proved right to build

[52]*New York Times,* May 19, 1969, and Ramazani, *Persian Gulf,* pp. 44-45.

[53]*New York Times,* May 19, 1969.

[54]The account is based on remarks made by several Iranian naval officers to the correspondent of the *Christian Science Monitor,* June 5, 1969.

up Iran's military strength to meet the challenge of "adventurist" regimes in the Middle East. "I was right in the past," he told the *Washington Post*'s correspondent; think what "the Iraqis could do today with their torpedo boats in the Persian Gulf if we did not have the power to retaliate."[55] Iran's firm stand against Baghdad was supported by Turkey also in June at the end of Prime Minister Hoveyda's visit to Turkey to explain the situation. King Hasan II of Morocco also supported Iran's stand on the Shatt al-Arab river dispute. Iran also continued to take initiative in offering ways of settling its differences with Iraq. The principal reason for this was Iran's fear that the conflict might push Iraq further and more rapidly toward the Soviet Union. On February 6, 1970, the Turkish deputy foreign minister gave a report to the Iranian Ministry of Foreign Affairs after his talks with the Iraqi minister, Mahdi Ammash, on his visit to Ankara.[56] Iran offered through the Turkish Deputy Foreign Minister Orhan Eralp to withdraw its troops from the Iraqi frontier provided Baghdad showed a willingness to take reciprocal action.

Iran's unresolved conflict with Iraq in light of the imminent departure of British forces from the Persian Gulf spurred Iran's efforts toward maintaining and creating further support for its position in the Persian Gulf within and outside the region. The Iranian Parliament's endorsement of the wish of the people of Bahrain to gain recognition of their identity in a "fully independent and sovereign State" on May 14-18, 1970, mentioned before, was followed by strenuous efforts to befriend Bahrain even before it was declared independent. Iran dispatched a goodwill mission, headed by Manuchihr Zilli, to the island in the same month, received a Bahraini mission for the first time on June 13, 1970; abolished visa requirements between the two countries on June 30; and finally a year later signed a continental shelf accord during the visit of the Iranian foreign minister to Bahrain. Tehran considered the agreement to be of major importance because of the number of offshore oil deposits in the demarcated area. Manama also regarded the agreement as significant, and it was believed that the two countries might cooperate in searching for oil and its exploitation in several fields bordering the demarcation line. When Bahrain was declared independent on August 14, 1971, Iran was "the first nation" to recognize it only one hour after its announcement.[57]

Qatar was the other gulf state that eventually gained its independence outside the framework of the Union of Arab Emirates (UAE), as will be seen. Iran also tried to befriend Qatar before the British withdrawal; it signed a

[55] *Kayhan* (Weekly English), June 14, 1969.

[56] *Ittila'at Hava'i*, Feb. 7, 1970.

[57] Ramazani, *Persian Gulf*, pp. 55-56.

continental shelf agreement with the sheikhdom on September 20, 1969, similar to the agreement with Saudi Arabia.[58] In April 1970 Sheik Ahmad bin'Ali al-Thani, the ruler of Qatar, paid his first state visit to Iran, speaking, on his arrival, of the "common objective" between Iran and "Qatar in stability and security and welfare in the Persian Gulf region. When Qatar declared its independence from Britain on September 1, 1971, barely one hour later, as in the case of Bahrain, the shah recognized it by cable. And as in the case of Bahrain, Iran styled itself as the first state in the world to recognize the independence of Qatar.

In his concerted effort to gain supporters for Iran's policy within the gulf and the Middle East area, the shah created further ties with Kuwait and resumed diplomatic relations with Lebanon. During a two-day visit to Kuwait of the Iranian foreign minister, Ardishir Zahidi, beginning July 5, 1970, Iran and Kuwait finally agreed to sign a continental shelf agreement. More important, the foreign minister's visit at the time was precipitated by Iran's strong opposition to the possibility of the British Conservative government's change of mind, as will be seen, in withdrawing from the Persian Gulf. None of the Arab states of the gulf had yet revealed its reaction to the British news, and Iran sought to insure that like-minded states, such as Kuwait and Saudi Arabia, would also oppose a new British position. The Kuwaiti foreign minister declared at the time that his country "supported Iran's policy in regard to the departure of British forces from the Persian Gulf."[59] The Iraqi's dormant claim to Kuwait and the prospective termination of Britain's defense agreement with Kuwait made Kuwait a particular object of Iran's attention at the time. Iran's diplomatic rupture with Lebanon had occurred over the problem of the extradition of Gen. Taimur Bakhtiar, former head of the Iranian security police. In light of the imminent British withdrawal, the shah preferred to resume diplomatic relations with old friends of Iran, like Lebanon. Camille Chamoun, former president of Lebanon, who had enjoyed Iran's support in the 1950s, had an audience with the shah in July 1971. He stated at a press conference that the shah "has graciously ordered that relations between Iran and Lebanon should be resumed." "The bad times" in the relations of the two countries were over, and "the doors" were open for "fresh fruitful co-operation," he declared.

Iran's most dramatic tactical move before the British departure, however, was the resumption of diplomatic relations after ten years of rupture with Nasir's Egypt. As noted previously, the clash between the shah and President Gamal 'Abd al-Nasir dated back to the early 1950s, although the rupture of

[58]For the text of the continental shelf agreement with Qatar, see *Ittila'at Hava'i,* Nov. 30, 1969.

[59]*Kayhan* (Weekly English), July 11, 1970, and *Ittila'at Hava'i,* July 6-9, 1970.

diplomatic relations between the two countries finally took place in 1960, ostensibly over Israel. As also noted Iran's policies in the Persian Gulf collided with the Pan-Arab aspirations of President Nasir in the area. As late as May 1967, before the Arab-Israeli war, the shah disclaimed any "hostility" toward the Egyptian "people" in an interview with a German correspondent, but he singled out President Nasir, charging that his policies in the past ten years or so had "always been aggressive, dangerous, inhuman," and then proceeded to state that "the Persian Gulf is a vital area and our life depends on it. All the northern Gulf areas are in our hands. Egypt is hundreds of kilometers away from this area; it has no business here. We have enough experience with Egyptian imperialism, or better yet, the Egyptian leader's imperialism."[60]

Against such a background of psychological warfare, the decision to resume diplomatic relations with Egypt in 1970 called for an explanation. One explanation was that the attitude of Iran in the Arab-Israeli conflict of 1967 had helped to heal old wounds. In the wake of the June war the shah had called for the restoration of Arab territories to Arab states by Israel, and simultaneously the "Red Lion and Sun," the Iranian equivalent of the Red Cross (*shir va khorshid-i sorkh*), dispatched medical and similar aids to Iraq and Jordan. When the managing director of the "Red Lion and Sun" was asked whether similar aid could be sent to Egypt and Syria, he declared that it would be done as a humanitarian responsibility regardless of political attitudes of their governments.[61] The other explanation of the resumption of diplomatic relations with Egypt pointed to the impact of the conflict between Cairo and Baghdad. The Egyptian-Iraqi relations had deteriorated ever since the rise of al-Bakr to power in Iraq and President Nasir's acceptance of the United States Middle East cease-fire initiative of June 19, 1970 (the "Rogers Plan," named after Secretary of State William Rogers).[62]

Both these explanations make sense and probably contributed to the resumption of diplomatic relations, but neither really explains the fundamental consideration underlying the Iranian attitude. In the context of this study, it is quite apparent that the Iranian move fitted perfectly the pattern of the shah's determined efforts to seek accommodation with as many Middle Eastern states as possible with a view to the departure of the British in 1971. Egypt had always been considered the principal Arab state and one whose friendship could serve Iran's best interests. At the moment Iran's greatest interest was to insure that if its negotiations with Britain for the acquisition of the islands of Abu Musa and the two Tumbs failed, its planned unilateral military action for regaining the islands would not be roundly condemned by Arab states. The

[60]*Ittila'at Hava'i,* May 11, 1967.

[61]Ibid., June 11, 12, 1967.

[62]Ibid., Aug. 25, 1970.

pattern of cultivating Arab states was perfectly clear by 1970, as evidenced by the ties already established with Saudi Arabia, Kuwait, Bahrain, Qatar, Lebanon, and the Trucial States. The same consideration undergirded Iran's search for Indian, Pakistani, and Turkish support for its Persian Gulf policy. As we shall see, the resumption of diplomatic relations with Egypt, the leading Arab state, paid off handsomely when Iran finally landed troops on the three disputed islands in the Persian Gulf; Egypt evinced a moderately adverse reaction as compared with Iraq, Libya, Algeria, and South Yemen.

The earliest signal for resumption of diplomatic relations was given by the shah himself. In an exclusive interview granted to the Tunisian daily *L'Action*, it was reported by *Kayhan* on January 7, 1970, that the shah said since it was Egypt that "insulted" Iran and broke off diplomatic relations in 1960, Egypt should now come forward to make a resumption of relations possible. Upon arrival in Amman, the Iranian foreign minister, Ardishir Zahidi, stated on May 31, 1970, that considering the improved attitudes in Tehran and Cairo since the Arab-Israeli conflict of June 1967, and "particularly in the past few months," he would think that King Husain, like other interested leaders, could also be helpful in the resumption of relations between Iran and Egypt.[63] On June 16, 1970, Amir Muhammad Isfandiari, a high-ranking Iranian diplomat, arrived in Cairo to pave the way for resumption of relations with Iran while his Egyptian counterpart was already doing the same in Tehran. Finally, on August 29, 1970, the two nations formally resumed diplomatic relations. At the time it was reported that this had followed the mediation efforts by the Libyan foreign minister, which had been preceded by similar efforts by Turkey, Afghanistan, Jordan, and Kuwait at different intervals. Immediately after the announcement of the resumption of diplomatic relations in Cairo, Radio Baghdad launched a "violent" attack on President Nasir, accusing him of "stabbing Iraq in the back." Nasir was accused of pursuing "a policy of compromise with imperialism [that is, acceptance of the Rogers Plan] over Palestine and with Iran over the Persian Gulf."[64] Iran was not tardy in seeking Egyptian support for its Persian Gulf policy. As was suggested, this was the basic reason for resumption of diplomatic relations. Premier Hoveyda did not miss the opportunity to broach the Persian Gulf question with the Egyptian leaders while in Cairo attending Nasir's funeral. The Egyptian foreign minister reportedly stated that his government supported the Iranian policy in the Persian Gulf and it, too, demanded the withdrawal of the British troops from this area.[65] More important, during his five-day official visit to Egypt in May

[63]Ibid., May 31, 1970.

[64]*Kayhan* (Weekly English), Aug. 29, 1970.

[65]See *Ittila'at Hava'i,* Oct. 13, 1970.

1971, the Iranian foreign minister said everything that could reveal Iran's determination to "regain" the islands of Abu Musa and the two Tumbs. He stated that Iran would not allow Britain to undermine its sovereign rights over three key islands in the gulf. He stated that these islands had been taken by force over seventy years ago, that this occupation did not change their status, and that London's efforts aimed at involving certain small emirates (Sharja and Ras al-Khaima) in the question would fail, and that the dispute was one solely concerning Iran and the United Kingdom.[66] This last point was aimed at separating Arab concern from the future of the three islands by playing up the struggle against the British.

As noted, from the very outset Iran had linked its claims to Bahrain and the islands of Abu Musa and the two Tumbs to the recognition of the British-sponsored Arab federation. Once the Bahrain problem was tactfully settled, Iran then made the settlement of its claim to the three islands the prerequisite of its recognition of the prospective Arab federation, and all these, of course, had been premised on the British timetable to withdraw forces from the Persian Gulf in 1971. For a brief period, however, this premise was called into question when it was made known that the new British Conservative government might reverse the plans of the previous Labour government for the withdrawal. Iran's opposition was made abundantly clear by Iranian leaders. Premier Hoveyda told a UPI correspondent, when asked about the news of a possible change in British policy, that he was "inclined to believe that the present government realizes full well that the historical situation which led to a British military presence in the Persian Gulf has changed." He also reiterated that the "security of the region must rest only in the hands of the littoral states and emirates of the Persian Gulf and no outside interference should be allowed there."[67] The specific reference to the emirates was intended to warn that Iran was opposed to the British stay there and the islands that Iran claimed. The shah himself opposed the British stay in July 1970 at a press conference in Helsinki. He simply stated that "the era of colonialism is over" and did not see by what "right" one country could stay in another country without invitation, without a mandate from the United Nations, or without a treaty. Upon his return from the United Nations General Assembly meeting in 1970, the Iranian foreign minister gave the impression in Tehran that he had reached an "understanding" with his British counterpart, Sir Alec Douglas-Home, on the question of foreign troops in the Persian Gulf. That is, the British had finally come around to agreeing with Iran's firm opposition to any attempts at continuing British military presence in the Persian Gulf. And Iran finally declared its satisfaction in

[66]*Kayhan* (Weekly English), May 22, 1971.

[67]Ibid., June 27, 1970.

March 1971 over the Conservative government's upholding of its predecessor's decision to withdraw from the gulf in 1971.

Having overcome this momentary hurdle, Iran once again reiterated its claims to the three islands in June 1971, but this time with the first public indication of its intention to regain these islands by force if negotiations with the British failed. The year of decision was 1971. The shah stated on June 24, 1971, that the islands belonged to Iran; they had been "grabbed" some eighty years ago when Iran had no central government; his father had sent gunboats to recover them, but the British assured Iran that neither side would raise the flag till the question was settled. He then added: "I hope this happens now. Otherwise we have no alternative but to take the islands by force." In the same interview, the shah denied the applicability of his approach to Bahrain to Iran's claim to these islands, claiming that Bahrain had a population, but these islands "have no such problem." The same warning about Iran's intention to resort to force if it could not settle the problem with Britain before their departure was voiced soon thereafter by Premier Hoveyda and Foreign Minister Zahidi. As I have shown elsewhere, Iran continued negotiations with Britain as late as November 21, 1971, but because negotiations were secret it was impossible when I was writing to state whether an agreement had been reached with the British before their departure.[68] Nearly two years later 'Abbas Masudi, the well-known editor of the semiofficial *Ittila'at* and senator, who had repeatedly visited the heads of Persian Gulf states, declared on May 12, 1973, that he would "divulge" the events regarding the three islands. He referred to the long history of Iran's claim to these islands and admitted that it was intensified after the settlement of the Bahrain dispute with Britain. He then stated that Iran continued negotiations with Britain regarding the "restoration" (*istirdad*) of these islands to Iran, with Sir William Luce representing Britain in these discussions. These discussions led to an agreement between Iran and Sharja concerning the island of Abu Musa, "but regarding the two Tumbs neither Iran nor Britain considered the consent of the sheikh of Ras al-Khaima necessary. For this reason the negotiations between Iran and Britain concluded that Iran could regain its two islands after the British withdrawal. But Iran wished to regain its islands at the time of the British presence, it did so a day before the British departure."[69]

On November 30, 1971, Iran landed forces on the three islands, only twenty-four hours after Sharja announced agreement with Iran on the island

[68] For details see Ramazani, *Persian Gulf,* pp. 59-60.

[69] My translation from the Persian report. See *Ittila'at Hava'i,* May 12, 1973. I have difficulty in concluding, from an informal conversation with Sir William Luce on Sept. 29, 1973, that Masudi's account can necessarily be construed as reflecting the British view on the matter as well.

of Abu Musa. Later Iran claimed that not only Sharja but also Ras al-Khaima "were aware of the landing of Iranian forces." The Iranian foreign minister, 'Abbas'Ali Khal'atbary, stated subsequently that Iran's entire undertaking to retrieve the islands through long negotiations was designed to avoid bloodshed, and regretted the incident on Greater Tumb. Still in keeping with its drive to maintain influence with gulf states, Iran was quick to recognize the government of the Union of Arab Emirates in the wake of its formation. Britain had departed, and Iran was already in possession of the three islands, and thus there was no further reason to stand by the tactical negative attitude toward the federation. Abu Dhabi, Dubai, Sharja, Ajman, Fujaira, and Umm al-Qaywayn formed the union on December 2, 1971, without Ras al-Khaima at the time, but it, too, later joined the union. On the same day the shah recognized the union within an hour, as with Bahrain and Qatar previously.

The Arab reaction was not uniformly intense, although it was universally adverse.[70] Understandably the swiftest and most violent reaction came from Baghdad, which immediately broke diplomatic relations with Iran and Britain, accusing the latter of failing its obligations toward the Arab emirates and of collusion with Iran. Algeria, Libya, South Yemen (in addition to the sheikh of Ras al-Khaima) denounced Iran and joined Iraq in lodging a complaint with the United Nations Security Council.[71] Libya also nationalized British oil interests on December 7, 1971, charged Irano-British collusion, and created a Libyan state-controlled oil concern by the name of the Arabian Gulf Company Ltd. It had also planned, reportedly, to land troops on the three islands before the Iranians moved in. The most significant reaction, however, emanated from Cairo. Preoccupation with the conflict with Israel might have been responsible for Egypt's moderate stand, but Iran's previous resumption of diplomatic relations with Cairo after a ten-year break had been a farsighted and timely move. Although Egypt called for the evacuation of Iranian troops from the islands and although it pledged cooperation with other Arab states for the preservation of the "Arab character" of the islands, it refused to join the several Arab states mentioned above to complain to the United Nations; it also chose not to follow the example of Iraq in breaking diplomatic relations with Iran. The same Egyptian moderation held within the Arab League, which called for an emergency session on December 2 and met December 5-7. The Iraqi proposal within the league for rupture of diplomatic relations with Iran by all Arab states equally failed. Egyptian leadership within the league was also helpful on this score as well, not to speak of the attitudes of Saudi Arabia and other Arab states whose friendship Iran had cultivated so carefully for a day such as this.

[70] For details see Ramazani, *Persian Gulf,* pp. 63-66.

[71] For details see ibid., pp. 66-67.

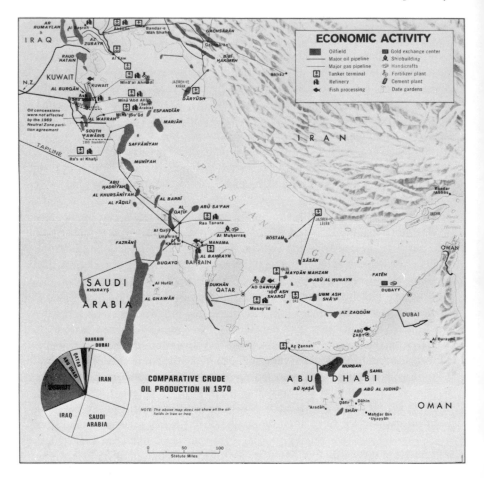

Kuwait, Bahrain, Qatar, and United Arab Emirates. U.S., Central Intelligence Agency, Washington, D.C.: Government Printing Office, April 1972.

In preparation for the British withdrawal, Iran quietly built up its military strength, as seen, with the assistance of the United States, particularly after 1969.[72] It should also be recalled from previous discussions that the American contribution of squadrons of the late-model Phantom jet fighter-bombers was matched by British tanks and naval units. Secret deliveries of American and British weapons to Iran in 1969-70 was matched by Iran's open diplomacy ever since the announcement of the British decision in January 1968 for gaining support for its policies in the Persian Gulf and the Middle East. Despite all the sincere talk about Iran's willingness to maintain the security of the Persian Gulf collectively with other gulf states, Iran realized the serious limits of such an undertaking in light of the realities of the gulf situation. The Iranian security policy in the region, therefore, showed that Iran would maintain gulf security in cooperation with other gulf states if it could but would go it alone if it must. The diverse interpretations of Iran and Sharja of their agreement regarding Abu Musa and the absence of Ras al-Khaima's consent in landing Iranian troops on the two Tumbs remained as potential sources of Iranian difficulties in the future.[73] At the time the overriding concern with security prevailed in the lower part of the Persian Gulf close to the strategic Strait of Hormuz, which was not only Iran's lifeline but also the petroleum artery of the Western world and Japan.

Consolidation of Iran's Position after the British Withdrawal

After the British departure, Iran's Persian Gulf policy began to undergo dramatic changes. The first serious and public indication of this change was given by the shah in an interview granted to three Swiss and two American journalists on January 15, 1972. When asked whether he considered the defense of the Persian Gulf as separable or inseparable from the defense of the Indian Ocean in general, he replied: "Naturally, if the Indian Ocean becomes troubled we shall feel the effects and counter-effects. There is no doubt about that." Furthermore, when asked if he intended to establish bases farther afield, in the Gulf of Oman, for example, he replied: "The reinforcement of our military position on our own territory—which borders on the Gulf of Oman—will depend on the situation prevailing in the Gulf of Oman, the Arabian Sea and the Indian Ocean."[74] Subsequently, in a major speech on the fortieth anniversary of the Iranian navy in November 1972, the shah for

---

[72]See chapter 15 of this study.

[73]For details see Ramazani, *Persian Gulf,* pp. 67-68.

[74]For the text see *Kayhan* (Weekly English), Jan. 29, 1972.

the first time definitely indicated the expansion of Iran's "security perimeter."
He stated that the frontiers of Iran went beyond the Persian Gulf and the
Gulf of Oman into the Indian Ocean. He told the Iranian navy that its "strik-
ing power" would increase "several times over" within the next two years.
The changes, he indicated, would be qualitative as well as quantitative. For
Iran to be safe it should look far beyond its own immediate region. He
admitted that until three or four years before he only had the defense of the
Persian Gulf in mind, but "then came events that forced us to think of the
Gulf of Oman and Iran's coast there. Then other events in the world taught us
that the sea contiguous to the Gulf of Oman, and I mean the Indian Ocean,
recognizes no frontiers." Hence, Iran was no longer merely thinking of
defending Abadan, Khosrowabad, Bushire, or even Hormuz and Bandar Abbas.
"We are not even thinking merely of defending Jask and Chah-Bahar," the
shah declared. "We are thinking of Iran's security perimeter [*harim-i amniyat*]
and I am not speaking in terms of a few kilometers. Anyone versed in
geographical, strategic matters and especially in possibilities of naval and air
forces of today would guess how distant that frontier could be from Chah-
Bahar."[75]

The shah did not elaborate what events specifically prompted the decision
to spread the Iranian defense umbrella beyond the Persian Gulf and the Gulf
of Oman, but *Kayhan's* "political correspondent" revealed the rationale of
the Iranian decision. Four main reasons were given for the shah's new
declaration: the Indian invasion of Pakistan and the implications of it for
South Asia; a South Yemeni-supported attack on an oil tanker off the island
of Perim; the Dhofari rebellion supported by South Yemen; and the role of
the Soviet Union in the Indian Ocean. The last consideration—that is, the role
of the Soviet Union—was played down by citing simply two divergent views
on the Soviet role in the Indian Ocean: the British view that the Soviets were
"all out to dominate the ocean as a means of encircling China while also
holding Western trade interests in ransom"; and the view that held that "the
Soviet Union is neither in a position nor urgently interested in getting involved
in a nineteenth century style power struggle in the Indian Ocean." The
writer then concluded that Iran was determined to play it safe by spreading
the defense umbrella of the navy and the air force to the whole of the Gulf of
Oman. "Beyond that little is known of Iran's intentions. But it is certain that
from now on Iran will seek a position from which it will be able to operate
much further afield. That is necessary for nipping in the bud any threat that
might appear on the horizon without waiting for it to reach our very
doorsteps."[76]

[75] For the text of the shah's statement, see *Ittila'at Hava'i,* Nov. 6, 1972. See also
Kayhan (Weekly English), Nov. 11, 1972.

[76] *Kayhan* (Weekly English), Nov. 18, 1972.

The shah's silence on the fundamental consideration underlying the expansion of Iran's "security perimeter," like the *Kayhan* political correspondent's playing-down of the role of the Soviet Union in the Indian Ocean, only represented the kind of dilemma in which Iran found itself. It had developed, by November 1972 when the shah announced his new "security perimeter," unprecedented commercial, technical, and economic ties with the Soviet Union after its missile bases pledge of 1962 and the normalization of relations with Moscow. Expansion of Soviet stakes economically in Iran would, it was hoped, place a brake on the development of close ties between Moscow and Baghdad. But as it turned out the process of Soviet-Iraqi rapprochement was intensified with the announcement of the British decision in 1968 and the rise of the al-Bakr regime in Iraq in the same year. That process finally resulted in the Soviet-Iraqi treaty of April 9, 1972, which, as seen, dealt the single heaviest blow to Irano-Soviet relations since the crisis of 1958-59.

Iran's deep concern with the expansion of Soviet influence at the head of the Persian Gulf began to be paralleled by its growing alarm with the expansion of Soviet naval power in the Indian Ocean and the Arabian Sea, with far-reaching implications for the Persian Gulf. Iran's traditional concern with Russia had always been primarily land-centered—whether the Russian move southward focused in Azerbaijan or Khorasan. Iran had traditionally thought of Russia as a land-power, challenging the security of extensive Iranian frontiers primarily in the north. But ever since 1968 the Iranian navy had been observing Soviet activities in the Indian Ocean. Iranian naval officers did not wish to identify the Soviets as "the enemy," but when pressed, they revealed concern over the Soviet Union's advances in the Indian Ocean. The Soviet navy had made six appearances in the gulf since 1968, when Britain announced its decision to withdraw, according to Iranian naval sources. On each occasion the Soviet ships paid courtesy calls at the Iraqi base of Um Qasr. Soviet freighters, however, passed "continuously" through the gulf, mostly with arms and oil equipment for Iraq, Iranians believed.[77] After the landing of Iranian forces on the Persian Gulf islands of Abu Musa and the two Tumbs, Iran began to conceive of its security in terms of not only the strategic Strait of Hormuz, in the lower part of the gulf, but also the waters that lay beyond. To Iran the strait was one of many choke points in the vast area from the Straits of Malacca to Bab al-Mandab, at the southern entrance to the Red Sea. The transfer of the headquarters of Iran's gulf fleet from Khoramshahr, forty-five miles upriver from the head of the gulf on the Iraqi border, to Bandar Abbas at the mouth of the gulf would be a helpful strategic move, but the security of the Strait of Hormuz could hardly be conceived in isolation from the connecting international waterways on which Iranian trade and communication interests depended. With the Soviet naval presence in the Indian Ocean on the increase,

[77] *New York Times*, Jan. 25, 1972.

Iran feared that it might have to face Russia for the first time in history in the south as well as the north, if the Soviet presence in the Indian Ocean were to be extended into the Persian Gulf.

Iran's desire to see the Indian Ocean kept free of great-power rivalry first found expression in Premier Hoveyda's extension of Iran's hands-off policy in the Persian Gulf to the Indian Ocean. Speaking on December 4, 1972, at a banquet in honor of the visiting premier of Mauritius, he declared. We hope that the Indian Ocean which forms so important a world maritime trade route will remain free of big power hegemony and competition."[78] Meanwhile, Iran was seeking naval facilities from Mauritius, whose premier told reporters in Tehran that although Mauritius was not allowing big powers to have military bases on the island, it would welcome Iran's request for naval facilities. The Iranian prime minister was properly expressing a "hope," because in Washington it was believed by at least one high official that the Soviet naval presence in the Indian Ocean was already "an established fact." The statement was made by Ronald I. Spiers, director, Bureau of Politico-Military Affairs, to the Subcommittee on National Security Policy and Scientific Developments of the House Committee on Foreign Affairs, on July 28, 1972, only a few months before the shah's statement on the Indian Ocean.[79]

While it remained to be seen what, in fact, Iran could do to keep the vast waterways of the Indian Ocean free of Soviet hegemony or great-power competition, Iran reached far beyond the Persian Gulf region for the support of the People's Republic of China as a counterbalance to the Soviet Union in the Persian Gulf area. The earliest public indication of the shah's changing attitude toward China was his statement to the Karachi newspaper *Dawn,* in September 1969. "Although we do not recognize the People's Republic of China," he stated, "we believe that China must be admitted into the United Nations."[80] To be sure, Iran's changing attitude toward the admission of China into the United Nations reflected in part the attitudes and policies of an increasing number of states about the Chinese admission. But Iran also had its own reason and timetable. The British forces were to withdraw in 1971 from the Persian Gulf and Iran wished to have the support of China for its Persian Gulf policy. Given the fact of Soviet presence in the Indian Ocean and frequent naval visits to the Persian Gulf and the Iraqi port of Um Qasr, the establishment of friendly relations with Moscow's arch-rival seemed desirable.

[78]*Kayhan* (Weekly English), Dec. 9, 1972.

[79]
    For the text of the statement by Ronald I. Spiers, see U.S. State Dept. *Bulletin* 65, no. 1678 (Aug. 23, 1972): 199-203.

[80]*Kayhan* (Weekly English), Sept. 6, 1969.

Within the United Nations Iran abstained from voting on the China question in 1970, but it explained its vote by stating that it did so because the resolution for admission of the People's Republic of China also called for the expulsion of the Nationalist Chinese. The sisters of the shah, Princess Ashraf and Princess Fatimih, visited China on separate occasions in 1971, as the first step in the direction of establishing diplomatic relations with China. In a press interview with a Japanese newspaper, the shah stated that the Chinese invitation to his sister Princess Ashraf had come at the time the American pingpong players were invited to China. In the same interview, in April 1971, he stated that Iran had been studying the problem of recognition of China because a nation of some eight hundred million people could not be overlooked. How could one ignore, he asked, a country with such a population and thermonuclear capability?[81] Iran's decision to establish diplomatic relations with China came only a few months before the departure of British forces from the Persian Gulf. The decision was announced officially on August 17, 1971, in Tehran and Peking simultaneously. According to the joint statement, Iran and China had agreed to exchange ambassadors "in the shortest possible time."[82] Iranians also believed that Iran thus recognized the People's Republic of China as "the only lawful government of China."[83] Shortly before noon on August 16 the Taipei government was informed of Iran's decision. Iran had also committed itself to voting in favor of Peking's admission to the United Nations but had said that it would not approve of the expulsion of Taiwan from the world organization.

The exchange of ambassadors between Iran and China did not take place as quickly as Iran had wished, but when the time finally came some seven months after the establishment of diplomatic relations, Iran appointed one of its foremost diplomats and a former foreign minister as its first ambassador to China. 'Abbas Aram was appointed Iranian ambassador to China on March 12, 1972, and the Chinese ambassador to Tehran presented his credentials to the shah on April 4, 1972. Even before the actual exchange of ambassadors, Iran and China began to explore expanding their relations in a variety of fields, including air communication, trade, and petroleum sale to China. On April 17, 1972, Iran signed an important air agreement with China. China would thereby open its first international airline, in a linkup with Europe via Tehran. It was expected that air services between Tehran and Peking would link the two capitals through a seven-hour direct flight. On September 17, 1972, Empress Farah left Tehran for a visit to China. During her visit Iran and China declared

---

[81]*Ittila'at Hava'i,* Apr. 21, 1971.

[82]For the text of the statement see ibid., Aug. 17, 1971.

[83]*Kayhan* (Weekly English), Aug. 21, 1971.

their firm intention to build up their friendship and expand cooperation in all fields. Empress Farah and Premier Chou En-lai cited the ancient "Silk Road" as an indication of the historic commercial and cultural ties between the two nations dating back some two thousand years. Exchanges of study missions and high-ranking officials were intensified after the empress's visit to China. During a five-day visit to China, the Iranian minister of economy, Hushang Ansari, succeeded in signing in Peking on April 8, 1973, the first trade and payment agreement between Iran and China. Although a barter agreement, for the first time rials were accepted as the basis of accounts.[84] Iranian exports to China included chemical fertilizers, agricultural equipment, and buses and trucks, while Chinese exports to Iran included papers, stationeries, tea, and fabrics.

The linkage between Iran's bilateral relations with China and the Persian Gulf situation was beginning to become increasingly apparent as time went on. According to Ambassador Aram, both Iran and China were considering, for example, the creation of a shipping line linking the Persian Gulf to China. With the signing of the first trade and payments agreement, Irano-Chinese trade was expected to increase rapidly during the following five years. A shipping line of that kind then would make all the more sense. There was, nevertheless, little doubt in Tehran that it was not so easy to expand the Chinese trade in view of the limited number of commodities that the two nations could barter. The question of oil sale to China was studied, and it remained to be seen what would become of it. Meanwhile, Iran reaped the first direct benefit of its new relations with China. On June 16, 1973, the shah received for the first time the Chinese foreign minister in Tehran. No communiqué was issued at the end of his visit, but there was little doubt among well-informed observers in Iran that the discussions were significantly political in nature and ranged over a variety of subject matters of concern to Third World countries. More important, the Chinese foreign minister publicly and "unreservedly" (*bi choon-o chira*) endorsed Iran's policy in the Indian Ocean and the Persian Gulf, commending Iran for its steadfast determination to strengthen its forces in light of the existing situation in the region and the expansionist and conflicting ambitions of great powers.[85] From the Chinese standpoint establishing relations with Iran was a logical step in its westward move in the Middle East. With China firmly established in Pakistan, the move to establish diplomatic relations with Iran was matched in the same year by similar moves in Turkey, Kuwait, Libya, and Ethiopia. All these Chinese efforts aimed at challenging the Soviet Union in the Third World.[86] For

[84] See *Ittila'at Hava'i,* Apr. 9, 1973.

[85] Ibid., June 16, 1973.

[86] *New York Times,* Oct. 17, 1971.

example, the air agreement with Iran provided Peking with a direct air route to its allies in Rumania and Albania, bypassing the Soviet Union. But from the standpoint of Iran's foreign policy in general and the Persian Gulf policy in particular, China could prove a useful counterbalance to increasing Soviet bilateral ties with Iraq and particularly to Soviet advances in the Indian Ocean and the Persian Gulf.

Closer at home Iran's conciliatory attitude toward Afghanistan was also influenced by the situation in the Persian Gulf following the announcement of the British decision in 1968. During most of the 1950s Iran's alliance policy clashed with Afghanistan's policy of strict neutralism. The Iraqi revolution called for friendship with Iran's other neighbors. Pakistan and Turkey were Iran's allies, but Afghanistan had to be wooed. As early as 1959 the shah appointed Gen. Amanullah Jahanbani to search for a solution to the ancient dispute over the Helmand River between Iran and Afghanistan.[87] The discussions were followed up in 1960, when Premier Sardar Muhammad Daud Khan visited Iran; they were further pursued by the Iranian premier, Sharif-Imami. New agreements were reached on two major questions, one concerning Iran's oil sale to Afghanistan, December 4, 1960, and one on transit, February 1, 1962. But no agreement was reached on the Helmand River dispute.

Almost as in the case of Iran's ancient dispute with Britain over Bahrain, and more recent continental shelf disputes with Saudi Arabia, Kuwait, Qatar, and Bahrain, the Helmand River dispute with Afghanistan was nearly resolved fundamentally in the light of the Persian Gulf situation. After the British withdrawal from the gulf and the Indo-Pakistani war in 1971, the settlement of the age-old dispute with Afghanistan seemed all the more important. Iran wished to concentrate attention on difficulties in the gulf area and to be able to mediate, as the shah had done in 1962, the differences between Afghanistan and Pakistan over the problem of Pushtunistan. This festering Afghan-Pakistan problem spelled difficulties for already dismembered Pakistan. Pakistani vulnerability to the separatist movement in Baluchistan was, however, a more direct challenge to Iranian security; Baluchistan straddled the Irano-Pakistani border. The Iraqi treaty with the Soviet Union signed April 9, 1972, further intensified Iran's determination to remove the ancient Helmand River problem from its relations with Afghanistan. After some seven months of strenuous negotiations, on March 13, 1973, Iran and Afghanistan signed a treaty in Kabul in order to settle the ancient dispute. For Premier Hoveyda, who signed the treaty, it was an "unforgettable" moment. The Iranian Majlis approved it July 17, 1973. On the same day the Afghan army toppled

---

[87] For the background of the Helmand River dispute, see Ramazani, *Foreign Policy of Iran*, pp. 266-69.

vacationing King Muhammad Zahir Shah in a bloodless coup d'etat and declared Afghanistan a republic. The coup was led by former Premier Sardar Muhammad Daud Khan. On July 21, 1973, Iran recognized the new republic, and on August 1, 1973, the Iranian Senate approved the Helmand River treaty. But it remained to be seen whether the new republic would ratify the treaty because as 1973 drew to an end no favorable action was yet taken by Afghanistan in spite of improving relations between Kabul and Tehran. Meanwhile, Iran envisaged a railway link between the Persian Gulf port of Bandar Abbas and landlocked Afghanistan under its Fifth Plan.

Just as the Persian Gulf situation undergirded the resolution of so many disputes between Iran and its neighbors, it intensified Iran's friendship with Turkey and Pakistan, with which Iran already had close ties within and outside CENTO and the Regional Cooperation Development (RDC). The relations with Pakistan particularly called for strengthening in light of the Persian Gulf situation. The Indo-Pakistan war of 1971 alarmed Iran considerably because it left Iran's ally dismembered and vulnerable to the Baluchi separatist movement, as mentioned before. The real alarm bell was rung on February 10, 1973, when Pakistani police raided the Iraqi embassy and seized an estimated three hundred machine guns and sixty thousand rounds of ammunition smuggled in as diplomatic baggage from Baghdad. The arms were clearly destined for Baluchistan, which straddled the Irano-Pakistani border, but Iraq's real target was Iran.[88] Baghdad had been the haven for the Baluchi Liberation Front since 1968, and Iran's cold war with Iraq after the Iranian capture of the three Persian Gulf islands in 1971, as will be seen, had deteriorated severely. This event seemed to call for some kind of commitment by Iran to the maintenance of Pakistani security. The first indication of this was given by the Iranian ambassador to Pakistan, Manuchihr Zilli, who stated in a newspaper interview in April 1973 in Pakistan that Iran considered Pakistan's safety "vital" to its own security. During the state visit of President Zulfiqar Bhutto to Iran, the shah stated on May 11, 1973: "Once again I repeat that we shall always be on your side: we are compelled to mention that what happens to our neighbor in the east, that is, the State of Pakistan, is vitally important to us; and should another event befall that country we would not tolerate it. The reason for this is not only our fraternal affection for you as a Muslim nation, but because of Iranian interests we would not be able to tolerate other changes or difficulties in Pakistan. It is quite natural that we strongly affirm that we will not close our eyes to any secessionist movement—God forbid—in your country."[89] The semiofficial *Ittila'at* characterized the shah's informal commitment as a "defensive agreement" (*ahdnamih-ye*

[88]*Middle East Monitor,* Mar. 1, 1973, p. 1.

[89]Ibid., June 1, 1973, p. 2.

difa'i) between Iran and Pakistan. Like Iran's military aid to Oman, mentioned previously, this was another example of Iran's use of its newly acquired military capability toward the achievement of its basic objectives in the Persian Gulf area.

Iran's relations with Iraq after the capture of the three islands and the British departure took a turn for the worse. As already noted, Iraq broke its diplomatic relations with Iran immediately after the landing of Iranian forces on Abu Musa and the two Tumbs and denounced Iran violently in the Arab League and the United Nations. After the British departure a tour by a group of Western journalists of the sheikhdoms in 1972, from the important communications center of Bahrain to the poor Emirate of Ras al-Khaima, revealed that there was "no real power vacuum in the area but rather a new balance of power with the British remaining in the dominant position."[90] This view was based in part upon the fact that Britain signed friendship treaties with rulers in the lower part of the gulf and retained responsibility for training and arming the local defense. Bahrain and Qatar, as seen, declared themselves independent and stayed outside the Union of Arab Emirates. The British Forces Gulf Command, situated at Jufair, was turned over to Bahraini authorities, and only the United States Navy continued to occupy one corner of the Jufair base under an executive agreement signed on December 23, 1971, with Bahrain. Most American authorities claimed that the Middle East Force was merely a "flag-showing operation" and reflected "no change in the U.S. Naval presence in the Persian Gulf and involves no defense or security commitment of any sort to the Government of Bahrain."[91] Nevertheless, the shah did not seem to welcome the American agreement with Bahrain. "We have declared before that we would not want to see any foreign presence in the Gulf. England, the United States, or China—our policy hasn't changed," he told a group of journalists on January 15, 1972.[92]

If from all this Iraq could have concluded that Britain remained the dominant power in the entire Persian Gulf, it would have directed its attacks more against Britain than Iran. But the fact was that this assessment of the remaining British power in the gulf was true only in regard to the lower gulf, Iran was the chief power in the Persian Gulf as a whole after the British withdrawal. This more comprehensive and accurate assessment of the power situation was made public, after an on-the-spot check, in these terms: "The 470-mile cruise from Kharg Island at the head of the gulf to Bandar Abbas at the Strait of Hormuz showed that the Iranians control the key sites along the

[90]*New York Times,* Jan. 12, 1972.

[91]U.S., Congress, House, Subcommittee on the Near East, *U.S. Interests in and Policy toward the Persian Gulf,* 92d Cong., 2d sess., 1972, p. 23.

[92]From the text of the shah's interview. See Ramazani, *Persian Gulf,* pp. 143-48.

vital oil route and are building up their defenses at the entrance to the gulf."[93] This was an entirely new element in Iran's relations with Iraq. The challenge of real Iranian power in the gulf was added for the first time to the traditional Irano-Iraqi jockeying for position at the head of the gulf, particularly along the Shatt al-Arab river.

This sharp Irano-Iraqi power rivalry in the Persian Gulf undergirded the intensity of Iraqi deportations and border clashes that followed the British withdrawal. "A helpless mass of human beings [was] being used as a political instrument by two unfriendly powers," it was reported on January 9, 1972.[94] Thousands of expatriate Iranians were forced out of Iraq in the bitter cold of the winter. According to one of them, the Ba'thist regime accused Tehran of using them as "a fifth column" in Iraq. An on-the-spot report from Khosravi, a border town, estimated that if all those who were waiting for permission to enter Iran were admitted, the "number of people of Iranian origin expelled from Iraq during the past two years would amount to over 100,000."[95] By January 1, 1972, some seven thousand five hundred new deportees had been settled at the Nasrabad camp near Qasr-i Shirin while over four thousand others were being cared for at various mosques in Kermanshah. Several prominent Shi'i religious leaders, such as Ayatollah Haj Mustafa Mishkat, were among the refugees, a factor stirring up a great deal of religious sentiment in Iran. From another border town, Nasrabad, the shah expressed deep regret about Iraq's expulsion of some sixty thousand Iranians and warned Baghdad "not to go beyond certain limits." He then added that a "country which is sure of itself and is strong must always have enough forebearance."[96] Western reports, however, estimated the number of deportees at the time at forty-eight thousand. Nevertheless, this was more than twice the number of Iranians that Iraq had expelled in the 1969 crisis.

The acrimonious relations between Tehran and Baghdad took a turn for the worse after Iraq and the Soviet Union formalized their growing rapprochement in a fifteen-year treaty of political and economic cooperation, April 9, 1972, mentioned previously. The signing of the treaty might indeed have been precipitated by the capture of the three islands and the emergence of Iran as the dominant power in the Persian Gulf. But the fact still remained that the American assistance to Iran in building up its "credible deterrent," and the Soviet arms aid to Iraq over the years had already injected Soviet-American rivalry into the gulf area indirectly. No matter who started what first between

[93] *New York Times,* Jan. 25, 1972.

[94] Ibid., Jan. 31, 1972.

[95] *Kayhan* (Weekly English), Jan. 1, 1972.

[96] Ibid., Jan. 8, 1972.

the two superpowers, the Soviet treaty with Iraq clearly accentuated Soviet alignment with Iraq and further globalized the Irano-Iraqi power conflict. The immediate consequence of this for the two local powers was the outbreak of "the most serious clash" between Iran and Iraq. Border clashes broke out on April 10, 1972, in the Qasr-i Shirin-Khanaqin region, and by May 13 sniping incidents were almost daily occurrences. For example, raiding parties from Iraq blew up an oil pipeline, placed charges under the bridge at Qasr-i Shirin, fired on vehicles on a border road, and carried off into Iraq three Iranian gendarmes. More important, Iraqi regular forces, according to Iranians, attacked four Iranian posts, using armored personnel carriers, artillery, mortars, rockets, and small arms.[97] Meanwhile, Iraq complained to the United Nations of border clashes, and Iran accused Baghdad of being a "haven and a training center" for subversive groups throughout the region. Outside the United Nations, Iraq persuaded Kuwait to join it in claiming the three Persian Gulf islands, while Iran ridiculed the claim. By July 1972 the Iraqi regime began to broach the possibility of talks with Iran, but a month later the Ba'thist regime accused Iran of supplying heavy weapons to the Kurds in Iraq. The capture of Iraqi arms smuggled into the Iraqi embassy in Pakistan for Baluchistan, mentioned before, further exacerbated Iran's relations with Iraq.

By summer 1973 it was becoming increasingly apparent that the Irano-Iraqi power rivalry in the Persian Gulf not only had become intermeshed with indirect Soviet-American rivalry but also was further complicated by the activities of other outside powers in the gulf area. Iran believed that the Russians were behind a systematic campaign to break up Pakistan and to elevate India to the dominant position in South Asia and on the Indian Ocean, while supporting subversion on Iran's western flank in the gulf as well.[98] An alleged secret agreement signed between Iraq and India on April 8, 1973, occasioned this Iranian view in June of that year. According to this agreement, a small Indian air force mission in Baghdad was training Iraqi pilots to fly Russian-supplied Mig fighters, although India denied the report.[99] Meanwhile another non-Persian Gulf power, Cuba, was beginning to provide military training to South Yemen, whose aid to the Dhofari rebels had led to Iran's military aid to the sultan of Oman. It was revealed in Washington June 25, 1973, that Cuba was beginning to train South Yemeni pilots to fly the advanced Mig-21 jet fighters that the Soviet Union was supplying to them.[100] More than one hundred Cubans were reportedly in South Yemen, many of

[97] See *New York Times,* May 14, 1972, and *Kayhan* (Weekly English), Apr. 22, 1972.

[98] *Washington Post,* June 22, 1973.

[99] Ibid., June 24, 1973.

[100] Ibid., June 25, 1973.

them advisers to the militia and air force of Yemen, a source of deep concern to North Yemen and Saudi Arabia. It was speculated that the presence of the Cuban pilots might explain the previous South Yemeni attack on Saudi Arabia by two Migs flown by "unidentified" pilots. This attack and the Saudi realization that the South Yemenis were obtaining Mig-21s were understood to have triggered the Saudi decision to procure Phantom jet fighter-bombers from the United States. The Soviet-American rivalry was thus interlocking not only with the Irano-Iraqi power conflict at the head of the gulf but also with the intra-Arab and Arab-Iranian conflicts on the approach to, and at the entrance of, the Persian Gulf.

XVII

Conclusion

LET US SEE what this study has tried to say to area specialists interested in Iran and the Middle East and foreign policy analysts in general. The generalizations that follow are *propositions* based primarily upon the findings of the empirical analysis of the foreign policy of Iran from 1941 to 1973, and the key concepts set forth in the Introduction toward the study of foreign policy in modernizing societies.

Memories and Perceptions

Memories of a glorious ancient civilization and an imperial past have a significant bearing on the foreign policy of Iran. Contemporary policymakers such as Foroughi, Qavam, Sa'id, Musaddiq, and Muhammad Riza Shah, like such earlier rulers as Shah Isma'il, Shah 'Abbas, and Riza Shah, in one way or another reveal the abiding influence of past memories on foreign policy behavior. Muhammad Riza Shah, for example, celebrated Iran's 2,500th anniversary later than it was due but in time for the historic British withdrawal from the Persian Gulf in 1971, when Iran's resurgence as the chief power in the gulf could also be hallowed by the legitimacy that international prestige on this occasion could bestow on Iran and the monarchical regime.

Perceptions, attitudes, and personal idiosyncrasies of individual policy-makers are influential in Iran's foreign policy. Shah Isma'il's religious zeal, Nadir Shah's military ambitions, Riza Shah's abiding suspicion of foreign powers, to cite a few earlier examples, left their imprints on Iran's foreign policy. The perceptions of Musaddiq and the shah influenced their respective foreign policies. Musaddiq perceived the root cause of the Iranian malaise to be the British interference in Iranian affairs that led to the coup d'etat of Riza Khan in 1921 for the primary purpose of aiding the British oil interests through the Anglo-Iranian Oil Company (AIOC). Nationalization, to Musaddiq and his leading National Front colleagues, was a "political necessity," to recall the words of Allahyar Salih, before the decision was made. Assuming that Iran could not do so well as the AIOC in extracting and selling oil, Musaddiq advocated that the "oil should stay in the ground until the future generation could make better use of it." The nationalist perception was as influential in the implementation of the decision to nationalize as it was in its formulation, as evidenced by the breakdown of every attempt at settlement fundamentally over the control of the industry. To Musaddiq and his colleagues nationalization was, as they told the Security Council, the International Court of Justice, the AIOC, the British government, the United States, and the World Bank, "an act of self-determination." It was not idle talk when Musaddiq wrote President Truman that during "the half century of the former company's domination it has never been possible for the Iranian Government to make a free decision in its internal affairs and its foreign policy." And it was against such a perception that Musaddiq portrayed the choices before his government to the very end in terms of what he called "real independence and happiness" (*sa'adat va istiqlal-i vaqa'i*), or "surrender and submission" (*inqiyad va taslim*).

In contrast the shah perceived the nature of the Iranian malaise more in terms of the threat of Russian, rather than British, imperialism. He criticized Musaddiq for crying out against British imperialism while forgetting "another even more lethal kind of imperialism." This perception emphasized military security as "the first essential" of Iranian domestic and foreign requirements. Domestically it meant suppression of political opposition and internationally it meant Iran's alliance with the West in the cold war. In spite of normalization of relations and economic cooperation with the Soviet Union after the early 1960s, the shah's nationalism still emphasized the threat of Soviet imperialism. As late as 1973 he stated that in negotiations with Moscow Iran must always remember the chief dilemma of "Russian imperialism." "There exists what I call," he said, "the USSR's pincer movement. There exists their dream of reaching the Indian Ocean through the Persian Gulf." At bottom, both Musaddiq's and the shah's perceptions are variations of the modernizing nation's quest for autonomy, that is, the drive for freedom of action in the international system. Musaddiq's nationalization has been repeated time and again in a wide variety of new nations in the Middle East, in Latin America, and by the shah himself in Iran in 1973. The new nations' demand for control of their natural resources voiced consistently within and outside the United Nations, specialized agencies of the United Nations, and regional organizations are too well known to require mention. In terms of foreign policy in general, Musaddiq tried to pursue the path of nonalignment while the shah saw Iran's interest in alliance with the West. Since the early 1960s the shah's regime has found it possible to cooperate more fully with the Soviet Union, a policy that the National Frontists advocated in the tumultuous days of 1961.

Systemic Influences

Few factors influence the foreign policy of Iran more profoundly than the structure of power in the international system. Historically, the Anglo-Russian rivalry constituted the single most influential systemic factor in Iran's foreign policy. The Anglo-Russian invasion of Iran in 1941 brought on the shift in Iran's policy of neutrality in favor of what Premier Foroughi called "defensive alliance" (*itihad-i tadafo'i*) with the Soviet Union and Britain in 1942, declaration of war on Germany in 1943, persistent defiance of Soviet interference in Iranian affairs, and consistent pressures for the evacuation of Soviet troops from Iranian territory. The dramatic change in the international environment as the result of the Anglo-Russian invasion also revived Iran's historic interest in the United States, principally as counterweight to the Soviet Union and only secondarily to Britain. When Soviet pressures, first for oil concessions and subsequently for a joint-stock company, were defied, an open cold war with Moscow was triggered. The interlocking of Moscow's cold war against Iran with the Soviet-American cold war in the Middle East after the announcement of the Truman Doctrine, on the one hand, and the British government's tacit support of the AIOC's adamant position in protracted negotiations with Iran, on the other, constituted the main systemic influences that lay back of the idea, the demand, and the decision to nationalize the oil industry.

The Soviet-American cold war was the single most important systemic influence in complicating the implementation of Musaddiq's nationalization policy, in pursuing the general strategy of negative equilibrium, and in the downfall of his government. The American perception of the Iranian situation, which, according to Acheson, differed from that of Britain and the AIOC at first, was changed as the result of British persuasion, according to Eden. President Eisenhower viewed Musaddiq as a "semi-invalid" who carried on a "fanatical campaign," but the shah had always impressed him as a man of "good intent" who was concerned with the welfare of his people and enjoyed "much more authority than any constitutional monarch of Europe." In the course of the nationalization crisis, said the president, he "conferred daily with officials of the State and Defense Departments and the Central Intelligence Agency and saw reports from our representatives on the spot who were working actively with the Shah's supporters." Direct or indirect, intervention of great powers in new nations' affairs is an aspect of systemic influences too well known to require repetition. The Dominican Republic, Guatemala, Cuba, Indonesia, Egypt, and the Communist-dominated new nations of Hungary and Czechoslovakia are only the most obvious cases. Just as the cold war impaired Muaddiq's foreign policy, it assisted the shah's during most of the 1950s. And just as the cold war influenced the shah's foreign policy of positive nationalism, the détente movement lay at the root of his new independent national policy.

Changes in the power structure of various subsystems influence Iran's foreign policy. New power configurations in the Persian Gulf after 1968 and, in South Asia particularly after the Indo-Pakistani war of 1971 and the Soviet treaty with India; in Sino-Soviet and Sino-American relations, particularly after President Nixon's visit to China, and in the Middle East after the Arab-Israeli war of 1967 and particularly the war of 1973—all exerted profound effects on Iran's foreign policy. The convergence of changes in various subsystems with changes in the East-West subsystem presented Iran with the most complicated international system with which it has ever had to deal. The Soviet Union, for example, is not only Iran's neighbor, as in the past, but also a Middle Eastern power and a South Asian power. In the past Iran was concerned with the Soviet Union primarily as a land-centered power pressuring Iran from the north. In the 1960s Iran began to face the Soviet Union from north and south and from the sea as well as overland. Given the Soviet-Indian rapprochement, Iran feared in the early 1970s that it might have to face the Soviet Union in the East as well, if Pakistan were further dismembered through the establishment of an independent Baluchistan at the expense of both Iran and Pakistan and as a corridor for Soviet access to the Indian Ocean. These subsystem changes have also affected the foreign policy of numerous other new nations, as evidenced, for example, by the dramatic change in Egypt's posture vis-à-vis Israel after the 1973 war, the Saudi Arabian oil embargo against the United States, Indian friendship with Iraq, and the decision of a great number of new nations to welcome China into the United Nations and establish diplomatic relations with it.

The Ubiquity of Political Modernization

Problems of political modernization influence Iran's foreign policy. Every major foreign policy objective and decision of Iran has its domestic counterpart. Political stability, or authority, is the most persistent problem of political modernization that interacts with foreign policy objectives and actions. The quest for autonomy in the international system is inseparable from the elite's drive to maintain control over the polity. Whether the elite hired Millspaugh, established commercial ties with the United States, employed Colonel Schwartzkopf, Major Greely, or General Ridely, hired American Overseas Consultants (OCI), engaged in a cold war or normalized relations with the Soviet Union, formed an alliance with, or pursued an independent course from, the United States, quarreled with Iraq or cultivated friendship with other Persian Gulf and Middle East states, the objective of domestic political control played a part in all these and similar foreign policy actions. More than any other single factor this ubiquity of politics in Iran's foreign policy was an influence in the failure of such economically oriented missions as those of Millspaugh and the OCI group. These American economic efforts were solicited by the political elite primarily for political reasons. The same was true of the employment of military missions. But the relative success of the military advisory groups was partly the outcome of the greater compatability of their efforts with what the political elite really wanted—greater domestic political authority rather than genuine economic reforms, because the elite itself would lose if such reformers as Millspaugh and OCI groups had their way.

To take up another problem of political modernization as it relates to foreign policy, let us recall that of identity. After the Anglo-Russian invasion, the eruption of the Kurdish revolt of Hama Rashid led to the fall of the Foroughi government at a difficult time in Iran's relations with the Allied powers. Later the government was caught between fighting the Qashqa'i and Buir Ahmadi tribes at Semirom and simultaneously resisting pressures from the British and Soviet ambassadors, who claimed German infiltration of tribal groups. The most difficult identity problem complicating Iran's objective of limiting Soviet interference was the Azeri and Kurdish rebellions. Even after the Soviet forces withdrew from northern Iran, Husain 'Ala kept the "Iranian Question" before the United Nations Security Council because of uncertainty surrounding the Soviet reaction when the central government moved to return Azerbaijan and Kurdistan to its authority.

Iran's ability to cope more effectively with economic development, to cite another example, exerted a profound influence on its foreign policy beginning in the 1960s. The regime's ability to penetrate Iranian society by means of both political suppression and economic reforms increased Iran's domestic capacity to the point that it influenced the rise of its international economic and military capabilities. Successes in increasing the level of oil production and revenues from petroleum as the result of prolonged negotiations with the international consortium undergirded the ability of Iran to earmark an increasing amount of revenues for economic development. During the past three decades, particularly the last one, Iran has developed economically and militarily at a favorable pace in comparison with not only the less developed nations of the Middle East and other areas but also with Turkey and Egypt, as evidenced, for example, by its energy production *and consumption* as compared with both these nations, and as compared with Egypt in terms of the gross national product and per capita income. As one of the fastest growing nations in the world, Iran's gross national product increased about 12 percent per year in the late 1960s and early 1970s and its per capita income reached the level of $500 and was expected in 1973 to reach $1000 by the end of the Fifth Plan in 1978.

Militarily, Iran spent more on defense than many developing nations. With a Gross National Product less than that of Turkey in 1971, for example, Iran spent more on defense, but with a Gross National Product higher than that of Egypt in the same year it spent less than Egypt on arms. By the end of 1973, however, Iran seemed to show signs of surpassing even Egypt in military expenditures. In any event, by the end of 1973 the passive, occupied, and economically backward and militarily destitute Iran of the 1940s had risen as the chief power in the Persian Gulf and an active member of the international community of nations. In spite of the British presence in the lower gulf, Iran controlled the key sites along vital routes of communication and oil transportation and sat astride the Strait of Hormuz, through which some twenty-five million barrels of Arab and Iranian oil passed every day, largely to the industrialized world.

The twofold quest for autonomy in the international system and authority in domestic politics has, depending on the circumstances, competed with, contradicted, postponed, and reinforced Iran's other impulses toward political modernization. In spite of spectacular achievements in economic development, the problems of identity, legitimacy, distribution, participation, and penetration complicate Iran's quest for optimal freedom of action in the international system. Iran's modern historical experience reveals that objectives of autonomy and authority overshadow other objectives, such as distribution and participation. In spite of the White Revolution maldistribution of wealth continues to be a major problem of economic development; the Fifth Plan partly tries to address itself to this problem by allotting heavy investment in the agricultural and social sectors, including education, in order to cope with ubiquitous imbalances. The result remains to be seen. The democratization of the polity is repeatedly proclaimed as an objective of the regime, but controlled local and national elections, the controlled party system, and the "participation" of peasants and workers in rural cooperatives and factories are not regarded by the politically awakened as proper responses to demands for political participation. The political assassinations, riots, terror, and individual and mass arrests of the 1940s and 1950s were repeated in the 1960s and early 1970s as well. The rise in Iran's international military and economic capabilities and greater freedom of action in the international system may or may not be balanceable by attempts at satisfying other impulses of political modernization, but there is little doubt that the twin goals of autonomy abroad and authority at home are the most salient features of interaction between foreign policy and domestic politics in Iran.

Objectives and Strategies

In the decades covered by this study Iran pursued four major strategies in achieving its foreign policy objectives. These were third-power strategy, negative equilibrium, positive nationalism, and independent national policy. The third-power strategy was in principle inherited from the interwar period when Riza Shah favored Germany as a counterweight to Britain and the Soviet Union. Once the Anglo-Russian pressures on Iran began to build up as a result of the German invasion of the Soviet Union, Iran began to look to the United States as a substitute for Germany, as evidenced by its appeals to the United States, culminating in Riza Shah's personal plea to President Roosevelt. The Anglo-Russian invasion intensified Iranian efforts at fostering American interests in Iran as a way of countering the presence of the Soviet Union and Britain on Iranian soil.

It is mistaken to speak of Iran's having a foreign policy in wartime as a "misnomer." The presence of great powers on Iranian territory placed serious limitations on Iran's freedom of action, but by no means did it eliminate that freedom. The foreign policy of no nation is completely free from both internal and systemic restraints, especially that of a small and occupied nation. Conscious of the Allied powers' need of Iranian territory as a communication link, Iran managed to extract maximum assurances from them regarding its political independence and territorial integrity, as evidenced by its flat denial of Iran's prior agreement to an oil concession to the Soviet Union in its response to the Soviets shortly after the invasion; by Premier Foroughi's ability to get the Allied powers to spell out their assurances regarding Iran's territorial integrity and political independence in a solemn treaty; by his acquisition of a more specific timetable for the withdrawal of the Allied troops, instead of their open-ended "after the war" proposal; by obtaining the Allied commitment to consult with Iran in matters directly affecting its interests, even after the expiration of the treaty and before the conclusion of peace; and by impressing upon them the sacrifices that Iran had to bear and its expectation of their economic assistance. In pursuing its third-power strategy Iran also took the initiative in numerous instances both during and after the war, as evidenced by its persistent efforts in acquiring technical-military and technical-financial aid from the United States as a means of both strengthening the elite's domestic control on the polity and countering the pressures of Britain and, particularly, the Soviet Union. Iran's ability to acquire American diplomatic, advisory, military, and economic assistance before the Truman Doctrine and at a time when it was possible that the United States might withdraw to its traditional isolationism, was clearly indicative of the success of its third-power strategy.

"Negative equilibrium" (*muvazinih-ye manfi*) has been known as a "policy" (*syasat*) as well as a "principle" (*asl*) in discussions of Iran's foreign relations. The leading proponent of the conception was Musaddiq. As early as 1944, in opposing the Soviet demand for oil concessions and in introducing his bill against the government's grant of, or negotiations for, foreign oil concessions, he also called for the exploration and exploitation of Iranian oil by "Iranian hands." The idea of nationalization was from inception associated with the strategy of negative equilibrium; it was rooted in the notion that rejection of the Soviet demand for an oil concession (1944) and proposal for a joint-stock company (1947) should be matched by redressing Iran's claims against the AIOC. By the time the idea crystallized into demands and finally into the decision to nationalize the AIOC altogether, it enjoyed the most widespread social support in comparison with any other decision in the history of Iran's foreign policy.

The inability of Musaddiq to implement the nationalization decision and the downfall of his government in 1953 were, in the last analysis, partly the result of the conjunction of international and domestic conditions. Briefly, they were in part the outcome of the conjunction of the rigidity of the Anglo-American cold war perception of their interest in Iran and the Soviet and Tudeh opportunistic exploitation of the nationalist struggle, on the one hand, and Musaddiq's obsessive distrust of the British and his struggle with the shah for power, on the other. But these conditions were also partly the result of difficulties arising in implementing the strategy of negative equilibrium. Given the combination of Iran's geographic location and the emergent Soviet-American cold war in the Middle East, despite its theoretical plausibility the strategy of negative equilibrium in practice seemed so full of contradictions as to expose it to criticism from all sides. The Tudeh attacked it, for example, when it claimed that Musaddiq's acceptance of Harriman's mediation amounted to submission to the imperialist camp, and the Soviet Union denounced it when it attacked his acceptance of the extension of American military aid to Iran in 1952. And segments of the nationalist faction denounced Musaddiq's "deviation" from pursuing negative equilibrium strictly and hence advocated the adoption of "absolute equilibrium" (*bitarafi-ye mutlaq*) as an alternative strategy. As difficulties in implementing negative equilibrium gradually interlocked with the emergence of a determined Anglo-American front against the Musaddiq government, the United States could no longer be used by Iran to pressure the British, and thus expedient reliance on the Soviets and the Tudeh seemed unavoidable on occasions. This, in turn, emboldened the Tudeh to seek the destruction of the monarchy by August 1953, while the Soviet Union awaited anxiously the triumph of the "anti-imperialist forces" first, and that of the Tudeh over the "bourgeois nationalists" next.

Just as the cold war distorted Musaddiq's negative equilibrium into something anti-Western and pro-Soviet and pro-Tudeh, it portrayed the shah's positive nationalism as blindly pro-Western and anti-Soviet. The resumption of diplomatic relations with Britain, the signing of the 1954 oil agreement, entry into the Baghdad Pact, endorsement of the Eisenhower Doctrine, and the signing of the 1959 defense agreement with the United States were all designed to help the shah's regime consolidate power domestically and offer the Soviet Union maximum resistance. The acquisition of economic and military aid directly from the United States and indirectly through the Baghdad Pact, and subsequently CENTO, was matched by allowing unprecedented participation of American interests in Iranian oil and American investment in the Iranian economy, as evidenced by the terms of the 1954 oil agreement and the comprehensive Treaty of Amity and Economic Relations and Consular Rights (1957) for fostering and protecting private American interests in Iran. Yet neither the oil agreement of 1954 nor the alliance with the United States did in fact escape Iran's serious reservations about both. The oil agreement was regarded as a lesser evil in light of domestic and international conditions, but an evil nevertheless, as evidenced by the shah's own subtly qualified acceptance of the agreement "under the circumstances" and by his permitting, if not encouraging, severe criticism of the agreement by Deputy Darakhshish and Senator Divanbaigy. The alliance, too, was subjected to criticism from inception because of American nonparticipation and the meagerness of aid through it. The Iraqi revolution intensified Iran's dissatisfaction with the alliance, as did subsequently the American position in regard to the Indo-Pakistani war.

The strategy of positive nationalism did not amount to blind hostility with the Soviet Union, just as it did not result in uncritical friendship with the United States. The post-Stalinist Soviet policy toward Iran before the early 1960s was viewed as twofold in character—"intimidation and ingratiation" (*tahdid va tahbib*), and Iran responded to both. Soviet diplomatic and propaganda attacks were defiantly resisted in the 1954-62 period, as in the decade before 1951, particularly the 1946-51 period, when they were occasioned by Iran's participation in the Western-sponsored alliance, by endorsement of the Eisenhower Doctrine, and by its defense agreement with the United States, which twice unleashed Premier Khrushchev's personal wrath upon the shah. But Iran also tried to respond positively to Soviet overtures of peaceful coexistence from the very inception of the strategy of positive nationalism, as evidenced by unprecedented agreements with the Soviet Union regarding boundary problems (1954 and 1957), and transit and joint utilization of boundary rivers (1957), and the visits of Iranian parliamentarians, the shah, and the queen to the Soviet Union. Iran's entry into negotiations with the Soviet Union for a Treaty of Friendship and Non-

Aggression (1958-59) was not merely a pressure tactic to secure a satisfactory defense agreement with the United States or to forestall future Soviet pincer movements from the north and from the south through Iraq in the Persian Gulf. It was also in keeping with Iran's determination to probe and test Soviet gestures of peaceful coexistence and offers of economic cooperation.

Finally, the strategy of "independent national policy" (*syasat-i mustaqill-i melli*), adopted by the shah's regime in the early 1960s, was not simply a pro-Western, "de facto nonalignment" posture. This strategy was adopted as a result of the combination of a variety of complex domestic and international factors, including intensification of the détente movement, specific changes in Soviet and American strategic thought and policies, Iran's own persistent differences with the United States over the magnitude and kind of military and economic aid, Soviet preparedness to accept Iranian definition of "bases" and to offer Iran substantial economic cooperation opportunities, Iran's mounting concern with the Iraqi, Egyptian, and Syrian policies in the Persian Gulf, the regime's shaky economic and political position domestically in spite of increasing oil revenues and massive American aid, and severe suppression of the National Front and the Tudeh throughout the post-Musaddiq 1950s. The principal objectives of the new strategy were (1) to further consolidate the regime's control over the polity and launch unprecedented measures of economic reforms and (2) to further explore possibilities of (*a*) cooperation with the Soviet Union, (*b*) a more independent policy toward the United States, and (*c*) a more active policy in the Persian Gulf. These last three constituted the major components of Iran's strategy of "independent national policy."

First, normalization of relations with the Soviet Union was primarily economic in character. "Cooperation" (*hamkary*) resulted in stabilization and expansion of trade and transit relations and inauguration of new technical and economic ties with the Soviet Union. Even in economic terms, however, cooperation with the Soviet Union encountered difficulties, as evidenced by Iran's persistent concern with its trade deficit with the Soviet Union, which was reduced over time. But it remained to be seen whether the Soviet commitment to "balanced trade" in the 1972 treaty would overcome this difficulty. Iran's complaints about the slow pace of construction of the steel mill, the heavy cost of building the gas pipeline, and the poor quality of the steel mill and the Aras Dam projects, as contrasted with the Dez Dam, reflected other economic difficulties. The overall policy of Iran toward the Soviet Union, however, was troubled more severely by political considerations. During the 1963-73 decade, as in the post-Musaddiq 1950s, Iran continued to resist Soviet pressures, but in the later period resistance was offered more in deference than in defiance, in keeping with the more subtle and nonviolent tenor of Soviet policy and propaganda. Nevertheless, Iran refused to (1) abandon its alignment with the United States, (2) nationalize its oil industry in a manner prejudicial to the West, or (3) countenance a Soviet bid for dominant influence in the Persian Gulf area.

Second, paralleling this pattern of continuity and change in Iran's policy toward the Soviet Union during the 1963-73 decade, alliance with the United States was for all practical purposes intensified after the 1968 British decision to withdraw from the area east of Suez. To be sure, the 1950s legacy of disappointment with CENTO was intensified as the result of disenchantment with the United States position in the 1965 Indo-Pakistani war, but Iran's alignment with the United States was unprecedentedly strengthened beginning in 1969. Iran's independent national strategy fitted the tenets of the Nixon Doctrine, as its positive nationalism strategy had suited the Truman Doctrine and the United States cold war containment policy. Although the shah called for reappraisal of CENTO during its Twentieth Session of the Council of Ministers, he affirmed that "the basic philosophy and objectives of our alliance remain unaltered." At the same time the CENTO members affirmed their concern with "subversion" in the Persian Gulf area, declared their determination to meet subversive threats to their independence and territorial integrity "with all the means at their disposal," and witnessed Secretary Rogers's admission of "dangers of subversion" in the area by means of Soviet ideology in spite of détente. Secretary Kissinger's specification of conditions of peaceful coexistence with the Soviet Union announced during the 1973 Arab-Israeli war brought the Nixon Doctrine even closer to Iran's independent national strategy. The United States would oppose (1) Soviet predominance globally or regionally, (2) Soviet exploitation of détente to weaken American alliances, and (3) Soviet manipulation of relaxation of tensions as a "cover to exacerbate conflicts in international trouble spots." Intensification of Iran's alignment with the United States was further evidenced by not only the magnitude of its purchase of American arms but also its ability to breach the traditional reluctance of the United States to provide Iran with sophisticated modern weapons. Iran's determination and ability to play the leading role in the Persian Gulf, an area of increasing economic and strategic significance to the United States and its allies, especially in light of the energy crisis, suited the Nixon Doctrine's reliance on local powers to protect their own as well as American interests without United States involvement.

The third and final component of Iran's independent national strategy during the 1963-73 decade was its new assertive position in the Persian Gulf and the immediately contiguous areas of the Middle East and South Asia. Iran's Persian Gulf policy before the 1968 British decision to withdraw from the area east of Suez was primarily an extension of its alliance with the West, as evidenced by its attempts to counter Egyptian and Syrian positive neu-tralism by its own positive nationalism, which was manifested not only in its alliance with Iraq but also its diplomatic efforts to cultivate the friendship of Saudi Arabia, Chamoun's Lebanon, and most Persian Gulf sheikhdoms as a counterweight to the Syrian-Egyptian power bloc. By 1968 Iran's primary objectives in the Persian Gulf area had crystallized into (1) protection of the regime from internal subversion sponsored directly or indirectly by hostile Arab states or groups or by Soviet proxy; (2) preservation of free transit through the Strait of Hormuz, the gulf, and the Shatt al-Arab; and (3) the protection of Iranian oil resources and facilities on shore and off against any deliberate or accidental disruptions. Considering the insufficiency of the alignment patterns of the cold war days for the attainment of these objectives, on the one hand, and the improbability of a new regional security arrangement embracing the littoral states of the gulf, on the other, Iran was determined to maintain the gulf security collectively if it could and individually if it must.

Before and after the British withdrawal in 1971 it launched a twofold strategy of (1) strengthening its military capability with the help of the United States and Britain and (2) cultivating friends and allies, not only in the gulf area, but also in the Middle East and in South and East Asia as well. Iran received British and American assistance not only in building up its "credible deterrent" but also their support within and outside CENTO for its warnings against the interference of outside powers in the gulf, in the lower part of which the British presence on the Arab side was helpful to Iran's effective preservation of freedom of navigation through the strategic Strait of Hormuz. Iran also cultivated the support of regional members of CENTO, Turkey, and Pakistan for its Persian Gulf policies both within and outside that organization. Except for Iraq, relations with which were troubled, particularly after the rise of the Bakr regime and the Soviet-Iraqi treaty of 1972, in spite of Baghdad's patch-up work with Tehran after the outbreak of the 1973 Arab-Israeli war, Iran managed to cultivate in the gulf area the friendship of all other gulf states by economic, diplomatic and military means. Beyond the immediate gulf area, it scrapped a decade of diplomatic rupture with Egypt, resumed diplomatic relations with Lebanon, and tried to settle its historic dispute with Afghanistan over the Helmand River (as it did with Britain over the ancient Bahrain dispute), committed its support to the integrity of Pakistan in the face of the Baluchi separatist movement (as it committed forces in Oman in the face of the Dhofari rebellion), extended its "security perimeter" (*harim-i amniyat*) to the Gulf of Oman and the Indian Ocean, and established diplomatic and economic ties with China as a counterbalance to Indian and Soviet bids for influence in South Asia, the Middle East, the Indian Ocean, and the Persian Gulf.

Stripped of local labels, variations of all these four major strategies are found in other modernizing societies. Aspects of third-power strategy could be found, for example, in Pakistan's flirtation with China in the face of the Soviet-American cold war, on the one hand, and Pakistan's disappointment with the American attitude in its dispute with India over Kashmir, on the other; or in Saudi Arabia's oil-sale deal with France in the face of disappointment to reach a long-term oil agreement with Washington in 1972, on the one hand, and the fear of Soviet ambitions in the Persian Gulf, on the other, or in a number of gulf states' economic and even military ties with a variety of West European states and Japan. Similarities between Musaddiq's negative equilibrium and the nonalignment strategies of a great many modernizing societies can be even more easily detected. The Bandung Conference and subsequent conferences held by nonaligned nations symbolized their common strategies. Musaddiq himself was attracted to Nehru's nonalignment, but he enjoyed neither the domestic political stability nor the benevolent attitudes of the great powers to sustain that policy. Iran's alliance strategy was also paralleled in the 1950s by the other regional members of CENTO, namely, Turkey and Pakistan, which, like Iran, signed almost identical defense agreements with the United States in 1959. Finally, the resemblance between Iran's independent national policy and Turkish "foreign policy with personality" is striking; their cooperation with the Soviet Union is primarily economic, and they both continue to sustain their military alliance with the United States.

Foreign Policy and Style

Throughout most of Iran's modern history the person of the king has played the key role in the making of Iran's foreign policy. Muhammad Riza Shah began to control the policy firmly after the downfall of the Musaddiq government (1953), but he did play a major role in Iranian foreign policy before that. From his accession to the throne he displayed a pervasive influence on Iran's third-power strategy, as evidenced by his personal and persistent interest in fostering American interest in Iran militarily, economically, and diplomatically, by his major role in internal matters crucially related to Iran's foreign relations, such as the rejection of Muzafar Firuz's agreement with the Azerbaijan government, the crucial cabinet shake-up of 1946, and above all his personal role in the making and execution of the decision to destroy the Azeri and Kurdish rebel regimes. Premier Qavam himself acknowledged the shah's major role in the Azerbaijan crisis before the Majlis. The decision to nationalize the oil industry, however, was from inception the result of the initiative of nationalist deputies of the Majlis led by Musaddiq. Although the Majlis technically made the decision, the record clearly shows that it was primarily the result of the initiative, perseverance, and dedicated campaigning of a handful of National Front deputies who enjoyed widespread social support. The personal leadership of the charismatic Musaddiq was clearly decisive in its formulation and subsequent attempts at execution. Other prime ministers in Iran's modern history, such as Mushir al-Dowlih, Mustofi al-Mamalik, and Ahmad Qavam played major roles in Iran's foreign policy, but none so dramatically as Musaddiq.

Muhammad Riza Shah's personal control of Iran's foreign policy after the downfall of the Musaddiq government became supreme and unchallenged. In foreign policy even more than in domestic politics the shah plays the central role. His all-pervasive personal role is evidenced in all major decisions, ranging from the oil agreement (1954), the entry into the Baghdad Pact alliance, insistence on the definition of "bases" in Irano-Soviet negotiations (1958-59), dramatic reversal of Iran's position on the Bahrain dispute, nonrenewal of the oil agreement, and his personal agreement with the oil companies in Saint-Moritz (1973), to mention only a few. Personal diplomacy at the summit is most often associated with the making, and implementation of, major decisions, such as the shah's frequent visits to the United States, the Soviet Union, Pakistan, and Turkey as well as numerous visits to East and West European as well as Southeast Asian nations. Members of the royal family also make important goodwill visits to foreign countries and participate actively in international universal organizations. The prime minister, too, engages in major foreign visits in pursuance of the shah's decisions and performs a critical role in matters with which the shah himself prefers not to get directly involved. The same is true of the role of the Parliament. Under the constitution the Majlis in particular can play a decisive role in certain vital areas of foreign affairs, as indeed the First, Second, Third, Fourth, Fourteenth, Fifteenth, and Sixteenth Majlis did; in the past two decades it has acted primarily as the arm of the political elite. As such, it has played important roles in postponing, criticizing, reneging on, modifying, and even rejecting foreign policy proposals on which the elite itself did not wish to take a public stand, as evidenced by the parliamentary debate over the 1954 oil agreement, the Eisenhower Doctrine, the status of forces agreement with the United States, and other matters.

The sheer scope, complexity, and diversity of Iran's expanding ties with an ever-widening circle of nations, corporations, and regional and universal organizations involve an increasing number of ministries and agencies in the actual conduct of Iran's foreign policy. The list of these agencies and ministries is headed by the Ministry of Foreign Affairs, with its distinguished record of performance in world affairs ever since Iran opened its first major embassies along modern lines in London, Saint Petersburg, and Constantinople in the 1850s and is followed by the National Iranian Oil Company, the Ministry of Economy, and Ministry of Defense, to mention only the most important ones. In reporting, representing, and other functions, the Iranian diplomatic service inevitably makes direct and indirect contributions in the making and execution of Iranian foreign policy, but the tone, direction, and expectations of performance in the Ministry of Foreign Affairs as in others are set usually by men who are trusted by the shah, as evidenced by the appointment of Iqbal to the NIOC, Ardishir Zahidi to the Foreign Ministry, and Alikhani to the Ministry of Economy. Furthermore, most often important contributions to the decision-making process are made by the least expected and formal sources, such as Husain 'Ala, or Assadullah 'Alam, not so much as ministers of court or prime ministers but as trustees of the shah.

The overriding importance of personality in foreign-policy-making in Iran, be it the shah, Ahmad Qavam, or Musaddiq, is observable in other modernizing nations. The roles of Nasir, Sukarno, Sadat, Nkrumah, Nehru, King Faisal, Bourguiba, and many others are, to be sure, not identical with that of the shah or of able Iranian prime ministers; nevertheless, individual leaders in modernizing societies play a far more pervasive role in making foreign policy than in developed societies. Like most other modernizing nations Iran enjoys a greater degree of flexibility of action in world affairs than such ultramodern societies as the United States, which are burdened by the colossal machinery of government, the perennial problem of coordination of functions within the executive, and the ancient tensions in the executive-legislative relationship in foreign affairs. The pragmatic thrust of such veteran Iranian statesmen as Foroughi, Qavam, and the shah are manifest in Iran's performance in world affairs. President Nixon probably had this quality in mind when he characterized the shah as a "world statesman."

Challenges Ahead

The foreign policy of Iran is penetrated by the quest for autonomy. The aristocratic, sectarian, and dynastic conceptions of Iranian foreign policy may compete theoretically with the nationalist conception of autonomy, but empirically the quest for freedom of action in the international system permeates Iran's foreign policy decisions and actions regardless of the principal actors. The emergence of the concept of "national interests" (*manafa'-i milli*) as a guide for foreign policy decisions and actions is accompanied by an inverted concept of balance of power. This concept underlies all the four major strategies pursued by Iran in the international system in the past three decades or so. It lay at the heart of the third-power strategy, negative equilibrium, and positive nationalism, as it now lies at the core of independent national policy. They have all been designed to maximize Iran's freedom of action in the international system, either by relying upon the United States as a counterweight to Britain and the Soviet Union, by trying to pursue a nonalignment course, by allying Iran with the United States against the Soviet Union, or by continuing to rely ultimately on the United States for security against the Soviet Union while engaging in limited economic-technical and commercial cooperation with it.

The most profound future challenge to Iran's foreign policy will be philosophical. This will be true whether or not the emerging concept of national interest as the guiding principle of Iranian foreign policy is intertwined with monarchical and dynastic interest. It will also be true whether the international system is bipolar, tripolar, or multipolar. To be sure, preservation of self-interest, to borrow Reinhold Niebuhr's words, is "tentatively necessary," and the balancing of power can serve higher interests. Nevertheless, the question is asked, What does this resurgence of Iranian power mean? Will Iran, for example, try to dominate, or cooperate with, other Persian Gulf states? In other words, is there any scheme of higher values that Iran's emergent national foreign policy will try to serve? The founding fathers of the United States, for example, are said to have sought to use foreign policy as a means to such higher ends and purposes as individual rights to life, liberty, and the pursuit of happiness. What are those higher ends beyond self-interest to which Iran aspires? How does Iran define the "self" it tries to realize at home and within the international system?

The founders of ancient Iran were also concerned with normative problems. In fact, according to Adda B. Bozeman, the Iranians posed "for the first time in historically known terms" the problem of moral principles and national interest in foreign policy. She says that in the sixth century B.C. when the tyranny of empires plagued the fabric of community life everywhere, the Persian Empire, vaster than any preceding empire west of China, attained "universal" peace for some two hundred years in a large part as the result of a tolerant respect for the cultural diversity of the subjugated peoples, and "this Persian policy of tolerance probably was suggested by the statesmanship rather than by the religious ethics of the sixth century B.C." I suggest that the Iranian heritage contains the germ of the notion that Santayana calls "the harmony of the whole which does not destroy the vitality of the parts." The incessant quest for national autonomy within the international system inclines Iran, like all modernizing nations in this age of nationalism, to emphasize today the vitality of the parts. But the real question may be whether Iran can develop out of its own rich and cosmopolitan heritage and the realities of an increasingly interdependent world a concept of order that would simultaneously contribute to greater harmony of the international community as well as Iranian self-realization.

Appendix

Comparative Statistics on Iran's Social, Economic, and Military Capabilities

Table 1. Demographic indicators

Country	Population estimates (in thousands)					Density				Birthrates (per 1000)			
	1937	1947	1963	1968	1971	1947	1954	1968	1971	1945-49	1955-59	1959-69	1971
Iran	16,200	17,000	23,649	27,345	29,783	–	13	16	18	48	48	40.9	45.4
Canada	11,045	12,582	18,925	20,772	21,786	1.3	2	2	2	27	27.8	23.7	17
Egypt	16,009	19,179	27,947	31,693	34,130	20	23	32	34	42.4	40.6	39.3	34.9
Iraq	–	4,800	7,660	8,634	9,750	11	11	20	22	48	–	49.3	49.3
Jordan	300	400	1,793	2,103	2,383	4	14	22	24	–	40.1	–	49.1
Lebanon	925	1,179	2,285	2,580	2,873	100	133	248	276	–	28.6	30.6	26.5
Mexico	18,737	23,432	39,871	47,267	50,830	11.9	15	24	26	44.4	44.9	43.5	43.4
Saudi Arabia	–	6,000	6,530	7,100	7,965	–	4	3	4	–	–	–	50.0
Syria	–	–	4,969	5,701	6,451	–	20	31	35	19.8	24.4	33.2	47.5
Turkey	16,823	19,250	29,655	33,539	36,162	25.1	30	43	46	43	–	43	39.6
U.S.A.	128,825	144,034	189,417	201,152	207,006	18.4	21	21	22	23.4	24.6	18.2	17.3
USSR	–	194,000	224,789	237,796	245,066	–	10	11	11	–	25.3	17.8	17.8

SOURCE: U.N., Statistical Office, Department of Economic and Social Affairs, *Demographic Yearbook* 1-24 (1949-73).

Table 2. Wheat Production (in thousands of metric tons)

Country	1940	1945	1952-56 Aug.	1963	1968	1969	1970	1971
Iran	1,868	2,080	2,279	3,000	4,977	4,200	3,800	3,700
Canada	14,702	8,669	15,024	19,691	17,686	18,623	9,023	14,412
Egypt	1,190	1,182	1,471	1,493	1,518	1,277	1,519	1,729
Iraq	478	400	726	488	1,361	1,183	1,236	822
Jordan	–	–	176	76	111	159	54	168
Lebanon	–	–	57	60	48	33	50	45
Mexico	–	–	823	1,703	1,894	2,377	2,436	1,853
Saudi Arabia	–	–	59	135	150	150	–	–
Syria	459	390	845	1,190	600	1,064	625	662
Turkey	4,068	2,187	6,649	10,137	9,602	10,593	10,081	13,594
U.S.	22,171	30,161	29,425	31,211	42,740	39,740	37,291	44,620
USSR	–	–	48,449	74,399	93,393	79,917	97,734	98,700

SOURCE: U.N., Department of Economic and Social Affairs, *Statistical Yearbook* 1-24 (1949-73).

Table 3. Natural gas consumption (apparent) (in thousand million cubic meters)

Country	1960	1963	1968	1969	1970	1971
Iran	0.95	1.14	1.570	2.781	10,258	9.945
Canada	11.89	21.68	33.345	38.110	43.066	45.640
Egypt	–	–	–	–	–	–
Iraq	0.60	0.72	0.721	0.895	0.785	0.870
Jordan	–	–	–	–	–	–
Lebanon	–	–	–	–	–	–
Mexico	7.04	8.54	15.250	16.177	17.949	17.961
Saudi Arabia	–	0.01	2.161	2.590	2.852	3.000
Syria	–	–	–	–	–	–
Turkey	–	–	–	–	–	–
U.S.	361.99	424.90	560.062	601.932	630.713	650.738
USSR	45.06	89.52	168.872	180.487	198.201	215.971

SOURCES: U.N., Statistical Office, Department of Economic and Social Affairs, Statistical Papers, Series J, *World Energy Supplies, 1960-63* (1965) and *World Energy Supplies, 1968-71* (1973).

Table 4. Crude petroleum production (in thousands of metric tons)

Country	1940	1945	1953	1963	1968	1969	1970	1971
Iran	8,765	17,108	1,489*	73,557	140,480	168,488	191,740	223,921
Canada	1,105	1,091	10,941	34,845	51,197	54,112	60,624	64,418
Egypt	929	1,350	2,690	5,599	900	12,350	16,406	14,718
Iraq	2,514	4,607	28,185	56,669	73,775	74,485	76,448	83,775
Jordan	–	–	–	–	–	–	–	–
Lebanon	–	–	–	–	–	–	–	–
Mexico	6,217	6,187	10,362	16,433	20,345	21,508	21,501	21,412
Saudi Arabia	700	2,872	41,544	81,049	141,004	148,846	176,850	223,412
Syria	–	–	–	–	833	2,620	4,243	5,289
Turkey	–	–	26	746	3,104	3,623	3,542	3,452
U.S.	182,867	231,575	318,535	372,001	449,885	455,602	475,289	466,704
USSR	–	–	52,777	206,069	309,150	328,373	353,039	377,075

SOURCE: U.N., Statistical Office, Department of Economic and Social Affairs, *Statistical Yearbook* 1-24 (1949-73).

*Reflects change to National Iranian Oil Company

Table 5. Energy production and consumption

Country	National Production (in million metric tons coal equiv.)					National consumption (in million metric tons coal)					Per capita consumption (in kilograms)		
	1965	1968	1969	1970	1971	1965	1968	1969	1970	1971	1965	1968	1971
Iran	124.33	185.28	223.21	264.95	317.28	9.42	12.93	15.01	25.64	26.66	383	478	895
Canada	133.87	169.41	179.64	206.03	233.70	148.86	176.21	177.30	192.59	201.38	7593	8483	9326
Egypt	8.67	12.08	16.56	21.92	18.81	9.02	9.43	7.11	8.76	9.69	307	298	-38
Iraq	84.30	96.96	98.02	100.43	110.07	4.13	5.56	5.76	5.82	6.34	504	644	650
Jordan	–	–'	–	–	–	0.58	0.59	0.68	0.68	0.76	301	279	318
Lebanon	0.06	0.10	1.11	1.11	1.10	1.47	1.17	2.02	2.00	2.42	611	687	841
Mexico	41.97	50.78	56.86	58.54	59.20	41.07	50.30	54.62	57.34	64.70	962	1064	1270
Saudi Arabia	132.71	185.19	196.95	233.70	295.35	2.47	3.62	5.23	6.40	7.87	366	510	988
Syria	0.01	1.09	2.98	5.51	6.88	1.83	2.48	2.90	2.85	3.13	348	434	485
Turkey	7.68	10.55	11.23	11.05	11.01	10.92	15.12	16.06	16.87	18.65	350	450	516
U.S.	1633.26	1876.06	1452.40	2062.52	2029.19	1790.76	2078.17	2143.01	2218.90	2727.64	9202	10331	11244
USSR	925.48	1087.44	1139.10	1189.00	1256.26	829.40	965.22	1010.60	1054.65	1112.19	3597	4059	4535

SOURCE: U.N., Statistical Office, Department of Economic and Social Affairs, *Statistical Yearbook* 1-24 (1949-73).

Table 6. World trade (in millions of U.S. $)

Country	Imports (CIF)							Exports (FOB)						
	1938	1953	1963	1968	1969	1970	1971	1938	1953	1963	1968	1969	1970	1971
Iran	92	168	518	1,386	1,582	1,658	1,879	160	90	917	1,879	2,099	2,355	2,642
Canada	691	4,317	6,085	11,431	13,071	13,360	15,458	865	4,220	6,466	12,602	13,773	16,119	17,582
Egypt	188	516	916	666	638	787	920	153	409	520	622	705	762	789
Iraq	46	191	319	404	440	509	694	–	392	781	1,028	1,042	1,093	1,529
Jordan	6	52	143	161	190	184	215	3	6	18	40	41	34	32
Lebanon	–	143	385	474	646	625	650	–	26	57	119	170	198	253
Mexico	110	808	1,240	1,960	2,076	2,461	2,407	159	585	968	1,254	1,430	1,402	1,471
Saudi Arabia	–	–	–	–	127	143	–	–	–	–	–	14	13	–
Syria	–	131	235	303	368	357	438	–	103	189	172	207	203	195
Turkey	119	533	691	770	754	894	1,087	115	396	368	496	537	589	677
U.S.	2,180	10,915	17,072	33,066	35,863	39,756	45,510	3,064	15,661	23,104	34,199	37,463	42,590	43,482
USSR	273*	2,769*	7,059*	9,410*	10,327	11,732	12,479	255	2,948	7,272	10,634	11,655	12,800	13,806

SOURCES: U.N., Conference on Trade and Development, *Handbook of International Trade and Developmental Statistics* (1972); U.N., *Statistical Office, Department of Economic and Social Affairs, Statistical Yearbook* 1-24 (1949-73) and *Yearbook of International Trade Statistics 1968* (1969)

* FOB.

Table 7. National income

Country	National income (millions of U.S. $)						Per capita income (U.S. $)					
	1958	1963	1968	1969	1970	1971	1958	1963	1968	1969	1970	1971
Iran	2,916	4,256	6,812	8,852	9,764	—	143	183	252	312	334	—
Canada	25,732	30,317	46,677	65,316	69,402	81,421	1,503	1,602	2,247	3,097	3,246	3,769
Egypt	2,730	3,904	4,828*	6,392	—	—	111	140	156*	197	—	—
Iraq	1,048	1,471	1,922*	2,574	—	—	161	192	228*	278	—	—
Jordan	222	338	507*	655	623	663	141	189	249*	294	270	279
Lebanon	417	865	1,156	1,367	1,454	—	208	378	448	566	521	—
Mexico	9,167	13,904	24,190	28,358	32,016	—	272	349	511	580	632	—
Saudi Arabia	760	1,467	2,383	—	—	—	127	225	336	—	—	—
Syria	669	815	1,226	1,548	1,589	—	155	164	214	256	254	—
Turkey	4,666	6,621	10,783	13,589	12,249	—	180	223	321	396	348	—
U.S.	369,962	485,264	719,796	838,961	879,702	946,778	2,115	2,562	3,578	4,139	4,294	4,573
USSR	—	—	—	—	—	—	—	—	—	—	—	—

SOURCES: U.N., Statistical Office, Department of Economic and Social Affairs, *Statistical Yearbook* 1-24 (1949-73) and *Yearbook of National Account Statistics* 1 (1970).

* Unavailable for 1968. The figure is for 1967, the closest year for which data are available.

Table 8. Gross domestic product

Country	National GDP (millions of U.S. $)						Per capita GDP (U.S. $)					
	1958	1963	1968	1969	1970	1971	1958	1963	1968	1969	1970	1971
Iran	3,431	5,046	8,059	10,198	11,249	–	168	217	299	359	384	–
Canada	30,231	35,797	54,449	74,393	79,696	92,910	1,766	1,892	2,621	3,529	3,738	4,301
Egypt	2,723	3,999	4,989*	6,831	–	–	110	143	161*	210	–	–
Iraq	1,358	1,929	2,403*	3,141	–	–	209	252	258*	343	–	–
Jordan	220	330	495*	609	598	–	139	184	243*	273	259	–
Lebanon	446	895	1,196	1,400	1,488	–	223	391	463	519	533	–
Mexico	9,832	14,928	26,160	29,992	33,496	36,432	292	374	553	632	682	717
Saudi Arabia	1,187	2,126	3,458	–	–	–	198	326	487	–	–	–
Syria	695	849	1,282	1,570	1,684	1,930	161	171	223	259	269	307
Turkey	4,899	7,001	11,347	13,367	12,127	11,890	189	236	338	389	344	328
U.S.	412,873	540,800	796,636	927,876	972,581	1,045,753	2,361	2,855	3,960	4,578	4,797	5,051
USSR	–	–	–	–	–	–	–	–	–	–	–	–

SOURCES: U.N., Statistical Office, Department of Economic and Social Affairs, *Growth of World Industry, 1938-61* (1965), *Growth of World Industry, 1953-65* (1967), and *Statistical Yearbook* 1-24 (1949-73).

*Unavailable for 1968. The figure is for 1967, the closest year for which data are available.

Table 9. Gross National Product

Country	National (million U.S. $)				Per capita (U.S. $)			
	1958	1963	1968	1969	1958	1963	1968	1969
Iran	3,362	4,899	7,960	9,110	165	210	295	327
Canada	33,889	40,134	62,254	68,710	1,979	2,121	2,997	3,260
Egypt	3,061	4,331	5,736*	6,100	124	155	186*	188
Iraq	1,222	1,733	2,171*	2,693	188	226	257*	294
Jordan	254	385	575*	595	161	215	282*	259
Lebanon	485	999	1,336	1,435	242	437	518	531
Mexico	10,176	15,376	26,744	29,370	302	386	566	600
Saudi Arabia	895	1,652	2,685	2,790	149	253	378	388
Syria	796	936	1,425	1,600	179	188	248	273
Turkey	5,304	7,669	12,750	13,016	204	259	380	380
U.S.	454,965	599,705	880,774	947,850	2,602	3,166	4,379	4,664
USSR	—	—	—	285,710	—	—	—	1,188

SOURCES: U.N., Conference on Trade and Development, *Handbook of International Trade and Developmental Statistics* (1972); U.N.,Statistical Office, Department of Economic and Social Affairs, *Yearbook of National Account Statistics* 1 (1970).

*Unavailable for 1968. The figure is for 1967, the closest year for which data are available.

Table 10.   Military indicators

Country–Year		Estimated population	Military service	Total armed forces	Estimated GNP	Defense expenditure
Iran	1968-69	26,000,000	2 years	221,000	$7 billion	$495 million
	1969-70	27,500,000	2 years	221,000	$8.5 billion	$505 million
	1970-71	28,400,000	2 years	161,000	$8.9 billion	$779 million
	1971-72	29,500,000	2 years	181,000	$10.9 billion	$1.023 billion
Egypt	1968-69	31,500,000	3 years	211,000	$5.1 billion	$690 million
	1969-70	32,100,000	3 years	207,000	$5.5 billion	$805 million
	1970-71	33,300,000	3 years	288,000	$6.3 billion	$1.272 billion
	1971-72	34,150,000	3 years	318,000	$6.43 billion	$1.495 billion
Iraq	1968-69	8,500,000	2 years	82,000	$2.2 billion	$252 million
	1969-70	8,700,000	2 years	78,000	$2.25 billion	$280 million
	1970-71	9,000,000	2 years	94,500	$2.8 billion	$424.76 million
	1971-72	9,250,000	2 years	95,250	$3.12 billion	$237.16 million
Israel	1968-69	4,000,000[a]	30 months[b]	40,000[c]	$3.6 billion	$628 million
	1969-70	2,800,000	36 months	22,500	$3.9 billion	$829 million
	1970-71	2,900,000	36 months	75,000	$4.5 billion	$1.075 billion
	1971-72	3,040,000	36 months	75,000	$5.4 billion	$1.4837 billion
Jordan	1968-69	1,250,000	2 years	55,000	$0.5 billion	$81 million
	1969-70	2,150,000	2 years	55,000	$0.5 billion	$126 million
	1970-71	2,225,000	2 years	60,250	$0.7 billion	$117.6 million
	1971-72	2,225,000	2 years	60,250	$0.64 billion	$90.44 million
Saudi	1968-69	4,000,000	voluntary	36,000	$2.4 billion	$321 million
Arabia	1969-70	6,000,000	voluntary	34,000	$2.7 billion	$343 million
	1970-71	7,300,000	voluntary	36,000	$3.9 billion	$387 million
	1971-72	7,400,000	voluntary	41,000	$4.1 billion	$383 million
Syria	1968-69	5,600,000	2 years	60,500	$1.05 billion	$137 million
	1969-70	5,800,000	2 years	70,500	$1.09 billion	$195 million
	1970-71	6,025,000	30 months	86,750	$1.35 billion	$221 million
	1971-72	6,200,000	30 months	111,750	$1.46 billion	$176 million
Turkey	1968-69	33,000,000	2 years[d]	514,000	$10.1 billion	$472 million
	1969-70	34,000,000	2 years	483,000	$12 billion	$510 million
	1970-71	35,200,000	20 months	477,500	$14 billion	$401 million
	1971-72	36,100,000	20 months	508,500	$13.7 billion	$446 million

SOURCES: Data are from the International Institute for Strategic Studies, *The Military Balance, 1968-69* (London, 1968), *The Military Balance, 1969-70* (London, 1969), *The Military Balance, 1970-71* (London, 1970), and *The Military Balance, 1971-72* (London, 1971).

Army: total strength	Navy: total strength	Air Force: total strength	Paramilitary: total strength	Country–Year	
200,000	6,000	15,000	25,000	Iran	1968-69
200,000	6,000	15,000	25,000		1969-70
135,000	9,000	17,000	40,000		1970-71
150,000	9,000	22,000	40,000		1971-72
180,000	12,000	15,000	90,000	Egypt	1968-69
180,000	12,000	15,000	90,000		1969-70
250,000	14,000	20,000	90,000		1970-71
275,000	14,000	25,000	120,000		1971-72
70,000	2,000	10,000	10,000	Iraq	1968-69
70,000	2,000	6,000	10,000		1969-70
85,000	2,000	7,500	20,000		1970-71
85,000	2,000	8,250	20,000		1971-72
29,000	3,000	8,000	not listed	Israel	1968-69
11,500	3,000	8,000	not listed		1969-70
11,500	3,500	8,000	10,000		1970-71
11,500	3,500	8,000	10,000		1971-72
53,000	250	1,750	not listed	Jordan	1968-69
53,000	250	1,750	not listed		1969-70
58,000	250	2,000	37,500		1970-71
58,000	250	2,000	37,500		1971-72
30,000	1,000	5,000	20,000	Saudi	1968-69
28,000	1,000	5,000	28,000	Arabia	1969-70
30,000	1,000	5,000	24,000		1970-71
35,000	1,000	5,000	30,000		1971-72
50,000	1,500	9,000	158,000	Syria	1968-69
60,000	1,500	9,000	108,000		1969-70
75,000	1,750	10,000	256,500		1970-71
100,000	1,750	10,000	6,500		1971-72
425,000	39,000	50,000	40,000	Turkey	1968-69
400,000	40,000	43,000	40,000		1969-70
390,000	37,500	50,000	40,000		1970-71
420,000	38,500	50,000	75,000		1971-72

[a]Jewish population only.   [b]Service for men; women serve 20 months.
[c]Figures on armed forces and various services represent regular cadres that when mobilized to full strength far exceed these figures.

[d]Army and navy; air force 3 years.

Bibliography

Index

Bibliography

A few words may make this Bibliography more useful. Since this is the first systematic study of Iran's foreign policy from 1941 to 1973, I hope my research experience will help to stimulate further research on Iranian foreign policy. As a first step consultation of my early article "Research Facilities in Iran" will prove helpful. This article was prepared at the invitation of the Middle East Studies Association while I was in Iran, and its publication has been followed by similar articles by other scholars on Algeria, the United Arab Republic, Morocco, Tunisia, Lebanon, and others. Students of Iranian foreign policy may well profit by these other articles as well, especially those who are interested in Iran's relations with Arab states.

Documentary research on Iranian foreign policy can profit from United States government publications. First and foremost, the State Department volumes on the foreign relations of the United States contain data seldom available elsewhere, including Iran. Presidential public papers, congressional studies, and treaties and international agreements series are also useful. Sporadic publications of the Iranian Ministry of Foreign Affairs, such as *Iran's Foreign Policy*, and of course the annual "Report of the Ministry of Foreign Affairs" (*Gozarish-i Salianih-ye Vizarat-i Kharijih*) can be found useful. Without implying that access is guaranteed to all scholars, the library of the Iranian Ministry of Foreign Affairs can provide unclassified "Reports" (*Gozarish-ha*) by Iranian diplomats that are difficult to match. Researchers interested in foreign trade statistics will find the Finance Ministry's "annual statistics" (*Amar-i Salianih*) indispensable. Researchers who cannot read Arabic will find two publications of the Department of Political Studies and Public Administration of the American University of Beirut most convenient. These are *Arab Political Documents* and the related *Chronology of Arab Politics*. Among British sources two in particular stand out: *Documents on International Affairs,* published by the Royal Institute of International Affairs, and *The Military Balance,* published by the International Institute for Strategic Studies. Finally, United Nations publications are useful, as evidenced, for example, by the official records of the Security Council, United

Nations *Treaty Series,* publications of the International Court of Justice, and statistical data, all used in this study.

Students of contemporary Iranian foreign policy will have to rely upon a great variety of other primary sources as well. The *Current Digest of the Soviet Press* is indispensable for researchers who are unable to read Russian. The use of this source together with *International Affairs* (Moscow), *New Times,* the *Mizan Newsletter,* and the United States Foreign Broadcast Information Service volumes, *USSR International Affairs,* can be rewarding indeed. On the actions and reactions of Arab states, the most convenient and perhaps thorough journalistic source is the well-known *Al-Ahram;* in addition to Egyptian perspectives it often runs interviews with other Arab leaders on a variety of issues. The Lebanese *Al-Anwar, Daily Star,* and *Le Jour* are also helpful. Two other publications from the Middle East in English contain considerable material of interest to foreign policy analysts; *Mid-East Commerce* and the *Middle East Economic Digest.* The usefulness of the *Middle East Monitor* is becoming well known. Among Iranian journalistic sources, *Ittila'at,* and *Ittila'at Hava'i* are too well known to require elaboration, as is *Kayhan,* daily in Persian and English as well as weekly in English. Interpretative essays published occasionally in *Khandaniha* are sometimes insightful, as are those published in the *Tihran Ikonomist,* although the latter is relatively recent as compared with *Khandaniha,* which is one of the few Iranian publications of its kind to be published for decades without major interruption. The publications of the Central Bank of Iran, especially its *Bulletin* in English (*Majallih,* in Persian) and the annual report, contain valuable data on economic matters in general and occasionally the full text of major economic agreements, such as those with East European countries. Finally, the United States Department of State's *Bulletin* together with the *New York Times,* the *Washington Post,* and occasionally the *Christian Science Monitor* provide valuable research materials, especially on Iran's relations with the United States.

Documents and Official Publications

Dennet, Raymond, and Turner, Robert, eds. *Documents on American Foreign Relations.* Vol. 8. Princeton: Princeton University Press, 1948.

Goodrich, Leland M., and Caroll, Marie J., eds. *Documents on American Foreign Relations.* Vol. 4. Boston: World Peace Foundation, 1942.

Great Britain. Central Office of Information. *Paiforce: The Official Story of the Persia and Iraq Command, 1941-1946.* London: H.M. Stationery Office, 1948.

Hurewitz, J. C. *Diplomacy in the Near and Middle East: A Documentary Record.* Vol. 2. Princeton: Van Nostrand, 1956.

International Court of Justice. *Anglo-Iranian Oil Co. Case (United Kingdom v. Iran). Judgment,* July 22, 1952.

——. *Pleadings, Oral Arguments, Documents.*

Iran. Idarih-ye Kull-i Intisharat va Tabliqat. *Asnad-i Naft.* Tehran: n.p., 1951/52.

Iran. Majlis. *Bakhshi az Parvandih-ye Naft-i Iran, Matn-i Nutqha-ye Senator Divanbaigy dar Majlis-i Sina.* Tehran: Chapkhanih-ye Majlis, n.d.

——. *Nutq-i Aqa-ye Muhammad Darakhshish dar Mukhalifat-i ba Qarardad-i Naft-i Amini-Page keh dar Majlis-i Shora-ye Milli Irad Shodih.* Tehran: Chapkhanih-ye Majlis, 1954.

——. Majlis-i Panzdahum. *Ruznamih-ye Rasmi.*

Iran. Makki, Husain (Rapporteur of the Oil Commission). *Kitab-i Siyah.* Tehran: Muhammad 'Ali 'almi, 1951/52.

Iran. Ministry of Finance. *Salnamih-ye Amar-i Bazargani-i Khariji-i Iran;* and *Nashriyih-ye Bazargani-i Khariji-i Iran.* 1964-1973.

Iran. Ministry of Foreign Affairs. *Iran's Foreign Policy: A Compendium of the Writings and Statements of His Imperial Majesty Shahanshah Aryamehr.* Tehran: Iranchap, n.d.

——. *Ravabit-i Khariji-i Iran dar Sal-i 1346.* Tehran: Chap-i Matbu'ati-ye Iran, 1968/69.

Iran. *Prime Minister's Reports.* Tehran: Bank Melli Iran Press, 1952.

Iran. Shah. Nikpay, Gholamriza, ed. *Surat-i Jalasat-i Showray-i Iqtisad, ya Majmu'aih-ye Az Asnad-i Tarikh-i Mu'asir-i Iran.* 2 vols. Tehran: Chap-i Vizarat-i Farhang va Honar, 1964-68.

Royal Institute of International Affairs. *Documents on International Affairs, 1951.* London: Oxford University Press, 1954.

——. *Documents on International Affairs, 1952.* London: Oxford University Press, 1955.

——. *Documents on International Affairs, 1953.* London: Oxford University Press, 1956.

——. *Documents on International Affairs, 1954.* London: Oxford University Press, 1957.

——. *Documents on International Affairs, 1955.* London: Oxford University Press, 1958.

——. *Documents on International Affairs, 1959.* London: Oxford University Press, 1963.

Turkey. Central Treaty Organization. *CENTO Conference on National and Regional Agricultural Development Policy.* Ankara: Office of the United States Economic Coordinator for CENTO Affairs, 1968.

——. *Progress through CENTO: Communications.* Ankara: CENTO Public Relations Division, n.d.

United Nations. Security Council. *Official Records* (S/2357). 6th Year: 559th meeting; 560th meeting; 561st meeting; 563d meeting; 565th meeting, Oct. 1, 15, 16, 17, 19, 1951.

——. *Official Records.* First Year: First Series, no. 1; First Year: First Series, *Supplement* no. 1; First Year: First Series, no. 2; First Year: First Series, *Supplement* no. 2.

——. Secretariat. *Treaty Series.* Vols. 11, no. 171 (1947); 31, nos. 176, 484 (1949); 204, no. 2754 (1955); 233, no. 3264 (1956); 272, no. 3934 (1957); 303, no. 1057 (1958); 327, no. 4725 (1959); 335, no. 4788 (1959); 342, no. 4898 (1959); 393, no. 5288 (1961); 398, no. 5717 (1961); 433, no. 6249 (1962); 451, no. 6497 (1963); 457, no. 6586 (1963); 633, no. 9037 (1968); 643, no. 9192 (1968).

United States Congress. House. Committee on the Judiciary. *Hearings* before Antitrust Subcommittee of the Committee on the Judiciary. House of Representatives, Pt. 1, 84th Cong., 1st sess., 1955.

——. Subcommittee of the Committee on Government Operations. *Hearings.* 84th Cong., 2d sess., 1956.

——. Committee on Armed Service. *Hearings on Military Posture.* 88th Cong., 1st sess., 1963.

——. Subcommittee on the Near East. *U.S. Interests in and Policy toward the Persian Gulf.* 92d Cong., 2d sess., 1972.

——. Department of Commerce. *International Commerce.* March 31, 1969.

——. Department of State. *Foreign Relations of the United States,* Diplomatic Papers, *The Conference of Berlin (The Potsdam Conference), 1945.* Vol. 2. Washington, D.C.: Government Printing Office, 1960.

——. *Foreign Relations of the United States,* Diplomatic Papers, *The Conference at Malta and Yalta, 1945.* Washington, D.C.: Government Printing Office, 1955.

——. *Documents on German Foreign Policy, 1918-1945.* Series D. Washington, D.C.: Government Printing Office, 1962.

——. *Foreign Relations of the United States,* Diplomatic Papers, *The Conferences at Cairo and Tehran, 1943.* Washington, D.C.: Government Printing Office, 1961.

——. *Foreign Relations of the United States, 1940.* Diplomatic Papers. Vol. 3. *The British Commonwealth, The Soviet Union, The Near East and Africa.* Washington, D.C.: Government Printing Office, 1958.

——. *Foreign Relations of the United States, 1941.* Diplomatic Papers. Vol. 3. *The British Commonwealth, The Near East and Africa.* Washington, D.C.: Government Printing Office, 1959.

——. *Foreign Relations of the United States, 1942.* Diplomatic Papers. Vol. 4. *The Near East and Africa.* Washington, D.C.: Government Printing Office, 1963.

——. *Foreign Relations of the United States, 1943.* Diplomatic Papers. Vol. 4. *The Near East and Africa.* Washington, D.C.: Government Printing Office, 1964.

——. *Foreign Relations of the United States, 1944.* Diplomatic Papers. Vol. 5. *The Near East, South Asia, and Africa; the Far East.* Washington, D.C.: Government Printing Office, 1965.

——. *Foreign Relations of the United States, 1945.* Diplomatic Papers. Vol. 8. *The Near East and Africa.* Washington, D.C.: Government Printing Office, 1969.

——. *Foreign Relations of the United States, 1946.* Vol. 7. *The Near East and Africa.* Washington, D.C.: Government Printing Office, 1969.

——. *The Suez Canal Problem, July 26-September 22, 1956: A Documentary Publication*: Washington, D.C.: Government Printing Office, 1956.

——. *United States Treaties and Other International Acts Series 1666.*

——. *United States Treaties and Other International Acts Series 1924.*

——. *United States Treaties and Other International Acts Series 1941.*

——. *United States Treaties and Other International Agreements.* Vols. 1, TIAS nos. 2068, 2071, 2139 (1950); 8, pt. 1, TIAS no. 3853 (1955); 14, pt. 2, TIAS no. 5451 (1963); 18, pt. 1, TIAS no. 6219 (1964); 19, pt. 4, TIAS no. 6487, and pt. 6, TIAS no. 6594 (1968); 20, pt. 1, TIAS no. 6694 (1968), and pt. 2, TIAS no. 6726 (1969).

——. Executive Department. *Executive Agreement Series 361.* Washington, D.C.: Government Printing Office, 1944.

——. *Executive Agreement Series 410.* Washington, D.C.: Government Printing Office, 1944.

——. President. *Public Papers of the Presidents of the United States.* Dwight D. Eisenhower, 1953. Washington, D.C.: Government Printing Office, 1960.

—. *Public Papers of the Presidents of the United States.* Dwight D. Eisenhower, 1954. Washington, D.C.: Government Printing Office, 1960.

—. *Public Papers of the Presidents of the United States.* Dwight D. Eisenhower, 1959. Washington, D.C.: Government Printing Office, 1960.

—. *Public Papers of the Presidents of the United States.* John F. Kennedy, 1962. Washington, D.C.: Government Printing Office, 1963.

—. *Public Papers of the Presidents of the United States.* John F. Kennedy, 1963. Washington, D.C.: Government Printing Office, 1964.

Books and Pamphlets

Acheson, Dean. *Present at the Creation: My Years in the State Department.* New York: W. W. Norton & Co., 1969.

Adamiyat, Fereydoun. *Bahrain Islands: A Legal and Diplomatic Study of the British-Iranian Controversy.* New York: Frederick A. Praeger, 1955.

Afsheen, Kazim. *Naft va Khuzistanian.* Tehran: Firdowsi, 1333 (1954/55).

Al-'Aqqad, Salah. *Isti'mar fi al-Khalij al-Farisi.* Cairo, 1956.

Algar, Hamid. *Religion and State in Iran, 1785-1906: The Role of the Ulama in the Qajar Period.* Berkeley and Los Angeles: University of California Press, 1969.

Al-i Ahmad, Jalal. *Gharbzadigi: Maqalih.* Tehran: n.p., 1965/66.

'Ali al-Daud, Mahmud. *Muhadarat 'an al-tatawwur al-siyasi al-hadith li Qadiyat'Um.* Cairo, 1964.

Almond, Gabriel A. *Political Development: Essays in Heuristic Theory.* Boston: Little, Brown & Co., 1970.

Almond, Gabriel A., and Powell, G. Bingham, Jr. *Comparative Politics: A Developmental Approach.* Boston: Little, Brown & Co., 1966.

Al-Tikriti, Salim Taha, *Al-Sira' 'an al-Khalij al 'Arabi.* Baghdad, n.p., 1966.

Amini, Davoud, M. *Iran Ba'd Az Jang.* Tehran: Chapkhanih-ye 'Almi, 1944/45.

Amuzegar, Jahangir, *Technical Assistance in Theory and Practice: The Case of Iran.* New York: Frederick A. Praeger, 1966.

Amuzigar, S. H. *Naft va Havadis-i Azarbaijan.* Tehran: Shirkat-i Matbu'at, 1326 (1947/48).

Arfa, Hassan. *The Kurds: An Historical and Political Study.* London: Oxford University Press, 1966.

Bahar, Doktor Mehdi. *Miras-khar-i Ist'amar.* Tehran: n.p., 1966/67.

Baldwin, George B. *Planning and Development in Iran*. Baltimore: Johns Hopkins University Press, 1967.

Barnet, Richard J. *Intervention and Revolution*. New York: World Publishing Co., 1969.

Behzadi, Hassan. *Bahrih-bardari Az Manab'a-I Khalij-i Fars*. Tehran: Chihr, 1345 (1966/67).

Bihniya, 'Abdulhusain. *Pardih-hay-i Siyasat: Naft, Nihzat, Musaddiq, Zahidi*. Tehran: Chap-i Rangin, n.d.

Bill, James Alban. *The Politics of Iran: Groups, Classes and Modernization*. Columbus, Ohio: Charles E. Merrill Publishing Co., 1972:

Bina, 'Ali Akbar. *Tarikh-i Siyasi va Diplomacy-i Iran*. Tehran: University Press, 1337 (1958/59).

Binder, Leonard. *Factors Influencing Iran's International Role*. Santa Monica, Calif.: Rand Corporation, October 1969.

—. *Iran: Political Development in A Changing Society*. Berkeley and Los Angeles: University of California Press, 1962.

—. Coleman, James S.; Palombara, Joseph La; Pye, Lucian; Verba, Sidney; and Weiner, Myron. *Crisis and Sequences in Political Development*. Princeton; Princeton University Press, 1971.

Bozeman, Adda B. *Politics and Culture in International History*. Princeton: Princeton University Press, 1960.

Bushihri, Nozadih. *Falat-i Qarrih va Jazayir-i Khalij-i Fars*. Tehran: Tabish, 1338 (1959/60).

Campbell, John C. *Defense of the Middle East: Problems of American Foreign Policy*. New York: Frederick A. Praeger, 1960.

Center for Mediterranean Studies. *The Changing Balance of Power in the Persian Gulf*. New York: American Universities Field Staff, 1972.

Churchill, Winston. *The Second World War*. Vol. 3. *The Grand Alliance*. Boston: Houghton Mifflin Co., 1948.

Copeland, Miles. *The Game of Nations: The Amorality of Power Politics*. London: Weidenfeld and Nicolson, 1969.

Cottam, Richard W. *Nationalism in Iran*. Pittsburgh: University of Pittsburgh Press, 1964.

Danishpoor, A. *Nairangbazan-i Naft ya 'Allal-i Shikast-i Misyon-i Garner*. Tehran: Chapkhanih-ye Musavi, 1953/54.

Deutsch, Karl W. *Nationalism and Social Communication: An Inquiry into the Foundations of Nationality*. Cambridge, Mass.: M.I.T. Press, 1953.

Eagleton, William, Jr. *The Kurdish Republic of 1946.* London: Oxford University Press, 1963.

Eden, Anthony. *Full Circle.* Boston: Houghton Mifflin Co., 1960.

Eisenhower, Dwight D. *Mandate for Change, 1953-1956.* Garden City, N.Y.: Doubleday & Co., 1963.

Eisenhower, Dwight D. *Waging Peace, 1956-1961.* Garden City, N.Y.: Doubleday & Co., 1965.

Ellwell-Sutton, L. P. *Persian Oil: A Study in Power Politics.* London: Laurence and Wishart, 1955.

Engler, Robert. *The Politics of Oil.* New York: Macmillan Co., 1961.

Farrell, Barry R., ed. *Approaches to Comparative and International Politics.* Evanston, Ill. Northwestern University Press, 1966.

Fatih, Mustafa. *Panjah Sal Naft-i Iran.* Tehran: Shirkat Sahami-i Chap, 1957/58.

Gehlen, Michael P. *The Politics of Coexistence: Soviet Methods and Motives.* Bloomington: Indiana University Press, 1967.

Ghosh, S. D. *Anglo-Iranian Oil Dispute.* Calcutta: Firma K. L. Mukhopadhyay, 1960.

Gudarzi-i Tabrizi, Rahim. *Lozum-i Hifz-i Bitarafi.* Tehran: Chapkhanih-ye Musavi, 1955/56.

Hizb-i-Iran. *Jarayan-i Muzakirat-i Naft dar Majlis-i Panzdahom.* Tehran: Hizb-i Iran, n.d.

Hull, Cordell. *The Memoirs of Cordell Hull.* Vol. 2. New York: Macmillan Co., 1948.

Huntington, Samuel P. *Political Order in Changing Societies.* New Haven: Yale University Press, 1968.

Iranian Government. *Sayr-i Komonism dar Iran.* Tehran: Kayhan, 1956/58.

——. *Kitab-i Siyah dar Barih-ye Saziman-i Afsaran-i Tudeh.* Tehran: n.p., 1954/55.

Jahanbani, Sipahbud Amanullah. *Marzha-ye Iran va Showravy.* Tehran: Chapkhanih-ye Majlis, 1958/59.

——. *Sargozasht-i Baluchistan va Marzha-ye An.* Tehran: n.p., 1338 (1959/1960).

Jukes, Geoffrey. *The Indian Ocean in Soviet Naval Policy.* London: International Institute for Strategic Studies, May 1972.

Kayostovan, Husain. *Syasat-i Muvazinih-ye Manfi dar Majlis-i Chahardahom.* Tehran: Ibn Sina, 1329 (1950/51).

Khadduri, Majid. *Republican 'Iraq: A Study in 'Iraqi Politics since the Revolution of 1958.* London: Oxford University Press, 1969.

——. *The Islamic Law of Nations: Shaybani's Siyar*. Baltimore: Johns Hopkins University Press, 1966.

——. *War and Peace in the Law of Islam*. Baltimore: Johns Hopkins Press, 1955.

Khajih-Nuri, A. *Bazigaran-i 'Asr-i Tala'i*. Tehran: n.p., n.d.

Kianfar, Mihdi. *Siyasat-i Amrika dar Iran*. Tehran: Kitabkhanih-ye Khayyam, 1949/50.

Kirmani, Husain Kuhi. *Az Shahrivar 1320 ta Faja'ih-ye Azerbaijan va Zanjan*. Vol. 1. Tehran: Mazahiri, n.d.

——. *Az Shahrivar-i 1320 ta Faja'ih-ye Azerbaijan va Zanjan*. Vol. 2. Tehran: Mazahiri, 1950/51.

Lenczowski, George. *Russia and the West in Iran, 1918-1948: A Study in Big-Power Rivalry*. Ithaca, N.Y.: Cornell University Press, 1949.

Lepawski, Albert; Buehrig, Edward H.; and Lasswell, Harold D., eds. *The Search for World Order: Studies by Students and Colleagues of Quincy Wright*. New York: Appleton-Century Crofts, 1971.

Lewis, Bernard. *The Middle East and the West*. Bloomington: Indiana University Press, 1964.

Lissani, Abulfazl. *Talay-i Siyah ya Balay-i Iran*. Tehran: Chap-i Mihr. 1950/1951.

Lohbeck, Don. *Patrick J. Hurley*. Chicago: Henry Regnery, 1956.

Malik (Yazdi), Muhammad Khan. *Ghoghay-i Takhlieh-ye Iran*. Tehran: Shirkat-i Sahami-i Tab'i Kitab, 1947/48.

Maliki, Ahmad. *Tarikhchih-ye Jibhi-ye Milli, Chira Jibhi-ye Milli Tashkil Shod? Chigonih Jibhi-ye Milli Monhal Gardid?* Tehran: Chap-i Taban, 1332 (1952/53).

Masudi, Qasim. *Jarayan-i Musafirat-i Misyon-i I'zami-i Iran be-Mosko*. Tehran: Shirkat-i Sahami-i Chap, 1946/47.

Middle East Institute. *The Arabian Peninsula, Iran and the Gulf States: New Wealth, New Power: A Summary Record*. 27th Annual Conference of the Middle East Institute. Washington, D.C.: Middle East Institute, September 28-29, 1973.

——. *World Energy Demands and the Middle East*, pts. 1 & 2. 26th Annual Conference of the Middle East Institute. Washington, D.C.: Middle East Institute, September 29-30, 1972.

Millspaugh, Arthur C. *Americans in Persia*. Washington, D.C.: Brookings Institution, 1946.

Mohammad Reza Shah. *Mission for My Country*. New York: McGraw-Hill, 1961.

Mughraby, Muhamad A. *Permanent Sovereignty over Oil Resources: A Study of Middle East Oil Concessions and Legal Change*. Beirut: Middle East Research and Publications Center, 1966.

Munshizadih, Doktor. *Komonism va Liberalism*. Tehran: Sumka, 1957/58.

Musaddiq, Muhammad. *Matn-i Difa'a-i Doktor Muhammad Musaddiq*. Tehran: Bongah Sarsar, n.d.

Naiyyir Nuri, Hamid. *Sahm-i Iran dar Tammadon-i Jahan*. Tehran: Shirkat-i Milli Naft-i Iran, 1966/67.

Nirumand, Bahman. *Iran: The New Imperialism in Action*. New York: Monthly Review Press, 1969.

Parsons, Talcott, and Shills, Edward A., eds. *Toward a Theory of Action*. New York: Harper & Row, 1951.

Pisyan, Najafquli. *Az Mahabad-i Khunin ta Karanih-ha-ye Aras*. Tehran: Shirkat-i Sahami-i Chap, 1948/49.

——. *Marg Bood Bazgasht Ham Bood*. Tehran: Shirkat-i Sahami-i Chap, 1948/49.

Pye, Lucian W. *Aspects of Political Development*. Boston: Little, Brown & Co., 1966.

Ramazani, Rouhollah K. *The Foreign Policy of Iran, 1500-1941: A Developing Nation in World Affairs*. Charlottesville: University Press of Virginia, 1966.

——. *The Middle East and the European Common Market*. Charlottesville: University Press of Virginia, 1964.

——. *The Northern Tier: Afghanistan, Iran and Turkey*. Princeton: Van Nostrand, 1966.

——. *The Persian Gulf: Iran's Role*. Charlottesville: University Press of Virginia, 1972.

Rosenau, James N., ed. *International Politics and Foreign Policy*, New York: The Free Press, 1969.

——. *The Scientific Study of Foreign Policy*. New York: The Free Press, 1971.

Royal Institute of International Affairs. *Survey of International Affairs. 1939-46: The Middle East in the War.* London: Oxford University Press, 1952.

—. *Survey of International Affairs, 1951.* London: Oxford University Press, 1954.

—. *Survey of International Affairs, 1952.* London: Oxford University Press, 1955.

—. *Survey of International Affairs, 1953.* London: Oxford University Press, 1956.

—. *Survey of International Affairs, 1954.* London: Oxford University Press, 1957.

Rustow, Dankwart A. *A World of Nations: Problems of Political Modernization.* Washington, D.C.: Brookings Institution, 1967.

Shajia'i, Zahra. *Namayandigan-i Majlis-i Showra-ye Milli dar Bist va Yek Dowrih-ye Qanun-gozari: Motala'ih Az Nazar-i Jama'ih Shinasi-i Siyasi.* Tehran: Mu'assihsih-ye Motali'at va Tahqiqat-i Ijtima'i, 1965/66.

Shulze-Holthus, Bernard. *Daybreak in Iran: A Story of the German Intelligence Service.* London: Staples Press, 1954.

Skrine, Sir Clarmont. *World War in Iran.* London: Constable & Co., 1962.

Sorenson, Theodore. *Kennedy.* New York: Harper & Row, 1965.

Sprout, Harold and Margaret. *Foundations of International Politics.* Princeton: Van Nostrand, 1962.

Thomas, Lewis, and Frye, Richard. *The United States and Turkey and Iran.* Cambridge, Mass.: Harvard University Press, 1952.

Truman, Harry S. *Memoirs by Harry S. Truman.* Vol. 2. *Years of Trial and Hope, 1946-1952.* Garden City: Doubleday & Co., 1956.

Tully, Andrew. *CIA: The Inside Story.* New York: William Morrow, 1962.

Van Wagenen, Richard W. *The Iranian Case, 1946.* New York: Carnegie Endowment for International Peace, 1952 (in consultation with T. Cuyler Young).

Von Grunebaum, G. E. *Modern Islam: The Search for Cultural Identity.* Berkeley and Los Angeles: University of California Press, 1962.

Yar-Shater, Ehsan, ed. *Iran Faces the Seventies.* New York: Praeger, 1971.

Zabih, Sepehr. *The Communist Movement in Iran.* Berkeley and Los Angeles: University of California Press, 1966.

Zonis, Marvin. *The Political Elite of Iran.* Princeton: Princeton University Press, 1971.

Periodical Articles and Parts of Books

Abrahamian, Ervand. "Communism and Communalism in Iran: The Tudeh and the Firqah-e Dimukrat." *International Journal of Middle East Studies* 1, no. 4 (1970):291-316.

Almond, Gabriel A. "Political System and Political Change." *American Behavioral Scientist* 6, no. 10 (1963):3-10.

Avery, Peter. "Iran 1964-8: The Mood of Growing Confidence." *World Today* 24, no. 11 (1968):453-66.

——. "Trends in Iran in the Past Five Years." *World Today 21, no. 7 (1965): 279-90.*

Belgrave, Sir Charles. "Persian Gulf—Past and Present." *Journal of the Royal Central Asian Society* 55, pt. 1 (Feb. 1968):28-34.

Bharier, Julian. "A Note on the Population of Iran, 1900-1966." *Population Studies* 22, no. 21 (1968):273-79.

Binder, Leonard. "Iran's Potential as a Regional Power." In Paul Y. Hammond and Sidney S. Alexander, eds. *Political Dynamics in the Middle East,* pp. 355-94. New York: American Elsevier Publishing Co., 1972.

Bullard, Sir Reader. "Persia in Two World Wars." *Royal Central Asian Journal* 50, pt. 1 (Jan. 1963):6-20.

Campbell, John C. "The Communist Powers and the Middle East." *Problems of Communism* 21 (Sept.-Oct. 1972):40-54.

D. L. M. "Soviet Interest in Middle East Oil." *Mizan* 13, no. 1 (1971):30-34.

Enayat, Hamid. "Iran and the Arabs." In Sylvia G. Haim, ed. *Arab Nationalism and a Wider World,* pp. 13-25. New York: American Academic Association for Peace in the Middle East, 1971.

Frye, Richard N. "Iran and the Unity of the Muslim World." In Richard N. Frye, ed. *Islam and the West,* pp. 179-93. The Hague: Mouton & Co., 1957.

Gittinger, Price. "Planning and Agricultural Policy in Iran—Program Effects and Indirect Effects." *Economic Development and Cultural Change* 16, no. 1 (1967):107-16.

Grady, Henry F. "What Went Wrong in Iran?" *Saturday Evening Post*, Jan. 5, 1952, p. 30.

Halpern, Manfred. "Perspectives on U.S. Policy in Iran." *SAIS Review* 6 (Spring 1962):25-30.

Hambly, Gavin. "Attitudes and Aspirations of the Contemporary Iranian Intellectual." *Journal of Royal Central Asian Society* 51, pt. 2 (Apr. 1964):127-40.

Harkness, Richard and Gladys. "America's Secret Agents: The Mysterious Doings of CIA." *Saturday Evening Post*, Nov. 6, 1954, p. 34.

Jacobs, Norman. "Economic Rationality and Social Development: An Iranian Case Study." *Studies in Comparative International Development* 2, no. 9 (1966):137-42.

Jobri, Marwan. "Dilemma in Iran." *Current History* 48, no. 285 (1965):277-307.

Kazemzadeh, F. "Ideological Crisis in Iran." In Walter Z. Laqueur, ed. *The Middle East in Transition*, pp. 196-203. New York: Frederick A. Praeger, 1958.

Keddie, Nikki R. "The Iranian Power Structure and Social Change 1800-1969: An Overview." *International Journal of Middle East Studies* 2, no. 1 (1971):3-20.

Khaleeli, Abbas. "Some Aspects of Iran's Foreign Relations." *Pakistan Horizon* 21, no. 1 (1968), pp. 14-20.

Kingsley, Robert. "Premier Amini and Iran's Problems." *Middle Eastern Affairs* 13, no. 7 (1962):194-98.

Lambton, Ann K. S. "Some of the Problems Facing Persia." *International Affairs* (London) 22, no. 2 (1946):254-72.

—. "The Impact of the West on Persia." *International Affairs* 33, no. 1 (1957):12-25.

Lee, Christopher D. "The Soviet Contribution to Iran's Fourth Development Plan." *Mizan* 11, no. 5 (1969): 237-57.

——. "Soviet and Chinese Interests in Southern Arabia." *Mizan* 13, no. 1 (1971):35-47.

Mclane, Charles B. "The Soviet Union and the Developing Countries: A Sample of Recent Western Research." *Mizan* 12, no. 3 (1970):153-59.

Mahdavy, Hossein. "The Coming Crisis in Iran." *Foreign Affairs* 44, no. 1 (1965):134-46.

Marlowe, John. "Arab-Persian Rivalry in the Persian Gulf." *Journal of the Royal Central Asian Society* 51, pt. 1 (Jan. 1964):23-31.

Melson, Robert and Wolpe, Howard. "Modernization and the Politics of Communalism: A Theoretical Perspective." *American Political Science Review* 64, no. 4 (1970):1112-30.

Morison, David. "USSR and Third World: II. Questions of Foreign Policy." *Mizan* 12, no. 2 (1970):124-52.

——. "USSR and Third World: III. Questions of Economic Development." *Mizan* 12, no. 3 (1970):69-79.

Page, Stephen. "Moscow and the Persian Gulf Countries, 1967-1970." *Mizan* 13, no. 2 (1971):72-88.

Paul, H. G. Balfour. "Recent Developments in the Persian Gulf." *Journal of the Royal Central Asian Society* 56, pt. 1 (Feb. 1969):12-19.

Pranger, J. Robert. "Currents in Iranian Nationalism." *Current History* 36, no. 210 (1959):102-6.

Qureshi, Khalida. "Pakistan and Iran—A Study in Neighbourly Diplomacy." *Pakistan Horizon* 21, no. 1 (1968):33-39.

Ramazani, Rouhollah K. "Afghanistan and the U.S.S.R." *Middle East Journal* 12, no. 2 (1958):144-52.

——. "The Autonomous Republic of Azerbaijan and the Kurdish People's Republic: Their Rise and Fall." *Studies on the Soviet Union* 11, no. 4 (1971):401-27.

——. "Changing United States Policy in the Middle East." *Virginia Quarterly Review* 40, no. 3 (1964):369-82.

——. "The Choice-of-Law Problems and International Oil Contracts: A Case Study." *International and Comparative Law Quarterly* (London) 11, pt. 2 (1962):503-18.

——. " 'Church' and State in Modernizing Society: The Case of Iran." *American Behavioral Scientist* 7, no. 5 (1964):26-28.

—. "Cultural Change and Intellectual Response in Algeria, Tunisia and Iran." *Comparative Studies in Society and History: An International Quarterly* 6, no. 2 (1964):219-29.

—. "Images of Arab Unity and the Soviet Union." *Free World Forum* 2, no. 1 (1960):16-20.

—. "Iran, CENTO and the Soviet Union." *Free World Forum* 2, no. 4 (1960):52-55.

—. "Iran's Changing Foreign Policy: A Preliminary Discussion." *Middle East Journal* 24, no. 4 (1970):421-37.

—. "Iran's 'White Revolution': A Study in Political Development." *International Journal of Middle East Studies* 5, no. 2 (1974):124-39.

—. "Islamic Studies: A Concept and Approach" (Guest Editorial). *Muslim World* 58, no. 4 (1968):279-83.

—. "The Kurdish Problem." *Quarterly Review* (London), Jan. 1967, pp. 71-79.

—. "A Lesson of the Anglo-Iranian Oil Relations." *World Affairs Interpreter* 26, no. 2 (1955):201-10.

—. "Modernization and Social Research in Iran." *American Behavioral Scientist* 5, no. 6 (1962):17-20.

—. "Oil and Law in Iran." *Journal of John Basset Moore Society of International Law* 2, no. 2 (1962):56-70.

—. "Pan-Arabism and the Soviet Policy: Today and Tomorrow." *Proceedings of the Middle East Institute,* Fourteenth Annual Conference, 1960, pp. 53-61.

—. "Research Facilities in Iran." *Middle East Studies Association Bulletin* 3, no. 3 (1969):53-61, and 4, no. 1 (1970):51.

—. "Self-Determination and Settlement of the Arab-Israeli Conflict." Comments in *Proceedings of the American Society of International Law,* Sixty-Fifth Meeting, Apr. 29-May 1, 1971, 50.

—. "The Settlement of the Bahrain Dispute." *Indian Journal of International Law* 12, no. 1 (1972):1-14.

—. "The Shi'i System: Its Conflict and Interaction with Other Systems." *Proceedings of the American Society of International Law,* 1959, pp. 1-7.

—. "Soviet Military Assistance to the Uncommitted Countries." *Midwest Journal of Political Science* 3, no. 4 (1959):356-73.

——. "Syria and the Soviet Bloc." *World Affairs Quarterly* 30, no. 1 (1959): 34-45.

——. "Toward a United States Policy in the Middle East." *Quarterly Review* (London) Jan. 1960, pp. 1-7.

——. "Treaty Relations: An Irano-Soviet Case Study." In Albert Lepawsky, Edward H. Buehrig, and Harold D. Lasswell, eds. *The Search for World Order: Studies by Students and Colleagues of Quincy Wright*, pp. 298-311. New York: Appleton-Century-Crofts, 1971.

——, and Robert Loring Allen. "Afghanistan Wooed But Not Won." *Swiss Review of World Affairs* 7, no. 7 (1957): 16-19.

——, and Oles M. Smolansky. "Iran." In Thomas T. Hammond, ed. *Soviet Foreign Relations and World Communism: A Selected, Annotated Bibliography of 7,000 Books in 30 Languages*, pp. 825-60. Princeton: Princeton University Press, 1965.

Roosevelt, Archie, Jr. "The Kurdish Republic of Mahabad." *Middle East Journal* 1, no. 3 (1947): 247-69.

Rossow, Robert. "The Battle of Azerbaijan." *Middle East Journal* 10, no. 1 (1956): 17-32.

Shafaq, S. Rezazadeh. "The Iranian Seven Year Development Plan: Background and Organization." *Middle East Journal* 4, no. 1 (1950): 100-105.

Tarokh, Ahmed. "Iran and the Arab States." *New Outlook* 9, no. 1 (1966): 23-27.

Watt, D. C. "The Decision to Withdraw from the Gulf." *Political Quarterly* (London) 39, no. 3 (1968): 310-21.

——. "The Persian Gulf—Cradle of Conflict." *Problems of Communism* 21 (May-June 1972): 32-40.

Wheeler, Geoffrey. "Soviet Interests in Iran, Iraq, and Turkey." *World Today* 24, no. 5 (1968): 197-203.

Young, T. Cuyler. "Iran in Continuing Crisis." *Foreign Affairs* 40, no. 2 (1962): 275-92.

——. "The Social Support of Current Iranian Policy." *Middle East Journal* 6, no. 2 (1952): 125-43.

Zabih, Sepehr. "Iran's International Posture: De Facto Non-Alignment within a Pro-Western Alliance." *Middle East Journal* 24, no. 3 (1970): 302-18.

Zonis, Marvin. "Political Elites and Political Cynicism in Iran." *Comparative Political Studies* 1, no. 3 (1968): 351-69.

Newspapers, Bulletins, Digests, and Radio Broadcasts

Al-Ahram, 1968-1973.

Bank Markazi Iran. *Bulletin*, 1963-1973.

Bisoy-i Ayandih, 1950-1953.

Current Digest of the Soviet Press, 1949-1973.

Daily Star (Beirut) 1967-1969.

International Affairs (Moscow), 1963-1973.

Ittila'at, 1941-1958.

Ittila'at Hava'i, 1958-1973.

Kayhan (Daily and Weekly, English) 1968-1973.

Khandaniha, 1941-1973.

Mid-East Commerce, 1961-1966.

Middle East Economic Digest, 1957-1966.

Middle East Monitor, 1971-1973.

Mizan Newsletter, 1959-1964.

New Times (Moscow), 1968-1973.

New York Times, 1941-1973.

United States, Department of State, *Bulletin*, 1941-1973.

United States, Foreign Broadcast Information Service, *U.S.S.R. International Affairs*, 1968-1973.

Washington Post. 1968-1973.

Index